Windows Server 2008 All-in-One Desk Reference For Dummies

W9-BTM-771

Common Windows Keyboard Shortcuts

Shortcut	Description
– (On numeric keypad)	Collapses current selection in a hierarchical display
* (On numeric keypad)	Expands everything under the current selection in a hierarchical display
+ (On numeric keypad)	Expands the current selection in a hierarchical display
Alt+– (hyphen)	Displays the selected child window's system menu, which includes the Restore, Move, Resize, Minimize, Maximize, and Close commands
Alt+double-click	Displays the Properties dialog box for the selected object when the object provides a Properties dialog box
Alt+↓	Opens a drop-down list box
Alt+Enter	Displays the Properties dialog box for the selected object when the object provides a Properties dialog box
Alt+F4	Quits the program that has focus
Alt+F6	Switches between windows of the same application (for example, between multiple documents opened in Excel)
Alt+space	Displays the main window's system menu, which includes the Restore, Move, Resize, Minimize, Maximize, and Close commands
Alt+Tab	Switches between open programs
Backspace	Switches to the parent folder when the application provides the required support
Context menu key	Displays the context menu for the selected object
Ctrl+A	Selects all items or objects in the current window
Ctrl+B	Bold
Ctrl+C	Copy
Ctrl+Esc	Displays the Start menu
Ctrl+F4	Closes the selected child window in an application that uses an MDI
Ctrl+I	Italic
Ctrl+Shift+Tab	Shifts to the previous window in an application that uses a Multiple Document Interface (MDI) or to the previous tab in a Properties dialog box
Ctrl+Tab	Shifts to the next window in an application that uses a Multiple Document Interface (MDI) or to the next tab in a Properties dialog box
Ctrl+U	Underline
Ctrl+V	Paste
Ctrl+Windows key+F	Displays the Search Results – Computers window, where you can perform searches for computers
Ctrl+Windows key+Tab	Changes the focus between the Start menu, Quick Launch toolbar, and System Tray
Ctrl+X	Cut
Ctrl+Z	Undo
Ctrl+Z	Undo the last command

Windows Server 2008 All-in-One Desk Reference For Dummies®

Shortcut	Description
F1	Help
F10	Activates the menu bar options
F2	Renames the selected object
F3	Finds all files or repeats the selected search
F4	Opens the Address drop-down list box
F5	Refreshes the displayed content
F6	Switches between panes in the active application when the application provides the required support (such as the support provided by Windows Explorer and other Windows Server 2008-specific applications)
Left Alt+Left Shift+Num Lock	Toggles MouseKeys on and off
Left Alt+Left Shift+Print Screen	Toggles high contrast on and off
← (On numeric keypad)	Collapses the current selection in a hierarchical display when the selection is expanded; otherwise, it places the cursor on the parent element
Num Lock key for five seconds	Toggles ToggleKeys on and off
→ (On numeric keypad)	Expands current selection in a hierarchical display when the selection is collapsed; otherwise, places the cursor on the next child element
Shift	Bypasses the start of a CD or the execution of applications in the Startup folder
Shift five times	Toggles StickyKeys on and off
Shift key for eight seconds	Toggles FilterKeys on and off
Shift+Delete	Deletes the selected object permanently (no Recycle Bin)
Shift+double-click	Runs the secondary default command (the second command on the context menu)
Shift+F1	Displays context-sensitive Help when the application provides the required support
Shift+F10	Displays the context menu for the selected object
Shift+right-click	Displays an alternative context menu for the selected object
Shift+Windows key+M	Displays all the windows you previously minimized
Windows key	Displays the Start menu
Windows key+Break key	Displays the System Properties dialog box
Windows key+D	Minimizes all windows so that you see the desktop
Windows key+E	Opens a copy of Windows Explorer
Windows key+F	Displays the Search Results window, where you can perform searches for files
Windows key+F1	Displays the Help and Support Center window no matter which application is active
Windows key+M	Minimizes all windows so that you see the desktop
Windows key+R	Displays the Run dialog box
Windows key+Tab	Selects the individual taskbar buttons without selecting the corresponding application

For Dummies: Bestselling Book Series for Beginners

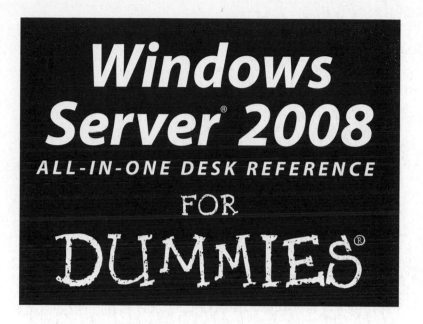

Windows Server® 2008
ALL-IN-ONE DESK REFERENCE
FOR
DUMMIES®

by John Paul Mueller

WILEY

Wiley Publishing, Inc.

Windows Server® 2008 All-in-One Desk Reference For Dummies®

Published by
Wiley Publishing, Inc.
111 River Street
Hoboken, NJ 07030-5774

www.wiley.com

Copyright © 2008 by Wiley Publishing, Inc., Indianapolis, Indiana

Published by Wiley Publishing, Inc., Indianapolis, Indiana

Published simultaneously in Canada

For general information on our other products and services, please contact our Customer Care Department within the U.S. at 800-762-2974, outside the U.S. at 317-572-3993, or fax 317-572-4002.

For technical support, please visit www.wiley.com/techsupport.

Wiley also publishes its books in a variety of electronic formats. Some content that appears in print may not be available in electronic books.

Library of Congress Control Number: 2008924084

ISBN: 978-0-470-18044-0

Manufactured in the United States of America

10 9 8 7 6 5 4 3 2 1

WILEY

About the Author

John Mueller is a freelance author and technical editor. He has writing in his blood, having produced 78 books and over 300 articles to date. The topics range from networking to artificial intelligence and from database management to heads-down programming. Some of his current books include a Windows power optimization book, a book on .NET security, and books on Amazon Web Services, Google Web Services, and eBay Web Services. His technical editing skills have helped over 52 authors refine the content of their manuscripts. John has provided technical editing services to both *Data Based Advisor* and *Coast Compute* magazines. He has also contributed articles to a number of magazines, including *CIO.com, DevSource, InformIT, Informant, DevX, SQL Server Professional, Visual C++ Developer, Hard Core Visual Basic, asp.netPRO, Software Test and Performance,* and *Visual Basic Developer.*

When John isn't working at the computer, you can find him in his workshop. He's an avid woodworker and candlemaker. On any given afternoon, you can find him working at a lathe or putting the finishing touches on a bookcase. He also likes making glycerin soap, which comes in handy for gift baskets. You can reach John on the Internet at JMueller@mwt.net. John is also setting up a Web site at http://www.mwt.net/~jmueller/; feel free to look and make suggestions on how he can improve it. Check out his weekly blog at http://www.amazon.com/gp/blog/id/AQOA2QP4X1YWP.

Dedication

This book is dedicated to the beauty of nature around my home and what it means to me. No, it has nothing to do with computers, but that's what makes nature so amazing. Snow falling, crisp winter days, trees in spring, tomatoes in the garden, falling leaves, deer and quail, and all of the other things that I might miss if I never left my desk to see them leave me awestruck at the diversity of our earth and the God who created it.

Author's Acknowledgments

Thanks to my wife, Rebecca, for working with me to get this book completed. I really don't know what I would have done without her help in researching and compiling some of the information that appears in this book. She also did a fine job of proofreading my rough draft.

Russ Mullen deserves thanks for his technical edit of this book. He greatly added to the accuracy and depth of the material that you see here. I really appreciate the time that he devoted to checking my procedures for accuracy. I also spent a good deal of time bouncing ideas off Russ as I wrote this book, which is a valuable aid to any author.

Matt Wagner, my agent, deserves credit for helping me get the contract in the first place and for taking care of all the details that most authors don't really consider. I always appreciate his assistance. It's good to know that someone wants to help.

A number of people read all or part of this book to help me refine the approach, test the procedures, and generally provide input that every reader wishes they could have. These unpaid volunteers helped in ways too numerous to mention here. I especially appreciate the efforts of Eva Beattie, who read the entire book and selflessly devoted herself to this project. I'd love to thank by name each person who wrote me with an idea, but there are simply too many.

Finally, I would like to thank Katie Feltman, Nicole Sholly, Rebecca Whitney, and the rest of the editorial and production staff for their assistance in bringing this book to print. It's always nice to work with such a great group of professionals.

Publisher's Acknowledgments

We're proud of this book; please send us your comments through our online registration form located at www.dummies.com/register/.

Some of the people who helped bring this book to market include the following:

Acquisitions, Editorial

Project Editor: Nicole Sholly

Sr. Acquisitions Editor: Katie Feltman

Copy Editor: Rebecca Whitney

Technical Editor: Russ Mullen

Editorial Manager: Kevin Kirschner

Editorial Assistant: Amanda Foxworth

Sr. Editorial Assistant: Cherie Case

Cartoons: Rich Tennant
(www.the5thwave.com)

Composition Services

Project Coordinator: Erin Smith

Layout and Graphics: Claudia Bell, Stacie Brooks, Melissa K. Jester, Christine Williams

Proofreader: Catie Kelly, Tricia Liebig

Indexer: WordCo Indexing Services

Publishing and Editorial for Technology Dummies

> **Richard Swadley,** Vice President and Executive Group Publisher

> **Andy Cummings,** Vice President and Publisher

Mary Bednarek, Executive Acquisitions Director

> **Mary C. Corder,** Editorial Director

Publishing for Consumer Dummies

> **Diane Graves Steele,** Vice President and Publisher

> **Joyce Pepple,** Acquisitions Director

Composition Services

> **Gerry Fahey,** Vice President of Production Services

> **Debbie Stailey,** Director of Composition Services

Table of Contents

Introduction

Microsoft is determined to make a better operating system, and the company accomplished that goal with Windows Server 2008. Reliability, performance (as long as you have the required hardware), and security are all improved. In fact, security takes a front seat with Windows Server 2008. In *Windows Server 2008 All-in-One Desk Reference For Dummies*, you discover just how profound these changes are. I found myself impressed by many of the new features that Microsoft added and feel that the company has done a good job of putting together this version of Windows.

You come across many things to like in Windows Server 2008. Of course, you find the usual new features. Anyone who hasn't seen IIS 7 should look because Microsoft finally provides a cleaner, easier-to-use interface with lots of good changes underneath. The new, managed version of IIS provides better performance because it doesn't load everything (whether you need it or not). In addition, you find significant security improvements, better reliability, and full support for ASP.NET. That's right! You can finally work with the developer to create a fully configurable managed Web application that can produce impressive results.

Security is a front-line consideration for Windows Server 2008. Microsoft attempts to secure everything in this version of Windows. For example, BitLocker encryption helps ensure that your data remains safe, even when someone sends an old computer to the dump without erasing the hard drive first. Reliance on User Account Control (UAC) ensures that even administrators can't accidentally thwart an organization's efforts to maintain a secure environment. Everything is also locked down better. No longer does Microsoft leave all the security doors open and hope that you lock them later. *Windows Server 2008 All-in-One Desk Reference For Dummies* makes a special effort to describe all the security changes.

Unfortunately, nothing comes free. Spend more than a little time with Windows Server 2008 and you'll find that some changes break applications and cause other problems. This book also helps you overcome any potential obstacles that can interfere with your Windows Server 2008 computing experience. The thing that impressed me most, however, was that the number of breaking changes is quite small, especially when you consider the considerable number of good changes you receive. Even so, *Windows Server 2008 All-in-One Desk Reference For Dummies* won't leave you in the lurch to figure out the small number of changes that break applications — this book is all about finding the solutions you need.

About This Book

Windows Server 2008 All-in-One Desk Reference For Dummies provides everything needed to perform common administration tasks with Windows Server 2008. No, you won't find arcane material in this book, because I took extra time to ensure that you have the material you need for everyday tasks. Everything from installation to figuring out why a user can't gain access to resources on the server appears in this book in considerable detail. You also see procedures for all common tasks — everything from setting up Internet Connection Sharing (ICS) to promoting your server to a domain controller.

Procedures and topical information are nice, but this book goes much further. Sometimes it's hard to know how to proceed with Windows Server 2008. This product contains so many features that you can easily become lost and install the wrong features for your needs. This book provides insights into when you need a feature and how best to use the feature to meet your organization's needs. Although I can't guess about every need you might have, you find common needs addressed in this book. For example, when you need to decide between installing a workgroup or a domain controller, you find the pros and cons of both setups in this book.

My main goal in writing this book is to provide you with useful tools and information. Windows Server 2008 is an amazing piece of software, despite what many people may think about it. Navigating the labyrinth of features requires a good tool, and *Windows Server 2008 All-in-One Desk Reference For Dummies* is the tool you need. In reading this book, you discover the good, the bad, the overlooked, the surprising, and everything else that makes Windows Server 2008 unique.

Conventions Used in This Book

I always try to show you the fastest way to accomplish any task. In many cases, this means using a menu command, such as Start⇨Programs⇨ Accessories⇨Windows Explorer. When working with dialog boxes, I tell you which tab to access first and then which feature to use on that tab.

Whenever possible, I use shortcut keys to help you access a command faster. In some cases I provide multiple methods for accessing a feature so that you can use the method that's most convenient at the time. For example, you can display the Task Manager by pressing Ctrl+Alt+Delete and clicking Task Manager on the Windows Security dialog box or by right-clicking the Taskbar and choosing Task Manager from the context menu.

This book also uses special type to emphasize some information. For example, entries that you need to type appear in **bold**. All code, Web site URLs, and on-screen messages appear in `monofont type`. Whenever I define a new word, you see that word in *italics*. Italics are also used to denote placeholders.

Because you use multiple applications when you're working with Windows Server 2008, I always point out when to move from one application to the next. When a chapter begins, I introduce the main topics for that chapter, which likely includes a combination of theory, usage suggestions, best practices, and procedures.

What You Should Read

Windows Server 2008 has a considerable array of new features, and Microsoft has changed the way many features work. Even experienced administrators will want to begin by reading Book I, Chapter 1 because it contains an overview of Windows Server 2008 features and tells you where to find details about these features in the book. You can find features by reviewing the table of contents and the index, but Book I, Chapter 1 provides a short description of each feature that helps you determine whether you need to read more information about that feature.

Anyone who hasn't performed a number of Windows installations in the past will definitely want to read the rest of Book I because it's easy to get lost without this information. Microsoft provides a number of new tools as part of the boot manager, so you want to read about these tools in case you experience an error during installation.

Everyone will want to read Book II, Chapter 1 next because it provides a description of every role and feature that Windows Server 2008 provides. If you don't know the difference between a role and a feature, this chapter explains it to you. Older versions of Windows don't include the concept of roles and features, so this information is exceptionally important even to the experienced administrator.

Where you go next depends on how you plan to use your server. Before you spend a lot of time configuring your server, however, you may want to read Book II, Chapter 4 and Book II, Chapter 5 to determine whether you want to create a workgroup or a domain. The choice may seem obvious, but Windows Server 2008 provides enough surprises that you want to make your decision based on the new functionality that Windows Server 2008 offers. In some cases, you can use a simpler workgroup configuration where you may have needed a domain controller in the past.

The names of many administrator tools are the same as in past versions of Windows. In some cases, the tools even look like those past versions. Even so, you want to review Book III, Chapter 1 next to ensure that you understand how the various administrator tools have changed. Some tools, such as those provided with IIS 7, are so different that everyone will want to read about them before installing the associated role or feature.

What You Don't Have to Read

The best way to approach this book is to read the overview of a topic first. When you find that you need additional information, proceed next to the sections that contain best practices and then to the procedures that describe how to work with the feature. In most cases, you don't gain anything of value by reading everything about the topic when you don't plan to use the target feature.

Most chapters contain some advanced material that will interest only some readers. In most cases, this material appears in sidebars or in separate sections. The introductory text tells you that the section contains advanced material. When you see an advanced-material warning, you can feel free to skip the entire section without missing anything valuable for less-skilled readers.

You can also skip any material marked with a Technical Stuff icon. This material is helpful, but you don't have to know it to work with Windows Server 2008. I include this material because I find it helpful in my administration efforts and hope that you will, too.

Foolish Assumptions

You might find it difficult to believe that I've assumed anything about you — after all, I haven't even met you! Although most assumptions are, indeed, foolish, I made these assumptions to provide a starting point for the book.

I'm assuming you've worked with Windows long enough to know how the keyboard and mouse work. You should also know how to use menus and other basic Windows features. If you haven't worked with Windows and Windows applications for a while, you may find some concepts in this book difficult to understand.

You must also have some level of administrative privileges. Many of the procedures and configuration tips in this book won't work without the proper rights. Windows may not even make the required feature visible to you.

It's important that you test new procedures and configuration tasks on a test server. Don't use a production server to perform the task the first time because even with the best instructions, you can make mistakes. I'm also assuming that you have the minimum hardware required to work with Windows Server 2008, that you have drivers and software compatible with Windows Server 2008, and that you perform proper maintenance (such as backups) on your server.

How This Book Is Organized

This book contains several minibooks. Each minibook demonstrates a particular Windows Server 2008 concept. In each minibook chapter, I discuss a particular topic and include examples of how to perform required configuration tasks.

Book 1: Installation and Setup

The first minibook contains everything you need to install Windows Server 2008 and perform a basic setup. This book describes the new Windows Server 2008 features and helps you understand why they're important. You also discover the requirements for working with various editions of Windows Server 2008 and even the new Windows version, Windows Server 2008 Server Core. You want to at least skim this minibook because Windows Server 2008 includes boot diagnostics and a new way of setting the boot settings, among other changes that could confuse even experienced administrators.

Book 11: Configuration

After you install and perform a basic setup of Windows Server 2008, you want to perform some configuration tasks. Unlike with previous versions of Windows, Microsoft doesn't assume anything about you. Consequently, when you start Windows Server 2008 the first time, you don't have any functionality — not even a file server. This minibook introduces you to the vast array of roles and features that Windows Server 2008 provides. You also see how to install and configure your hardware, work with the Control Panel, create workgroups, and promote your server to a domain controller.

Book 111: Administration

When you reach this minibook, your server is running and configured. This minibook describes the next step, which is to perform basic administration tasks. You first discover the tools found in the Administrative Tools folder of the Control Panel and then move on to setting group policies and configuring the registry. All these tasks are common to any Windows Server 2008 setup.

This minibook also provides information on working with Active Directory that you can use when working with a domain controller. A special chapter on performing standard maintenance tasks will help you keep your server at peak performance. Finally, this minibook contains some basic information about working at the command line. Although you can perform most administration tasks without ever seeing the command line, you still need to know about the command line to perform a few special tasks discussed in other places in this book.

Book IV: Networking

A server isn't much good if you can't use it to share resources with other computers, printers, users, and any other entity you can think of. This minibook provides some good theoretical information about how networks work, best practices you can use to ensure that your network works as intended, and procedures you can use to install required roles and features. You also find techniques you can use to maintain your network, discover errors when they exist, and verify that your network interacts with others safely.

Book V: Security

If you find Microsoft's security confusing, you're not alone. Just about every administrator finds Microsoft's security strategy confusing, which is why many servers lack proper security controls. This minibook helps clear away the confusion. You get good theoretical information on how security works, best practices for implementing security in your organization, a complete description of both standard and managed security, and procedures for working with both kinds of security. When you complete this minibook, you have the tools required to create a secure environment, and you understand what you're doing (no more confusion).

Book VI: Windows PowerShell

Let's face it: The command prompt provided with previous versions of Windows has been around since the days of DOS. Just in case you don't remember DOS, it was Microsoft's original cash cow in the days of the early computer. (You can see an interesting history of DOS at `http://www.computerhope.com/history/dos.htm`.) Windows PowerShell is the new command prompt. It provides better security, a complete scripting language, access to the .NET Framework (and all it provides), and better access to the operating system. In addition, Windows PowerShell comes with truly useful help.

This new command line is such a radical change from what has gone in the past that I decided to devote an entire minibook to the topic. What you can do with Windows PowerShell will amaze you and, more importantly, save you a lot of time. This minibook provides you with a helpful overview of Windows PowerShell, describes how to use it, provides some examples that you can use on your own server, and even describes how to implement your own scripts and Cmdlets.

Book VII: IIS

Forget everything you know about IIS of the past because IIS 7 has nothing in common with those earlier products. In fact, Microsoft should have come up with a different name for this application. IIS 7 is a new Web server with so many neat features that you'll want to install it even if you don't need a Web server, just to see how this new product works. Everything from the user interface to the underlying technology is different. The best part about IIS 7 is that it works better than any previous version of IIS. This is the must-have feature of Windows Server 2008! This minibook describes the new interface, tells you a little about the inner workings of IIS 7, and describes how to perform common configuration tasks.

Book VIII: Services

Services may not seem interesting, and they don't normally receive much coverage in books. Unfortunately, services are at the center of everything that Windows Server 2008 does. You can't even start the operating system without the proper services in place. This minibook seeks to right a wrong in the services coverage you may have seen in the past. Rather than make services a second-class citizen, this minibook helps you understand the true value of services to your server. In addition, you discover some interesting new best practices for services and even learn about a dirty secret concerning services and viruses. That's right: Viruses can hide on your server in the form of services, and this minibook tells you all about it.

Icons Used in This Book

As you read this book, you see icons in the margins that indicate material of interest (or not, as the case may be). This section briefly describes each icon used in this book.

Tips are nice because they help you save time or perform some task without a lot of extra work. The tips in this book are timesaving techniques or pointers to resources that you should try in order to get the maximum benefit from Windows Server 2008.

I don't want to sound like an angry parent or some kind of maniac, but you should avoid doing anything marked with a Warning icon. Otherwise, you could find that your server melts down and takes your data with it.

Whenever you see this icon, think *advanced* tip or technique. You might find these tidbits of useful information just too boring for words, or they could contain the solution that you need to get a program running. Skip these bits of information whenever you like.

If you don't get anything else out of a particular chapter or section, remember the material marked by this icon. This material usually contains an essential process or bit of material that you must know to work successfully with Windows Server 2008.

Where to Go from Here

It's time to start your Windows Server 2008 adventure! I recommend that everyone start with Book I, Chapter 1 because Windows Server 2008 contains so many new features that you need to know about to receive the full benefit of this product.

Part I

Installation and Setup

The 5th Wave · By Rich Tennant

"So, what's this breakthrough in virtualization you wanted to show me?"

Contents at a Glance

Chapter 1: An Overview of Windows Server 2008

Microsoft tries to improve each version of Windows Server. Most new versions offer improved reliability, performance, and security. They also include a wealth of new features. Windows Server 2008 is no different in this regard. You'll find that it includes many new capabilities, some of which you'll use today, some tomorrow, and some you'll never need. The only problem is figuring out what the new features are and whether you really do want them. This chapter provides an overview of Windows Server 2008 features and helps you understand their importance to your organization. Of course, you'll need to decide how these features answer your organization's needs.

You're probably expecting many of the new features. For example, Microsoft is introducing yet more new printing and storage management features. Depending on your hardware configuration, you may consider some of these features long overdue.

Windows Server 2008 also includes a new version of Internet Information Server (IIS) that's so different from what you used in the past that you might not even recognize it as the same product. (For this reason, you'll find an entire minibook, Book VII, dedicated to the topic.) Of course, Microsoft does something different with IIS in every version of Windows, so you probably expected this change in part.

The most radical change is the new Windows Server 2008 Core Services, which is a Windows without windows. That's right: All you get is a command prompt with this version of Windows. Fortunately, Microsoft has a good reason for creating this version of Windows Server 2008, and you should read about it in the "Understanding Windows Server 2008 Server Core" section of this chapter. With all these changes in mind, you find that the following sections help you prepare for the new Windows Server 2008 update.

An Overview of Major New Features in Windows Server 2008

Windows Server 2008 includes a host of new features, and I explore all of them somewhere in this book. However, some features warrant a special mention because they're more substantial than some of the tweaks that Microsoft usually makes. The following sections don't provide a complete list of every new feature you'll find in Windows Server 2008; rather, they provide an overview of the features that really make a difference.

BitLocker drive encryption

BitLocker, a new feature in Vista, has also made its way into Windows Server 2008. This particular feature has the potential to improve system security immeasurably when it comes to tampering. Because Windows encrypts the entire hard drive, anyone attempting to read the hard drive outside the server won't get very far. In addition, someone can't even start the server without the required information because the hard drive encryption keeps the data completely locked (including the Windows boot code) until you provide the required code.

This feature makes a lot more sense on a laptop or other machine that leaves your premises regularly. Someone leaving a laptop sitting in a public location won't then compromise all that precious data you worked so hard to accumulate. However, using BitLocker does mean that you don't have to worry as much about someone gaining access to company data when you perform an upgrade of the hardware. Even if your assistant forgets to wipe the hard drive, no one can get to the data at the recycling center. You'll find a complete discussion of this topic in the "Encrypting Your Hard Drive Using BitLocker" section of Book II, Chapter 2.

Enhanced Windows Firewall

Microsoft has been working hard to improve the security of Windows. One method it's employing is to make it harder for outsiders to gain entry to the server while making it easier for the network administrator to perform the required configuration. The Windows Firewall in Windows Server 2008 is considerably easier to use than in previous versions of Windows, and it provides additional functionality. The initial display says it all by providing you with a quick indicator of firewall status, as shown in Figure 1-1.

Windows Firewall is also considerably easier to configure than in the past. Click Change Settings and you'll see the dialog box shown in Figure 1-2. The General tab lets you turn the firewall on or off. You use the Exceptions tab to configure Windows Firewall to allow individual applications to communicate with the outside world. The Advanced tab lets you configure individual network connections. You'll find a complete discussion of this topic in the "Configuring the Windows Firewall" section of Book V, Chapter 4.

Figure 1-1:
The new firewall makes it easy to detect its current status.

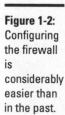

Figure 1-2:
Configuring the firewall is considerably easier than in the past.

Federated rights management

Windows Server 2008 includes a number of new roles, one of which is Active Directory Federation Services (AD FS). This feature lets an administrator define an access identity across a network even if the access occurs over the Internet. In addition, this feature relies on the role-based security built into the .NET Framework. Consequently, when someone logs in to the system, they have the rights defined by their role. A manager may have only manager rights when logging in from a local system — they may actually appear in the user role logging in from the Internet.

The AD FS role works across platforms, so it no longer matters if your network contains a mix of Windows, Linux, and Macintoshes. The administrator can also provide role-based authorization to Windows SharePoint Services (WSS) and Rights Management Services (RMS) for a federated partner. A new Group Policy feature lets the administrator limit federation service deployment. It's also possible to check on certificates by using the certificate-revocation-checking settings.

A second Windows Server 2008 role is Active Directory Rights Management Services (AD RMS). This service provides the means to attach usage rights to the data on your server. The rights to that data remain persistent no matter where someone moves it. You would use this feature to provide security for sensitive documents, such as financial reports.

The combination of AD FS and AD RMS form the Federated Rights Management feature. The use of these two server roles together provides a package of persistent, secure data management. You'll find a complete discussion of this topic in the "Configuring an Access Solution with Federated Rights Management" section of Book V, Chapter 2.

Improved failover clustering

Failover clustering is an important feature for a multiserver network, where one server can take over for another when a failure occurs. Of course, you have to have the right hardware and software to create a clustered network, which means having knowledge of precisely what Windows is looking for in a cluster. Unfortunately, it was very difficult to make this determination in the past. Microsoft has fixed this problem in Windows Server 2008 by providing validation tests you can use to ensure that your setup will work as a cluster. You now have access to node, network, and storage tests that determine whether a cluster will work and provide you with tips on resolving any potential issues.

After you determine that your hardware will work, you need to perform the setup. The new cluster software performs a configuration validation before it attempts to install the cluster. When the validation passes, the administrator can use a single-step setup process to install the cluster. Of course, you have to configure the cluster after the setup is complete, which is the most time-consuming part of the process. Fortunately, Microsoft also provides a migration tool now that makes it easy to copy or move an existing setup to another cluster.

Daily maintenance is a requirement for any clustered setup. The new software provides easy methods for adding and removing clustered resources as needed. It's also possible to perform management tasks from the command line (using standard cluster utilities) or with Windows Management Instrumentation (WMI). In fact, you can combine the two and use the command line WMIC tool to work with WMI at the command line.

The biggest improvement in failover cluster management is the way in which you can interact with hard drives. For example, you can now add a hard drive resource while the cluster is serving applications. The actual hard drive interactions are also improved. Microsoft has made changes that improve performance, such as not relying on SCSI hard drive resets. In addition, the software no longer leaves the hard drives in an unprotected state, which reduces the risk of corruption. You can even use a GUID Partition Table (GPT), as contrasted with the standard master boot record (MBT) partition, for increased hard drive space and reliability.

Internet Information Server (IIS) 7

Internet Information Server (IIS) 7 is so completely different from what has gone in the past that you probably won't recognize it. The interface is different, the configuration is different, and the internal workings are different. The reason for the massive change is that the old IIS just wasn't keeping up with the latest Web technologies. In addition, at least some of the problems that administrators experience with IIS are due to the older design. Figure 1-3 shows how IIS 7 differs.

The biggest difference you'll find in IIS 7 is that it places a new emphasis on administrators working with developers to create a Web solution. You can now configure ASP.NET applications in ways that you could only imagine in the past. Developers can also include new settings in applications to make the applications more responsive to enterprise needs.

Microsoft has also placed an emphasis on .NET development in IIS 7. Yes, you can still provide static content, and most scripted applications will work as well as they did before. However, you'll also notice that a considerable number of the settings shown in Figure 1-1 emphasize ASP.NET in one way or another. The result is that your ASP.NET applications will perform better than ever.

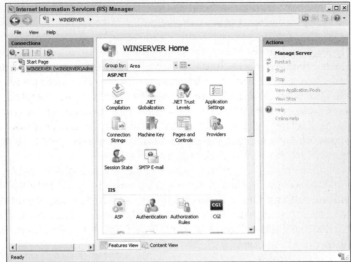

Figure 1-3:
IIS 7
provides a
significant
array of new
features.

IIS 7 includes a wealth of other changes that you'll find make your job easier. For example, all the configuration files are now based on XML instead of relying on an arcane database that's prone to corruption and other problems. You can configure IIS easily from the command prompt, from within the Internet Information Services (IIS) Manager, or by using a simple text editor to change the files directly.

The changes in IIS 7 are so significant that it's not possible to discuss them in any detail in one section of a book. Book VII tells you all about IIS 7 and how the changes it provides affect you.

Internet Protocol version 6 (IPv6)

The world is running out of Internet Protocol (IP) addresses because every device seems to require one these days. When IP version 4 (IPv4) originally appeared on the scene with 4,294,967,296 possible address combinations, the standards groups thought that no one could ever use that many addresses. (The original standard appears at `http://www.faqs.org/ rfcs/rfc791.html`.)

Unfortunately, the standards groups were wrong, and we now need IPv6, which provides a significantly larger address space of

```
3.4028236692093846346337460743177e+38
```

possible addresses. Of course, the standards groups also took this opportunity to improve performance, add support for mobile devices, and make IP more secure. You can discover more about the differences between the two versions of IP at `http://www.opus1.com/ipv6/whatisipv6.html`.

Just because Windows Server 2008 supports IPv6 doesn't mean that everyone supports it. Before you can gain the benefits of IPv6 on your own network, you need to update older machines to use it. Microsoft has no plans to support IPv6 on Windows 2000 or Windows 98 machines, as outlined in the FAQ at `http://www.microsoft.com/technet/network/ipv6/ipv6faq.mspx`. The same FAQ tells you how to install IPv6 support for Windows XP and Windows 2003. Fortunately, both Vista and Windows Server 2008 include IPv6 as part of their default configurations.

Adding IPv6 to your own network won't do anything for external connections. To gain the full benefits of IPv6, you must also encourage your Internet service provider (ISP) to upgrade, which may be more difficult than you think. At some point, you can expect IPv6 to become a reality across the Internet, but the wait may be a long one.

.NET Framework 3.0

The .NET Framework is now part of Windows when you install it. The main reason for this change from previous versions is that Microsoft is using the .NET Framework more and more within Windows applications. For example, you'll find that the Internet Information Services (IIS) Manager relies on the .NET Framework. In fact, you may very well find that many parts of Windows Server 2008 rely on the .NET Framework, which means that you have to get used to some new rules for setting security.

The .NET Framework 3.0 isn't much different from the .NET Framework 2.0 in many respects — at least, not in ways that you'd notice immediately. The main difference is that this new version of the .NET Framework provides access to some new features that Microsoft includes in both Vista and Windows Server 2008. These features appear as part of new foundations that Microsoft provides for making development easier, as shown in the following list (you can obtain a detailed, developer-level overview of this product at `http://msdn2.microsoft.com/en-us/library/ms687307.aspx`):

✦ **Windows Presentation Foundation (WPF):** Lets you create interesting graphics displays. In general, this feature applies only to client machines because it provides access to features such as the Aero Glass display in Vista. A server developer could possibly use this feature to provide graphs, charts, and other graphical elements in an application, but it's unlikely.

✦ **Windows Communication Foundation (WCF):** Provides access to Web services. A *Web service* is a special kind of external connection to resources on another machine. For example, an application on your server could request a database update from another server through a Web service.

In most cases, you won't even know that the application is using a Web service to perform its work, because everything happens in the background.

✦ **Windows Workflow Foundation (WF):** Provides a means of creating an application that relies on a workflow to perform a long-running task. *Workflow* is a new marketing term from Microsoft that essentially means performing a task using a specific process. Using this feature, a developer can create an application where activities must proceed in a specific order based on various conditions, such as the successful completion of another activity. Using workflows tends to reduce human error, which is the entire point of using this functionality.

✦ **Windows CardSpace:** Maintains user digital identity information in a secure environment that provides an ease of use equal to working with identity or credit cards. These virtual identity cards make it easier to gain access to resources online. In addition, because the user doesn't actually have to remember much, the digital identity can rely on complex passwords and other means of identifying the user to the server.

Generally speaking, all the existing .NET applications you have will run just fine under Windows Server 2008. About the only time you notice a change is if the application requires a new .NET Framework 3.0. In most cases, these changes appear only under the new operating systems. You'll find a discussion of how the .NET Framework affects security in the "Working with .NET Security" section of Book V, Chapter 1. The information in Book VI, Chapter 2 tells you how the .NET Framework interacts with applications.

Some people have begun teaching Windows XP as many Vista tricks as possible, and many of these new tricks require the .NET Framework 3.0. For example, Stardock's Object Desktop (http://www.stardock.com/products/ odnt/) can make your desktop look like Vista. A complete look at the various things you can do to Windows XP by adding the .NET Framework 3.0 is outside the scope of this book, but you can learn more at http://ezine articles.com/?Windows-XP-Revisited---Teaching-the-Faithful-Old-Dog-Some-New-Tricks&id=610102.

Network access protection (NAP) and enforcement

Every time other people access your network, they interact with it in ways that could cause contamination on their systems to also appear on your server. For example, if a laptop user gets a virus, your server will very likely get the virus too, unless you have a number of safeguards in place. Of course, most organizations today have all kinds of spam, virus, and other types of protection in place, even for internal contacts. The problem remains one of unhealthy clients — clients who lack the required updates or have some other fault that makes them a risky connection.

NAP provides the means to check the health of any client connecting to your network. When NAP detects an unhealthy client, it can act by limiting access until the client receives the necessary updates and configuration changes. In addition, you can specify a means of fixing the client to place it in a healthy state again. The bottom line is that your system gains another layer of protection from outside influences. You can learn more about NAP in the "Working with Network Access Protection (NAP)" section of Book V, Chapter 3.

New printer and storage options

Microsoft has provided a number of new printer and storage options in Windows Server 2008. Most of these features fall into the required upgrade category. For example, Microsoft really needed to provide a means to access devices from the Web, so it provided a means to do that. Administrators have complained for years about the management tools in Windows, so Microsoft has also addressed that requirement. The following list provides some details on these new features:

✦ **XML Paper Specification (XPS) Document Support:** XPS is a new open document format that Microsoft is promoting. It relies on XML to store document data so that you can theoretically retrieve the data even if the application used to create it no longer exists.

✦ **New print paths:** A *print path* defines the software and actions that the operating system uses to process a document and send printer-ready data to the printer for output. In the past, the only print path relies on the Graphics Device Interface (GDI) originally found in Windows 3.*x* (albeit modified with each version of Windows). Microsoft now provides the XPS Driver (XPSDrv) software to process XPS documents more efficiently than ever. This new print path includes a host of features, such as direct support for transparencies, but you have to have the WPF installed to get it (see the ".NET Framework 3.0" section of this chapter for details). You find a number of other useful additions to Windows Server 2008 in support of the XPS specification.

✦ **New printer driver model:** XPSDrv software represents a new way of outputting data. However, it also supports older output methodologies using the new print path. Even though XPSDrv software provides support for newer technologies, such as WPF, you can still use the driver without the .NET software. Of course, you won't get any of the new features, but you will gain the performance benefits.

✦ **Scalability improvements:** Normally, when a client makes a print request, the server performs all the required processing. Of course, placing the burden on the server reduces overall performance of the system for a very small gain in network performance. Windows Server 2008 now places the burden of printing on the client.

✦ **Web Services on Devices (WSD):** This new feature relies on a common framework to describe and manage network devices. The concept is the same as a Web service, where you can query the device for specific information by sending it an XML request. Because this technology hides the details of working with the device, it greatly simplifies device interaction and reduces the potential for error.

✦ **Improved print server management tools:** Anyone who has used Windows 2003 R2 has to appreciate the Print Management Console (PMC). Microsoft has improved this tool in Windows Server 2008. For example, you can now use PMC to migrate a printer from Windows 2000 or Windows 2003 to Windows Server 2008. The suite of tools also includes an improved Printer Installation Wizard that reduces the number of steps that an administrator must perform to detect and install a printer.

As you can see from the list, Microsoft has provided some necessary and some nice-to-have printer and storage features in Windows Server 2008. It's important to note that you still have to work pretty hard to obtain drivers for some hardware, but at least the support will be there after you find the drivers. You'll find a complete discussion of these improvements in Book II, Chapter 2.

Read-only domain controller (RODC)

Even though you consider your domain controller safe from external influences, someone could potentially break into it and make changes to your setup. In addition, errant applications can cause havoc to your system. These are just two of the reasons for having a read-only domain controller (RODC). Using an RODC makes Active Directory a read-only environment, which means that any changes that anyone makes are automatically overwritten with the original data. No changes occur to the server unless you make them.

The main reason to use an RODC is that you can't guarantee the physical security of the domain controller or have other concerns about the maintenance of server data. For example, the RODC could appear in a branch office where a less-skilled administrator performs application installation or other tasks. In most cases, this less-skilled administrator won't have access to any other server and won't appear as part of the Domain Administrators group.

Don't worry that an RODC automatically becomes outdated either. Unlike with a writeable domain controller, you can't make changes directly to Active Directory, but the server can make requests for data from a writeable domain controller. For example, when a user tries to authenticate against the domain controller the first time, the RODC sends the authentication request to a writeable domain controller. If the authentication is successful, the RODC can request a copy of the credentials from the writeable domain controller and store them locally.

Using an RODC improves security by making it impossible to write data to the local copy of Active Directory. However, it also provides benefits to the branch office. A special feature allows nonadministrators to gain a temporary increase in privileges to install applications and perform some limited management tasks so that an administrator doesn't have to continually run to the branch office. In addition, because the RODC provides a local cache of Active Directory data, users will notice a performance increase because the network doesn't continually experience the latency issues found in a standard wide area network (WAN).

Windows Deployment Services

Microsoft wants to make it easier for you to get its product on your machine, and Windows Deployment Services (WDS) is another in a long line of features designed to make that happen. The theory is that you use this new service to deploy Windows over a network on systems that have no operating systems installed. This feature originally appeared in Windows Server 2003 as a separate install, but you get it as part of Windows Server 2008. One especially nice addition is that you can perform the deployment without being physically present at the remote machine. You also find these features included with the new WDS in Windows Server 2008:

✦ **Enhanced Trivial File Transfer Protocol (TFTP) performance:** Windows Deployment Services relies on TFTP to download network boot programs and the Windows Preinstallation Environment (PE) images to the client. TFTP now includes a configurable windowing mechanism that reduces the number of packets that clients send, improving performance.

✦ **Diagnostics:** Windows Deployment Services now provides a considerable amount of information about the client install in the form of Crimson logs. You can use any Crimson-compatible product, such as Microsoft Office InfoPath, to process the logs and perform data mining on them.

✦ **Multicast deployment:** Using a multicast deployment technique lets the server install Windows on more than one client at a time using the same transmission thread. This approach improves overall performance and makes it possible to update the clients quickly. You have a choice between ScheduledCast (a task-based deployment where the client must join the session before the start of the download) or AutoCast (available at any time) deployment. Windows Server 2008 provides monitoring so that you can see how much of the multicast deployment the individual clients have received.

You can find an overview of this topic at `http://msdn2.microsoft.com/EN-US/library/aa967394.aspx`. As previously mentioned, WDS originally appeared as an update for Windows 2003, and you can find a step-by-step guide for using it in that environment at `http://technet2.microsoft.com/WindowsVista/en/library/9e197135-6711-4c20-bfad-fc80fc2151301033.mspx`. The Vista guide appears at `http://technet.microsoft.com/en-us/windowsvista/aa905118.aspx` and `http://technet.microsoft.com/en-us/windowsvista/aa905061.aspx`. As of this writing, the Windows Server 2008 version of the guide isn't complete, but you can find it at `http://technet2.microsoft.com/windowsserver2008/en/library/b279dfef-892e-4b12-bb6b-c250cf8c95f41033.mspx` and `http://www.microsoft.com/windowsserver2008/deployment/services.mspx`. Complete coverage of this topic is outside the scope of this book.

Considering the Windows Server 2008 Editions

Windows Server 2008 comes in a number of versions and a number of editions. A *version* affects functionality in some way. For example, if your server requires a 32-bit operating system, you use the 32-bit version of the product. Likewise, anyone with an Itanium processor will require the Itanium version of the product.

Windows Server 2008 breaks with tradition in that it also offers a Server Core version. This new lightweight version is Windows without the windows; you can read more about it in the "Understanding Windows Server 2008 Server Core" section of this chapter. The Server Core version comes in Standard, Enterprise, and Datacenter editions. You can't get Server Core in the Web or Storage Server editions because these editions require the use of a graphical interface and Server Core doesn't provide the required support.

The Itanium Processor version is specifically designed to run on the Itanium processor. Except for not supporting a 32-bit version (because this processor doesn't come in a 32-bit format), the features of the Itanium Processor version are much like those found in the Enterprise edition. Consequently, this chapter discusses the Itanium Processor version as part of the Enterprise edition.

An *edition* defines the feature set of a particular version of the operating system. The Standard edition offers a different feature set from the Enterprise edition. You can get both editions in 32-bit versions. Consequently, you need to know which version and which edition you want before you purchase Windows Server 2008. Although figuring out which version you want is relatively easy because you already know about your hardware, figuring out the edition is a lot harder because you have to consider features that you may not know about. The following sections describe each of the editions that Microsoft is offering for Windows Server 2008.

Memory considerations

The edition you choose determines how much memory the server will support. Sometimes, the memory limits aren't a problem. If you have a small company with basic needs, you'll never exceed the limits of even the 32-bit version of the Standard edition. However, if you're working in a large enterprise and your server is part of a server farm, you'll probably need something more robust than the Standard edition. Table 1-1 provides you with the memory limitations for various editions of Windows Server 2008.

Table 1-1	Memory Limits for the Windows Server 2008 Editions	
Edition	*32-bit Limit*	*64-bit Limit*
Standard	4 GB	32 GB
Enterprise	64 GB	2 TB
Datacenter	64 GB	2 TB
Itanium Processor	N/A	2 TB
Web	2 GB	32 GB
Storage Server	4 GB	32 GB

Other hardware considerations

You're going to need a relatively large hard drive for Windows Server 2008. Even though Microsoft says that you can get by with a 10 GB hard drive, that's hardly realistic. Even the 40 GB hard drive that Microsoft recommends is quite small for a Windows Server 2008 setup. A real setup is going to have as much hard drive space as you can afford. Because hard drives are inexpensive today, you should consider getting a 500 GB or larger hard drive and make sure to include a Redundant Array of Inexpensive Disks 1+0 or 0+1 setup in your plans, for reliability reasons. (You can read more about the various RAID levels at http://en.wikipedia.org/wiki/Standard_RAID_levels, http://www.pcguide.com/ref/hdd/perf/raid/levels/multLevel01-c.html, and http://www.acnc.com/04_01_0_1.html.)

In addition to having hard drive support, you must have a Video Graphics Array (VGA) display adapter (or better) capable of at least 800 x 600 resolution. It's important to remember that this is a server, not a workstation. In many cases, you won't need a super-high-resolution display adapter and monitor for a server. In fact, in some cases, it's detrimental to provide too much screen real estate because moving all those bits around will simply consume processing cycles you could use for some other task.

You normally need a mouse too when working with Windows Server 2008. It's possible to get by without a mouse by using hardware shortcuts, but you may find that some tasks become difficult when you go this route. As with the display adapter, you don't need a fancy mouse to work with the server.

Standard

The Standard edition provides functionality that the average work center, small business, or even medium-size business requires. You receive all the virtualization, enhanced Web, and new security features described in this book as part of the Standard edition. In addition, you'll see the tools described in this book for managing your server. The main limitations for the Standard edition are the number of processors (up to four processors in a single server) and the amount of memory you can use. (See the "Memory considerations" section of this chapter for details.)

Enterprise

The Enterprise edition provides functionality that a medium-size business will normally require for a centralized server. You also find this edition in larger businesses as part of a large workgroup. In addition to all the functionality that the Standard edition provides, the Enterprise edition also provides greater memory support and the ability to use more processors (up to eight processors in a single server). Additional features include clustering and hot-add memory support.

Datacenter

The Datacenter edition provides support for large businesses as part of the centralized server setup. It provides the maximum processor (up to 64 processors in a single server) and memory support allowed by Windows Server 2008. You receive, in addition to the features found in the Enterprise edition, improved clustering support and the ability to dynamically partition hardware. Additional features include hot-replace memory and hot-add/replace processor support.

Web

The Web edition is a special Windows Server 2008 setup for the sole purpose of supporting Web sites. Consequently, you won't find many of the features found in other editions in the Web edition. This edition focuses on .NET Framework, IIS 7, and ASP.NET support. The reason you want to get this edition for Web sites is that it uses resources more efficiently and helps you support Web sites with fewer resources. In addition, having fewer features translates into a more reliable and secure server because there are fewer ways in which the server can fail. The memory and processor limits for the Web edition are the same as for the Standard edition. You can't use the Web edition to create virtualized images.

Understanding Windows Server 2008 Server Core

Microsoft is doing something new with Windows Server 2008. You can now get Windows without windows. That's right — Windows Server 2008 Server Core starts with nothing more than a command prompt. It doesn't include much in the way of graphical tools for interaction, so you need to know the command line utilities to use it. In fact, you can't even shut down Windows Server 2008 Server Core without knowing the `Shutdown /r` utility command — it's much like going back to the command line interfaces of old, as shown in Figure 1-4.

Figure 1-4:
Using
Windows
Server 2008
Core
Services
requires
moving
back to the
old
command
line.

Of course, the big question is why Microsoft would produce such a project. The answers are numerous. One of the most important is resource usage. Microsoft recommends 2 GB of RAM for Windows Server 2008, but you can get by with 1 GB in Windows Server 2008 Server Core. The hard drive requirements are also less — you need only 10 GB for Windows Server 2008 Server Core, but Microsoft recommends 40 GB for Windows Server 2008. The GUI in Windows Server 2008 consumes a considerable amount of resources, so the Windows Server 2008 Server Core is a bargain from the resource usage perspective.

In addition, Windows Server 2008 Server Core can execute some tasks considerably faster because it doesn't have the overhead of a GUI to consider. Consequently, most applications perform better on Windows Server 2008 Server Core than they do when working with Windows Server 2008. Of course, you don't have a GUI to use for management tasks, which means that you have to type everything at a command prompt. Neither version of the product is demonstrably better — only better for a given set of tasks.

Microsoft has a couple of specific uses in mind for Windows Server 2008 Server Core, as described in the sections that follow. This book contains some additional overview information on Windows Server 2008 Server Core, but complete coverage of this version of Windows Server 2008 is outside the scope of the book. You can obtain detailed information about working with Windows Server 2008 Server Core in my book *Administering Windows Server 2008 Server Core* (Sybex, 2007).

Creating lightweight servers with specific roles

The initial, and probably most important, use of Windows Server 2008 Core Services is as a lightweight server — one that lacks all the usual Windows baggage. Some organizations don't require a server with every bell and whistle that Windows Server 2008 has to offer. A small organization may simply require a file or print server. Windows Server 2008 Server Core contains only the software required to create a server that has Active Directory (domain controller), Active Directory Lightweight Directory Services (AD LDS) (formerly known as Active Directory Application Mode), Domain Name System (DNS), Dynamic Host Configuration Protocol (DHCP), File, Media Services, or Print roles. Because Windows Server 2008 Server Core includes all these roles, smaller organizations may not need anything else.

In addition to creating standard roles, you can create an Internet Information Server (IIS) setup that performs a limited number of tasks. This IIS setup limits you to static and some scripted content. You won't be able to use any of the advanced IIS features, including ASP.NET, IIS Management Console version 7 (because it requires a graphical interface), IIS Management Service, IIS Legacy Snap-In or IIS Management Console version 6 for managing legacy Web sites, IIS FTP Management, and the Windows Activation Service. Consequently, this IIS setup probably won't meet the needs of larger organizations.

Working with Windows Server Virtualization (WSV)

Many organizations today need to run multiple servers to provide separation between groups of users. A server may serve specific roles. In some cases, the server may use a different operating system than Windows, such as Linux. It's important to note that the WSV won't ship with Windows Server 2008 Server Core, but you should see it by the second half of 2008. The Microsoft site at `http://www.microsoft.com/windowsserver system/virtualserver/techinfo/virtualization.mspx` also offers an overview of WSV.

Virtualization offers a number of benefits, including the ability to run multiple servers on a single piece of hardware. Using virtualization software also offers other benefits, such as being able to start a new copy of a fully functional server whenever necessary and gaining some level of both reliability and security over a single server on a single piece of hardware. The virtual server is more reliable and secure because it has an underlying operating system monitoring it. The underlying, or *host,* operating system isn't visible to the outside world, so no one can tamper with it. The host operating system is also invisible to a guest operating system (the virtual server), so no one can gain access to the host through the guest.

In the past, an organization had to purchase virtualization software separately for Windows, and the virtualization software ran on the GUI version of the product, which meant wasting resources. An administrator doesn't need a GUI to work, create, and manage virtual servers, because the administrative tasks occur on the server itself. Consequently, having a minimal environment in which to run the virtual server saves considerable resources and helps the virtual server run faster. Of course, the administrator must create the virtual servers by using commands at the host command prompt, but this is a small price to pay for all the benefits that the host provides.

Defining the Benefits of Windows Server Manager

The main purpose of Windows Server Manager is to help administrators install, configure, and manage server roles and features. A *server role* is a major part of the server, such as Active Directory support. A *server feature* is a less-inclusive part of the server that supports a server role, such as Failover Clustering. You can also use this utility to perform diagnostics and configuration and to manage storage, as shown in Figure 1-5. In many respects, Server Manager is a version of Computer Management (found in client Windows systems) for the server. You'll find a complete discussion of this topic in the "Using the Server Manager Console" section of Book II, Chapter 1.

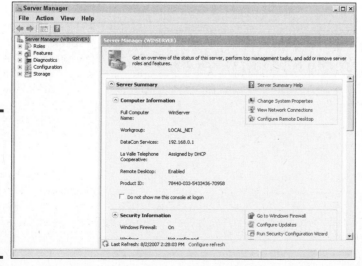

Figure 1-5:
Windows
Server
Manager
promises to
reduce
adminis-
trator
workload.

You can also perform tasks with Server Manager at the command line. The ServerMgrCmd utility provides access to all the Server Manager functionality. You can use this utility to automate most server configuration tasks.

Considering Windows PowerShell

Windows *PowerShell* is a new kind of command prompt based on .NET technology. If you worked with the Windows command prompt in the past, you already have a very good idea of how to use Windows PowerShell because they both fulfill some of the same purposes. Of course, the two text environments aren't precisely the same — Windows PowerShell overcomes some of the problems of the old command prompt by adding additional security and significantly enhancing your ability to create both batch files and scripts.

One of the features you'll like best about Windows PowerShell is the Help system. Figure 1-6 shows an example of what you'll see. No, Microsoft hasn't perfected Help just yet, but the help provided by Windows PowerShell is a vast improvement over the help provided at the command line. You still won't see many examples, but you will see consistent information about each command and even a list of related commands.

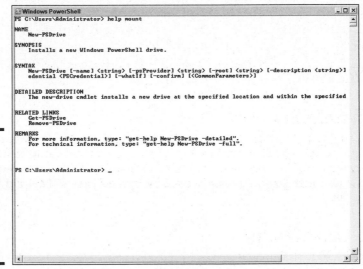

Figure 1-6: Windows PowerShell is a new command line based on .NET technology.

Microsoft makes a big deal about telling you every little thing that Windows PowerShell can do (and then forgetting a bunch of major things). It's true that Windows PowerShell can perform a vast number of tasks. However, the easy way to remember what Windows PowerShell can do is to think about the .NET Framework. Anything you can do with the .NET Framework, you can also do with Windows PowerShell (sometimes you need to perform some coding to access the functionality, but at least it's there). You'll find a complete discussion of this topic in Book VI.

Communicating with Terminal Services (TS)

Terminal Services (TS) is an essential part of any server setup because it's part of the software that lets you work from a remote location. Given that many people don't like to work in the same closet that holds the server (it's dark and stuffy in there), TS is an incredibly important application.

Windows Server 2008 improves on TS considerably. Microsoft's goal seems to be to provide remote access to applications and data in a way that makes it unnecessary to provide these features on the client in many cases. It's a nod to the centrally managed mainframe computer of days gone by. The following sections provide a brief description of the special TS features for Windows Server 2008. You'll find a complete discussion of this topic in the "Working with Terminal Server" section of Book IV, Chapter 3.

TS Easy Print

Most users need to print their data at some point. In the past, many printing solutions let the user print locally or remotely, but not both. TS Easy Print lets the user print the data from the TS RemoteApp application either locally or remotely. The server doesn't even have to have the printer driver installed as long as the printer driver is installed on the client machine. Group policies help administrators control which printers users can access and how they can use them.

TS Gateway

Users can still rely on the Remote Desktop application to create a connection to the server. The Remove Desktop application must support Remote Desktop Connection (RDC) 6.0 to receive full functionality, but otherwise the user doesn't notice any difference between Windows Server 2008 and any previous version of Windows.

TS RemoteApp

The TS RemoteApp feature makes it possible for the user to interact with TS without really knowing it. The user can start an application, as always, by double-clicking an icon or selecting an option on the Start menu. Of course, the user will see a delay in starting the application because a network can't react as fast as the local machine can, but the application otherwise will run as normal. As with a locally installed application, the user can also start a remote application by double-clicking an associated file.

In addition to the transparent methods of starting a remote application, the user can also choose to start the application by clicking a TS RemoteApp link on a Web site. This second method relies on the TS Web Access functionality described in the "TS Web Access" section of this chapter.

TS Session Broker

The TS Session Broker offers an alternative to Microsoft's Network Load Balancing for Terminal Services. (Read more about this product at `http://www.microsoft.com/technet/prodtechnol/windows2000serv/reskit/deploy/dgbm_win_dvec.mspx`.) This product works well for smaller server farms consisting of two to five servers. TS Server Broker automatically sends new requests to the least loaded server so that the caller always receives the best possible performance. The caller need not know anything about the server setup because TS Session Broker automatically addresses any needs in the background.

Interestingly enough, TS Session Broker also provides a modicum of fault tolerance. If a particular server in the server farm becomes unavailable, TS Session Broker automatically addresses any new requests to the least loaded server.

TS Web Access

The TS Web Access feature makes it possible to offer TS RemoteApp applications from a Web site. When the user clicks the TS RemoteApp link, TS starts a new session and creates a gateway to the application on the server. The TS Web Access feature also provides a default Web page that you can customize with your applications by using a Web Part. (A *Web Part* is a special Microsoft control for offering content — it relies on .NET technology to perform its job.)

Chapter 2: Using the Boot Diagnostics

In This Chapter

✓ Locating the boot diagnostics

✓ Starting Windows using a special boot mode

✓ Using tests to check memory performance

✓ Restoring Windows after a significant failure

✓ Relying on the command prompt to perform specific tasks

*O*ne of the problems in running an operating system when you try to perform diagnostics is that the operating system can get in the way of accomplishing the task. The operating system uses memory, so part of the memory is unavailable for testing. The operating system also locks parts of the hard drive and uses files on it, so you can't always access every file you need. The need to hide hardware access from view is also a problem because you don't know whether an error is the fault of the operating system or the hardware itself. In short, the operating system can cause false positives and prevent some types of testing. For many years, administrators have asked for an alternative to testing when the operating system is running, to overcome these and other problems. In fact, a thriving third-party software market has long supported testing that doesn't require you to start the operating system.

Third-party products still fill an important niche in your testing toolkit, so don't throw away any products you have now. However, a third-party product can't help you perform operating-system-specific tasks. That's where the boot diagnostics described in this chapter come into play. You use the boot diagnostics supplied with Windows Server 2008 to perform operating-system-specific tests. Of course, the most common testing need is checking memory for errors, and the new diagnostics can help you do just that. The memory tests may not provide the level of testing that a third-party product does, but they do provide enough information that you should be able to weed out the most common memory errors.

Many of the Windows diagnostics don't cover the same ground as the third-party utilities. For example, Windows has always had the Safe Mode booting feature, which lets you start Windows with fewer pieces of software installed. In many cases, Safe Mode booting lets you find errant drivers and other pieces of software quickly. Using Safe Mode with the command prompt lets you use command line utilities to perform analysis of your system and discover flaws that the operating system may ordinarily hide. Likewise, boot logging is a tool that helps you determine how the system is booting so that you can find errors in the actual boot sequence. Windows has always included support for a number of boot scenarios, and this chapter describes them all.

New to Windows Server 2008 is the ability to disable automatic restart after a failure. Many administrators complained that the automatic restart destroyed information they needed to learn more about a particular problem. In addition, you can also disable the requirement to use signed drivers. Microsoft has added this requirement to Windows Server 2008 to reduce the risk of loading a driver. However, you may find the need to use an unsigned driver to locate a particular problem.

Obtaining a third-party diagnostic

Microsoft has taken great strides in creating diagnostic tools for Windows Server 2008. However, these tools aren't complete. For example, the memory diagnostic finds common problems, but may not find unusual memory problems with your system. Of course, you could just yank all the memory out of your system and replace it, but you still wouldn't be sure of a complete fix.

You'll encounter a number of other difficult hardware problems that the Windows diagnostics don't even touch. For example, the Windows diagnostics don't tell you whether your hard drive is starting to fail. To obtain that kind of information, you need a third-party product that you can boot and use to test the hard drive without any interference from the operating system. Likewise, network interface cards (NICs) and ports can prove difficult to troubleshoot while the operating system is running. Many of these pieces of hardware require a third-party product in order to troubleshoot.

One thing that software can't do for you is tell you about the Power On Startup Test (POST) codes for your system. These codes can help you locate many hardware problems in seconds rather than

force you to spend hours testing them. A few high-end motherboards actually display the POST codes for you, but you normally need a third-party hardware solution, such as Millennium Solutions' PCI POST Diagnostic ReaderCard (http://www.millennium-solutions.co.uk/diagnostic-tool-pc-computer/post-probe-code-reader-card.html).

To obtain a detailed picture of your server hardware, you need a third-party product, such as Touchstone's CheckIt (http://www.touchstonesoftware.com/) and related products. As an alternative, you might want to check out PC Diag Inc.'s PC Diagnostics Software (http://www.pc-diagnostics.com/). This company also offers hardware-based solutions that can help you locate especially difficult problems. Some companies, such as Freshdevices' Fresh Diagnose (http://www.freshdevices.com/freshdiag.html), offer free products that lack significant depth but can get you started. The point is that you shouldn't have to guess the source of a particular hardware problem — you should be able to rely on tools to help you locate the precise cause.

Two final diagnostic features described in this chapter are the ability to restore a complete PC backup and access to the command prompt from the boot CD. Both of these features help you recover from devastating system failures quite quickly and without any interference from the operating system. This chapter provides you with an overview of how these features work. The "Performing a system backup" section of Book III, Chapter 5 tells you how to create the backup used for the restoration process. You can also find an alternative to using the boot restore option in the "Performing a system restore" section of Book III, Chapter 5.

Accessing the Boot Diagnostics

The method you use to access the boot diagnostics depends on which boot diagnostic you want to use and how you want to use it. You can access the memory diagnostic from either the boot CD or the boot menu. In fact, you can access the memory diagnostic from within Windows Server 2008 as well, but the effect is the same as accessing it from the boot menu, because the test restarts the machine.

When you access the memory diagnostic from the CD, you receive results that aren't affected by the operating system in any way. However, the results are harder to read because you don't see the results graphically. When you're using the boot menu approach, the diagnostic has to contend with having a small part of the operating system loaded, but you gain the advantage of seeing the results graphically, which can make them easier to understand. The "Performing a Memory Test" section of this chapter provides additional details on this topic.

Some diagnostics appear in one setting only. For example, you can't use any of the options described in the "Using a Special Boot Mode" section of this chapter when booting from the CD. This restriction makes sense because the CD installs the operating system, so, theoretically, the operating system isn't booting — the installation program is booting. Likewise, you don't see an option to perform a complete PC restore on the boot menu. You have to perform this task when the operating system isn't running, because the operating system always opens files on the hard drive. That's why you see the complete PC restore option when you boot the CD.

The command prompt is accessible in a number of ways (see the "Using the Command Prompt" section of this chapter, for details). It's the one boot diagnostic that you can access anywhere. Of course, the method you use to access the command prompt determines what you can do while there. Now that you have a better idea of how access affects the features and functionality of the diagnostics, it's time to discover how to access the features. The following sections describe how to start the diagnostics from either the boot CD or the boot menu.

Using the boot diagnostics during installation

Some administrators are under the impression that they use the boot diagnostics only after they successfully install Windows Server 2008. Actually, you can start using them immediately after the initial boot occurs, which is why this information appears in this chapter rather than later in the book. Windows Server 2008 incorporates a number of new features, including the use of signed drivers that could cause your installation to fail every time, even if it would normally succeed. You can see how to overcome this problem in the "Disabling driver signature enforcement" section of this chapter.

The diagnostics found in this chapter work any time after the initial software installation, and you can even use them before you begin the installation, when necessary. For example, you can open a command prompt after booting from the installation CD. You can perform many diagnostic and configuration tasks at the command prompt. You may decide to check the partition information by using the DiskPart utility. Diagnostics aren't just part of the package after you install Windows — they're also part of the package before and during installation.

Starting diagnostics from the boot CD

Starting diagnostics from the boot CD keeps the operating system out of the picture. What you're really starting is the specialized setup program, and it doesn't affect your system in any significant way. Your system must provide the means to boot from a CD. Fortunately, most modern systems provide this capability and you shouldn't experience any problems. The following steps get you started using this technique:

1. **Place the boot CD in the CD drive and restart the system.**

2. **Press Enter when you see the message to boot from a CD or DVD.**

The setup program tells you that it's installing some device drivers and other software. The drivers and other software represent the minimum required to interact with your system. For example, the setup program may have to install a driver to access the hard drive. When the initialization completes, you see the Install Windows dialog box, shown in Figure 2-1.

3. **Select the appropriate options in the Language to Install, Time and Currency Format, and Keyboard or Input Method fields. Click Next.**

The setup program displays a different set of options. The main option shown in Figure 2-2 is Install Now, but you don't want to install the operating system at this point. What you want to do is access the diagnostic programs. Look at the options in the lower-left corner of Figure 2-2.

4. **Click Repair Your Computer.**

You see a System Recovery Options dialog box.

5. **Select the partition that contains the copy of Windows you want to manage.**

Figure 2-1:
Choose the
language
and input
options for
using
Windows
Server 2008.

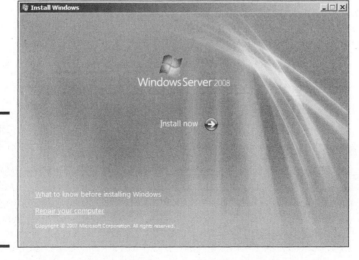

Figure 2-2:
The Install
Windows
options
include
access to
the repair
features.

6. **Click Load Drivers, if necessary, to load the drivers for your hard drive. Place the disk containing the required drivers in the disk drive and click OK.**

   You should need to perform this step only for older devices, such as Small Computer System Interface (SCSI) drives. Follow the vendor instructions to load the driver.

7. **Click Next.**

   You see a System Recovery Options dialog box containing three diagnostic options, as shown in Figure 2-3. See the "Performing a Windows Complete PC Restore" section of this chapter for instructions on using the Windows Complete PC Restore option. See the section "Performing a Memory Test" for instructions on using the Windows Memory Diagnostic Tool option. See the "Using the Command Prompt" section of this chapter for instructions on using the Command Prompt option.

Figure 2-3:
Choose the diagnostic features you want to use with Windows.

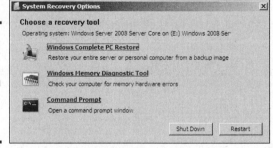

When you finish performing diagnostics, click Restart or Shutdown. The Shutdown option actually turns your system off unless it lacks the required functionality. The Restart option always restarts the system. Make sure you don't press Enter when you see the Boot from CD or DVD message when you want to start the system normally.

Starting diagnostics from the boot menu

Starting diagnostics from the boot menu is considerably simpler than starting them from the boot CD. In this case, you want to start your system normally. However, when you see the boot menu, press F8 to display the Advanced Boot Options menu. The "Using a Special Boot Mode" section of this chapter describes all these options.

You may want to start the memory diagnostic rather than use an advanced boot option. In this case, press Tab to access the Tools menu. The only selection in the current version of Windows is Windows Memory Diagnostic. Press Enter to choose this option. The "Performing a Memory Test" section of this chapter describes this option in detail.

Undocumented boot options

Sometimes, Microsoft provides an undocumented boot option. When you see the boot menu, you can highlight a boot option and press F10. The Boot Manager displays the Edit Boot Options screen, where you can edit the boot options for the selection you made. The main menu doesn't document this key, so Microsoft can change it at any time. In addition, be sure that you understand the boot options fully before making any changes. The default Windows Server 2008 option is /NOEXECUTE= OPTOUT, which means that all the Data Execution Prevention (DEP) options are on by default and you must explicitly disable them. DEP is a security measure that keeps viruses from performing certain kinds of attacks. You can read more about it at `http:// support.microsoft.com/kb/875352`.

Exercise care when changing boot options on your system. An incorrect setting can cause a lot of grief. That's the reason you want to know about this undocumented feature, so that you can modify the boot options when something goes wrong. Windows Server 2008 no longer uses the BOOT.INI file that you may have used in the past to make these changes. Instead, it uses the Boot Configuration Data (BCD) technique, so you can't make changes directly because these files are always locked when the operating system is running. Even though the storage method has changed, the options haven't. You can find a complete list of options at `http://www.microsoft.com/tech net/sysinternals/information/ bootini.mspx`.

Using a Special Boot Mode

Windows Server 2008 provides a number of special boot modes. Most of these modes are the same as those found in previous versions of Windows, but a few of them are new. All of these special boot modes help you diagnose problems with your system in a certain way. For example, you can get rid of all the non-essential device drivers to ensure that they aren't causing the boot problem. You can even boot with a command prompt to use command line utilities to check for certain problems. The following sections describe the various special boot modes that Windows Server 2008 provides.

Working with the Safe Mode options

Safe Mode is one of the oldest diagnostic features of Windows, and it's still one that you find used quite often to locate problems. The idea behind Safe Mode is that the operating system boots with the minimal number of features in place that are necessary for the operating system to work. By removing all the extraneous features, you can determine whether the operating system will even boot. If Windows doesn't boot in Safe Mode, you can more or less guarantee that something terrible has happened and it won't boot at all.

Safe Mode also makes it possible to fix problems. You can uninstall a problem device driver, service, or application in order to boot the system. It's also possible to undo registry changes that may have looked good at the time but ultimately caused Windows to stop booting properly. This mode normally lets you restore a backup that you made as long as the backup device has the proper drivers installed. In short, even though you don't want to use Safe Mode to perform any actual work, it can clear the way to fixing your system and making it possible to boot it again.

Windows actually provides three kinds of Safe Mode. Each form serves a specific purpose, so you should choose the form that best suits your needs. The following sections describe each form.

Using standard Safe Mode

Standard Safe Mode is the most restrictive form: None of the non-essential device drivers, services, or applications load. In fact, you can't even access the network. Your system becomes a standalone machine that really can't do much except recover from whatever problem has affected it. Use standard Safe Mode when you don't need network access but you do need to use the graphical interface to perform a task. For example, you can use this mode for the following tasks:

✦ Restore a backup.

✦ Perform a backup.

✦ Modify the registry.

✦ Uninstall an errant application, device driver, or service.

✦ Perform GUI-based diagnostics.

Using Safe Mode with Networking

The Safe Mode with Networking option performs the normal Safe Mode setup and then adds any drivers, services, and applications required to create a network connection. The resulting network connection lets you access other machines. Windows also restores any device mappings for your system so that you have access to hard drives on other systems. Whether you have access to printers depends on which drivers and application software the printer requires. You shouldn't count on using a printer in Safe Mode because Windows doesn't load the printer software in most cases.

Use the Safe Mode with Networking option when you need the extra capability that network support can provide and you're certain that the network isn't the cause of your problem. You may actually want to start the system in the standard Safe Mode first to ensure that it boots at all before you use this option. You can use this mode for the following tasks:

✦ Install an application, device driver, or service update using a file on a server.

✦ Connect to another machine to compare its setup with the local setup.

✦ Use a shared Internet connection to obtain updates online.

✦ Use a shared Internet connection to search for troubleshooting help, leave help messages on newsgroups, and search vendor Web sites for additional information.

✦ Troubleshoot a network connectivity problem in an environment free of other software.

✦ Make the troubled system available for collaborative troubleshooting.

You should never place a machine with questionable software on the network. In some cases, a virus, some adware, or another type of malicious software can load, even using the Safe Mode with Networking option. When a system has a potential infection, you should isolate it from the rest of the network and perform any required cleanup before you reattach it. Otherwise, you risk giving the same problem to other machines on the network.

Using Safe Mode with Command Prompt

The Safe Mode with Command Prompt option starts the system in Safe Mode but doesn't start the graphical user interface (GUI). What you see instead is a command prompt where you can run utilities to determine the system status.

You may not think that the command prompt has much to offer, but you can perform nearly any configuration task at the command prompt without GUI interference. In fact, Windows Server 2008 includes a new utility named Server ManagerCmd that makes it considerably easier to configure your server from the command prompt (see the "Using the ServerManagerCmd Utility" section of Book II, Chapter 1 for details on using this utility). You can use this mode for the following tasks:

✦ Verify that the graphical components aren't causing a system failure.

✦ Perform configuration tasks outside the GUI to determine whether the GUI is keeping them from completing normally.

✦ Use batch files or other character-based tools to troubleshoot your system faster than you can when using the GUI (this mode provides a significant performance boost).

The Safe Mode with Command Prompt option doesn't start most of the GUI features that you may have used in the past. You can't even use a mouse. Consequently, make sure you know how to perform tasks using just the keyboard. In addition, you don't have access to the Start menu. If you start in this mode, you need to type **Shutdown /s** and press Enter. This command shuts off the system completely. If you decide that you want to restart the computer instead, type **Shutdown /r** and press Enter.

When working at the command prompt, use the pipe symbol (|) followed by the More command to display long screens of Help information. For example, if you want to see all the help information for the Shutdown command, you type **Shutdown /? | More** and press Enter. Windows displays the Help information one screen at a time. You can find this and a wealth of other helpful information about the command line in my book *Windows Administration at the Command Line* (Sybex, 2007).

Enabling boot logging

Whenever you start your computer in Safe Mode, you'll notice a number of messages scrolling by that tell you which file Windows is loading. Unfortunately, the list can scroll by so fast that you can't read it. Knowing which file Windows is loading is important because loading the wrong file at the wrong time can prove fatal when getting the operating system to work. Selecting the Enable Boot Logging option slows the Windows loading process considerably because the operating system records everything it loads into the NTBtLog.TXT file, located in the %SystemRoot% folder (normally C:\Windows) of your system. You can open this file using Notepad and see a list of the files that Windows loads, as shown in Figure 2-4.

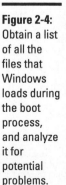

Figure 2-4: Obtain a list of all the files that Windows loads during the boot process, and analyze it for potential problems.

Of course, all those filenames may not mean much to you. Sure, you might recognize a few of them, but for the most part, the meaning isn't clear. Fortunately, you can check most of these filenames online. A simple Google search is enough to provide everything you need in most cases. You can also go to sites such as the ones in the following list to view information about the files:

✦ **Program Checker:** `http://www.programchecker.com/`

✦ **Spyware.net:** `http://www.fbmsoftware.com/spyware-net/`

✦ **Software Tips & Tricks:** `http://www.softwaretipsandtricks.com/necessary_files/`

✦ **eConsultant:** `http://www.econsultant.com/windows-tasks/`

You have another option for obtaining information about the individual files that load during the boot process. Because the `NTBtLog.TXT` file contains the full path to each of the files, you can quickly locate an individual file that Windows loaded. Right-click the file and choose Properties from the context menu. On the Digital Signature tab, you can verify the digital signature of the company that signed the file. The Details tab, shown in Figure 2-5, provides significant information about the file that you can use for verification purposes on the many Web sites that provide this information.

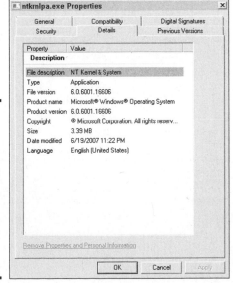

Figure 2-5:
Verify the digital signature and detailed information about the file as part of finding out more about it.

The whole point of working through the NTBtLog.TXT file is to ensure that you know what's loading and to look for potential sources of problems. In most cases, the log tells you when files haven't loaded and tells you about errors that Windows experienced during the boot process. Although it's perfectly normal to see some drivers fail to load, the failure of an essential driver is something you should note and fix.

Enabling low-resolution video

Choosing the Enable Low-Resolution Video (640 X 480) option places Windows in what most administrators know as Video Graphics Array (VGA) mode. When working in VGA mode, Windows doesn't load any of the standard video drivers, which may not seem like a very big deal. However, many Windows problems are the result of errant video drivers. Because the video drivers take part in every activity, they have a big effect on overall system operation, so this debugging mode is helpful in overcoming problems you have with video drivers.

In addition to handling errant video drivers, using VGA mode can help you reset your system to use a display mode that works with your monitor. For example, you may have your system set for a high-resolution mode and your monitor fails. If you obtain a lower-resolution monitor as a replacement, you may not be able to bring the system to full readiness because the monitor can't accept the input signal. Of course, your system may simply get set to the wrong resolution caused by an application or other error. It's good to know that you can get your display back by using this simple setting.

Using the last known good configuration

Many errors occur due to a configuration change. For example, you might install a new device driver and find that the system suddenly doesn't boot because of it. A new application can cause the system to fail as well. Any change that affects the boot sequence can cause problems that seem impossible to fix. The Last Known Good Configuration (Advanced) option lets you use the configuration from the last time that Windows booted successfully without using any of the special options. Think of it as an undo feature — you can reverse the effects of a single bad decision, configuration change, or installation.

Of course, this feature isn't the same as creating a system restore point. You can use it only to reverse changes that prevent the system from booting properly. A *system restore point* is an automatic or manual process of saving the system settings when a major system change occurs or simply because you want to save your system setup (always a good idea when you install a new application). Never count on the Last Known Good Configuration (Advanced) option as a replacement for creating a system restore point.

You can't undo the use of the Last Known Good Configuration (Advanced) option. Any changes that you reverse using this feature are gone, which makes this option a hammer when you really wanted a screwdriver. Always use this option with care. It's really a last-ditch effort to get your server going again when all other options have failed.

Using Directory Services Restore mode

Active Directory is a special kind of hierarchical database that stores system settings, computer information, user information, application configuration, and a wealth of other information and statistics about your network. In fact, Active Directory is the most important database on your server, and you find out more about it in Book III, Chapter 4. When this database becomes corrupted, it can prevent your server from booting because Windows can't find the settings it needs. Choosing the Directory Services Restore Mode option tells Windows to attempt to fix Active Directory — at least enough to let you boot the server. After you boot the server, you can restore any backup you have to fix the problem completely.

You find Active Directory used only on domain controllers (see Book II, Chapter 5 for details on working with domain controllers). If your server isn't a domain controller, it doesn't have Active Directory installed and you should never use this option with it. When you use the Directory Services Restore Mode option, Windows performs the following tasks:

1. **The server begins booting as if you had selected a Safe Mode option.**

2. **The server then performs a check of the hard drives on your system. This check looks for any problems with the hard drive that could have caused the Active Directory corruption (using the ChkDsk utility).**

3. **After a few more configuration tasks take place, you see a normal login screen. Supply your credentials and you see a Safe Mode screen — not the normal GUI.**

4. **Use any Active Directory GUI or command line tool to make repairs to Active Directory. You can also restore any backup you made (assuming the backup is available in Safe Mode).**

5. **After you finish the repairs, type** Shutdown /r **and press Enter at the command prompt or choose Start⇨Shutdown.**

   When you're working at the command line, Windows displays a You Are About to be Logged Off dialog box. After about a minute, the server reboots. When working with the GUI shutdown, you see the normal Shut Down Windows dialog box, where you can choose any of the standard shutdown options. You can use Windows Server 2008 in its normal mode at this point and continue any repairs you need to make to Active Directory.

Using debugging mode

Debugging mode is an option where Windows boots a special version of itself called the kernel debugger. A developer can use this mode to troubleshoot errant code either locally (when the system is generally working) or from a remote location. Unlike Remote Desktop or other methods of connecting remotely, debugging mode requires a serial connection, normally using COM2.

A description of the actual use of this mode is outside the scope of this book. This is a developer tool, and you probably won't want to use it unless you know how to work with the kernel debugger. Overall, this mode looks and acts like the standard display. The big difference is that the server runs considerably slower because the kernel debugger is in operation. The debugger contains a lot of extra code to make debugging possible. In addition, you may notice a number of oddities in how Windows works. For example, the mouse on my system failed to work for whatever reason (unexplained by a support request to Microsoft).

If you start this mode accidentally, log in as usual. When you see the command prompt, type **Shutdown /r** and press Enter. Windows displays a You Are About to be Logged Off dialog box. After about a minute, the server reboots.

Keyboard shortcuts to know about when your mouse fails

Many debugging modes can cause your mouse to fail. The mouse cursor appears as normal, but moving the mouse no longer moves the cursor. You can always try rebooting your system and entering debugging mode again, but sometimes this technique doesn't work. When you can't get the mouse to work, you need to use the keyboard exclusively.

Of course, most people know that you can move from field to field in an application by pressing the Tab key. Pressing Alt+Menu Letter accesses menu options in an application. Move between applications by pressing Alt+Tab. Move between options on the Taskbar using a combination of the Tab key (to move between major areas) and the arrow keys. Clear or check an option by pressing the spacebar. If you need to display a list of options in a list box or combo box, press Alt+Down Arrow, select the option you want, and then press Enter. Of course, you can press the Windows key to select the Taskbar and then the Context menu key (between the Windows key and the Ctrl key on the right side of the keyboard) to display context menus. You can find a host of additional keyboard shortcuts in the Microsoft Knowledge Base article at `http://support.microsoft.com/kb/126449`.

Disabling the automatic restart on system failure

Windows is set up to restart automatically during a major system failure. This behavior makes it possible to recover from a major failure without having to perform a hard boot (essentially pulling the plug or pressing the Reset button on the front of the system), which can cause damage to your hard drive. There are two problems with this feature:

✦ Windows can reboot before you can record all the information you need about the major failure.

✦ Some viruses rely on the reboot feature and can actually prevent you from using the server by causing the server to constantly crash.

The Disable Automatic Restart on System Failure prevents the Windows reboot feature from working. When the system crashes after you use this option, it remains unusable. Of course, using this feature also means that you can potentially damage the hard drive or lose data due to the error and the emergency shutdown method you'll need to use. Consequently, you should use this option only when other approaches have failed and you're certain you have a current system backup.

Disabling driver signature enforcement

Many of the virus, adware, security, and crash problems with Windows occur when someone installs a driver of dubious origin. The driver supposedly provides some special feature for Windows but in reality makes Windows unstable and can open doors for people of ill intent who want your system for themselves. Of course, Microsoft's solution is to lock down Windows so that you can use only signed drivers. A *signed driver* is one in which the driver creator uses a special digital signature to "sign" the driver software. You can examine this signature (as can Windows) to ensure that the driver is legitimate.

Windows 2008 doesn't load a driver that the vendor hasn't signed. Unfortunately, you'll find more unsigned than signed drivers on the market right now. Vendors haven't signed their drivers, for the most part, because the process is incredibly expensive and difficult. Many vendors see the new Windows 2008 feature as Microsoft's method of forcing them to spend money on something that they dispute as having value. Theoretically, someone can forge a signature, which means that the signing process isn't foolproof and may not actually make Windows more secure or reliable. Of course, the market will eventually decide whether Microsoft or the vendors are correct, but for now you have to worry about having signed drivers to use with Windows.

Sometimes, not having a signed driver can cause your system to boot incorrectly or not at all. The Disable Driver Signature Enforcement option lets you override Microsoft's decision to use only signed drivers. When you choose this option, Windows boots as it normally does. The only difference is that it doesn't check the drivers it loads for a signature. You may even notice that Windows starts faster. Of course, you're giving up a little extra reliability and security to use this feature — at least in theory.

You can't permanently disable the use of signed drivers in the 64-bit version of Windows Server 2008 — at least, not using any Microsoft-recognized technique. It's possible to disable the use of signed drivers in the 32-bit version by making a change in the global policy (more on this technique later in the section). A company named Linchpin Labs has a product called Atsiv (`http://www.linchpinlabs.com/resources/atsiv/usage-design.htm`), which lets you overcome this problem, even on 64-bit systems. Microsoft is fighting a very nasty war to prevent people from using the product. (They recently asked VeriSign to revoke the company's digital certificate and had the product declared malware; read more about this issue at `http://avantgo.computerworld.com.au/avantgo_story.php?id=69104626`.)

Using the boot method of permanently disabling signed driver checking

An undocumented method of disabling the signed driver requirement for both 32-bit and 64-bit versions of Windows Server 2008 is to use the BCDEdit utility to make a change to the boot configuration. Because this feature isn't documented, Microsoft could remove it at any time. This procedure isn't something that a novice administrator should attempt to do, but it's doable. The following steps describe the process:

1. **Choose Start⇨Programs⇨Accessories.**

You see the Accessories menu.

2. **Right-click Command Prompt and choose Run As Administrator from the context menu.**

Windows opens a command line with elevated privileges. You can tell that the privileges are elevated because the title bar states that this is the *administrator's* command prompt rather than a standard command prompt.

3. **Type** BCDEdit /Export C:\BCDBackup **and press Enter.**

BCDEdit displays the message This Operation Completed Successfully. This command saves a copy of your current boot configuration to the `C:\BCDBackup` file. Never change the boot configuration without making a backup.

4. **Type** BCDEdit /Set LoadOptions DDISABLE_INTEGRITY_CHECKS **and press Enter.**

BCDEdit displays the message This Operation Completed Successfully. Your command prompt should now look like the one shown in Figure 2-6.

Figure 2-6:
Modify the
boot options
for the
current
configur-
ation so that
Windows
doesn't
check driver
signing.

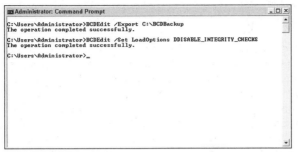

The Driver Disable (DDISABLE) option tells Windows not to check the signing of your drivers during the boot process. Be sure to type the BCDEdit command *precisely as shown.* The BCDEdit utility is very powerful and can cause your system not to boot when used incorrectly. If you make a mistake, you probably have to use the technique described in the "Using the Command Prompt" section of this chapter to open a command prompt using your boot CD and then fix the problem by using the BCDEdit / Import C:\BCDBackup command. This technique modifies only the current boot configuration. If your server has multiple boot partitions, you must make this change for each partition individually.

5. **Restart your system as normal to use the new configuration.**

Using the group policy method of permanently disabling signed driver checking

Users of the 32-bit version of Windows Server 2008 also have a documented and Microsoft-approved method of bypassing the signing requirement. (This technique will never work on the 64-bit version of the product.) In this case, you set a global policy that disables the requirement for the local machine (when made on the local machine) or the domain (when made on the domain controller). The following steps describe how to use the Global Policy Edit (GPEdit) console to perform this task.

1. **Choose Start⇨Run.**

You see the Run dialog box.

2. **Type GPEdit.MSC (for Group Policy Edit) in the Open field and click OK.**

Windows displays the Local Group Policy Editor window.

3. **Locate the `Local Computer Policy\User Configuration\ Administrative Templates\System\Driver Installation` folder.**

   You see the policies shown in Figure 2-7.

4. **Double-click the Code Signing for Device Drivers policy.**

   You see the Code Signing for Device Drivers Properties dialog box, shown in Figure 2-8.

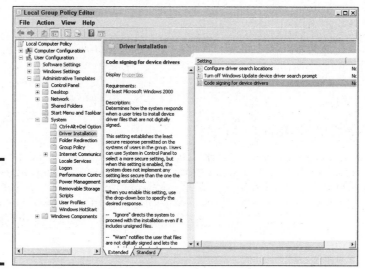

Figure 2-7:
A view of the driver installation policies for users.

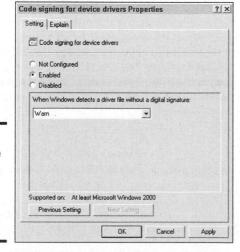

Figure 2-8:
Change the policy for installing unsigned drivers as needed.

5. **Select Enabled.**

6. **Choose Ignore (installs unsigned drivers without asking), Warn (displays a message asking whether you want to install the unsigned driver), or Block (disallows unsigned driver installation automatically) from the drop-down list.**

7. **Click OK.**

   The Local Group Policy Editor console sets the new policy for installing device drivers.

8. **Close the Local Group Policy Editor console.**

9. **Reboot the server.**

   Theoretically, the changes you made should take effect immediately after you log back in to the system. However, to make sure the policy takes effect for everyone, reboot the server.

Performing a Memory Test

Modern computers contain a significant amount of memory, and it isn't easy to know whether the memory is usable. Because of the way that Windows manages memory, it's impossible to test memory correctly in Windows. A few products on the market try, but the results are probably inaccurate or memory isn't fully tested. Windows Server 2008 comes with a new memory testing diagnostic that you can access from one of three locations:

✦ The Control Panel

✦ The boot menu

✦ The CD diagnostics

The diagnostic behaves about the same no matter where you access it. To access the memory diagnostic from within Windows, open the Control Panel and double-click the Memory Diagnostics Tool entry within the Administrative Tools folder. To start the diagnostic at the boot menu, press Tab, select the Windows Memory Diagnostic option from the Tools menu, and press OK. You can find the procedures for working with the CD in the "Starting diagnostics from the boot CD" section of this chapter.

When you start the Windows Memory Diagnostics tool from the CD or from within Windows, it displays a dialog box where you choose between performing the test immediately or waiting until the next time you boot the machine. Performing the test immediately is the preferred option when you suspect that your system is having memory problems. Starting the Windows Memory Diagnostic tool from the boot menu begins the test immediately.

If you're starting this test from the CD, don't boot from the CD when you want to run the test. The test starts when you attempt to boot from the hard drive. Of course, this means you have to have a bootable partition on the hard drive and that this isn't one of the diagnostics you can run exclusively from the CD. All you can do is start the test from the CD when you can't start it for whatever reason by using the boot menu or directly from Windows.

When the test begins, you see a Windows Memory Diagnostic Tool screen. Windows isn't booted at this point, so you can't do anything with the machine. You can use the default settings for most situations. However, if you want a faster or more comprehensive test, press F1 to enter the Windows Memory Diagnostics Tool – Options window, where you can set any of these options:

- ✦ **Test Mix:** Determine the tests that Windows runs on memory. Extended tests can help you locate even subtle memory problems, but they require a significant amount of time. Basic tests are good for a very quick check when you want to verify system health.

- ✦ **Cache:** Enable or disable the memory cache. The default setting uses the configuration found in the BIOS settings for your machine. In general, you want to use the Default setting unless you have a reason to suspect that the cache is damaged.

- ✦ **Pass Count:** Define the number of times that the test runs. The default setting of 2 finds most problems. You can miss intermittent problems by using a value of 1. The settings let you run the tests up to 99 times, which is probably overkill.

Configure the settings you want to use and then press F10. The Windows Memory Diagnostic Tool screen displays the test progress for you. When the test completes, your machine boots as normal. If you started the test from the boot menu or within Windows, you see in the notification area a status message from the Windows Memory Diagnostic tool. Click the associated Notification Area icon to remove the message. If you start the test using the CD, you don't see the status message when you boot Windows — you need to watch the test as it runs.

Performing a Windows Complete PC Restore

At some point, your server will experience some type of major hard drive failure and won't boot. Yes, you can keep track of the event log, configure the hard drive's Self-Monitoring, Analysis, and Reporting Technology (SMART) capability in the BIOS configuration, and run your own diagnostics, but sometimes the hard drive will fail even with all this vigilance in place. In addition, bad configurations, viruses, adware, and other issues can force you to perform a complete restore of your hard drive to get the system back into a usable state. Of course, all these issues point to the need for a good backup. The "Performing a system backup" section of Book III, Chapter 5 tells you more about this requirement.

Assuming that you have a good backup, you can restore it using either the standard approach or the Windows Complete PC Restore option of the System Recovery Options dialog box, shown in Figure 2-3. Starting the restoration by using the CD ensures that any virus, adware, or other type of nefarious software isn't running when you begin the restore, which tends to ensure that the restoration process will succeed as expected. In addition, you must use the CD approach when the hard drive fails completely.

When you first click Windows Complete PC Restore, the program searches your hard drive for a backup. If it doesn't find one, you see an error message telling you that the application can't find the backup. Click Cancel and you see the Restore Your Entire Computer from a Backup dialog box, shown in Figure 2-9. Insert the CD or DVD containing your backup into the drive and then click Next. At this point, this feature uses the same approach to restoring the system as the standard system restore. You can find out more about a standard system restore in the "Performing a system restore" section of Book III, Chapter 5.

This section should tell you something important about backups. Placing a backup on your local hard drive is always a bad idea because if the hard drive fails, you don't have any means to restore the backup. You can place the backup on a CD, DVD, removable drive, flash drive, network drive, or second drive in the same machine. The point is to store the backup in another location — one that a hard drive failure won't affect.

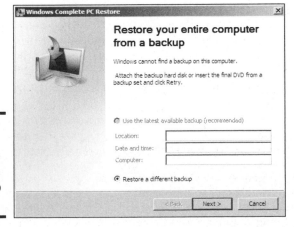

Figure 2-9:
Provide a
location for
the backup
you want to
use.

Restore your entire computer
from a backup

Windows cannot find a backup on this computer.

Attach the backup hard disk or insert the final DVD from a
backup set and click Retry.

○ Use the latest available backup (recommended)

Location:

Date and time:

Computer:

● Restore a different backup

< Back   Next >   Cancel

Using the Command Prompt

At one time, everyone worked at the command prompt. Windows didn't exist, and you used DOS or another character-based application that didn't have much (if anything) in the way of graphics. Many things have changed over the years, but the need for a character-based environment for managing your applications hasn't. You've already seen several examples of using the command line to perform tasks in this chapter, such as using BCDEdit to change the boot configuration of the machine.

As handy as the command prompt is, you really don't want to have to work without one. Fortunately, the command prompt is accessible in a number of forms. You should use the form that makes the most sense for the task you want to perform. Here are the three most common methods to access the command prompt:

✦ **Boot CD:** You can use the boot CD to open a command prompt that doesn't have any access to any operating system resources but can perform tasks without any operating system interference. This option is the best one to use for low-level tasks. For example, you use this option to replace operating system files or repartition the disk. However, this option may not be available when the hard drive relies on BitLocker encryption. Yes, you can still open the command prompt, but the BitLocker encryption prevents you from performing any useful tasks.

✦ **Boot menu:** Using the boot menu option provides a command prompt that includes some operating system functionality but none of the normal drivers. The system has booted into Safe Mode. All the normal paths are in place, but you may notice that some devices are unavailable. Use this option when you need to perform diagnostics with command line utilities. For example, you can verify that the system has specific services running. You can start or stop services to observe their effect on the system and determine whether a particular service is causing the system to fail.

✦ **Within Windows Server 2008:** When you open a command prompt from within Windows Server 2008, you normally have full access to the system features. In addition, you can work with all the normal drivers loaded and services running. Use this option when you want to perform configuration or other maintenance tasks at the command line. Be aware, however, that the operating system may actually hide some system features from view.

You may find other ways in which to open the command prompt. Some people have actually created a special boot disk that has the sole function of creating a command prompt. The idea is to create a command prompt in the manner that best reflects what you want to do. In general, adding more operating system features provides you with better management capability, and keeping the operating system out of the picture makes hardware diagnostics easier to perform.

Windows Server 2008 actually provides a number of levels of command prompt access. Because even administrators have fewer privileges, you generally need to elevate your privileges to use the command prompt, by right-clicking the Command Prompt entry in the Start menu and choosing Run As Administrator from the context menu. Otherwise, many of your commands will fail. Most command line utilities assume that you have administrator privileges and don't provide you with any hints about the lack of privileges when they fail to work.

The command prompt is an unforgiving place to work. You must be certain that you know what you're doing when you work there because the utilities at the command prompt are notorious for performing tasks in precisely the way you ask. Consequently, you need a good reference for using the commands. One of the easiest ways to learn about a particular utility is to type the name at the command prompt along with the /? (help) switch. For example, when you type Dir /? and press Enter at the command prompt, you can find out all about the Dir (directory) command. It's also possible to use one of many online resources, such as at the Microsoft Web site at http://www. microsoft.com/resources/documentation/windows/xp/all/prod docs/en-us/ntcmds.mspx, to find out more about commands. You can read more about using the command prompt in Book III, Chapter 6.

Chapter 3: Performing the Basic Installation

In This Chapter

✔ Defining the installation requirements

✔ Performing pre-installation checks

✔ Initiating a DVD installation

✔ Initiating a Windows installation

✔ Determining when to use an alternative installation technique

✔ Creating an initial configuration

*B*efore you can do anything with Windows Server 2008, you have to install it. Of course, you don't simply stick the installation media in the drive, turn the machine on, and hope for the best. A good installation requires planning and then proper execution in order to work. You must choose the version, processor platform, and edition that will work best for your needs. It's important to ensure that your hardware will actually work with the configuration you choose. You also have to decide how to perform the installation because a poor installation choice can produce unexpected results.

Microsoft provides a number of methods for installing Windows Server 2008. Most people choose to install Windows Server 2008 while actually sitting at the machine they're configuring. However, over the years Microsoft has worked to provide alternatives to the on-site installation. For example, you can potentially install Windows Server 2008 over a network. In addition, because every company has special needs, you can create your own specialized *slipstream* installation, in which you prepare special installation media that contains all the required setups for your organization so that the administrator doesn't need to interact with the system after the installation begins. Most companies also provide all current fixes with their slipstream installations.

If you do decide to sit in front of the machine and perform a manual installation, you still have a number of choices to make. First, you must consider how to perform the installation. You can insert the installation media into the drive and use it to boot a special version of Windows used for installation. As an alternative, you can perform the installation using a Windows-based setup, as you would when working with an application. Within these two manual installation techniques are many other choices you need to make.

After you perform the basic installation, you have to plan for the initial configuration. Planning for the initial configuration ensures that the server remains secure and has all the features you need, but nothing extra. This chapter helps you through the planning stages — Book I, Chapter 4 takes you through the actual configuration process. The important issue is not to cause problems for yourself by performing the basic installation correctly and then failing to plan for the configuration. (The result is that you normally have to reinstall the operating system again, to get the configuration right.)

An Overview of the Installation Prerequisites

Few administrators would attempt to perform an installation without first considering the installation requirements of the operating system. For example, you need to know that the system has enough memory and that the processor is fast enough to run the operating system. Of course, the hard drive has to have sufficient room to store the operating system, provide for features such as indexing, and still include enough room left over to hold any applications you want to run. Sometimes you need to consider the special features of your hardware, such as a Redundant Array of Inexpensive Disks (RAID) setup, as part of discovering whether the operating system will install.

The installation prerequisites include a number of other factors. The version (Server Core or GUI) of Windows Server 2008 that you choose makes a difference in the hardware requirements. The edition you choose also presents tradeoffs in flexibility and performance. A system that works fine with the Enterprise edition may not work at all with the Data Center edition, so you need to consider with care which version to purchase for your hardware. (See the "Considering the Windows Server 2008 Editions" section of Book I, Chapter 1 for details on the various editions.)

Sometimes you run into an unexpected issue. For example, you might have a 64-bit processor and want to use the 64-bit version of Windows. However, before you perform the installation, make sure that the 64-bit version of Windows Server 2008 provides the device driver support you need. Unlike the 32-bit version, where you can choose to install unsigned drivers, the 64-bit version requires that you install only signed drivers, and many vendors don't provide signed versions of their drivers (when they support 64-bit drivers at all).

It doesn't take long to figure out that you really need to examine Windows in depth before you begin the installation. You have many issues to consider before you can even make a purchasing decision, much less stick the media in the drive. With these needs in mind, the following sections examine some of the installation prerequisites you should consider.

Keeping an eye on enterprise needs

A book can only help you discover the requirements for an operating system; it can't help you assess the particular requirements of your company. For example, you don't find specific recommendations for setting up a custom application in this chapter because there isn't any way to obtain this information in advance. Consequently, you must consider the needs of your particular organization when reading this book. If you need to run Exchange Server 2007 with specialized applications, then you have to consider those specialized applications as part of your prerequisites planning.

Also consider the growth curve of your company. A company with a significant growth curve will require additional computing resources quickly, and a shortsighted server configuration won't do the job. Always plan for growth as part of the prerequisites. Unfortunately, this chapter can't help you predict growth — you need to discover this requirement on your own.

The skills of the members of your IT team are also important. Many organizations today have a mixed environment that can include Linux, Mac, or other platforms. Consider this mixed environment as part of the prerequisites because your Windows Server 2008 installation must work in this environment, and the staff you have today will manage the installation. A staff member who knows how to work in the 32-bit environment will likely have a large learning curve when moving to 64-bits.

Choosing a processor configuration

Windows Server 2008 comes in two processor configurations: 32-bit (also known as x86) and 64-bit (also known as x64). If you have a 64-bit processor installed in your system (and you probably do), it's tempting to choose the 64-bit processor immediately to gain the perceived benefits that 64-bits can provide. However, the question of whether to use the x86 or x64 version isn't always an easy one to answer because there are hidden pitfalls to consider.

Microsoft has also made it difficult to determine the benefits of 64-bit processing, which tends to make your decision considerably harder. The benefits of 64-bit processing always help the operating system, but you may not even notice these benefits in some cases because they're slight when compared to the applications you run. To obtain the benefits of 64-bit processing, you must have 64-bit applications, so using a 64-bit operating system may not yield many benefits.

To make things more interesting, the 64-bit version of Windows requires signed drivers. This requirement can actually cause three problems. First, many vendors don't have 64-bit versions of their drivers, so you don't have a driver to install. In the past, resource administrators used third-party equivalents to overcome this deficiency, but these third-party products may not run in Windows Server 2008. Second, the vendors who provide 64-bit drivers may not have signed them. Because the 64-bit version of Windows Server 2008 doesn't allow you to use unsigned drivers and there isn't a way to get around this requirement, unsigned drivers are akin to having no drivers at all. Third, when a vendor does offer a signed 64-bit driver, you may find that the performance of that driver is lacking and that it doesn't work as well as the 32-bit equivalent because it has received less testing. Providing a signature for a driver tells you only who produced the driver — it doesn't signify that the driver has great performance and runs error-free.

Before you decide to use the 32-bit version of Windows Server 2008, you need to know that Microsoft has embarked on a campaign to move certain of its applications to the 64-bit environment. For example, when you read the requirements for Exchange Server 2007 carefully (see `http://www.microsoft.com/technet/prodtechnol/exchange/2007/evaluate/sysreqs.mspx` for details), you notice that you must run this product on a 64-bit version of Windows. Yes, the tools run on a 32-bit system, but the product itself doesn't. As part of your evaluation, you must consider the current and future support plans of the application vendors you rely on for server applications.

You may encounter a situation where you don't have a good processor decision to make. Every potential solution is equally bad. Although this book doesn't discuss the process, you may find that you have to run multiple copies of Windows Server 2008 to meet all your needs. Some organizations meet this need by purchasing multiple physical servers and installing Windows Server 2008 on each one. However, one of the reasons that Microsoft has provided Server Core is its ability to run multiple copies of Windows Server 2008 on one physical server by using a virtual server setup. In fact, Microsoft plans to release specialized virtual server software for Server Core sometime after it releases the actual product. (The current rumor says that the virtualization software will appear about 180 days after the Windows Server 2008 release.) You can read more about using virtual servers to solve potential processor problems at `http://blogs.dirteam.com/blogs/sanderberkouwer/archive/2007/07/09/virtual-server-core.aspx`. It's also important to read the administrator's guide at `http://www.microsoft.com/technet/prodtechnol/virtualserver/2005/proddocs/default.mspx`.

The important issue to consider about virtual servers is that they don't use resources as efficiently as physical servers. The underlying operating system uses resources, as does the virtual server software and each of the operating systems is used as a virtual server. A virtual server setup provides flexibility. It can also improve security by reducing the attack surface of your system and can make your setup more reliable. However, the cost in resources of using a virtual server setup is considerable.

Considering the version and edition requirements

The "Considering the Windows Server 2008 Editions" section of Book I, Chapter 1 tells you about the differences between the Windows Server 2008 versions and editions. The features that each version and edition provide require resources. For example, when you install Internet Information Server (IIS) 7 on your system, the system requires additional resources to support IIS 7. Every feature, in fact, consumes resources, and you need to plan for those resources as part of the installation prerequisites. Load your server too heavily and it can't respond to user requests — and your company will lose money on the installation.

Choosing the right version and edition is important because different version-and-edition combinations provide you with a different mix of features and performance. A Server Core installation can provide an excellent setup as long as you need it to perform only certain roles, including the following:

✦ Active Directory (domain controller)

✦ Active Directory Lightweight Directory Services (AD LDS), formerly known as Active Directory Application Mode

✦ Domain Name System (DNS)

✦ Dynamic Host Configuration Protocol (DHCP)

✦ File server

✦ Media Services

✦ Internet Information Services without ASP.NET support, but with both scripted (such as ASP) and static content support

✦ Print server

The problem with Server Core is that it also lacks functionality, so it may not be a good choice. An Enterprise edition of Server Core doesn't have the same functionality as an Enterprise edition of the full (GUI) version. In fact, it's missing these features:

✦ ASP.NET

✦ The IIS Management Console version 7 (because it requires a graphical interface)

✦ The IIS Management Service

✦ The IIS Legacy Snap-In or IIS Management Console version 6, for managing legacy Web sites

✦ IIS FTP management

✦ The Windows Activation Service

Because of the limitations that Server Core has, you can't use it for roles such as an application server, even though you might be using the Enterprise edition of the product. Offsetting this lack of functionality is that Server Core uses resources very efficiently and runs considerably faster than a comparable full-version installation of the product. Consequently, you must consider not only the edition you want but the version as well. The tradeoffs between versions and editions are considerable, and they affect how you install the product and what you can expect from the product later.

Understanding the minimum requirements

Every piece of software you install on your system uses resources, including the operating system. The three most important resources are memory, processing cycles, and hard drive space. You can use Windows Server 2008 without a mouse — it might not be very easy sometimes, but it's possible. Theoretically, you need a DVD drive to work with Windows Server 2008, but you can even get around this requirement by booting from a network drive and installing from it. However, you can't hope to run the operating system without three essential resources — it may not even start.

Of course, installing a server operating system and then just staring at it isn't very exciting. You'll want to install databases and applications on your server and use them to perform useful work. Consequently, you can't install Windows Server 2008 on a machine with the minimum requirements and hope that it will do something useful. In addition to providing the minimum requirements for the operating system, you must also consider the requirements for each application you want to use. The following sections examine the three essential resources you need for Windows Server 2008.

Memory

Microsoft will try to tell you that the minimum memory requirement for Windows Server 2008 is 512 MB. Theoretically, you can run Server Core with that amount of memory, but it doesn't perform many tasks. As a test, I tried this configuration on an older system and was able to install all the non-Active Directory roles. Active Directory really does require more memory. The full version of Windows Server 2008 doesn't run with 512 MB — at least not well enough to do any useful work, based on some basic tests.

The Microsoft-recommended amount of memory is 1 GB, and the optimal amount is 2 GB, which is less than many people have on their Vista work stations. A more realistic amount of memory for the full installation of Windows Server 2008 is 4 GB for a small business, and you'll want to move up from there as the size of your business increases. A small business that wants to save money may very well want to look at Server Core rather than obtain the hardware for the full installation; but as previously mentioned, Server Core doesn't work as an application server.

At 4 GB, your server will have enough memory to perform basic tasks, such as serve files, perform printing, act as a DNS or DHCP server, and even support a basic Active Directory setup. You may still find that some applications don't run. A 4 GB setup will probably support a small SQL Server installation, as long as you don't install too many other operating system features. The 4 GB level is really just a good starting point for a serious server setup. Unfortunately, 4 GB of memory is also the maximum amount that you can install for the 32-bit version of the Standard edition.

Always consider the installation requirements for your applications before you begin installing the operating system. For example, an Exchange Server 2007 installation requires 2 GB of memory and a minimum of 1.2 GB of hard drive space. (See the specifications at `http://www.microsoft.com/ technet/prodtechnol/exchange/2007/evaluate/sysreqs.mspx` for details.) In addition, Exchange Server 2007 requires a 64-bit version of Windows, so you're limited on which versions of Windows Server 2008 you can use. Most vendors make the memory requirements for their applications easily accessible because they want you to have a good install. However, you should always consider the minimum requirements as bare minimums and perhaps hardly usable. It's important to keep all the application installation requirements in mind as you work on your system.

Processor

Windows Server 2008 uses a lot of processing power to present the GUI. No, it doesn't have the fancy Areo Glass functionality of Vista, but the GUI still chews up a lot of processing cycles. Consequently, you need to have some serious processing power to accomplish tasks. In this case, Microsoft recommends a 1 GHz processor as a minimum, which definitely doesn't work unless you're using Server Core. The 2 GHz recommended level works as long as you don't expect the server to perform quickly. Microsoft recommends a 3 GHz processor for optimal performance.

During information testing, I found that a 1 GHz system runs Server Core adequately enough to provide basic services and even support Active Directory. (As with the memory test, this test relied on an older system.) It doesn't provide these services quickly — after about five users, you see even Server Core start to slow down significantly. The minimum full installation processor configuration you should consider for a small business with application server, domain controller, and database needs is a dual Xeon processor setup. The test system for this book relied on a dual processor setup running at 2 GHz (effectively giving the test system four processors).

Hard drive

Hard drive space is cheap. In fact, it's the least expensive component of your server, so this is one area where you don't have a good reason to cut corners. Get enough hard drive space for Windows Server 2008, your applications, data storage, a large paging file, and plenty left over for later expansion. (Computers with more than 16 GB of memory require more disk space for the paging file, hibernation, and memory dump files.)

Microsoft's recommendation of 8 GB for Server Core or a full installation doesn't work with today's application requirements, and no one should seriously consider it. The recommended amount of drive space is 40 GB for a full installation or 8 GB for Server Core (because Server Core requires so much less hard drive space). Even the optimal size of 80 GB for a full installation is probably too small. A more realistic setup for a small business has at least 250 GB. As your business becomes larger, you need to increase the amount of available hard drive space.

It's also important to consider the complexity of the hardware you use when estimating your resource requirements. For example, a Redundant Array of Inexpensive Disks (RAID) setup will cost you considerably more hard drive space than a standard setup does. Mirrored drive setups require twice as much space because everything appears twice. You should also consider the requirements of Storage Area Networks (SANs) and other storage technologies that your system uses.

Deciding between a DVD and Windows installation

The kind of installation you perform also affects some of your pre-installation decisions. Of course, you should always make a backup of your system before you begin any installation task. However, when you plan to reformat your hard drive, it doesn't hurt to export as many settings as you can to make the installation of the new operating system easier. The following sections provide insights into when you should choose one installation technique over another.

Installing on a new system

If you have a new system, or have upgraded the hard drive to something bigger, your only real choice is a DVD setup unless you want to rely on one of the more exotic solutions, such as a network installation. A manual DVD installation has the advantage of letting you configure Windows Server 2008 specifically for a particular system, but it can prove time consuming. Booting from the installation media has the advantage of ensuring that your system memory is as clean as possible. Having a clean environment greatly improves the chances of a successful installation and reduces the risk of encountering odd installation problems. The cleaner the environment in which you work when installing Windows, the better.

Understanding the benefits of using the Windows installation technique

The problem for any administrator who currently has the hardware to run Windows Server 2008 is figuring out which installation type to use. The one reason to perform a Windows installation is the need to keep the existing settings for your server. If you can install Windows Server 2008 right over the existing setup, you'll find that you don't have to work nearly as hard to get Windows Server 2008 ready for use. In fact, if your setup is simple enough, you may be ready to go immediately after you perform the installation. Having only one really good reason to use the Windows installation may not seem like much. However, considering that a complete installation can occupy the better part of a week (after you get your applications installed as well), it's a significant reason and you should consider it whenever possible.

Installing over an existing Windows installation may seem like a perfect solution for an administrator who is already short on time. If you've recently reinstalled Windows, you'll probably find that the environment is clean, as is the registry. You don't have remnants of other products around to confuse the installation program and cause you woe after the installation. However, when your system has run for a long time on the same installation or you've added and removed numerous applications, the environment is no longer clean and your registry probably contains many entries that can cause problems down the road. If you find yourself in this situation, then you should probably consider performing a DVD installation rather than an installation that begins with Windows.

Update installations, those commonly performed using the Windows installation method, generally require more time to complete than a DVD installation. The reason for the time difference is that the installation program must spend more time saving settings and working around configuration issues when performing an update. Make sure to set aside enough time to allow the manual installation to complete. The additional installation time is more than offset by the time you save configuring the system, so don't consider the additional time as a negative when it comes to using the Windows installation technique.

When you install over an existing Windows installation, you get one more benefit: The installation program can go online and check for updates before it begins the installation process, which means that your installation will have all required patches and fixes from the outset. When using the DVD installation method, you're stuck with whichever version of Windows Server 2008 appears on the media, which means that your server could be subject to infection immediately after installation. (At one time, a virus actually attacked new servers before they could get to Windows Update to install required fixes and patches.)

Understanding the benefits of using the DVD installation technique

There are a number of other scenarios where you must use a DVD installation. For example, if you currently have a 32-bit installation and need to install the 64-bit version of the product, you must perform a DVD installation. Because Microsoft is making a move toward 64-bit applications, now may be a good time to get rid of that old 32-bit installation and upgrade to 64 bits of power. Of course, you have to be sure that your hardware will work with a 64-bit setup and that you have all the required signed 64-bit drivers before you take this step.

Another DVD-only installation scenario is one in which you have the hard drive partitioned to provide a small boot drive and a larger data drive. When the boot partition is smaller than 10 GB, you should consider performing a DVD installation because the boot drive is barely adequate to hold Windows Server 2008.

Windows Server 2008 also spends more time checking your system for potential problems than did previous versions of Windows. It may detect an issue where you must perform a DVD installation. Someone will almost certainly put up a Web site that provides techniques for overcoming this "limitation," but you're better off performing the DVD installation. Windows Server 2008 really does do a better job than previous versions of Windows in detecting potential problems and helping you overcome them. If you try to overcome the installation program's safety features, the only one who loses is you — circumventing the safety features costs you time and potentially money somewhere along the way.

Considering Pre-Installation Requirements

Before you perform any server setup, including those exotic options that your organization may use, you need to perform some pre-installation steps. The following list describes some essential tasks you must perform. Make sure to also check the README file that comes with the installation media, and check Microsoft's Web site (`http://www.microsoft.com/windows/default.mspx`) before you perform the installation. Microsoft generally provides a lot of guidance on pre-installation steps because completing these steps greatly reduces the probability of a failed installation:

✦ **Perform application compatibility checks:** Because of the additional security that Windows Server 2008 provides, you may find that old applications don't work at all. You must check for compatibility problems before you perform the installation because Microsoft doesn't provide any means of reversing an installation after you complete it. You can learn more about application compatibility checks at `http://tech net.microsoft.com/en-us/windowsvista/aa905066.aspx`.

✦ **Disconnect the uninterruptible power supply (UPS):** The installation program normally looks for any devices connected to the ports and immediately installs support for them. Unfortunately, the installation program often confuses UPSs for other devices, especially when you connect them to the serial port (where the installation program insists that it has detected a mouse). Forgetting this step isn't fatal — the installation will probably work fine, but you have less fix up work to do later if you disconnect the UPS now.

✦ **Perform a complete system backup:** Because your server affects every part of the network, it's usually a good idea to perform a complete backup. Creating a complete backup, including all the workstations, is a good idea because you never know when something will go wrong. It's better to have a complete backup of everything now than to wish for one later. Make sure your backup includes boot, system partition, and system state data, to make it easier to restore the backup later.

✦ **Disable the virus protection software:** Microsoft has a long history of causing all kinds of problems for virus protection software. Just about every Microsoft installation program will tell you that you should disable the virus protection software, and you should heed that warning. The virus protection software can not only prevent the installation from completing properly but also increase the installation time significantly. In some cases, you end up with a partial installation that appears to work but causes you nothing but trouble. If you have any doubts about applications, especially virus protection software that you installed on your system, it's a good idea to perform a DVD installation rather than a Windows installation.

✦ **Check the system memory:** A minor glitch in system memory can cause all kinds of problems for the installation, and it's likely you won't see them immediately. In fact, your system could run just fine for weeks and suddenly start performing oddly. You may even lose data and find that Windows doesn't save system settings changes correctly. Bad memory can cause a true disaster for your data — and you. Microsoft recommends using the Windows Memory Diagnostic tool to check your system's memory. Check out the site at `http://oca.microsoft.com/en/windiag.asp`, and see the "Performing a Memory Test" section of Book I, Chapter 2 for additional details about the Windows Memory Diagnostic tool. If you choose not to use the Windows Memory Diagnostic tool, make sure to check memory using a third-party diagnostic.

✦ **Don't assume the installation has failed — check the firewall:** The installation program turns on the Windows Firewall by default for Windows Server 2008. This default setting may make it appear that your installation has failed or caused a number of other problems. Make sure to verify that the Windows Firewall is set to allow inbound connections before you assume the installation has failed. You can find out more about the Windows Firewall at `http://technet.microsoft.com/en-us/network/bb545423.aspx` and in the "Configuring the Windows Firewall" section of Book I, Chapter 4.

✦ **Prepare the Active Directory environment for the update:** Windows Server 2008 provides additional features, and you can't use it directly with a Windows 2000 or Windows 2003 server in the same forest or domain without preparation. Fortunately, the update procedure is relatively painless because Microsoft provides the tools you need to do it. The "Preparing a forest for installation" and "Preparing a domain for installation" sections of this chapter help you perform the required preparation tasks.

Preparing a forest for installation

An Active Directory *forest* is a group of domain controllers that are working together to service user needs. All the members of the forest share data and update each other so that the loss of a single domain controller doesn't cause a complete failure of Active Directory or result in lost settings. However, because the members of the forest rely on each other, you must be sure that the forest can work with all the domain controllers it supports and that the addition of a new domain controller won't cause problems.

You must prepare the forest to receive a Windows Server 2008 system because Windows Server 2008 provides additional functionality not found in previous versions of Windows. The following steps tell you how to prepare a forest to receive a Windows Server 2008 installation. (If you don't precisely understand these steps, make sure to read the content of Book II, Chapter 5.)

1. **Log on to the machine that you have set up as the schema master as a member of the Enterprise Admins, Schema Admins, or Domain Admins group.**

You must have the required permissions in order to work with the forest files and save them to another location. If you don't have the required group access, ask someone who does have the required permission to perform this task.

2. **Copy the contents of the `\sources\adprep` folder from the Windows Server 2008 installation media to the folder used by the schema master role holder.**

It's possible to use Windows Explorer to perform this task. You can also rely on command line utilities, such as these:

- *The Copy command:*
  `http://www.microsoft.com/resources/documentation/windows/xp/all/proddocs/en-us/copy.mspx`

- *The XCopy utility:* `http://www.microsoft.com/resources/documentation/windows/xp/all/proddocs/en-us/xcopy.mspx`

- *The RoboCopy utility:* `http://www.ss64.com/nt/robocopy.html`

  Make sure to verify the copy after you complete it, to ensure that all the files have copied successfully.

3. **Choose Start⇨Programs⇨Accessories⇨Command Prompt.**

   If you're working with Vista using a remote connection, make sure to right-click the Command Prompt entry and choose Run As Administrator from the context menu, or else you won't have the proper rights.

4. **Use the DVD command to change directories to the folder used by the schema master role holder.**

5. **Type** AdPrep /ForestPrep **and press Enter.**

   The AdPrep utility prepares your system to work with Windows Server 2008.

6. **If you plan to install a read-only domain controller, type** AdPrep /RODCPrep **and press Enter.**

7. **Allow the procedure to complete and the changes to replicate to the other domain controllers before you use the procedure in the "Preparing a domain for installation" section of this chapter.**

The AdPrep utility is a new application that Microsoft has added to the Windows Server 2008 media. You don't find this utility supplied with older versions of Windows. Microsoft provides details about this utility at `http://technet2.microsoft.com/windowsserver/en/library/bc5ebbdb-a8d7-4761-b38a-e207baa734191033.mspx`.

Preparing a domain for installation

A *domain controller* is a single computer set up for client server operation rather than for the workgroup operation that smaller networks use. The domain controller can appear as a single server in a smaller network or as part of a forest on a larger network.

You must separately prepare each domain controller to work with Windows Server 2008. If your domain controller appears as part of a forest, then you must prepare the forest first, using the procedure found in the "Preparing a forest for installation" section of this chapter. The following steps describe how to prepare a domain controller for user with Windows Server 2008:

1. **Log on to the domain controller as a member of the Domain Admins group.**

You must have the required permissions to work with the domain controller files and save them to another location. If you don't have the required group access, ask someone who has the required permission to perform this task.

2. **Copy the contents of the** `\sources\adprep` **folder from the Windows Server 2008 installation media to the folder used by the infrastructure master role holder.**

   It's possible to use Windows Explorer to perform this task. You can also rely on command line utilities, such as these:

   - *Copy command:* `http://www.microsoft.com/resources/documentation/windows/xp/all/proddocs/en-us/copy.mspx`

   - *The XCopy utility:* `http://www.microsoft.com/resources/documentation/windows/xp/all/proddocs/en-us/xcopy.mspx`

   - *The RoboCopy utility:* `http://www.ss64.com/nt/robocopy.html`

   Make sure to verify the copy after you complete it, to ensure that all the files have copied successfully.

3. **Choose Start⇨Programs⇨Accessories⇨Command Prompt.**

   If you're working with Vista using a remote connection, make sure to right-click the Command Prompt entry and choose Run As Administrator from the context menu, or else you won't have the proper rights.

4. **Use the DVD command to change directories to the folder used by the infrastructure master role holder.**

5. **Type** AdPrep /DomainPrep /GPPrep **and press Enter.**

   The AdPrep utility prepares your system to work with Windows Server 2008.

6. **Allow the procedure to complete and the changes to replicate to the other domain controllers.**

Performing a DVD Installation

The DVD installation provides the easiest method of getting Windows Server 2008 onto a system that doesn't include an operating system. You can also use this technique when you don't want to save the settings on a system (you want to perform a clean install) or when you want to perform diagnostics before performing the installation. For example, you may want to test system memory. The following steps describe how to perform a DVD installation:

1. **Start the system and place the DVD into the boot DVD drive as soon as possible before the system begins looking for a boot drive.**

The system displays a message asking whether you want to boot from the DVD. If you miss this sequence, you can always place the DVD into the drive and press the Reset button on the front of the computer system to restart it. You see the required message during the next boot sequence.

2. Press Enter to boot from the DVD.

You see a message that Windows is loading files. This message appears for several minutes, so be patient. After the initial file load completes, you see an Install Windows dialog box, as shown in Figure 3-1.

Figure 3-1:
Choose the installation language, time and currency format, and keyboard options.

3. Choose an installation language, time and currency format, and a keyboard or other input method. Click Next.

You see a dialog box with three options, as shown in Figure 3-2. The Install Now option helps you install the operating system immediately. The What to Know Before Installing Windows option displays a Help and Support dialog box, where you can discover information about the Windows release and pre-installation requirements. Make sure to pay close attention to requirements such as disconnecting your UPS serial cable before you begin the installation (or the installation may fail). Selecting the Repair Your Computer option displays the boot diagnostics. Book I, Chapter 2 provides a complete description of these essential tools.

4. Click Install Now.

The installation program performs some additional tasks and eventually displays a dialog box that asks for your product key. If you simply click Next at the product key dialog box, Windows displays a warning dialog box (click No to bypass it) and then displays a list of Windows editions you can install. You must eventually provide a product key for your installation, but this option lets you try a Windows operation system edition for a predefined timeframe (120 days as of this writing). Choose the edition you want to install, select the I Have Selected the Edition of Windows that I Purchased option, and click Next.

Figure 3-2:
Begin the installation by clicking Install Now.

5. **Type your product key. Select the Automatically Activate Windows When I'm Online option. Click Next.**

You see a list of options for the editions of Windows Server 2008 you purchased. Normally, these options include a GUI version and a Server Core version. The GUI version has all the features that you normally associate with Windows. This is the version of Windows Server 2008 described throughout most of this book. The Server Core version contains only a command prompt. You don't see most of the GUI features normally associated with Windows when working with this version, but this version does provide certain reliability, performance, and security features that offset the lack of a GUI. You can read more about the Server Core version of the product in the "Understanding Windows Server 2008 Server Core" section of Book I, Chapter 1.

6. **Select the GUI version of the operating system and click Next.**

You see the licensing dialog box.

7. **Check I Accept the License Terms and click Next.**

You see an installation type dialog box. An upgrade installation lets you keep your files, settings, and programs intact on the host system. The upgrade installation performs most tasks automatically. When you select

Upgrade, you can simply sit back and watch the installation program perform most of the work for you. (All you need to do is perform any custom configuration after the operating system installation completes — the topic of the rest of this book.) A custom installation lets you perform a clean install of the operating system. This procedure continues with the custom installation.

8. Click Custom (Advanced).

The installation program asks where you want to install Windows. In most cases, you use the entire hard drive for the Windows installation. If you have multiple hard drives, you can choose any drive to hold the Windows installation. It's also possible to create a special partition (a part of the hard drive allocated to hold Windows). A partition allows you to install multiple Windows versions on a single machine, a topic that doesn't appear in this book.

9. Choose the hard drive you want to use for Windows and click Next.

The installation program now has enough information to proceed. It begins copying and expanding the files needed for the operating system. Because this process can require quite a bit of time (depending on the capabilities of your server; my server required about ten minutes to complete the task), now might be a good time to get that cup of coffee. At some point, the server reboots, to continue the installation process. After the server reboots, it performs a number of additional tasks and may reboot again. (This sequence can occur multiple times, depending on the complexity of your setup.) At some point, you see a message telling you that you must change the user's password before logging in the first time. This new safety feature ensures that you have an opportunity to change the administrator password before you perform any other task with Windows Server 2008.

10. Click OK.

You see an Administrator screen, where you must type in a new password and then confirm it.

11. Type a new password and click the Right Pointing Arrow icon.

Windows tells you that it has changed the password.

12. Click OK.

You see a flurry of activity as Windows Server 2008 configures itself. Eventually, you'll see the message: "The user's password must be changed before logon on the first time."

13. Click OK.

You see the Administrator log in screen.

14. Type a password in the New Password field. Confirm it in the Confirm Password field. Click the right-pointing arrow.

You see a Changing Password message, followed by Your Password Has Been Changed.

15. Click OK to enter Windows the first time.

You see an Initial Configuration Tasks window, where you can perform the initial configuration. The "Performing an Initial Configuration" section of the chapter describes how to perform this task. You now have Windows Server 2008 installed.

Performing a Windows Installation

The main difference between the Windows installation method and the DVD installation method is where you begin the process. Rather than boot the system to use the operating system on the media disk, you use the existing copy of Windows as a starting point. Taking that approach normally lets you preserve your existing setup, unless the installation program encounters a problem. In many respects, this approach isn't much different from installing an application, because you begin by inserting the media in the drive and waiting for the automatic installation process to start. (You can also start the setup by locating Setup.exe on the installation media and double-clicking it in Windows Explorer.)

As previously mentioned, the main problem with this type of installation is that the environment and the registry aren't clean. Consequently, you can experience problems even if the installation should proceed flawlessly. Scrupulous attention to detail helps prevent problems — make sure to follow the guidelines in the "Considering Pre-Installation Requirements" section of this chapter before you start the installation. The following steps tell you how to accomplish the installation:

1. Place the installation media in the drive.

If you see the AutoPlay dialog box, click Run Setup.exe. You see the Install Windows dialog box, shown in Figure 3-3.

2. Click Install Now.

The installation screen shown in Figure 3-3 disappears while the installation program works in the background. Eventually, you see a gray background appear and then the Install Windows dialog box, shown in Figure 3-4. Always choose to go online and update the installation media because you don't want to get a virus immediately. The only time you should choose Do Not Get the Latest Updates for Installation is when you don't have an Internet connection to use or you rely on a local version of Windows Update for updates.

3. Clear the I Want to Help Make Windows Installation Better option if you don't have an Internet connection or don't want to share information about your installation with Microsoft.

Figure 3-3:
The Windows Server 2008 installation begins with this installation screen.

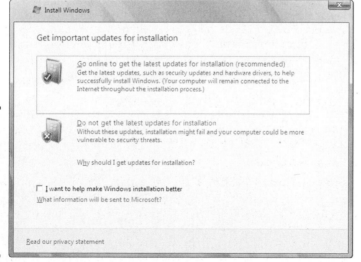

Figure 3-4:
Determine whether you want to get on the Internet to update the installation media.

4. **Click Go Online to Get the Latest Update for Installation (Recommended).**

The installation program tells you that it has searched for installation updates. If it finds installation updates, it tells you that it has downloaded them. At some point, the dialog box shown in Figure 3-4 disappears for a few minutes, and you eventually see the Type Your Product Key for Activation dialog box, shown in Figure 3-5.

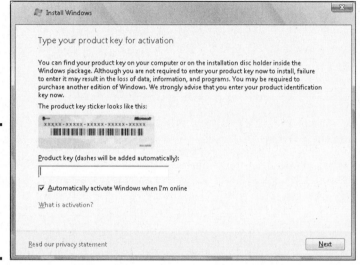

Figure 3-5:
Type your product key before proceeding with the Windows installation.

5. **Type your product key. Select the Automatically Activate Windows When I'm Online option. Click Next.**

You see a list of options for the editions of Windows Server 2008 you purchased, as shown in Figure 3-6. Normally, these options include a GUI version and a Server Core version. The GUI version has all the features that you normally associate with Windows. This is the version of Windows Server 2008 described throughout most of this book. The Server Core version contains only a command prompt. You don't see most of the GUI features normally associated with Windows when working with this version, but this version does provide certain reliability, performance, and security features that offset the lack of a GUI. You can read more about the Server Core version of the product in the "Understanding Windows Server 2008 Server Core" section of Book I, Chapter 1.

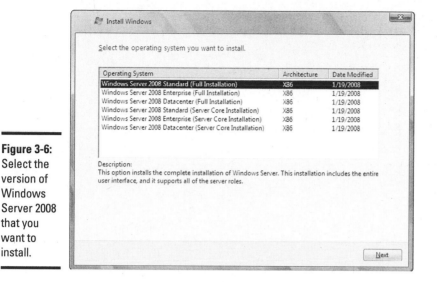

Figure 3-6:
Select the version of Windows Server 2008 that you want to install.

6. **Select the GUI version of the operating system and click Next.**

You see the licensing dialog box.

7. **Select I Accept the License Terms and click Next.**

You see an installation type dialog box, as shown in Figure 3-7. An upgrade installation lets you keep your files, settings, and programs intact on the host system. The upgrade installation performs most tasks automatically. When you select Upgrade, you can simply sit back and watch the installation program perform most of the work for you. (All you need to do is perform any custom configuration after the operating system installation completes, which is the topic of the rest of this book.) A custom installation lets you perform a clean install of the operating system. If you want to perform a custom installation, follow the steps, starting with Step 8, in the "Performing a DVD Installation" section of this chapter. This procedure continues with the upgrade installation.

8. **Click Upgrade.**

The installation program performs a compatibility check of your system. If the installation program finds errors, such as those shown in Figure 3-8, you must stop the installation process by clicking Close, fixing the errors, and then restarting the installation at Step 1. If you can't fix the errors, you must perform a DVD installation — see the "Performing a DVD Installation" section of this chapter for details.

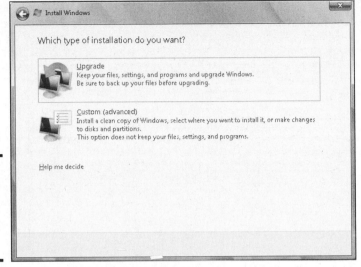

Figure 3-7:
Determine which type of installation to perform.

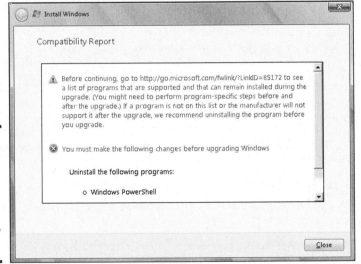

Figure 3-8:
The installation program checks for errors and displays any it finds.

9. **Click Next.**

The installation program now has enough information to proceed. It begins copying and expanding the files needed for the operating system, as shown in Figure 3-9. Because this process can require quite a bit of time (depending on the capabilities of your server; my server required about ten minutes to complete the task), now might be a good time to get that cup of coffee. At some point, the server reboots, to continue the installation process. After the server reboots, it performs a number of additional tasks and may reboot again. (This sequence can occur multiple times, depending on the complexity of your setup.) At some point, you see a message telling you that you must change the user's password before logging in the first time. This is a new safety feature that ensures you have an opportunity to change the administrator password before you perform any other task with Windows Server 2008.

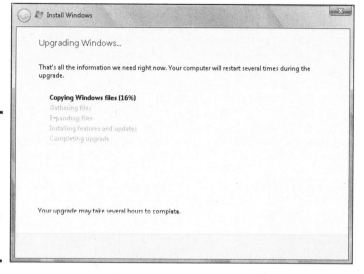

Figure 3-9: When the installation program has enough information, it copies the required files to disk.

10. **Click OK.**

You see an Administrator screen where you must type in a new password and then confirm it.

11. **Type a new password and click the right-pointing arrow.**

Windows tells you that it has changed the password.

12. **Click OK.**

You see a flurry of activity as Windows Server configures itself. Eventually, you'll see the message: "The user's password must be changed before logon on the first time."

13. **Click OK.**

You see the Administrator log in screen.

14. **Type a password in the New Password field. Confirm it in the Confirm Password field. Click the right-pointing arrow.**

You see a Changing Password message, followed by Your Password Has Been Changed.

15. Click OK to enter Windows the first time.

You see an Initial Configuration Tasks window, where you can perform initial configuration. The "Performing an Initial Configuration" section of this chapter describes how to perform this task. You now have Windows Server 2008 installed.

Considering the Windows Installation Alternatives

The two manual techniques for installing Windows that are described in this chapter are the standard methods that you use. Small and medium-size businesses commonly use these techniques because they don't have many servers to maintain. Even enterprises use these techniques when they begin working with Windows Server 2008 because they lack a configuration from other installations. However, the manual techniques are decidedly time consuming and require that an administrator spend time right in front of the computer, working with it. Most enterprises require something a little more exotic than the manual techniques described in this chapter if they want to roll out Windows Server 2008 quickly. The two most common alternative techniques that enterprises use are

✦ Creating a slipstream disk that the administrator can simply place in the server's drive and boot.

✦ Relying on a network install, where the server logs in to another server and downloads the required software across a network connection.

Both of these methods save time when you have a considerable number of servers to update. After you perform the required setups, you can almost perform the required tasks automatically. However, the key phrase here is "perform the required setups." It takes time and effort to create the required setup. The administrator must perform a number of tasks to create a viable setup that will work for any number of servers. The following steps provide an overview of a typical setup scenario:

1. Perform a manual installation.

2. Set up the initial server.

3. Test the installation.

4. Download and install any required fixes or patches.

5. Install any applications.

6. Create the slipstream disk or set up a network installation.

7. Test the installation on another server.

8. Debug the installation.

9. Perform Steps 1 through 8 again as needed to repair any problems.

Microsoft's new deployment technique for enterprises

Even though it's not strictly a method for deploying servers, you can probably use the Business Desktop Deployment (BDD) to create a disk for your Windows Server 2008 installation. Microsoft originally created this product to make it easier to install Windows on a workstation. You can read about the technique at `http://technet.microsoft.com/enus/desktopdeployment/default.aspx`.

The interesting part about BDD is that it doesn't really care about what software you want to install — it only wants to help you get it installed. Consequently, you can theoretically use BDD with Windows Server 2008 even if Microsoft doesn't necessarily advertise BDD

for this purpose. While writing this book, I used BDD to reconfigure my system quickly (and I did it often to try out various setups). It's interesting to note that the software worked well — not perfectly, but well enough.

You'll probably want to conduct some tests with BDD before you commit to using it in your enterprise environment. Fortunately, you can download this software for free at `http://www.microsoft.com/downloads/details.aspx?FamilyId=13F05BE2-FD0E-4620-8CA6-1AAD6FC54741`. The point is that you may need to think outside the box when you need an alternative to manual installations in your organization, and BDD may provide the right answer.

Only after the administrator has performed all of these steps does the alternative installation technique become usable. Because these steps require personalization and special configuration, it's impossible to demonstrate the techniques completely in a book. That's why you don't see any alternative installation techniques described in this book — they're simply too complex to describe satisfactorily unless you have an entire book devoted to the topic.

Performing an Initial Configuration

At some point, the installation program declares Windows Server 2008 installed, but it really isn't installed yet. Sure, you can begin working with it, but you wouldn't want to expose it to the outside world and you definitely wouldn't want to start inviting users to work with the server. Windows Server 2008 is a blank slate when you get to this point. This section of the chapter helps you get Windows Server 2008 to the point where you can begin adding roles and features to make the operating system completely usable.

One of the first tasks you should perform is setting up your desktop to make it usable. In most cases, you're looking at a low-resolution desktop that the installation program configured to provide a usable display no matter what happens during the video setup. Most of the dialog boxes and windows in

Windows Server 2008 are large enough that they don't fit in this default screen. In fact, you're probably looking at the initial configuration screen, which doesn't fit well at all within the default display.

Configuring a user account for yourself is the next step. The reason that you want to perform this step is that you don't want to use the Administrator account unless absolutely necessary during configuration due to the new rules that Windows Server 2008 implements. You work safer with an account of your own because Windows Server 2008 alerts you to potentially dangerous situations. Of course, the User Account Control (UAC) isn't fun to work with, but it does provide a safety net that you didn't have in the past.

In most cases, you want to activate your copy of Windows sooner rather than later. To perform this task, right-click Computer and choose Properties from the context menu. You see the Control Panel\System window, shown in Figure 3-10. At the bottom of this window, you see a Windows activation link. Click this link to see a Windows Activation dialog box. Click Activate Now and you see a success message in a few seconds.

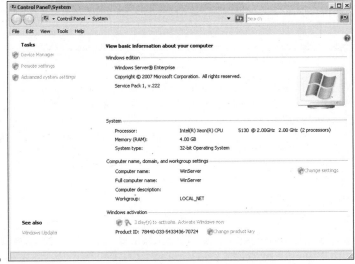

Figure 3-10: Activate your copy of Windows Server 2008 after installation.

It's important to verify that the installation was able to identify all your hardware because some configuration tasks don't work well without the required hardware access. The method for accessing the Device Manager has changed in Windows Server 2008. To display the device status, simply click the Device

Manager link on the left side of the Control Panel\System window, shown in Figure 3-10. You see a list of devices such as the one shown in Figure 3-11. If you see nonfunctional devices, you can use the techniques found in the "Working with Device Manager" section of Book II, Chapter 2 to repair the problem.

Windows Server 2008 ships with the strictest level of firewall protection in place, and this protection may even prevent you from accessing the Internet for updates, fixes, and device drivers that you need. You need to configure the Windows Firewall to allow access to the outside world. The "Configuring Windows Firewall with Advanced Security" section of Book V, Chapter 4 helps you perform this configuration task. Make sure that you have a clear path to the resources you need.

After you perform the initial configuration tasks, you can begin configuring the server. To perform this task, you perform tasks such as adding roles and features to the server so that it can do the work you want. This configuration of the server is the last step you perform before you begin adding users and then adding applications — after which your server is open for business. Book I, Chapter 4 provides all the information you need to perform the remaining server configuration tasks.

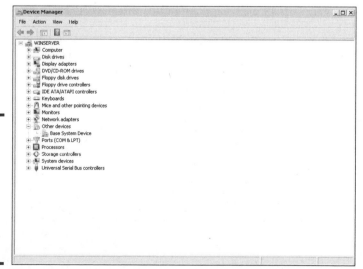

Figure 3-11: Verify that the installation program located all the devices on your machine.

Chapter 4: Performing Initial Configuration Tasks

In This Chapter

↙ **Understanding the Initial Configuration Tasks window**

↙ **Defining information about the computer**

↙ **Updating the server with patches and fixes**

↙ **Performing server customization tasks**

↙ **Changing how your server boots using BCDEdit**

After you finish installing Windows Server 2008, you see it start up for the first time and then it hits you that you haven't performed any of the configuration tasks you performed in the past. You haven't set the time zone, configured any server applications, or even performed any sort of an update. In fact, your system is truly a blank slate.

Microsoft now provides a new feature, the Initial Configuration Tasks window. This feature leads you through the task of configuring your server for use. The interesting part about the Initial Configuration Tasks window is that you can perform the tasks in any order. For example, if you don't know what do to about networking now but you do know that you want to add a particular role, you can configure the roles first and work on the networking as you gain information about the server configuration. You no longer have to follow a precise set of steps.

The Initial Configuration Tasks window suggests a particular configuration order, and you see that order described in this chapter. The only reason for the suggested set of steps is to ensure that you bring your server online with the correct features in place at the right time. For example, you don't want to expose the server to the public without first having set the required security level. Consequently, one of the first steps that Microsoft asks you to perform is to identify any domain affiliation so that you can start using the domain security immediately. Of course, you can always choose to perform the tasks in another order — the steps you follow are up to you in Windows Server 2008.

This chapter also provides some tips for using the Initial Configuration Tasks window efficiently. You may even decide to close the window for a while and then bring it back up when you need it. The chapter also tells you the secret words you need to type to make the Initial Configuration Tasks window reappear after you close it (it isn't on any of the Start Menu entries).

An Overview of the Initial Configuration Tasks Window

What you see in the Initial Configuration Tasks window depends on how you install Window Server 2008. A clean installation (see the "Performing a DVD Installation" section of Book I, Chapter 3) presents options that you don't see during an update (see the "Performing a Windows Installation" section of Book I, Chapter 3). Figure 4-1 shows how the Initial Configuration Tasks window appears after a clean installation, whereas Figure 4-2 shows the same window after an update. Notice that the update version of the window already has certain features configured, such as the time zone, and that you can't set the Do Not Show This Window at Logon option.

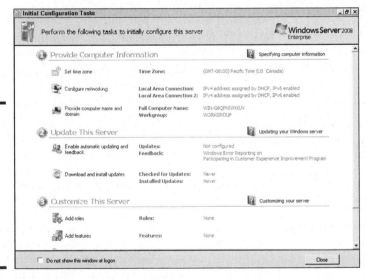

Figure 4-1: A clean installation presents additional options in the Initial Configuration Tasks window.

Figures 4-1 and 4-2 show that Microsoft has a definite process in mind when configuring the server. Of course, some of the options, such as Enable Automatic Updating and Feedback in Step 2, are purely optional, and you should configure these options with your company policies in mind. The following sections describe the default settings, provide an overview of the configuration process, and tell you how to display the Initial Configuration Tasks window if you close it accidentally.

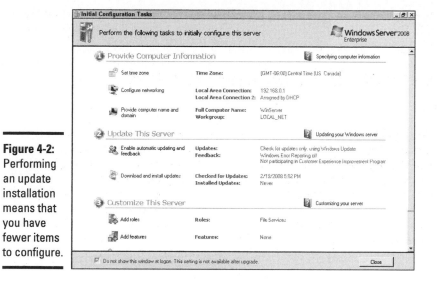

Figure 4-2:
Performing
an update
installation
means that
you have
fewer items
to configure.

Understanding the default Windows Server 2008 settings

Because the Windows Server 2008 installation doesn't perform any initial configuration, it's important to know about the default settings that could cause problems for your server. You'll want to address these settings to ensure that your server works as it should and doesn't open any security holes. Table 4-1 provides a listing of the essential default settings for Windows Server 2008.

Table 4-1	Essential Windows Server 2008 Default Settings	
Setting Name	*Default Setting*	*Description*
Administrator Password	Blank	Provides default access to the system. The system is wide open when you start, so setting the password is a must-do item.
Computer Name	Random Value	Defines the computer's name on the network and provides the name others will use to access the computer. The random name that Microsoft provides will be hard to use.

continued

Table 4-1 *(continued)*

Setting Name	Default Setting	Description
Domain Membership	The computer is joined to a workgroup named WORKGROUP	Defines the computer's connectivity on the network. For a small company or a group within an enterprise, a workgroup may work fine, but most organizations rely on a domain.
Windows Update	Off	Automatically updates the computer as needed. You need to turn on this feature after performing the initial update to ensure that the server receives required updates.
Network Connections	Set to obtain their IP address using Dynamic Host Configuration Protocol (DHCP)	Using DHCP is a standard for domains because you must have a DHCP server to set up a domain. A workgroup with a shared Internet connection also has a DHCP host. However, some workgroups still require manual IP configuration.
Windows Firewall	On	Provides security for incoming and outgoing network traffic. The default Windows Firewall configuration is set to disallow any form of network traffic, to ensure that no one can access the server while you configure it. Change this setting after the initial server configuration but before you attempt to download updates and fixes.
Roles	None Installed	Specifies the tasks that the server can perform. If you don't define any roles, the server looks more like a workstation than a server. In fact, it doesn't even make a good workstation.

An overview of the configuration process

The Initial Configuration Tasks window, shown in Figures 4-1 and 4-2, lists a series of steps in the order in which Microsoft thinks you should accomplish them. The steps you perform depend on the kind of installation you perform. Obviously, someone who is performing an update doesn't need to set the administrator password because they should have set it during the initial installation of the previous server software. The basic steps are

1. *Provide computer information.* You need to identify your computer in a way that others can identify it too. The random name that Microsoft provides for your computer isn't helpful to anyone. In addition, you can't access your workgroup or domain using the standard settings, unless your workgroup just happens to have the name WORKGROUP. If you're using the name WORKGROUP, you probably want to change it anyway to improve network security.

2. *Update this server.* A major concern for a new server is potential security problems due to missing patches and fixes. Adding the required patches and fixes makes it less likely that a virus will attack the server before you can even configure the various roles you want the server to perform. It doesn't matter when your company uses Microsoft's Windows Update or you run your own, local version of Windows Update (see `http://technet.microsoft.com/en-us/wsus/default.aspx` for details on Windows Server Update Services, or WSUS), you must get the patches and fixes in place fast after you install the server software. Of course, before you can perform updates, you must have connectivity to the network, which is why you first need to perform Step 1, provide computer information. Note that you may have to configure the Windows Firewall before you can gain access to Windows Update.

3. *Customize this server.* After you identify and patch your computer, you can begin configuring it to perform useful work. Microsoft separates the configuration items into two categories in Windows Server 2008: roles and features. A *role* is a major server activity, such as providing file services or acting as a DHCP server. A *feature* is software you add to help the server perform its tasks, such as Windows PowerShell or Group Policy Management.

It's important to remember that the Initial Configuration Tasks window is just that — for initial configuration. Even after you've worked with the server for a while, you may find that you need to add more roles or features to it. You can always display the Initial Configuration Tasks window as needed until the server is set up perfectly.

When you complete the configuration tasks you want to perform, you can close the Initial Configuration Tasks window by clicking the Close box in the upper-right corner of the window. If you don't want to see this window the next time you start Windows, make sure to check the Do Not Show This Window at Logon option before you close the window. Immediately after the Initial Configuration Tasks window closes, you see the Server Manager console appear. The "Using the Server Manager Console" section of Book II, Chapter 1 describes this feature in detail.

The Initial Configuration Tasks window helps you perform the initial server configuration — Microsoft doesn't intend for you to continue using it when you begin managing the server. When the server enters management mode, then you can use the Server Manager Console to perform any configuration tasks. Each of these configuration tools excels in the environment in which Microsoft designed them to work. Using the Server Manager Console provides better access to roles and features after you know the roles and features you want to work with. If you're a command line commando, you can use Server ManagerCmd (described in the "Using the ServerManagerCmd Utility" section of Book II, Chapter 1) in place of the Server Manager Console. Most administrators use a combination of the two tools.

Reopening the Initial Configuration Tasks window

The Initial Configuration Tasks window doesn't appear as an option on the Start menu or within the Control Panel (not even as part of the Administrative Tools folder). You can always restart the Initial Configuration Tasks window using the following steps:

1. **Choose Start⇨Run.**

   You see the Run dialog box, shown in Figure 4-3.

2. **Type** OOBE **in the Open field and press Enter.**

   You see the Initial Configuration Tasks window for the type of setup you performed.

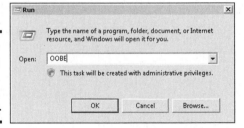

Figure 4-3:
Use the Run dialog box to start new applications.

Providing Computer Information

Setting the computer information helps identify your computer, its physical location, and its network affiliation. The Initial Configuration Tasks window contains three tasks for the computer. The following sections describe each of these tasks:

Setting the time zone

Microsoft assumes that everyone lives in Washington, so the default setting is for the Pacific time zone. Of course, not everyone does live in Washington, so you may need to change the time zone to match your area of the country. Use the following steps to configure the time zone to meet your specific needs:

1. **Click Set Time Zone.**

You see the dialog box shown in Figure 4-4.

Figure 4-4:
Modify the
time zone to
meet your
specific
needs.

2. **Click Change Time Zone.**

You see the Time Zone Settings dialog box, shown in Figure 4-5.

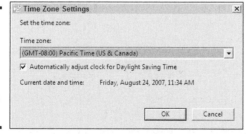

Figure 4-5:
Choose a
time zone
and the
Daylight
Saving Time
setting.

3. **Select a time zone from the Time Zone field.**

4. **Clear the Automatically Adjust Clock for Daylight Saving Time option
if you don't use daylight saving time in your time zone.**

5. **Click OK to close the Time Zone Settings dialog box.**

At this point, the time zone is set, but you don't know whether your
system clock is correct. The installation program has a tendency to
change the system time to match the time in Washington.

6. **Select the Internet Time tab.**

   Windows tells you when the next synchronization will occur (normally a week or more after the installation). If you don't have a usable Internet connection, skip to Step 10 because you can't synchronize your clock.

7. **Click Change Settings.**

   You see the Internet Time Settings dialog box.

8. **Click Update Now.**

   Windows automatically updates your clock to the correct time, as shown in Figure 4-6. If you don't see a Success message, then choose one of the other options in the Server drop-down list box and click Update Now again. Try each server in turn until you find one that works.

9. **Click OK to close the Internet Time Settings dialog box.**

10. **Click OK to close the Date and Time dialog box.**

    The time should now read correctly in the Notification Area of the Taskbar.

Figure 4-6:
Update the clock so that it has the correct time.

Providing a computer name and domain

The computer name and workgroup or domain name that Microsoft provides are unlikely to work with anyone's setup. These settings are simply place-holders for the unique values you provide. The following steps help you perform this configuration task:

1. **Click Provide Computer Name and Domain.**

   You see the System Properties dialog box, shown in Figure 4-7.

2. **Type a description for your server in the Computer Description field.**

3. **Click Change.**

   You see the Computer Name\Domain Changes dialog box, shown in Figure 4-8. Despite the name of this dialog box, you can also use this dialog box to configure your server for use with a workgroup.

4. **Type a name for your server in the Computer Name field.**

5. **Select either Domain or Workgroup in the Member Of field.**

Figure 4-7:
The
Computer
Name tab of
the System
Properties
dialog box
contains
identifying
information.

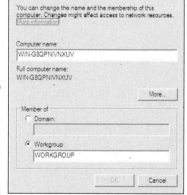

Figure 4-8:
Provide a
name and
network
affiliation for
your server.

6. **Type the name of the domain or workgroup in the Domain or Workgroup field (as appropriate).**

7. **Click OK to close the Computer Name\Domain Changes dialog box.**

   Windows makes the required configuration changes (it may require a few moments). You see at some point a Welcome dialog box that says you successfully joined a workgroup or domain.

8. **Click OK to clear the welcome message.**

   Windows displays a message telling you to restart your computer to make the changes permanent.

9. **Click OK to clear the restart message.**

10. **Click Close to close the System Properties dialog box.**

Windows asks whether you want to restart your system. You must restart it to have the name change take effect.

11. **Click Restart Now.**

Windows restarts your server. When your system reboots, it uses the new computer name you provided and is part of the chosen workgroup or domain.

Configuring networking

Even though the Configure Networking option appears second on the list, you probably want to perform the Provide Computer Name and Domain task first. Networking relies on the correct configuration of these two items, so it doesn't make sense to try to configure networking when you can't be sure of connecting to anything. After you configure the computer name and domain or workgroup, come back to this step.

When you click Configure Networking, you see the Network Connections window, shown in Figure 4-9. Each icon represents a network adapter that you can configure.

In general, the more you can allow Windows to perform the configuration dynamically for you, the better off you are. However, if you're part of a domain, you likely need to configure some network features, such as which Domain Name System (DNS) server to use. Likewise, if you're configuring a workgroup and this server has the Internet connection associated with it, then you need to configure Internet Connection Sharing. This chapter doesn't provide all the details you need to configure the network — check Book IV for these details instead. (ICS configuration appears in the "Performing an ICS Setup" section of Book V, Chapter 2.)

Figure 4-9: Modify the network setup to meet your networking needs.

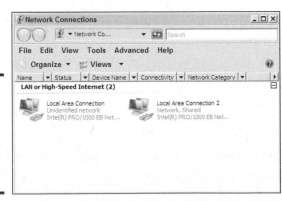

After you perform any required configuration, restart the server. Windows doesn't tell you to restart the server, but you need to restart it to see certain changes, such as a change of IP address, take effect. In addition, when you configure the system to use a particular DNS or DHCP server, you need to restart the system to ensure it obtains new configuration information based on these associations.

If you absolutely can't restart the server (a very rare event at this stage), right-click each of the adapter icons and choose Diagnose from the context menu. Windows displays a diagnostic screen and eventually tells you whether it found any problems with the connection. More importantly, you generally find that the server has reconfigured the adapters for use with the new settings you provided. Unfortunately, this technique doesn't always work and you may find that you have to restart the server, after all. If you see the dialog box shown in Figure 4-10, you very likely need to perform a restart to obtain the correct configuration.

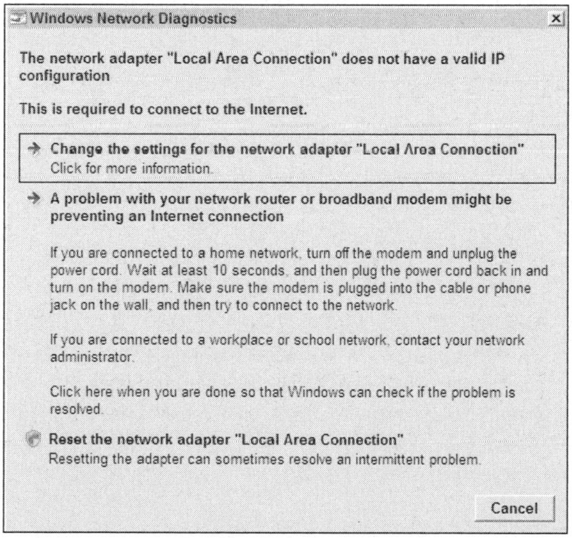

Figure 4-10:
Many network configuration changes require a restart before Windows will accept them.

Microsoft doesn't provide an option to make your server visible to the network as part of the Initial Configuration Tasks window. However, you need to provide this visibility to start testing your setup. The following steps tell you how to provide network visibility:

1. **Right-click Network and choose Properties from the context menu.**

You see the Network and Sharing Center window, shown in Figure 4-11.

2. **Click Off in the Network Discovery row.**

   The Network and Sharing Center window changes to show the Network Discovery option details.

3. **Select the Turn On Network Discovery option.**

Figure 4-11: The Network and Sharing Center window provides many configuration options.

4. **Click Apply.**

   Windows displays the Network Discovery dialog box, shown in Figure 4-12, which asks how you want to work with Network Discovery. It's normally unsafe to make your computer visible to public networks without all the proper configuration options in place. However, there's little, if any, risk on a private network because anyone accessing the server from a private network requires the proper rights.

Figure 4-12: Choose a level of interaction for Network Discovery on your server.

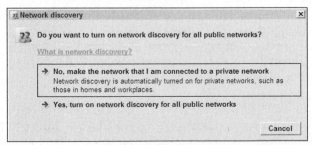

5. **Click No, Make the Network That I Am Connected To A Private Network.**

Windows makes the required configuration changes. The Network Discovery option now reads as having a Custom configuration rather than Off. Machines on your private network should be able to see the server but not use it. No one on the Internet will even see your network.

To ensure that the client can see the server, open a command prompt on the client and type **Ping ServerName**, where ServerName is the name of your server. Press Enter. You see the Ping utility try to contact the server and display connection messages, such as those shown in Figure 4-13, when it does. The fact that the client can see the server doesn't mean that the client can actually use any server resources. The client must have the proper permissions first.

Figure 4-13:
Test the
client
connection
with the
server.

```
D:\WINDOWS\system32\cmd.exe                                    _ □ ×

C:\>Ping WinServer

Pinging WinServer [192.168.0.1] with 32 bytes of data:

Reply from 192.168.0.1: bytes=32 time<1ms TTL=128
Reply from 192.168.0.1: bytes=32 time<1ms TTL=128
Reply from 192.168.0.1: bytes=32 time<1ms TTL=128
Reply from 192.168.0.1: bytes=32 time<1ms TTL=128

Ping statistics for 192.168.0.1:
    Packets: Sent = 4, Received = 4, Lost = 0 (0% loss),
Approximate round trip times in milli-seconds:
    Minimum = 0ms, Maximum = 0ms, Average = 0ms

C:\>
```

Updating Your Server

When you have some basic connectivity in place, you can begin updating your server. Attempting to update it before you have the required connectivity may prove futile because you can't connect to other systems on the network. These other systems may run a copy of WSUS or provide required connectivity to the Internet. The only time you can update your server without first creating the required connectivity is when the server has its own direct connection to the Internet or you have a disk with the required updates and fixes on it. The following sections describe how to configure your server for updates.

Enabling automatic updating and feedback

Whether you enable automatic updates depends on how your organization works with Windows Server 2008. If you're using a local update technique, then you may not want the server automatically downloading updates. Many organizations test any updates that Microsoft provides before allowing them on the server, so the automatic update technique doesn't work for them. On the other hand, if you own a small company and want to ensure that Windows Server 2008 is always up-to-date, then enabling automatic updates may be the optimal solution.

When you click Enable Automatic Updating and Feedback in the Initial Configuration Tasks window, you see an Enable Windows Automatic Updating and Feedback dialog box, as shown in Figure 4-14. The recommended option is to use the Microsoft defaults. Unfortunately, Microsoft doesn't tell you anything about those defaults. A second option lets you manually configure the settings, which is usually the best idea to ensure you get the settings you need.

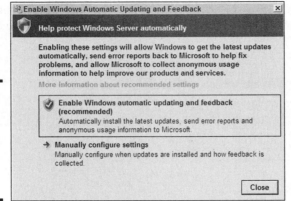

Figure 4-14: Configure your server to perform automatic updates as needed.

Click Manually Configure Settings and you'll see the Manually Configure Settings dialog box shown in Figure 4-15. As you can see, the automatic settings actually include three features:

✦ **Windows Automatic Updating:** This setting controls how and when Windows Server 2008 obtains updates from Microsoft. If you have a standalone server and don't use a local update procedure, then you should tell Windows Server 2008 to at least check for updates. You can still choose whether you want to install them or not.

✦ **Windows Error Reporting:** This setting determines whether Windows Server 2008 reports errors it encounters to Microsoft. In some respects, this setting is a two-edged sword. On the one hand, you have to provide information to Microsoft to use this feature. You hope anything you share isn't identifiable, but you don't know with absolute certainty that the information is safe. On the other hand, you obtain information about errors you're encountering automatically. Using this feature can save a significant amount of time and alert you to fixes that arrive after you've worked on the problem for a while. In most cases, the benefits of this feature outweigh the risks, so you should turn it on.

✦ **Customer Experience Improvement Program (CEIP):** Some administrators refer to this as the call home feature. What this feature does is record statistical information about your computer and determines how you use Windows Server 2008, and then sends the statistics to Microsoft. The information Microsoft collects supposedly helps create better products. According to Microsoft, they only collect statistics and never any personally identifiable information. Whether you believe Microsoft or not determines how you configure this feature.

The default settings for automatic updates and feedback favor Microsoft and its needs. The automatic updates aren't on by default. You'll find that Windows Server 2008 provides the maximum allowable error reporting to Microsoft and doesn't even ask you about it. The CEIP settings are also generous and give Microsoft everything it wants. If you want to change these defaults, use the information in the following sections.

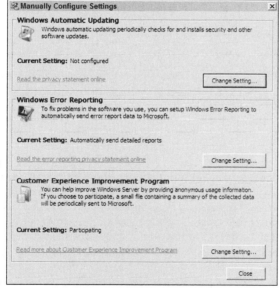

Figure 4-15:
Set the
settings
manually to
ensure you
get the right
setup.

Configuring Automatic Updates

Automatic Updates are an essential part of your server health. If you don't have a localized update solution, then you need to use the Microsoft solution of updating from their Web site. When you click Change Setting in the Windows Automatic Updating section of the Manually Configure Settings dialog box, you see the Change Settings window, shown in Figure 4-16.

As shown in Figure 4-16, you have access to four levels of settings. The Install Updates Automatically setting is the one that Microsoft recommends, and it works well as long as you trust Microsoft completely and always plan to install every update it provides without question. Most organizations aren't that trusting, so you probably won't use this setting. If you do use this setting, however, you must be aware that the server can boot any time after it downloads updates. Consequently, you must configure the update for a time when absolutely no one is using the server. Otherwise, your users could experience unexpected disruptions in service.

Figure 4-16:
Configure
Automatic
Update to
provide the
level of
service you
need.

The Download Updates But Let Me Choose Whether to Install Them option automatically downloads every update, but at least you have a choice about when to install them. This option consumes a lot of hard drive space, especially if you choose not to install all of the updates. However, you also don't have to wait for the updates to download, so this option provides a certain level of efficiency that you don't get with other options.

The Check for Updates But Let Me Choose Whether to Download and Install Them is optimal for organizations that don't plan to install every update because you waste fewer resources with this setting. However, you do have to wait for the updates to download after you do choose to install them. Because the update process is automatic to an extent, you'll probably find that the wait isn't that big of an issue unless Microsoft has a lot of updates during a particular update cycle.

The final option, Never Check for Updates (Not Recommended) is a very poor choice if you don't have a local update solution in place. Many virus writers now produce viruses that attack the latest Windows vulnerabilities on the day Microsoft makes them public. Even if the virus writers give you a few days before releasing their crud on the unsuspecting public, you still need to get an update in place.

Windows Update assumes that you want all the critical updates for your system. You can also choose to download recommended updates by checking the Recommended Updates option. The recommended updates can include updated device drivers and other software that doesn't fix a problem within Windows but can improve how it works. Generally, it's a good idea to get the recommended updates along with all the critical updates that Microsoft provides. Always be sure to back up your system before you install new low-level software, such as a device driver, because sometimes Microsoft's updates don't work as well as anticipated.

Configuring Windows Error Reporting

Some administrators are probably wary of the Windows Error Reporting feature. However, this feature can save you considerable time and effort spent looking for solutions to problems on your system. Because the information you provide to Microsoft is specific to your system, you can actually obtain some noteworthy help for your problem. Of course, you have to be willing to send the information about the problem to Microsoft, and some organizations aren't prepared to do this. Microsoft has said that it doesn't collect any personally identifiable information, but because it's possible to identify your system based on configuration alone, you should consider your decision carefully. You see the Windows Server Error Reporting Configuration dialog box (shown in Figure 4-17) when you click Change Setting in the Windows Error Reporting area of the Manually Configure Settings dialog box.

Microsoft provides several levels of error reporting. If you're pursuing this particular feature, then you should probably consider the first option: Yes, Automatically Send Detailed Reports. If you don't send detailed reports, the probability that you'll receive usable feedback from Microsoft is small.

Of course, you could always choose to send the information to help everyone out, without much thought about your own needs. In this case, choosing the Yes, Automatically Send Summary Reports option should work well. You're sending less information to Microsoft, in this case, so any information you send is less likely to compromise personal information.

The Ask Me About Sending Reports Every Time an Error Occurs option doesn't make a lot of sense for a server, especially if you don't sit in front of it all of the time, just waiting for an error to occur. You can use this option if you want absolute control over when your system reports errors, but the resulting dialog box could present problems for any application that creates it. Windows doesn't clear the errant application, in many cases, until you tell it what to do with the error report. In fact, if you want this level of control, it may simply be better not to participate in the program (the final option in the list).

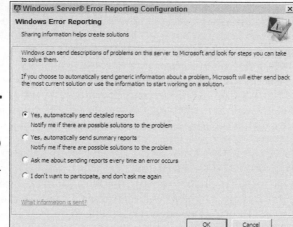

Figure 4-17:
Let
Windows do
the work of
checking for
fixes to
errors you
encounter.

Configuring Customer Experience Improvement Program (CEIP)

Unlike when you use the Windows Error Reporting feature, you get absolutely nothing from the CEIP. This feature records usage information and other statistics about your server and sends them to Microsoft. The statistics enter a black hole somewhere, go round and round for a bit, and finally, hopefully, produce better software, but you really don't know that for sure. No one will ever contact you about your contribution or thank you for making it. As far as you're concerned, the feature might not even work. When you click Change Setting in the Customer Experience Improvement Program area of the Manually Configure Settings dialog box, you see the Windows Server CEIP Configuration dialog box, shown in Figure 4-18.

You have a choice of whether you want to participate. This feature doesn't offer multiple levels of cooperation. However, you can choose whether you want to include additional information with the statistics. In this case, you can choose to tell Microsoft how many servers you have, how many desktop PCs you have, and what industry you work in. None of this information is personally identifiable and could possibly improve Microsoft's ability to use your statistics, but no one will ever know for sure because Microsoft never tells anyone about this feature.

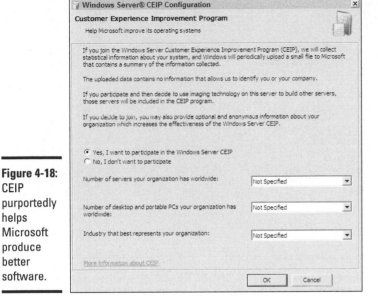

Figure 4-18:
CEIP
purportedly
helps
Microsoft
produce
better
software.

Downloading and installing updates

Microsoft makes a manual update process available for your use, and you access it by clicking Download and Install Updates. Normally, it's not a good idea to rely on your own memory to perform updates because it's too easy to get sidetracked performing other tasks. A server that isn't updated is an open target for anyone who wishes to gain access using the latest security holes that someone has discovered in Microsoft's software. However, updating immediately after you install your server is always a good idea, and that's the real reason to use this feature.

Click Download and Install Updates and you see the Windows Update window, shown in Figure 4-19. The interesting thing about this window is that it always tells you that your system is up-to-date, even when you know it isn't because Microsoft has released a service pack since the time you obtained the installation media. In other words, you can't believe the Windows Is Up To Date entry when you first install your server (you can believe it later). The following sections tell you more about the Windows Update window.

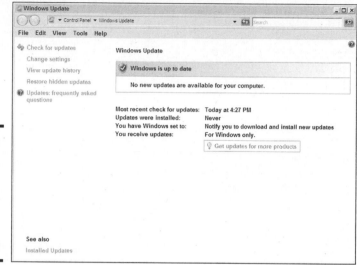

Figure 4-19:
Use
Windows
Update to
perform a
manual
update of
your server.

Checking for updates

When you click Check for Updates, Windows accesses the Windows Update site online to determine whether Microsoft has released any updates for your server. When Windows Update detects new updates, it processes them using the settings you configured for Windows Update. For example, if you choose automatic updates, then Windows Update simply downloads the updates, install thems, and reboots the system for you — all without any interaction on your part.

Changing the settings

Clicking Change Settings displays the same window shown earlier, in Figure 4-16. You use the "Configuring Automatic Updates" section of this chapter to make any necessary changes to the settings you need. All that this link provides is another way to access the settings.

Viewing the update history

In some cases, you may read about a potential virus or other issue and its corresponding fix. When you click View Update History, you see a window similar to the one shown in Figure 4-20. The View Update History window provides you with complete information about each of the updates you installed. You can sort the updates in various ways to make it easier to find the update you need to research. If you don't see the update listed in this window, then you haven't installed it on your machine. It's important to note that whereas many Microsoft products appear in this window, third-party products don't.

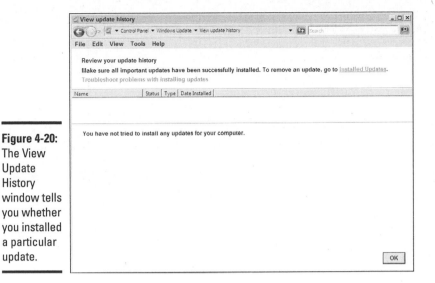

Figure 4-20:
The View
Update
History
window tells
you whether
you installed
a particular
update.

Restoring hidden updates

You may decide at some point that you don't need a particular update. Perhaps the update affects a feature you never use or appears in a language you don't speak. There are many reasons that you might not need a particular update, most of which have nothing to do with not wanting to install the update in the first place.

Unfortunately, you may find that you need a particular update that you didn't install. When this situation occurs, you can restore the update to the list of things to install, download the required update, and install it as you normally would. When you click Restore Hidden Updates, you see the Restore Hidden Updates window, shown in Figure 4-21.

The Restore Hidden Updates window provides various sort options to make it easier for you to find a particular update. When you locate an update you need, select it and click Restore. Windows Update adds the update back into the list of updates that you need to apply to your system.

Customizing Your Server

After you're sure that you have updated your server and that someone can contact it on your private network, it's time to begin adding roles and features to the server. This portion of the initial configuration task determines the capabilities of the server and defines how users will eventually interact with it. It's important to note that users still can't access the server, which is good because you're still configuring it.

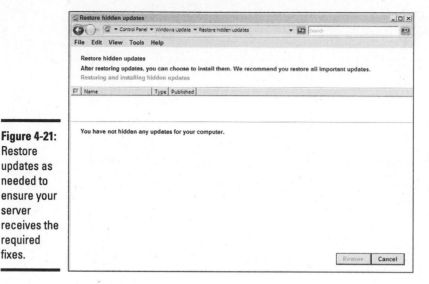

Figure 4-21:
Restore
updates as
needed to
ensure your
server
receives the
required
fixes.

When you complete this step, you thoroughly test your server to make sure it provides everything the user needs. After you're sure that the user will find everything needed, that all the hardware works, and that all the patches are applied, you can begin letting users access the server. Of course, you need to configure the server to allow this access. The "Performing User Configuration for a Workgroup" section of Book II, Chapter 4 tells you how to configure users for workgroup scenarios.

The following sections provide a quick overview of roles and features. In addition, you discover how you can use Remote Desktop to access your server from a client system. Finally, you find out a little about how Windows Firewall can help protect your server.

Adding roles

As previously mentioned, roles determine major functionality of a server. Fortunately, Microsoft provides a special wizard for installing roles on Windows Server 2008. You access this wizard by clicking Add Roles. Figure 4-22 shows the Add Roles Wizard.

Microsoft makes it easy to add new roles. All you need to do is check the roles you want to add and then click Next. The installation of new roles is nearly automatic. Notice how the Description field, at the right side of the Add Roles Wizard, tells you about the particular role you have highlighted. If you want additional information about the role, simply click the link. In addition, you find detailed information about each of the roles in this book. The "Working with roles" section of Book II, Chapter 1 tells you how roles enhance your server's functionality. The "Understanding the Server Roles" section of the same chapter tells you about all of the roles that Windows Server 2008 provides.

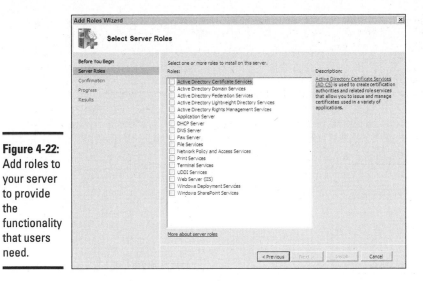

Figure 4-22:
Add roles to
your server
to provide
the
functionality
that users
need.

Whenever you choose a role that has additional requirements, the Add Roles Wizard displays an additional dialog box, such as the one shown in Figure 4-23. In this case, to install the Application Server role, you must also install the required .NET Framework functionality. The Application Server role relies on a managed application interface, so you have to have required software support to use it.

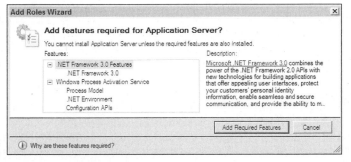

Figure 4-23:
Add roles
and features
as needed
to fully
support the
selected
role.

Adding features

As with adding new roles, Microsoft provides the Add Features Wizard to help you install new features, as shown in Figure 4-24. You find that the Add Features Wizard has many other similarities to the Add Roles Wizard. For example, when you highlight a particular feature, the Add Features Wizard shows a description of it in the Description field. Clicking the link displays additional help about the feature. The "Working with features" section of

Book II, Chapter 1 tells you how features extend the capabilities of your server. The "Understanding the Server Features" section of Book II, Chapter 1 tells you about all the features that Windows Server 2008 provides.

Working with the Add Features Wizard is the same as working with the Add Roles Wizard. When you want to install a feature, check its entry in the list and click Next to install it. As with roles, when a feature requires additional elements to install properly, you see a dialog box, similar to the one shown in Figure 4-23, that asks whether you want to install the additional role or feature.

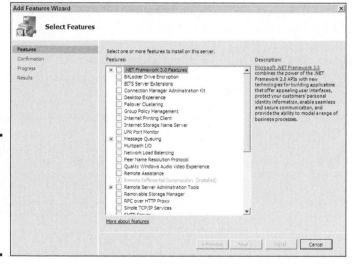

Figure 4-24: Add features to your server to enhance its capabilities.

Enabling Remote Desktop

Remote Desktop is possibly one of the best features an administrator can install because it lets you see the server desktop as if you're sitting in front of the server, without actually being there. When you click Enable Remote Desktop, you see the Remote tab of the System Properties dialog box, shown in Figure 4-25. To enable Remote Desktop, select one of the two connection options shown.

Remote Desktop allows two levels of connection. Select the first Allow Connections setting when you want to connect using an older Windows client, such as Windows XP. This setting is less secure because it doesn't provide the detailed security checks on the caller that newer versions of Windows can provide. Use the second Allow Connections setting when you want to connect using a Vista client. This option provides far greater security, and you should use it when you can. In all cases, the Administrators group automatically has access to the server using Remote Desktop. If you want to use Remote Desktop for administration tasks only, don't add any users to the list of people allowed to connect to the server.

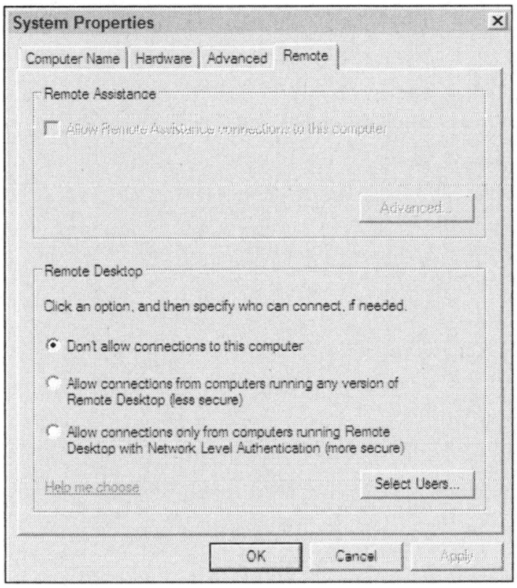

Figure 4-25:
Enable
Remote
Desktop
when you
want to
connect to
the server
from a
remote
location.

Remote Desktop provides considerable flexibility and has many convenience features you'll want to know about. The "Working with Remote Desktop" section of Book III, Chapter 5 provides detailed information about using Remote Desktop to manage your server.

Configuring the Windows Firewall

The Windows Firewall protects your system from outside intrusion. Unlike previous versions of Windows, Windows Server 2008 provides both incoming and outgoing protection. The two-way protection greatly reduces the potential for compromising data or allowing outsiders access to your server. The Windows Firewall is on by default when you install Windows Server 2008 and you'll find that it doesn't allow much interaction with the outside world. Figure 4-26 shows the Windows Firewall window you see when you click Configure Windows Firewall.

To a certain extent, Windows Firewall is self-configuring. When you add a role or feature that requires outside access, Windows automatically adds the required exception to Windows Firewall so that the role or feature works as expected. When you uninstall the role or feature, Windows automatically removes the exception so that Windows Firewall doesn't have an unneeded security hole. However, in many cases, you need to add or remove exceptions manually because Windows doesn't know what to do. You always have to add exceptions when working with third-party products. (Some newer products make the configuration changes for you, but not many of them are on the market as of this writing.) The "Configuring Windows Firewall with Advanced Security" section of Book V, Chapter 4 provides detailed information about configuring the Windows Firewall.

Figure 4-26:
Windows
Firewall
helps
protect your
system from
outside
intrusion.

Configuring the Startup Options with BCDEdit

The Boot Configuration Database Editor (BCDEdit) utility is a complex piece of software that you use occasionally to reconfigure the boot selections for Windows. Unlike previous versions of Windows, Windows Server 2008 doesn't provide a way to edit the boot configuration using the Startup and Recovery dialog box. This dialog box is nowhere to be found in Windows Server 2008.

To start working with BCDEdit, you need to have a command prompt with Administrator privileges. Choose Start➪Programs➪Accessories to display the Accessories menu. Right-click Command Prompt and choose Run As Administrator from the context menu. You see a command prompt that tells you it's opened in Administrator mode.

The first thing you want to do is export the boot settings to disk. The reason you want to perform this task is to ensure that you can recover from any incorrect changes. To save the settings, type **BCDEdit /Export C:\MyBCD** and press Enter. This command line places a copy of the current Boot Configuration Database (BCD) in the root directory of the C drive, where you can find it if you need to recover from an error. To restore the settings you saved, type **BCDEdit /Import C:\MyBCD** and press Enter. In both cases, you see the message "The operation completed successfully" when the command is successful.

This chapter doesn't provide usage instructions for every feature of BCDEdit because it's such a complex utility. However, you can see all the tasks that BCDEdit can perform by typing **BCDEdit /?** and pressing Enter. If you need additional information about a particular feature, such as exporting data, type **BCDEdit /CommandLineSwitch /?** and press Enter. Replace Command LineSwitch with a command line switch, such as /Export.

Before you can do anything with BCDEdit, you need to know about the contents of the BCD. To perform this task, type **BCDEdit /Enum** and press Enter. You see a listing of the current boot options, as shown in Figure 4-27.

Figure 4-27:
BCDEdit
provides
you with full
details
about your
boot
configur-
ation.

Figure 4-27 shows a server that has three boot partitions. The Windows Boot Manager entry determines which of these boot partitions boots by default and the order in which the boot entries appear. The Default property shows the default boot partition, which is {current} in this case. The Display Order property shows the actual boot order. You use the TimeOut property to determine how long the Boot Manager waits to choose a selection. All these entries are configurable. For example, if you want to change the TimeOut property to 35 seconds, you type **BCDEdit /Set {bootmgr} TimeOut 35** and press Enter. The command consists of five parts:

+ The BCDEdit command
+ The verb telling BCDEdit what you want to do
+ The name of the object that will receive the verb's action
+ The name of the property you want to change
+ The new property value

If you make a mistake with BCDEdit, your system may not boot at all. Whenever you complete a task, make sure you use the BCDEdit /Enum command to ensure that you made the correct change. Verify that the property you changed contains all the correct information.

The first partition on this system is a Windows 2003 server. You can quickly see these partitions because the BCDEdit /Enum output displays them as Windows Legacy OS Loader, as shown in Figure 4-27. Let's say you want to change the description for this operation system option (the way it will appear on the boot menu) to Windows 2003 Server. In this case, you type **BCDEdit /Set {ntldr} Description "Windows 2003 Server"** and press Enter. Notice that you must enclose the property value in double quotes. Whenever a property value contains one or more spaces, you must use double quotes or else BCDEdit will enter the property value incorrectly into the database.

Notice that each of the boot partition entries has an Identifier property. In some cases, the identifier is an easy-to-read name, such as {ntldr} or {current}. However, in other cases, you see a Globally Unique Identifier (GUID) instead. Every Identifier property is unique, so the GUID ensures this uniqueness. Notice that the third boot partition uses a GUID. To make changes to this partition, you must type the GUID without error. The following steps tell the easiest way to perform this task:

1. **Right-click the Command Prompt window and choose Mark from the context menu.**

2. **Drag the mouse across the GUID.**

   Windows highlights the GUID as you select it.

3. **Press Enter.**

   Windows places the highlighted information on the Clipboard.

4. **Type the beginning of the command, up to the point where you need to type the GUID.**

5. **Right-click the Command Prompt window and choose Paste from the context menu.**

   Windows pastes the GUID into the current cursor position on-screen.

Part II

Configuration

The 5th Wave   By Rich Tennant

EARLY STORAGE SOLUTION

"Configuring it has been a little tougher than we thought."

Contents at a Glance

Chapter 1: Configuring Server Roles and Features

In This Chapter

✔ **Performing management tasks using the Server Manager console**

✔ **Performing management tasks using the ServerManagerCmd utility**

✔ **Understanding the Windows Server 2008 roles**

✔ **Understanding the Windows Server 2008 features**

*M*ost administrators are used to working with Windows using the Add or Remove Programs applet in the Control Panel. You use this applet to locate the server functionality you want to install. However, the Add or Remove Programs applet can hide server functionality or, at least, make it difficult to install correctly. Consequently, Microsoft has used a different approach in Windows Server 2008, by dividing installation functionality into two areas — roles and features — and making both considerably more accessible than in the past.

Roles and features are very different from each other. They serve completely different functions in Windows Server 2008. A *role* is a major server activity, such as providing file services or acting as a DHCP server. A *feature* is software you add, such as Windows PowerShell or Group Policy Management, to help the server perform its tasks. This chapter describes each of the roles and features available in Windows Server 2008 Enterprise Edition. If you install one of the other editions of Windows Server 2008, you may find that you don't have all these roles and features available to you.

Book I, Chapter 4 describes how you can use the Initial Configuration Tasks window to manage roles and features in Windows Server 2008. After you complete the initial configuration of your server, you may still need to add or remove roles and features. Windows Server 2008 provides two additional methods of performing this task: the Server Management console and the ServerManagerCmd command line utility. This chapter describes both techniques.

Using the Server Manager Console

Book I, Chapter 4 describes the Initial Configuration Tasks window, which organizes management tasks in a suggested order for an initial configuration.

However, at some point, the initial configuration is complete and the server enters a management mode. At this point, the Initial Configuration Tasks window is no longer especially helpful because Microsoft hasn't arranged the tasks in an order that you would use to maintain the server.

The Server Manager console, shown in Figure 1-1, is the tool you should use for management tasks. As you can see, this tool organizes the management tasks in a different order — one that helps you to maintain the server after the initial setup. The Server Manager console automatically appears when you close the Initial Configuration Tasks window. When you check Do Not Show This Window at Login in the Initial Configuration Tasks window, the Server Manager console is the first window you see when you start Windows Server 2008.

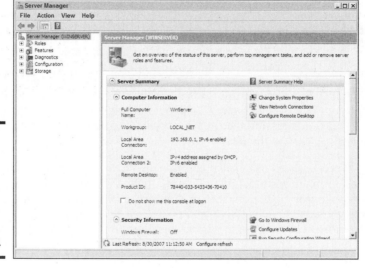

Figure 1-1:
The Server Manager console is the tool of choice for managing your server.

As with the Initial Configuration Tasks window, you can check Do Not Show Me This Console at Logon to keep the Server Manager console from appearing when you first start Windows Server 2008. However, unlike with the Initial Configuration Tasks window, you have many ways to display the Server Manager console:

✦ Double-click the Server Manager entry in the Administrative Tools folder of the Control Panel.

✦ Choose Start⇨Programs⇨Administrative Tools⇨Server Manager when using the Classic Start Menu option with Display Administrative Tools option selected.

✦ Choose Start➪Run, type **CompMgntLauncher** in the Open field, and
click OK.

✦ Locate the `\Windows\System32` folder in Windows Explorer and
double-click the `CompMgntLauncher.EXE` entry.

No matter how you open the Server Manager console, you see a summary
like the one shown in Figure 1-1 when you initially open the program. This
summary includes information such as the number of roles and features you
have installed, the security features you have in place, and the resources
you have available. In the left pane, you see a number of detail views you can
use to refine your understanding of the server configuration. The following
sections describe these detail views.

Working with roles

Windows Server 2008 comes with no roles installed. However, you'll find that
it supports a host of roles, as described in the "Understanding the Server
Roles" section of this chapter. When you select Roles in the left pane of
Server Manager, you see a summary of the roles installed on the server, as
shown in Figure 1-2. You can also drill down into configurable roles in the left
pane, as shown in Figure 1-2. The following sections describe in detail how to
work with roles.

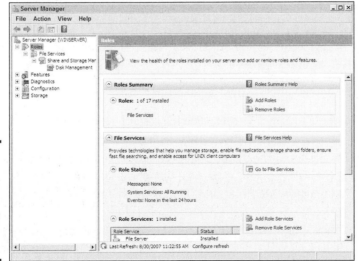

Figure 1-2:
Roles help
define the
major
functionality
of your
server.

Drilling down into a role

Whenever you drill down into a role, you see the details about that role. The further you drill, the more detailed the information becomes. For example, when you choose the File Services role, shown in 1-2, you see an overview of the File Services role, as shown in Figure 1-3.

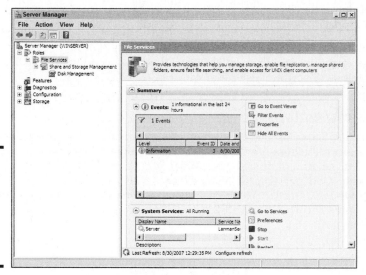

Figure 1-3:
Drilling down into a role shows details about that role.

The overview helps you understand the role better and configure it with greater ease. Some features help you maintain the role so that your organization gets maximum benefit from it. The precise information you see in this overview depends on the role, but the File Services role includes

✦ Access to Event Viewer. (See the "Event Viewer" section of Book III, Chapter 1 for details.)

✦ Details about the status of any related services. (See Book VIII for details.)

✦ A list of additional services related to the role. (For details, see the "Adding role services" and "Removing role services" sections of this chapter.)

✦ A listing of the resources and support that Microsoft provides for this role.

The right side of the summary pane provides a list of actions you can perform with a particular element. For example, when you select an event log entry, you can click Properties to see it. Likewise, when you want to view all the events associated with a role, click Go to Event Viewer. If you don't want to see all the events related to a particular role, you can click Filter Events to filter the entries. If you really don't want to see any events, you can click Hide All Events to hide them (they still exist within the event log and you can click Show Hidden Events to display them again).

One of the major improvements that Microsoft has made is to make you aware of resources and support at your disposal. Microsoft provided considerable resources in the past, but finding them was difficult at best (quite often impossible, in fact). Each role summary now includes a Resources and Support section, similar to the one shown in Figure 1-4.

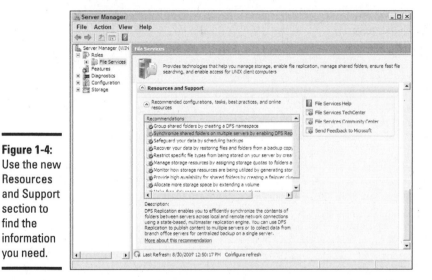

Figure 1-4:
Use the new Resources and Support section to find the information you need.

When you see a help topic you want to investigate, highlight its entry in the list and click More About This Recommendation. You see a Help file open with the required information selected. Each of the roles also provides a Help overview. For example, when you click File Services Help, shown in Figure 1-4, you see a Help file open with a File Services role overview. You also see a list of online resources as part of the Resources and Support section. In this case, the File Services role provides links to

✦ File Services TechCenter (provides articles and downloadable resources)

✦ File Services Community Center (where you can ask questions about the File Services role)

✦ Send Feedback to Microsoft (lets you tell Microsoft that you didn't find the information you need or that it was easy to find or helpful)

As you drill further down into the File Services hierarchy in the left pane, you see additional overviews in the right pane. For example, when you choose Share and Storage Management, you see a listing of shares on the local server. You can also determine who's using the shares and see how they logged in to the system. At the next level down, you can see the physical devices that support the shares. In short, you can drill down into the File Services role as far as needed to perform required management tasks without having to go to other utilities, as you did in the past. Although this section focuses on the File Services role, the same techniques apply to every other role you install.

Adding roles

You still have access to the Add or Remove Programs applet, as you did in the past, in Windows Server 2008. However, Microsoft has changed the name of this feature to Programs and Features. It's still possible to add or remove roles using this approach. Server Manager provides another option that you might want to try, however: Adding and removing roles can now rely on a wizard that helps you create a complete role rather than install a particular piece of software and find that you didn't install enough.

This section describes the process of adding roles using the wizard. You'll find the removal process described in the "Removing roles" section of this chapter. The following steps describe how to add a role:

 1. **Open Server Manager and choose Roles in the left pane.**

 You see a Role Summary view, as shown in Figure 1-2.

 2. **Click Add Roles.**

 Server Manager displays the Before You Begin page of the Add Roles Wizard dialog box. Make sure you read the instructions on this page before you proceed. You can avoid displaying this page every time you start the wizard by checking Skip This Page by Default.

 3. **Click Next.**

 The Add Roles Wizard displays a list of available roles, as shown in Figure 1-5. The wizard automatically grays out any installed roles so that you don't install them a second time.

 4. **Check each of the roles you want to install.**

 When you select some roles, you see an Add Roles Wizard dialog box, such as the one shown in Figure 1-6. It tells you that you must install another role to obtain the desired functionality.

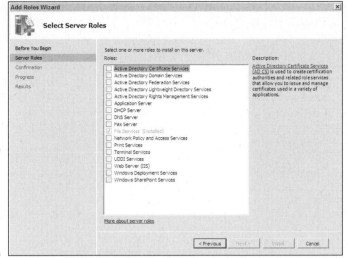

Figure 1-5:
Choose the
roles you
want to
install on
the server.

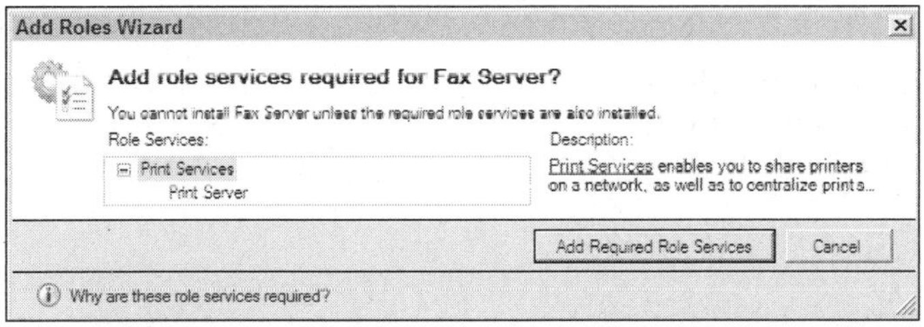

Figure 1-6:
Some roles
rely on other
roles to
work
properly.

5. **Click Add Role Service as needed to install dependent roles.**

As you add roles, the Add Roles Wizard also adds configuration steps, as
shown in Figure 1-7. These additional steps vary by role, so you may see
many steps in some cases and only one or two in others. An overview
page at the beginning of each configuration step (such as the one shown
in Figure 1-7) tells you what to expect and details the purpose of each
step. Individual steps perform specific configuration tasks for that role.

6. **Perform any required configuration. Click Next for each additional
configuration step.**

Sometimes a configuration step adds roles to the server. For example, if
you choose Internet Printing in the Role Services step for the Print
Services role, you see an Add Roles Wizard dialog box, like the one shown
in Figure 1-6, to add the Web Server (IIS) role and Windows Process
Activation Service feature when you don't have these elements installed.

Figure 1-7:
Adding roles
adds steps
to the
wizard to
provide role
configura-
tion.

7. Perform Step 6 as often as necessary to configure each role.

Eventually, you reach the Configuration Installation Selections page. This
page tells you what the wizard will install.

8. Verify the installation information, and then click Install.

You see the Installation Progress page. An indicator at the bottom of the
page provides information on how much of the installation is complete.
When the installation is complete, the Add Roles Wizard displays the
Installation Results page, where you can see the results of the installation.

9. Click Close.

Removing roles

At some point, you may decide to remove a role that you no longer need.
Removing a role in the past was error prone because you couldn't be sure
you had removed all the component parts. Windows Server 2008 improves
on this process through the Remove Roles Wizard. The following steps
describe how to remove a role you have installed on the server:

1. Open Server Manager and choose Roles in the left pane.

You see a Role Summary view, as shown in Figure 1-2.

2. Click Remove Roles.

Server Manager displays the Before You Begin page of the Remove Roles
Wizard dialog box. Make sure you read the instructions on this page
before you proceed. You can avoid displaying this page each time you
start the wizard by checking Skip This Page by Default.

3. **Click Next.**

The Remove Roles Wizard displays a list of roles, as shown in Figure 1-8. The wizard automatically grays out any roles you haven't installed.

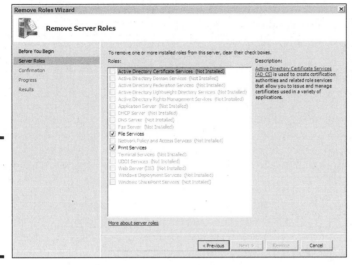

Figure 1-8:
Choose the roles you want to remove from the server.

Book II
Chapter 1

Configuring Server
Roles and Features

4. **Put a check mark next to the role you want to remove.**

The Remove Roles Wizard adds steps to the process as necessary to remove the role completely. Not every role requires that you perform additional steps, so you may not see any additional roles.

5. **Perform any required configuration. Click Next for each additional configuration step.**

6. **Perform Step 5 as often as necessary to configure the removal process for each role.**

Eventually you reach the Configuration Installation Selections page. This page tells you what the wizard will remove.

7. **Verify the removal information, and then click Remove.**

You see the Removal Progress page. An indicator at the bottom of the page provides information on how much of the removal process is complete. When the removal process is complete, The Remove Roles Wizard displays the Removal Results page, where you can see the results of the removal process. In most cases, this page also tells you that you must reboot the server to complete the removal process.

8. **Click Close.**

The Remove Roles Wizard asks whether you want to restart the server now. To prevent damage to your server, you normally should reboot immediately.

9. **Click Yes.**

The server reboots. After the server reboots, you see a Resuming Configuration dialog box. Eventually, the Removal Results dialog box returns and you see the results of the configuration process.

10. **Click Close.**

Adding role services

Sometimes a role provides multiple services. For example, when you install the print server, you can choose multiple print services, such as printing from the Internet. The File Server role includes the services shown in Figure 1-9.

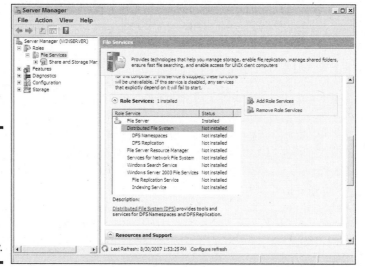

Figure 1-9: Most roles include role services that enhance role functionality.

Sometimes you must install a role service to install another role, but in many cases you can choose to install the service as necessary to enhance role functionality. You can determine the functionality of a particular role service by highlighting its entry in the Role Services list, shown in Figure 1-9. The Description field tells you about the role service. Click the associated link and you see additional information about the role service in the Help file. The following steps describe how to add a role service:

1. **Select the role you want to modify in Server Manager.**

2. **Locate the Role Services entry.**

If you don't see this entry, the role doesn't provide any role services and Microsoft doesn't provide anything to add to the role.

3. **Click Add Role Services.**

You see the Add Role Services dialog box. Figure 1-10 shows a typical example, but the entries in this dialog box vary by role. Any role services that you already installed appear grayed out.

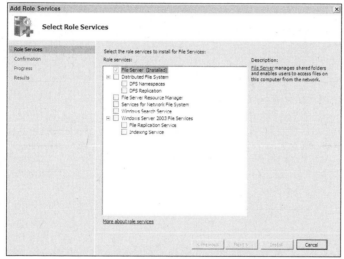

Figure 1-10:
Choose
the role
services you
want to add.

4. **Check each of the role services you want to add.**

In some cases, the wizard adds steps to configure the role services you choose, as shown in Figure 1-11. Unlike roles, the role services don't provide overview pages. They provide only specific configuration steps (as needed), such as the one shown in Figure 1-11.

5. **Perform any required configuration tasks.**

Eventually, you see the Confirm Installation Selections page.

6. **Click Install.**

You see an Installation Progress dialog box that contains a progress indicator. After the installation is complete, you see an Installation Results dialog box. At this point, the role services are ready to use.

7. **Click Close.**

Figure 1-11:
The specific configuration steps help you ensure a role service works as anticipated.

A successful installation of a role service doesn't necessarily mean that the role service will work immediately. In some cases, you may see errors in the event log. When this problem occurs, clear the event log entries, reboot the server, and check the event log again to make sure the errors are gone. If they aren't gone, troubleshoot the problem immediately before you install any other roles, role services, or features.

Removing role services

Removing a role automatically removes all role services that the role supports. You don't need to remove role services that you installed individually when you want to remove the role as a whole. However, you may find that you need to remove an individual role service at times. In this case, you can use the following steps to remove one or more individual role services without removing the role itself:

1. **Select the role you want to modify in Server Manager.**

2. **Click Remove Role Services.**

You see the Remove Role Services dialog box. Figure 1-12 shows a typical example, but the entries in this dialog box vary by role. Notice that role services you haven't installed appear grayed out.

3. **Clear the check next to each role service you want to remove.**

Clearing the uppermost entry, File Server, in Figure 1-12, removes the entire role. You lose all configuration options for the role. In many cases, you also need to perform extra work if you use this approach. If you want to remove the entire role, be sure to use the procedure found in the "Removing roles" section of this chapter.

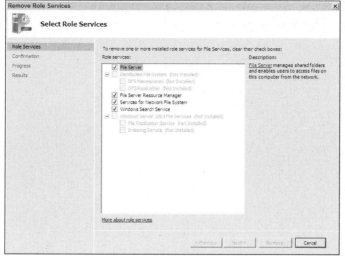

Figure 1-12:
Choose
the role
services you
want to
remove.

4. **Click Next.**

   You see the Confirm Removal Selections page, which shows which role services the wizard will remove for you.

5. **Verify the role services you want to remove and click Remove.**

   The Remove Role Services wizard displays a Removal Progress dialog box that contains a progress indicator. When the removal process is complete, the Remove Role Services Wizard displays a Removal Results window, where you can see the results of the removal process. In most cases, this page also tells you that you must reboot the server to complete the removal process.

6. **Click Close.**

   The Remove Roles Services Wizard asks whether you want to restart the server now. To prevent damage to your server, you normally want to reboot immediately.

7. **Click Yes.**

   The server reboots. After the server reboots, you see a Resuming Configuration dialog box. Eventually, the Removal Results dialog box returns, and you see the results of the configuration process.

8. **Click Close.**

Working with features

Windows Server 2008 comes with no features installed. However, you find that it supports a host of features (some of which are required to support roles), as described in the "Understanding the Server Features" section of this chapter. When you select Features in the left pane of Server Manager, you see a summary of the features installed on the server, as shown in Figure 1-13.

Figure 1-13: Features help extend the functionality of your server.

In a few cases, you also need entries you can use to drill down into specific features. Unlike roles, features rely on standard consoles that you would normally access from the Control Panel for configuration. Consequently, you don't find a description of the drill-down feature in this chapter. Look for each feature configuration console description in the appropriate section of the book.

Adding and removing features is almost the same as adding and removing roles (see the "Adding roles" and "Removing roles" sections of the chapter for details). The main difference is that you see the Add Features Wizard, shown in Figure 1-14, or the Remove Features Wizard in place of the Add Roles Wizard or Remove Roles Wizard. The basic concepts are the same, however.

As with roles, some features require you to add or remove other roles or features. For example, when you install the full .NET Framework 3.0 feature, you also need to install the Web Server (IIS) role and the Windows Process Activation Service feature. You even see the same dialog box shown in Figure 1-6 (except that the title bar says Add Features Wizard). In short, if you know how to add or remove a role, you also know how to add or remove a feature.

Performing diagnostics

Diagnostics help you locate and repair errors on your server. These tools help you measure your server's ability to perform useful work and through those measurements tell you when something is wrong. For example, Event Viewer provides you with a list of informative messages about your server. The three levels of message — error, warning, and information — tell you about the significance of the message and help you understand the effect of the message content on your system. The performance and reliability measuring tools provide a gauge of system state and help you determine when the system is no longer working as it should. You can see a list of these tools in Figure 1-15.

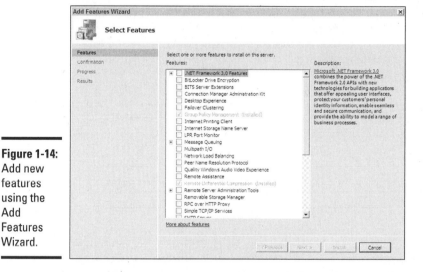

Figure 1-14:
Add new features using the Add Features Wizard.

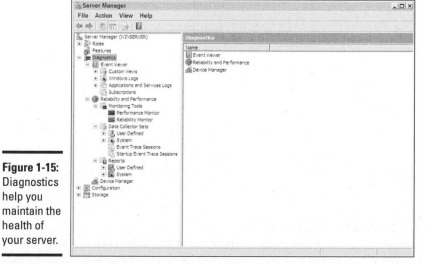

Figure 1-15:
Diagnostics help you maintain the health of your server.

Book III provides additional information about most of the diagnostic features that Windows Server 2008 provides. For example, you find information about Event Viewer in the "Event Viewer" section of Book III, Chapter 1. The "Measuring Reliability and Performance" section of Book III, Chapter 5 tells you how to use the Reliability and Performance feature. You find the Device Manager details in the "Working with Device Manager" section of Book II, Chapter 2.

Performing configuration tasks

Configuration can cover a lot of ground. You already discovered the configuration tasks to initially configure your server in Book I, Chapter 4. This chapter also includes a considerable amount of configuration information, but of the sort used to manage the server. However, the Configuration section of Server Manager includes a different kind of configuration from what you've seen. In this case, *configuration* means the changing of existing server settings. You don't even have to install anything special to perform this configuration. Figure 1-16 shows the tasks you can perform using the Configuration section of Server Manager.

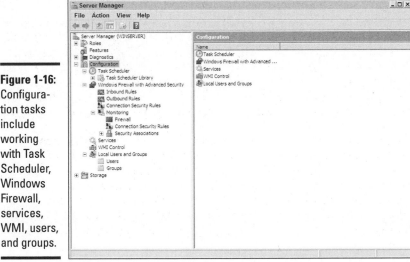

Figure 1-16: Configuration tasks include working with Task Scheduler, Windows Firewall, services, WMI, users, and groups.

It's important to note that many of these features are simple settings. For example, when you want to add a new user or group to the server, you use the Local Users and Groups entry. However, other features affect the system in a unique way. When you want to automate tasks so that they run at a specific time without your intervention, you rely on Task Scheduler. In many respects, Task Scheduler doesn't change anything the user would ever notice, but you notice its effect. By setting tasks to execute automatically, you make it more likely that the system will receive proper maintenance, download and install both patches and updates, and even configure itself as needed on a specific schedule. Using automation makes you more efficient and ensures that the user always receives the expected service. The point is that configuration, in this case, may mean thinking outside the box if you plan to obtain the maximum benefit from it.

Books III and VIII provide additional information about most of the configuration task features that Windows Server 2008 provides. For example, you find details on using Task Scheduler in the "Automating Diagnostic Tasks with Task Scheduler" section of Book III, Chapter 5. The Windows Firewall with Advanced Security feature appears in the "Windows Firewall with Advanced Security" section of Book V, Chapter 4. Because services can be a complicated topic, you find them discussed in Book VIII. Even though you can use the Windows Management Interface (WMI) to configure all aspects of Windows Server 2008, you find the major elements of this feature described in Book VIII, Chapters 1 and 2. Book II, Chapter 4 tells you how to configure users and groups for workgroups. You find the same information for domains in the "Configuring Objects in Active Directory" section of Book III, Chapter 4.

Configuring and managing storage

The storage options supported by your server are possibly the most important and expensive part of the server. If you lose an entire server, you might lose some money and a little time. However, if you lose your data, you might cost your company contracts and certainly the good will of any clients. When the data loss is severe enough, a company can actually shut down because the loss is too expensive to overcome. Data is a difficult concept to understand in many ways because it isn't something you can touch — data is abstract.

Considering the impact that data has on your organization, you must manage storage on the server carefully. Windows Server 2008 has gone a long way toward making data storage considerably safer. Data encryption ensures that the data is safe from prying eyes, diagnostics help ensure the integrity of the data, backups provide a means of overcoming disasters, and other tools help manage the structure of the data itself. Figure 1-17 shows the storage management features you can access from Server Manager itself.

Figure 1-17: Storage features help you perform backups and manage disks.

Book III, Chapter 5 tells you all about configuring and managing storage on your server. The "Performing a system backup" and "Performing a system restore" sections tell how to manage your data safely. You find the details of managing your hard drive setup in the "Performing Disk Management Tasks" section of that chapter.

Unlike many of the other Server Manager features described so far, the storage management functionality is incomplete. You find storage management features spread throughout this book. For example, if you want to protect your data, you might consider using BitLocker (see the "Encrypting your hard drive using BitLocker" section of Book II, Chapter 2 for details). Make sure to examine this book in detail for the storage strategies it provides. You may be surprised at the kinds of tools that Microsoft provides to help you make storage management both easier and more reliable.

Using the ServerManagerCmd Utility

Server Manager is the graphical interface that you normally use to interact with the server. However, you may find that you want to automate some configuration tasks. Using the graphical utility isn't the best way to automate tasks, so you want another method of performing the task. The command line utility equivalent of Server Manager is the ServerManagerCmd utility. This utility provides much of the same functionality as the graphical version. More importantly, it lets you automate tasks.

Before you can use the ServerManagerCmd utility, you must open a command prompt. The command prompt must have full administrator privileges. The "Opening an Administrative Command Line" section of Book III, Chapter 6 tells you how to open an administrator command prompt so that you can perform tasks at the command line.

Many command line utilities rely on commands or modes to accomplish tasks. Using one mode may help you retrieve the values that the command line utility supports while another mode helps you change a setting. The ServerManagerCmd utility provides six modes of operation. The first mode you commonly use is -query, as shown here.

```
ServerManagerCmd -query [<query.xml>] [-logPath <log.txt>]
```

When you use this mode, it displays all the roles and features that the server can support. All the entries have a box next to them, as shown in Figure 1-18. A check mark in this box shows that you installed the role or feature on the system. When you supply the name of an XML file, this mode also places the information in the named file for you. The ServerManagerCmd always logs the results of the -query mode. You use the -logPath command line argument to specify a different location for this log.

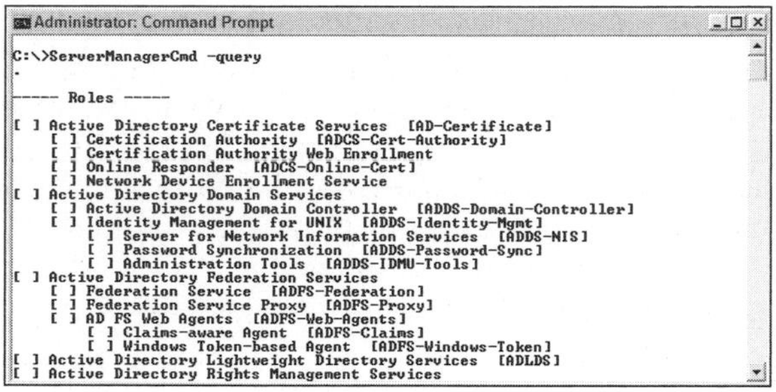

Figure 1-18:
Determine
the status of
the server
by using the
-query
mode.

After you determine the status of your server, you likely want to install or remove roles or features. The -query mode tells you the names of all roles and features that the server supports. You can install roles or features only when you haven't installed them already. Likewise, you can remove only features that you have installed. The ServerManagerCmd utility tells you when you make an error. Here's the command line you use to install or remove roles or features:

```
ServerManagerCmd -install <name>
    [-setting <setting name>=<setting value>]*
    [-allSubFeatures] [-resultPath <result.xml> [-restart]
    | -whatIf] [-logPath <log.txt>]

ServerManagerCmd -remove <name> [-resultPath <result.xml>
    [-restart]   | -whatIf] [-logPath <log.txt>]
```

The -install and -remove modes contain a lot of optional arguments. If you don't understand what an optional argument is, see the "Understanding Command Line Symbols" section of Book III, Chapter 6. In this case, all you have to provide is the name of the role or feature you want to install or remove. However, you may find that you also want to install all subfeatures for the role or feature. In this case, add the -allSubFeatures command line switch to the command line as well. Let's say you want to install the Fax Server role. That's its display name. However, the real name of this role is Fax, so you would type **ServerManagerCmd –install Fax** and press Enter. Figure 1-19 shows what happens.

Figure 1-19:
Install or remove roles and features as needed by providing the role or feature name.

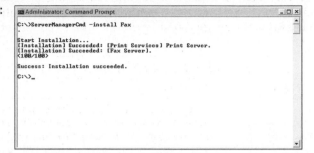

Notice that ServerManagerCmd automatically installs the required Print Server features because Fax Server needs them in order to function. ServerManagerCmd doesn't ask you about these support features — it assumes that you want to install them. Consequently, you have to review the output of any installation or removal that you perform because otherwise you could end up with features you never intended to install on the system. Use the –logPath argument to create a log of the installation so that you can review it later.

You may find that you want to install a number of roles and features at one time. It's possible to use a batch file or script to perform this task. However, the ServerManagerCmd utility provides a better way. Simply create an XML file that contains a list of the roles and features you want to install and provide this file as input to the –inputPath mode. Here's the command line for the –inputPath mode:

```
ServerManagerCmd -inputPath <answer.xml>
    [-resultPath <result.xml> [-restart] | -whatIf]
    [-logPath <log.txt>]
```

Sometimes you need a bit of help with the ServerManagerCmd utility. Most people don't memorize all the command line switches and arguments. Fortunately, you can obtain help quickly and easily by using the –help or -? modes shown here:

```
ServerManagerCmd -help | -?
```

Finally, for those times when you're not sure you have the most recent version of ServerManagerCmd, try the –version mode. Here's all you need to type:

```
ServerManagerCmd -version
```

Now that you have a better idea of how this utility works, you'll want to know more about the command line switches it uses. Table 1-1 describes the command line switches you need to perform any task.

Table 1-1	ServerManagerCmd Arguments and Switches
Argument or Switch	*Description*
Name	Specifies the name of the role or feature that you want to install. Make sure to use the feature's ID rather than its display name. For example, the Active Directory Certificate Services role has an ID of AD-Certificate.
-setting <setting name>= <setting value>	Provides any required settings to perform an installation. These settings are the same ones you provide using the various pages in the graphical interface. If you don't provide settings, ServerManagerCmd configures the role or feature using default settings.
-allSubFeatures	Specifies that you want to install all subordinate role services and features along with the role, role service, or feature. The ServerManagerCmd utility automatically installs required roles, role services, and features. You use this option only when you want to install optional elements as well.
-resultPath <result.xml>	Saves the result of performing a particular task with ServerManagerCmd to the file specified by `result.xml`. You can use any filename; however, you should ensure that the file has an XML filename so that you can read it properly with an application.
-restart	Automatically restarts the computer when ServerManagerCmd determines that a restart is necessary to complete the operation. Use this option carefully when installing new roles or features on a production server, because you can disconnect users accidentally.
-inputPath <answer.xml>	Defines the path and filename that holds the list of roles, role services, and features you want to install.
-whatIf	Displays the operations that the system will perform to install or remove a particular feature without actually performing them. The output is the same as the format for the `answer.xml` file, so you can use this command line switch to help create an `answer.xml` file.
-logPath <log.txt>	Species a nondefault location for the log file. Even though ServerManagerCmd always creates a log file, you may want to place the file in a location that you can reach with greater ease.

Of course, there's one final issue to consider about the ServerManagerCmd utility — the format of the `answer.xml` file. Microsoft strove to keep the format of this file very simple. All you really need to provide is a list of what you want to install or remove. For example, if you want to install the Web Server role, you create an `answer.xml` file with the following content:

```
<ServerManagerConfiguration Action="Install"
    xmlns="http://schemas.microsoft.com/sdm/Windows/
        ServerManager/Configuration/2007/1">
            <Role Id="Web-Server" />
</ServerManagerConfiguration>
```

Even though the `<ServerManagerConfiguration>` element appears on multiple lines in this book, it should appear on a single line in your file. The `Action` attribute tells ServerManagerCmd which task to perform. You can specify `Install` or `Remove` as the actions. The `<Role>` element tells ServerManagerCmd that you want it to install a new role with an ID value of Web-Server. Notice that you must enclose the ID value in double quotes. Use the `<RoleService>` element to install role services and the `<Feature>` element to install features.

Understanding the Server Roles

The roles that you see defined for your server depend on which version of Windows Server 2008 you purchase. Advanced versions of the product include more roles. In addition, the GUI version of Windows Server 2008 provides more roles than does the Server Core version. The following sections describe the roles that come with the GUI version of Windows Server 2008 Enterprise Edition. The roles you see with your server setup may vary from this list.

Considering the Active Directory Certificate Service role

You install this role to create a new Certificate Authority (CA). A *CA* is a special server used to issue certificates, such as those used to sign applications or enhance the security of your e-mail. The certificate tells someone else who you are and helps them determine whether they can trust you. These certificates are the same ones you see when you go to a secure Web site. In fact, you can use this role to help you create a certificate for your Web server, making secure communications possible (see the "Obtaining a Certificate" section of Book VII, Chapter 6 for details).

This role has limited functionality in the real world, but the functionality it provides is extremely important. Normally, the CA is a trusted third party, such as VeriSign. A self-signed certificate of the kind created by this role is good only in situations where the person seeing your certificate already trusts you. The certificate acts only as verification that it really is you and not someone posing as you. Common uses for this kind of certificate include testing setups of Internet Information Server (IIS) and in-house applications. Using a self-signed certificate saves money and lets you preserve the third-party certificate you own for external, public use.

Considering the Active Directory Domain Services role

This role is the one that Windows Server 2008 installs when you promote the server to a domain controller. Active Directory is a special kind of database that holds all the settings for everything on your network. You find user, application, and system settings in this database. In addition to storing settings, Active Directory provides support for major applications such as Microsoft Exchange Server. The Domain Services portion of an Active Directory setup is essentially the Database Management System (DBMS) that provides access to the Active Directory database.

You can't install this role by itself. Windows Server 2008 looks for a number of additional features. In addition, the setup for this role is more complicated than just about any other role you can install. Book II, Chapter 5 contains complete instructions on how to promote your server to a domain controller.

An overview of the Active Directory Federation Services role

One problem with modern networks is that the user has to remember so many logons. Every time the user wants to access another resource, it requires a logon of some sort. When you install Active Directory Domain Services (AD DS), you obtain federated logon capability for the local network. A *federated* logon is one in which a Single Sign On (SSO) acts as a key to access all areas of the network for which the user has the appropriate credentials. Using SSO makes working with the network considerably easier.

Unfortunately, the federated services provided with AD DS don't extend to Web applications. When a user logs on to your server from a remote location through multiple Web applications, every Web application requires a separate logon. The Active Directory Federation Services (AD FS) role adds support for SSO to your server. The user can now log on once and access every application for which the user has the proper credentials. Of course, not just local users require these services. You can also use this feature to make things easier for your business-to-business (B2B) relationship. The more complex the B2B relationship, the more sense it makes to install this role on your server.

Microsoft uses standardized technologies to provide AD FS support, in the form of the WS-* standards. A complete discussion of all these standards is outside the scope of this book. However, you can read about them, and see how they relate to each other, at `http://www.ws-standards.com/`.

Working with the Active Directory Lightweight Directory Services role

Most of the applications on your network don't use Active Directory for data storage. Only the large applications, such as Exchange Server, require extensive data storage in Active Directory. However, some applications fall between these two extremes of needing no Active Directory support and requiring the complete package. In this case, the application may need Active Directory Lightweight Directory Services (AD LDS).

You may know AD LDS by a different name, Lightweight Directory Access Protocol (LDAP). *LDAP* is a standardized technology that you find on many platforms, not just on Windows (see the LDAP standards at `http://www.ietf.org/rfc/rfc1777.txt` and `http://www.faqs.org/rfcs/rfc1823.html` for further information). It provides a standardized method of accessing directory information using TCP. AD LDS is an LDAP implementation that doesn't depend on AD DS. In other words, you can use this feature without promoting your server to a domain controller. You can find a listing of LDAP resources at `http://dir.yahoo.com/Computers_and_Internet/Communications_and_Networking/Protocols/LDAP__Lightweight_Directory_Access_Protocol_/`.

Working with the Active Directory Rights Management Services role

The whole purpose of Active Directory Rights Management Services (AD RMS) is Digital Rights Management (DRM). The features that this role provides help you protect your data by checking the credentials of each user requesting data access. It doesn't matter where the access occurs — the user must have proper rights to work with it.

Using this role implies that you want to protect access to your data when that access occurs outside your network. Consequently, you must install the Web Server (IIS) role to use this role. In addition, the software requires access to a DBMS. Microsoft naturally suggests that you use SQL Server to provide the DBMS services. These three pieces of the software combine to let a document "call home" and verify that someone opening it has the required permissions. When a user doesn't have the required permissions, the document doesn't let the user see anything.

The only problem with DRM is the speed with which people find ways around it. Microsoft's DRM solution was already hacked before Windows Server 2008 made it out the door (see `http://www.windowsitpro.com/Article/ArticleID/23000/23000.html` and `http://news.com.com/2100-1023-274721.html` for details). Of course, Microsoft will repair this hack, only to have someone else come along and hack it again. Generally speaking, the best way to keep a secret is not to tell anyone. When you have data that you must share, placing it on your Web server probably isn't the best idea. Restricting access — not telling the secret — is always the best first line of defense at your disposal.

Working with the Application Server role

An *application server* is a special way of providing services to a client machine. The application executes partially on the server and partially on the client. Precisely how the application works depends on where the developer determines the particular piece of code works best. The Application Server role provides this functionality to Windows Server 2008 users. The following list provides additional resources you can use for this topic:

Book II
Chapter 1

Configuring Server
Roles and Features

✦ Discover the Enterprise Service Bus (ESB) at `http://www.microsoft.com/biztalk/solutions/soa/esb.mspx`.

✦ See the Microsoft Enterprise Services Overview at `http://www.microsoft.com/downloads/details.aspx?FamilyId=B4FF0934-2CF1-423B-B273-D482E60442BA`.

✦ Discover .NET Framework 3.0 resources at `http://www.microsoft.com/events/series/msdnnetframework3.aspx`.

✦ Obtain an overview of the .NET Framework 3.0 at `http://msdn2.microsoft.com/en-us/library/ms687307.aspx`.

Considering the DHCP Server role

The Dynamic Host Configuration Protocol (DHCP) is a standard means for client computers to request an Internet Protocol (IP) address from a server. You normally need just one such server for a small to medium-size network. You must have a DHCP server installed before you can promote your server to a domain controller. (See the "Installing DHCP" section of Book II, Chapter 5 for details. You should also review the "Understanding DHCP" section of Book IV, Chapter 1.)

Considering the DNS Server role

The Domain Name System (DNS) is a standard means of converting IP addresses into a human readable form. For example, when you want to access Microsoft's main page, you type `http://www.microsoft.com`, not the IP address of the Microsoft Web site. The DNS server converts this human readable name into the IP address. You must have a DNS server installed before you can promote your server to a domain controller (see the "Installing DNS" section of Book II, Chapter 5 for details). You should also review the "Understanding DNS" section of Book IV, Chapter 1.

An overview of the Fax Server role

Installing the Fax Server role lets you use your server to send and receive faxes, if you have the required hardware and software installed. This role also requires that you install the Print Server role.

An overview of the File Services role

Installing the File Services role lets you share files on the network. This role is the one you *always* install on the server because a server isn't much good if you can't share files. Adding the File Services role provides basic file sharing only.

File services haven't changed much over the years. The first peer-to-peer network provided this basic functionality. However, file services have increased in functionality. You can install a number of role services to enhance the capability of this particular role. For example, Microsoft provides a role service that indexes content to make it easier and faster to find.

Considering the Network Policy and Access Services role

The name of this particular role is a bit misleading because it provides a lot more functionality than its name implies. In fact, installing this particular role provides the following services:

✦ Network Policy Server (NPS)

✦ Network Access Protection (NAP) Health Policy Server

✦ Secure Wireless Access (IEEE 802.11)

✦ Secure Wired Access (IEEE 802.3)

✦ Central Network Policy Management

✦ Remote Access Dial-In User Server (RADIUS) Server and Proxy

✦ Remote Access Service (RAS)

✦ Routing

✦ Health Registration Authority (HRA)

✦ Host Credential Authorization Protocol (HCAP)

✦ Tools Required to Manage All Access Services

The scope of this particular role is incredible. It provides many of the features that modern servers must provide for outside communication. You can discover more about these features in the "Working with Remote Access Services" section of Book IV, Chapter 3.

Considering the Print Services role

Providing print services is another common role for servers. At one time, printers were extremely expensive (and good printers still are), so issuing one to each user wasn't cost effective. This role helps you manage all printers connected to the server and offers their use to any users with the required access. You can learn more about printer-related tasks in the "Performing Printer-Related Tasks" section of Book II, Chapter 2.

Considering the Terminal Services role

Terminal Services offers remote connectivity to anyone who needs to work with the server directly. In many cases, this activity means using a light client or involves an administrator performing configuration tasks. The two most common ways to use Terminal Services is by using Remote Desktop or by using RemoteApp applications.

Using Terminal Services offers many benefits, including reducing client costs and ensuring that applications remain updated. Of course, many issues arise from working with Terminal Services as well, such as increased server load. You can discover more about these features in the "Working with Terminal Server" section of Book IV, Chapter 3.

**Book II
Chapter 1**

**Configuring Server
Roles and Features**

Considering the UDDI Services role

The Universal Description, Discovery, and Integration (UDDI) service is the Microsoft method of making Web services and their associated applications easily accessible from the server. For the most part, you never install this role unless you have a custom application that relies on it.

Considering the Web Server (IIS) role

Web servers traditionally serve content over the Internet or an intranet. Users view the content by using a browser or a special application. Modern Web servers provide fully distributed application support in addition to dynamic and static content. IIS 7.0 is a completely new version of IIS with many changes that will surprise you if you haven't worked with it yet. Book VII provides complete details on working with IIS 7.0.

Working with the Windows Deployment Services role

If you normally install Windows through your server, you need to install this role. The Windows Deployment Services lets a client log in to the server and install a complete copy of Windows without any interaction on the part of the user or administrator. Of course, you have to perform a number of configuration tasks to make this feature work. You can learn more about Windows Deployment Services at `http://msdn2.microsoft.com/en-us/library/aa967394.aspx`.

Working with the Windows SharePoint Services role

The SharePoint Services technology lets application users share data through the server. The application must provide the functionality required to work with SharePoint Services. For example, advanced versions of Office 2007 provide the functionality required to use SharePoint Services. Of course, before you can use SharePoint Services, you must have a server with the SharePoint Services role installed in order to provide the required connectivity, which is the only reason that you would install this role. You can learn more about SharePoint Services at `http://www.microsoft.com/technet/windowsserver/sharepoint/default.mspx`.

Understanding the Server Features

You normally add server features as needed to address a specific requirement. For example, when your server needs to provide support for Windows PowerShell so that you can use the new scripting features Microsoft provides, you normally install the .NET Framework 3.0 features as well. The combination of these features lets you perform additional tasks, even though the actual role of the server hasn't changed. In some, the server has augmented capability but doesn't have a change in role. The following sections describe each of the features you can install in Windows 2008 Enterprise Edition. The features you can install on your server depend on the Windows Server 2008 version, as well as the Windows Server 2008 edition that you install.

Considering the .NET Framework 3.0 features

The .NET Framework provides all the managed functionality that you need to run managed applications. Microsoft is promoting *managed* applications, those that rely on the .NET Framework as safer, more reliable, and more secure. Theoretically, managed applications offer all these features, but many of these features are available only when the developer provides the proper support within the application code.

The .NET Framework 3.0 builds on the functionality of the .NET Framework 2.0 to provide additional features. Some of these features you don't need on a server, such as the Aero Glass interface provided on Vista machines. However, other features provide interesting functionality for servers, such as the improved access to Web services offered by the Windows Communication Foundation (WCF). Make sure to talk with the application developer to determine whether you need to install the .NET Framework 3.0 features to support an application and which level of support the application requires. You can learn more about the .NET Framework 3.0 in Book VI, Chapter 2.

Considering the BitLocker Drive Encryption feature

BitLocker is a full drive-encryption technology that relies on one of several key technologies to unlock the drive during the boot process. Many servers have a Trusted Platform Module (TPM) chip installed (see the Web site at `https://www.trustedcomputinggroup.org/groups/tpm/` for details on this technology). This chip holds the key to unlocking the drive. You must provide a personal identification number (PIN) to activate the key. As an alternative, you can place the key on a flash drive (those little key fob devices that contain several gigabytes of storage). Placing the flash drive (see `http://www.usbflashdrive.org/` for details on this technology) in a Universal Serial Bus (USB) port provides the key to access the encrypted hard drive during the boot process.

**Book II
Chapter 1**

**Configuring Server
Roles and Features**

The theory behind BitLocker is that the drive is secure unless you provide someone with the key. Even removing the drive from the system and placing it in another system doesn't provide access to the required key. No one can boot the drive and gain access to your data, at least in theory. So far, implementations of BitLocker affect only the boot drive, so you must encrypt other drives in the system by using other technologies. In addition, BitLocker may not be a good solution for your server. If you lose the key, the drive's data is locked forever — no recovery is possible. For the most part, locking up your server and securing the hard drive in other ways seems like a prudent way to encrypt the drive.

Don't get the idea that BitLocker is a somewhat useless technology in search of a problem. Just because it isn't the optimal technology for your server doesn't mean that you can't use it in other places. This technology is the option of choice for laptops because you can't lock up your laptop in a secure room, and people do simply pick them up when they see them in public places, such as airports. You can learn more about the process for using BitLocker in the "Encrypting your hard drive using BitLocker" section of Book II, Chapter 2.

Considering the BITS Server Extensions feature

If you've ever used Windows Update, you've used the Background Intelligent Transfer Service (BITS). BITS provides the means to continue an upload or download despite poor line conditions, disconnections, and even reboots. The BITS Server Extensions feature lets clients upload files to your server by using the BITS technology. The server can also send files to the client by using BITS technology. If your server provides files to client systems or requires the client to perform uploads, this feature is an excellent one to install because you already have access to it on the client.

Working with the Connection Manager Administration Kit (CMAK) feature

The CMAK functionality helps you define connection scenarios for clients accessing your server. Connection scenarios can include everything from a dial-up connection used on the weekend to upload or download files to a full Virtual Private Network (VPN) connection used to conduct business from a remote location. Here are some basic reasons to use CMAK:

✦ Avoid creating connections manually.

✦ Create secure connections that users can't change.

✦ Preconfigure Web Proxy connections so that users don't need to guess about them.

✦ Define firewall policies so that the connection works with the firewall rather than against it.

✦ Update telephone numbers automatically using the server's Phone Book Service.

✦ Rely on the Routing and Remote Access Quarantine service to protect your network from inappropriate scripting.

Obviously, creating a connection is the most basic reason to use CMAK, but all these other features are useful too. This is a complex feature that requires that you perform custom connection setups and is outside the scope of this book. For further details, see the documentation online here:

```
http://technet2.microsoft.com/windowsserver/en/Library/
    be5c1c37-109e-49bc-943e-6595832d57611033.mspx
```

Defining the Desktop Experience feature

You install this feature to make your server look a lot more like Vista, rather than like an improved version of Windows 2003. The problem is that all the Vista "eye candy" consumes a lot of resources, yet doesn't really provide any improvement in operating system functionality, reliability, security, or performance. Given that you probably don't use your server as a workstation, installing this feature is probably the worst thing you can do. Installing it gives you lots of Vista eye candy, but also reduces server performance and response time as a minimum.

Considering the Failover Clustering feature

If your organization has multiple Windows Server 2008 installations, you can use failover clustering to improve overall system reliability. When a server fails, the load that server was carrying is transferred to another server. The user likely notices a drop in performance but still continues using the network, oblivious to the failure. The servers must communicate with each other to implement this feature, so you see the effects of the additional overhead. Generally, the servers become a little less responsive. Depending on your setup, no one may even notice that change. In essence, you trade some performance to obtain additional reliability.

Failover clustering can't overcome certain kinds of failures. For example, if your entire network goes down, failover clustering doesn't help. In fact, if you lose more than one server on a cluster with five servers set up, you probably experience performance degradation severe enough to render the failover clustering useless. Even so, this technology can help you overcome situations where a single server fails and you still want to maintain your business.

Considering the Group Policy Management feature

Group policy management is an important part of the enterprise. You can use it to control everything from the local machine to network connections to the server. Everything on your entire network probably has a setting you can use to control policy for it. Of course, this feature works only with Active Directory because you need the Active Directory database to store the settings.

Considering the Internet Printing Client feature

Sometimes clients need to print from the Internet using the local server. The Internet Printing Protocol (IPP) helps the client perform this task with relative ease. Using this feature lets the client send a report to a collaborator or perform other printing-related tasks.

Considering the Internet Storage Name Server feature

The Internet Storage Name Server (iSNS) feature lets you make your local system hard drive available to Internet clients as an Internet Small Computer System Interface (iSCSI) drive. A correctly configured iSCSI drive looks like a local drive to the client system.

Considering the LPR Port Monitor feature

You need this feature only when working with a Unix system. The Line Printer Remote (LPR) port monitor tracks printers that are running the Line Printer Daemon (LPD) on a remote system. When this service is available, the local machine can use the remote printer as though it were a locally attached device. You can learn more about this feature in the "Configuring an LPR printer" section of Book II, Chapter 2.

Considering the Message Queuing feature

Message queuing is akin to using the post office: Someone sends a letter, the post office delivers it, and the recipient picks up the letter. No one has to see anyone else in this entire scheme. The sender need not see anyone at the post office, the people at the post office need not see the recipient, and the recipient doesn't have to retrieve the letter at any particular time. Even so, this system of delivering mail is consistent and relatively reliable.

Working with Message Queuing in Windows Server 2008 is even more reliable than at the post office — in fact, the post office guarantees delivery. You configure a server to use Message Queuing when you have one or more applications installed that use this feature. The application sends messages to the message queue (the post office). A second application (or perhaps part of the same application) retrieves the message and processes it. In some cases, the recipient sends a response, but in other cases, the transfer is a one-way process.

The only time you should install and configure this service is when you have an application that relies on the Message Queuing feature. In many cases, the application installation performs many of the configuration tasks for you, but you still need to manage the resulting queues.

Considering the Multipath I/O feature

This feature, along with the Microsoft Device Specific Module (DSM), provides the means to support multipath Input/Output (I/O) on the server. A multipath solution is similar to clustering, in that it provides a high reliability solution. However, it differs from clustering by focusing on the storage device rather than on an entire system. Consequently, Microsoft Multipath I/O (MPIO) has some significant advantages from a cost perspective. You can read more about MPIO in the "Working with Multipath I/O" section of Book II, Chapter 2.

Considering the Network Load Balancing feature

Network Load Balancing (NLB) distributes an application load across several servers. A main server accepts requests from the caller and then sends that request to the server in a server farm that has the smallest load. Using NLB helps your server farm scale better by distributing the load evenly. It also provides many of the same reliability benefits of clustering, but you use this solution (along with MPIO) in different circumstances.

Considering the Peer Name Resolution Protocol feature

Finding resources on a network relies on someone providing an identifier and someone else providing a name for that identifier. Sometimes the identifier is simply part of a search and, in other cases, the caller is looking for something specific. Most networks rely on DNS to resolve names, such as www.mycomputer.com, into an IP address, which is essentially an identifier. Sometimes DNS doesn't work as well as it should, so Microsoft came up with Peer Name Resolution Protocol (PNRP) to overcome DNS problems and to augment the DNS functionality. You can read more about PRNP in the "Working with Peer Name Resolution Protocol" section of Book II, Chapter 4.

Considering the Quality Windows Audio Video Experience feature

The Quality Windows Audio Video Experience (Qwave) provides a number of Audio Visual (AV) performance enhancement and management features. For example, using the Quality of Service (QoS) feature guarantees a specific level of performance, assuming that your network can support the performance level in the first place. In addition to general management, Qwave provides these management functions:

✦ Admission control

✦ Runtime monitoring and enforcement

✦ Application feedback

✦ Traffic prioritization

This isn't a run-of-the-mill corporate feature — Microsoft designed it with the home enthusiast in mind. However, it can work in the corporate setting for delivering training materials and engaging in conference calls, among other tasks.

Working with the Remote Assistance feature

The Remote Assistance feature works the same on the client system as it does on Windows Server 2008. You use this feature to provide remote assistance to the person using the computer. Generally, this feature makes sense on a workstation, especially workstations used by less-experienced users, but it's probably not a feature that you need on Windows Server 2008 very often. Don't confuse this feature with Remote Desktop, which lets you control the server from a remote location. You can read more about this feature at `http://technet.microsoft.com/en-us/library/bb457004.aspx` and `http://www.microsoft.com/windowsxp/using/helpand support/learnmore/remoteassist/intro.mspx`.

Working with the Remote Differential Compression feature

In times past, whenever an application sent data across the network, it sent the entire dataset. Because the dataset was small, the cost of sending the entire dataset was also small. However, as the size of the dataset for any given transfer has increased, so has the cost of sending them. The Remote Differential Compression (RDC) feature makes it possible to send just the information that has changed, rather than the entire dataset, across the network, which saves considerable time and resources.

You don't have to perform any special configuration to obtain the performance benefits of this feature. The applications you install must have special coding to use this feature. Consequently, you may find that this feature is already installed on Windows Server 2008 as the result of installing an application. In most cases, you never need to install or uninstall this feature because an application does it for you. Never uninstall this feature unless you know that the server doesn't have any applications that require it.

This book doesn't discuss the low-level details of how this technology works, but it can make for interesting reading. You can find more information about RDC at `http://msdn2.microsoft.com/en-us/library/aa372948.aspx`. The Web site at `http://technet2.microsoft.com/windowsserver/en/library/8c4cf2e7-0b92-4643-acbd-abfa9f189d031033.mspx` tells you how the Distributed File System (DFS) feature relies on RDC to perform its work.

Considering the Remote Server Administration Tools feature

Installing this feature installs a number of Microsoft Management Console (MMC) snap-ins you can use to perform remote server administration of roles and features. Microsoft lets you install all the snap-ins, just the snap-ins for roles or features, or individual snap-ins for roles or features. You can learn more about this feature in the "Installing and Using the Remote Server Administration Tools" section of Book III, Chapter 1.

Considering the Removable Storage Manager feature

The Removable Storage Manager (RSM) catalogs any removable media you use on your server. It's also possible to use this feature to manage the catalogs that RSM creates. You can learn more about this feature in the "Working with the Removable Storage Manager" section of Book II, Chapter 2.

Working with the RPC over HTTP Proxy feature

The Remote Procedure Call (RPC) technology has been around for many years. It's a technique for distributing an application across multiple systems. An application on one system calls a procedure found in a component on another system. Although the application is distributed and the client doesn't even necessarily know where it's calling for assistance, the entire system appears as a local application to the user. This technology is so old and stable that you can find a 1988 specification for it at `http://www.faqs.org/rfcs/rfc1050.html`.

Unfortunately, RPC doesn't work very well across the Internet. Firewalls and other obstacles tend to break connections and cause other problems. An application that works perfectly might break due to the new methods by which computers connect. The RPC over HTTP Proxy feature helps correct these problems by making it possible to use HTTP to perform the actual data transfer rather than rely on older technologies to perform the task.

RPC over HTTP Proxy is a technology that you install to meet specific application needs. In fact, the application may install it for you automatically. Never uninstall this feature unless you know that you don't have any applications installed that require it. You can learn more about RPC over HTTP Proxy at `http://technet.microsoft.com/en-us/library/bb124035.aspx`. The Web site at `http://www.computerperformance.co.uk/exchange2003/exchange2003_rpc_http.htm` tells how Microsoft Exchange Server can use RPC over HTTP.

Working with the Simple TCP/IP Services feature

The Simple Transmission Control Protocol/Internet Protocol (TCP/IP) Services feature is a compatibility support item. You don't normally need to install this feature because it's unlikely that you need the services it provides. This feature provides support for these TCP/IP requests:

✦ Character generator

✦ Daytime

✦ Discard

✦ Echo

✦ Quote of the day

If these requests are unfamiliar, you definitely don't require this particular feature. In fact, you probably should avoid this feature because it comes with several well-known security issues. Over the years, people of ill intent have discovered methods of using these features to gain access to your server. You can find additional information about these requests at `http://www.tcpipguide.com/free/t_MiscellaneousTCPIPTroubleshooting ProtocolsEchoDisc.htm`.

Considering the SMTP Server feature

The Simple Mail Transfer Protocol (SMTP) is the basis for e-mail systems. You can actually combine various pieces of Windows Server 2008 to create a rudimentary e-mail system. However, most people use this feature with a full-featured e-mail program.

Generally, you install this feature to support a role such as the Web Server (IIS) role or you install it as part of your setup for a third-party e-mail product. In some cases, the e-mail program installs this feature for you automatically. Some e-mail programs now include their own built-in SMTP support, so you don't need to install this feature at all. Make sure to check the vendor documentation to understand the program's requirements. You can learn more about working with SMTP in the "Installing and Configuring SMTP Support" section of Book VII, Chapter 2.

Considering the SNMP Services feature

The Simple Network Management Protocol (SNMP) is one of a number of methods you can use to manage your server. Windows Server 2008 provides a number of management technologies, and the one you choose depends on your server and network setup. The advantage of SNMP is that it's standardized across many platforms. In fact, you can read the SNMP standard at `http://www.cse.ohio-state.edu/cgi-bin/rfc/rfc1157.html`.

However, *standardized* doesn't always equate to *complete*. The most complete method of managing a Windows server is to use the Windows Management Interface (WMI). SNMP fulfills the role of providing standardized interactions across multiple platforms, but to provide configuration in detail, use WMI.

Considering the Storage Manager for SANs feature

A Storage Area Network (SAN) provides a means for maintaining hard drive storage external to a server. The SAN provides hard drives to a server, and you can configure specific servers to rely on certain hard drives. By placing the hard drive external to the server, you can move storage around as needed to meet specific requirements. In addition, when a server becomes unavailable, you can quickly move its storage to another server. You can read more about SANs in the "Working with SANs" section of Book II, Chapter 2.

Working with the Subsystem for UNIX-based Applications feature

The Subsystem for UNIX-based Applications (SUA) feature provides a level of cross-platform compatibility support. This support is relatively limited, and you find that most modern UNIX applications can't use it. A discussion of cross-platform compatibility is outside the scope of this book. You can read more about SUA at `http://technet2.microsoft.com/WindowsServer/en/library/695ac415-d314-45df-b464-4c80ddc2b3bc1033.mspx`.

Book II
Chapter 1

Configuring Server
Roles and Features

Considering the Telnet Client feature

Telnet is an ancient (in computer terms) technology for creating a connection between computers. It provides a basic connectivity option that works across most platforms today. In fact, you find Telnet used with devices such as routers too. Although Telnet doesn't provide much in the way of functionality, it provides a rudimentary connectivity option that you should consider when other options are either inaccessible or not working. Generally, you can run most command line applications on the remote system using Telnet. Of course, this means knowing the command line utilities you want to use.

Considering the Telnet Server feature

A Telnet client requires a Telnet server to gain access to any system. The Telnet server doesn't provide access to everyone. In fact, Windows Server 2008 allows access to only members of the Administrators group when using the default setup. However, you can configure Telnet for other scenarios as needed. You can read more about Telnet in the "Working with Telnet" section of Book VIII, Chapter 2.

Considering the TFTP Client feature

The Trivial File Transfer Protocol (TFTP) client feature helps you perform file transfers from remote systems. This technology is standardized across platforms — you can read the specification for it at `http://www.faqs.org/rfcs/rfc1350.html`. In most cases, you use TFTP to work with embedded devices or other specialty devices using TCP/IP as the communication medium. You can read more about this technology at `http://www.tcpipguide.com/free/t_TrivialFileTransferProtocolTFTP.htm`.

An overview of the Windows Internal Database feature

You never need to install the Windows Internal Database feature. That's because this feature provides a relational database for other Windows Server 2008 roles and features. Consequently, leave this particular feature alone because after it's installed, you will need it to meet particular needs. The roles and features that rely on the Windows Internal Database include

✦ Active Directory Rights Management Services

✦ Windows Server Update Services

✦ Windows SharePoint Services

✦ Windows System Resource Management

✦ Universal Description Discovery and Integration (UDDI) Services

Considering the Windows PowerShell feature

Windows PowerShell is the new command line. Unlike the command line that you probably used in the past to manage Windows, this command line includes additional security features and provides access to managed applications (those supported by the .NET Framework). As with the command line you used since the days of DOS with only a few changes, Windows PowerShell supports scripting. However, you find that the scripts you create using Windows PowerShell are significantly more powerful than those created for the command line and more reliable as well. You can read more about Windows PowerShell in Book VI.

Considering the Windows Process Activation Service feature

Microsoft has rebuilt IIS from the ground up. In fact, the IIS in Windows Server 2008 bears little resemblance to the IIS that you worked with in the past. IIS has a completely new interface, and the inner workings are equally different. One of the changes that Microsoft made was to implement a new process activation strategy — one that doesn't necessarily rely on an HTTP request. The Windows Process Activation Service feature is the new way to make your applications run with IIS, and you find that it has a lot to offer. As with everything else Microsoft is doing these days, the Windows Process Activation Service also relies on managed code, so it relies on the Windows Communication Foundation (WCF) to accomplish tasks.

Considering the Windows Recovery Disc feature

At some point, a catastrophe will occur on your system and you'll find that it has reduced capability or may not boot at all. You may not receive any warning about the problem or even have a feeling of impending doom, but it will happen. A Windows Recovery Disc can help you overcome massive system failures. Although you can't rely on this strategy to recover your data, you can use it to recover your system quickly. Consequently, you also want to have a good system backup to help restore your data. You can read more about the Windows Recovery Disc feature in the "Creating a Windows Recovery Disc" section of Book III, Chapter 5.

Considering the Windows Server Backup features

It's impossible to have a good maintenance strategy without including a good backup. Any maintenance you perform must include a backup because a backup is the only good form of data protection at your disposal. Although Windows backup no longer provides the flexibility you obtained with previous versions of Windows, it's better than nothing at all. You can read more about creating and using system backups in the "Performing a system backup" section of Book III, Chapter 5.

Considering the Windows System Resource Manager feature

Your server has a number of valuable resources. It's possible for one application to attempt to grab all those resources and for other applications to become resource starved. Users may notice that the server is slow on some days but not on others, and for apparently no reason. The Windows System Resource Manager (WSRM) feature helps you manage the CPU and memory resources on your server to improve performance and ensure that applications work reliably. You can read more about this feature in the "Working with the Windows System Resource Manager (WSRM)" section of Book II, Chapter 5.

Considering the WINS Server feature

The Windows Internet Naming Service (WINS) is another in a long line of methods of mapping a human readable name for an object into something the computer can understand. In this case, WINS maps a Network Basic Input/Output Service (NetBIOS) name into an IP address. Depending on your organization, you may not even use WINS any longer because other mapping services have replaced it. However, you may still need WINS, in some cases, especially when working with multiple platforms on the same network.

Installing a WINS server is an optional component that you can provide before you promote your server to a domain controller (see the "Installing WINS" section of Book II, Chapter 5 for details). You also want to review the "Understanding WINS" section of Book IV, Chapter 1.

Considering the Wireless LAN Service feature

Most organizations have some number of wireless devices today. The Wireless Local Area Network (WLAN) service helps you configure your server to automatically poll for and configure wireless devices.

Chapter 2: Configuring Server Hardware

In This Chapter

✔ **Understanding how Windows scalability improves hardware support**

✔ **Using Device Manager to configure hardware**

✔ **Adding hardware using the Add Hardware Wizard**

✔ **Working with hard drives**

✔ **Working with printers**

✔ **Configuring the hardware on your system**

*O*ne task that you perform almost immediately after installing Windows is to check your hardware. Even if Windows recognizes all your hardware and configures it properly, you'll probably install vendor-specific software to improve the flexibility and performance of the hardware. In addition, vendor-specific software often accesses features that the vendor recognizes but the generic Microsoft drivers don't. For example, display adapters commonly provide, in the Notification Area, special icons you use to access special display modes.

Sometimes Windows doesn't recognize a piece of hardware and you want to make the hardware work before you install any applications. Device Manager and the Add Hardware Wizard can help you install support for devices that Windows doesn't recognize by default. In many cases, Windows Server 2008 won't install a driver, even when one exists, because the vendor hasn't signed the driver. You can override this behavior on 32-bit systems to get the piece of hardware up and running.

Hardware isn't much good without software to access it. In many cases, obtaining that access means installing a special Windows Server 2008 feature. The feature provides the software required to access the hardware. A display adapter comes with its own, special software that you normally want to use, but Microsoft supports special software for hard drives and printers that you read about in this chapter.

Along with knowing how to get software support, you need to know how to configure the hardware for optimal performance in your environment. Microsoft tends to use generic settings that work for everyone but provide the least amount of functionality. By configuring your hardware, you can obtain additional flexibility and realize the true potential of your hardware for daily tasks. Although you use this chapter immediately after you complete the basic system configuration, you come back to it every time you experience a hardware failure or install a new piece of hardware on your system.

Considering the Windows Scalability Improvements

You've probably heard the term *scalability*, but few people take the time to define it for themselves. In this book, scalability is the ability of a server to handle an additional load without significant performance degradation. When you add a second user, the server may slow a little, but not enough for anyone to notice. Adding three or more users also incurs a small, barely noticeable performance degradation.

Even when a server is scalable, it eventually reaches a maximum load where it can't handle even one more user. When every resource is used, albeit used as efficiently as possible, the server has reached a maximum load and can't handle another user no matter how you might try to coax it. Many people feel that scalability is limitless. All scalability really does is make the server perform better across its load range — there isn't any magic involved in the process. Of course, a scalable server can extend its load slightly because it uses resources more efficiently.

Windows Server 2008 provides many levels of additional scalability over previous editions of Windows. The focus of this chapter is hardware, and you'll find many scalability improvements in this area. You can categorize the improvements in three ways:

✦ **Improved software support:** Using drivers and support software that improves overall server performance also improves scalability. Every time Windows Server 2008 uses a resource more efficiently, the resource availability extends to users, processes, drivers, and other entities that need it. The new XML Paper Specification Driver (XPSDrv) is an example of improved software that provides a performance and scalability boost.

✦ **Direct device participation:** Many devices now include some level of intelligence. By leveraging that intelligence, Windows Server 2008 can offload part of the processing requirements to the device, which frees server resources for other uses. The new Web Services on Devices (WSD) functionality is an example of how Windows Server 2008 supports device participation.

✦ **Direct client participation:** Clients make many requests and then wait for the server to respond to them. While the client sits and idles, many of the processor cycles that it could use end up wasted. Providing ways for the client to participate in handling a particular request makes the server more scalable.

The amount of scalability that a server achieves often depends on the cooperation of these three elements. For example, the amount of processing burden that the server can offload to the client depends on the Page Description Language (PDL) that the print job uses and the content of the document itself. Some forms of PDL and content require a certain level of server participation. Printing a report that depends on content from a database using PostScript is far less likely to enhance scalability than a plain-text print job that relies solely on the content in Word.

The client also affects how scalable the server becomes. Microsoft's technology appears to depend on communicating with a Vista client to achieve maximum scalability. Obviously, someone has to run tests, at some point, to demonstrate this reliance because Microsoft isn't saying much (although its marketing literature often fails to mention Windows XP as a client). My own tests indicate that Windows Server 2008 prefers Vista as a client.

Windows Server 2008 also uses Remote Procedure Calls (RPCs) more efficiently. An *RPC* is a call from the client to the server for specific needs, such as the print spooler. By using RPC calls more efficiently and relying on fewer of them, Windows Server 2008 gets a scalability boost, especially in a medium to large company environment (where even small differences can mean a lot).

Working with Device Manager

Device Manager is a special tool you can use to check the status of any devices that Windows Server 2008 sees on your system. In addition, you can use it to manage devices, work with device drivers, and perform some configuration tasks. In most respects, nothing has changed in Device Manager from previous versions of Windows. If you knew how to use it in the past, you probably know how to use it in Windows Server 2008.

You can access Device Manager in a number of ways. For example, you can access it through the `Diagnostics\Device Manager` folder of Server Manager. (See the "Using the Server Manager Console" section of Book II, Chapter 1 for details.) You can also access Device Manager from the Desktop by using these steps:

1. **Right-click Computer and choose Properties from the context menu.**

You see the System window, as shown in Figure 2-1. You can also open this window by opening the System applet in the Control Panel.

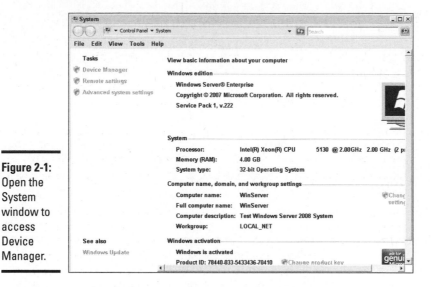

Figure 2-1:
Open the
System
window to
access
Device
Manager.

2. **Click Device Manager in the Tasks area.**

Windows opens the Device Manager window, as shown in Figure 2-2.

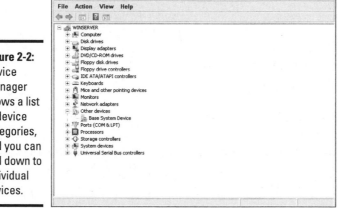

Figure 2-2:
Device
Manager
shows a list
of device
categories,
and you can
drill down to
individual
devices.

Another alternative for opening Device Manager is to open the Device Manager applet in the Control Panel. You also find Device Manager in the Computer Manager console and in many other places. It's hard not to run into Device Manager when you're an administrator. The following sections describe Device Manager in detail.

Managing the Device Manager display

Many people use Device Manager in a single view, the Devices by Type view shown in Figure 2-2. This view is quite convenient for finding a particular device quickly, which is why people use it often and the reason that Microsoft made this view the default. All the view options appear on the View menu. Device Manager includes these four views:

✦ **Devices by Type:** When using this view, Device Manager categorizes the devices on the system and places each device into a folder containing other devices of the same type. For example, the Disk Drives folder contains all hard drives and flash drives on the machine. However, CD and DVD drives appear in a separate DVD/CD-ROM Drives folder.

✦ **Devices by Connection:** Everything in the computer is connected in some way. The connections form a hierarchy, with the computer as a whole sitting at the top of the hierarchy. As you move down the hierarchy, you begin seeing support devices and, finally, devices such as hard drives. For example, your server may use the hierarchy shown in Figure 2-3 to display the connectivity required to access the hard drive.

Figure 2-3:
Everything
in a
computer
system is
connected.

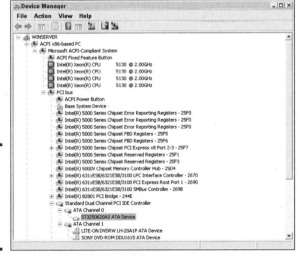

✦ **Resources by Type:** The resources provided by your computer come in four forms: memory, input/output (I/O) addresses, interrupt requests (IRQs), and direct memory access (DMA). The "Understanding resources" section of this chapter provides a complete discussion of resources. However, this view provides a listing of resources used by various devices and categorizes them by resource type.

✦ **Resources by Connection:** You may run into a situation where it appears that multiple devices have a resource conflict. All the devices appear to have problems, but you can't discover the source of that problem. Viewing resources by connection helps you see the interaction between devices based on the resources they use. You may find that a device doesn't work because a device that's higher in the hierarchy doesn't have the resources it requires. A single device misconfiguration can cause multiple device failures.

The views determine what you see. However, *you* can also choose what you see. Choose the View➪Customize command and you see the Customize View dialog box, as shown in Figure 2-4. Choosing options in this dialog box shows or hides the Device Manager features.

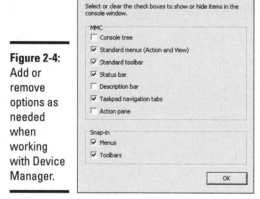

Figure 2-4: Add or remove options as needed when working with Device Manager.

You can remove any of the toolbars or menus. If you remove everything, you end up with the File and Help menus. When you're working in this view, it's impossible to change the view and perform many other tasks. However, you can still perform many tasks by right-clicking the object you want to work with (such as a hard drive) and choosing the appropriate option from its context menu.

If you remove enough options, you find that the View menu disappears completely, which may leave you wondering how to get it back. When this problem occurs, right-click the title bar and choose Customize View from the context menu. You see the Customize View dialog box shown in Figure 2-4, where you can add the view features you need.

Viewing broken devices

You may have noticed in Figure 2-2 the device (Base System Device) with the odd-looking yellow triangle containing an exclamation mark. This device is broken. The yellow triangle tells you that the device isn't functioning at all (rather than partially) for whatever reason. Whenever you open Device Manager, it shows you all broken devices automatically, by expanding the hierarchy to show these devices and displaying the little yellow icon. Another term for a device in this condition is *banged out.* Categories that have broken devices also display a special icon, a circle with a blue question mark.

The method you use to fix a broken device depends on the problem it has. Fortunately, Device Manager normally provides some kind of clue to the problem. To see this clue, right-click the device entry and choose Properties from the context menu. Select the General tab and you see a Properties dialog box, such as the one shown in Figure 2-5. Notice that this device is broken because it lacks device drivers.

Book II
Chapter 2

Configuring Server
Hardware

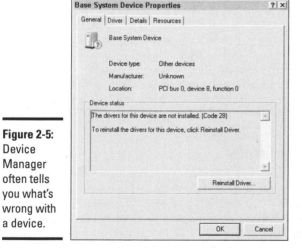

Figure 2-5: Device Manager often tells you what's wrong with a device.

In this case, you can usually fix the problem by clicking Reinstall Driver. Device Manager shows you the Update Driver Software Wizard. You can find out more about this wizard in the "Updating drivers" section of this chapter.

Drivers are the most common problem you encounter, other than a device that has completely failed. When a device fails completely, you have to replace it and let Windows recognize the new device.

Sometimes a device won't even appear on the list. You installed it, but Windows simply doesn't recognize it. When this problem occurs, make sure to verify that you installed the device correctly. A missed connector or a connector that isn't firmly seated can cause all kinds of problems. If you're certain that the device is installed correctly, choose Actions⇨Scan for Hardware Changes, and Windows checks for the new device.

To go along with the act of scanning for a device, sometimes uninstalling and then reinstalling a device can work wonders. Right-click the device and choose Uninstall from the context menu to remove its driver from the system. Reboot and Windows normally detects the device automatically. Make sure that you use the latest signed drivers to reinstall the device.

Other errors include resource conflicts or a device that simply isn't receiving what it needs to work properly. Although manual resource configuration is rarely needed when working with newer versions of Windows, you may still have to do it. (See the "Understanding resources" section of this chapter for a discussion of resources.)

When all else fails, you may have to disable a device to get the rest of your system working. Generally, this is a last-ditch effort because the device becomes completely unusable and Windows won't scan for updates for you. It's as though the device doesn't exist on your system. Of course, you can always enable the device later when you discover a fix for the problem. To disable a device, right-click its entry and choose Disable from the context menu. When you want to re-enable the device, right-click its entry and choose Enable from the context menu.

Understanding resources

Computers provide a number of resources. Some resources are dynamic. When you start an application, it allocates memory from a pool of memory that the server provides. However, other resources are static. The server allocates the resources to address specific needs. Most hardware uses static resources in one of four categories:

✦ Memory

✦ I/O

✦ IRQ

✦ DMA

The hardware relies on the memory to perform tasks, just as applications do. For example, a display adapter uses memory to store images that you eventually see on the monitor. The processor communicates with a particular piece of hardware using a specific I/O address. When a piece of hardware needs to communicate with the processor, it relies on an IRQ. Hardware may also need to transfer data from its own, "personal" memory to the system memory using DMA. DMA provides data transfers between main memory and device memory without interrupting the CPU. You can view resources by type or connection. Figure 2-6 shows an example of resources listed by type.

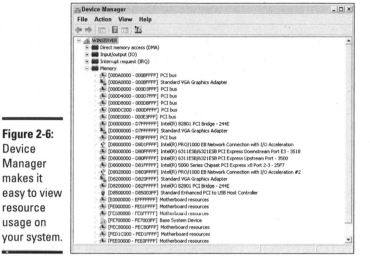

Figure 2-6: Device Manager makes it easy to view resource usage on your system.

**Book II
Chapter 2**

Configuring Server Hardware

Sometimes you want to view the resources used by a particular device. In this case, right-click the device you want to view and choose Properties from the context menu. Select the Resources tab and you see a listing of the resources used by that device, as shown in Figure 2-7.

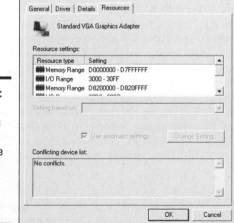

Figure 2-7: Use the Properties dialog box to view the resources used by a particular device.

An easy technique for converting between hexadecimal and decimal

Most people don't think about numbers in hexadecimal. In fact, making the transition can prove difficult, even when you need to use hexadecimal for every task. Fortunately, Windows provides an easy method of converting between decimal and hexadecimal: the Calculator utility.

To start this utility, choose Start⇨Programs⇨ Accessories⇨Calculator. When you see the Calculator utility, choose View⇨Scientific. Notice that Calculator view changes to include a number of new features, including Hex and Dec options.

Conversions are easy: To convert a number from decimal to hexadecimal, click Dec, type the decimal value you want to convert, and then click Hex. The number automatically changes from decimal to hexadecimal form. Likewise, if you want to convert a number from hexadecimal to decimal, click Hex, type the hexadecimal value you want to convert, and then click Dec.

Notice that this device, the Standard VGA Graphics Adapter, has both memory and I/O range resource requirements. In addition, the system tells you that this device isn't conflicting with any other device on the system, which means that no two devices require the same memory or I/O range.

All the entries you see are in hexadecimal (base 16) because that's how the computer thinks about the resources. If you ever need to change any of the resource settings, you also need to think in hexadecimal. Normally, hexadecimal entries appear with 0x in front of them. For example, 0xF is a hexadecimal value with the decimal value 15. However, all values in Device Manager are in hexadecimal, even if they aren't preceded by 0x.

Most devices have standardized settings. For example, communications port 1 (COM1) normally uses an I/O range of 0x03F8 to 0x3FF and an IRQ of 4. A standard computer can have up to four COM ports, each of which has its own standard settings. The same statement holds true for parallel (LPT) ports and many other devices. Windows stores these settings in the information (INF) files associated with the device. If you need to use an alternative setting, clear the Use Automatic Settings option and you find that you can choose from one of the recognized alternatives, as shown in Figure 2-8. In this case, the COM port can use one of eight alternative settings.

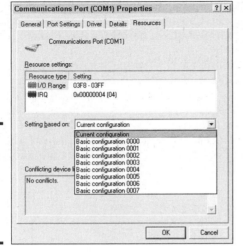

Figure 2-8:
Modify
devices
to use
alternative
settings as
needed.

In very rare circumstances, you can provide custom settings for a particular device. To make this happen, you must clear the Use Automatic Settings option and choose one of the resources. For example, you might choose to change the IRQ for the COM port. Click Change Settings and you see an Edit Interrupt Request dialog box, where you can choose a different IRQ. Device Manager tells you whether any other devices are using the setting you choose. In some cases, you might have to disable one device to make room for another — although this, too, is extremely rare when working with Windows Server 2008.

The settings you change in Device Manager aren't arbitrary. The hardware must have the required configuration to accept the new settings. For example, if a serial card has settings for only IRQ 3 and IRQ 4, then you can't set the card for IRQ 5 in Device Manager and expect it to work. The settings in Device Manager define the physical interface between the Windows drivers and the hardware. Normally, you want to stick with the automatic settings when you can, and use the standard configurations provided by the device vendor when the automatic configuration fails. Avoid providing custom settings unless you truly know which settings the device accepts.

Viewing hidden devices

Your system has hidden devices. Device Manager hides devices that aren't in use or likely to ever require your attention. For example, if you use a Universal Serial Bus (USB) mouse but your system also has a Personal System/2 (PS/2) mouse connector, Device Manager hides the PS/2 mouse connector because you aren't using it. The PS/2 mouse connector appears banged out because you don't have a mouse attached to it. Hiding the device keeps you from having to troubleshoot hardware that doesn't require it.

Device Manager makes it possible to view hidden devices. Simply choose View⇨Show Hidden Devices. You see some other devices that you normally don't see. For example, my system shows the PS/2 Compatible Mouse entry, as shown in Figure 2-9. Because I don't have a PS/2 mouse attached to my system, the entry appears banged out. One new device type you always see when you view hidden devices is Non-Plug and Play Drivers, which contains all the device drivers that don't rely on plug-and-play technology to work (normally older devices).

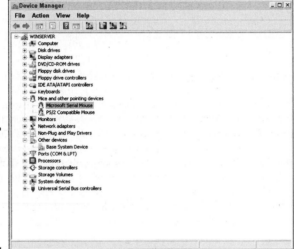

Figure 2-9: Most hidden devices are hidden because you aren't using them.

Unfortunately, Device Manager still hides certain types of devices. For example, if you have a ghosted USB device — one that's normally present but is disconnected at the moment (say you removed your laptop from the docking station), you don't see it in the list. You have to do something special to see these devices. Device Manager looks for a special environment variable when it starts to determine which devices it sees. Use the following steps to enable this additional level of hidden device viewing:

1. **Right-click Computer and choose Properties.**

You see the System window.

2. **Click Advanced System Settings.**

Windows displays the Advanced tab of the System Properties dialog box, as shown in Figure 2-10.

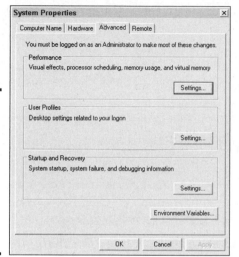

Figure 2-10:
The Advanced tab lets you configure special properties of your Windows setup.

3. **Click Environment Variables.**

You see the Environment Variables dialog box, as shown in Figure 2-11. Notice that this dialog box contains two environment variable listings. The top listing contains environment variables that affect only your user account. The bottom listing contains environment variables that modify the system globally. The list you modify depends on whether you want everyone to see the full list of devices or want to reserve this privilege to yourself. It's important to realize that only people who have access to the server console and can log in to it locally see the effect of the environment variable change.

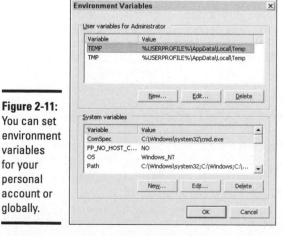

Figure 2-11:
You can set environment variables for your personal account or globally.

4. **Click New.**

   You see either a New User Variable or New System Variable dialog box. The fields are the same in both cases. The only difference is that the New User Variable dialog box works with your personal environment variables and that the New System Variable dialog box works with global environment variables.

5. **Type** devmgr_show_nonpresent_devices **in the Variable Name field.**

6. **Type** 1 **in the Variable Value field.**

7. **Click OK.**

   Windows adds the new environment variable to the list you chose to modify.

8. **Click OK twice to close the System Properties dialog box.**

9. **Start a new copy of Device Manager to see the changes.**

   Don't forget to choose View➪Show Hidden Devices to display the hidden devices. Device Manager always hides these devices by default.

Scanning for new devices

Any new devices you add to your system are unlikely to lack plug-and-play capability. In fact, devices that administrators once associated with legacy hardware, such as third-party parallel ports, now include plug-and-play capability. Using plug-and-play means that the device tells the system about itself. If the device lacks jumpers and other characteristics of old hardware, you can usually try working with it as plug-and-play hardware.

To scan for new plug-and-play hardware, choose Action➪Scan for Hardware Changes. If Windows Server 2008 knows anything at all about the device, you need to look fast because it installs the software automatically. Only when Windows can't find the required driver does it display a wizard asking you for information about the hardware. In this case, the process for working with the new device is precisely the same as the procedure described in the "Updating drivers" section of this chapter.

Working with older devices

Because Windows Server 2008 requires signed drivers and is not likely to provide drivers for older devices, you should consider replacing older hardware that Windows Server 2008 doesn't understand. In fact, you'll find that the 64-bit version of Windows Server 2008 probably won't work with that old hardware, but you can have success with the 32-bit version by using your older (Windows XP or Windows 2003 or better) driver. To install support for older hardware, choose Action➪Add Legacy Hardware. You see the Add Hardware Wizard. Use the steps in the "Using the Add Hardware Wizard" section of this chapter to install the hardware.

Viewing individual device settings

Every device installed on your system has a number of settings you can view. The number of settings depends on the device, but you need to realize that Device Manager may provide the only place to see and modify these settings. To display the settings for any device, right-click the device entry and choose Properties from the context menu. You see a device Properties dialog box.

The only tab common to every device is General. The General tab tells you the device type and vendor name and shows whether the device is working. If the device isn't working, the General tab provides information about what Windows thinks is wrong with the device, which may or may not always help you locate the source of the problem. You also see three common tabs: Resources, Driver, and Power Management. The "Understanding resources" section of this chapter describes the Resources tab for you. You find out about drivers in the "Updating drivers" section of this chapter. The "Configuring power management" section of this chapter describes power issues.

A device commonly includes another tab: Details. You can see this tab in Figure 2-12. Selecting an entry from the Property field shows that value in the Value field. The value tells you something about the device. For example, when you choose Inf Name in the property field, you see the name of the INF file containing the settings for the device. The Inf Section property tells you where to look in the INF file for configuration information for the selected device. You find many common properties, such as Inf Name and Inf Section, and many device-specific properties in the list. For example, a Network Interface Card (NIC) may contain the name of a service that supports it. The important issue to remember is that the Details tab contains a lot of good configuration information that you can use to locate problems with your hardware.

If you ever need to retain information you see on the Details tab, you can copy it to the Clipboard. Simply right-click the Value field and choose Copy from the context menu. You can paste the text information anywhere you need it.

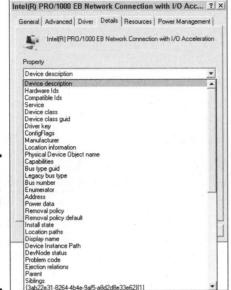

Figure 2-12:
The Details
tab provides
consider-
able
information
about each
device.

The other tabs you see in a device Properties dialog box rely entirely on the
kind of device. For example, when working with NICs, you see an Advanced
tab that contains hardware-specific settings for the device. For example, the
Advanced tab commonly lets you set the size of the receive and send buffers
for the NIC. You can also choose special features, such as whether to use
flow control.

It can be interesting to look through the various devices on your system to
see what kinds of configuration settings the device offers. For example, when
you open a disk drive entry, you commonly see a Policies tab and a Volumes
tab, as shown in Figure 2-13.

The Policies tab is interesting because it provides settings you can use to
obtain a significant performance boost from your hard drive. Getting this
boost normally involves some risk, so Microsoft chooses the most reliable
option.

The Volumes tab provides information about the volumes on the hard drive.
You have to click Populate to obtain this information as shown in Figure 2-13.
Device Manager enables the Properties button whenever you highlight a particular volume. Clicking Properties displays the same volume Properties
dialog box you see when you right-click the drive in Windows Explorer and
choose Properties.

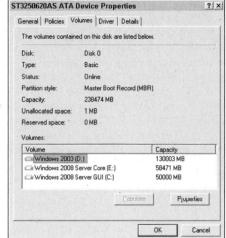

Figure 2-13:
Work through the devices on your system to discover the settings they offer.

Book II
Chapter 2

Configuring Server Hardware

Updating drivers

Most devices require a driver in order to work — get the wrong driver and the device won't work. The Driver tab of the device Properties dialog box, shown in Figure 2-14, helps you manage the drivers for a particular device.

Figure 2-14:
Drivers provide the basis for interacting with most devices.

You use these options on different occasions. For example, when you call technical support or want to check the version of your driver online, you click Driver Details, which shows you information about the driver, as shown in Figure 2-15. The Driver Files field contains a list of driver filenames and their locations. Many devices require just one driver file, but you may see more files for complex devices.

Figure 2-15: The list of driver files tells you the location of the driver on disk.

When you select a particular driver, you can determine the name of the vendor that produced it, the driver version, its copyright information, and whether the driver is signed, along with other information that the vendor provides. The driver version is the critical piece of information in most cases. You can use this information to determine whether you have the most current driver installed on your system. Of course, there's an easier way to check the driver version. The following steps tell you how to perform an automatic update of the device driver:

1. **Click Update Driver.**

You see the Update Driver Software dialog box, as shown in Figure 2-16. This dialog box gives you two options for looking for drivers. Unless you have a CD or DVD with the driver or you already downloaded it from the vendor's Web site, you normally choose the Search Automatically for Updated Driver Software. Because you use this option most often, this section uses the automatic-update approach. (If you have a driver, simply select the Browse My Computer for Driver Software option and tell Windows Server 2008 where to find it.)

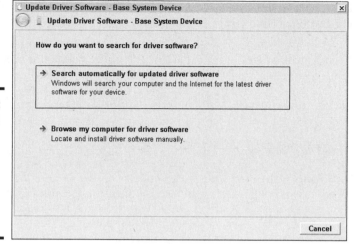

Figure 2-16:
The Update
Driver
Software
dialog box
provides
options for
locating a
driver.

2. **Click Search Automatically for Updated Driver Software.**

   The Update Driver Software Wizard gives you three options for searching for the driver, as shown in Figure 2-17. Normally, you want to search
   online to ensure that you get the latest driver. If you choose Don't
   Search Online, you need to provide the Update Driver Software Wizard
   with a local source for the driver.

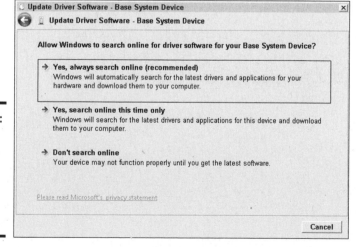

Figure 2-17:
Tell the
Update
Driver
Software
how you
want to
search.

3. **Click Yes, Always Search Online (Recommended) or Yes, Search Online This Time Only.**

The Update Driver Software Wizard searches for the required driver. If the wizard finds the driver, it automatically installs it for you. Otherwise, you see an error message. If you have a local driver you can use, click the back arrow twice in the upper-left corner of the dialog box and choose the Browse My Computer for Driver Software option.

Configuring power management

All the hardware on your system uses power, but you can manage the power for only some of the devices. For example, because you don't always need your hard drive, it's possible to turn it off. Of course, this policy may not be a good one to adopt on a server where users want service and they want it fast. Even though a power management setting is available, you can't always use it on a server.

Figure 2-18 shows a typical example of a Power Management tab. Notice that you can set the device to allow the system to turn it off, to save power. In this case, the hub has a flash drive attached, so turning off the power may cause problems, depending on how you set the performance options for the flash drive.

Figure 2-18: Set the device to allow the computer to turn it off to save power whenever possible.

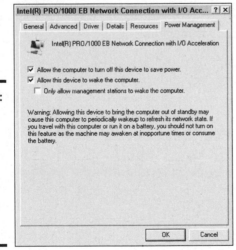

In many cases, you can also set the device to wake the computer when it receives the proper signal. This feature is especially helpful with NICs. You can set the computer to turn itself off to conserve power when the system isn't in use (over the weekend, for example, for a business with a five-day workweek). A central server can wake up the system for automated maintenance and updates as needed by using the Wake on LAN feature of the NIC.

You have to consider other kinds of power indicators in Device Manager. The most common of these power indicators is the amount of power that devices plugged into a USB hub use, as shown in Figure 2-19. The USB hub is the only device that provides this particular tab. Notice that it tells you that a device is plugged into the hub and is using 200 milliampere (mA). The hub can supply up to 500 milliampere, so you can plug other devices into it. The tab also tells you that this hub can accept seven more devices.

Figure 2-19:
Monitor the
power
usage of
USB hubs
to prevent
potential
power
problems.

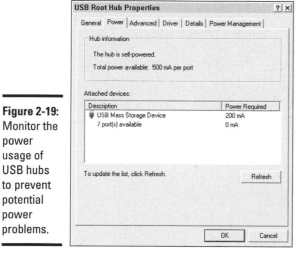

One problem that administrators can encounter is a USB port that burns out. Sometimes, people assume that the presence of a port automatically means that the hub can accept another device. However, you need to account for the power that the device uses to ensure that you don't overload the hub.

Using the Add Hardware Wizard

Windows Server 2008 does an amazing job of automatically detecting devices you add to the system. In fact, sometimes it installs the required software so fast that you don't see it and may think that the device is working by magic. The fact is that most hardware requires a driver in order to work, and sometimes Windows Server 2008 doesn't know what to install.

If the vendor provides an installation CD or DVD for your device and the installation program is compatible with Windows Server 2008, use the vendor-supplied media to install your hardware. The vendor's installation program generally provides additional software that you need to manage the device. In addition, the vendor's installation program makes settings changes to the registry that the Add Hardware Wizard doesn't provide.

Assume that you don't have a vendor CD or DVD. In this case, you need to use the Add Hardware Wizard to install the hardware. You can access this wizard in a number of ways, but the most direct method is to double-click the Add Hardware applet in the Control Panel. The following steps tell you how to use this wizard:

1. **Click Next to get past the Welcome screen.**

The Add Hardware Wizard presents you with two choices for installing the hardware. Because both options eventually lead to the same place, it's a good idea to rely on automation as much as possible.

2. **Choose the Search For and Install the Hardware Automatically (Recommended) option and click Next.**

The Add Hardware Wizard searches for new devices on your system. If it finds a new device, it begins searching for a driver for the device. Otherwise, you see an error message saying that the wizard couldn't find the hardware and you need to provide the device information manually. You always have to provide the device information for non-plug-and-play devices.

3. **Click Next.**

The wizard displays a list of potential hardware types to install, as shown in Figure 2-20.

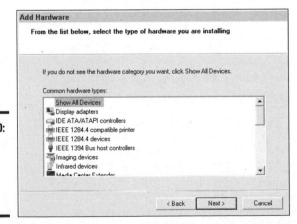

Figure 2-20: Select the kind of hardware you want to install.

4. **Select a hardware category and click Next.**

The wizard displays a list of vendors and the devices that Windows Server 2008 natively supports for each vendor, as shown in Figure 2-21. If you don't see the vendor for your device or don't see the vendor in the device list and have a disk for the device, click Have Disk. Supply the location of the disk, and then follow the vendor instructions for installing the device driver.

**Book II
Chapter 2**

Configuring Server
Hardware

Figure 2-21:
Select a
vendor and
a device for
that vendor.

5. **Choose a vendor in the Manufacturer list, a device in the Model list, and then click Next.**

The wizard tells you that it's ready to install the required support.

6. **Click Next.**

The Add Hardware Wizard installs the device driver. Some drivers require that you perform additional steps, depending on the requirements for that driver. Follow the steps that the vendor provides.

Performing Hard-Drive-Related Tasks

Your hard drive contains all the valuable information for your server, yet it's perhaps the least reliable part of your system. The moving heads and platter are a source of concern because they can fail in ways that solid-state components never encounter. Unfortunately, your hard drive is also easily compromised — even throwing it out when you get done using it can cause problems.

Over the years, vendors have introduced all kinds of software to overcome these issues, and you still need some of it. For example, Microsoft still hasn't come up with a good backup program. It apparently gave up on creating one because you won't find one in Windows Server 2008. (See the "Performing a system backup" section of Book III, Chapter 5 for details.)

However, Microsoft has come up with some utilities that can make your hard drive more secure, make it perform better, and provide connectivity that you didn't have in the past. The following sections describe these software options and tell you how to use them.

Encrypting your hard drive using BitLocker

Perhaps the best new feature of Windows Server 2008 is *BitLocker,* a drive encryption technology that promises to keep your data safe even if you lose the drive somehow. Of course, losing the drive is admittedly harder when you have it installed in a server in a locked room. BitLocker is an exciting technology for laptop owners, but some server owners are wondering whether they should install it. The problem with BitLocker is that if you lose the key (the PIN or the flash drive containing the key), you also lose access to your data. Whether BitLocker makes sense for your server depends on where you have the server installed. However, if you want to provide maximum protection for your data, you really should install BitLocker and ensure that you keep the key somewhere safe (and not in one of those places that you also easily forget).

Installing BitLocker

You install BitLocker support as you would any other feature — the "Working with features" section of Book II, Chapter 1 describes how to perform this task. BitLocker is one of the few features you can install that requires a reboot (Microsoft has worked hard to eliminate reboots from most of its software). Consequently, when you install this feature, you should do it at a time when no one else is using the server. The optimal solution is to install BitLocker as part of the initial server setup rather than waiting until later, when you've already placed it in production.

Performing BitLocker configuration tasks

After you install the BitLocker support, you see a new applet in the Control Panel: BitLocker Drive Encryption. When you open this applet, you see the BitLocker Drive Encryption window, as shown in Figure 2-22. If you have a Trusted Platform Module (TPM) installed on your server, all you need to do is select the drives you want to encrypt.

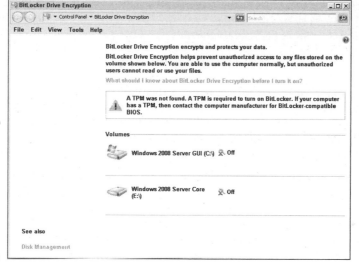

Figure 2-22:
Enable or
disable
BitLocker
drive
encryption
for each of
your drives.

**Book II
Chapter 2**

**Configuring Server
Hardware**

When you click the Turn On BitLocker link, you see a dialog box that asks whether you're sure you want to perform BitLocker encryption. Encrypting a drive changes it so that no one can read it without proper credentials. If you're certain that you want to encrypt the drive, click Continue with BitLocker Drive Encryption. The system performs a number of tasks, encrypts the drive, reboots the system, performs a few additional tasks, and then lets you begin working as before. You don't even notice the encryption when you have the proper credentials. If you aren't sure about using BitLocker encryption, click Cancel BitLocker Drive Encryption.

Unlike with Vista, you can encrypt any drive that uses the version of NTFS that comes with Windows Server 2008 — you can't encrypt drives that use an older version of NTFS, such as the version that comes with Windows Server 2003. However, you must always encrypt the boot drive before you encrypt any other drives on the system. Consequently, you don't see the Turn On BitLocker link for any other drive until after you encrypt the boot drive on your system. To ensure that you can encrypt a Windows Server 2003 partition on your server, always set up and format the partition by using the Windows Server 2008 installation disk. Windows Server 2003 is installed as normal but uses the newer version of NTFS.

Understanding the TPM chip

A *TPM* is a special piece of hardware on your system that provides storage for security information. When working with Windows Server 2008, you can use the TPM to store the credentials used to access an encrypted drive on your system, but TPM provides more functionality than you may see Microsoft implement in the future.

Most machines today don't include the TPM chip, but you can read about it at `https://www.trustedcomputinggroup.org/home`. A TPM provides standardized security; you can see the specification for it at `https://www.trustedcomputinggroup.org/groups/tpm/`.

The TPM also requires special management. Microsoft provides these management tips for your TPM at `http://technet2.microsoft.com/WindowsVista/en/library/29201194-5e2b-46d0-9c77-d17c25c56af31033.mspx`.

Overcoming the TPM chip requirement

Unfortunately, most administrators will be surprised to find out that their new servers lack TPMs. The error message seems to say that you can't use BitLocker on the system. Fortunately, you have a way around this issue: You need to set a group policy that tells Windows to allow you to use a flash drive, rather than a TPM, to store the credentials for the encrypted hard drive. Although the flash drive option isn't as secure as using a TPM, it's still a lot more secure than leaving the drive unencrypted. Use the following steps to overcome the BitLocker TPM chip requirement:

1. **Choose Start⇨Run.**

Windows displays the Run dialog box.

2. **Type** GPEdit.MSC **in the Open field and click OK.**

Windows starts the Local Group Policy Editor, as shown in Figure 2-23.

3. **Select the Local Computer Policy\Computer Configuration\ Administrative Templates\Windows Components\BitLocker Drive Encryption folder.**

You see a number of BitLocker policies in the right pane as shown in Figure 2-23.

4. **Double-click the Control Panel Setup: Enable Advanced Startup Options policy.**

The Local Group Policy Editor displays the policy shown in Figure 2-24. I already configured this policy as needed to use a flash disk, so your initial screen shot will look different from mine.

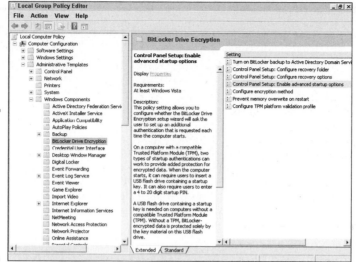

Figure 2-23: Change policies as needed to allow advanced system configuration.

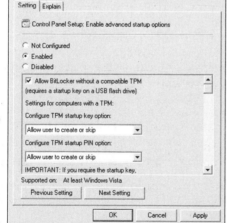

Figure 2-24: Modify the group policy to allow the use of a flash disk.

5. Select Enabled.

Your dialog box now matches the one shown in Figure 2-24.

6. **Click OK.**

Windows creates the new group policy. At this point, you can configure BitLocker using the information found in the "Performing BitLocker configuration tasks" section of this chapter. Using a flash drive is no different from working with a TPM except that you don't have to provide a PIN to use the flash drive.

Working with Multipath I/O

The Multipath I/O (MPIO) feature of Windows Server 2008 provides you with the means of supporting multiple data paths to a storage device. To obtain this support, you must install the Microsoft Device-Specific Module (DSM) or the third-party DSM that came with your device. Installing the Multipath I/O feature works the same as any other feature on your system — see the "Working with features" section of Book II, Chapter 1 for details. The following sections describe the MPIO feature in more detail. However, you want to consult the vendor documentation for your storage device for additional information and device-specific requirements.

Understanding how MPIO works

The basic concept behind MPIO is to make your data storage more reliable. An MPIO setup uses multiple adapters, connectors, switches, and other components to create more than one way to reach a particular storage device. Consequently, if one path becomes unusable, you can always use another path to access the storage. Only when all paths become inoperable do you lose contact with the storage path.

Some administrators confuse clustering and multipathing. A cluster relies on multiple computers, associated storage, and required clustering hardware and software to provide high application reliability. The goal is to make the application reliable and the use of multiple servers transparent. A multipathing solution focuses on storage. It seeks to make the storage reliable by providing multiple paths to it. A single server can rely on multipathing to improve the overall data reliability, but if the server fails, the user still sees a loss of application availability.

The primary reason to use MPIO is to ensure that an application can always access its data. For example, you might use MPIO with a mission-critical database application. You can discover more about MPIO at http://www.microsoft.com/WindowsServer2003/technologies/storage/mpio/default.mspx.

Performing MPIO configuration

After you install the Multipath I/O feature, you see a new MPIO console in the Administrative Tools folder of the Control Panel. Opening this console displays the MPIO Properties dialog box, as shown in Figure 2-25.

Figure 2-25:
Set up the device you want to use with MPIO, and then discover the paths you can use with it.

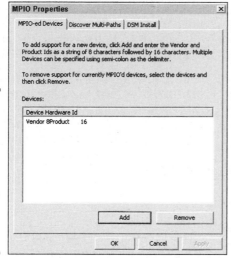

The first step of the configuration process is to add a storage device that possesses the multipathing capability. Use these steps:

1. **Click Add.**

You see an Add MPIO Support dialog box.

2. **Type the vendor's name using 8 characters.**

Add spaces, if necessary, to ensure that the first entry consumes exactly 8 characters.

3. **Type the product identifier using 16 characters.**

Add spaces, if necessary, to ensure that the second entry consumes exactly 16 characters.

4. **Click OK.**

Windows automatically searches for the device and adds it to the list shown in Figure 2-25.

At this point, you can begin searching for the multiple paths. Normally, Windows performs this task for you by querying the storage devices. If you don't see the paths you expected, you can click Add in the Discover Multi-Paths tab and add them manually. Optionally, you can also add support for Internet Small Computer System Interface (iSCSI) devices on this tab, so you can also use devices that are accessible by using an Internet connection.

You may have to perform an additional step when working with some storage devices. The DSM Install tab contains fields for installing a third-party DSM when necessary. Follow the instructions that come with the third-party product when performing this task.

Working with the Removable Storage Manager

The Removable Storage Manager (RSM) helps you work with storage that isn't a permanent part of the server. You use the RSM to monitor removable storage on your server (or any other machine, for that matter) such as DVDs, CDs, and flash disks. These devices work, even if you don't install RSM. All the RSM does is provide a monitoring capability. The following sections describe how to work with RSM.

Creating the RSM console

One oddity of the RSM installation is that Microsoft doesn't create a console for you in the Administrative Tools folder of the Control Panel. A monitoring feature isn't much good without some means of performing the monitoring, so you need to create a console on your own. The following steps tell you how to perform this task:

1. **Choose Start⇨Run.**

You see the Run dialog box.

2. **Type MMC in the Open field and click OK.**

Windows displays a blank console window. It doesn't contain any snap-ins, such as the consoles in the Administrative Tools folder of the Control Panel do. You need to add the required snap-in before you see anything.

3. **Choose File⇨Add/Remove Snap-In.**

The Microsoft Management Console (MMC) displays the Add or Remove Snap-Ins dialog box, as shown in Figure 2-26. Notice that this dialog box already has the Removable Storage Management entry selected.

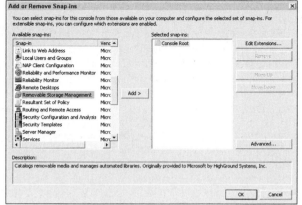

Figure 2-26:
Add the
Removable
Storage
Manage-
ment
snap-in to
the console.

4. Locate the Removable Storage Management entry and then click Add.

MMC displays the Select Computer dialog box, as shown in Figure 2-27. You choose the computer you want to monitor using this dialog box. In fact, a single console can contain multiple copies of the same snap-in, all of which are monitoring a different computer. You can also configure the snap-in to let you specify a particular computer when you start it from the command line.

Figure 2-27:
Choose the
computer
you want to
monitor.

5. Select the Local Computer option.

6. (Optional) Check the Allow the Selected Computer to Be Changed When Launching from the Command Line option.

7. **Click Finish.**

   MMC adds the snap-in to the Selected Snap-Ins list.

8. **Click OK.**

   The blank console now contains the Removable Storage Management snap-in you configured.

9. **Choose File⇨Save.**

   Windows displays the Save As dialog box. Notice that this dialog box automatically chooses the Administrative Tools folder as the storage place for the console you just created. Unless you have a good reason for not sharing the console with other administrators, maintain this storage location.

10. **Type** Removable Storage Manager.MSC **and click Save.**

    MMC changes the title of the console to match the name of the Microsoft Console (MSC) file, as shown in Figure 2-28. In addition, you now see the Removable Storage Manager in the Administrative Tools folder of the Control Panel, where you can access it as needed. You can use this same set of steps to create any console you need.

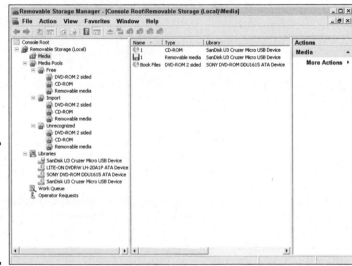

Figure 2-28:
The new console provides complete information about RSM.

Using the RSM console

The new RSM console shown in Figure 2-28 provides information about the RSM on the target machine. In this case, you're looking at the removable storage on a test server. The removable storage on your server looks similar but contains all the information about your server.

When you choose the Media folder, as shown in Figure 2-28, you can see a number of statistics about the media, including the media type. When you select a particular media entry, that media appears in the Actions pane. Choose More Actions⇨Properties, and you see a Properties dialog box for the media you chose, as shown in Figure 2-29.

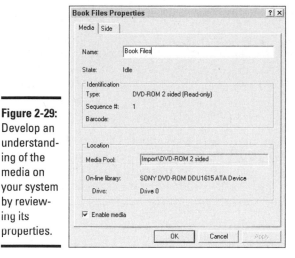

Book II
Chapter 2

Configuring Server Hardware

Figure 2-29: Develop an understanding of the media on your system by reviewing its properties.

You can perform several tasks in the Properties dialog box, but most of the entries are only for informational purposes. If the media allows it, you can change the media name. In addition, you can clear the Enable Media option. When you clear this option, Windows disables the media, making it unavailable for anyone to use.

The Side tab contains additional information about the media. For example, you can discover whether the operating system has ever mounted or allocated the media. You can also type a description for the media.

The More Actions menu contains a number of other options. You can click Eject when you want to eject the media from the system. Of course, this option works only when the media has an ejection device — you can eject a DVD, but you can't eject a flash disk.

The Free option frees the media for use by other applications. This action is the same as formatting the media, so using the Free option destroys any data that already appears on the media. Don't think of Free as making the drive itself available, but rather as a means of quickly removing any data on the drive so that another application can format the drive and use it for some other task.

The Media Pools folder contains a list of polls where RSM can store information about the media. Think of this folder as an organizational aid. If you want to find free media, check the Free folder. The Import folder contains lists of media that already has data on it that RSM has imported into a library. The Unrecognized folder contains lists of media that RSM didn't recognize (usually flash disks). Beneath each of these status folders are the media type folders, including DVD-ROM 2 Sided, CD-ROM, and Removable Media.

The Work Queue folder contains the status of any actions you attempt to perform with the media, such as disabling it, and the action status. It also contains RSM actions, such as identifying media, as shown in Figure 2-30. Failed actions can point to illegal actions, such as attempting to disable media that users are using, or problems with the device or media, such as a broken drive.

Figure 2-30: Determine the status of actions performed using RSM.

The Operator Requests folder tells you about pending actions. You see the requested action, when the operator requested it, and the associated application. In most cases, this folder is empty (or changing rapidly) unless there's a problem with the media or device.

Working with SANs

This section provides, at best, an incomplete view of the Storage Area Network (SAN). The SAN that you attach to Windows Server 2008 has specific requirements. Although Windows Server 2008 recognizes SANs that it supports, you still need to perform vendor-specific configuration. Because I have no way to discuss every vendor's solution in this book, you need to reference the vendor documentation for installation and support requirements before you begin this section.

After you install the SAN hardware and software, you can install the Storage Manager for SANs feature. This feature provides a graphical utility for managing your SAN, as shown in Figure 2-31. As you can see from the figure, the utility helps you manage the Logical Unit Number (LUN), subsystems, and drives for your SAN. This utility supports SANs in the traditional sense and iSCSI drives.

Figure 2-31:
Manage
the SANs
connected
to your
system
using this
special
console.

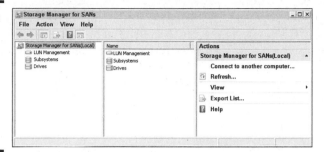

As with many other administrator tools, you find the Storage Manager for SANs console in the Administrative Tools folder of the Control Panel. When you first open the Storage Manager for SANs console, the snap-in looks for any Virtual Disk Service (VDS) setups on your system. When it finds a compatible VDS, the snap-in queries it for configuration information, including the number and setup of drives. The VDS has been around for a long time, but the new Storage Manager for SANs feature looks for particular VDS setups used to support SANs. Consequently, it doesn't work or act like the older VDS tools found in Windows 2003, including the Disk Management console.

The information that the console receives depends on the capabilities of the VDS, so you need to refer to your vendor documentation for configuration specifics. Microsoft provides a general overview of how the VDS works, at `http://technet2.microsoft.com/windowsserver/en/library/ dc77e7c7-ae44-4483-878b-6bc3819e64dc1033.mspx`. You can discover more information about the Storage Manager for SANs console at `http:// technet2.microsoft.com/windowsserver/en/library/25257b2a- 6d72-4adb-8f43-e3c0d28471d01033.mspx`.

Performing Printer-Related Tasks

Everything you connect to your server is relatively standard, except for the printer. Over the years, printers have added features and defined new methods of connectivity. Depending on your organization, you could conceivably have printers that connect using serial, parallel, or USB ports. The printer may provide simple output, have special features (such as a duplexer), or provide spectacular color output. It may rely on print cartridges or other means of coloring the page, which can change how the printer appears to Windows. Unfortunately, the more Microsoft fiddles with the printer support in Windows, the more ways the printer vendors find to complicate matters.

Understanding why your old printer driver doesn't work

Printer vendors have gone to great lengths to make their printer perform special tasks. For example, if you have an ink jet printer, you may find that the vendor software tells you how much ink the cartridges contain and even how to clear the nozzles without leaving your desk. Many of these features rely on changes to kernel mode DLLs. These DLLs are special because they control how the operating system works. Someone with ill intent could also modify these files to hide viruses on your system — in fact, they already did just that with rootkits. (See `http://en.wikipedia.org/wiki/Rootkit` for details on how rootkits work.) Microsoft wants to keep your system safe, so it has made it harder in Windows Server 2008 to modify these special kernel mode DLLs. Whereas this new protection helps keep your system safe, it can also make it impossible to install your old printer driver software.

Printer drivers also suffer from the same problems as other old drivers you might try. For example, you can't install an unsigned driver on the 64-bit version of Windows Server 2008, and you must override the signing requirement on the 32-bit version. In addition, your old printer driver can't make use of the new Windows Server 2008 printer driver model, much like other old drivers can't use other Windows Server 2008 features. For these, and many other reasons, it's a good idea to either use the generic printer drivers that Microsoft supplies with Windows Server 2008 or request a Windows Server 2008 specific driver from the printer vendor.

Working with the Printer Installation Wizard

In most cases, Windows Server 2008 automatically installs your printer. No matter how you connect the printer, the second that Windows Server 2008 sees it, it installs the proper generic driver. You look in your Printers folder, as shown in Figure 2-32, and find that the printer is already there. (Select the Printers applet in the Control Panel to open the Printers folder.) The printer may be using a generic driver, but you can use it immediately. In fact, when you work with a USB device, you want to follow the vendor instructions carefully because many installation routines require you to start with the printer disconnected from the system.

If you want to remove an existing printer, simply highlight the printer entry in the list and press Delete. Windows Server 2008 asks whether you're sure that you want to remove the printer. Press Yes and the printer entry goes away. At this point, you can install a custom printer if the printer is still attached to the system. You can also remove the printer from the system when you no longer need it. In either case, it helps to turn off the printer before you remove the printer driver, or else Windows Server 2008 may add it back into the Printers folder for you.

Figure 2-32:
The Printers folder contains a list of printers on your system.

Installing local printers

At some point, you may encounter a printer that Windows Server 2008 doesn't recognize automatically. For example, the generic printer driver may almost, but not quite, match the printer connected to your system. In some cases, the connection method may prevent proper identification or you may not have the printer configured to provide bidirectional communication. Any number of problems can occur. In this case, you can use the Printer Installation Wizard to install the printer. The following steps tell you how to perform this task:

1. **Double-click Add Printer in the Printers folder.**

You see an opening dialog box, like the one shown in Figure 2-33, that asks about the printer connection. Local printers have a physical connection to the server through a FireWire, parallel, serial, or USB connector.

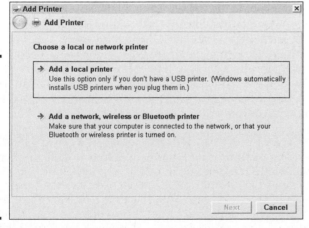

Figure 2-33:
Choose the local option to connect to a printer that's physically connected to your server.

2. Click Add a Local Printer.

The Add Printer Wizard asks you which port to use for the printer, as shown in Figure 2-34. Normally, you choose the existing physical connection you created for the printer. However, when you connect the printer to the network using a network connection (the printer has its own NIC) you need to choose the Create a New Port option and follow the directions to create a new Standard TCP/IP Port. The TCP/IP options let you connect to a standard TCP/IP device or through a Web service. Always obtain the required connection information from the vendor documentation or the Web service provider.

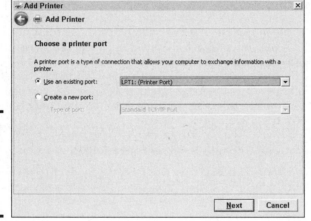

Figure 2-34:
Select the kind of port used to connect to the printer.

3. Select a printer port and click Next.

In some cases, Windows Server 2008 automatically detects the printer at this point, and the procedure is finished. However, in other cases, you see the dialog box shown in Figure 2-35, where you choose the printer driver to use for the attached device. If you have a printer disk, you can click Have Disk to install the driver from the disk. You can also click Windows Update to tell the Add Printer Wizard to search for the required software online.

4. Highlight the printer manufacturer in the Manufacturer list.

5. Highlight the printer model that best matches your printer in the Printers list and click Next.

The Add Printer Wizard asks you to supply a name for the printer. It supplies a default name based on the name of the print driver, which works in most cases. You can also choose to make this printer the default printer.

Figure 2-35:
Choose
the printer
that best
matches
your printer.

6. **Type a name for the printer in the Printer Name field. Optionally, check the Set As the Default Printer option. Click Next.**

   The Add Printer Wizard tells you that it's installing the printer. When the printer software installation is finished, you see the dialog box shown in Figure 2-36, which asks whether you want to share this printer. Sharing the printer makes it available to other people on the network. Because this is a server, you likely share the printer, which is why Add Printer Wizard automatically chooses this option for you.

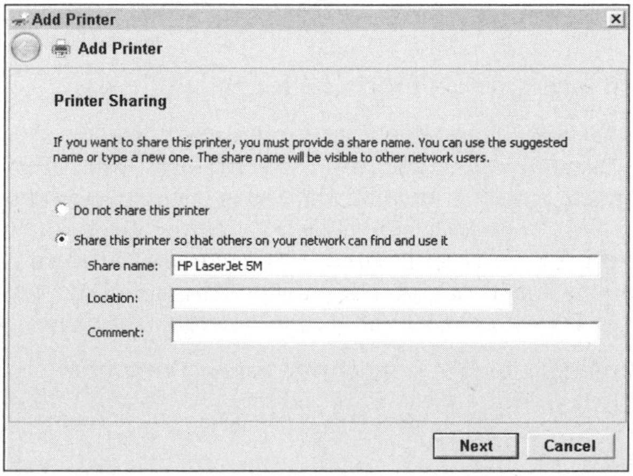

Figure 2-36:
Determine
whether you
want to
share the
printer on
the network.

7. **Type a name for the printer in the Share Name field as a minimum. You can, optionally, type additional share information in the Location and Comment fields. Click Next.**

   The Add Printer Wizard shows a success message. However, you really aren't successful yet. You must test the printer to ensure that it works.

8. **Click Print a Test Page.**

   You see a dialog box telling you about the printer test. In a few seconds, you should see the test page coming out of the printer. If you see this test page, the printer driver installation is successful. Otherwise, you need to troubleshoot the printer problem.

9. **Click Close and then click Finish.**

   The printer is ready for use.

Installing network, wireless, or Bluetooth printers

Not all printers you want to use from the server have a local connection. Sometimes you want to use a network, wireless, or Bluetooth printer. Windows Server 2008 never detects wired network printers, but it may automatically detect wireless or Bluetooth printers. When you want to connect to one of these printers, you use the following steps:

1. **Double-click Add Printer in the Printers folder.**

   You see an opening dialog box shown in Figure 2-33 that asks about the printer connection. Network, wireless, and Bluetooth printers all share the characteristic that they don't have a physical connection to the server.

2. **Click Add a Network, Wireless, or Bluetooth Printer.**

   The Add Printer Wizard searches for any network, wireless, or Bluetooth printers. In some cases, this process can require a lengthy wait. When you see your printer in the list, click Stop (or get a cup of coffee and enjoy reading *War and Peace*). The list includes printers you shared because they're network printers. For example, in Figure 2-37, the HP Office 5600 is a networked printer on another machine, while the HP LaserJet 5M is a networked printer on the local machine.

   If you don't see the printer you want listed, the printer setup may have a problem. Make sure that you shared the printer and that it provides proper rights for people to access it. The host system must have the Server service running. After you ensure that everything is set up correctly and you still don't see the printer in the list, click The Printer That I Want Isn't Listed. Use the Find a Printer by Name or TCP/IP Address dialog box to provide the wizard with the information it needs to locate your printer.

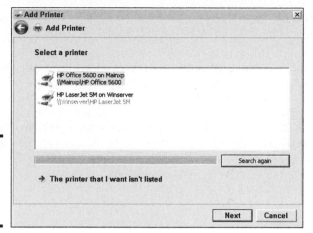

Figure 2-37:
Select one
of the
printers in
the list.

3. Highlight the printer you want to use and click Next.

You see a message that the Add Printer Wizard is connecting to the remote printer. After a few moments, you see a Type a Printer Name dialog box, but you can't type a name. The Add Printer Wizard uses the name selected by the remote system to identify the printer. You can also choose to make this printer the default printer.

4. Optionally, check the Set As the Default Printer option. Click Next.

The Add Printer Wizard shows a success message. However, you really aren't successful yet. You must test the printer to ensure that it works.

5. Click Print a Test Page.

You see a dialog box telling you about the printer test. In a few seconds, you should see the test page coming out of the printer. If you see this test page, the printer driver installation is successful. Otherwise, you need to troubleshoot the printer problem.

6. Click Close and then click Finish.

The printer is ready for use.

The Add Printer Wizard uses the generic driver supplied with Windows Server 2008 when you add the networked, wireless, or Bluetooth printer to your system. Even if the host system provides additional features, the driver on the Windows Server 2008 machine doesn't support these features, so you don't see them in the Properties dialog box. You can always update the printer driver by using the options on the Advanced tab of the printer's Properties dialog box. You can learn more about these options in the "Modifying the printer's Advanced tab options" section of this chapter.

Configuring the printer options

After you install a new printer on your system and ensure that you can print to it, you should configure the printer to meet your specific needs. In many cases, the settings that Microsoft provides work just fine, but you still want to check them, to be sure. To configure any printer on your server, right-click its entry in the Printers folder (refer to Figure 2-32) and choose Properties from the context menu. You see a printer Properties dialog box, like the one shown in Figure 2-38. The following sections describe each of the printer configuration tabs.

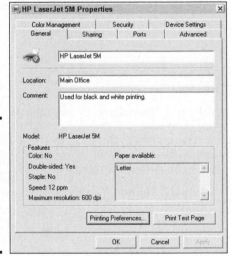

Figure 2-38: Use the General tab to find more about the printer and perform a basic test.

Modifying the printer's General tab options

The General tab provides basic information about the printer, such as the features it provides. You can see a typical example of the General tab in Figure 2-38. Notice that the general information includes a few items you can change, such as the printer's name and location and comments about the printer.

Clicking Print Test Page sends a test page from Windows to the printer so that you can verify that the printer is functioning correctly. This simple test is your assurance that you can work with the printer. Unfortunately, this test doesn't always tell you what's wrong with the printer. Your printer also comes with diagnostics that you can run at the printer. The vendor manual that comes with your printer tells you about these tests. Run these tests to verify that the printer is working, and then work your way back from the printer by checking the cable connecting the printer to the server (when there is one), and, finally, checking your Windows setup.

Click Printing Preferences when you want to change how the printer works with the data you send it. Figure 2-39 shows a typical setup, but your printer may include additional features. The tabs you see depend on the kind of printer you're using. For example, color printers provide additional tabs that help you set the color for the printer at a basic level.

Figure 2-39:
Perform basic configuration of how your printer works with data you send.

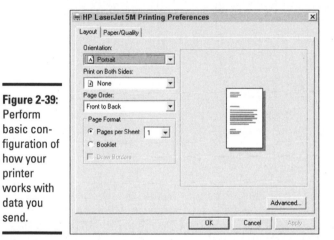

All these tabs provide essential settings, but you have to refer to your vendor documentation to set most of them because they vary by printer. The Layout tab generally tells the printer whether you want to print in landscape (horizontal) or portrait (vertical) mode. In this case, the printer also provides a duplexer so that you can print on both sides, so the Layout tab contains features to set the duplexing options. The Paper/Quality tab normally contains options for setting the printer's output resolution, defines which paper tray to use, and controls the paper type.

Configuring the printer's Sharing tab options

The Sharing tab tells the system how to share your printer, as shown in Figure 2-40. Simply checking the Share This Printer option is enough to share it with anyone else on the network. The *share name,* which is the name that people who want to use the printer must provide, appears next to the Share This Printer option. Use a short but descriptive option whenever possible, to ensure that people know where they're connecting.

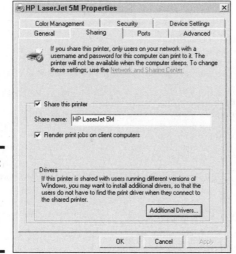

Figure 2-40:
Use these options to share your printer with others.

The Render Print Jobs On Client Computers option is new for Windows Server 2008. This option tells the system to force the client to create the printer-ready output, rather than use server resources to perform the task. The result of this change in workload is that the client system may notice a slight performance degradation, but the server gains a performance boost. Windows Server 2008 checks this option by default so that your server gains the performance boost automatically.

In some cases, your network may consist of a mix of x86 (32-bit), x64 (64-bit), and Itanium computers. The drivers you install on your server may not work with these other machines. When you must support a range of machine types, click Additional Drivers. You see the Additional Drivers dialog box, where you can check the other configuration options you need. When a machine with the alternative configuration wants to share the printer, the drivers already appear on the server, making it much easier to install the required support.

Viewing the printer's Ports tab options

Normally, you never need to change the settings on the Ports tab, shown in Figure 2-41. The Add Printer Wizard adds your printer to a free port during installation, and you use that port to access the printer from the command line. You don't need the port to be able to access the printer from within Windows, but having the printer accessible available from the command line is beneficial and doesn't impair your server's performance or functionality in any way.

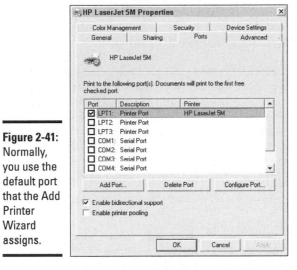

Figure 2-41: Normally, you use the default port that the Add Printer Wizard assigns.

Book II
Chapter 2

Configuring Server Hardware

Printers can communicate with Windows, in most cases, to provide status information. For example, a printer can tell Windows that it's out of paper or the toner cartridge is empty. However, to obtain this support, you must enable bidirectional communication by checking the Enable Bidirectional Support option. Windows automatically checks this option for you when it detects that the printer provides the required support.

The Enable Printer Pooling option serves a special purpose. When you check this option, Windows Server 2008 lets you assign more than one port to a particular printer, which may not seem beneficial. However, let's say you have a printer attached to a USB port. You can't use a USB port from the command line. In this case, you can check Enable Printer Pooling and assign a second port to the printer that the DOS application can see, such as LPT1.

The default setup includes a number of standard ports. In most cases, you have enough ports to meet any need. However, if you do run out of ports, you can click Add Port, select Local Port, and click New Port to create a new one. Simply give the port a name and click OK. Later, if you decide that you no longer need the port, you can highlight its entry and click Delete Port. Windows Server 2008 asks whether you're certain that you want to delete the port. Clicking OK removes it. Make sure that you assign a new port to the printer after you complete this task.

Many modern printers come with their own network cards. In this case, you may have to add a special port to connect to the printer using a TCP/IP connection. In this case, click Add Port, select Standard TCP/IP Port, and click New Port to create a new one. You must provide the printer name or IP address to use this feature, along with a name for the port.

The parallel (LPT) and serial (COM) ports also provide configuration options. The default configuration options work fine for most needs. However, you might find that the printer doesn't communicate properly or constantly times out. In this case, highlight the port and click Configure Port. You see a dialog box for configuring that port type. Make sure to check the vendor documentation for your printer for any special configuration requirements. This feature may work with other special port types, but there aren't any configuration options for the Text File, USB, or XML Paper Specification (XPS) ports.

Modifying the printer's Advanced tab options

The Advanced tab, shown in Figure 2-42, provides access to the advanced features of the printer's device driver. The first two options control the print driver availability. You can tell Windows to make the print driver accessible during specific timeframes or to let everyone use it at any time. Controlling the print driver access normally controls printer access as well, unless you have multiple drivers or driver copies installed for a particular printer. The Priority setting controls how Windows interacts with the printer driver. If two drivers require service at the same time, the driver with the lowest number priority receives service first.

At some point, you may need to change the driver used with the printer. To perform this task, click New Driver. You see a dialog box similar to the one shown earlier, in Figure 2-35. Choose the manufacturer and model of the printer you want to install. You can also click Have Disk when you have a third-party disk containing the new driver you want to use.

Using a print spooler provides performance benefits for the host computer, requires additional resources, and tends not to affect the printer much unless you have a very fast printer. If you want to obtain the fasted possible performance from your printer, select the Print Directly to the Printer option. However, if you want to optimize the server to receive maximum benefit from spooling, check the Start Printing After Last Page Is Spooled option. (This option also requires the greatest amount of system resources, such as memory and hard drive space.) Microsoft chose the middle ground for performance by checking the Start Printing Immediately option.

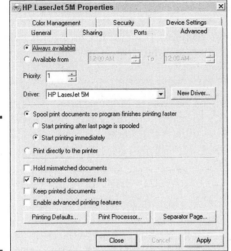

Figure 2-42: Modify the way the print driver works by using the Advanced options.

Book II
Chapter 2

Configuring Server Hardware

You can tailor the performance of the print driver in a number of other ways. How much these performance options help depends on how you use your printer. The following list describes the four additional performance enhancements that Microsoft provides for printing:

✦ **Hold Mismatched Documents:** Checking this option means that Windows holds documents that don't match the current setup. The server prints all documents that match the current setup and then requests that you make the required changes to the setup for the first document with a mismatch. This feature can improve overall performance when you use multiple forms and other special printer features. However, be prepared to hear user complaints when their documents don't print in order.

✦ **Print Spooled Documents First:** This option is the only one that Microsoft enables by default. Checking this option tells Windows to service any spooled print jobs first, and then those that print directly to the printer. Using this approach tends to maximize the benefits of using a print spooler.

✦ **Keep Printed Documents:** Normally, Windows deletes a document from the print queue immediately after it prints it. Some documents require a lot of time to create because they have graphics or other special features. Selecting this option means that Windows retains the document in the print queue, which lets you reprint it without re-creating it. The document prints significantly faster. Of course, this option also consumes hard drive space — the hard drive space is the tradeoff you make for obtaining better performance. To use this feature effectively, create a special printer entry for common documents and print only those documents to that entry. Printers can have multiple entries, each of which has special configuration options. This is one time where the multiple printer entry feature is especially useful.

✦ **Enable Advanced Printing Features:** Many printers include special features, such as the ability to print multiple pages of data per physical sheet of paper. Using this option can make printing significantly faster or at least more efficient. However, it can also introduce compatibility problems, so use it with care.

Modifying the printer's Color Management tab options

When you select the Color Management tab, you see a single button labeled Color Management. Clicking this button is the same as opening the Color Management applet in the Control Panel. When you either click Color Management or open the Color Management applet, you see the Color Management dialog box, as shown in Figure 2-43.

Figure 2-43:
The Color Management dialog box helps you control the color output of devices on your system.

Color management helps control the color output of various devices on your machine. The display uses a different process to create color than your printer. Applications interpret colors differently based on the capabilities that the developer provided. Without a color management system, the colors of each device and even applications would differ, making color significantly less useful. Unfortunately, color management is an incredibly difficult task to perform because of all the variables you must consider. A complete explanation of color management could require another entire book. If you want to learn more about the Windows color management system, see the article at `http://www.microsoft.com/whdc/device/display/color/icmwp.mspx`.

Fortunately, you don't really need to worry about color management unless you have very special printing needs. Microsoft provides color management functionality with Windows, and vendors who produce color-capable devices provide color management files with the drivers for the device. In most cases, you never even need to worry about the color management settings, no matter how complex your color printing requirements are.

Modifying the printer's Security tab options

You probably don't want everyone to manage the printers on your server because that would lead to chaos. However, it's important that users manage their own documents. Consequently, security for a printer is a bit different from security for a file. In some cases, a user is a creator of a document, but in other cases a user hasn't created the document and doesn't own it, so the user shouldn't be able to modify it either. The default security settings for your printer consider these differing requirements. Figure 2-44 shows the Security tab.

In most cases, the settings that are shown should work just fine for a printer that everyone can access. Using the default setup, everyone can print to the printer. The owner of a document (the person who printed it) can also manage documents. Only a member of the Administrators group can manage printers, which means that only administrators can change the printer setup.

You may need to change these settings when you want to restrict printing access to particular groups or give specific users additional access to the printers. The security settings work very much like those for files and folders. Use the techniques found in the "Configuring File and Folder Security" section of Book V, Chapter 1 to configure security settings for your printer.

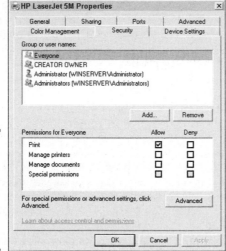

Figure 2-44:
The default
security
settings
generally
work well
for printers.

Modifying the printer's Device Settings tab options

The Device Settings tab provides access to the majority of the configurable special features for your printer. For example, you can configure the envelope feeder on the printer, modify the duplexer options, set up font cartridges, and perform other tasks. Figure 2-45 shows a typical view of the Device Settings tab. However, unless you have the same printer model as I do, the contents of your Device Settings tab will likely differ from the one shown in Figure 2-45.

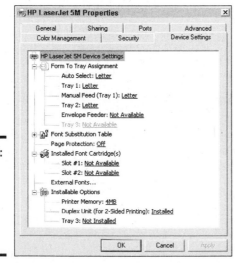

Figure 2-45:
Set the
device-
specific
settings to
meet your
needs.

The content of the Device Settings tab changes to match the printer you have installed and the optional features that the printer provides. Consequently, when you change your printer setup or buy a new add-on, check this tab for changes too. Consult the vendor documentation for the special settings that your printer supports.

Configuring an LPR printer

Line printers are ancient history. Unfortunately, the *concept* of the line printer is still around, and you might eventually need to work with it when you manage older Unix systems (you don't need to worry about it with Linux). In fact, this technology is so embedded that some vendors, such as Hewlett-Packard, provide print servers to provide Line Printer Daemon (LPD) services. (See http://h20000.www2.hp.com/bizsupport/ TechSupport/Document.jsp?objectID=bpj02836 for details.)

The Line Printer Remote (LPR) port monitor tracks printers that are running the Line Printer Daemon (LPD) on a remote system. A *daemon* is a kind of service, just like the services that Windows uses. It provides the background tasking required to perform a service, such as spooling documents to a printer.

You still need to set Windows to provide the LPR port. When you use the Add Printer Wizard to add a printer (see the "Working with the Printer Installation Wizard" section of this chapter for details), you notice that a new LPR port option is available when you add a printer, as shown in Figure 2-46. Select this port to create an LPD setup.

Book II
Chapter 2

Configuring Server Hardware

Figure 2-46:
Create an LPR port for your printer to provide LPD services.

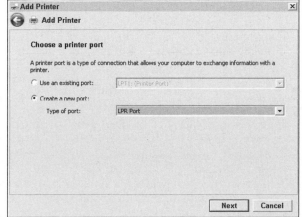

When you click Next, the Add Printer Wizard asks you to provide details of the LPD setup, including the name of the server providing this service and the name of the printer to use.

You don't notice any change to the Start menu or Control Panel when you install the LPR Port Monitor feature. Rather than install a new graphical feature, you obtain two new command line utilities: LPQ and LPR.

The Line Printer Queue (LPQ) utility provides status information that you can use to troubleshoot a LPD server. You can use this utility to display the status of each document in the queue. This utility uses the following syntax:

```
LPQ  -Sserver -Pprinter [-l]
```

The Line Printer Request (LPR) utility sends a print job to the printer. When working at the command line, you normally send text files, but the LPR utility can also accommodate binary files and PostScript. This utility uses the following syntax:

```
LPR -S server -P printer [-C class] [-J job] [-o option] [-x] [-d] filename
```

You can gain general information about using either of these utilities by using the /? command line switch. My book *Windows Administration at the Command Line* (Sybex, 2006) also provides full details on working with these utilities.

Performing Configuration Tasks

You may need to perform a number of additional configuration tasks on your server that aren't precisely hardware related but do affect the hardware you use. The following sections describe the most common tasks you perform. You should also review other minibooks in this book, such as Book IV for additional configuration information.

Working with fonts

One of the more interesting aspects of working with Windows is that you must place the fonts you want to use on the client, not on the server. More than a few administrators have lost sight of that rule and installed a number of fonts on their servers. In fact, you should keep the number of fonts on your server to a minimum because you don't need many of them to be able to display text on-screen. You definitely don't want to install any extra fonts when an application offers the opportunity.

To see the fonts installed on your system, open the Fonts applet found in the Control Panel. You see a list of fonts like the ones shown in Figure 2-47. Many of the fonts are so small that you don't really need to do anything with them. For example, Aharoni Bold, shown in the figure, is only 50 KB, a pittance for today's huge hard drives. However, some of the fonts in the list top 33 MB. Even though this number doesn't seem like much, having several hundred of these huge fonts makes a definite dent in your hard drive space.

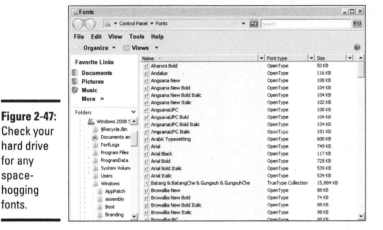

Figure 2-47: Check your hard drive for any space-hogging fonts.

Removing a font is easy: Simply highlight the font you want to remove and press Delete. Windows Server 2008 asks whether you're sure that you want to remove the font. Click Yes to complete the process.

Configuring the keyboard

Nothing is worse than trying to type on a keyboard that doesn't provide the right feel. Type too fast and you might find yourself duplicating keys. Set the repeat rate too slow and you spend a lot of time waiting for the keyboard to do something. To change the settings for the keyboard, open the Keyboard applet of the Control Panel. You see the configuration options shown in Figure 2-48.

The Repeat Delay setting controls how long Windows waits to begin repeating a keystroke after you press the key. The Repeat Rate setting controls how fast Windows repeats the keystroke. The combination of the two options provides a comfort level for working with repeated keys on the keyboard. You can try different combinations and then test the setup in the test area.

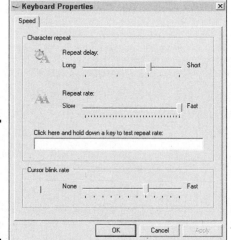

Figure 2-48: Modify the keyboard settings so that you can type comfortably.

The cursor blink rate isn't usually much of an issue. However, some people are susceptible to blink rates at certain speeds. If you have a medical condition that requires you to adjust the blink rate or you simply prefer a different setting, make sure to adjust the Cursor Blink Rate slider. This setting is one of the few that affects your view of the server, even if you access it using the Remote Desktop application.

Configuring the mouse

The mouse settings help you make your mouse more useful. For example, you can choose special pointers or tell the mouse to display a mouse trail so that you can see it easier. You can adjust all the mouse settings by opening the Mouse applet of the Control Panel. The Mouse Properties dialog box, shown in Figure 2-49, contains all the settings required to configure your mouse.

Changing the Buttons tab settings

The Buttons tab contains settings that adjust the position of the buttons. If you're left-handed or prefer to use the mouse left-handed, click Switch Primary and Secondary Buttons.

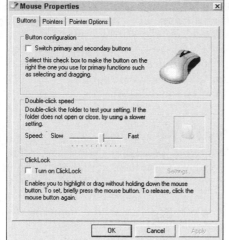

Figure 2-49:
Adjust your
mouse to
make it
more human
friendly.

Not everyone double-clicks at the same speed. Some people double-click
slower, and others double-click faster. The problem is that Windows has to
detect your double-click as a double-click. If you have problems getting
Windows to react to your double-clicks, change the slider position in the
Double-Click Speed section.

The ClickLock feature is interesting because it lets you hold the mouse
button for a few seconds, simply move the mouse, and then click quickly
to create the same effect as a drag. This feature is very nice for tired hands
because you don't have to hold down the mouse button the entire time
you drag the mouse. Even so, it takes a while to get used to this feature.

When you check the Turn On ClickLock option, Windows enables the
Settings button. Clicking Settings displays the Settings for ClickLock dialog
box, where you can adjust the length of time you must hold down the mouse
button to start a drag.

Changing the Pointers tab settings

The Pointers tab contains a list of the mouse cursors you normally see when
using Windows. You can use the options on this tab to change the appearance of the mouse cursors and make them more interesting. When you find a
combination of mouse cursors you like, you can save them as a scheme so
that you can call them up at any time.

Microsoft provides a number of default schemes you can test. The Windows Black (Extra Large) scheme is especially nice when working in a sunny room or from a laptop. Try the Windows Standard (Large) or Windows Standard (Extra Large) schemes if you have trouble seeing the mouse cursors normally. Given that this is a server operating system, Microsoft doesn't include any of the fancy, me-based schemes you find on the client operating systems, but you can always install them if desired.

Changing the Pointer Options tab settings

The Pointer Options tab contains options for making the mouse pointer (the *cursor*) work better. For example, if you have a high-precision mouse, check the Enhance Pointer Precision option to ensure that you gain the full benefit of your hardware. You can also set the pointer speed to make the mouse move faster or slower across the display. In some cases, an overactive mouse can make it difficult to select options on-screen.

The Snap To section of the tab contains an interesting feature: When you check the option in this section, Windows automation moves the pointer to the default button in a dialog box or window. You can then simply click to accept the default settings when they're correct. Although this feature might not seem like an important one, it can save you time, especially if you regularly have to hunt through complex dialog boxes to locate the default button.

You also have the option of making the pointer more visible. The default Hide Pointer While Typing option can become a nuisance because the mouse may have a tendency to remain "hidden." You may want to clear this option on a server to ensure that the mouse cursor remains visible at all times. Check the Display Pointer Tails option if you have a hard time following the mouse cursor in motion. The pointer tails tend to draw your eye toward the mouse cursor, so you can track it with greater ease. Finally, if you really have a hard time finding the mouse, check the Show Location of Pointer When I Press the Ctrl Key option. This option displays a surrounding bull's-eye that makes it significantly easier to find the mouse on a busy display.

Configuring the phone and modem options

Most servers today don't have a phone or modem installed. The use of broadband has all but doomed the modem. However, when you open the Phone and Modem Options applet in the Control Panel, you see the Location Information dialog box, as shown in Figure 2-50.

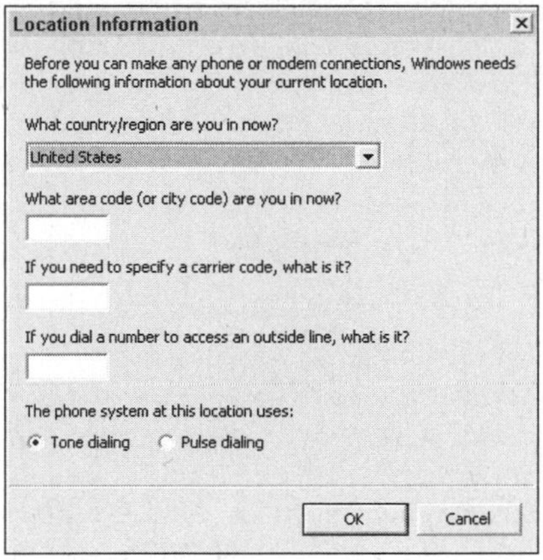

Figure 2-50:
Provide your
location
information
so that
applications
can find it
as needed.

This dialog box accepts information about your location, such as your area code. Many Microsoft and third-party applications rely on the location information to interact with your system correctly. For example, you probably need this information if you set up a fax on your server.

Setting the power management options

The power management features that Windows provides are a great idea for your workstation, but possibly not the best idea for your server. The problem is that you can easily configure the server to conserve energy and then find that no one can use the printer because it becomes unavailable when certain conditions occur (such as the server goes into a low power state). Microsoft tells you about some of these problems when you configure the service, such as sharing a printer, but not when you configure the power management setup, which makes it quite easy to create problems in trying to save energy.

When you open the Power Options applet of the Control Panel, you see the Power Options window, as shown in Figure 2-51. The default plan is High Performance, as shown in the figure. You should probably maintain this setting because using one of the other settings turns off parts of your server that should remain active, such as the hard drives.

You can adjust the settings, if you want. Click the Change Plan Settings link, and you see an option for turning off the display. The default setting is 20 minutes. However, if you mainly work with your server using Remote Desktop, you can easily change this setting to 1 or 2 minutes and save some energy. Unfortunately, 1 minute is the lowest setting available.

Figure 2-51:
Use the power manage-ment options carefully.

If you click Change Advanced Power Settings, you see the Power Options dialog box, as shown in Figure 2-52, which provides you with precise control over your server power management. Notice that the figure shows that the system never turns off the hard drives — a good setting for a server. If you ever find that you made an error in setting the power management policy, you can click Restore Plan Defaults to return your server to a usable state.

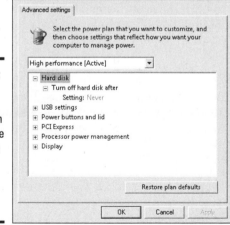

Figure 2-52:
The advanced settings can help you eke a little more power savings from your server.

Configuring the sound options

Most servers don't have sound devices installed. Consequently, Windows Server 2008 may not even have the Windows Audio service enabled. If you attempt to open the Sound applet in the Control Panel and Windows asks you to enable the Windows Audio service, click No. You don't have any accessible audio devices.

If you have an audio device installed, you configure the sound options as you do with a standard workstation. You find tabs for selecting a recording and playback device. In addition, you find a tab for choosing system sounds. In general, all these features work as specified in the vendor manual, and you should follow the vendor instructions for setting up your audio device.

Chapter 3: Using the Control Panel

In This Chapter

✔ Obtaining access to the Control Panel

✔ Configuring the Control Panel to meet your needs

✔ Accessing individual Control Panel applets

The Control Panel provides access to some of the most important configuration tools for Windows Server 2008. Most of these tools appear at least once in this book, and some of them appear several times. The simple act of adding or removing applications appears as one of the applets in the Control Panel. An *applet* is a special kind of file that you access by using the Control Panel. It provides you with the means to perform many configuration tasks.

This chapter focuses on the Control Panel. You discover many interesting new ways to interact with the Control Panel and a few methods for bypassing it. However, this chapter doesn't tell you how to use each of the applets — this information appears throughout the book, and you find mentions of the sections where this information appears as part of the applet descriptions.

Accessing the Control Panel

Gaining access to the Control Panel is easy because you can do it from so many locations. Most people know that you can access the Control Panel by selecting its entry on the Start menu. The details vary according to whether you use the new or classic Start menu, but the entry is there either way.

When you choose the Show Control Panel in My Computer option on the View tab of the Folder Options dialog box, you also see the Control Panel when you open My Computer. The Folder Options dialog box appears when you open the Folder Options applet in the Control Panel.

You can also access the Control Panel from Windows Explorer. The Control Panel entry always appears near the bottom of the list. Clicking this entry grants access to the Control Panel and you see the familiar applet icons in the right pane. Except for the pane configuration, Windows Explorer view looks like any other view of the Control Panel you've seen.

It's not even necessary to access the Control Panel using any of these direct methods. Choose Start⇨Run to display the Run dialog box, type **Control** in the Open field, and click OK. You see a copy of the Control Panel open. This trick also works at the command line.

Bypassing the Control Panel to access applets

Some people think it's necessary to open the Control Panel to access the applets it contains. One method to bypass this requirement is to check the Expand Control Panel option in the Customize Classic Start Menu dialog box. You can access this dialog box by clicking Customize on the Start Menu tab of the Taskbar and Start Menu Properties dialog box. After you make this change, you see the Control Panel as a menu, where you can choose the applet you want to open. If you're using the new Start menu, you can obtain the same benefit by choosing the Display As Menu option for the Control Panel entry on the Advanced tab of the Customize Start Menu dialog box.

Using CPL files to open applets

You can also open the applets directly if you know the applet name. For example, if you open the Run dialog box, type **Desk.CPL** in the Open field and click OK; you see the Display Properties dialog box. You can also type the name of the file at the command line to access the applet. Table 3-1 contains a list of common applets, the associated filename, and a description of that applet.

Table 3-1	Common Windows Applets	
Applet Name	*Filename*	*Description*
Add Hardware	HdwWiz.CPL	Displays the Add Hardware Wizard. This feature is unchanged from previous versions of Windows. You can also access this window using the Microsoft.AddHardware command object.
Date and Time	TimeDate.CPL	Displays the Date and Time dialog box (the Date and Time Properties dialog box in previous versions of Windows). The tasks that this dialog box helps you perform are the same, but some of the techniques for using it are different from previous versions of Windows. You can also access this window using the Microsoft.DateAndTime command object.

Applet Name	Filename	Description
Display Settings	Desk.CPL	Provides access to the Display Settings dialog box (Display Properties dialog box in previous versions of Windows), which consists of the Monitor tab in Windows Server 2008. Use the Microsoft. Personalization command object to access the new personalization settings.
Internet Options	InetCPL.CPL	Displays the Internet Properties dialog box. This feature is unchanged from previous versions of Windows. You can also access this window using the Microsoft. InternetOptions command object.
Mouse	Main.CPL	Displays the Mouse Properties dialog box. This feature is unchanged from previous versions of Windows. You can also access this window using the Microsoft. Mouse command object.
Network Connections (not in the Windows Server 2008 Control Panel)	NCPA.CPL	Displays the Network Connections dialog box. You could access this applet directly in previous versions of Windows. However, now you must access it through the Network and Sharing Center window. You can't access this dialog box directly using a command object, but you can access it indirectly using the Microsoft.NetworkAnd SharingCenter command object.
Phone and Modem Options	Telephon.CPL	Displays the Location Information dialog box (the Phone and Modem Options dialog box in previous editions of Windows). This feature is unchanged from previous versions of Windows. You can also access this window using the Microsoft.PhoneAndModemOptions command object.
Power Options	PowerCfg.CPL	Displays the Power Options window. This feature used to be the Power Options Properties dialog box in previous versions of Windows. The new window contains many new features and doesn't work anything like the old dialog box did. You can also access this window using the Microsoft.PowerOptions command object.

continued

**Book II
Chapter 3**

**Using the
Control Panel**

Table 3-1 *(continued)*

Applet Name	Filename	Description
Programs and Features	AppWiz.CPL	Displays the Programs and Features window, which replaces the Add or Remove Programs applet. You can also access this window using the Microsoft. ProgramsAndFeatures command object.
Regional and Language Options	Intl.CPL	Displays the Regional and Language Options dialog box. Although the name of the dialog box is the same, you find some changes to the Windows Server 2008 version of the dialog box from previous versions of Windows. You can also access this window using the Microsoft.RegionalAndLanguageOptions command object.
Sound	MMSys.CPL	Displays the Sounds and Audio Devices Properties dialog box. This feature is unchanged from previous versions of Windows. This dialog box is one of the few that you can't access directly with a command object, but you can access it indirectly using the Microsoft. Personalization command object.
System	SysDM.CPL	Displays the System Properties dialog box. The System Properties dialog box in Windows Server 2008 contains far fewer tabs than older versions of the dialog box because you can access these features as part of the Personalization window (Microsoft.Personalization command object). The new dialog box contains only the Computer Name, Hardware, Advanced, and Remote tabs.
Windows Firewall	Firewall.CPL	Displays the Windows Firewall window (a dialog box in previous versions of Windows). You can also access this window using the Microsoft.Windows Firewall command object.

Using command objects to open applets

You may have already noticed that Table 3-1 is missing quite a few applets. Microsoft actually provides three methods of implementing applets:

+ *CPL file,* discussed earlier in the chapter.

+ *Shell folders,* a special kind of applet that requires a registry entry (you can't access these applets from the command prompt).

✦ *Command objects,* special applications written to replace the CPL files. Any developer can create a command object and register it with the Control Panel.

You access a command object with a new and mostly undocumented command line switch: /Name. For example, to access the User Accounts applet, you type **Control /Name Microsoft.UserAccounts** and press Enter at the command prompt (or use it within the Open field of the Run dialog box). The name of the command object matches the name of the applet, so using command objects is easy. Here's a list of the command objects that Windows Server 2008 provides by default — you can access any of them using the /Name command line switch:

Microsoft.AddHardware	Microsoft.ParentalControls
Microsoft.AdministrativeTools	Microsoft.PenAndInputDevices
Microsoft.AudioDevicesAndSoundThemes	Microsoft.PeopleNearMe
Microsoft.AutoPlay	Microsoft.PerformaceInformationAndTools
Microsoft.BackupAndRestoreCenter	Microsoft.Personalization
Microsoft.BitLockerDriveEncryption	Microsoft.PhoneAndModemOptions
Microsoft.Bluetooth	Microsoft.PowerOptions
Microsoft.CardSpace	Microsoft.Printers
Microsoft.ColorManagement	Microsoft.ProblemReportsAndSolutions
Microsoft.DateAndTime	Microsoft.ProgramsAndFeatures
Microsoft.DefaultPrograms	Microsoft.RegionalAndLanguageOptions
Microsoft.DeviceManager	Microsoft.ScannersAndCameras
Microsoft.EaseOfAccessCenter	Microsoft.SecurityCenter
Microsoft.FolderOptions	Microsoft.SpeechRecognitionOptions
Microsoft.Fonts	Microsoft.SyncCenter
Microsoft.GameControllers	Microsoft.System
Microsoft.GetPrograms	Microsoft.TabletPCSettings
Microsoft.GetProgramsOnline	Microsoft.TaskbarAndStartMenu
Microsoft.IndexingOptions	Microsoft.TextToSpeech
Microsoft.Infrared	Microsoft.UserAccounts
Microsoft.InternetOptions	Microsoft.WelcomeCenter
Microsoft.iSCSIInitiator	Microsoft.WindowsAnytimeUpgrade
Microsoft.Keyboard	Microsoft.WindowsDefender
Microsoft.MobilityCenter	Microsoft.WindowsFirewall
Microsoft.Mouse	Microsoft.WindowsSidebarProperties
Microsoft.NetworkAndSharingCenter	Microsoft.WindowsSideShow
Microsoft.OfflineFiles	Microsoft.WindowsUpdate

Configuring the Control Panel

The Control Panel provides a number of viewing methods. These methods make it considerably easier to find the applet you need based on a number of criteria. The two methods you use most often are Category view and Classic view. The normal view for someone using the standard Start menu setup is Category view. Likewise, the normal view for someone using the classic Start menu setup is Classic view. The following sections tell you about the various views.

Using Category view

Category view automatically presents applets in categories, as shown in Figure 3-1. The categories make it easier for you to locate a particular applet based on the task you're performing. Microsoft has found that many people work better with task-oriented displays than with menus, and this view reflects this new strategy.

When you use this view, you select applets by type. For example, the System and Maintenance category contains applets such as Open Device Manager and View Event Logs. You don't have any other viewing options when using Category view — the presentation you see in Figure 3-1 is the one you get to use.

Figure 3-1: Category view groups the Control Panel applets by type.

If you find that Category view doesn't provide enough information about the category or applet, you can hover the mouse over the applet and the system displays a tooltip with additional information. This technique also works in Classic view, described later in this section.

The list of applets you see in Figure 3-1 isn't complete. The category contains just the applets that Microsoft thinks you use most often. When you click one of the category links, such as System and Maintenance, you see a complete list of the applets that Microsoft provides with this group, as shown in Figure 3-2.

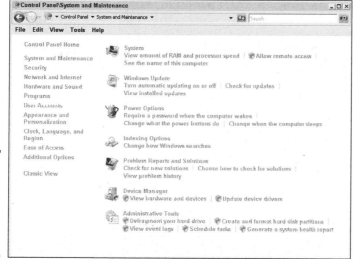

Figure 3-2:
Click on a group to see all the applets it contains.

Along the left side of the display, you see links for each of the categories shown in the initial display in Figure 3-1. Click on one of these links and you see the applets for that category.

Each applet link opens a window or dialog box that lets you perform a particular task. For example, when you click System, you see the System window. The links below the System link tell you about tasks you can perform with the System window. Clicking a specific link takes you to the window as well. However, when working with a dialog box, you often see the particular tab you must use to accomplish the task you clicked.

At the bottom of the display, on the left side, you notice a Recent Tasks area. These quick links help you go back to a recent task quickly, even if it doesn't appear in the current category.

Understanding the Control Panel groups

Microsoft provides plenty of grouping strategies for the Control Panel, but doesn't manage to provide you with an overview so that you can see how the categories work. The following list shows the categories and their associated applets; you may see some applets twice because Microsoft places them in more than one category:

Category	Associated Applets and Folders
Additional Options	Personalization Power Options
Appearance and Personalization	Folder Options Fonts Taskbar and Start Menu Personalization Ease of Access Center
Clock, Language, and Region	Date and Time Regional and Language Options
Ease of Access	Ease of Access
Hardware and Sound	Personalization Printers Add Hardware AutoPlay Color Management Keyboard Mouse Phone and Modem Options Sound Text to Speech Device Manager Power Options
Network and Internet	Network and Sharing Center Offline Files Windows Firewall Internet Options
Programs	Default Programs Programs and Features
Security	Windows Firewall Internet Options Windows Update
System and Maintenance	Device Manager Power Options Administrative Tools iSCSI Initiator Problem Reports and Solutions System Indexing Options Windows Update
User Accounts	User Accounts

Using Classic view

Many people prefer Classic view because they've worked with Windows for years and already know which applets perform a particular task. Notice that Figures 3-1 and 3-2 both contain a Classic View link. Classic view is the one that appeared in past versions of Windows. It displays the applets as simply a list of applets rather than as categories, applets, and tasks. Figure 3-3 shows a typical example of Classic view. To get back to Category view, click the Control Panel Home link.

Figure 3-3: Classic view sorts the Control Panel by the specified criteria.

Category view shown in Figure 3-1 is definitely friendlier than Classic view shown in Figure 3-3. However, Classic view provides some benefits over Category view. For example, when you choose View⇨Details, you can see the category of each applet, as shown in Figure 3-4.

You can choose to sort the applets by category in this view by clicking the Category column. To sort the applets when using a different view, such as Tiles, choose one of the options on the View⇨Sort By menu.

You can also group the applets in Classic view. Grouping provides an additional level of sorting. For example, Figure 3-5 shows how Classic view looks when you choose to display the applets as tiles, sort them by name, and group them by category. You can't use groups when you choose to display the applets as a list.

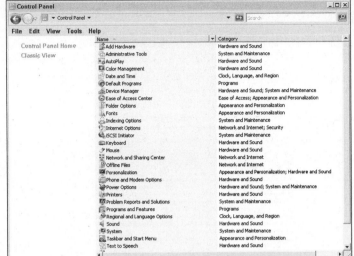

Figure 3-4:
Classic view
provides
category
information
for each
applet.

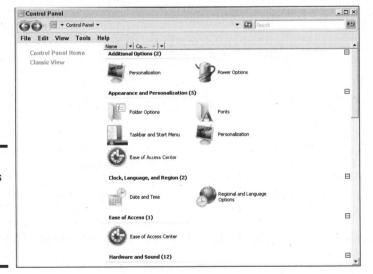

Figure 3-5:
Use groups
to make it
easier to
find
particular
applets.

Groups also make it easier to hide unwanted detail. Choose View⇨Collapse All Groups and you see just the groups shown in Figure 3-5. You can choose to open individual groups to display just those applets. Figure 3-6 shows Classic view using large icons, sorted by category, and grouped by name, with just the A–H group open.

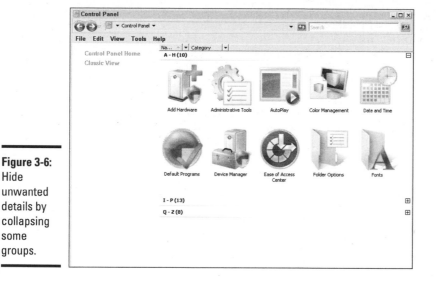

Figure 3-6:
Hide
unwanted
details by
collapsing
some
groups.

You may have never realized that the Control Panel provides this much flexibility, but you can use this flexibility to your benefit. By ordering the applets in a particular way — the way that matches the way you work — you can find applets quickly and easily.

Understanding the Control Panel Applets

A chapter on the Control Panel wouldn't be very helpful without a description of the applets it contains. The sections that follow provide a description of the standard Control Panel applets — the ones you commonly see when using Windows. You may also see other applets. For example, an application or a new piece of hardware may install another applet on your system. Refer to the vendor documentation when you have questions about any custom applets. These sections may not provide complete information about each applet, but provide a pointer to the place in this book where you can obtain additional information.

Add Hardware

The Add Hardware applet helps you add hardware when Windows Server 2008 doesn't discover it automatically. In many cases, the hardware you install using this applet is older hardware that doesn't provide the required identification information. Some hardware may not provide signed drivers, so replacing it with hardware that does provide the required drivers is a good idea for protecting your server setup. You can learn more about this applet in the "Working with Device Manager" section of Book II, Chapter 2.

Administrative Tools

The Administrative Tools folder isn't an applet in the conventional sense. This shell applet is the only one Microsoft provides, and it contains all the Microsoft Management Console (MMC) consoles you use to maintain your server. You can find an overview of this important folder in Book III, Chapter 1. This book shows you how to use most of the default consoles. For example, the Server Manager console appears in the "Using the Server Manager Console" section of Book II, Chapter 1.

You don't have to use the Control Panel to access the Administrative Tools folder when you perform the required setup. You can also access the Administrative Tools folder directly from the Start menu. When working with the standard Start menu, select the Display on the All Programs Menu and the Start Menu option in the System Administrative Tools folder. When working with the classic Start menu, check the Display Administrative Tools option. Making the Administrative Tools folder available on the Start menu increases productivity because you don't have to open the Control Panel first. For even quicker access, drag and drop a copy of the Administrative Tools folder from the Start menu or Control Panel onto your desktop.

AutoPlay

The AutoPlay applet opens the AutoPlay window, shown in Figure 3-7, where you choose the actions to perform with media that can have an automatic-play feature. Each media type can have a different default action.

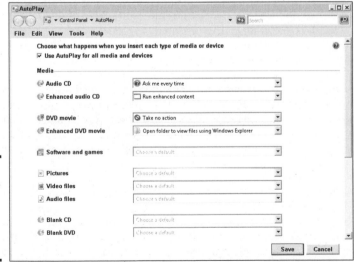

Figure 3-7: Choose how Windows reacts to media you provide.

The number of actions you can take depends on the kind of media you're using. The four common actions are described in this list:

✦ **Ask Me Every Time:** Windows asks you what to do every time you insert media of this type. Because many people perform the same action every time with a particular kind of media, this option can become annoying. Choose this option only if you do something different with the media each time you insert it.

✦ **Run Enhanced Content:** Many kinds of media include both standard media (such as music) and enhanced content (such as data or an application). This option tells Windows that you want to run the enhanced content rather than use the standard media. In some cases, you may have access to only the enhanced content.

Some recording companies use Digital Rights Management (DRM) software from companies such as Cactus Data Shield, Key2Audio, Doc.Loc, and Logo's that prevent you from playing the standard media on your computer. The copy protection never affects the enhanced content designed to run on your computer — just the standard media that you're not supposed to copy (at least according to the recording companies). Yes, it's a pain and there are ways to overcome it, but a description of the techniques is outside the scope of this book.

✦ **Take No Action:** Windows ignores the fact that you installed new media in the device and does nothing. If you want to do something with the media, you have to initiate the action manually.

✦ **Open Folder to View Files Using Windows Explorer:** This action opens a copy of Windows Explorer and automatically sets Windows Explorer to view the content on the media. This option is the best one to use with data files. Given that you probably perform this action most often on a server, you may simply want to set all media types to open a copy of Windows Explorer at the outset.

Servers normally aren't used for playing multimedia locally. However, if you install an application such as Nero (`http://www.nero.com/enu/index.html`), the application very likely installs other default actions you can perform. In short, you should check your AutoPlay defaults after you install any media-specific application, to ensure that the configured choices are still the ones you want.

Color Management

The Color Management applet opens the Color Management window. The settings in this window determine how Windows interacts with color devices attached to the system, to ensure consistent color output. You can read more about this applet in the "Modifying the printer's Color Management tab options" section of Book II, Chapter 2.

Date and Time

The Date and Time applet opens the Date and Time dialog box, as shown in Figure 3-8, where you can adjust the system date and time. It's important to maintain the correct date and time for your server because many security and other system operations depend on a correct date-and-time synchronization. For example, Kerberos requires relatively precise time synchronization to work properly. When the time varies by more than 20 seconds between c omputers, Kerberos begins taking certain protective measures. You can read more about the criticality of time for Kerberos at `http://search windowssecurity.techtarget.com/originalContent/0,289142, sid45_gci1014049,00.html`.

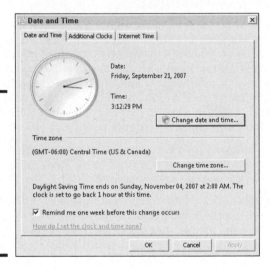

Figure 3-8:
Make sure
the system
time is
correct, or
else
services
may fail to
work
properly.

One of the most common time problems is setting the time zone incorrectly. The "Setting the time zone" section of Book I, Chapter 4 tells you how to configure the time zone on your server.

You notice in Figure 3-8 that Windows Server 2008 makes it impossible to set the time on the Date and Time tab. This new feature makes it possible for users to change their time zones as needed, but not the date and time. Security policies control how a user can interact with the time setting (see the group policy management information in Book III, Chapter 2 for details). To set the current time, click Change Date and Time. You see the Date and Time Settings dialog box, where you can change the time directly.

A better way to set the time is to use a time source. If this is your only server, you need to use an external time source. The easiest way to configure an external time source is to select the Internet Time tab and click Change

Settings. You can choose a default time source and update from it immediately. The "Setting the time zone" section of Book I, Chapter 4 provides additional details on this feature.

The final interesting feature in the Date and Time dialog box is the Additional Clocks tab, shown in Figure 3-9. You can tell Windows to provide up to two additional clocks. These clocks are quite useful when you must work with multiple time zones. Each time zone can have its own clock.

To select a clock, check its entry, select a time zone for it, and give it a name, as shown in Figure 3-9. Now when you click the time entry in the Notification Area, you see the additional clocks you defined, as shown in Figure 3-10.

Figure 3-9:
Use multiple clocks as needed to track multiple time zones.

Figure 3-10:
The Notification Area shows the additional clocks you defined.

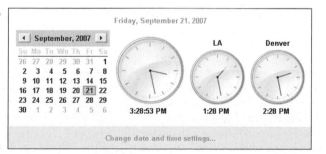

Default Programs

The Default Programs applet opens the Default Programs window. This window contains three links:

✦ Set Your Default Programs

✦ Associate a File Type or Protocol with a Program

✦ Change AutoPlay Settings

The "AutoPlay" section of this chapter tells you about the Change AutoPlay Settings link. The other two links may or may not contain everything you expect for default programs settings, but the new setup is considerably easier to use than editing the registry by hand.

When you click Set Your Default Programs, you see the Set Default Programs window, shown in Figure 3-11. This window usually lists every Microsoft application on your system and lets you specify it as the default application for all file types it supports. You probably won't see any third-party applications in this list until those vendors figure out how to place their applications there. Consequently, you probably want to avoid this window unless you're using only Microsoft applications and know that you want the Microsoft application to handle all file types that it supports.

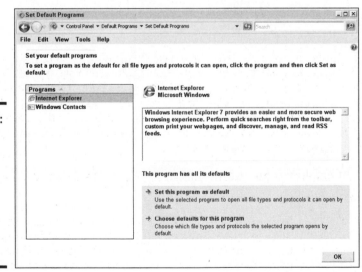

Figure 3-11: Setting the default programs usually means accepting the Microsoft solution.

When you click Associate a File Type or Protocol with a Program, you see the Set Associations window, shown in Figure 3-12. This window lists every file extension and protocol registered on your server. Changing the default application using this approach is considerably easier than modifying the registry directly. However, you can't use this window to add new file extensions or protocols, so you may still need to work with the registry on some occasions.

Figure 3-12:
Modify the file associations on your computer as needed to support the installed applications.

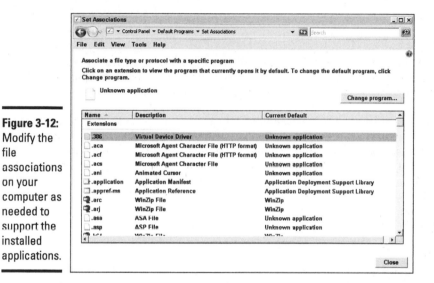

Most applications create the file extensions and protocols they require. In addition, these applications create all the required registry entries to support the associations they require. The problem occurs when you can use more than one application to work with a particular file extension or protocol. In most cases, the last application you install controls the file extension or protocol, which may not be the choice you want. The following steps tell you how to modify an association:

1. **Highlight the file extension or protocol that you want to change.**

2. **Click Change Program.**

Windows displays the Open With dialog box, where you can choose one of the existing applications associated with the file extension or protocol. If the application you want to use doesn't appear on the list, click Browse, locate the program you want to use, and click Open.

3. **Select the program you want to use as a default.**

4. **Click OK.**

You see the program you selected in the Current Default column.

Device Manager

The Device Manager applet opens the Device Manager dialog box, which you use to manage the hardware installed on your system along with the associated drivers. This dialog box also provides you with hardware status information so that you can quickly resolve hardware and driver problems. You find the Device Manager details in the "Working with Device Manager" section of Book II, Chapter 2.

Ease of Access/Ease of Access Center

The Ease of Access and Ease of Access Center applets both open the Ease of Access Center window, shown in Figure 3-13. You use the features in this window to configure your computer to meet special needs.

Although some people associate these features with disabilities, many features are useful for everyone. For example, if you need to see something small, such as an icon, in detail, you can use the magnifier. Some people use the screen reader to hear, rather than read, Web site content when they have tired eyes. Using an extra large mouse cursor can help when you have problems seeing it. A high-contrast display can also make life easier at the end of a busy day.

The best way to work with the Ease of Access Center is to try the various options to determine whether they work for you. You may find that some features work well, even when you don't have a particular need. For example, many people aren't very good at drawing on-screen, and you may seldom need to do it. Using some of the mouse features can make drawing considerably easier for the non-artist, and they're free — you don't have to buy anything.

Figure 3-13: Try out the accessibility features to meet your own, special needs.

Folder Options

The Folder Options applet opens the Folder Options dialog box. Microsoft hides a lot of Windows Server features from view by default on the assumption that most people don't need to see everything. Although this viewpoint is probably correct on a client machine, it's downright dangerous on a server, so you should configure your display to show everything. See the "Defining the Folder Options settings" section of Book III, Chapter 5 for additional information.

Fonts

In general, the fewer fonts you have on your server, the better. You need only a few fonts to accomplish Administrator tasks on a server. The Fonts applet displays all fonts installed on your system, and you should prune the fonts to just those you need. See the "Working with fonts" section of Book II, Chapter 2 for additional information.

**Book II
Chapter 3**

**Using the
Control Panel**

Indexing Options

Creating an index of the information on your hard drive can speed searches considerably. Of course, you need to trade some background processing time and some hard drive space to obtain this benefit because Windows has to create and store the index.

Indexing affects local searches, not networked searches. Consequently, you need to enable indexing on your server only when you plan to work with your server extensively using a local connection. To provide the benefits of indexing to the client machine, enable indexing on the client machine and add the networked drives to the list of indexes the client maintains.

Microsoft disables indexing by default on your server. If you want to index the local drives, you must install the Indexing Service role service of the File Services role. After you install this role service, you can open the Indexing Options applet. This applet controls which drives you index on your system.

Internet Options

The Internet Options applet controls how you interact with the Internet when using Internet Explorer. This applet doesn't affect third-party solutions, such as Firefox. Because your server contains a large amount of valuable data, set the Internet options conservatively and then tell Internet Explorer which sites to trust (such as Windows Update). See the "Defining the Internet Options settings" section of Book III, Chapter 5 for additional information.

iSCSI Initiator

Some organizations are slowly moving to online storage. One method for providing access to online storage is to use the Internet Small Computer System Interface (iSCSI) protocol. You configure this protocol using the iSCSI Initiator applet.

Keyboard

The Keyboard applet opens the Keyboard Properties dialog box, where you can adjust the settings for your keyboard. See the "Configuring the keyboard" section of Book II, Chapter 2 for additional information.

Mouse

The Mouse applet opens the Mouse Properties dialog box, where you can adjust the settings for your mouse. See the "Configuring the mouse" section of Book II, Chapter 2 for additional information.

Network and Sharing Center

Clicking the Network and Sharing Center applet opens the Network and Sharing Center window, which provides access to the majority of the networking features in Windows Server 2008. Considering the complexity of networking, you find the Network and Sharing Center described throughout Book IV. However, if you just want a quick overview of this important feature, check out the "An Overview of the Network and Sharing Center" section of Book IV, Chapter 1.

Offline Files

Offline files exist on the network but can also appear on your system when you don't have a network connection. The system copies these files to your local drive so that you can always access them. When you have network access, the system automatically updates the files on the network to reflect your local copy. Likewise, if you lose network contact, the system automatically updates the network copy of the files when you regain access. The Offline Files applet helps you configure offline file access — a feature that's definitely intended for use with a client system (likely a laptop) because you always have network access for your server. Microsoft disables this feature by default, and you should probably leave it disabled.

Personalization

The Personalization applet displays the same Personalization window that you see when you right-click the desktop and choose Properties from the context menu. No matter how you access the Personalization window, it provides you with access to the settings that control your user environment and make Windows more fun to use. See the "Defining the Personalization settings" section of Book III, Chapter 5 for additional information.

Phone and Modem Options

The Phone and Modem Options applet opens the Location Information dialog box, where you can set the area code and other dial-up information for your system. Even with the use of broadband applications, applications on your system may need this information for uses such as fax services. See the "Configuring the phone and modem options" section of Book II, Chapter 2 for additional information.

Power Options

Setting the power options for your server can net a big gain in power efficiency and save your company money. However, setting the power options incorrectly can also cause network delays and other unwanted side effects. The Power Options applet helps you configure the power settings for your server to obtain the best power use with minimum delays. See the "Setting the power management options" section of Book II, Chapter 2 for additional information.

Printers

Most servers have one or more printers connected at some point. The Printers applet helps you configure the printers attached to your server. See the "Working with the Printer Installation Wizard" section of Book II, Chapter 2 for additional information.

Problem Reports and Solutions

Information exchange with Microsoft can be important if you want to obtain answers for your server problems without spending a lot of money to do it. The Problem Reports and Solutions applet opens the Problem Reports and Solutions dialog box, where you can maintain a list of problem reports you send to Microsoft. When Microsoft comes up with a fix for your problem, you automatically see it as a solution. Of course, you must send the initial information, which means exposing some part of your server to Microsoft (even if its intent is completely benevolent). See the "Defining the Problem Reports and Solutions settings" section of Book III, Chapter 5 for additional information.

Programs and Features

The Programs and Features applet opens a modified form of the Programs and Features window that you've used in the past. However, you no longer manage Windows features using this window — you use the Server Manager instead. If you want to manage the Windows features for your server, see the information found in Book II, Chapter 1. However, if you want to manage third-party applications on your server, see the "Adding and Removing Standard Applications" section of Book III, Chapter 5 instead.

Regional and Language Options

The Regional and Language Options applet opens the Regional and Language Options dialog box, where you manage anything to do with language for the local system. The settings offered by this dialog box control everything from the layout of your keyboard to the formatting of numbers. See the "Defining the Regional and Language Options settings" section of Book III, Chapter 5 for additional information.

Sound

Most servers don't have sound cards because most servers don't need one. In many cases, no one interacts with the physical server, so a sound card is a waste of money. However, if your server has a sound card, you use the Sound applet to configure it. See the "Configuring the sound options" section of Book II, Chapter 2 for additional information.

System

The System applet opens the System window, where you can see an overview of your system setup. (As an alternative, right-click Computer and choose Properties from the context menu to see the System window.) This window also contains a number of links you use to manage the specifics of your system. See the "Interacting with the System Applet" section of Book III, Chapter 5 for additional information.

Taskbar and Start Menu

The Taskbar and Start Menu applet opens the Taskbar and Start Menu Properties dialog box. You can also open this dialog box by right-clicking the Taskbar and choosing Properties from the context menu. The options in this dialog box control the appearance of the Taskbar and Start menu. The Start menu appearance is especially important because it determines the steps you use to perform tasks such as starting applications. See the "Defining the Taskbar and Start Menu settings" section of Book III, Chapter 5 for additional information.

Text to Speech

Given that most servers don't have sound cards, the text-to-speech feature doesn't work either. If you have a sound card installed on your server and you decide that you want to enable text-to-speech functionality, open the Text to Speech applet to configure the text-to-speech feature. This dialog box helps you choose a voice for your computer, fine-tune the voice presentation, and choose a method for outputting the audio.

User Accounts

Before anyone can use your server, they need to have an account on it. The User Accounts applet provides access to any of the accounts on your system (assuming that you have Administrator rights). You can use the User Accounts windows to quickly configure features such as the user picture and environmental variables. See the "Performing User Configuration for a Workgroup" section of Book II, Chapter 4 for additional information.

Windows Firewall

Windows Firewall protects your server from unexpected incoming and outgoing Internet traffic. You can find out more about the Windows Firewall at `http://technet.microsoft.com/en-us/network/bb545423.aspx` and in the "Configuring the Windows Firewall" section of Book I, Chapter 4.

Windows Update

The Windows Update applet opens the Windows Update window, where you can check the status of updates on your system. Windows Update has a number of important purposes in Windows. For example, you should run it as part of the installation. (See the "Performing a Windows Installation" section of Book I, Chapter 3 for details.) Windows Update is turned off by default (see Table 4-1 in Book I, Chapter 4 for system defaults), so you need to run it as soon as possible to update your server. The "Configuring Automatic Updates" section of Book I, Chapter 4 tells you how to obtain updates automatically using Windows Update. You should monitor the Windows Update window to verify that your server is up-to-date. Discover more about this requirement in the "Downloading and installing updates" section of Book I, Chapter 4.

Chapter 4: Working with Workgroups

In This Chapter

✔ Working with workgroups

✔ Creating a workgroup

✔ Determining whether to use centralized or group sharing

✔ Performing the required server configuration

✔ Performing the required user configuration

✔ Using the Peer Name Resolution Protocol

A *workgroup* is a cluster of networked machines that normally rely on only one or sometimes no server — a workgroup normally relies heavily on shared resources that exist on multiple machines. A workgroup can consist of just two machines, each of which has resources that the other machine requires. The key to the workgroup is that each member of the workgroup is a peer of all the other machines — no single machine is in charge of the network.

Some people associate workgroups with small configurations. However, it's possible to create large workgroups, and sometimes they have multiple central servers. One of the defining workgroup elements is that workgroups lack Active Directory support. If you don't elevate your server to a domain controller and don't install Active Directory (the Active Directory support is automatic when you promote the server to a domain controller), then you have a workgroup.

This chapter helps you understand workgroups, prepare to create a workgroup, set up a server and users for a workgroup, and then perform some workgroup-specific configuration tasks. When you finish this chapter, you should know how to create a workgroup configuration. The workgroup won't have all the features you need to support a production environment, but it will function as a workgroup. (A *production environment* is one in which users can perform useful work, such as editing a document, accessing a database, or using an intranet.) Each machine can then access other machines on the network, and you can share resources as needed.

Make sure to review Book II, Chapter 1 for a listing of all the roles and features that you can install. These roles and features help determine what you can do with your workgroup. You also need to install third-party applications (see Book III, Chapter 5), set up printers and other hardware (see Book II, Chapter 2), and perform other configuration tasks to turn your basic workgroup from this chapter into a fully functioning production environment.

Understanding Workgroups

The workgroup was the original form of networking supported by Windows, and it's really still the basic form of all Windows networking. The concept of a workgroup was originally defined around peer-to-peer networking, where any machine on a network can act as a server and any machine can act as a workstation. Even today, Windows Server 2008 has both the Server and the Workstation services that provide these two roles. You can use your Windows Server 2008 server as a workstation if you want — no one can honestly say that this functionality is unavailable. Of course, Microsoft now has the Server Core version of Windows Server 2008. Theoretically, you can use Server Core as a workstation, but I don't know of anyone who'd want to.

The other standard form of networking is *client/server*. In this form of networking, you don't use the server as a workstation. In fact, when working with operating systems such as NetWare (`http://www.novell.com/products/netware/`), you can't use the machine that has the operating system installed as a workstation. It's simply impossible to use a NetWare server as a workstation because no functionality exists to do it. The advantage of client/server setups is that they're very light and reliable. The server uses all its resources to perform tasks on behalf of the client. However, this form of networking lacks flexibility. All workstations are always workstations, and all servers are always servers. As you discover in the "Understanding Domains" section of Book II, Chapter 5, domains aren't really a true client/server architecture — they're a hybrid form of networking that mimics a client/server setup.

Understanding the pros of workgroups

Workgroups are convenient because you don't have to have one super machine to handle everyone's requests. Any workstation can also act as a server, so you can attach a laser printer to one workstation and an inkjet to another workstation. With the proper settings, everyone has access to both printers even though the printers appear on different machines. Sharing occurs on many levels. A workstation with an exceptionally large hard drive can share some of that hard drive space with everyone on the network. Likewise, a workstation with an Internet connection can share the connection with everyone else. Peer-to-peer networking is all about sharing whatever a workstation has in excess with everyone else on the network so that everyone benefits from that excess.

Most administrators also find workgroups easier to manage, at least when they're small. If someone wants access to a particular workstation, their name must appear on the list of users for that workstation. When a workstation wants to share a particular asset, you must configure that asset for sharing and define who can use it. All of the settings are localized and easy to understand. You don't have to worry about global security policies, Active Directory, or anything else that's overly complicated.

A workgroup need not exist as a separate entity. You can use a workgroup network setup at the departmental level and a domain or client/server setup at the enterprise level. The concepts behind a workgroup work equally well in the departmental environment as they do in standalone mode.

One question with workgroups is finding out how large can you make them before they reach their limit. The best way to answer this question is to determine how the administrator configures the workgroup, know whether the workgroup contains the proper number of dedicated servers, and what you expect the workgroup to do. If your only goal for the workgroup is to share files and print documents, a workgroup of any size is possible. As you add tasks, such as database management, the potential size for a workgroup decreases because you're asking it to perform more work. A workgroup configuration that includes e-mail, file, print, and database management services is probably limited to 100 nodes. However, a skillful administrator could potentially increase that size.

Understanding the cons of workgroups

Using a workgroup becomes less advantageous when you begin using a number of custom applications and require centralized management for help desk support and other needs. Adding remote users and other enterprise requirements increase complexity and the need for centralized management, which usually means obtaining a central management application. For example, if you plan to use Microsoft's System Center Operations Manager, or SCOM (`http://www.microsoft.com/systemcenter/opsmgr/default.mspx`), you need a domain. Consequently, the workgroup meets its match in complexity, not necessarily in size.

Workgroups also tend to provide poorer security than does a centralized network (client/server or domain). Because everyone is sharing resources freely, it can be difficult to lock down those resources and ensure that they're shared only as required to accomplish tasks within the workgroup. Because of the poorer security, workgroups often encounter problems with adware and viruses where one machine's woe automatically becomes every machine's woe.

Preparing to Create a Workgroup

The "Understanding Workgroups" section of this chapter describes workgroups and how you can benefit from them and avoid their limitations. A workgroup isn't always the right solution to your networking needs, even when it provides the ease-of-configuration that you need. Consequently, your first step in preparing to create a workgroup is determining whether a workgroup is the right solution. If your network meets these requirements, you can probably use a workgroup to solve your basic networking needs:

✦ It provides basic file and printer sharing.

✦ (Optional) It provides basic database management support with no more than two custom applications.

✦ (Optional) It provides e-mail support with a product such as Exchange Server.

✦ (Optional) It provides centralized Internet access.

✦ It has no need for complex mission-critical applications involving large databases.

✦ It has no need for centralized resource management.

✦ It requires no remote access.

✦ It has no need to support external applications, a Web site, or Web services.

✦ It needs no more than 100 nodes in most cases.

After you determine whether you actually need a workgroup configuration, it's time to spend some time figuring out the details. Remember that a workgroup is made up of peers. Consequently, you don't have to have one machine that does everything. Don't be afraid to create a plan that emphasizes the strengths of each machine in the workgroup, even if you plan to use a server. The server should provide centralized storage, but any other machine can support any other task. In fact, it may be beneficial to spread out the tasks so that the server doesn't become overwhelmed trying to perform every task.

Create a list of the machines you plan to connect, the resources each machine can provide, and the location of each machine. You can use this list as a planning guide for configuring the network later. Make sure to consider the tasks that each machine will normally perform so that you don't overload it. If the workstations in a workgroup are overloaded, consider getting a dedicated server to reduce some of the load. Obtain a server that can handle the current load plus at least twice as much additional load for future expansion. Most companies find that their server becomes too small, quite quickly if they don't obtain enough capacity for future needs.

Although the topic is outside the scope of this book, you also need to consider the physical requirements of the network. The network will likely require switches, NICs, cabling (unless you plan to go wireless), and other physical elements. The kind of cabling you choose is also important because the cable must provide support for the network speed you choose or you'll experience errors in transmitting the data. Whenever possible, use switches instead of hubs because switches have intelligence built into them that makes them more reliable and faster. Some companies don't consider these issues and end up with cost overruns as a result. If you use a consultant to perform the physical configuration, make sure to plan for the consulting costs and add a little cushion in case the consultant encounters unanticipated problems.

Survey all the applications you need to run and consider these applications as part of the network setup. In many cases, you need to reconfigure the applications to run properly on the network. For example, Office users will likely want to store their data files in a central location so that everyone in the workgroup can access them. The centralized storage requires additional configuration time, and you need to plan for it as part of your preparation.

One of the issues that administrators tend to run into is that everyone wants to add special gizmos to the network simply because they can and not because they require the gizmos. Avoid gizmos when you can because they usually spell trouble. The more gizmos you have, the more complex your network becomes and the more time you spend securing, configuring, and maintaining it. Gizmos add to support costs and usually make users less productive. In short, gizmos are usually a waste of time, effort, and money, so you should avoid them.

Considering Centralized versus Group Sharing

One of the most important preparation steps for your server is determining how to store the data you create. The two common methods are centralized and group sharing:

✦ *Centralized sharing* involves placing all data in one location. You can organize the data into folders to keep various projects separate, but everything appears under one main folder or on a particular hard drive.

✦ *Group sharing* involves placing data in multiple locations based on who creates it and who needs to work with it next. Every workstation could have an inbox to hold files that the person needs to work on next. Each person can also have private data stores for files that no one else will need.

The sharing methods aren't mutually exclusive: You may choose to provide centralized sharing for your word-processed files but provide group sharing for graphics files. The technique you choose depends greatly on how your organization uses the data. If everyone collaborates on word-processed files, then centralized sharing makes sense.

Centralized sharing provides advantages over group sharing. For example, it's easier to locate files when everyone knows where the files appear on the network. In addition, you can back up and restore centralized files with greater ease. Security also becomes less cumbersome because you don't have to open as many areas to common access.

Before you get the idea that group sharing isn't useful, you should know it also provides some essential workgroup functionality. A group sharing strategy can prove quite useful in workflow scenarios where data flows from one person to the next. Only the two people involved in the data transfer actually need access to the data storage area, so this approach reduces potential security problems by reducing the number of people with access to the data. When working with private data, only the person who actually needs to work with the data has access to it. You can therefore secure confidential documents with greater ease.

It's easy to find reasons to use one or the other sharing strategy in a particular situation. In some cases, you won't find a perfect strategy unless you mix elements of both. For example, when working with word-processed files, you might collaborate on a document with your peers and then move the document from the centralized sharing area to the inbox of someone who will prepare the document for printing. An editor might review the document for grammar and spelling issues and then move the file to the inbox of a compositor who prepares the document in PDF form. Eventually, someone prints the final document. In this case, you use a combination of strategies to ensure the document is prepared in a timely manner.

Configuring the Server for a Workgroup

Preparation is important, but eventually you consider all elements of your workgroup and create a plan for the network it requires. At this point, you want to *configure* the server, which means to set up users, groups, and resources for use. The server can be standalone or used as a workstation. How you set up the server depends on the plan you created for your workgroup. After you create this plan, be sure to stick with it as much as possible. Of course, you may have to make the occasional change when you encounter an issue you didn't consider.

You perform most of the configuration tasks in this chapter by using the Computer Management console, found in the Administrative Tools folder of the Control Panel. Open this console and you see folders for scheduling tasks, viewing entries in the event logs, creating new shares, managing users, monitoring the system, working with system storage, and managing services. The folders in the left pane show a hierarchy of tasks you perform. The right pane shows the task you selected. Figure 4-1 shows a typical view of the Computer Management console.

**Book II
Chapter 4**

**Working
with Workgroups**

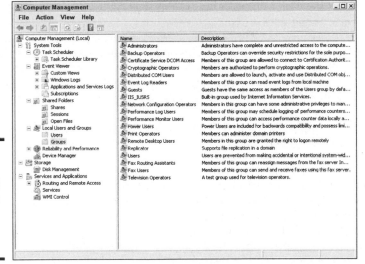

Figure 4-1: Windows Server 2008 comes with many default groups.

This section discusses only the server configuration for workgroup use; it doesn't tell you about security requirements. Obviously, a workgroup requires security to ensure that the workgroup shares resources in the way you intended. In addition, improper security settings can aid in the distribution of adware and viruses. Security serves many purposes — even though many users view it as a means to keep them from using resources they want. You can discover more about security in Book V, especially Chapter 1. Make sure to set both workgroup security and local security policies to maximize the effectiveness of the security settings. The following sections describe the configuration process.

Adding groups to the workgroup

One remaining organization task is to create groups for your workgroup. For example, you might create a group of writers who work on developing new promotional documents. You could give such a group the simple name Writers. Another group you probably need is managers, the people who manage projects on the network. The reason these groups are so important is that they help you think about the various roles that each member of the group fulfills. In addition to organizing the people on your network, the use of groups makes it easier to secure your workgroup.

To provide maximum functionality for your workgroup, always create the groups before you create the users. You assign users to groups, not groups to users. Sometimes you need to create a group or two after you set everything up — it's certainly possible to forget a potential requirement, but you should create as many of the groups as possible before you begin to create users.

You don't start with a blank slate when it comes to groups. Windows Server 2008 comes with a number of predefined groups. To see the default groups, open the Computer Management console, found in the Administrative Tools folder of the Control Panel. Select the `Computer Management\System Tools\Local Users and Groups\Groups` folder. You see the listing of groups shown in Figure 4-1 as a minimum. These are the default groups.

As shown in Figure 4-1, Windows Server 2008 provides a number of default groups that address many operating system needs. Of course, the group with the most power is the Administrators group. Notice that these defaults include a special group for reading the event logs and the Users group that has everyone as a member. You can also use the various operators groups (such as Print Operators) to provide access to special features of the server for those who need it.

These default groups all address the operating system requirements, not your special company requirements. For example, notice that the default groups don't include managers or writers. You won't find a group for advertisers or any other special group in your organization either. To address these custom needs, you must create new groups. As previously mentioned, it's always a good idea to create the groups you need before you create any users so that you can assign the users to the groups as you create the user entries. The following steps tell how to create a new group:

1. **Right-click the Groups folder, shown in Figure 4-1, and choose New Group from the context menu.**

   You see the New Group dialog box, as shown in Figure 4-2.

2. **Type a name for the group in the Group Name field.**

   Use a descriptive name for the group. For example, when you want to create a group for managers, use the name Managers. One- or two-word group names are best because they're easiest to remember. Don't try to describe the group using the name. Although you should use a descriptive name, you don't need to provide a lengthy name that will prove difficult to remember later.

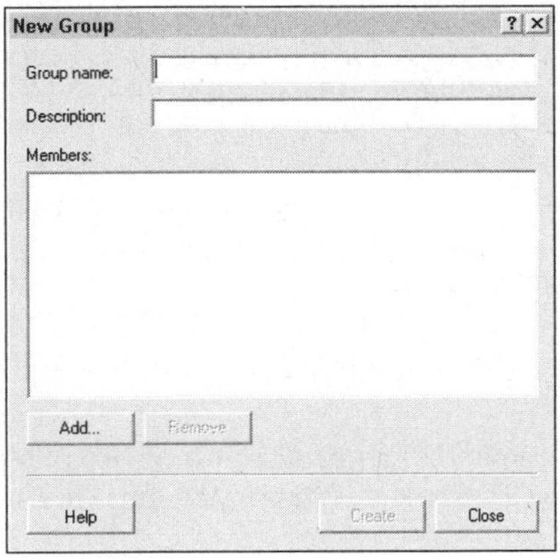

Figure 4-2:
Use the New Group dialog box to create new groups for your server.

3. **Type a description for the group in the Description field.**

   Use as many words as necessary to describe the group completely. You should include what the group is for, who is typically in it, why you created it, how to use the group, and when the group should dissolve if you created it for a particular project only. Describing the group completely helps prevent misuse and makes it easier for other administrators to use the group correctly. If all you want to do is create a new group, proceed to Step 8.

4. **Optionally, click Add to add users to the group.**

   You need to perform this step only when you create the group after you create the users. Windows displays the Select Users dialog box, shown in Figure 4-3, where you can choose users as members of this group.

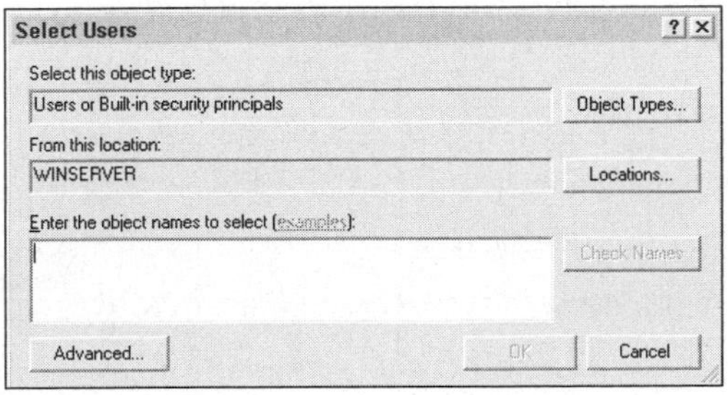

Figure 4-3:
Provide the names of users and groups that should appear as members of a group.

5. **Type the names of the users or groups that belong to this group.**

   That's right — groups can contain other groups. For example, if all users from a particular project are also managers, you can place the project group within the Managers group. The only group you can't add to another group is Administrators, and that's because administrators already have full access to everything on the machine. You normally add only usernames to the group. Separate each name in the list with a semicolon. For example, typing `George; Amy` adds users George and Amy to the group. Follow these steps if you don't remember the name of a user or group:

   a. **Click Advanced to display a larger version of the Select Users dialog box, shown in Figure 4-4, where you can find names based on specific criteria.**

   b. **Click Find Now to display a list of names and groups.**

   c. **Highlight the names you want and then click OK.**

   The names you want to use appear in the list in the smaller Select Users dialog box.

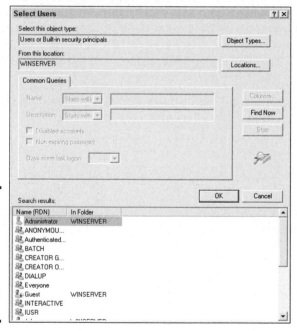

Figure 4-4: Find the names you need in the larger Select Users dialog box.

6. Click Check Names.

Windows checks all the names, to ensure that they're correct. If Windows finds an incorrect name, you see a Name Not Found dialog box, where you can choose to correct the name or remove it from the list.

7. Click OK.

You see all user and group names you provided added to the Members list of the New Group dialog box.

8. Click Create.

Windows creates the new group and displays a blank group for you. Follow Steps 2 through 8 to create another group if you want.

9. Click Close.

Windows closes the New Group dialog box and you see all the new groups you added in the Computer Management console.

Adding users to the workgroup

After you create the groups for your server and as your company hires new workers, you add new users to the workgroup. Windows Server 2008 has only two default users: Administrator and Guest. Because the Guest account is the target for so many viruses and security breaches, Microsoft disables it by default. Consequently, unless you want everyone to use the Administrator account (creating a huge security hole), you want to create new accounts for your machine. The following steps tell how to create a new user:

1. Right-click the Users folder, shown earlier in Figure 4-1, and choose New User from the context menu.

You see the New User dialog box, shown in Figure 4-5.

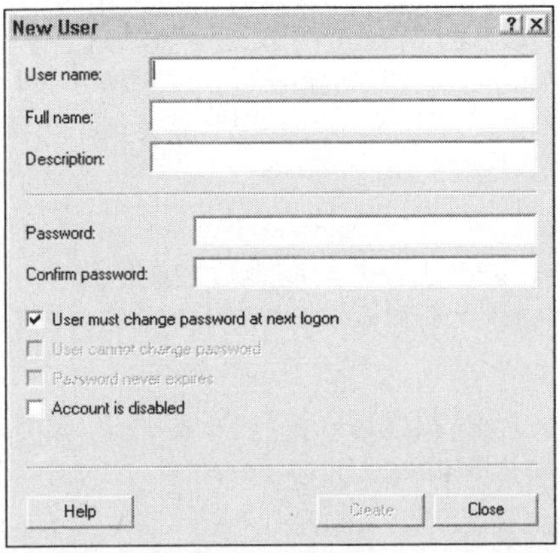

**Book II
Chapter 4**

Working
with Workgroups

Figure 4-5:
Use the
New User
dialog box
to create
new users
for your
server.

2. **Type a username in the User Name field.**

This name is the one the user will use to log in to the system. You should use a single word for the username because most users don't work well with multiple-word usernames. Windows requires a unique name, so you can use something like the user's last name, first initial, and middle initial. Unfortunately, in very large organizations, you may not find that this combination is unique, so you may have to add special identifiers, such as a number or special user characteristic.

3. **Type the user's full name in the Full Name field.**

Use the full name that appears on the user's employment record so that you know how the company refers to the user. For example, some companies don't use a middle initial, some use a middle initial, and some use the full middle name. The Full Name field should contain the same name that appears on the user's employment record so that you can refer to the user precisely when necessary (such as when you launch an investigation into unwanted user interaction with the system).

4. **Type a description for the user in the Description field.**

This entry is freeform. You can type anything needed here to describe the user. For example, you might use the user's office number, department name, job title, or other information. Anything that describes the user is useful. However, it's important to describe all users in the same way so that the Description field provides truly useful information — don't use a location for one user and a job title for another, for example.

5. **Type a temporary password in the Password field. Repeat this temporary password in the Confirm Password field.**

Use the same temporary password for everyone, to make it easier for the help desk to support new users. However, if you use the same temporary password for everyone, make sure to force the user to change the password the first time they log in to the system. In fact, this is the default setup for a new user account, so you generally want to leave alone the other settings shown in Figure 4-5. Never let the administrator assign the user password. If you do, users can legitimately say that they don't have exclusive access to their accounts, and any nefarious deeds they commit are hard to prove.

6. **Click Create.**

Windows creates the new user and displays a blank user dialog box for you. Follow Steps 2 through 6 to create another user, if you want.

7. **Click Close.**

Windows closes the New User dialog box, and you see all the new users you added in the Computer Management console.

The user creation process is designed to create a standard user with limited privileges. All users begin by belonging to the Users group, which means that anything the Users group can access, the new user can also access. If all you want to create is standard users, then the new user creation process works perfectly. Otherwise, you eventually want to modify the users by following the procedures in the "Performing User Configuration for a Workgroup" section of this chapter.

Removing users and groups from the workgroup

At some point, you need to remove users from your server as employees leave the organization. In some cases, you also need to remove groups from the workgroup as projects end and company needs change. To remove either a user or a group, highlight the user or group entry in the Computer Management console, and press Delete. Windows asks whether you're sure that you want to delete the user or the group. Verify the user or group entry and click Yes (or click No if you selected the wrong user or group).

Whenever you remove a user from the system, the user is gone for good. The user ceases to exist. Even if you create another user with precisely the same name, settings, and defaults, it's a different user as far as the system is concerned because the new user account has a different Security Identifier (SID). Consequently, any special security settings are also gone when you delete the user. In addition, if the user has encrypted files on the system, the files remain encrypted and you can't decrypt them. Because the process is one-way, you want to ensure that you're deleting the right user.

Group deletions can have even more significant implications on the server because you're working with the rights for a number of users. Whenever you delete a group, anyone in the group loses the rights that the group provided to them. Consequently, if you accidentally delete some groups, you may find that your server becomes unusable. Unfortunately, Windows doesn't provide any safeguard for the Administrators group. If you delete this group, you'll have a very tough time recovering and may well need to start your server setup from scratch. *Delete groups with extreme care.*

Sharing storage resources in the workgroup

The two main resources that administrators need to share in a workgroup setting are printers and storage. The "Installing local printers" and "Configuring the printer's Sharing tab options" sections of Book II, Chapter 2 tell you about printer sharing. This section of the chapter describes how to share storage resources. You have a number of ways to share storage resources in a workgroup.

The two most common methods are using the Computer Manager console and Windows Explorer. When you select the `Computer Management\ System Tools\Shared Folders\Shares` folder, you see a list of the current shares, as shown in Figure 4-6. Windows Explorer uses a special icon that has a hand under the drive or folder icon to indicate a share. However, most administrators find the list shown in the Computer Manager console more helpful than scouring individual entries in Windows Explorer.

Make sure to always check the list of shares before you create a new one. After you determine that you need a new share, follow these steps to share a storage resource using the Computer Manager console:

1. **Right-click the Shares folder and choose New Share from the context menu.**

You see the Welcome screen of the Create a New Shared Folder Wizard.

2. **Click Next.**

You see the Folder Path dialog box, as shown in Figure 4-7.

3. **Type the location of the storage resource you want to share, such as** C:\ **for a drive or** C:\MyData **for a folder. Click Next.**

You see the Name, Description, and Settings dialog box, as shown in Figure 4-8. Notice that the wizard suggests a share name based on the resource path.

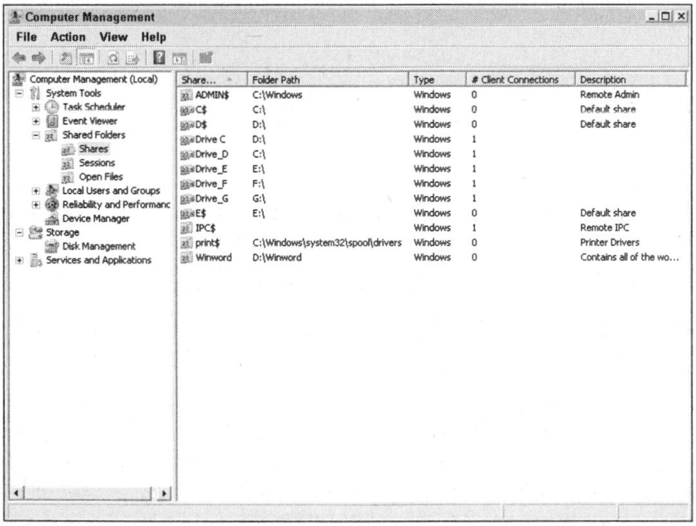

Figure 4-6:
See a list of the current shares on your server.

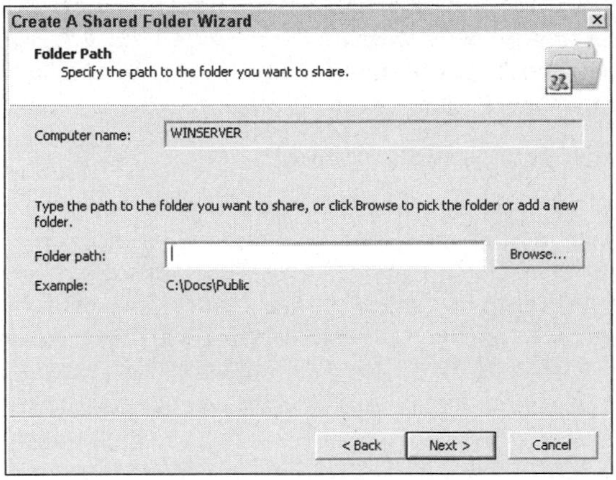

Figure 4-7:
Define the
folder path
for the new
share.

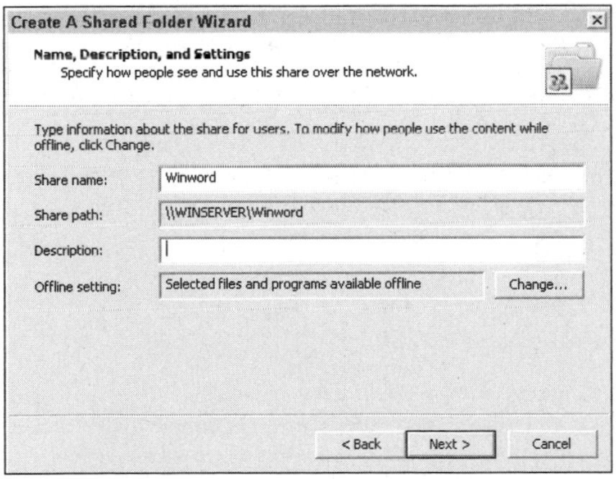

Figure 4-8:
Provide a
name and
description
for the
shared
resource.

4. **Type a share name in the Share Name field if you don't want to use the default name that the wizard has provided.**

5. **Type a description in the Description field.**

6. **(Optional) Click Change to change the offline setting of the shared resource.**

   The offline setting determines whether the user can share the folder as an offline folder. Offline folders provide the user with extra flexibility by letting them copy the folder contents to their local drive. Any changes they make to the folder contents are synchronized to the server storage. When the user has a connection, synchronization occurs immediately. When the workstation is disconnected, synchronization occurs when the workstation resumes contact with the server. Offline folders can result in lost data. When two users modify a folder in an offline state, the last changes to any modified files overwrite any previous changes. Consequently, you shouldn't provide offline status to folders where simultaneous edits can cause problems, such as database folders. You see the Offline Settings dialog box, as shown in Figure 4-9.

a. Choose an offline storage option.

The default option of letting the user make a choice provides optimal performance in most cases because most users don't use offline folders unless they're using laptops. The second option of forcing all users to use the folder in an offline mode is helpful when everyone using the folder has a laptop and you don't want users to forget to take their data with them. The third option disallows offline folder use; you normally use it in cases where you don't want to risk data loss when two users change the same file in an offline mode. You always use this option when sharing a folder with databases (such as an Access database) in it.

b. Click OK.

7. Click Next.

You see the Shared Folder Permissions dialog box, as shown in Figure 4-10. The standard permissions allow users and administrators specific levels of usage permission. In many cases, you have to set a custom permission strategy to account for specific folder requirements, such as a collaboration by a particular group of users.

a. (Optional) Choose Customize Permissions.

b. Click Custom.

You see the Customize Permissions dialog box, as shown in Figure 4-11, where you can add or remove special permissions as needed. To add a new permission, click Add, provide the name of the user or group you want to add, and then click OK. Highlight the new entry and set the permissions for that user or group by checking options in the lower dialog box. To remove a permission, highlight the user or group entry and click Remove.

Figure 4-9:
Determine which offline storage strategy to use for the folder.

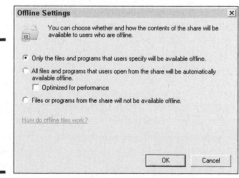

Figure 4-10:
Choose a
set of
permissions
for the
share.

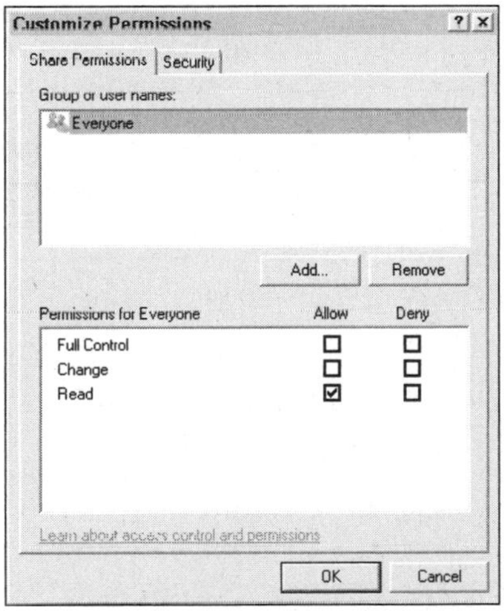

Figure 4-11:
Add and
remove
permissions
as needed.

You must also provide rights to the drive or folder for the user or group you add. Share security provides remote access to the resource only. To add security access, select the Security tab and add or remove users and groups as necessary to provide the proper rights to the folder. See the "Configuring File and Folder Security" section of Book V, Chapter 1 for additional details on file and folder security.

c. **Click OK.**

8. **Click Finish.**

You see a success dialog box that summarizes the share you created. Verify that the sharing information is correct. Notice the check box at the bottom of the success dialog box. Checking this option runs the Create New Shared Folder Wizard again. Simply follow Steps 2 through 8 to create the new share.

9. **Click Finish.**

You see the share added to the list, as shown in earlier, in Figure 4-6.

Creating a share using Windows Explorer is a little less structured. Windows Explorer depends on your knowing what to do from the outside and provides less help. Use these steps to share a folder with Windows Explorer:

1. **Choose Start⇨Programs⇨Accessories. Right-click the Windows Explorer entry and choose Run as Administrator from the context menu.**

You see a copy of Windows Explorer open.

2. **Locate the drive or folder you want to share in the Windows Explorer hierarchy. Right-click the entry and choose Share from the context menu.**

Windows displays the drive or folder Properties dialog box. Figure 4-12 shows a typical example. Notice that the dialog box tells you whether this resource is already shared. If the resource is shared, you can click Share to determine more information about the share.

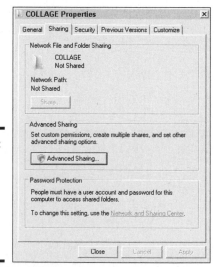

Figure 4-12:
Use the Sharing tab feature to share a drive or folder resource.

3. **Click Advanced Sharing.**

   You see the Advanced Sharing dialog box, shown in Figure 4-13. This dialog box already has entries in it, to show you how they would appear on your system.

4. **Check the Share This Folder option.**

5. **Type a name for the share in the Share Name field.**

6. **Define the number of simultaneous users you want to allow for this resource in the Limit the Number of Simultaneous Users To field.**

   Normally, you set limitations on resource usage by limiting the number of users that the server supports. This feature gives you the additional option of limiting access to a particular resource. For example, you might have a licensing limitation for a database or an application. Setting a limit here helps ensure that you don't go over the licensed limit.

7. **Type a description of the share in the Comments field.**

8. **Click Permissions.**

   You see a Permissions dialog box quite similar to the one shown in Figure 4-11, and you set the permissions using the same approach as for that dialog box. Remember that this dialog box sets the share permissions only. You must still set the access permissions by using the techniques found in the "Configuring File and Folder Security" section of Book V, Chapter 1.

9. **Click OK.**

Book II
Chapter 4

Working
with Workgroups

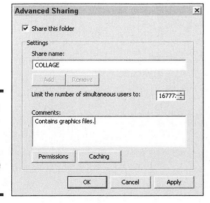

Figure 4-13: Define the share information for the drive or folder.

10. **(Optional) Click Caching.**

You see an Offline Settings dialog box such as the one shown in Figure 4-9. Configure this dialog box using the same approach that you do when using the Create a New Shared Folder Wizard. Click OK when you finish configuring the Offline Settings dialog box.

11. **Click OK.**

The information on the Sharing tab, shown in Figure 4-12, changes to show the shared status of the resource.

12. **Click Close.**

The resource icon in Windows Explorer changes to show the shared state of the resource.

Eventually, you need to change the sharing information for a particular resource. The groups that use the resource will change, you might need to stop sharing completely, or the share may require different permissions (perhaps you provided too many or not enough permissions at the outset). In all these cases, you can change the share settings by right-clicking the share in the Shares folder of the Computer Management console and choosing Properties from the context menu. You see a share Properties dialog box such as the one shown in Figure 4-14, where you can change any of the settings you configured using the wizard or Windows Explorer.

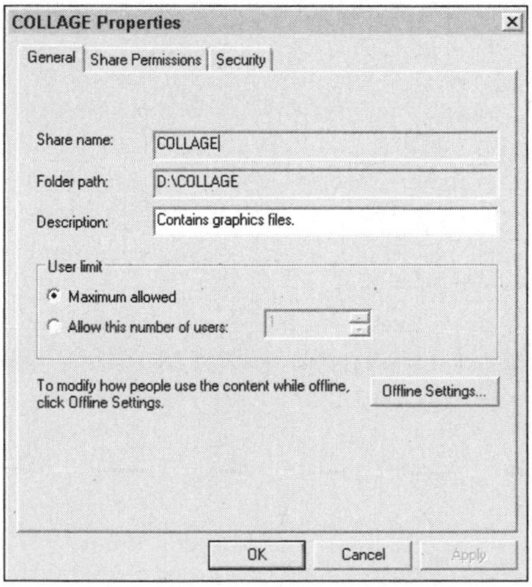

Figure 4-14:
Modify the
share
settings as
required to
provide a
balance
between
user needs
and
security.

If you choose to stop sharing the resource, right-click the share in the Shares folder of the Computer Management console and choose Stop Sharing from the context menu. Windows asks whether you're sure that you want to stop sharing the resource. Click Yes and the system stops sharing the share. You can use the same steps as before to re-create the share when necessary.

Performing User Configuration for a Workgroup

User roles and activities change as a user spends more time in an organization. A promotion may mean providing additional access to sensitive resources or adding the user to other groups. When a user forgets a password, you have to provide a temporary password so that the person can get into the system. The following sections describe two techniques for performing user configuration within a workgroup.

**Book II
Chapter 4**

Working with Workgroups

Using the User Account window

The User Account applet in the Control Panel provides access to user account information, as shown in Figure 4-15. The Tasks list on the left side of the window shows the various tasks you can perform, such as changing user environmental variables. You can find a discussion of the user password management tasks in the "Managing User Passwords" section of Book V, Chapter 3. The "Managing user encryption file certificates" section of Book V, Chapter 1 discusses how to work with encryption certificates you need to save before you delete a user. The User Account Control (UAC) settings appear in the "Understanding and Using the User Account Control (UAC)" section of Book V, Chapter 3.

Figure 4-15:
Manage user account settings by using the User Account applet.

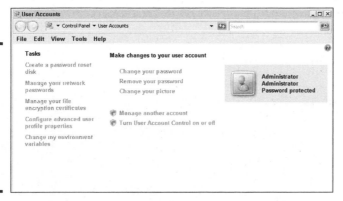

The User Account applet always opens your personal account. However, as an administrator, you normally want to manage someone else's account, so the first thing you do is click Manage Another Account. Windows displays the dialog box shown in Figure 4-16, where you can manage an existing account or create a new account. When you select another account, you see that user's account information — as long as you're an administrator with the correct security rights.

Figure 4-16:
Choose
another
user
account to
manage.

When you choose a different account, you see the limited choices shown in Figure 4-17. The User Account applet lets you change just about anything for your own account, but you can still change the account name, password, picture, or account type or simply delete the account.

Figure 4-17:
The User
Account
applet
provides
limited
access to
other
accounts.

Modifying users with the Computer Management console

When you need to perform tasks other than the limited set offered by the User Account applet, you need to work with the Computer Management console. To change a user account, right-click the user entry in the `Computer Management\System Tools\Local Users and Groups\Users` folder and choose Properties from the context menu. You see a user Properties dialog box similar to the one shown in Figure 4-18.

The General tab contains basic user information that you create in this chapter, such as name and description. You can also configure the user's password requirements on this tab. Notice that you can't reset the user's password on this tab — you must use the User Account applet to perform this task.

The Member Of tab contains a list of the user's group memberships. You can use the Add and Remove buttons to add or remove groups as needed.

The remaining tabs in this dialog box configure user network connectivity or Terminal Services settings. The Profile, Environment, and Session tabs appear in the "Configuring the User Settings Correctly" section of Book IV, Chapter 4. You find the Remote Control, Terminal Services Profile, and Dial-in tabs discussed in the "Configuring user-specific Terminal Services settings" section of Book IV, Chapter 3.

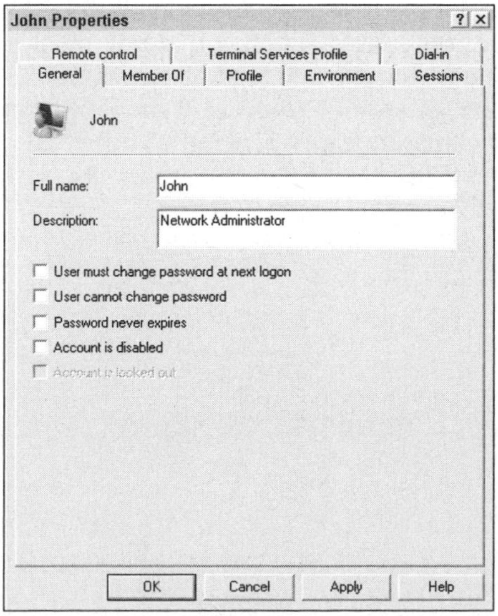

**Book II
Chapter 4**

Working with Workgroups

Figure 4-18: Perform detailed configuration using the user Properties dialog box.

Working with Peer Name Resolution Protocol

The Peer Name Resolution Protocol (PNRP) is the basis for connectivity between peers in a workgroup. Every computer in a network has to be able to identify every other computer. You wouldn't want to connect to Computer A one time and to Computer B another time because they both have the same name or the network confuses them in some way. Reliable connections ensure that everyone connects to the same machine every time.

A workgroup often experiences problems with standard methods of machine identification, such as using the Domain Name System (DNS). That's the reason Microsoft has created PNRP — to overcome identification difficulties. PNRP provides these benefits:

✦ Distributed identification that doesn't rely on a central server

✦ Support for as many names as the network requires

✦ Name publications without the use of third-party products or third-party servers

✦ Real-time identification updates

✦ Support for naming all device types, not just computers

✦ Protected name publication so that you don't have to worry about someone else grabbing your name

The best part about PNRP is that you normally don't have to do anything special to use it. The only potential problem is that you must ensure that the Computer Browser service is running and that all workstations that share resources also have the Server service running. If these two services are running, you probably won't experience any problems with PNRP. You can read the full technical details of PNRP at `http://technet.microsoft.com/ en-us/library/bb726971.aspx`.

Chapter 5: Promoting Your Server to a Domain Controller

*W*indows Server 2008 supports two kinds of network using two different server configurations. The first network is for smaller numbers of users, and it relies on the workgroup. Book II, Chapter 4 describes this form of network in some detail. The second network is for larger numbers of users, and it relies on the domain. The same machine can act as either a workgroup server or a domain controller. However, the choice you make is important because you trade some benefits for others when you create a domain.

After you make the decision to create a domain, which means promoting your server to a domain controller, you must perform some initial planning and install some new features on your server. The act of promoting your server to a domain controller also performs these preliminary tasks. However, performing the tasks as part of the domain controller promotion normally results in a less-than-useful setup. It's far better to perform the preliminary tasks as described in this chapter to ensure that you get a good setup.

The final task is to perform the actual promotion. At this point, the server has Active Directory installed, and you can use this centralized database to store all user information on your system. Unfortunately, Active Directory doesn't contain any user records, so one of your first configuration tasks is to add all users back into the system, which is one reason to make the decision to create a domain controller immediately after installing the server software.

Understanding Domains

Domains predate the workgroup by a considerable time-span in computer years. Older computer systems used a centralized mainframe and terminals attached to the mainframe to perform work. In many respects, a Windows domain works the same way as these systems of old. Yes, the workstations connected to the server have intelligence and perform some work locally, but the central computer maintains a firm grip on everything that goes on with the network. That's why administrators call servers that provide services in a domain a domain controller — the server controls the environment completely.

Don't get visions of "Big Brother" at this point. Yes, the domain controller exercises considerable control over the network, but many users won't even notice the difference. The difference is more noticeable to the administrator than it is to the user in most cases. Domains are extremely useful in some situations. You have many reasons for using a domain. These reasons include

- ✦ Better security
- ✦ Centralization of control over users, machines, and resources
- ✦ Improved organizational capability
- ✦ Enhanced performance through efficient resource usage
- ✦ Superior reliability on large networks

This list may lead you to believe that domains are far superior to workgroups, and they are, in some respects. However, you always have to consider both sides of the coin. Although domains provide you with all these benefits, you must also bear the cost of using them. These costs include

- ✦ Increased complexity, which can increase administration time and result in more errors
- ✦ Loss of certain Windows Server 2008 features, such as Internet Connection Sharing (ICS)
- ✦ Required use of some features, such as Active Directory
- ✦ Significantly increased training costs
- ✦ Decreased flexibility in some areas, such as the ability to create ad hoc connections when required

Domains are a good networking solution, but only in certain situations. In some cases, a workgroup is the right choice because the number of users doesn't warrant a domain. Of the factors that you should consider when choosing between a domain and a workgroup, the centralized management capability is the most significant reason to use a domain, whereas the increase in complexity is the most significant reason not to use a domain. No magic number of users exists for determining when to use a domain. The point at which a domain becomes necessary is a combination of the following user factors:

✦ The number of users makes a difference. (I've seen networks of up to 100 users work just fine as a workgroup, but 75 users is probably a more practical upper limit.)

✦ Application types, such as databases, require better security and control, which means that you may need a domain with fewer users.

✦ High-network-bandwidth applications require additional resources, which means you may need a domain with fewer users.

✦ High-security applications normally require a domain no matter how few or many users you have.

✦ Shared resource applications, such as word processing, don't require a domain in most cases unless you have a large number of users that must collaborate on content.

✦ Services such as file sharing and printing don't usually require a domain.

✦ Power users generally work better in a workgroup setup.

✦ Novice users may not require a domain, but the domain environment can sometimes prevent them from making as many mistakes.

✦ Scientific and other highly collaborative applications don't require a domain unless the application has significant security requirements. (The use of a domain will inhibit the users in this case.)

✦ Networks with high growth rates may not require a domain today, but will likely need one tomorrow, so installing the domain at the outset is less confusing for end users.

Preparing to Create a Domain

Every Windows Server 2008 machine starts life as a workgroup server. You must make the conscious choice to move to a domain. Although it's easy to move from a workgroup to a domain, the reverse isn't true. Moving from a domain to a workgroup requires considerable reworking of your server. Consequently, one of the first steps you must take when moving to a domain is determining whether you actually need one. The overriding question to answer is whether your network has enough users who require sufficient resources and functionality to demand a domain.

The planning process should include a time for making the upgrade. The easiest time to promote your server to a domain controller is before you place it in the production environment. In fact, you should perform the task immediately after installing Windows — before you perform any configuration tasks. The sooner you make a decision to promote the server to a domain controller, the easier the task becomes. If you must promote a production server to a domain controller, you must perform the task when no one is working on the server, perform any required configuration tasks to make the server operational, and reconfigure all workstations to use the domain controller before you allow users back onto the server.

Considering the prerequisites for your domain comes next. The first task is to remove every feature that could conflict with the domain. Every domain requires Domain Name System (DNS) and Dynamic Host Configuration Protocol (DHCP) support. Consequently, you must include these features on your list of tasks to perform unless your network already has these features configured. The Windows Internet Naming Service (WINS) is supposedly optional, but you'll find that many Microsoft features require it to work properly. You could always try to work with the server without WINS installed, but odd behavior generally indicates that something's missing and one of the items you must consider is WINS.

When you finally promote your server to a domain controller, the Promotion Wizard asks a number of questions. Some of these questions are exceptionally important because you can't change the entries later. The most important question is what you want to call your domain. If you plan to make your server accessible from the Internet, you must provide the domain name you registered. In addition, you must provide the machine name you want to use because you can't change the machine name later. Less pressing (because you can configure them later) are issues such as installing a server certificate that you can use for security purposes and precisely how you want to configure Active Directory. For example, you need to consider whether this is a standalone server or part of an existing domain.

Performing the Domain Configuration Prerequisites

After you create a plan for promoting your server to a domain controller but before you perform the actual update, you should perform some prerequisites. The promotion wizard performs these steps for you, but you generally get better results when you perform them yourself. For example, you can depend on the wizard to install DNS support for you, but you receive a generic setup that can prove difficult to modify later. Likewise, you can let the wizard remove ICS for you, but sometimes the results are imperfect — it's as though the wizard leaves behind some pieces of ICS to cause problems later. Now that you have a better idea of why you want to perform these tasks before you begin the promotion, it's time to look at the details of each task in the following sections.

Checking for unsupported roles and features

Workgroups and domains have a few mutually exclusive features. For example, you can't use Active Directory in a workgroup. No matter what you do, the second you try to install Active Directory, Windows also promotes the server to a domain controller. Likewise, domain controllers can't have ICS installed. ICS provides built-in DNS and DHCP support that conflicts with the DNS and DHCP support provided by the domain controller, so you can't have ICS installed.

Most roles and features work just fine on either a workgroup or a domain controller. For example, you can install Internet Information Server (IIS) on either configuration. Likewise, file sharing and printing work just fine in both environments. However, leaving an incompatible role or feature in place can cause problems later because the various wizards can leave behind pieces of the role or feature.

Some administrators attempt to guess at which roles and features are incompatible. (Microsoft doesn't publish a list because it assumes that its wizards are perfect.) Unfortunately, such an approach is error prone. The following steps provide a better way to accomplish the task:

1. **Perform a complete server backup, including a backup of the registry settings.**

2. **Uninstall all roles and features one at a time.**

Some roles and features require a reboot. Don't uninstall all roles and features at once because the system could miss some components of an individual role or feature, such as registry settings, that will come back to haunt you later.

3. **Perform the domain controller promotion.**

4. **Reinstall required roles and features.**

Configure each of the roles and features as needed. You may be surprised to see that the domain configuration requires different role or feature settings. These differences are hidden compatibility problems that you wouldn't have addressed without taking the extra step of uninstalling and then reinstalling the roles and features.

5. **Restore any data that you backed up.**

Exercise care in restoring registry settings. In some cases, you can save time and effort by restoring registry settings, but you can also end up overwriting settings that differ from the workgroup setup and cause problems for the server. You should also exercise care when restoring data to a system directory, especially data found in the \Windows\ System32 folder.

Installing DNS

The Domain Name System (DNS) server translates IP addresses on your network into human readable names. Every node on the network has a human readable name in most cases. When working with a system, you use that system's name to access it. DNS provides the service required to translate the human readable name you use into an IP address the computer can use. The following sections get you started.

Performing the DNS installation prerequisites

Windows Server 2008 does a few things differently from previous versions of Windows. For example, when working with a previous version of Windows, setting up ICS would also assign a static IP address to your server, but this action doesn't occur under Windows Server 2008. In addition, Windows Server 2008 natively supports IPv6, which can prove difficult to configure in DNS. With this in mind, most administrators will find that performing the following steps before installing DNS makes the installation and configuration process considerably easier.

1. **Right-click Network on the Desktop and choose Properties from the context menu. (This action is the same as opening the Network and Sharing Center applet in the Control Panel.)**

   You see the Network and Sharing Center window.

2. **Click Manage Network Connections.**

   You see the Network Connections window, which contains all the network connections for your system. In most cases, you see one connection for the local network and perhaps a second connection for the Internet, as shown in Figure 5-1. The number of connections normally reflects the number of Network Interface Cards (NICs) installed on your server. Although having two NICs is becoming standard, some servers have more and occasionally you see only one.

Figure 5-1: The network connections normally reflect the NICs installed on your system.

3. **Right-click the Local Area Network Connection entry (or the connection that corresponds to your LAN) and choose Properties from the context menu.**

    You see the Local Area Network Connection Properties dialog box, shown in Figure 5-2. This dialog box contains a listing of the clients, services, and protocols used by this connection. Changing an entry here affects only the connection in question and doesn't affect any other connection on the machine.

Figure 5-2:
Modify the
connection
clients,
services,
and
protocols as
needed.

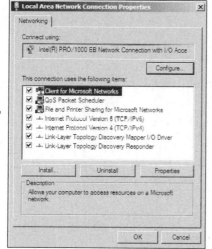

4. **Clear the check mark next to the Internet Protocol Version 6 (TCP/IPv6) entry.**

    Creating a DNS setup without IPv6 installed is considerably easier than trying to perform multiple-protocol DNS setups. Later, you can always add IPv6 back in when you need it.

5. **Highlight the Internet Protocol Version 4 (TCP/IPv4) entry. Click Properties.**

    You see the Internet Protocol Version 4 (TCP/IPv4) Properties dialog box, shown in Figure 5-3.

6. **Choose Use the Following IP Address, as shown in the figure.**

7. **Type an IP address for the connection.**

    The standard entries are 192.168.0.1 and 10.0.0.1, but you can choose any IP address that conforms to your network setup.

8. Type an appropriate subnet mask in the Subnet Mask field.

Windows generally suggests the correct subnet mask value when you use one of the standard entries. Make sure that the subnet mask matches other systems on the network.

9. Click OK and then Close.

10. Restart your system.

This preliminary configuration helps you obtain a better DNS server installation by setting the system to a simple default configuration that the DNS wizard will understand.

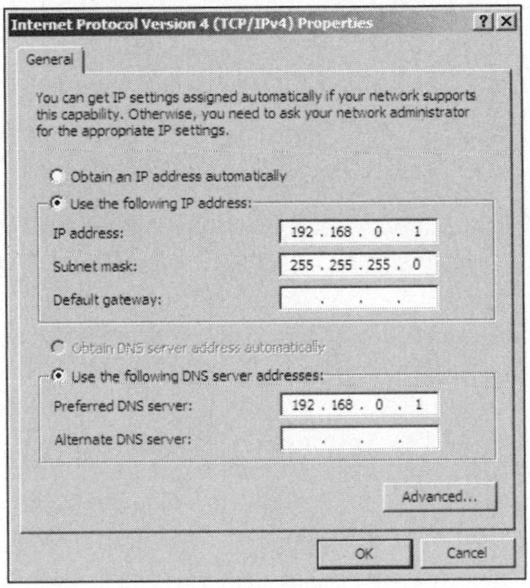

Figure 5-3:
Set IPv4 to use a static IP address.

Installing the DNS server role

Now that you have your system set up for DNS, it's time to add the DNS role. You can use the instructions found in the "Working with roles" section of Book II, Chapter 1 to add the DNS role. The DNS Server link found in the Add Roles Wizard includes some useful links that help you learn more about working with DNS in Windows Server 2008. You don't need to perform any special configuration inside the Add Roles Wizard to install the DNS role.

Configuring the DNS server

DNS isn't ready for use when you install it. Look in the Administrative Tools folder of the Control Panel, and you notice a new DNS entry. Open this entry and you see the DNS Manager console, similar to the one shown in Figure 5-4. You use this console to configure DNS before you begin using it the first time.

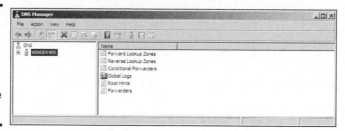

Figure 5-4:
Configure
the DNS
settings
before you
use DNS the
first time.

Fortunately, you don't have to spend time trying to configure everything manually. Microsoft provides a wizard to help you configure DNS for first use. The following steps help you perform the configuration tasks:

1. **Right-click the server entry (WINSERVER in Figure 5-4) and choose Configure a DNS Server from the context menu.**

    You see the Welcome page of the Configure a DNS Server Wizard dialog box.

2. **Click Next.**

    You see the Select Configuration Action page, as shown in Figure 5-5. The options are ranked from easiest to hardest to implement. The final option is intended for advanced administrators, and you don't find any coverage for root hints in this book because the settings are server specific.

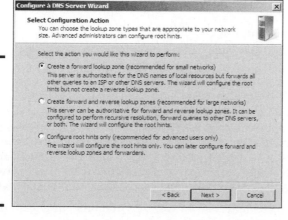

Figure 5-5:
Choose the
level of
configur-
ation that
makes the
most sense
for your
network.

In most cases, if your network has a single level of DNS servers, you can use the first option no matter how many other nodes your server might contain. Microsoft's use of small or large networks doesn't really reflect actual size, but is more related to network structure complexity. Always use the least complex setup that you can for your network because additional complexity always translates into reliability issues and additional administration time. This procedure assumes that you chose the first level of configuration.

3. **Choose a level of configuration and click Next.**

   You see the Primary Server Location page of the wizard. The wizard gives you a choice between maintaining the DNS information locally or relying on the DNS information provided by an Internet service provider (ISP). Unless every machine on your network has a connection to the ISP and you want the ISP to issue the IP addresses for your network, you should choose the first option, This Server Maintains the Zone. This chapter assumes that you have a standard network setup and will use the local server to maintain the DNS information.

4. **Choose a server location and click Next.**

   The wizard asks you to provide a name for the zone on your server. If you have a public domain name and this server is the one that provides the public presence on your network, you should use the public domain name. Otherwise, you should provide a zone name that reflects the purpose of the zone, such as accounting.mycompany.com. The zone name isn't the same as the server name — you won't use this zone name to reach the server. Every zone name on the network must be unique.

5. **Type a zone name and click Next.**

   You see the Zone File page of the wizard. Every zone has a file that contains settings for it. These settings determine how the DNS server translates human readable node names into IP addresses. If you have multiple DNS servers on a network with nearly the same configuration, you can save time by copying that DNS file to your server and using the settings it contains as a starting point for the new DNS server. Otherwise, if this server is new or you don't have another server with similar settings, you must create a new zone file. The zone file normally has the zone name followed by a .dns extension. For example, if your zone name is accounting.mycompany.com the zone filename is accounting.mycompany.com.dns.

6. **Type a zone filename, use an existing filename, or accept the default name. Click Next.**

   You see the Dynamic Update page of the wizard. In this case, the wizard is asking you how to update DNS records. A DNS record associates a node name with an IP address. When the DNS server can't find a particular node name in its list, it forwards the request to the next server in line. If your server is connected to the Internet, the request is automatically forwarded to the ISP's DNS server.

In the past, DNS servers accepted record updates from any machine on the network. This sounds like a good idea, and it is on a closed network. Letting clients update their records saves administration time and ensures that the DNS records are always up-to-date. However, when a server also has an outside connection, a nefarious individual can add their node to the DNS record and use this advantage to do terrible things to your network. Consequently, Microsoft sets the default to not allow dynamic updates. You can use the Allow Both Nonsecure and Secure Dynamic Updates option on any closed network (one without an outside connection) with perfect safety. The third option, Allow Only Secure Dynamic Updates, becomes available after you promote your server to a domain controller.

7. **Choose a dynamic update option and click Next.**

You see the Forwarders page of the wizard, as shown in Figure 5-6. (The figure shows two forwarders already in place.) A *forwarder* is a DNS server that receives requests that the current DNS server can't handle. The local DNS server contains only records for your network subnet. When someone requests an external DNS address (one outside the subnet), another server must handle the request. If this machine is connected to an ISP, you can simply forward the requests for external resources to the ISP's DNS server (available as part of the Network Connection Details dialog box for the external connection).

Book II
Chapter 5

Promoting Your
Server to a Domain
Controller

Figure 5-6:
Use
forwarders
to pass
requests on
to other
network
subnets.

```
Configure a DNS Server Wizard                                              x

  Forwarders
  Forwarders are DNS servers to which this server sends queries that it cannot
  answer.

  Should this DNS server forward queries?
  ⦿ Yes, it should forward queries to DNS servers with the following IP addresses:

     IP Address       Server FQDN      Validated          Delete
       <Click here to ...
     ⊘ 207.190.94.2    ns1.mwt.net      OK                  Up
     ⊘ 207.190.94.129  ns2.mwt.net      OK
                                                           Down

  ○ No, it should not forward queries
     If this server is not configured to use forwarders, it can still resolve names using
     root name servers.


                                      < Back    Next >      Cancel
```

8. **(Optional) Highlight the Click Here to Add an IP Address or DNS Name entry. Type the IP address or DNS name of the server to which you want to forward requests.**

   The wizard automatically checks your entries. When the wizard can reach the requested address, it displays OK in the Validated column, as shown in Figure 5-6. If you make a mistake in entering an IP address or DNS name of the server, highlight the errant entry and click Delete. Sometimes you want to use a particular server as the primary server. Highlight that server's entry and click Up until it appears first in the list. You can also click Down to move a server's entry down in the list. The DNS server always forwards requests based on the position of the server. When the first server can't answer a request, the DNS server queries the second server in the list, and so on, until it runs out of forwarders. You see a "not found" error message when the DNS server can't find a particular node name.

9. **Click Next.**

   You see a summary dialog box, where you can verify all the information you entered for the DNS server.

10. **Verify the DNS information and click Finish.**

    The DNS server now has a basic configuration and is useable. Depending on the configuration of your network, you may have to perform additional configuration tasks by manually changing entries in the DNS Manager.

Testing your DNS server

You may wonder whether your DNS server is actually working. Yes, you checked the event log and didn't see anything there and the service is certainly running, but you still aren't sure that the DNS server is working, and the network seems to have trouble locating resources. Use the following steps to test the DNS server:

1. **Right-click the server entry, shown in Figure 5-4, and choose Properties from the context menu.**

   You see the server Properties dialog box.

2. **Select the Monitoring tab.**

   You see the testing display shown in Figure 5-7. (This figure shows two test results.)

3. **Check the A Simple Query Against this DNS Server option.**

4. **(Optional) Check the A Recursive Query to Other DNS Servers option when you have forwarders configured.**

5. **Click Test Now.**

   You see the pass or fail status of the tests in the Test Results list. Figure 5-7 shows the results of both a simple and recursive test.

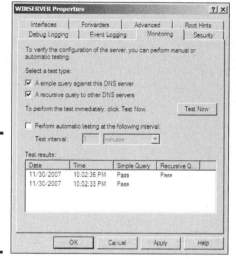

Figure 5-7: Verify that your DNS server works by using a simple test.

Installing WINS

WINS is an older protocol that you may need on your server when you have older applications that requires it. Windows Server 2008 doesn't require this protocol and works just fine without it. In most cases, you won't install this protocol on new systems that have newer applications because you simply don't need it, and Microsoft is trying to phase out support for WINS due to a number of problems with the protocol. Verify the need to install WINS before you install it on your server. Never install WINS if you use IPv6 because IPv6 doesn't support this protocol.

Always install WINS support after you perform the DNS installation, to ensure that you get a good installation (one that lacks errors in the addresses). You can use the instructions found in the "Working with features" section of Book II, Chapter 1 to add the WINS feature.

Installing DHCP

DHCP helps your server assign and manage IP addresses for every node on the network. Every node must have a unique IP address, so it makes sense to have a central server issue those addresses. In addition, using a central management authority ensures that every node receives the correct address and subnet mask. Incorrect and conflicting IP addresses cause more problems on networks than you might initially think.

Normally, it's a good idea to configure DNS and (optionally) WINS before you configure DHCP because some DNS and WINS settings affect DHCP. After you have DNS configured, you can perform the DHCP setup with greater ease. You can use the instructions found in the "Working with roles" section of Book II, Chapter 1 to add the DHCP role. However, DHCP includes a few additional settings you need to consider, as shown in Figure 5-8.

The Network Connection Bindings link in the Add Roles Wizard shows you the connections that DHCP will manage. If you have multiple connections on your machine, you must ensure that the wizard has recognized the local connection as the one it should manage. A common error in Windows is for the server to try to manage the wrong connection. When you see this problem, temporarily disable the errant connections in the Network Connections window (refer to Figure 5-1) and restart the Add Roles Wizard.

Depending on how you configure your network connections and DNS, you may see a number of steps grayed out. Figure 5-8 shows the results of the suggested configuration in this chapter. Notice that the IPv6 settings are grayed out and you don't have to configure them. You do need to provide a parent domain entry on the IPv4 DNS Settings tab. Normally you use the same domain name provided for the DNS server when working with a single domain or a subset of the domain you used for DNS when working in a larger domain. For example, if your DNS zone name is `accounting.mycompany.com`, you type `mycompany.com` in the Parent Domain field when working on a large network.

Figure 5-8:
Installing the DHCP role requires that you make some initial setup choices.

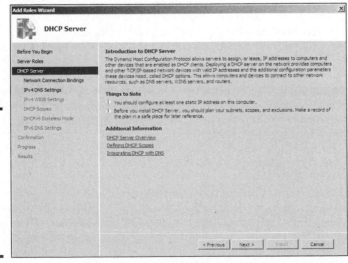

After you type the parent domain, you see that the wizard enables other options in the list. These other entries are optional, depending on how you want to configure your server. For example, if you use WINS, you must select the IPv4 WINS Settings and provide the required WINS address information. Likewise, when you choose to use IPv6, you must configure the IPv6 settings.

One feature you must configure is DHCP Scopes. When you select DHCP Scopes, you see the Add or Edit DHCP Scopes page. Click Add to add a new scope. You see the Add Scope dialog box, as shown in Figure 5-9, where you must provide the scope name, starting IP address, ending IP address, and subnet mask. If you want the client to access resources external to the current subnet, you must also define a default gateway.

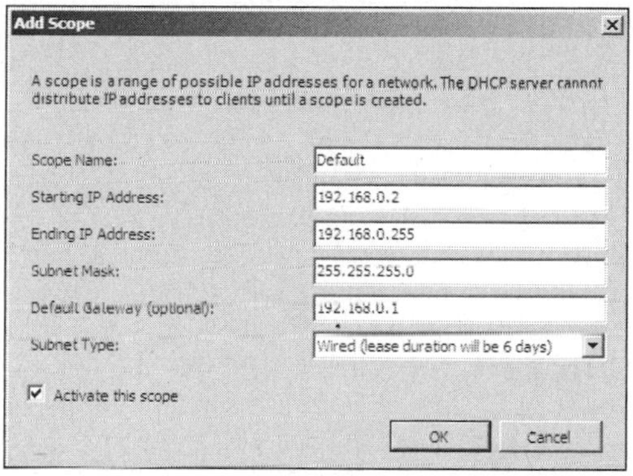

Figure 5-9:
Provide the
DHCP scope
for your
server.

Figure 5-9 shows some sample entries for a scope. The scope must not include the server's IP address. However, the scope must match the server's IP address configuration. For example, when the server has an IP address of 192.168.0.1, then the scope can include the range of addresses from 192.168.0.2 to 192.168.0.255. The subnet mask must also match the server's subnet mask. After you configure the DHCP scope, click OK.

After you perform the required configuration for your DHCP server, choose the Confirmation entry. Review the settings and click Install. The wizard installs your DHCP server. Unlike in previous versions of Windows, you normally don't need to authenticate the DHCP setup because you performed all required tasks during initial setup. However, you can use the DHCP console, found in the Administrative Tools folder of the Control Panel, to perform any required management tasks.

In some cases, the system doesn't authorize the DHCP server. You can verify this problem by reviewing the entries in the System event log. When DHCP isn't authorized, you see a number of other event log entries as well that could lead you to believe your server has major configuration problems. Use these steps to authorize DHCP on your server:

1. **Open the DHCP console found in the Administrative Tools folder.**

2. **Open the folder containing the root DHCP entry for your server.**

You see entries for both IPv4 and IPv6 below this root entry.

3. **Right-click the root entry and choose Authorize from the context menu.**

Windows displays a message that it's authorizing the server.

4. **After a few moments, right-click the root entry and verify that the Authorize entry is gone from the context menu and that Windows has replaced it with an Unauthorize entry.**

5. **Close the DHCP console.**

After you authorize DHCP on your server, you should verify that everything is working as anticipated. Clear the event logs, restart the server, and then check the event logs for new entries. This process helps you locate real problems left over after you authorize DHCP.

Configuring the Server for a Domain

At some point, you complete all the required planning and preparation steps for your new domain controller. At this point, you can promote your server to a domain controller. The following sections help you turn your workgroup server into a domain controller.

Performing the domain controller promotion

The actual task of promoting your server to a domain controller isn't hard if you completed all the required work. You have a couple of options for performing this task. Simply installing the Active Directory Domain Services role can promote your server. However, the better way of performing this task is to use the Domain Controller Promotion (DCPromo) utility. The following steps show how to use this second method:

1. **Choose Start⇨Run. Type** DCPromo **in the Open field of the Run dialog box and click OK.**

The system displays a message that it's performing some checks on the system configuration. These checks can require several minutes, depending on the complexity of your setup. After the system completes all required checks, it displays the Welcome page of the Active Directory Domain Services Installation Wizard.

2. **Click Next.**

You see the Choose a Deployment Configuration dialog box. If this server is the first one you're promoting, you'll always choose the Create a New Domain in a New Forest option because no forest currently exists. When you already have a configured server on the network, you must choose how to add the new server to the existing forest (the one in which the configured server exists). You can create a new forest, but then the two servers can't share information. Normally, you add the new server to the existing forest. This chapter assumes that this server is the first one you're configuring for your network.

3. **Choose a deployment option and click Next.**

The wizard asks you to provide a Fully Qualified Domain Name (FQDN) for the domain. In most cases, you use the same name that you did for the DNS server for a smaller network. In some cases, you have a FQDN already in place and need to use it to obtain connectivity between servers.

4. **Type the new FQDN and click Next.**

The wizard performs a number of checks on the name you provide. For example, it checks for a conflicting forest name on the network. Be patient: The checks require only a minute or two. Eventually, you see the Set Forest Functional Level dialog box. The *forest functional level* determines which Active Directory features your domain controller provides. The default setting of Windows 2000 provides minimal Active Directory support and probably isn't a good choice for your domain controller, unless you must support older Windows 2000 servers. Whenever possible, choose the Windows Server 2008 level because it provides the most functionality and the best security. The current best compatibility selection is Windows Server 2003, which may help prevent problems with older clients, such as Windows XP.

5. **Choose a level in the Forest Functional Level field and click Next.**

The wizard asks you to provide a domain functional level. This functional level works much like the forest functional level, except that it affects only the current server. The domain functional level is dependent on the forest functional level. For example, if you choose Windows Server 2003 for the forest functional level, the domain choices are Windows Server 2003 and Windows Server 2008. You can always provide more support for Active Directory within the local domain, but you can't choose less.

**Book II
Chapter 5**

Promoting Your
Server to a Domain
Controller

6. Choose a level in the Domain Functional Level field and click Next.

The wizard performs a few additional checks on your selections. This process is normally so fast that you may not even see the dialog box. At this point, you see the Additional Domain Controller Options dialog box, but you shouldn't have to do anything because you already configured these options, earlier in this chapter.

7. Click Next.

At this point, you may see the Static IP Assignment dialog box, such as the one shown in Figure 5-10, when your server has an external connection to an ISP. In some respects, this dialog box is confusing because it makes it sound as though you should change the information for the ISP connection. If you take the advice of the dialog box, you end up losing connectivity to the ISP. Click No to avoid this problem. However, if you truly do have adapters with dynamic IP addresses that aren't assigned by a third party, you should set them to a static value. In this case, click Yes.

8. (Optional) Click a static IP address setup option.

If you click No, the wizard stops and waits for you to reconfigure any dynamic IP addresses by using the Network Connections window (refer to Figure 5-1). After you perform the required configuration change, perform Step 7 again. If you click Yes, the wizard takes you to the next step, which asks you to provide location information for the various logs and Active Directory configuration information, as shown in Figure 5-11. In most cases, you don't want to change this location information unless you have a good reason for doing so. For example, you may want to put the SYSVOL folder on another drive to improve performance.

9. Accept the default locations for each of the Active Directory elements by clicking Next.

The wizard asks you to provide a restore mode administrator password. This account is different from the standard administrator account. Microsoft recommends that you use a complex and easily forgotten password. Whatever you do, make sure that you record the password and place it in a safe location, such as the company vault. You don't want anyone accessing this password without authorization.

Figure 5-10:
Verify that any dynamic IP addresses are truly necessary.

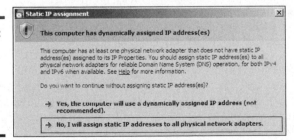

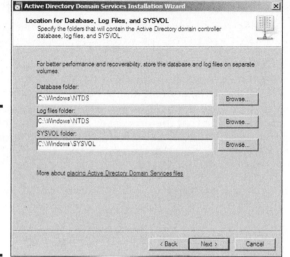

Figure 5-11:
Provide the
locations
used to
store
various
Active
Directory
features.

10. **Type a password and confirm it. Click Next.**

You see a summary dialog box. Notice the Export Settings button. Click this button if you want to save your settings for future use. Doing so can save you a lot of time later.

11. **Verify the settings in the Summary dialog box and click Next.**

At this point, you can go get a cup of coffee because the promotion process seems to take forever (and sometimes longer than that). You should see little messages as the process continues. For example, the wizard tells you that it's securing various directories and setting up policies. Eventually, you see a completion dialog box.

12. **Click Finish.**

You see a dialog box asking whether you want to reboot the machine.

13. **Click Restart Now.**

The system reboots. When the system comes back online, you have a domain controller. You can't access the server from any client machine at this point because you need to re-create user accounts, share resources on the server, and join the clients to the domain.

Configuring the user accounts

As previously mentioned, when you promote the server to a domain controller, it doesn't preserve any of the users you created for a workgroup. You must enter the users again by using a different console because the users now appear in the Active Directory database. Open the Active Directory

Users and Computers console, and you see a display similar to the one shown in Figure 5-12.

Adding a new user is almost precisely the same as when working with a workgroup. The "Configuring the Server for a Workgroup" section of Book II, Chapter 4 describes this process. In this case, you right-click the Users entry and choose New⇨User from the context menu. The New Object – User dialog box, shown in Figure 5-13, also contains a few new entries. However, don't let the difference make you think that the process is any different from what you did in workgroups. Yes, Active Directory can store more information, but the process of creating a user is the same.

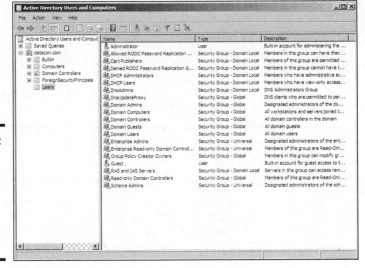

Figure 5-12: Active Directory relies on a different utility to manage users.

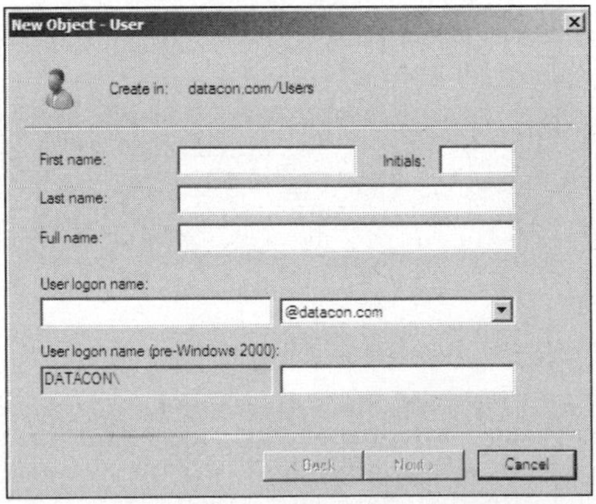

Figure 5-13: Manage users using the same techniques you used for workgroups.

Sharing resources on the domain

You share resources on a domain by using the same techniques you use with a workgroup. For example, to share a drive, folder, or file, you right-click the required object in Windows Explorer and choose Properties from the context menu. The Sharing and Security tabs provide everything you need to provide access to the resource. Book V, Chapter 2 provides additional information on this configuration task.

The only difference that you do need to consider is that you can augment some sharing and security choices through group policies on a domain. These group policies become available when you promote the server to a domain controller. Book III, Chapter 2 describes how to work with group policies on your server. Take time to explore the available group policies because your server may provide unique configuration options that will make it easier to share resources without opening security holes.

Joining clients to the domain

After you set up the domain, you can test it out by connecting to it with a client. The client need not be a member of the domain to access it. The purpose of this simple test is to verify that the client can access the server. However, when the client connects in this way, you don't obtain the full benefits of the domain. For example, you don't see the client's machine information entered into Active Directory, nor do you get most of the other benefits of using Active Directory.

Because the purpose of using a domain is to obtain the centralized control that Active Directory provides, you want to set up the client to join the domain. The fastest way to perform this task is to open the Computer Name tab of the System Properties dialog box, as shown in Figure 5-14. To access this dialog box in Windows XP and earlier systems, right-click My Computer and choose Properties from the context menu. When working with Vista or Windows Server 2008, right-click Computer to display the System window and then click Advanced System Settings.

When you see the System Properties dialog box, shown in Figure 5-14, click Change. Choose the Domain option and type the name of the domain you set up. Click OK. After Windows verifies that the domain exists and that the client has rights to access it, you see a welcome message. You must reboot the machine to let the changes take effect.

Book II
Chapter 5

Promoting Your
Server to a Domain
Controller

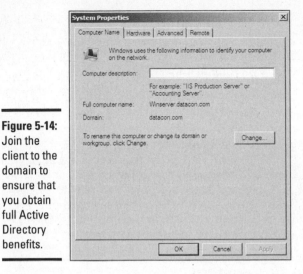

Figure 5-14:
Join the client to the domain to ensure that you obtain full Active Directory benefits.

Working with the Windows System Resource Manager (WSRM)

The Windows System Resource Manager (WSRM) is a tool that you can install and use no matter which configuration of Windows Server 2008 you use. When you're working in a workgroup setting, the main purposes for WSRM are to monitor Terminal Services connections and to manage resource usage by applications. In a domain environment, WSRM also helps you keep tight control over how the system and users work with resources. Using this tool helps you create an environment where everyone gets their fair share of resources. Of course, you can weight the usage depending on the criticality of the resource need.

To use WSRM, you must install the Windows System Resource Manager feature using the techniques found in the "Working with features" section of Book II, Chapter 1. WSRM relies on the Windows Internal Database. When you check the Windows System Resource Manager feature, you see the Add Features Wizard dialog box, telling you that you must install the Windows Internal Database feature as well. Click Add Required Feature to add this feature, if you haven't already installed it.

After you install WSRM, you see a new Windows System Resource Manager entry in the Administrative Tools folder. Opening the Windows System Resource Manager console displays the Connection to Computer dialog box, where you can choose the local computer or another computer on the network to manage. This section uses the local computer as an example, but the techniques shown work with other Windows Server 2008 computers as well.

Choosing a connection displays the resources for the computer you select, as shown in Figure 5-15.

The functionality provided by WSRM is new for Windows Server 2008. WSRM is such a useful console that you want to consider using it for heavily loaded systems or for networks that tend to become overwhelmed. The following sections describe why you need WSRM and how to use it.

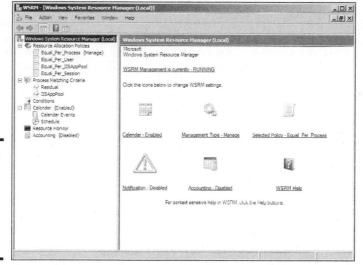

Figure 5-15: Use WSRM to manage local or remote computer resources.

Understanding how WSRM works and what you gain from it

WSRM provides automatic resource management based on predefined or custom policies. You use WSRM to manage both CPU and memory resources. Of course, you can already manage storage resources using the quota system that has appeared in all versions of Windows Server. In many respects, WSRM follows the policy setup used by Windows security. The policy modifies how the system interacts with entities using the resource.

The policies used by WSRM don't take effect until the server reaches 70 percent capacity in the affected area. For example, when the server is at only 20 percent CPU usage, the policy isn't used. Microsoft never tells why it chose the 70 percent level, but anecdotal evidence suggests that contention becomes troublesome at that level on Windows servers. You use WSRM to manage resources in the following ways:

✦ Manage system resources on a constant or scheduled basis using predefined or custom policies.

✦ Use calendar rules to specify different policies at different times.

✦ Select the appropriate policy based on server properties, events, changes to the amount of memory installed, or changes to the number of available processors.

✦ Obtain resource usage data and store it locally or within a centrally located SQL Server database.

The biggest benefit of resource management is to help make the server available even under significant load. Although a server that has a single role probably won't need WSRM, adding additional roles complicates the server setup and makes management valuable. In addition, using WSRM can help extend the useful life of older servers by reducing contention for valuable resources. Users tend to see slower, but consistent, response times with the appropriate policies in place. Processes don't end up starved for resources, which makes the server more reliable.

The Resource Allocation Policies folder contains all the policies used to manage resources on the server. WSRM comes with four predefined policies, as shown in Figure 5-15. The following list describes these four policies:

✦ **Equal_Per_Process:** Each running process receives an equal portion of CPU and memory resources. This default policy limits each process to a maximum of 10 percent of the available resources while the resource usage remains above 70 percent (the contention level). This is the default managing policy. You normally use this policy for service-related servers, such as those that provide file and print services.

✦ **Equal_Per_User:** Each user receives an equal share of CPU and memory resources. For example, if the server is servicing ten users, each user receives 10 percent of the available resources while the resource usage remains above 70 percent. You normally use this policy for application servers.

✦ **Equal_Per_IISAppPool:** Each Internet Information Server (IIS) application pool receives an equal share of CPU and memory resources. Applications that aren't part of an IIS application pool receive any resources that are left over from IIS activities. In some cases, this means that services and server-based applications won't receive any resources while IIS is under heavy load. You normally use this policy for Web servers or for servers that provide Web services.

✦ **Equal_Per_Session:** Each session receives an equal share of the CPU and memory resources. For example, if the server is servicing ten sessions, each session receives 10 percent of the available resources while the resource usage remains above 70 percent. Because a user can have multiple sessions, this policy isn't the same as the Equal_Per_User policy. Users with multiple sessions receive preferential treatment when using this policy. You normally use this policy for servers that support Terminal Services.

These default policies serve as a basis for common resource management scenarios, but may not meet your needs. The "Creating new policies" section of this chapter describes how to create new policies that meet specific needs. For example, you may want to give a particular application preferential treatment to ensure that users can always access it — address this requirement using a custom policy.

Policies also have a scope. You can assign a policy at the system level so that it affects every application, session, or user on the system. As an alternative, you can create a conditional scope specifying that WSRM uses a policy to meet a specific need. The "Assigning system policies" section at the end of this chapter describes how to set policies at the system level. Setting conditional policies can become quite complex and usually reflects a special setup on your server. This book doesn't discuss conditional policies.

In some cases, the server doesn't have the same load placed on it every day. A server may need to perform specific tasks based on calendar requirements. For example, an accounting computer may have to give priority to performing end-of-month calculations at the end of the month. To set a one-time or recurring policy event, choose the Calendar folder. This feature works precisely the same way as the Calendar feature in Outlook. Simply right-click the calendar area, choose the kind of event you want to create, and set the date and time parameters.

At some point, you need to know whether the policies you create work as anticipated. Choose the Resource Monitor folder to check the results of policy changes. This feature works precisely the same as the Reliability and Performance Monitor console, described in the "Measuring Reliability and Performance" section of Book III, Chapter 5.

Creating new policies

You create new policies when you want to define how to manage resources at either the system or conditional levels and one of the predefined policies doesn't fit. Custom policies provide you with significant flexibility in how the server allocates resources to users, sessions, or processes that request them. The following steps describe how to create a new policy:

1. **Right-click the Resource Allocation Policies folder, shown in Figure 5-15, and choose New Resource Allocation Policy from the context menu.**

   You see the New Resource Allocation Policy dialog box, shown in Figure 5-16.

2. **Type a policy name in the Policy Name field.**

3. **Click Add.**

   You see the Add or Edit Resource Allocation dialog box, shown in Figure 5-17. The three tabs help you create a resource management policy. You must fill out the information on at least the General tab to create a resource policy. The Memory and Advanced tab information is optional.

4. Choose an option in the Process Matching Criteria field.

A *process matching* criteria defines the process in some way. For example, if you want to define a policy that matches all executables that begin with the letter *A,* you use a matching criteria of A*.EXE. The only default process matching criteria is IISAppPool. Unless you have defined other criteria, you normally select <New...> from the list. The following steps describe how to create a new process matching criteria:

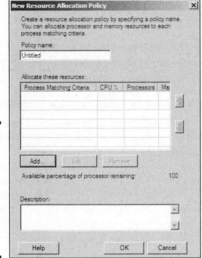

Figure 5-16: Create new WSRM policies as needed to manage server resources.

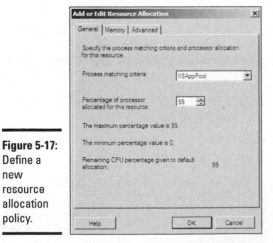

Figure 5-17: Define a new resource allocation policy.

a. **Choose <New...> in the Process Matching Criteria field.**

You see the New Process Matching Criteria dialog box, shown in Figure 5-18.

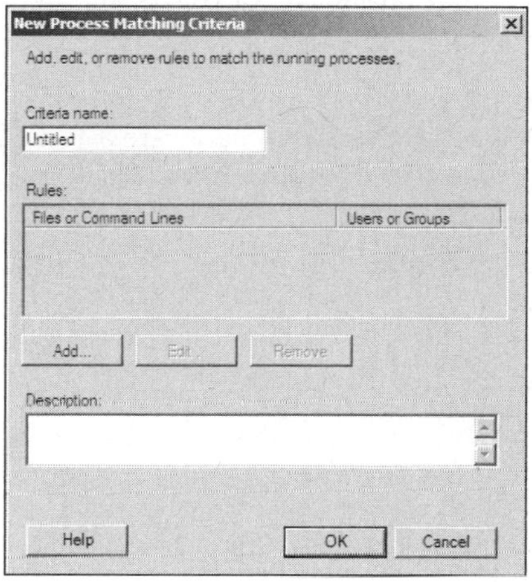

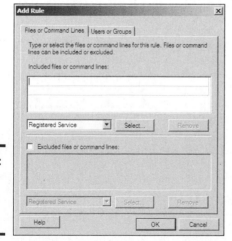

Figure 5-18:
Add a description of the process you want the resource allocation policy to match.

b. **Type a name for the criteria in the Criteria Name field.**

c. **Click Add.**

You see the Add Rule dialog box, shown in Figure 5-19. Process matching criteria can use as many rules as needed to define the match fully.

Figure 5-19:
Rules specify the matching criteria.

The Files or Command Lines tab contains options that let you choose registered services, running processes, applications, and IIS application pools. To choose any executable, locate the executable type in the drop-down list, click Select, choose the executable from the list that's provided, and click OK. You can use wildcard characters (* and ?) to define specific executables. Simply type the specification in the Included Files or Command Lines list.

The Users or Groups tab lets you choose rules based on a particular user or group. For example, you may add a rule for TERMINAL SERVER USER group. The resulting process matching criteria would affect that group only.

d. **Add rules as necessary to the Add Rule dialog box.**

e. **Click OK.**

You see the rule added to the Rules list.

f. **Perform Steps c through e for as many rules as required to create the process matching criteria.**

g. **Type a description for the process matching criteria in the Description field.**

h. **Click OK.**

You see the new process matching criteria added to the Process Matching Criteria field of the Add or Edit Resource Allocation dialog box.

5. **Define the amount of processor resources allocated to the process matching criteria in the Percentage of Processor Allocated for this Resource field.**

6. **(Optional) Select the Memory tab and use the options to set a memory policy for the resource allocation.**

You see the options shown in Figure 5-20. The options let you choose a particular action when a process exceeds its maximum memory allocation. For example, you can choose to stop the application or add an entry to the event log. You can also set the maximum memory that each process can use. Remember that this setting affects only the executables selected by the process matching criteria.

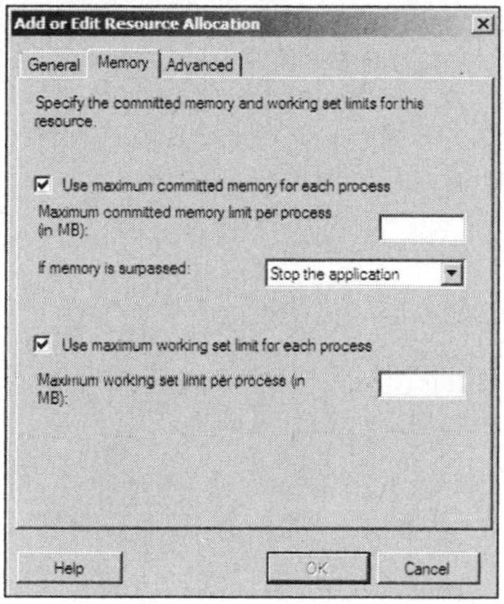

Figure 5-20:
Set the
memory
management
policy to
ensure that
executables
use memory
within
defined
limits.

7. **(Optional) Select the Advanced tab and use the options to select
   advanced settings for the policy.**

   You see the options shown in Figure 5-21. These settings let you choose
   which processors the selected executables can use. Choosing particular
   processors frees other processors to perform other tasks. You can also
   perform resource suballocation based on specific criteria. For example,
   you can use the process matching criteria to choose a group of executables
   and then use suballocation to specify the resource allocation for each
   process individually.

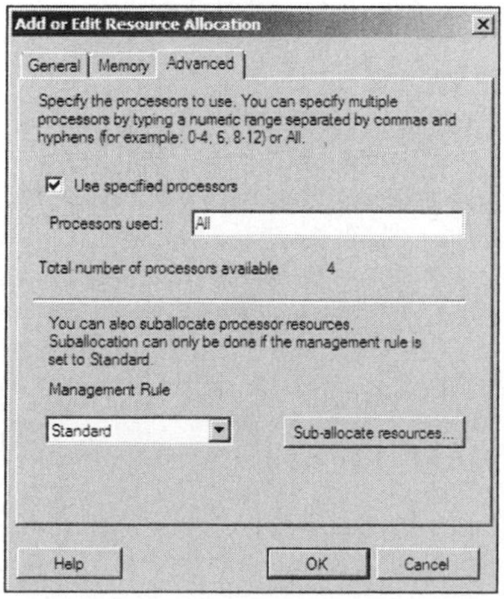

Figure 5-21:
Define
advanced
criteria as
needed to
ensure that
the policy
works as
anticipated.

8. **Click OK.**

You see the new resource allocation added to the Allocate These Resources list of the New Resource Allocation Policy dialog box.

9. **Repeat Steps 3 through 8 for additional resource allocations as needed.**

10. **Type a description for the resource allocation policy in the Description field.**

11. **Click OK.**

You see the new resource allocation policy added to the Resource Allocation Policies folder of the WSRM console.

Modifying and deleting policies

WSRM allows you to modify or delete only policies you create. The predefined policies don't allow any type of modification. To modify a policy, right-click its entry in the Resource Allocation Policies folder and choose Properties from the context menu. To remove a policy you no longer need, right-click the entry in the Resource Allocation Policies folder and choose Delete from the context menu. WSRM displays a warning dialog box. Click Yes to complete the deletion process.

Assigning system policies

System policies affect the server as a whole rather than individual processes based on a condition you set. The criteria you set as part of the policy still apply, but on a system level. A system policy performs management based on the management type you choose. WSRM supports two management types:

✦ **Manage:** WSRM performs active resource management based on the criteria within the policy.

✦ **Profile:** WSRM logs the resource management events based on the criteria within the policy, but doesn't perform any active management.

To change the system policy, right-click the policy you want to use. Select Set As Managing Policy from the context menu if you want to set the management type to Manage. Select Set As Profiling Policy from the context menu when you want to set the management type to Profile.

Part III

Administration

The 5th Wave   By Rich Tennant

"We mapped our corporate value stream, Phillip, and your department was such a mudflat that we're going to eliminate everything but the clams and scallops."

Contents at a Glance

Chapter 1: An Overview of the Administrative Tools Folder

In This Chapter

✔ Obtaining access to the Administrative Tools folder

✔ Considering the common Administrative Tools folder features

✔ Configuring the Remote Server Administration Tools

The Administrative Tools folder is the central location for all the graphical management tools that Windows Server 2008 provides. Some third-party vendors also place their tools in the Administrative Tools folder, and your custom tools appear in there. In fact, the "Creating the RSM console" section of Book II, Chapter 2 describes one technique for creating a custom tool. However, you can create any number of custom tools that you need using the techniques found in that section.

Given the importance of the centralized tool source in the Administrative Tools folder, it makes sense for an administrator to know a number of ways to access these tools. As with the Control Panel (see the "Accessing the Control Panel" section of Book II, Chapter 3), you have multiple methods at your disposal for accessing the Administrative Tools folder. In fact, you don't even have to open the Administrative Tools folder to locate the tools when you know the tool's filename.

This chapter also provides you with an overview of all the tools you find in the Administrative Tools folder. You see some of the tools all the time, but other tools depend on the roles and features you have installed. For example, there's little reason to provide an Internet Information Server (IIS) configuration tool when you don't have IIS installed. Consequently, you see descriptions of many specialty tools throughout this book. This chapter concentrates on the tools that are commonly available.

Continuing the theme of administration, the final part of this chapter discusses how you can install and use the Remote Server Administration Tools. These tools make it possible for you to connect to your server in San Diego, California, from Milwaukee, Wisconsin, and perform useful work. In fact, using the correct setup, you may not notice much of a difference between this remote connection and your local connection, except for speed. A remote connection always provides poorer speed than a local connection simply because the signal has to move farther.

Accessing the Administrative Tools Folder

Gaining access to the Administrative Tools folder is easy because you can do it from many locations. Most people know that you can access the Administrative Tools folder by selecting its entry in the Control Panel. The details vary according to whether you use the new or classic Control Panel setup, but the entry is there. However, many people don't know that you can fully access the Administrative Tools folder from the Start menu when you configure the Control Panel for Start menu access using the techniques found in the "Accessing the Control Panel" section of Book II, Chapter 3.

You can also access the Administrative Tools folder from Windows Explorer. The Control Panel entry always appears near the bottom of the list. Clicking this entry grants access to the Control Panel and you see the familiar applet icons in the right pane. Double-click the Administrative Tools entry, and you see the usual console tools.

Another way to gain access to the Administrative Tools folder is to place it on the Start menu. The technique you choose depends on which Start menu you used:

✦ **If you're using the classic Start menu:** Check the Display Administrative Tools option in the Customize Classic Start Menu dialog box. You can access this dialog box by clicking Customize on the Start Menu tab of the Taskbar and Start Menu Properties dialog box. After you make this change, you can open consoles by choosing Start⇨Programs⇨Administrative Tools.

✦ **If you're using the new Start menu:** You can obtain the same benefit by choosing the Display on All Programs Menu and Start Menu option in System Administration Tools entry on the Advanced tab of the Customize Start Menu dialog box. After you make this change, you can access the Administrative Tools folder by choosing Start⇨Administrative Tools.

Now that you have a better idea of how to access the Administrative Tools folder, it's time to consider how to bypass it. The following sections describe how you can bypass the Administrative Tools folder to access various consoles installed on your system. Some of these consoles are hidden and don't appear in the Administrative Tools folder, so you may find some unexpected goodies in these sections.

Understanding consoles

A *console* is a special kind of application defined by a Microsoft Console (MSC) file. The file is written using XML. For example, if you open the COMExp.MSC file using Notepad, you see the XML shown in Figure 1-1 for the Component Services console. This XML defines how the file appears when you open it.

```
comexp.msc - Notepad                                                    _ □ x
File  Edit  Format  View  Help
<?xml version="1.0"?>
<MMC_ConsoleFile ConsoleVersion="3.0" ProgramMode="UserMDI">
  <ConsoleFileID>{81E71BDC-85A7-4FC0-B4F1-B0B20A148515}</ConsoleFileID>
  <FrameState ShowStatusBar="true" LogicalReadOnly="true">
    <WindowPlacement ShowCommand="SW_SHOWNORMAL">
      <Point Name="MinPosition" X="-1" Y="-1"/>
      <Point Name="MaxPosition" X="-1" Y="-1"/>
      <Rectangle Name="NormalPosition" Top="71" Bottom="674" Left="177" Right="1040"/>
    </WindowPlacement>
  </FrameState>
  <Views>
    <View ID="1" ScopePaneWidth="196" ActionsPaneWidth="-1">
      <BookMark Name="RootNode" NodeID="1"/>
      <BookMark Name="SelectedNode" NodeID="2">
        <DynamicPath>
          <Segment String="Computers"/>
        </DynamicPath>
      </BookMark>
      <WindowPlacement WPF_RESTORETOMAXIMIZED="true" ShowCommand="SW_SHOWMAXIMIZED">
        <Point Name="MinPosition" X="-1" Y="-1"/>
        <Point Name="MaxPosition" X="-4" Y="-23"/>
        <Rectangle Name="NormalPosition" Top="0" Bottom="429" Left="0" Right="793"/>
      </WindowPlacement>
      <ViewOptions ViewMode="Report" ScopePaneVisible="true" ActionsPaneVisible="true" Des
    </View>
  </Views>
  <VisualAttributes>
    <String Name="ApplicationTitle" ID="1"/>
    <Icon Index="0" File="d:\Windows\System32\comres.dll">
      <Image Name="Large" BinaryRefIndex="0"/>
      <Image Name="Small" BinaryRefIndex="1"/>
    </Icon>
  </VisualAttributes>
  <Favorites>
    <Favorite TYPE="Group">
      <String Name="Name" ID="2"/>
      <Favorites/>
```

Figure 1-1:
An MSC file
is a special
kind of XML
file.

WARNING!

Unfortunately, the XML in these files is undocumented, so you modify them manually at your own risk. Always make a copy of any file before you modify it.

The host application for consoles is the Microsoft Management Console (MMC). When you open an MSC file, the MMC application reads the MSC file and configures the view you see appropriately. The MMC application is only a host — you can't use it by itself.

The basis of all consoles is the snap-in. An MMC *snap-in* is a special kind of DLL file that relies on the Component Object Model (COM) to perform tasks such as reading the status of your hard drives. By separating the code that does the work (the snap-in) from the code that presents information (the MMC application), Microsoft has made it possible to create complex administration tools with a consistent look and feel. In addition, the developer can usually create such a tool in less time because many of the user interface elements appear as part of MMC. You can create your own MMC consoles using the techniques found in the "Creating the RSM console" section of Book II, Chapter 2.

Using MSC files to open consoles

You can open the consoles found in the Administrative Tools folder directly if you know the applet name. For example, if you open the Run dialog box, type **COMExp.MSC** in the Open field, and click OK, you see the Component Services console. You can also type the name of the file at the command line to access the console (unlike with the Control Panel, Microsoft hasn't added any odd tricks for consoles yet). Table 1-1 lists common consoles, their associated filenames, and briefly describes the consoles.

Table 1-1	Common Administrative Tools Folder Consoles	
Console Name	*Filename*	*Description*
Component Services	COMExp.MSC	Provides support for COM, Distributed COM (DCOM), and COM+ applications. You use this tool to manage access to components that applications need to run properly. Because this console works with custom applications for the most part, you don't find a detailed discussion of it in this book. The developer who creates your custom application will help you with any Component Services configuration tasks.
Computer Management	CompMgmt.MSC	Helps you manage your computer resources, especially in a workgroup scenario. See Book II, Chapter 4 for additional details on configuring workgroups using the Computer Management console.
Data Sources (ODBC)	ODBCAd32.EXE	Configures sources of data for Database Management Systems (DBMSs) that rely on Open Database Connectivity (ODBC) to create connections to applications. Because this console works with custom applications for the most part, you don't find a detailed discussion of it in this book. The developer who creates your custom application will help you with any Data Sources (ODBC) configuration tasks. (ODBC stands for Open Database Connectivity.)
Event Viewer	EventVwr.MSC	Displays a list of the events that the system has experienced. The messages provide informational, warning, and error content. You can learn more about this tool in the "Event Viewer" section of this chapter.
iSCSI Initiator	iSCSICPL.EXE	Provides the same functionality as its Control Panel counterpart.
Local Security Policy	SecPol.MSC	Configures local security policies for the machine. These settings affect only the current machine and are normally used in workgroup scenarios. Domains normally rely on group policies set on the server. You can learn more about this feature in the "Creating a Local Security Policy" section of Book V, Chapter 1.

Console Name	Filename	Description
Memory Diagnostics Tool	MdSched.EXE	Schedules a test of system memory during the next boot cycle. This tool works only outside the Windows environment because Windows must be out of memory to conduct the test. See the "Performing a Memory Test" section of Book I, Chapter 2 for additional details.
Reliability and Performance Monitor	PerfMon.MSC	Provides both manual and automatic monitoring of system performance and reliability. In this case, performance equates to some type of speed measurement. The console also provides resources for development reports. You can discover more about this console in the "Measuring Reliability and Performance" section of Book III, Chapter 5.
Remote Desktops	TSMMC.MSC	Helps you manage remote desktops from one location. See the "Working with Terminal Server" section of Book IV, Chapter 3 for additional information.
Security Configuration Wizard	SCW.EXE	Creates new security policies by using a wizard approach rather than manual option settings. You can find out more about this feature in the "Using the Security Configuration Wizard" section of Book V, Chapter 1.
Server Manager	CompMgmt Launcher.EXE	Launches a copy of the Server Manager window, used for administration tasks throughout this book. Discover many of the Server Manager features in the "Using the Server Manager Console" section of Book II, Chapter 1.
Services	Services.MSC	Displays a list of all services installed on the computer and their status. You use the console to manage and configure services as needed. The "Services" section of this chapter provides additional information about this console.

continued

Book III
Chapter 1

An Overview of
the Administrative
Tools Folder

Table 1-1 *(continued)*

Console Name	Filename	Description
Share and Storage Management	StorageMgmt.MSC	Manages local storage and associated shares. In some respects, this console is another version of the `Computer Management\System Tools\ Shared Folders\Shares` folder of the Computer Management console. (See the "Sharing storage resources in the workgroup" section of Book II, Chapter 4 for details.) You can discover more about this console in the "Performing Disk Management Tasks" section of Book III, Chapter 5.
Storage Explorer	StorExpl.MSC	Configures various forms of external storage for your server, including iSCSI and Fibre Channel.
System Configuration	MSConfig.EXE	Displays and helps you configure system configuration information that affects the boot cycle of the local system. See the "System Configuration" section of this chapter for additional information about this console.
Task Scheduler	TaskSchd.MSC	Automates administrative, operating system, and application tasks by performing the requested task at a specified date and time. You can configure the tasks to provide completion information and notification as required. See the "Automating Diagnostic Tasks with Task Scheduler" section of Book III, Chapter 5 for additional information about Task Scheduler.
Terminal Services Configuration	TSConfig.MSC	Performs Terminal Services configuration tasks, such as managing connections and setting licensing options. See the "Working with Terminal Server" section of Book IV, Chapter 3 for additional information.
Terminal Services Manager	tsadmin.MSC	Performs Terminal Services management tasks such as tracking users and the groups to which they belong. See the "Working with Terminal Server" section of Book IV, Chapter 3 for additional information.

Console Name	Filename	Description
Windows Firewall with Advanced Security	WF.MSC	Determines how Windows Server 2008 reacts to incoming and outgoing communication with the Internet. Windows Server 2008 includes many features not found in previous Windows products. See the "Configuring Windows Firewall with Advanced Security" section of Book V, Chapter 4 for additional information.
Windows Server Backup	WBAdmin.MSC	Helps you schedule, manage, and perform system backups. See the "Performing a system backup" section of Book III, Chapter 5 for additional information about using Windows Server Backup.

Considering the undiscovered MSC file

Most of the consoles you want to work with appear in the \Windows\System 32 folder of your system. However, MSC files can appear anywhere on your hard drive, so you may eventually want to search for them. You may be surprised at how many management tools are lurking below the surface, just waiting for discovery. In fact, one of these undiscovered MSC files, GPEdit.MSC, is essential for domain maintenance, and you see it in Book III, Chapter 2. Table 1-2 lists hidden consoles that you commonly find on your system. Because these consoles are hidden and don't appear in the Administrative Tools folder, the table lists them in filename order.

Table 1-2	Hidden Consoles	
Console Name	**Filename**	**Description**
Authorization Manager	AzMan.MSC	Helps you manage authorization-store information about the local computer. The authorization store provides role-based security management for applications where user access is based on their roles within an organization. See the "Understanding role-based security" of Book V, Chapter 1 for additional information about role-based security.
CertMgr [Certificates – Current User]	CertMgr.MSC	Provides access to all certificates for the current user. The certificates are grouped according to type, and you can even search for specific certificates. In addition, you can export certificates to save them for future needs. See the "Managing User Certificates" section of Book V, Chapter 3 for additional information about this console.

continued

Book III Chapter 1

An Overview of the Administrative Tools Folder

Table 1-2 *(continued)*

Console Name	Filename	Description
Device Manager	DevMgmt.MSC	Provides access to the Device Manager. See the "Working with Device Manager" section of Book II, Chapter 2 for additional information about Device Manager.
Disk Management	DiskMgmt.MSC	Loads a simplified version of the Disk Management folder, found in the Computer Management console. This console is useful if you want to work only with the disks and to use the screen real estate more efficiently. Find out more about this console in the "Performing Disk Management Tasks" section of Book III, Chapter 5.
Shared Folders	FSMgmt.MSC	Loads a simplified version of the Shared Folders folder, found in the Computer Management console. This console is useful when you want to work only with shares and to use the screen real estate more efficiently. Find out more about this console in the "Sharing storage resources in the workgroup" section of Book II, Chapter 4.
Group Policy Editor	GPEdit.MSC	Creates policies that affect the entire network when created on a domain controller and changes security and configuration policies on the local machine when used in a workgroup or on a local machine. You can find out more about group policies in Book III, Chapter 2.
LUsrMgr (Local Users and Groups)	LUsrMgr.MSC	Loads a simplified version of the Local Users and Groups folder, found in the Computer Management console. This console is useful if you want to work with only the disks and to use the screen real estate more efficiently. Find out more about working with local users and groups in the "Configuring the Server for a Workgroup" section of Book II, Chapter 4.
NAPCICfg (NAP Client Configuration)	NAPCICfg.MSC	Configures the Network Access Protection (NAP) feature for Windows Server 2008.

Console Name	*Filename*	*Description*
Resultant Set of Policy	RSOP.MSC	Shows the results of policy decisions made at the group and local levels. As you create policies at various levels, it becomes difficult to determine the cumulative effects of those policies. The Resultant Set of Policy (RSoP) provides one solution to the problem by showing the results of policies set at all levels. You can learn more about this console in the "Viewing the Resultant Set of Policy (RSoP)" section of Book III, Chapter 2.
Server Manager	ServerManager.MSC	Provides an alternative method of displaying Server Manager. See the Server Manager entry in Table 1-1 for details.
Telephony	TAPIMgmt.MSC	Configures all types of Telephony Application Programming Interface (TAPI) access. The main purpose of this console is to configure remote communications and networking.
Trusted Platform Module	TPM.MSC	Manages the Trusted Platform Module (TPM) on systems that provide this support. Most computers today don't include a TPM chip. The main purpose for the TPM in Windows Server 2008 is for BitLocker encryption. You can find out more about BitLocker in the "Encrypting your hard drive using BitLocker" section of Book II, Chapter 2.
WMIMgmt (Console Root WMI Control)	WMIMgmt.MSC	Provides management support for the Windows Management Instrumentation (WMI) feature of Windows. *WMI* is a special method of configuring the system. You can use scripts or a special utility named WMIC (Windows Management Instrumentation Command line) to perform the management tasks. It's also possible to use a special application to perform this task. The "Understanding the Windows Management Instrumentation (WMI)" section of Book VIII, Chapter 1 shows how to use this console.

**Book III
Chapter 1**

**An Overview of
the Administrative
Tools Folder**

Working with Common Administrative Tools Folder Features

The Administrative Tools folder contains a certain number of entries, even if you don't install any roles or features. These features are common to all configurations. Any time you install a role or feature, you might see additional entries, but you don't see fewer entries in the Enterprise Edition of the product used for this book. (Other editions may contain fewer features than are listed here.) Here are the common Administrative Tools features:

+ Component Services

+ Computer Management

+ Data Sources (ODBC)

+ Event Viewer

+ iSCSI Initiator

+ Local Security Policy

+ Memory Diagnostics Tool

+ Reliability and Performance Monitor

+ Security Configuration Wizard

+ Server Manager

+ Services

+ Share and Storage Management

+ Storage Explorer

+ System Configuration

+ Task Scheduler

+ Windows Firewall with Advanced Security

+ Windows Server Backup

Detailed discussions of most of these features appear in other places in this book. You can find the locations for these discussions in Table 1-1. The following sections describe consoles that you use often within Windows Server 2008 but that don't necessarily have specific tasks associated with them.

Event Viewer

Most administrators probably remember Event Viewer, found in older versions of Windows. It provides a simple interface for viewing event messages from a minimum of three log files: Application, Security, and System. Newer versions include two additional logs: Internet Explorer and PowerShell. Some third-party products add a log or two, but overall these five logs are the limit to what you see. Each log contains a list of messages. The new version of Event Viewer provides these logs, but it provides significantly more, as shown in Figure 1-2.

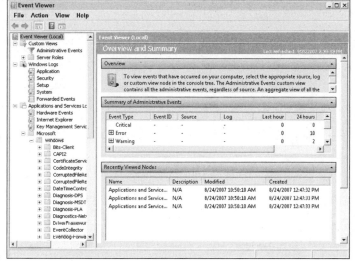

Figure 1-2:
Event Viewer is packed with new features and new logs.

The new interface provides you with considerably more information. For example, as shown in Figure 1-2, you see a lot more summaries and overviews that help you manage the information that Event Viewer provides.

Working with the Summary of Administrative
Events pane and viewing event messages

The Summary of Administrative Events pane shows the number of critical, error, warning, information, success audit, and success failure messages that appear on the system. Across the pane, you see the number of events in the past hour, past 24 hours, and past seven days. Click the plus sign next to any of the event types and you see the messages for that event type. Double-click an entry and the event log takes you directly to that event log entry, as shown in Figure 1-3. Notice that you didn't review any logs to move to (display) this message — the Event Viewer console takes you directly to the message and shows you a complete summary of it. If you need additional information, select the Details tab and you can see all the information used to create the event log message.

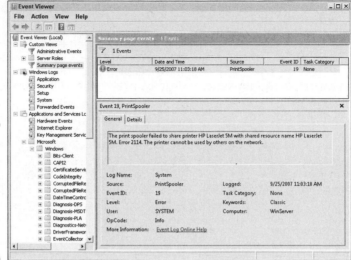

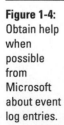

Figure 1-3:
You can see information much faster using the new event log summaries.

In general, all you really need when viewing event log messages is the summary shown in Figure 1-3, unless you need to supply information to the vendor for technical support. In this case, you know that the event message is an error, which means that something is wrong and that you have to fix it, but it isn't critical. (The system won't suddenly freeze or something of that nature.) The text tells you everything you need to know: The print spooler wasn't able to share the printer with the rest of the network.

If you want to know more about the error, you must look up the error code, 2114, in the vendor manual or within the Microsoft documentation. Notice the Event Log Online Help link. Click this link and you see a dialog box such as the one shown in Figure 1-4, which asks whether it's okay to send the error information to Microsoft. Click Yes, and you see a copy of Internet Explorer open with additional event-specific help.

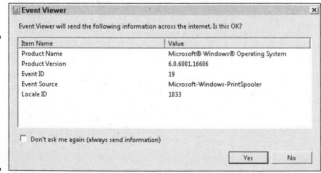

Figure 1-4:
Obtain help when possible from Microsoft about event log entries.

Working with the Summary of Administrative Events pane

Below the Summary of Administrative Events pane (refer to Figure 1-2) is the Recently Viewed Nodes pane. This pane maintains a list of nodes you visited most recently; in the order you visited them. You can use this list to get to places you visited recently by double-clicking the entry. Notice that you can also return to a previous node by clicking the left-pointing arrow or move to the next node in a historical list by clicking the right-pointing arrow. The console disables the arrows when there isn't any historical information to see.

Working with the Log Summary pane

The final pane in the Overview and Summary window doesn't appear in Figure 1-2. The Log Summary pane contains a list of event logs. It tells you about the setup for each log. Double-clicking a log entry takes you to that log so that you can view its events.

Working with custom views

The new version of the Event Viewer contains a folder that didn't appear in earlier versions of this console. Select the Custom Views pane and you see a list of custom views. These custom views are really just filtered output of all the messages that appear in every log. You can view some of the predefined views, such as Administrative Events, to see how these custom views work. What you see is a list of event log entries such as the one shown in Figure 1-5.

Book III
Chapter 1

An Overview of the Administrative Tools Folder

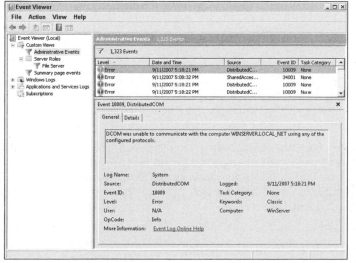

Figure 1-5:
Use custom views to see event log entries in new ways and to detect event patterns.

Creating a custom view

To create your own, custom views, right-click any node shown previously in Figure 1-2 and choose Create Custom View from the context menu. You see the Create Custom View dialog box, shown in Figure 1-6.

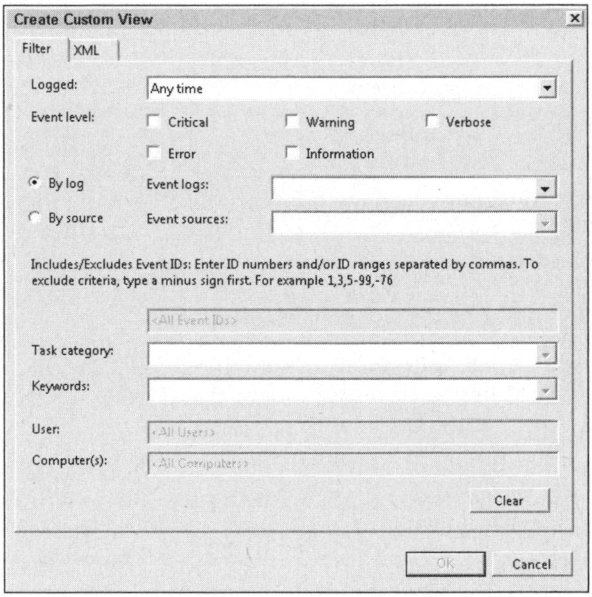

Figure 1-6: The Create Custom View dialog box provides entries you use to filter the event log data.

To create a new view, you select the items you want to use to filter the logs. These criteria determine what you see in your custom view:

✦ **Event Level:** Determines the kind of event message you want to check. Each level represents the severity of the message. For example, a critical message is more severe than an error message. The information message is the least critical type.

✦ **By Log:** You can choose to filter events based on specific logs. For example, you may want to see events from only the application and system logs. You find that Windows Server 2008 tracks a wealth of services and applications, so it probably has the log you need to track just about anything on the system.

✦ **By Source:** This option helps you locate messages based on a particular source. A *source* is a service, driver, or application that registers itself with Windows. Any application can register itself, but the developer must provide the code to do so. This entry is active even when you choose to focus on particular logs. However, the entries you see are based on the logs you choose. When software registers itself with

Windows, it must specify which logs it will use. When you choose to filter exclusively by source, you can choose from any of the sources that have registered themselves with Windows.

✦ **Event ID:** Every event has an event identifier — a number that specifies the kind of event that has occurred. You can choose to monitor only certain event IDs to obtain specific kinds of messages. Of course, you have to know which event IDs the application, driver, or service you want to monitor outputs. After you know the event IDs, you can apply them as an Event ID filtering criterion.

✦ **Task Category:** Filters event messages by task. You must have Task Scheduler configured for tasks to use this option.

✦ **Keyword:** Many of the events you can filter have keywords associated with them that further identify specific events. For example, when you select the application log, one of the keywords you can select is *Classic,* which means that you want to choose event messages created using the techniques found in older versions of Windows.

✦ **User:** Use this entry to monitor a particular user. This option is helpful when you think that user activities may cause errors on the server or when you want to monitor the activities of a particular user for other reasons.

✦ **Computer(s):** Use this entry to choose a particular computer to monitor. This option is helpful when you suspect that a problem on a client computer is causing errors on the server. You can also use this option to help you monitor unusual activities on the computer.

Book III
Chapter 1

After you fill in the Create Custom View dialog box, click OK and you see the Save Filter to Custom View dialog box, shown in Figure 1-7. This dialog box helps you save the filter you created in a permanent form. Use the following steps to fill out this dialog box:

An Overview of the Administrative Tools Folder

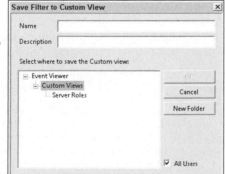

Figure 1-7:
Save the custom view that you created in a permanent form.

1. **Type a name for the filter in the Name field.**

   Choose a short, descriptive name that you'll recognize quickly.

2. **Type a description for the filter in the Description field.**

   Type a longer description that includes details about the filter. For example, you might include the logs you want to monitor, the event types, the keywords you've monitored, and so on. Make sure that someone else can understand the purpose of the filter.

3. **Highlight the folder where you want to store the view.**

   The default setting is to store the view in the Custom Views folder, which can make this folder quite crowded when you decide to create a number of custom views. A better option is to create subfolders you can use to store the custom views by category. These steps help you create a custom storage folder.

   a. **Highlight the parent folder for the new folder in the Select Where to Save the Custom View list.**

   b. **Click New Folder.**

      You see the Enter Name of the New Folder dialog box.

   c. **Type the name of the custom folder you want to create in the Name field and then click OK.**

      Event Viewer creates the custom log you requested and automatically selects it for you.

4. **Click OK.**

   Windows creates the custom view for you and stores it in the folder you requested.

Modifying a custom view

You may find at some point that the custom view you created performs many, but not all, of the filtering you want. In this case, you can simply modify the filter as needed. To perform this task, right-click the custom view's entry in the folder and choose Properties from the context menu. You see a filter Properties dialog box, where you can change the filter name and description.

If you need to change the details of the custom view, click Edit Filter. You see the Custom View Properties dialog box, such as the one shown in Figure 1-6, where you can change the filtering characteristics. Click OK twice when you complete any changes to the filter.

Exporting a custom view

Exporting a custom view lets you share it with other users or create a backup so that you can restore it later. To export a custom view, right-click the custom view's entry and choose Export Custom View from the context menu. You see a Save As dialog box. Type a name for the backup file in the File Name field and click Save to complete the process.

Importing a custom view

Importing a custom view lets you restore a custom view that you saved earlier or received from a friend. To import a custom view, right-click the folder where you want to store the custom view and choose Import Custom View from the context menu. You see the Import Custom View dialog box. Highlight the file containing the custom view you want to import, and click Open. You see an Import Custom View file that looks similar to the dialog box shown in Figure 1-7. You fill out the information using the same approach that you do when creating a new custom view.

Copying a custom view

It's possible to use an existing custom view as a basis for a new custom view and save yourself some time. Copying a custom view lets you create as many versions of a custom view as you need. To copy a custom view, right-click the custom view's entry and choose Copy Custom View from the context menu. You see a Copy Custom View file that looks similar to the dialog box shown in Figure 1-7. You fill out the information using the same approach that you do when creating a new custom view.

Deleting a custom view

Eventually, you need to delete custom views when you no longer need them. To delete a custom view, highlight its entry in the list of nodes in the left pane of Event Viewer. Press Delete. Event Viewer asks whether you're sure that you want to delete the custom view. Click Yes, and Event Viewer removes the entry for you.

Attaching tasks to event logs and custom views

One problem with older versions of Event Viewer is that you have to remember to check the log for new entries. Unfortunately, many administrators are too busy to check Event Viewer for new entries until a disaster occurs. At that point, the information is still helpful, but it doesn't help avoid a catastrophe, as it was originally intended to do. Event Viewer in Windows Server 2008 helps you avoid this problem by letting you attach a task to an event log or a custom view. The following steps tell you how to perform this task:

1. **Right-click the event log or custom view and choose Attach a Task to This Log or Attach Task to This Custom View from the context menu.**

   Event Viewer displays the Create a Basic Task Wizard dialog box, as shown in Figure 1-8.

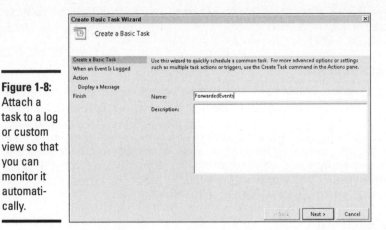

Figure 1-8:
Attach a task to a log or custom view so that you can monitor it automatically.

2. Type a name and description for the task and click Next.

You see the When an Event Is Logged dialog box, which lets you perform filtering on the events that trigger the task. Because a custom view already provides filtering, you won't be able to change any settings for a custom view. However, when working with a log, you can choose the source and event ID that triggers the task.

3. (Optional) Choose a source and event ID that will trigger the task and click Next.

You see the Action dialog box. This dialog box determines the action that the task will perform. A task can start a program, send an e-mail, or display a message on-screen. You can perform only one of these actions with a particular task. Consequently, if you want to perform two of the actions, you must create two tasks — one for each action.

4. Choose one of the actions in the list and click Next.

Event Viewer displays a form that matches the action you want to perform, as shown in Figure 1-9.

5. Fill out the required action information and click Next.

Event Viewer displays a summary of the actions you want to perform.

6. Verify that the action information is correct and click Finish.

Event Viewer creates the task within the `Task Scheduler\Task Scheduler Library\Event Viewer` folder. You won't see the task within Event Viewer. See the "Automating Diagnostic Tasks with Task Scheduler" section of Book III, Chapter 5 for more details on working with Task Scheduler.

Figure 1-9:
Event
Viewer
provides a
form
specifically
designed for
the action
you choose.

**Book III
Chapter 1**

**An Overview of
the Administrative
Tools Folder**

Setting the event log properties

The event logs have some properties you can set. Most importantly, you can enable or disable many of the logs. You can also determine how much space the log can use on the hard drive, the location of the log on disk, and the method it uses to get rid of old messages to make space for new messages. To set event log properties, right-click the event log and choose Properties from the context menu. You see the Log Properties dialog box, as shown in Figure 1-10.

Notice that the Log Properties dialog box contains properties similar to those you'd find for a file. For example, you can determine the current log file size and find out when it was last modified. These statistics can help you determine how the system is using the log and whether you even need to keep it active. (Fewer logs use fewer system resources.)

The three methods you can use to work with logs that have too many event messages is to overwrite the older messages, create a log archive, or manually clear the log. When you choose to create an archive, the system renames the current log and creates a new one every time the old log becomes too full. Unless you're careful, this setting can quickly fill your hard drive with log archives. The manual method isn't a good idea either because it retains all the old log entries and doesn't let in any new entries after the log reaches its full size. Any new log entries end up in the bit bucket. The default option of over-writing old log entries provides the best mix of efficient hard drive usage and ensuring that the event log always functions as intended.

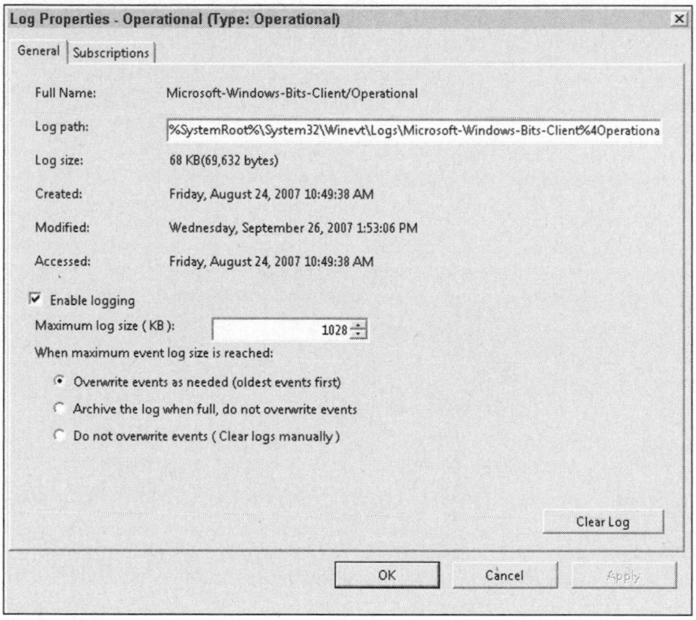

Log Properties - Operational (Type: Operational)

General | Subscriptions

Full Name: Microsoft-Windows-Bits-Client/Operational

Log path: %SystemRoot%\System32\Winevt\Logs\Microsoft-Windows-Bits-Client%4Operationa

Log size: 68 KB(69,632 bytes)

Created: Friday, August 24, 2007 10:49:38 AM

Modified: Wednesday, September 26, 2007 1:53:06 PM

Accessed: Friday, August 24, 2007 10:49:38 AM

☑ Enable logging

Maximum log size (KB): 1028

When maximum event log size is reached:

◉ Overwrite events as needed (oldest events first)

○ Archive the log when full, do not overwrite events

○ Do not overwrite events (Clear logs manually)

Clear Log

OK   Cancel   Apply

Figure 1-10:
Set event
log
properties
to match
your
organiza-
tion's
require-
ments.

When you click Clear Log, you see an Event Viewer dialog box. Event Viewer gives you the opportunity to archive the existing log. Click Save and Clear, and you see the Save As dialog box, where you can type the name of an archive file. Click Save to complete the action. Click Clear, and Event Viewer clears the log without saving the current log contents. You can't save just part of the log — it's an all-or-nothing proposition. Click Cancel whenever you choose not to clear the log after all.

Services

Services are an essential part of Windows. They're applications that monitor the system and run in the background. Most of the Windows features you take for granted are services. Consequently, the services running on your system partially determine the functionality your system provides. The Services console, shown in Figure 1-11, helps you configure and manage the services on your system.

Figure 1-11 shows the default view, which relies on the Extended tab. When you choose a service, the left side of the display shows the service description and a list of tasks you can perform with the service, such as starting or stopping it. Because the description already appears on the display, you can save a little screen real estate by right-clicking the Services entry and choosing View⇨Add/Remove Columns. You see the Add/Remove Columns dialog box, such as the one shown in Figure 1-12. Highlight the Description entry and click Remove so that the dialog box appears, as shown in Figure 1-12. Click OK. The display is now optimized for use with the Extended tab.

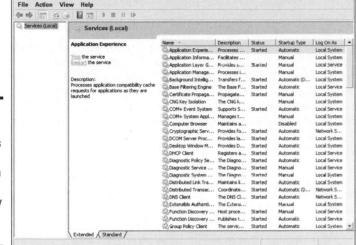

Figure 1-11: Configure the services on your system for a balance of functionality and efficiency.

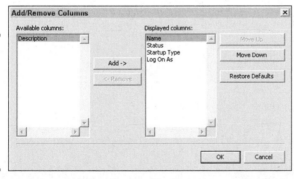

Figure 1-12: Remove the Description column when you plan to use Extended view.

As with any other application, a service consumes system resources. The service requires processing time and memory as a minimum, and may require hard drive space as well. A service may need other resources, depending on the job it performs. For example, a service designed to help you download files from the Internet requires network bandwidth. Consequently, you must balance the need for the services that a service provides and the resources it uses. In some cases, you may choose to keep a service in the stopped state when you're not using it and start it only when you need to perform a particular task.

Understanding the Services console display

A service can provide functionality only when started. The Status column of the Services console tells you the started state of the service. If you want to start a service, click Start. When you suspect that a service isn't working as it should, you can often correct the problem by clicking Restart. This action stops the service and starts it again, to clear up any problems with corrupted memory.

The Startup Type column tells you whether the service starts automatically. You very likely see many services that say they start manually, yet the Status column shows Started, despite the fact that you didn't start them. A manual startup simply means that the operating system must start the service based on a request rather than assume that the operating system needs the service at all times. Sometimes you see a service stop after a short interval because the operating system needs it for only a short time. The only time a service can't start is when you disable it.

The final column, Log On As, determines the account the service uses to log on to the system. Just like you, the service can't perform any work until after it has logged on. In some cases, the system can refuse to log the service on, and the service can't start for that reason. The account that the service uses determines the rights it has. The Local System account, which is the most common account, indicates that the service will interact with only the local system. The Network Service account, the next most commonly used account, assumes that the service will also perform tasks on the network. You can read more about which account to use for a particular service in the Services and Service Accounts Security Planning Guide at `http://www.microsoft.com/technet/security/guidance/serversecurity/serviceaccount/default.mspx`.

Configuring service properties

In most cases, starting and stopping services as needed is all you need to do with the Services console. However, in some cases, you need to configure the service or view additional information about it. To see the properties for a service, right-click the service entry and choose Properties from the context menu. In most cases, you see a service Properties dialog box, such as the one shown in Figure 1-13.

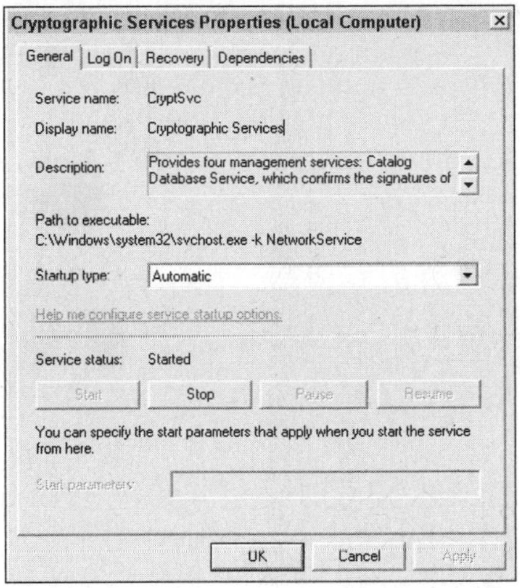

Figure 1-13:
Use the Properties dialog box to configure and manage the service.

The General tab of the service Properties dialog box, shown in Figure 1-13, lets you perform tasks such as starting and stopping the service. You can also set the startup type by using the options in the Startup Type field. Setting a service to start manually may help you save system resources by forcing the operating system to start the service only when needed. However, changing the setting can also cause the system to act strangely or not provide functionality that you require to perform useful work. Disabling a service can cause all kinds of problems if you disable something the system requires. Notice that Figure 1-13 also shows the executable file used for the service. This information comes in handy if the service's application file ever becomes corrupted.

The Log On tab contains the login information for the service. If you want to use the local system account, all you need to do is select the Local System Account entry. Otherwise, you need to select the This Account option, type a name and password, and then configure the password. If you don't choose an account that has the rights needed to perform a task, the service may not start or may not work correctly when it does start.

The Recovery tab, shown in Figure 1-14, determines how the system recovers when a service fails to start. It also takes these actions in some cases when the service fails for other reasons. You can define different actions for the first and second errors and for subsequent errors. The normal default action is to restart the service after the first failure. Restarting the service means stopping it (if it's currently in a started state) and starting the service again.

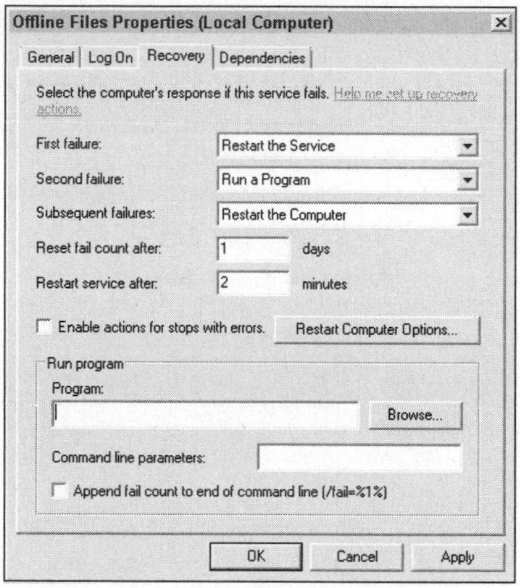

Figure 1-14:
Define
recovery
options for
the service
that match
your
corporate
policy.

It's also possible to run a program or restart the computer when a service fails. If you choose to run a program, you must provide the program name and any command line arguments it requires. Although you can run any program with a command line interface, using a non-GUI command or utility works best because you can't ensure that anyone will see the server display to work with a GUI application.

In rare cases, when you know that the system can't work without the service, you may choose to restart the server. In this case, you can optionally choose to send to all computers on the network a message telling everyone that the server is restarting. Simply click Restart Computer Options and type a message in the Restart Computer Options dialog box. This dialog box also lets you specify the length of time before the server restarts. A longer interval gives users time to close any data files they opened.

The Recovery tab contains two additional fields. The Reset Fail Count After field determines how long the system waits to reset the fail count. The system must reset this number at some point, or else the service would always have failures and use only the Subsequent Failures action. The Restart Service After field controls how long the system waits before it tries to restart the service. The interval is important because sometimes you have to wait for the server to accomplish other tasks before making the attempt. For example, if this service relies on another service that also failed, you must wait for the other service to restart before restarting this one.

Services depend on other services, as shown in Figure 1-15. Whenever you decide to stop a service, set it for manual start, or even disable it, you must consider the consequences for other services. The Dependencies tab shows (in the top list) which services the current service is required to run and (in the bottom list) the services that rely on this service. You can expand the lists to see entire hierarchies, as shown in the figure. The Dependencies tab is the place to look when you have any questions about the effect of a configuration decision.

Figure 1-15: Check dependencies before you make a configuration decision.

System Configuration

The System Configuration console shown in Figure 1-16 helps you create diagnostic startup scenarios. For example, when you want to determine whether a particular application is stopping the operating system from booting properly, you can disable the application and restart the machine to see the results. The System Configuration console provides a few standard alternative startup scenarios, but for the most part, you use specific troubleshooting steps, such as disabling a service. The following sections tell you more about this diagnostic aid.

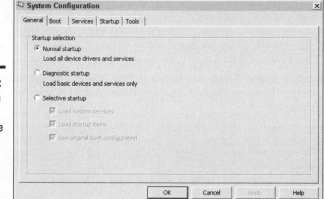

Figure 1-16:
The System Configuration console helps you create diagnostic startups.

Working with the general options

The General tab, shown in Figure 1-16, tells you the status of the system configuration and provides several standard diagnostic starts. When you see that the Normal Startup option is checked, you know that everything is normal — none of the options on any of the tabs is changed from its normal state.

The Diagnostic Startup option starts the system in what amounts to Safe Mode. Windows loads only the basic drivers and services that it must have to run. None of the startup applications runs either, which means that your system is relatively clean.

The Selective Startup option lets you choose which features (such as services and startup applications) Windows loads as part of the startup process. In addition, you can choose which INI files Windows processes as part of the startup process. For example, you can choose not to load the startup options so that you have a fully functional system, but you haven't loaded any of the extra utilities that may cause problems. The System Configuration console also selects this option when you modify any of the settings on the other tabs.

Working with the boot options

The Boot tab, shown in Figure 1-17, provides a number of boot options. You can set these options in a number of ways. For example, you could use the BCDEdit utility, described in the "Configuring the Startup Options with BCDEdit" section of Book I, Chapter 4 to perform the same tasks. All this tab does is provide a GUI front end for tasks you can perform in other places.

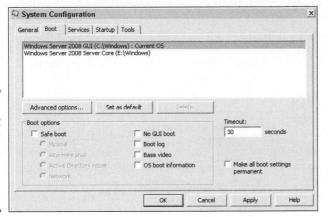

**Book III
Chapter 1**

An Overview of
the Administrative
Tools Folder

Figure 1-17:
Use the boot
options to
change the
way your
system
starts.

It's important to note that the System Configuration console doesn't provide
you with information about the Windows Legacy OS Loader section of the
boot configuration. The lack of information means that you can make changes
in System Configuration that won't account for your legacy Windows system
when you have a multiboot system. Use the options provided with the System
Configuration console with care in this situation. If you have a complex boot
configuration and need to modify it relatively often, you may want to obtain a
third-party utility, such as Vista Boot Pro (`http://www.pro-networks.
org/vistabootpro/`), to perform the task.

Configuring the services

The Services tab contains a list of all services on your system, along with the
vendors that created the services, and you see a list of the current state of
the services. This tab makes it possible to disable the service temporarily
for testing purposes. Simply clear the check next to the service, and it won't
start the next time you start the machine.

Working with the startup options

The Startup tab displays a list of all the applications that start when Windows
starts. The columns on this tab tell you the application vendor, the command
used to start the application, and the application's startup instruction location
(such as the Startup folder or a key within the registry). As with services,
you can disable a particular startup application by removing the check mark
next to its entry.

You can use the Startup tab for another purpose. Most viruses and adware don't bother to hide their entries on this tab. In fact, they can't unless they have rootkit potential. It's possible to use this list to locate every extra program that's running on your system and verify that it's a good application. Although this tab doesn't provide the resources to remove the virus or adware, it provides a clue that you can use to start researching a solution.

Using the tools

The Tools tab, shown in Figure 1-18, contains a number of interesting tools you can use to find out more about your system or perform certain configuration tasks. One of the more interesting features on this tab is a tool that helps you disable the User Account Control (UAC). You can use this tool to determine whether the UAC is causing an application to malfunction or the system to perform decreased functionality.

To use a particular tool, highlight its entry and click Launch. The tool starts automatically, using whichever default configuration Microsoft has provided.

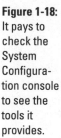

Figure 1-18:
It pays to check the System Configuration console to see the tools it provides.

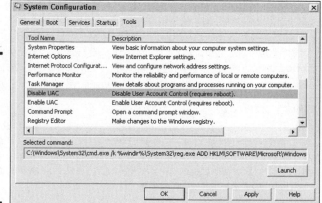

The Selected Command field is interesting because it can provide you with clues about how Windows performs certain tasks. For example, when you enable or disable the UAC, you're using the Reg.EXE program to perform the task. This program lets you change registry settings from the command line rather than use Registry Editor.

Installing and Using the Remote Server Administration Tools

The Remote Server Administration Tools feature, shown in Figure 1-19, helps you administer another server from the current location. The important issue to consider is that this feature makes it possible to administer other systems from the local server, not from a client machine. Of course, you can always use tools such as Remote Desktop (see the "Working with Remote Desktop" section of Book III, Chapter 5 for details) to perform remote administration using a console.

You install this feature as you would install any other feature on Windows Server 2008. After installation, you find additional consoles in the Administrative Tools folder of the Control Panel, unless the required functionality was already installed on your server. However, the most important change is that you can now work with other servers using those consoles.

In most cases, you connect to another server by right-clicking the root node of the console and choosing Connect To Another Server from the context menu. The terminology that the menu option uses varies by console. For example, when you open the WINS console, you choose the Add Server option instead. In all cases, you see a dialog box where you can provide the name of a remote computer to manage.

Figure 1-19:
Remote Server Administration Tools provide remote access to other servers.

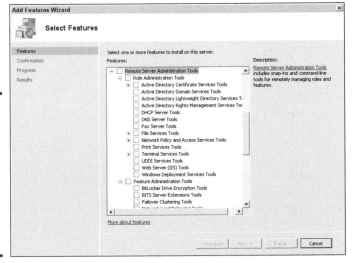

Chapter 2: Setting Group Policies

In This Chapter

✔ Discovering how policies work

✔ Opening the Group Policy Editor console

✔ Configuring the computer policies

✔ Configuring the user policies

✔ Working with the User Access Control (UAC) feature

✔ Determining the net effect of policies

*P*olicies are one of the bases for configuration in Windows Server 2008. A *policy* is a rule that tells the operating system how it can interact with callers or perform certain tasks. For example, you can tell the operating system that only administrators can change the time and date settings, or you can choose to create a policy that says users don't have to press Ctrl+Alt+Delete when they first start the system. A policy in Windows changes, to an extent, the way that the operating system works.

When a company has a large number of machines, it isn't reasonable to configure those machines one at a time. In most cases, a company will use a group policy instead. A *group policy* is a policy that exists on the server and affects all systems that use the network associated with that server. As with a policy, a group policy is simply a rule, but it has a broader effect on users.

This chapter discusses how you can use group policies to perform all kinds of configuration tasks on your network. Using group policies is a good way to control what users can do with their systems and apply that rule evenly for everyone. (Uneven application is a source of complaint for many users.) In addition, using a group policy makes it considerably easier to make changes because you have to make the change in one place only. In short, this chapter isn't just about controlling access or configuring your copy of Windows Server 2008; it's also about saving you time.

Understanding How Policies Work

As previously mentioned, a policy is simply a rule that you apply to users on the network. The Local Security Policy console, shown in Figure 2-1, confines itself to security and some application management. For example, you can choose to enable or disable the Administrator or Guest accounts. You can also configure the Windows Firewall with Advanced Security options. All these policies affect the local machine, and you configure them using the Local Security Policy console, which appears in the Administrative Tools folder of the Control Panel. (See Book III, Chapter 1 for details on the Administrative Tools folder.)

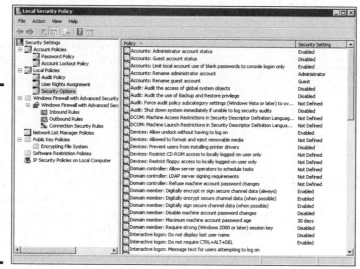

Figure 2-1:
Local security policies often revolve around security or application configuration.

Fortunately, you can set policies at various levels. It's also possible to set local security policies on the server that affect just that server. However, these policies also tend to affect anyone who logs in to the server because they control the tasks the server can perform. Consequently, even if you're in a workgroup, you can set policies at multiple levels by configuring them in the right place.

Group policies affect the network as a whole. When a client logs in to the server, it downloads the group policies supplied by the server. A group policy always overrides a local policy. When a group policy disallows an activity, the client won't allow the activity even if the local policy allows it. However, a local policy is still effective when the group policy isn't configured. In short, when the server doesn't have a policy, the client looks for a policy locally.

The combination of the various group and local policies has a cumulative effect. This Resultant Set of Policy (RSoP) determines what the user can do. In some cases, you may not even know what the RSoP is when you have multiple administrators working on a network and a few users with sticky fingers trying to gain rights they shouldn't have. Fortunately, Microsoft also provides a Resultant Set of Policy console you can use to determine the actual rights a user has. You can read more about this console in the "Viewing the Resultant Set of Policy (RSoP)" section of this chapter.

Starting the Group Policy Editor

The Group Policy Editor is different from the Local Policy Editor, which you can see in the Administrative Tools folder. Microsoft hides this editor from view, partly because not everyone needs access to this powerful tool and partly because those who need it will know where to find it (the same strategy the company uses for other tools, such as the Registry Editor). Use the following steps to start the Group Policy Editor:

1. **Choose Start⇨Run.**

You see the Run dialog box.

2. **Type** GPEdit.MSC **in the Open field and click OK.**

Windows starts the Group Policy Editor, shown in Figure 2-2. The precise title of this console can vary based on where you open the editor and which features you have installed on your server.

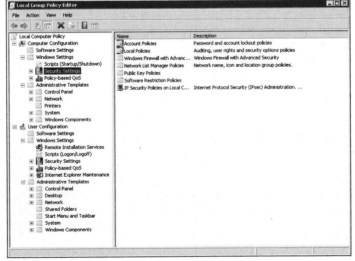

Figure 2-2:
The Group Policy Editor provides significantly more functionality than the Local Policy Editor.

When you compare Figures 2-1 and 2-2, you notice that the Group Policy Editor offers considerably more functionality. Rather than focus on just the individual user settings, you can also change computer settings. In addition, you can use the administrator templates to configure more than just security. For example, you can choose to deny users access to the Control Panel so that they can't make unfortunate changes to the system.

Performing Computer Management

The computer policies supported by the Group Policy Editor affect the system as a whole rather than individual users. Consequently, when you want to adjust the settings for everyone, you make the change in the Computer Configuration folder rather than in the User Configuration folder. The computer management policies fall into three major areas: software settings, windows settings, and administrative templates. This chapter doesn't describe every possible policy that you can set in these folders, but it does provide an overview of the changes you can make in the following sections.

Modifying computer Software Settings

The Computer Configuration\Software Settings folder contains the settings you use to control specific applications. These settings affect the computer system, such as the USB port to obtain information from an external source or the security when allowing people to log in to the application. When you first set up your Windows Server 2008 configuration, this folder won't contain any settings. A software vendor must provide special code with the application to use this configuration technique. Make sure that you check your vendor documentation for information on making configuration changes using the entries in this folder.

Modifying computer Windows Settings

When you select the Computer Configuration\Windows Settings folder, you see a view that looks very much like the Local Security Policy console, as shown in Figure 2-3. In fact, the view is very much the same, and you perform configuration tasks using the same techniques as you would in the Local Security Policy Editor console.

You see two additional entries. The first is Scripts, and the second is Policy-Based QoS (Quality of Service). When you select this folder, you see options for setting a startup or shutdown script. Double-click either of the entries, and you see a dialog box like the one shown in Figure 2-4, where you can enter the names of scripts to run.

The scripts can perform any task you desire. You could install new software or perform other jobs. The idea is that the scripts determine which events happen when you start or shut down the computer system.

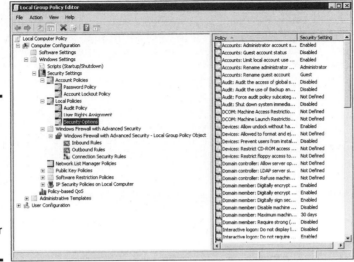

Figure 2-3:
The Windows Settings folder looks much like the Local Security Policy Editor console.

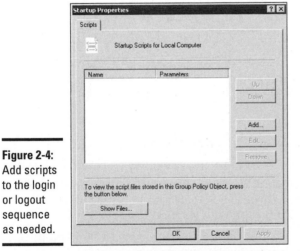

Figure 2-4:
Add scripts to the login or logout sequence as needed.

The Policy-Based QoS (Quality of Service) folder contains policies that determine how your server uses resources. For example, you may decide that you want a particular application to have a certain amount of network bandwidth so that it doesn't grab all the available bandwidth. You make entries in this folder using a wizard. The following steps describe this process:

1. **Right-click the Policy-Based QoS folder and choose Create New Policy from the context menu.**

You see the Policy-Based QoS Wizard, shown in Figure 2-5. This dialog box contains the name of the policy, the Differentiated Services Code Point (DSCP) value, and the level of throttling you want to employ. The DSCP value is a number attached to the Internet Protocol (IP) packet that determines which level of service it obtains from all the nodes that pass the packet on the network. You can read more about the DSCP at `http://technet2.microsoft.com/windowsserver/en/library/ d818f74b-de00-4590-a44f-56fce1b06f3c1033.mspx`. The Throttle Rate field defines the maximum amount of bandwidth the application can use to transfer data from the server to other nodes on the network. An application can always use less than the maximum amount.

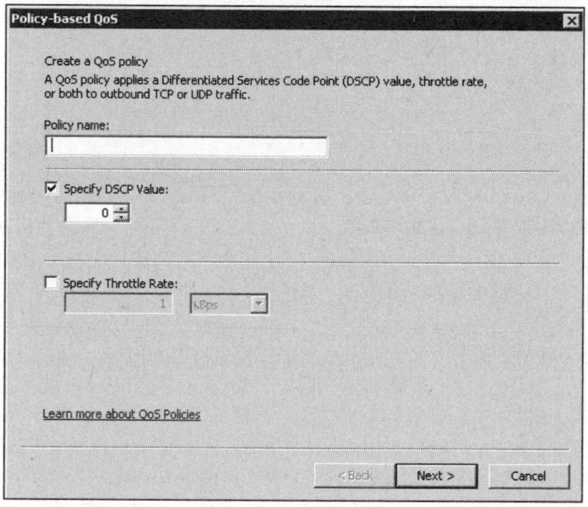

Figure 2-5:
Determine
the QoS
required for
a particular
application.

2. **Type, at minimum, a name for the policy. Optionally, you can define either a DSCP value, a throttle level, or both to provide a Quality of Service (QoS) measure for the policy. Click Next.**

   The Policy-Based QoS Wizard asks you whether this policy should apply to all applications or to a particular application.

3. **Choose an application option. When you choose the Only Applications with This Executable Name option, you must also provide the name of the executable. Click Next.**

   The Policy-Based QoS Wizard asks that you define the incoming (source) and outgoing (destination) IP address to use with this policy, as shown in Figure 2-6. You may also choose to apply the policy to all IP addresses. If an application uses multiple IP addresses to perform its work and you need to throttle only one of them, you can choose an individual IP address and let the other address work as normal.

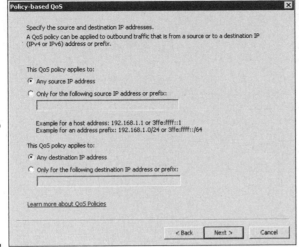

Figure 2-6:
Choose the incoming and outgoing IP address values.

4. **Choose an IP address option for both the incoming (source) and out-going (destination) entries. If you choose to work with specific IP addresses, you must type a valid Internet Protocol version 4 (IPv4) or Internet Protocol version 6 (IPv6) address. Click Next.**

The Policy-Based QoS Wizard asks that you define the protocol used to transport the data, as shown in Figure 2-7. You can choose the Transaction Control Protocol (TCP) or User Datagram Protocol (UDP) or both. This dialog box also lets you type a single port or a port range to use for the policy. Make sure to separate the two port numbers with a colon, such as 143:145. As with the IP address values, you can choose individual incoming (source) and outgoing (destination) values.

5. **Click Finish.**

Windows creates the policy for you based on the input you provided. You can edit this policy at any time by right-clicking the policy entry and choosing Edit Existing Policy from the context menu.

Using computer Administrative Templates

The Computer Configuration\Administrative Templates folder contains entries that match Windows Server 2008 features, as shown in Figure 2-8. You configure the usage of a particular feature by defining a policy for that feature. However, it's not just an on or off kind of configuration. For example, the Domain Name System (DNS) policies, shown in Figure 2-8, control everything from the DNS suffix to the use of dynamic updates.

**Book III
Chapter 2**

**Setting Group
Policies**

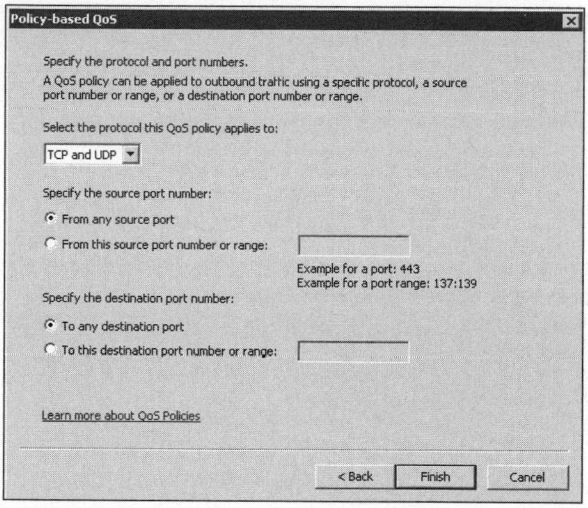

Figure 2-7:
Choose the incoming and outgoing TCP or UDP port values.

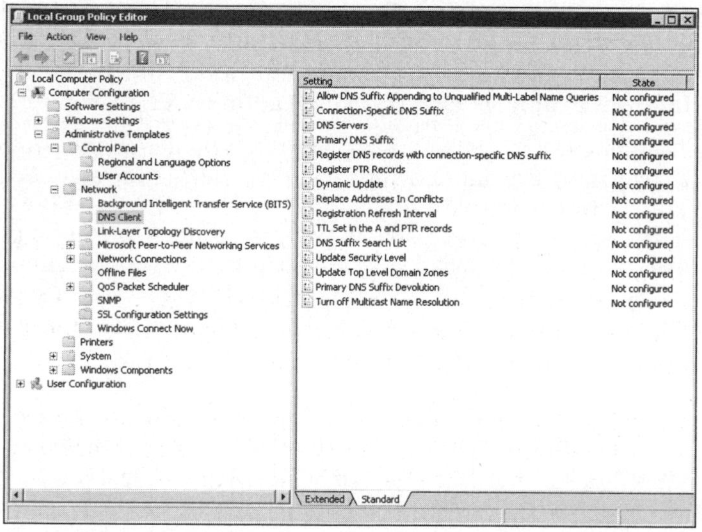

Figure 2-8:
Polices can affect many aspects of a single Windows feature.

Whenever you want to define a policy, double-click its entry. You see a dialog box like the one shown in Figure 2-9. Most of the dialog boxes offer similar features. You can enable, disable, or not configure a particular policy. When a policy is enabled, you usually have other configuration choices to make. In this case, you can provide the DNS suffix for the server.

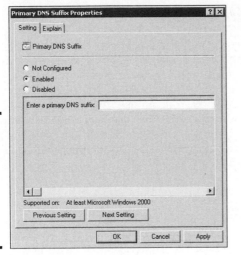

Figure 2-9:
Configure
policies for
particular
Windows
features
based on
your needs.

You should pay special attention to one of the features in this dialog box. Notice that the bottom of the dialog box contains an indicator of the operating system functionality for a policy. Not every policy works with every version of Windows. In this case, you must have Windows 2000 or greater installed to use the policy. Some policies go the other way. For example, the Connection-Specific DNS Suffix policy applies only to Windows XP, and you may find policies that affect only older versions of Windows.

The Group Policy Editor doesn't force you to open and close the dialog boxes to choose another policy. Click Previous Setting to see the previous policy, and Next Setting to see the next policy. The Group Policy Editor automatically saves any changes you make when you move from one policy to the next, so you don't need to worry about losing changes.

Unlike many parts of Windows, the Group Policy Editor provides help for each of the settings. Simply select the Explain tab to learn more about a particular policy. Even though the entry doesn't provide encyclopedic coverage of the setting, you usually learn enough to know whether you want to change the setting.

It's important to remember that these settings affect the machine as a whole. You can see precisely the same folder in the User Configuration folder and it will have different configuration settings in it. Consequently, if you don't see a setting in the Computer Configuration folder that you expected to find, look in the User Configuration folder as well.

Performing User Configuration

Many policies affect only the individual user. For example, administrators need more rights than standard users do, so configuring them the same won't work. The User Configuration folder contains settings that affect individual users, such as the ability to access the Control Panel or run an application using the Run dialog box. You can use these settings to control just about every aspect of the native Windows configuration that affects the individual user. As with the Computer Configuration folder, you find three major folders for configuring user settings: Software Settings, Windows Settings, and Administrative Templates. The following sections describe each of these folders.

Modifying user Software Settings

The User Configuration\Software Settings folder contains the settings you use to control specific applications. These settings affect individual users, such as the ability to use particular features based on role or the availability of certain kinds of data. When you first set up your Windows Server 2008 configuration, this folder won't contain any settings. A software vendor must provide special code with the application to use this configuration technique. Make sure to check your vendor documentation for information on making configuration changes using the entries in this folder.

Modifying user Windows Settings

The User Configuration\Windows Settings folder works very much like its counterpart in the Computer Configuration folder. Of course, all policies in this folder affect the individual user and not the computer as a whole. However, as shown in Figure 2-10, you get a couple of additional folders.

Figure 2-10:
The user configuration settings for the Windows Settings folder include additional policies.

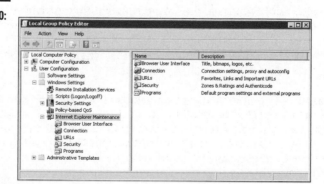

The Remote Installation Services folder contains a single entry: Choice Options. When you double-click this entry, you see the Choice Options Properties dialog box, shown in Figure 2-11. These settings control what the user can do when installing an application. For example, you may not want users to perform a custom setup, so you can disable that feature.

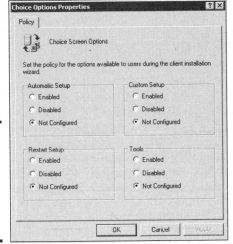

Figure 2-11: You can configure the user's application installation options.

Theoretically, users will have to install applications using the basic settings you provide. In some cases, savvy users can bypass these restrictions using any number of techniques, so you shouldn't count on this particular feature to provide airtight installation security.

The Internet Explorer Maintenance folder (refer to Figure 2-10) contains a number of interesting policies that affect the appearance and configuration of Internet Explorer. These settings affect only appearance and configuration — you find additional settings in the Administrative Templates folder. Consequently, as with many other Group Policy Editor policies, if you don't see the setting you need, look in another area for it because the setting probably exists.

You find a number of interesting settings in the Internet Explorer Maintenance folder. For example, look in the Connection folder and you find a User Agent String policy. You can use this policy to define the user agent string that the browser sends to remote sites. This feature can be helpful in hiding the browser's identity and could potentially reduce attacks meant specifically for Internet Explorer.

Book III
Chapter 2

Setting Group
Policies

It's also possible to use the policies in this folder to enforce both security and privacy settings, which will make it harder still for remote sites to burden the user with unwanted viruses and adware. Unfortunately, as well as these features work, a user will usually find a way to bypass them and get the virus or adware on their system anyway, so you must always combine the policy settings you make with training and vigilance. You have to assume that someone will find a way to bypass the security features you put in place.

Using user Administrative Templates

The User Configuration\Administrative Templates folder contains templates you can use to configure user access to Windows features. You interact with this folder using the same approach that you would use for the Computer Configuration\Administrative Templates folder. The only difference is the entries you see in this folder. For example, rather than set languages, you can specify how the user interacts with the Add or Remove Programs applet (the Programs and Features applet in Windows Server 2008). As with the other administrative templates, these templates often use names of features that appear in older versions of Windows, so you need to use the old names, rather than the new names, when you want to configure a policy.

Disabling UAC on the Server

You have several means at your disposal for controlling the UAC feature on your server. The first technique is to use the tools provided with the System Configuration console. This technique appears in the "Using the tools" section of Book III, Chapter 1. The problem with using the tool is that you don't have control over how the system enables or disables UAC. Consequently, this first approach may not do what you want, which is why you need the second approach described in this chapter.

The UAC actually relies on a number of policies — it isn't a simple on/off switch, as you might expect. All these policies are located in the `Computer Configuration\Windows Settings\Security Settings\Local Policies\Security Options` folder. You find them at the bottom of the list of options, and they all begin with the words *User Account Control*.

The policies include everything from running applications in secure locations to the method used to elevate permissions. In fact, you'll find that UAC provides separate policies for administrators and standard users, so you can literally turn off UAC for administrators while keeping it in place for standard users.

Interestingly enough, you can also make UAC even more demanding than the default setup. For example, you can tell UAC that it should elevate permissions only for applications that are properly signed and validated, which means that very few of your applications will run because most of them are neither signed nor validated. You can also place the administrator account into Admin Approval mode, which means that you spend most of your time telling UAC that it's okay to perform a task.

Viewing the Resultant Set of Policy (RSoP)

The Resultant Set of Policy console shows the effects of all policy decisions you make regarding Windows, no matter where you make those policy settings. To open this console, you use the Run dialog box just as you would for the Group Policy Editor. However, rather than type **GPEdit.MSC** in the Open field, you type **RSOP.MSC** instead. You see the window shown in Figure 2-12.

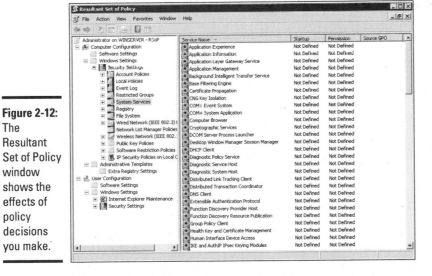

Figure 2-12: The Resultant Set of Policy window shows the effects of policy decisions you make.

The overall effect is the same as the Group Policy Editor. Any changes you make in any of the policy editors or through other means, such as the Services console or Windows Explorer, appear in the Resultant Set of Policy console. What you see is an overall view of every security policy in place on your system.

Unlike with the Group Policy Editor, you can't make any changes to policies in the Resultant Set of Policy console. The reason for this seemingly absurd restriction is that the Resultant Set of Policy console wouldn't know where to make the policy changes. In many cases, the console could make the policy change at several levels, and it would be impossible to make a choice. Rather than make things easier to understand, the Resultant Set of Policy console would actually end up making them harder.

Notice that the Resultant Set of Policy console also displays a number of extra folders that don't appear in the Group Policy Editor. These other folders come from information you define in other places. For example, you define the entries in the Services folder as part of the Services console. Likewise, the Registry folder contains policies that you make as part of working with the Registry Editor. In sum, the information you see in the Resultant Set of Policy console truly comes from every location on your system so that you can see the changes in one place.

Chapter 3: Configuring the Registry

In This Chapter

✓ Working with the Registry Editor

✓ Importing and exporting registry elements

✓ Locating a registry element

✓ Considering the registry data types

✓ Working with registry hives

✓ Configuring registry security

The registry is possibly the most complex and frustrating part of Windows. You have to treat this part of Windows with extreme caution because an errant entry can keep your system from booting. On the other hand, you can't ignore it either. All too often, you find a Microsoft Knowledge Base article or a third-party requirement for modifying the registry by hand. Of course, they all advise you to make a backup of the registry, without really telling you how to perform that task. (You'll find the instructions in the "Performing a registry backup" section of this chapter.) The registry has become so complex and fragile that Microsoft is constantly looking for new ways not to use it, and then failing. The latest method is to use a configuration file attached specifically to managed applications that rely on the .NET Framework. However, you'll find that the .NET Framework also supports a wealth of methods for interacting with the registry anyway.

In this chapter, you discover that the registry is huge and that you need ways to search it efficiently. Unfortunately, the registry provides only paltry methods to perform the task that often prove time-consuming at best and fruitless at worst. Even so, there are ways to make your searches for information reasonably effective, and this chapter discusses them.

The registry contains many kinds of data, and you need to know how to work with them. Some data types (a kind of data) are quite easy to work with. You won't find it hard to work with strings, in most cases, but other data types, such as double words (DWORDs), may prove difficult.

Even though the Registry Editor doesn't make it apparent, the registry isn't found in a single file. You find bits and pieces of the registry all over your hard drive. In fact, you can load and unload some of these bits and pieces as needed to edit the settings of other people who use the same machine as you do. It's also possible to connect to other machines and edit their registries from a remote location.

Finally, the registry provides security, and you may find a need to use it. As more organizations face adware, viruses, and generally nasty software from unknown locations, securing the registry becomes more important. You may be surprised to learn that the registry has the same kind of security as the files on your hard drive. Consequently, there isn't a good reason for someone to attack your registry unknowingly with the proper security in place. Fortunately, Microsoft has taken steps to secure the registry in Windows Server 2008.

Starting the Registry Editor

Like many of the more dangerous tools that Microsoft provides as part of Windows, the Registry Editor doesn't appear in the Start menu. It's another one of those utilities that you need to know about in order to access it. To start the Registry Editor, choose Start⇨Run to display the Run dialog box. Type **RegEdit** in the Open field and click OK. You see the Registry Editor, as shown in Figure 3-1.

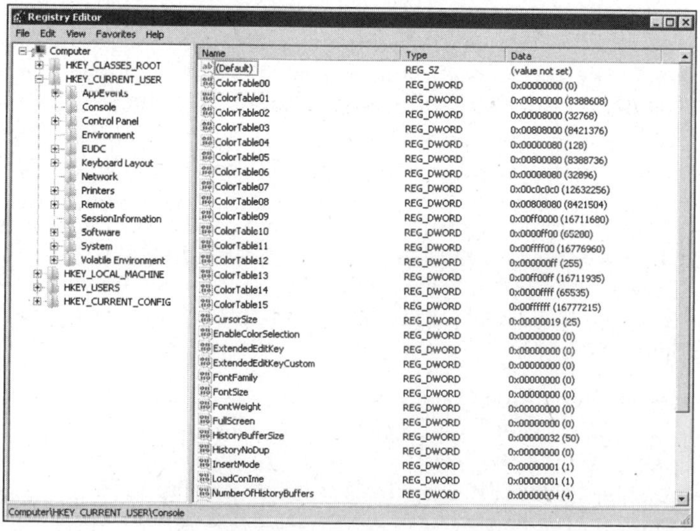

Figure 3-1:
The Registry Editor is a tool that provides access to the registry.

As you can see, the Registry Editor provides access to the entire registry database. The HKEY elements on the left side are *hives,* and the entries below these elements are *keys.* Values for the selected hive or key appear in the right-hand pane, and the registry supports a number of value data types. The remaining sections of this chapter describe all these elements in detail. For now, all you really need to know is that they exist and that you use them to make modifications to the registry.

Importing and Exporting Registry Elements

Importing and exporting registry elements lets you save and restore the registry on your system as needed. For example, you may want to save a section of the registry before you make changes to it. You can also use this approach, with care, to add registry entries to other systems or obtain registry entries from other systems for the current registry. Many application setups are simplified when you save the registry settings from a configured machine, modify the installation drive in the resulting file as needed, and restore the registry settings to a second machine.

Working with the registry is always problematic. It contains a great deal of fragile information. Even the act of moving data from one machine to another can backfire when the setup of the two machines differs. For example, if the two machines use different boot drives, some registry entries will fail to work when you move them from one machine to another. Consequently, you must always make a backup of the registry before you perform any activity on it. The following sections describe how to work with the registry using the Registry Editor.

Performing a registry backup

This section also provides the best way to back up your registry. Many backup applications claim to back up the registry, but they may not do the job well or successfully. This manual technique, while time-consuming, always works, and guarantees that you can restore your system after an accident. Use the following steps to perform the backup:

1. **Highlight the Computer entry at the beginning of the registry (refer to Figure 3-1).**

2. **Choose File⇨Export.**

The Registry Editor displays the Export Registry File dialog box, as shown in Figure 3-2. Notice that the All option is selected in the Export Range group. If you don't see All selected, you didn't choose the Computer entry in Step 1, and you need to press Cancel now. Begin again at Step 1.

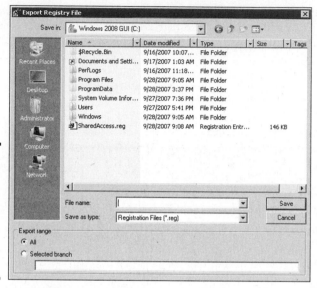

Figure 3-2:
The Export
Registry File
dialog box
contains
settings for
saving the
registry.

3. **Type a name for the file you want to use to save the registry in the File Name field.**

   Choose a name that's easy to remember. Make sure that you identify the user associated with the registry save because the HKEY_CURRENT_USER hive varies by user. Consequently, `Registry Save for John 03-01-2008.REG` is a useful filename, and `RegSave.REG` isn't.

4. **Click Save.**

   The Registry Editor saves the file to disk. Depending on your system characteristics and the size of the registry, you may notice a slight delay while the Registry Editor creates the file. Make sure that the Registry Editor completes the task (you see the original window reappear) before you do anything else.

You now have a complete copy of the registry, so you can make any changes needed to the registry and test them out. Because Windows continually makes changes to the registry, it's important to create backups whenever you want to make changes. Don't rely on an old backup of the registry because it could cause damage to your system by restoring old data. It's also important to create a copy of the registry before you perform a backup, so the registry file can appear as part of your backup. In most cases, you need this registry file to restore your applications to full functionality.

If you ever need to restore the entire registry, simply double-click the registry file you created in Windows Explorer. You can also type the name of the registry file at the command prompt and press Enter. In either case, the Registry Editor will display a warning message about merging the file with the existing registry. Click Yes to restore the backup you made and reboot the machine.

Working with branches

In many cases, you don't need to make a complete backup of the registry to create a useful file. Sometimes all you really need is to back up a particular registry branch. Whenever you find a Microsoft Knowledge Base article that asks you to edit the registry, make sure that you make a copy of the affected registry branch before you perform the changes. If you find the changes don't work, you can always double-click the file you created to restore the original settings on your machine.

Saving branches has other purposes. For example, you may find some application settings you want to move from one machine to another. Some applications provide a method of exporting these settings, and you should always use the application feature when provided. However, when the application doesn't provide the feature, you can usually locate the application settings in the registry. Applications normally store registry settings in three areas:

✦ First, you find file associations in the HKEY_CLASSES_ROOT hive. Don't attempt to re-create these settings on a second machine because you won't normally find all the required entries, and even if you do, the entries are probably specific to the first machine. Install the application on the second machine first to create the HKEY_CLASSES_ROOT entries, but don't start the application after installation.

✦ Second, you find the user-specific settings in the HKEY_CURRENT_USER\ Software key under the vendor or application name. For example, if you install Office, you find the settings for it in the HKEY_CURRENT_USER\ Software\Microsoft key because Office is made by Microsoft. Make sure to drill down into the particular Office key you need before exporting the data.

✦ Third, you find the global application settings (those used by everyone) in the HKEY_LOCAL_MACHINE\SOFTWARE key. As with the user settings, you need to drill down into the vendor and then the application keys to locate the precise information you need.

Make sure that you know where every piece of data you want to save is located in the registry before you begin saving it. You may need to create multiple files for the data — one for each branch that you want to save. Use a distinct filename so that you don't confuse these registry settings with other registry settings you may have stored. For example, using `Office 2003 User Settings.REG` is a good choice. You may want to add the date as part of the filename, to ensure that you use the correct version when restoring registry settings. The following steps tell how to create a branch backup:

1. **Highlight the registry entry you want to save.**

   Make sure that you verify the branch against your list.

2. **Choose File⇨Export.**

   The Registry Editor displays the Export Registry File dialog box, as shown in Figure 3-2. Notice that the Selected Branch option is selected in the Export Range group. If you don't see Selected Branch selected, you didn't choose the right branch entry in Step 1 and you need to click Cancel now. Begin again at Step 1.

3. **Verify that the branch shown next to the Selected Branch option is the branch that you want to export.**

   If the branch is incorrect, click Cancel now. Begin again at Step 1.

4. **Type a name for the file you want to use to save the registry in the File Name field.**

   Choose a name that's easy to remember.

5. **Click Save.**

   The Registry Editor saves the file to disk. Make sure that the Registry Editor completes the task (you see the original window reappear) before you do anything else.

6. **Repeat Steps 1 through 5 for any remaining branches.**

You can restore the registry files on the current machine or another one by double-clicking them. The order you use doesn't matter. However, if a registry setup requires multiple files, such as when configuring an application, make sure to restore all the registry files before you attempt to use the application or Windows feature. When moving a registry file from one machine to another, make sure the registry file matches the target machine's setup by using the information in the "Modifying the REG files" section of this chapter.

Modifying the REG files

In most cases, you won't want to modify the REG files that the Registry Editor produces because doing so can cause errors within the registry file. If you try to restore the file later, you can introduce errors into your registry as well. When the errors become severe enough, you may find that you lose functionality or that your machine may not boot. In short, the REG file is complex and you want to treat it with the required care.

Unfortunately, you may find yourself in a situation that requires a certain amount of editing by hand, such as when you move application settings from one machine to another. Always make a backup of the registry file before you make any changes to it. If you make a mistake, you can always use the backup to start again.

One of the few settings changes you should consider making to a REG file is the boot, or installation, drive. The directory structure is probably the same because Microsoft has gone to great lengths to standardize it, but the boot, or installation, drive can change between machines. When this situation occurs, you can modify the drive within the REG file easily. The following steps tell you how to perform this task using Notepad:

1. **Right-click the REG file entry in Windows Explorer and choose Edit from the context menu.**

Never double-click the REG file because that action will merge it with the current registry. You see a copy of Notepad open with the REG file loaded, as shown in Figure 3-3. Notice that the top of the file tells you that the Registry Editor has created this file and that it includes the Registry Editor version number.

Figure 3-3:
REG files
are pure
text, so use
Notepad to
edit them.

2. **Choose Edit⇨Find.**

You see the Find dialog box.

3. **Type the boot drive of the source machine, followed by a colon and two backslashes, such as** C:\\, **in the Find What field and click Find Next.**

If the file contains the boot drive reference, you see it highlighted, as shown in Figure 3-4.

Figure 3-4:
Locate any drive references within the file to ensure that you modify it for the target machine.

4. **When you locate a boot drive entry, choose Edit⇨Replace.**

   You see a Replace dialog box.

5. **Type the source (original) drive, followed by a colon and two back-slashes, such as** C:\\, **in the Find What field.**

6. **Type the target (new machine) drive, followed by a colon and two backslashes, such as** D:\\, **in the Replace With field.**

7. **Click Replace All.**

   Notepad replaces all the drive entries, as anticipated.

8. **Click Cancel.**

   Notepad closes the Replace dialog box.

9. **Perform Steps 2 through 8 for the installation drive and the data drive as needed.**

   Applications may have multiple drive specifications. Carefully replace each drive specification on the source machine with the appropriate drive specification on the target machine. Use the installation options you provided when you installed the application as a source of information.

10. **Choose File⇨Save to save the file.**

11. **Move the file from the source machine to the target machine.**

12. **On the target machine, open a copy of Windows Explorer, locate the REG file, and double-click it.**

   The Registry Editor asks whether you want to open the REG file.

13. **Click Yes.**

The Registry Editor merges the REG file with the existing registry.

14. **Perform Steps 1 through 13 for each of the REG files you created for a Windows feature or application.**

Even though this seems like a lot of work, you can save considerable time spent moving application settings instead of re-creating them on every machine, as long as you perform the task carefully. Of course, you need to edit only the REG file when the configuration of the two machines differs. Never edit the REG file unless you really need to do so. In corporate settings, you may find that you never need to edit a REG file at all because the machines contain approximately the same hardware configured the same way on each machine.

Using the Registry Editor at the command line

Many administrators automate tasks using batch files and scripts. It's possible to automate many registry tasks as well by using the RegEdit command line switches. You can use the -e command line switch within a batch file to save user settings before a system change. For example, typing **RegEdit -e "Microsoft User Settings.REG" "HKEY_CURRENT_USER\Software\ Microsoft"** and pressing Enter at the command prompt will save the Microsoft application user settings to a file named `Microsoft User Settings.REG`. Notice that you must enclose information with spaces in double quotes to ensure that the RegEdit utility will interpret them correctly.

You can accomplish a complete registry save at the command line by typing **RegEdit –e "Registry Save for John 03-01-2008.REG"** and pressing Enter. Notice that you don't supply the name of a hive or branch when you want to save the entire registry. When you want to restore the entire registry, simply type the name of the REG file. For example, if you type **"Registry Save for John 03-01-2008.REG"** and press Enter, the system will display a dialog box asking whether to add the information to the registry. Click Yes and the system will complete the task.

Finding Registry Elements

You often find that the registry isn't as logical as you might want it to be. A setting may appear in a different location than you thought because the vendor was trying to be clever. In some cases, you may not find all the required registry entries unless you search for them. Information can appear in multiple locations, and locating just one entry may not provide the results you were expecting. The following sections tell you how to perform and save searches.

Performing the search

Locating information in the Registry Editor means performing a search. The act of searching is relatively straightforward: Choose Edit➪Find. You see the Find dialog box, as shown in Figure 3-5. Type the information you want to find in the Find What field and click Find Next. The Registry Editor will highlight the information you requested when and if it finds the information in the registry. Pressing F3 will show you additional entries that match the criteria you provided.

Figure 3-5:
Locate the information you need within the registry.

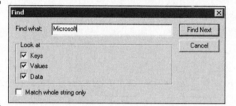

The problem of finding what you need is a matter of providing the correct criteria. For example, the Registry Editor can search in keys (which include the hives), values, and data. The default setting checks all three. However, you may need to search only for the data or the value. Here are some suggestions on how to search more efficiently:

✦ The keys describe the registry organization, so search on keys when you need to know how Microsoft has configured the registry or when you're looking for a particular area of the registry.

✦ The values describe properties. The properties may affect an application or a Windows feature, so use values when you need to locate something such as an application setting.

✦ The data determines the property setting. Every value has an associated data value that defines it. When you're looking for a particular setting, check for data values.

✦ Use combinations of key, value, and data entries when you aren't sure how a vendor has constructed the settings for an application.

✦ Use all three options when you're looking for new, useful entries within the registry and aren't completely sure where to look.

Notice the Match Whole String Only check box at the bottom of Figure 3-5. A registry entry can contain the information you need as part of a much larger entry. In fact, this is more the rule than the exception. When you know that you have the entire string that you need, check this option so that you don't have to spend time looking through combination entries that contain the search string as part of something else.

Setting registry entry favorites

After you find the key, value, or data that you need, you probably want to save the location. The easiest way to perform this task is to create a Favorite using the following steps:

1. **Highlight the key or value entry.**

2. **Choose Favorites⇨Add to Favorites.**

You see an Add to Favorites dialog box.

3. **Type the name you want to use for the favorite (all favorites must have unique names) and click OK.**

The Registry Editor will add the favorite to the list of favorites in the Favorites menu.

To use a favorite you saved earlier, select its entry in the Favorites menu. The Registry Editor will take you directly to that the location in the registry. Of course, you may get to a point where you have too many favorites and the list is more confusing than helpful. Use the following steps to remove a favorite from the list:

1. **Choose Favorites⇨Remove Favorite.**

You see a Remove Favorites dialog box.

2. **Highlight the favorite you want to remove and click OK.**

The Registry Editor will remove the selected favorite from the Favorites menu.

Understanding the Registry Data Types

You can't edit data in the registry without understanding the registry data types. Various kinds of data have different data types depending on the needs of Windows or the application that creates it. For example, the registry will likely store your name as a string. However, it may store the number of special entries in a folder as a number, rather than as a string, because the number is easier for Windows to use. The following sections provide a description of the various data types.

Working with strings

Strings are the most common form of data in the registry. In most cases, strings hold human-readable data. You can use strings to hold any other data type, but many applications choose specific data types to avoid having to convert the string to the data type they need. It's easy to see a string in the registry because its icon looks like a sheaf of paper with the letters *ab* in it. In contrast, all numeric values use an icon that has the numbers 011 110 in it. Strings come in three different forms, as described in the following sections.

Standard strings

The standard string contains plain text that Windows doesn't interpret in any way. It passes the string directly to the application or Windows feature that needs it. Consequently, standard strings usually hold textual configuration information, such as your name. When you double-click a standard string value, you see an Edit String dialog box, like the one shown in Figure 3-6, where you can change the string value.

Figure 3-6:
Standard strings contain plain text that Windows doesn't interpret.

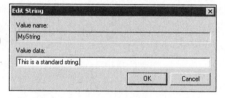

Expandable strings

An expandable string is just like a standard string, except that Windows will interpret the information the string contains before it passes it along to the application or Windows feature. Whenever Windows sees a name within percent signs, such as `%UserProfile%`, it interprets that name and replaces it with an actual value, such as `C:\Users\Administrator`. Most applications and Windows features use expandable strings to hold locations on the hard drive. You use the same Edit String dialog box shown in Figure 3-6 to edit an expandable string as you use to edit a standard string.

Multiple strings

Sometimes a value requires multiple strings to describe it. The multiple string data type can provide multiple strings for one value. Windows interprets these strings, just as it does the expandable string, so you could create a list of file locations using a multiple string. Because this string type provides multiple values, you need a different editor to work with it. Double-clicking a multiple string value shows the Edit Multi-String dialog box, as shown in Figure 3-7. Each string appears on a separate line, as shown in the figure.

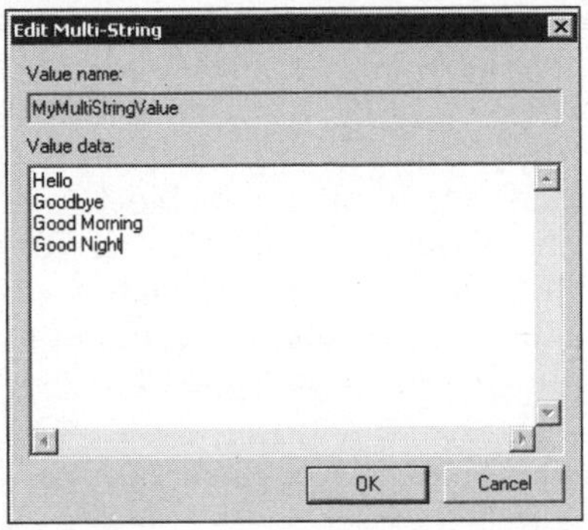

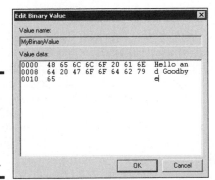

Figure 3-7:
Enter each
string on a
separate
line for a
multiple-
string data
type.

Working with binary data

Binary data can represent nearly anything in the registry. Normally, applications use binary data when they need to present information as the computer sees it rather than as a human would see it. The data may contain control keys, such as a carriage return or tab. In some cases, the data is something that a human can't understand in written form, such as an icon. You won't normally edit binary data unless a vendor provides you with precise instructions for doing so. Double-clicking a binary value presents the Edit Binary Value dialog box, as shown in Figure 3-8.

**Book III
Chapter 3**

**Configuring
the Registry**

Figure 3-8:
Binary data
focuses on
computer-
readable
information.

This dialog box shows three kinds of entry. On the left side you see a value that indicates the position of the data. The data begins at 0000, and each line increases the number by 8 for the number of DWORDs (32-bit values) that can appear in each line.

The middle section shows the hexadecimal values that the registry actually stores. These values can range from 00 to FF. You can edit the hexadecimal values directly by typing the appropriate numbers. Whenever you enter a new DWORD value, the human-readable form of that value (if any) appears on the right side.

The right side shows the information in human-readable form whenever possible. In this case, you can see that the entry is simple text (for demonstration purposes). Most binary data will contain a combination of control characters and human readable text. Even though you can edit the data on the right side, editing it in the middle area provides better results.

Working with DWORD and QWORD data

A computer works with bits. Any information you may have heard to the contrary is mere rumor. The bits actually perform tasks, such as turning switches on or off. Engineers found that working with bits is nearly impossible for the average human and unnecessary in most situations. Consequently, you see the bits that the computer uses grouped together into nibbles (4 bits), words (16 bits), DWORDs (double words, or 32 bits), and QWORDs (quad words, or 64 bits). If you want to learn the ins and outs of this kind of data, check out the tutorial at `http://www.learn-c.com/data_lines.htm`.

The DWORD and QWORD values in the registry hold numbers in most cases. The registry uses these numbers to indicate the number of something that appears in the registry or an application setting that defines the number of something that appears in the application. No matter how the DWORD or QWORD value is used, it usually represents a numeric value of some sort.

You may find that you edit DWORD and QWORD values on occasion to tell the computer how much of something it should provide. When you double-click either a DWORD or QWORD value, you see the Edit DWORD (32-bit) Value dialog box, as shown in Figure 3-9, or the Edit QWORD (64-bit) Value dialog box, which looks precisely the same as the DWORD version.

Figure 3-9:
Edit DWORD
or QWORD
data to
change a
number
within the
registry.

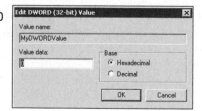

The Registry Editor lets you enter the DWORD or QWORD value as a decimal or hexadecimal value. Make sure to choose the correct option before you begin typing the number. The option you choose depends on the source of information you use to edit the value. Some sources will tell you to type a certain hexadecimal value, and others will provide a decimal value.

Working with special data types

All the data types discussed in this section are common throughout the registry. However, you may run into some truly odd data types while working with some applications. These special data types require special editors and handling. Never edit a special data type unless you have the instructions required to do so.

Understanding the Hives

Just why Microsoft chose the term *hive* for a particular element of the registry is a mystery. However, as previously mentioned, the hive is the basic storage unit for the registry. Knowing where to find a setting that you want to change begins with an understanding of the hives. In addition, when you need to connect to another location, you need to know which hive it belongs to or else you won't be able to do it. In short, the hive is a kind of focus for the registry. The following sections help you understand hives.

Locating the registry files

The registry is a hierarchical database, which means that it doesn't rely on the relational database technologies that you may have used with products such as SQL Server. You can see an overview of the various database structures used on computer systems at `http://blogs.ittoolbox.com/eai/implementation/archives/an-overview-of-database-management-systems-15615`. The Registry Editor also combines a number of files. Each of these files presents a different element of the registry database. For example, the HKEY_CURRENT_USER hive is contained within the individual user folders found in the Users folder of the boot drive. Table 3-1 shows each of the hives and its associated file on the hard drive; some hives use different files based on the user, and some rely on multiple files.

Table 3-1		Registry File Locations	
Hive	*Abbreviation*	*Folder*	*Filename*
HKEY_CLASSES_ROOT	HKCR	Symbolic Link to HKEY_LOCAL_MACHINE\ SOFTWARE\ Classes	N/A
HKEY_CURRENT_USER	HKCU	%UserProfile%	`NTUser.DAT` (Symbolic Link to the User Security Identifier; SID, for this user)
HKEY_CURRENT_USER\ Software\Classes	None	%UserProfile%\ Local Settings\ Application Data\Microsoft\ Windows	`UsrClass.DAT`
HKEY_LOCAL_MACHINE	HKLM	Various	Various
HKEY_LOCAL_MACHINE\SAM	None	%SystemRoot%\ System32\Config\	`Sam`
HKEY_LOCAL_MACHINE\ SECURITY	None	%SystemRoot%\ System32\Config\	`Security`
HKEY_LOCAL_MACHINE\ SOFTWARE	None	%SystemRoot%\ System32\Config\	`Software`
HKEY_LOCAL_MACHINE\ SYSTEM	None	%SystemRoot%\ System32\Config\	`System`
HKEY_USERS	HKU	%UserProfile%	`NTUser.DAT`
HKEY_USERS\.DEFAULT	None	%SystemRoot%\ System32\Config\	Default
HKEY_CURRENT_CONFIG	HKCC	Symbolic Link to HKEY_LOCAL_ MACHINE\ SYSTEM\ CurrentControl Set\Control\ID ConfigDB\ Hardware Profiles	N/A
HKEY_PERFORMANCE_DATA and HKEY_DYN_DATA	None	N/A	These hives aren't visible in the Registry Editor, but they exist, and you may see references to them. Microsoft doesn't provide the locations of these hives on the hard drive.

Hive	Abbreviation	Folder	Filename
N/A	None	%SystemRoot%\ System32\Config\	UserDiff (Used only when upgrading the operating system, so it doesn't appear as a hive.)

As shown in Table 3-1, the registry appears in files all over your hard drive. For example, each user has their own NTUser.DAT file that contains their settings. You see these settings in the HKEY_USERS hive, but the HKEY_CURRENT_USER hive always reflects the settings of the user that has logged in to the system. Because these files appear all over the hard drive, you must make sure to select the right file when performing special tasks with the Registry Editor, such as loading or unloading hives.

You can use the abbreviations listed in Table 3-1 for a number of purposes, but you normally find them used in scripts. Scripts can automate any task you normally perform with the registry, but you must use them carefully. A full discussion of scripts is outside the scope of this book.

TIP

The entries between percent signs (%) in the table are *environment variables* that you can use on any system. To determine where the environment variable points, open a command prompt, and then type **Echo <Environment Variable>** and press Enter. For example, to see where %UserProfile% points, type **Echo %UserProfile%** and press Enter. On my system it points to C:\Users\Administrator; however, it may point to a different location on your system. That's the reason environment variables are so useful — the environment variables are the same on every Windows system, even though the locations are different. Here are the common environment variables:

Book III
Chapter 3

Configuring
the Registry

+ %UserProfile%

+ %AllUsersProfile%

+ %ProgramFiles%

+ %SystemRoot%

+ %SystemDrive%

Working with HKEY_CLASSES_ROOT

The HKEY_CLASSES_ROOT hive is important because it provides access to file associations and actions associated with those actions. In addition, this hive contains keys that define the shell extensions that appear throughout Windows. For example, when you right-click an area in Windows Explorer and see a list of actions you can perform, this hive contains the entries that make it possible for you to create a new text file. You also find entries for the Component Object Model (COM) associations for files in this hive. In short, if you have an association or a task you want to perform with a file or folder, you'll very likely find those settings here.

Normally, you won't want to edit HKEY_CLASSES_ROOT by hand because the applications you install provide default entries for you. You can also add settings using Windows Explorer and by right-clicking the file or folder and choosing the Open With option from the context menu. However, it's interesting to know more about this hive. The hive is actually divided into three areas:

✦ **File Extensions:** The file extension section at the beginning of the hive contains keys that use the names of file extensions, such as TXT. When you select this entry, the (Default) value normally contains the name of a file association, such as txtfile, for this file extension. You may see other entries as well, such as those used for shell extensions or for Multipurpose Internet Mail Extensions (MIME).

✦ **File Associations:** The file associations found at the end of the hive tell which actions to provide when a user right-clicks a file. The common actions include Open, Print, and PrintTo. However, you can find any number of actions for a file association. Each of these actions includes a command. For example, when you check the Open/Command key for the txtfile file association, you find %SystemRoot%\system32\NOTEPAD.EXE %1 as the command, which tells Windows to open Notepad and send it the name of the file.

✦ **Class Entries:** Between the file extensions and the file associations, you find a wealth of class entries. Most of these class entries provide a COM association for a particular file. For example, a particular file type may require an application that relies on COM, or you may see additional property pages for the Properties dialog box for that file type that are defined in this area. You also find managed entries for the .NET Framework and very old Object Linking and Embedding (OLE) entries that let you perform the Paste Special command in applications that support it.

Working with HKEY_CURRENT_USER

The HKEY_CURRENT_USER hive contains all the settings that affect only one user — the current user. Every application and user configuration setting you can think of appears in this hive. Most applications still use the registry to store their settings. However, you find applications that still use INI files, some that use newer CONFIG files (.NET managed applications), some that rely on XML files, and some that don't store any configuration settings at all. Consequently, you can't assume that an application doesn't provide user-level configuration settings if you don't see settings for the application in this section. However, this is a good place to start looking.

This hive contains the vast majority of your Windows settings. For example, every time you change the colors of the display, the new color settings appear in this hive. Likewise, when you choose a new scheme, wallpaper background, or any other personal setting, it appears in this hive. Windows also places your personal Internet Explorer settings here. In fact, this hive contains a myriad of settings you may not think about, but need to use in order to Windows.

It's often interesting to look through the keys in this hive to see what it contains. However, look but don't touch. Settings changes you make in this section can render your account unusable. Even if you make a mistake in this hive, you can still boot the machine because this hive affects only your personal account.

Working with HKEY_LOCAL_MACHINE

The HKEY_LOCAL_MACHINE hive contains the settings that affect everyone who uses the host machine. As with HKEY_CURRENT_USER, you find a combination of Windows and application settings in this hive. The important thing to remember is that these settings affect everyone who uses the machine. Making a mistake in modifying this hive can prevent your system from booting.

Working with HKEY_USERS

The HKEY_USERS hive contains the essential information for every user with an account on the current machine. However, you won't see user names. Instead, you see a Security Identifier (SID), such as S-1-5-19 or S-1-5-21-329068152-1563985344-839522115-1003. The first SID is a common, or universal, Windows SID; you'll find a list of them at `http://support.microsoft.com/kb/163846`. The S-1-5-19 SID is set aside for the NT AUTHORITY\LOCAL SERVICE account. The longer SID number, S-1-5-21-329068152-1563985344-839522115-1003, is a user account number. Every account has a unique SID, so your account number is unique across your entire company. You can determine your own account name and SID using the WhoAmI utility at the command line.

Notice that the HKEY_USERS hive contains most, but not all, of the keys found in HKEY_CURRENT_USER. The Network, SessionInformation, VolatileEnvironment, and other keys that are missing in HKEY_USERS aren't permanent keys. These keys appear only when the user is logged in to the system. The system re-creates them for every new session, so you never need to worry about them as permanent entries.

**Book III
Chapter 3**

**Configuring
the Registry**

Working with HKEY_CURRENT_CONFIG

This hive simply points to the HKEY_LOCAL_MACHINE\SYSTEM\ CurrentControlSet\Control\IDConfigDB\Hardware Profiles key. Microsoft created it to provide easier access to hardware profile information within Windows. Generally, you won't need to work with this hive unless specially directed to do so by Microsoft.

Loading and unloading hives

You may have a need to load a hive at some point. Perhaps you want to compare the settings on one machine with the ones on another machine. The machine you're using may have multiple boot partitions and you want to move settings from one partition to another. Whatever the reason, you can load registry files into the current Registry Editor view using the following steps:

1. Highlight either the HKEY_LOCAL_MACHINE or HKEY_USERS hive entry.

You can load or unload hives from these two hive entries only.

2. Choose File⇨Load Hive.

You see the Load Hive dialog box, which looks and acts the same as the standard Open dialog box.

3. Locate the registry file you want to open, such as an NTUser.DAT file.

It's an error to attempt to load anything but a registry file into the Registry Editor. The Registry Editor will simply tell you that it can't load the hive, but it won't tell you why.

4. Click Open.

The Registry Editor will display the Load Hive dialog box again.

5. Type the name of the key you want to open in the hive in the Key Name field.

You must supply a key name. If you want to load the entire SID of an NTUser.DAT file, you must supply the SID, in the form of {0f69446d-6a70-11db-8eb3-985e31beb686}. Notice that you must include the curly brackets and hyphens as shown. You can also load a particular branch. For example, if you're interested only in the AppEvents key, type **AppEvents**.

6. Click OK.

The Registry Editor loads the hive or branch you requested.

At some point, you'll want to unload the hive. In this case, all you need to do is highlight the hive you want to unload and choose File⇨Unload Hive. Click Yes when the Registry Editor asks whether you're sure you want to unload the hive.

Connecting to network registries

Sometimes you want to manage a registry remotely, which means creating a connection to it. To use this feature, you must start the Remote Registry service on the remote system. Interestingly enough, this act is somewhat dangerous because if you can connect to the remote registry, so can someone else. Consequently, you don't want to start the Remote Registry service unless you know that you can do so safely (the system has no connection to the Internet and you've secured it in other ways). As an alternative, you can always manage the registry using the Remote Desktop application, which is safer because it provides a secure connection. Use these steps to create a remote connection:

1. **Choose File⇨Connect Network Registry.**

   You see a Select Computer dialog box.

2. **Type the name of the remote system.**

   As an alternative, you can click Advanced and use the advanced features to search for a computer on the network.

3. **Click OK.**

   The Registry Editor creates a new top-level icon for the remote computer with that computer's name. The hives it loads include HKEY_LOCAL_MACHINE and HKEY_USERS, which is all you need to manage the remote registry.

At some point, you finish managing the remote computer. When you're finished, right-click the computer entry in the Registry Editor and choose Disconnect from the context menu.

Setting Registry Security

Securing the registry is an important task. In fact, you'll notice that the Windows Server 2008 registry is already more secure than registries of the past because Microsoft has taken steps to secure it. However, you may find a need to modify the security settings in the registry. The actual process for setting security is the same as it is for a file or folder. So, you can use the techniques found in the "Configuring File and Folder Security" section of Book V, Chapter 1 to perform the task.

To access the security settings for a hive or key, right-click the hive or key and choose Permissions from the context menu. You see the Permissions dialog box, where you can add or remove users or groups and set permissions for them. As with a file or folder, the rights you assign at an upper level flow down to lower levels, unless you specifically override the rights at a lower level.

Part of the problem with setting security in the registry is that it isn't as straightforward as you might expect. For example, it's quite reasonable to think that a user shouldn't have access to some Windows settings in the registry, such as the hardware settings. However, you might be surprised to learn that the applications the user relies on might need that information in order to work correctly. Strictly speaking, the user has no need to access that information, but because the application runs under the user's account, the application has a need for it and therefore the user can access it as well.

Incorrect registry security can cause a wide range of side effects. You may make a security setting and then discover that applications are failing in subtle and unexpected ways. Consequently, you want to maintain a log of every security change you make, to ensure that the secure registry doesn't become the unusable registry.

One way around some registry security problems is to set the security for a particular user — one that you specifically design for the application that uses the registry settings. You can then use the RunAs utility to run the application as that user. All you need to do is modify the shortcut in the Start menu to use the RunAs utility. The user will never know unless they look at the shortcut (and you can remove this privilege as part of a group policy).

Chapter 4: Working with Active Directory

In This Chapter

✔ Defining how Active Directory stores information

✔ Working with Active Directory objects

✔ Managing Active Directory using the ADSIEdit utility

Active Directory is one of the main features of a domain. Some administrators view it as some kind of management software, but what Active Directory truly provides is a database. Active Directory is the kind of database you use to store not company data but, rather, information about the computer network as a whole. The database contains information about users, groups, clients, and a host of other objects required in order to create a network of computers and other hosts, such as printers.

Just because Active Directory provides database support doesn't mean that all Active Directory installations are the same. Active Directory installations vary by the kind of support the user requires. Just as networks vary in size and complexity, so do Active Directory installations. This chapter reviews some of the differences in Active Directory installations. The basic consideration of Active Directory complexity is that it's always proportional to the complexity of the network as a whole.

After you understand that Active Directory is simply a special kind of database, you can begin working with it to configure your system. The most common method used to perform this task is to rely on the various Active Directory consoles that Microsoft provides. This chapter reviews the common Active Directory consoles you use to configure your system.

A second method of interacting with Active Directory is to use the Active Directory System Interface Editor (ADSIEdit) console. This tool provides you with an in-depth look at the Active Directory database and helps you better understand its structure. In some cases, you may actually have to edit the database directly by using ADSIEdit to repair problems that you can't fix using the other Active Directory consoles, but for many administrators, ADSIEdit simply acts as a learning tool.

Understanding How Active Directory Works

Active Directory is a special kind of database. Many administrators are familiar with Relational Database Management Systems (RDBMSs), such as SQL Server. An RDBM provides an excellent means of storing data for business use because such data often appears in tabular form or a database administrator can change its structure to a tabular format with relative ease.

Unlike most databases, Active Directory is a hierarchical database. Think of a tree structure where you add branches as needed for new kinds of objects and each instance of an object is a leaf. For example, you can have a computer branch that holds objects that describe each machine attached to your network. The branch can hold as many leaves as is necessary to describe each machine.

In many respects, Active Directory is nothing new. The registry on your machine is also a hierarchical database. You can add as many keys to the registry as needed to store all the settings for your machine. The keys can also go to any depth needed to provide complete data segregation. Active Directory works on the same basis as the registry, but on a network level, so it's more complex and considerably larger than the registry on your machine. Active Directory also requires more tools to manage it (unlike the registry, which requires only the RegEdit utility for maintenance tasks). Even with these differences, you can view Active Directory as simply a very large form of the registry.

Configuring Objects in Active Directory

The easiest way to work with Active Directory objects is to use one of the three consoles designed for the purpose. You already used the Active Directory Users and Computers console in the "Configuring the user accounts" section of Book II, Chapter 5 to add users to a new domain. Each of these consoles affects a different area of the Active Directory configuration. The following sections provide an overview of how they work and tell you which part of Active Directory each console affects.

Using the Active Directory Domains and Trusts console

The Active Directory Domains and Trusts console contains a list of all domains on your network. If you have only one server on your network, it's unlikely that you'll ever need to use this console. The main purpose of this console is to help you manage large networks that contain multiple domain controllers within a forest. The following sections describe three tasks you perform using this console.

Raising the domain functional level

The one task you may need to perform on a small network is to raise the domain functional level. This setting controls how the domain controller interacts with Active Directory and which features Active Directory provides. Use these steps to change the domain functional level:

1. **Right-click the domain controller entry you want to change and choose Raise Domain Functional Level from the context menu.**

   You see a Raise Domain Functional Level dialog box, where you can choose a new level.

2. **Select the new level in the Select an Available Domain Functional Level drop-down list box.**

   Active Directory lets you only increase the domain functional level. For example, you can go from Windows Server 2003 to Windows Server 2008, but you can't go from Windows Server 2003 to Windows Server 2000. The change is also irreversible. You can't go back to a previous level after raising the functional level.

3. **Click Raise.**

   Active Directory raises the functional level. You normally want to reboot the system to ensure that the change takes place as expected.

Managing a domain controller

When you work with multiple servers, you can use the Active Directory Domains and Trusts console as a means of selecting the server you want to manage. Right-click the domain controller you want to work with and choose Manage from the context menu. Windows opens the Active Directory Users and Computers console for the domain controller you selected.

Setting domain controller properties and trusts

Domain controllers have certain properties that you can manage from the Active Directory Domains and Trusts console. To see the properties for a particular domain controller, right-click the domain controller entry and choose Properties from the context menu. You see the domain Properties dialog box, as shown in Figure 4-1.

The General tab tells you about the domain controller functionality levels. You see the overall functionality for the domain and the functionality level of the forest that holds the domain. The General tab also provides a Description field, where you can provide a description for the domain.

Book III
Chapter 4

**Working with
Active Directory**

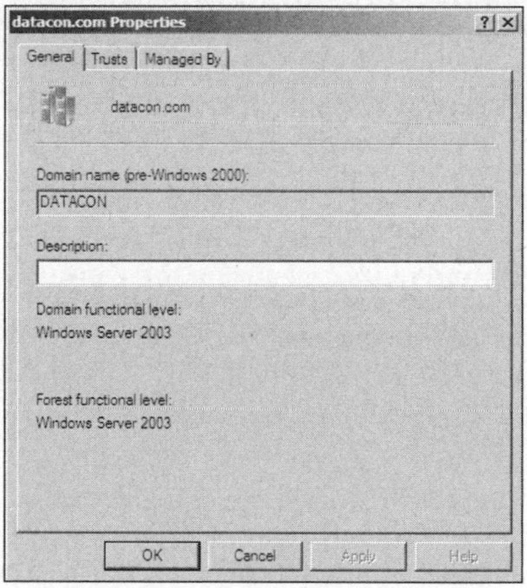

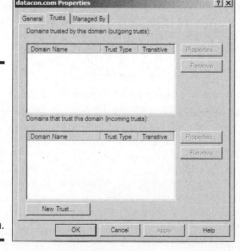

Figure 4-1:
Set the
domain
controller
properties
as needed.

The Trusts tab contains a list of trusts for the domain, as shown in Figure 4-2. A *trust* between two domains means that the domains can exchange data and perform other tasks together. The terms of the trust define specifically how the two domains trust each other. The upper list tells which domains trust the current domain. The lower list tells which domains the current domain trusts. The "Managing trusts" section of this chapter tells you more about working with trusts.

Figure 4-2:
Manage
trusts
between
various
domains to
ensure
proper
communi-
cation and
cooperation.

The Managed By tab contains information about the person who manages the domain. Depending on the content of the user's record in Active Directory, you can find the person's office location, address, telephone number, and fax number on this tab. Use this information to locate the administrator for the domain in question. For example, you might need to contact the administrator to create a trust between your domain and the domain the administrator manages.

Managing trusts

You can't generally add your domain to another domain's trust list. The administrator of the other domain must perform this task for you. However, you can add other domains to your trust list by using the following steps:

1. **Click New Trust on the Trusts tab of the domain Properties dialog box, as shown in Figure 4-2.**

You see the New Trust Wizard.

2. **Click Next.**

The wizard asks you to provide a trust name. The trust name can consist of either a DNS name or a NetBIOS name.

3. **Type the DNS name or NetBIOS name of the domain controller you want to trust. Click Next.**

The wizard asks you to provide a trust type. Active Directory supports two kinds of trusts:

- **Realm Trust:** Use this trust type when the server you want to trust doesn't have Active Directory installed. In this case, Active Directory relies on Kerberos version 5 to perform transactions with the remote system.

- **Trust with a Windows Domain:** Use this trust when working with another domain controller on your network.

4. **Choose a trust type and click Next.**

The wizard asks you to determine the transitivity of the trust. A *nontransitive* trust occurs within the current domain and realm — it's a straightforward connection between two machines on the same network. A *transitive* trust occurs when the trust relies on not only the current domain and realm but also the children of the domain and realm. This second form of trust is more encompassing and complex.

5. **Choose a level of transitivity and click Next.**

The wizard asks you to determine the direction of the trust. A two-way trust lets you pass information between two systems in either direction. A one-way incoming trust lets your domain controller accept input from the other server, but doesn't let your domain controller pass any information back. A one-way outgoing trust lets your domain controller pass information to the other server, but doesn't let your domain controller accept information from that server.

6. **Choose a direction of trust and click Next.**

   The wizard asks you to provide a trust password.

7. **Type and confirm the trust password. Click Next.**

   You see a summary of all the trust information you provided to the wizard.

8. **Verify the trust information and click Next. Click Finish.**

   Active Directory creates the new trust.

The domain Properties dialog box also provides the means for editing and removing trusts. To remove a trust, highlight its entry and click Remove. To edit a trust, highlight its entry and click Properties. You see a Properties dialog box for the trust where you can change the transitivity type and set the trust to use Kerberos encryption.

Using the Active Directory Sites and Services console

The Active Directory Sites and Services console, shown in Figure 4-3, contains information about the servers, services, and connection between machines on the network. You see a listing of subnets, intersite transports (IP and SMTP are the defaults), and servers that act as endpoints. You never need to use this console when working with a small network because Active Directory makes all required entries for you.

Figure 4-3:
Manage servers, services, and connections using this console.

Administrators need to use this console only occasionally on larger networks. You may need this console in order to

✦ Define new sites as needed

✦ Configure network subnets

✦ Delegate control of an object to a particular user or group

✦ Set server, site, transport, or other object properties

✦ Define site links and site bridges

✦ View Resultant Set of Policy (RSoP) for a site

✦ Add servers to or remove servers from a site

✦ Create new connections

Active Directory performs most of these tasks for you when working with local sites. For example, when you add a new server, the server automatically appears in the list — you shouldn't have to add it manually (and there's something wrong if you do). In most cases, Active Directory also performs subnet configuration correctly when you provide the correct information during domain controller promotion. Viewing RSoP is a manual process, but this is more of a maintenance function than a configuration task. The only time you perform these tasks manually is when communication between remote sites doesn't exist (or is intermittent). This chapter doesn't discuss the manual configuration tasks because you don't perform them often, the configuration for each network is unique, and an advanced administrator who already has the required knowledge usually performs these tasks.

Using the Active Directory Users and Computers console

Of the Active Directory consoles, the Active Directory Users and Computers console, shown in Figure 4-4, is the one that you use most often. This console helps you monitor and manage computers, domain controllers, foreign security principles (external objects that can administer the selected domain), and users. In addition, this console can manage a considerable number of optional objects that include contacts, Microsoft Message Queue (MSMQ) queue aliases, printers, and shared folders. In fact, you can't configure a domain without using this console. The following sections describe some of the tasks you can perform with this console.

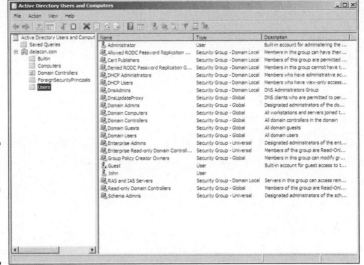

Figure 4-4:
Manage the
major Active
Directory
objects by
using this
console.

Configuring object properties

Every object within Active Directory has properties that describe it. *Objects* include anything you can right-click to see a Properties option on the context menu, which is everything but the root node of the console, shown in Figure 4-4. Defining these properties is essential if you want to obtain the maximum potential from Active Directory. For example, any query you want to define depends on these properties to locate particular objects. (See the "Defining an Active Directory query" section of this chapter for details.)

Folders tend to have simple Properties dialog boxes that consist of a General tab with a Description field. The Description field tells what information the folder contains. It's important to follow the same format for the description of every folder to ensure that other administrators understand how you created the hierarchy of the Active Directory installation. You can use the descriptions found in existing folders to obtain ideas for your own folder descriptions.

Active Directory contains a significant number of other object types, many of which you never see unless you work with the ADSIEdit console, described in the "Working with ADSIEdit" section of this chapter. The objects in the Active Directory Users and Computers console define the elements that most administrators work with daily, such as users, groups, printers, domain controllers, and client computers. Figure 4-5 shows the domain controller Properties dialog box, where you can define configuration information for a domain controller.

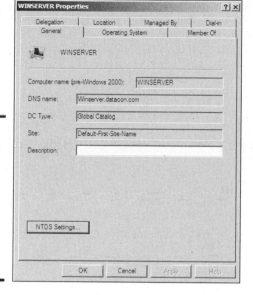

Figure 4-5: Most objects provide properties you use to define that object's configuration.

As you can see from Figure 4-5, Active Directory automatically polls the computer and defines certain properties for you. Properties generally fall into these categories:

◆ **Modifiable Configuration:** Active Directory often polls the object and provides this information for you. However, you can correct errors as needed by changing the property value. Properties in this category provide noncritical configuration information that Active Directory provides for your use, but normally doesn't use itself.

◆ **Non-modifiable Configuration:** Active Directory polls the object for some types of critical information, such as the operating system version, and stores it for later use. You can query against this information, but you can't change it by using the Properties dialog box. To change this information, you must change the object configuration.

◆ **Identification:** Some properties identify the object in some way, such as the address and telephone number of a user or the location of a computer. Active Directory never supplies this information. However, you want to input this information to make queries easier and more complete. It's important to create company policies regarding the format and content of these entries so that everyone makes them the same way.

◆ **Security:** You use security information to control access to resources by the object. Active Directory usually provides a minimal level of security entry. In some cases, the minimum entry works fine. However, you may need to add other security information to ensure that the object works properly.

✦ **Management:** Active Directory never assumes anything about object management. You should provide this entry so that other administrators know who is responsible for managing the object. The person responsible for the object should be the one to make any changes to its configuration.

✦ **Communication:** A few objects include communication properties. These properties define whether the object can interact with an object such as a server from a remote location. Communication arguments can determine when, where, and how an object communicates with another object. To use properties of this type, you must install some type of remote dial-in capability on the target object.

Defining an Active Directory query

Depending on your Active Directory setup, the database can become huge. In fact, it can become downright unwieldy, making it difficult to locate any particular piece of information. Fortunately, the Active Directory Users and Computers console makes it easy to locate objects using a query. The query asks the Active Directory questions, and Active Directory responds by showing objects that meet the criteria you specify. The following steps describe how to create a query:

1. **Right-click the Saved Queries folder and choose New⇨Query from the context menu.**

You see the New Query dialog box, shown in Figure 4-6. This screen shot shows a sample query. The dialog box you see at first doesn't contain any entries in the fields.

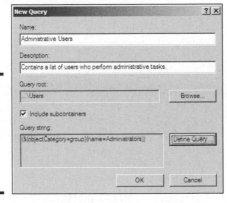

Figure 4-6:
Request information from Active Directory using a query.

2. Type a descriptive name for the query in the Name field.

Keep the name short but descriptive. Using a short name makes it easier to tell other administrators which query to use. A descriptive name makes the query self-describing.

3. Type a description in the Description field.

Include as much information as you need to document the query completely.

4. Click Browse.

You see a Browse dialog box, where you can choose a folder containing objects within Active Directory. The folders need not appear in the Active Directory Users and Computers console — you can choose any folder that Active Directory supports.

5. Highlight a folder you want to query and click OK.

The New Query dialog box contains the folder you chose in the Query Root field.

6. Click Define Query.

You see the Find dialog box, like the one shown in Figure 4-7. The Find dialog box changes to match the kind of query you want to create. Figure 4-7 shows the Find Common Queries dialog box. However, if you choose a different entry in the Find field, the dialog box changes to match the entry you choose.

Figure 4-7:
Define the kind of query you want Active Directory to perform.

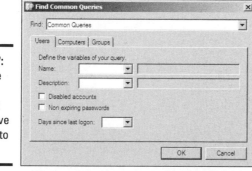

7. Choose a query type in the Find field.

The dialog box configuration changes to match the Find field value.

8. Click each tab in turn and define the values that specify the query arguments.

9. **Click OK.**

   You see the query added to the Query String field (refer to Figure 4-6).

10. **Click OK.**

    Active Directory saves the query, selects its folder in the console, and displays the results of the query on-screen.

If you decide that the query doesn't work as you want it to, right-click its entry and choose Edit from the context menu. Remember to choose Action⇨ Refresh whenever you edit a query to see the results of the change. When you no longer need a query, right-click its entry and choose Delete from the context menu.

Queries show three columns of information when you first create them. In many cases, the Name, Type, and Description fields don't provide the information you need. To add or remove columns from the display, right-click the query and choose View⇨Add/Remove Columns from the context menu. You see the Add/Remove Columns dialog box, as shown in Figure 4-8.

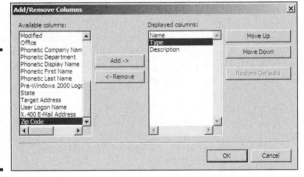

Figure 4-8: Choose the output of your query to match any special need.

Highlight columns you want to add or remove from the list, and then click Add or Remove as needed to change the content of the Displayed Columns list. Change the order of the entries by highlighting an entry in the Displayed Columns list and clicking Move Up or Move Down as needed.

Creating new groups

Developing a good security plan is easier when you use groups. Rather than manage individual users, you manage the group of users as a whole. The "Configuring the user accounts" section of Book II, Chapter 5 shows how to add users to a new domain. This section describes the other part of the process, adding new groups.

After you add a new group, you add users to it by using the options on the Member Of tab of the user Properties dialog box or the Members tab of the group Properties dialog box. Groups can also become members of other groups. You add groups as members of other groups using the same techniques you rely on for users. Use the following steps to create a new group:

1. **Right-click the Users folder and choose New⇨Group from the context menu.**

   You see the New Object – Group dialog box.

2. **Type a group name in the Group Name field.**

   This entry can contain spaces.

3. **Type a group name, without spaces, in the Group Name (Pre-Windows 2000) field.**

   The two group names should match each other as closely as possible to make management easier.

4. **Choose a group scope in the Group Scope field.**

   You choose between Domain Local, Global, and Universal. The scope determines the access level of the group. A local domain group appears on the local server only. A global group appears within the current forest. A universal group appears everywhere. You should avoid using universal groups unless necessary because they make management harder. You must consider the impact of a universal group change on an organization level, which can prove difficult at best.

5. **Choose a group type in the Group Type field.**

   You choose between Security and Distribution. Security groups control access to resources. Distribution groups control distribution of information.

6. **Click OK.**

   Active Directory creates the group, but doesn't assign any members to it. Consequently, the group is available but useless at this point.

7. **Double-click the group entry in the Users folder.**

   You see the group Properties dialog box.

8. **Choose the Members tab.**

9. **Click Add.**

   You see the Select Users, Contacts, Computers, or Groups dialog box.

10. **Type the names of users, contacts, computers, or other groups that should appear as members of this group.**

 11. Click OK.

You see the users, contact, computers, and other groups added to the Members list.

 12. Click OK.

Active Directory updates the group and makes it functional. You can now assign the group rights to resources by using the techniques found in the "Sharing Resources" section of Book V, Chapter 2.

Working with ADSIEdit

The ADSIEdit console provides special functionality. You use it to peer into the depths of Active Directory. The ADSIEdit console lets you see the entire database for a particular domain. When you initially open ADSIEdit, the display is blank. Before you can work with any of the entries, you create a connection to the domain or other context you want to see.

ADSIEdit doesn't provide much in the way of safety features. Microsoft assumes that you know how to work with Active Directory. You can always view entries without creating problems. However, changing an entry can have unexpected results. The following sections describe how to work with ADSIEdit.

Creating a connection

The first step in using ADSIEdit is to create a connection. ADSIEdit relies on the Lightweight Directory Access Protocol (LDAP) to create the connection. Fortunately, Microsoft provides an easy-to-use dialog box for creating the required connection. To access the dialog box, right-click the ADSIEdit entry and choose Connect To from the context menu. You see the Connection Settings dialog box, as shown in Figure 4-9.

The easiest connection to create is the Default Naming Context because Microsoft defines it for you. When you want to use the Default Naming Context, the context that connects you to your local domain, click OK. Use the following steps when you want to create another connection type:

 1. Type a name for the connection in the Name field.

 2. Choose a Connection Point option.

You may choose one of the well-known naming contexts (simple) or create a custom context (advanced). The best option is to work with the well-known naming contexts first to understand how LDAP works.

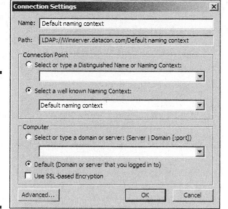

Figure 4-9:
Define the
connection
to a domain
or other
context
using this
dialog box.

3. **Provide a naming context.**

   When working with a well-known naming context, simply select an entry from the drop-down list box. Otherwise, you must type the LDAP statement that defines the naming context.

4. **Choose a Computer option.**

   If you choose a different domain than the default current domain, you must also provide the name of the server that hosts the domain or the domain name.

5. **(Optional) Check Use SSL-based Encryption for remote systems that support this feature.**

6. **(Optional) Click Advanced to provide advanced connection information.**

   The advanced information can include your user credentials on the remote system, the domain port number, and the protocol to use. (The default is LDAP because most systems recognize it, but you can also choose Global Catalog.)

7. **Click OK.**

   ADSIEdit creates the new connection for you. The ADSIEdit utility can support multiple connections. Figure 4-10 shows an example of ADSIEdit with two connections (the Default Naming Context and the Schema naming context for the current domain). Every time you reopen ADSIEdit, it automatically restores the connections that you had in place the last time you used the console, so depending on your setup, you may have to create the connection only once.

Book III
Chapter 4

Working with
Active Directory

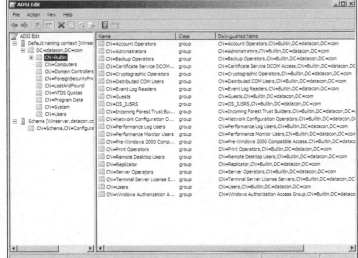

Figure 4-10:
ADSIEdit
displays any
connections
you create.

Viewing the database hierarchy

It's important to remember that Active Directory is a hierarchical database. You can drill down several levels before you find the root nodes of a particular node. The nodes all have identifiers associated with them. The most common identifiers include

✦ **DC:** Domain controller

✦ **OU:** Organization unit

✦ **CN:** Context

The distinguished name for a particular object depends on its level within the hierarchy. For example, the Builtin object, shown in Figure 4-10, has the distinguished name `CN=Builtin,DC=datacon,DC=com`. You use the distinguished name to access objects much as you use the path when working with a hard drive.

Every entry in ADSIEdit has a Properties dialog box associated with it, except for the ADSIEdit entry and the naming context entries. To access the object properties, right-click the object entry and choose Properties from the context menu. You see a dialog box like the one shown in Figure 4-11.

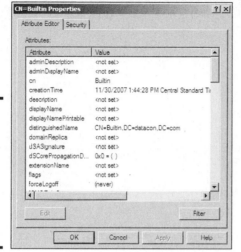

Figure 4-11:
The
Properties
dialog box
tells you
about the
Active
Directory
object.

It's always safe to view the properties. However, edit the properties at your own risk because you can easily damage the Active Directory database with the wrong changes. The Attribute Editor tab shows a list of properties that define the object. The Security tab contains security settings that determine who can access the object.

Managing objects

You may need to add new objects in some cases. It's always easier to add objects by using one of the consoles that Microsoft provides. So you won't want to use ADSIEdit unless you can't access the object in some other way. In all cases, you right-click the parent object and choose New➪Object to add a new child object. You see a Create Object dialog box, where you can choose the class of object you want to add. ADSIEdit shows you the legal object types for the parent context. After you choose an object class, click Next and follow the prompts to add the new class. In most cases, you double-click the new class after you complete it to use the Attribute Editor (refer to Figure 4-11) to modify the object properties.

When you want to remove an object, right-click its entry and choose Delete from the context menu. ADSIEdit asks whether you're sure you want to remove the entry. Click Yes to complete the process. You can also use ADSIEdit to rename objects and move them to other locations by using the appropriate context menu entries.

**Book III
Chapter 4**

**Working with
Active Directory**

Chapter 5: Performing Standard Maintenance

In This Chapter

✔ **Working with the System applet**

✔ **Defining the user interface**

✔ **Considering the effects of UAC**

✔ **Managing standard applications**

✔ **Checking system reliability and performance**

✔ **Backing up and restoring the system**

✔ **Managing and monitoring the hard drives**

✔ **Using Task Scheduler to automate tasks**

✔ **Managing remote systems with Remote Desktop**

✔ **Overcoming emergencies with a recovery disc**

Part of administering a server is performing maintenance on it. Of course, *maintenance* can mean many different things. Some people view it as performing the upkeep tasks needed to keep the server running. However, sometimes maintenance means looking around to see what's happening with your server. Sometimes you just need to observe it to ensure that everything is working as you anticipated it would. Otherwise, an emergency unfolds before you have any idea that it will occur. In some cases, you have to measure system status to ensure that you're viewing the system state accurately. This chapter discusses all of these kinds of maintenance.

You won't find every maintenance task discussed in this chapter. The sections in this chapter focus on common maintenance tasks, such as performing a system backup, creating a recovery disc, or monitoring system performance. You also discover a way to become more productive using Task Scheduler so that performing maintenance doesn't have to become a chore. In some cases, you may actually begin to look forward to some maintenance checks to determine whether the modifications you've discovered in this book have worked as anticipated. The best part is that users complain less about performance when they know you're already on top of things.

One of the things that most developers should discover early is that learning how to perform new tasks on a production system almost certainly causes problems at some point. Savvy administrators use a test server to practice new skills and discover any potential problems before moving on to the production server. To use this chapter most effectively, try out the various skills on a test server — really work with these new techniques to ensure that you understand them.

Interacting with the System Applet

In past versions of Windows, opening the System applet opened the System Properties dialog box, which contained a number of tabs for managing some major system features (such as computer name, hardware, System Restore, and Remote Access) and advanced features (such as the size of the paging file). Windows Server 2008 doesn't provide access to these features in the same way. Now you see the common general features first, as shown in Figure 5-1, and click links to obtain access to more advanced features.

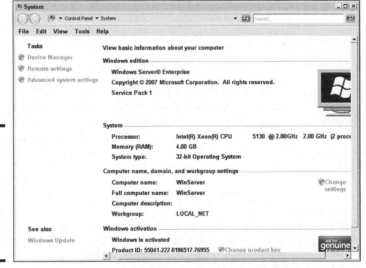

Figure 5-1:
The new System window shows the information you need most often.

This window shows you the basics, such as how much system memory Windows recognizes and which edition of Windows you own. You can also see the workgroup you belong to, the type of processor installed in your machine, and whether you have multiple processors installed (this machine has two). If you ever have questions about any of this information, click the question mark icon in the upper-right corner of the window, and you see a Help file that describes all the entries in this display.

Activating Windows

The System window also shows whether you've activated your copy of Windows. If you haven't activated it, you see a notice specifying how many days you have left to do so, as shown at the bottom of Figure 5-1. If you see this link, use the following steps to activate your copy of Windows:

1. **Click the activation time link.**

You see the Windows Activation dialog box.

2. **Click Activate Windows Online Now.**

Windows attempts to perform the activation process. If the process is successful, you see a success message.

3. **Click Close.**

You see that Windows is activated. (You also see the Genuine Windows logo in the lower-right corner of the window.)

If you ever decide to upgrade your Windows edition, you'll receive a new product key. Click Change Product Key to enter the new product key. You have to activate Windows again after you finish the upgrade because the original activation is attached to the original product key.

Using the System Properties dialog box links

The System window shown in Figure 5-1 has a number of links in it. Most of these links take you to the System Properties dialog box. For example, when you click Change Settings in the Computer Name, Domain, and Workgroup Settings section, you see the Computer Name tab of the System Properties dialog box, as shown in Figure 5-2. You can find a complete discussion of this tab in the "Providing a computer name and domain" section of Book I, Chapter 4.

At this point, you can change to any of the other tabs simply by clicking the tab you want. For example, clicking the Remote tab displays information about creating a Remote Desktop connection. You can see a discussion of this topic in the "Enabling Remote Desktop" section of Book I, Chapter 4. Click the Advanced System Settings link, and you see the Advanced tab of the System Properties dialog box. You'll find techniques for working with this tab throughout this book. For example, you'll find a technique for working with hidden system devices in the "Viewing hidden devices" section of Book II, Chapter 2. You'll also find sections for performance (see the "Configuring the Windows performance options" section in this chapter), startup and recovery options (the "Configuring Startup and Recovery Options" section of Book V, Chapter 3), and environment variables (the "Setting Environment Variables" section of Book III, Chapter 6).

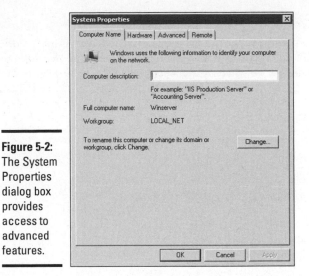

Figure 5-2:
The System
Properties
dialog box
provides
access to
advanced
features.

Clicking the Device Manager link doesn't take you to the Hardware tab of the System Properties dialog box, as you might think it would. Instead, it takes you to the Device Manager window. You can find a complete discussion of the Device Manager window in the "Working with Device Manager" section of Book II, Chapter 2.

The System window also provides a Windows Update link in the lower-left corner. Click this link, and you see the Windows Update window. Discover more about this feature in the "Downloading and installing updates" section of Book I, Chapter 4.

Configuring Your User Interface for Maximum Functionality

The user interface that you see when you begin using Windows Server 2008 probably isn't optimal. It represents the user interface that Microsoft thinks most people want, but it really doesn't provide everything you need. In fact, after you complete the basic setup of your server, you probably want to optimize the interface so that you can perform management tasks in greater comfort. The following sections describe the personalization options you have at your disposal. How you configure them is up to you because everyone has different comfort needs. Play around with these settings — have fun, try something new. After a while, you'll eventually find the settings that suit your particular needs.

Defining the Folder Options settings

The Folder Options applet of the Control Panel opens the Folder Options dialog box, as shown in Figure 5-3. Even though these settings may not seem very important, they can significantly affect your ability to perform useful work because they tend to affect most areas of Windows. For example, these settings affect how you interact with Windows Explorer and what you see in the various Windows Explorer panes. The following sections describe the three tabs of the Folder Options dialog box.

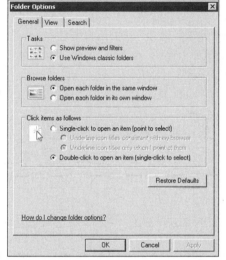

Figure 5-3:
Use the Folder Options dialog box to configure applications such as Windows Explorer.

Configuring the General tab

The General tab contains settings that affect how you interact with folders. For example, you can choose to display the previews that define the new version of Windows, or you can use the classic folders. The previews and filters can make it easier to find what you want, but they also consume resources and tend to slow Windows Explorer, making it harder to work quickly. Consequently, you need to consider whether using this feature will make you more efficient or using classic folders is worth the loss of information.

Likewise, you can choose how Windows handles new folders that you open and whether it provides a browser-like, single-click interface or the traditional double-click interface. The choices you make depend on what makes you feel comfortable — what makes you work most efficiently.

Configuring the View tab

The View tab, shown in Figure 5-4, helps you make display decisions. For example, you can choose whether Windows always shows application icons rather than thumbnails of the information within files. The application icons are helpful because they tell you which application opens the file, while the thumbnails can be helpful because you can use them to locate certain kinds of information. In most cases, you want to use application icons on a server unless you also use the server to modify data files (the main source of thumbnails).

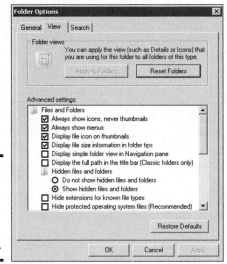

Figure 5-4:
The View tab helps you define what you want to see.

A few of the settings are counterproductive for administrators. For example, it's helpful to see file extensions for the sole reason that doing so makes it less likely that you'll attempt to open a file with a virus in it. Because you're an administrator, you also want to see all hidden files. Otherwise, you might not be able to access some types of system resources and management utilities. In fact, if you're anything like me, you even want to display the protected operating system files so that you can access them when needed. Most of the other settings are of the comfort variety, and you should experiment to determine which settings work best for you.

Configuring the Search tab

The Search tab defines how you search for items on the hard drive. The thing is, you must start the Indexing service before any of these settings makes a difference. The "Indexing Options" section of Book II, Chapter 3 tells you about the Indexing Options applet of the Control Panel. After you start the indexing service, you can use these settings to configure how Windows searches for items on the hard drive.

Before you decide to start the Indexing service and use the system resources to work with it, consider that the Indexing service indexes only items for the local drive. In other words, you must work at the server to gain any benefit from using it. In many cases, you find that the payback for using the Indexing feature on your server is so small that it's better to use other techniques to search for items you need.

Defining the Internet Options settings

The Internet Options applet opens the Internet Properties dialog box. (Yes, Microsoft did give the applet one name and the dialog box another name, making it possible to get confused. To avoid confusion, this chapter uses the name Internet Options when referring to the applet.) You can see this same dialog box by choosing Tools⇨Internet Options in Internet Explorer. No matter which way you open this dialog box, it does more than affect how Internet Explorer works.

You also find that Microsoft is using the Internet Properties dialog box when you interact with network drives and other remote locations. The security you set using this dialog box also affects your ability to use resources on other systems on your network because Microsoft now has all network resources defined in the Internet zone. Before you can use these resources, you must often place them in the Trusted zone. Consequently, the following sections help you do more than simply work with Internet Explorer.

Configuring the General tab

The General tab of the Internet Properties dialog box, shown in Figure 5-5, contains settings that affect the appearance of Internet Explorer and any other application that relies on these settings. To make Internet Explorer work faster, you can often get rid of some of the garbage, such as plug-ins, that Web sites toss your way. Click Accessibility and you see the Accessibility dialog box, where you can tell these applications to ignore colors, fonts, and font sizes. You can even define your own style sheet so that you don't have to wait for these Web sites to render fancy effects, such as special fonts or graphics. I normally set my initial page to about:blank so that Internet Explorer starts quickly. After all, this machine isn't your workstation and you want to get things done quickly.

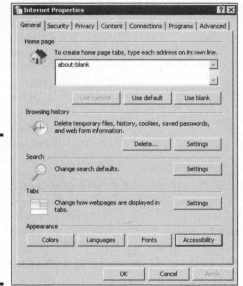

Figure 5-5:
Configure
Internet
Explorer for
speed
rather than
fanciness
whenever
possible.

Because you're not browsing with this copy of Internet Explorer, you may want to set the browsing features to a minimum and set the history feature to retain zero days of history. Anything you can do to make Internet Explorer work faster and use fewer resources is a good idea. Many features that provide convenience on a client system aren't practical on a server.

Click Settings in the Tabs area to change how tabs work in Internet Explorer. In some cases, you may actually have multiple tabs open, but it's more likely that you'll use the server copy of Internet Explorer to open Windows Update and perform other tasks that require a single pane. Even so, you should set the tabs up to provide comfortable use, just in case you need them.

Configuring the Security tab

As mentioned earlier, the Security tab provides input to more than just Internet Explorer. Windows Explorer also uses the settings when working with network drives, and you may find that other applications use these settings as well. Consequently, setting the Security tab (shown in Figure 5-6) correctly is important.

The icons at the top correspond to four security zones: Internet, Local Intranet, Trusted Sites, and Restricted Sites. Depending on your needs, you probably want to set all these zones, except Trusted, to High on a server because you won't use the server for browsing but you want to ensure that the server has maximum protection. When you find a location, such as a network drive or

Windows Update, that requires special privileges, you can add them to your Trusted Sites zone using the following steps:

1. **Select the Trusted Sites icon.**

2. **Click Sites.**

You see the Trusted Sites dialog box.

3. **Type the location of the site in the Add This Website to the Zone field.**

When working with standard Web sites, type the entire zone, including the protocol, such as `http://www.microsoft.com`. When working with a folder or drive, use the file protocol entry, such as `file:////D:\WINWORD` for the WINWORD folder on the D: drive. Notice that the file protocol uses four forward slashes in place of the two used for the http protocol.

4. **Click Add.**

You see the URL added to the list of URLs.

5. **Click Close.**

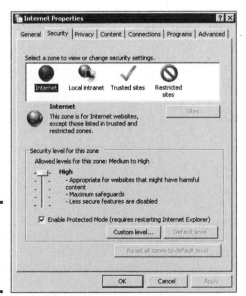

Figure 5-6:
Configure security carefully on your server.

If you find that the Trusted Sites zone doesn't provide the functionality you require on the server, try lowering the security slider. The security slider controls the strictness of the security for a particular zone. When the security slider doesn't provide sufficient rights, click Custom Level. You see the Security Settings – Trusted Sites Zone dialog box, where you can configure individual security options. Carefully test the security options one at a time until you find the settings you need to ensure that Web sites and network drives work as anticipated.

Configuring the Privacy tab

The Privacy tab, shown in Figure 5-7, controls the use of cookies and pop-ups as you move between Web sites. In most cases, you'll restrict browsing on the server anyway because you don't want to contaminate it with outside sources of information. Because privacy is important and you really don't care about the cookies from Web sites anyway, the best policy is to set the privacy setting to High and ensure that you don't allow pop-ups.

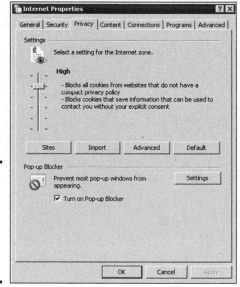

Figure 5-7:
Disallow most cookies and all pop-ups on your server.

Configuring the Content tab

The Content tab contains settings that control your interaction with information on Web sites, as shown in Figure 5-8. In most cases, your only interaction with this tab is to turn some features off and to work with any certificates on your machine. Your server should never need the Content Advisor because this tool helps you discover the content rating of Web pages that you visit (unless you plan to let children use your server to browse the Internet).

Normally, it's a good idea to turn off the AutoComplete and Feeds features as well because you really shouldn't use them on a server. You won't be using your e-mail program, so feeds aren't helpful and AutoComplete is dangerous on a server because you want to verify the content you provide in every field of every form you fill out. To disable these features, click Settings in each section and clear all the check boxes. Click OK to make the configuration change complete.

The Certificates section is the important part of the Content tab because you'll likely encounter secure Web sites when working with your server and you want to manage these certificates. In addition, you'll probably install your own certificate when working with features such as Internet Information Server (IIS). To see any certificates installed on your system, click Certificates. You see the Certificates dialog box, where you can import certificates on disk, export certificates to disk, and remove certificates. Microsoft groups the certificates by category.

When you experience problems accessing a secure Web site, click SSL State. This action clears the Secure Sockets Layer (SSL) cache and forces the browser to download new information from the server you're attempting to access.

In some cases, you may also need to know about the certificate publishers that your system accepts. Click Publishers and you see the Certificates dialog box again. However, in this case, the dialog box lists only the publishers that your system will accept. As with certificates, you can import, export, or remove publisher certificates. The publisher certificates fall into three categories: Trusted Root Certification Authorities (those allowed to issue certificates), Trusted Publishers (those allowed to send you a certificate), and Untrusted Publishers (those whose certificates you need to avoid).

Figure 5-8:
Define how
you'll work
with content
on Web
sites.

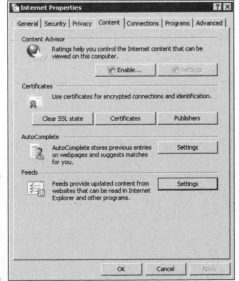

Configuring the Connections tab

The Connections tab determines how you connect to the Internet. If the server is the connection point for the Internet, you won't even need to view this tab. When you use another kind of connection, you need to use this tab to configure the connection requirements. Check with your Internet service provider (ISP) for details on working with this tab. In many cases, the best option is to try the Internet connection first after you've made the connection to the router, hardware firewall, switch, modem, server, or other piece of hardware that provides your connection to the Internet. In many cases, Internet Explorer will surprise you and work without any configuration of this tab.

Configuring the Programs tab

The Programs tab offers a means of setting the default applications to react to specific file types on the Internet. Because you won't use your server to view content, in most cases, the default settings should work fine. However, in the rare case that you need to install a helper application, you can click Set Programs to display the Default Programs window. You can learn more about this window in the "Default Programs" section of Book II, Chapter 3.

You also use the Programs tab to check whether Internet Explorer is the default browser on your machine. Unlike on your workstation, where you browse the Internet, you probably want to retain Internet Explorer as the default and only browser on your server.

Finally, this tab helps you manage any add-ons for Internet Explorer on your server. Again, as with many other features, you probably won't need any add-ons for your server. For example, Windows Update works just fine without any add-ons. You can probably visit most vendor update sites without installing any add-ons either. If you do install an add-on, do so carefully because it can contain viruses and adware that open up your server to those nefarious individuals outside.

Configuring the Advanced tab

The Advanced tab contains a host of advanced settings for Internet Explorer, as shown in Figure 5-9. The Advanced tab contains a host of interesting settings, some of which can help you create a more secure and efficient environment on a server. You probably wouldn't use some of these settings on a client system because you really do need them in order to browse properly.

Look through the list of Advanced tab options and you see features such as visual styles for buttons and other controls. Unless you want to wait for these features to load, you can easily disable them without any loss of functionality. You can also disable pictures and sounds on Web sites because your server will work just fine without the pictures, and it probably doesn't have a sound card installed for the sounds anyway. All of these features rob your system of performance when you enable them, and they don't serve any useful purpose on a server.

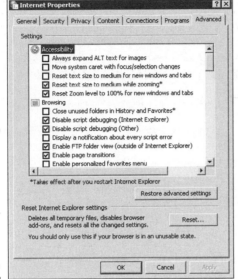

Figure 5-9:
Configure the advanced settings to provide a secure and efficient environment.

As far as security is concerned, you've already enhanced security by severely limiting what Web sites can do in a browser and by increasing privacy. However, the Advanced tab contains a few other settings you may want to try. Look in the Security section of the Settings list and you'll see that you can do things like enable the phishing filter and enable memory protection. (Although the memory protection uses some server resources and could potentially cause compatibility problems, it also tends to reduce the potential for online attacks.)

Defining the personalization settings

The personalization settings for Windows Server 2008 define the look of the display, the themes you use, and special features, such as the use of effects. You can access these settings in a number of ways. The easiest method is to right-click the Desktop and choose Personalize from the context menu. This window is also accessible by opening the Personalization applet in the Control Panel. No matter how you open the Personalization window, you see a list of options like the ones shown in Figure 5-10.

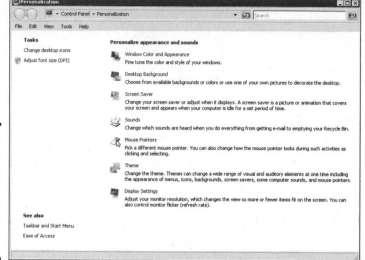

Figure 5-10:
Use the Personalization options to provide a nicer-looking display.

Microsoft provides a Spartan appearance for Windows Server 2008 for a good reason: Most administrators aren't very interested in fancy displays for a system they interact with for only a few minutes each day. The efficiency of the display is more important than how it looks. In fact, the special appearance of the client operating systems isn't even available. Unless you specifically install the Desktop Experience feature (not a good use of system resources or screen real estate), you won't find the Windows Server 2008 options available as one of the personalization settings. For the most part, the choices you have are very limited, as described in this list:

✦ **Window Color and Appearance:** You can choose from the Windows Classic, Windows Standard, or a number of high-contrast settings to define Windows color and appearance. However, the Appearance and Settings dialog box, which appears when you click the Window Color and Appearance link, contains an Effects button. When you click Effects, you see a listing of effects that you can use to enhance your display, such as Use the Following Method to Smooth the Edges of Screen Fonts. Selecting these effects uses system resources, but you can make the display easier to see in some cases by using them.

✦ **Desktop Background:** The Windows background setting is limited to a number of colors and a few pictures.

✦ **Screen Saver:** The screen savers are limited to the Blank and Windows Logo screen savers. Of course, you can always add screen savers (files that have the SCR file extension) from other systems. You must place these additional files in the \Windows\System32 folder of the server.

✦ **Sounds:** In most cases, you won't have access to any sounds on the server unless you have a sound card installed and start the Windows Audio service. See the "Configuring the sound options" section of Book II, Chapter 2 for details.

✦ **Mouse Pointers:** Windows Server 2008 provides a full range of mouse features. You can switch the buttons, change the double-click speed, and even use all the accessibility features you my have used in the past. See the "Configuring the mouse" section of Book II, Chapter 2 for details.

✦ **Theme:** You can create and save themes in Windows Server 2008. In addition, the Windows Server 2008 setup includes the Windows Classic theme, and you can use other themes you've obtained from other sources. However, the standard theme support in Windows Server 2008 is very thin, and you really don't need themes to manage your server efficiently.

✦ **Display Settings:** Clicking this link displays the Display Settings dialog box, where you can view the current display resolution and number of colors for your monitor. Use the Resolution slider to change the display resolution, and the Colors drop-down list box to change the number of colors that your server displays. When you click OK, Windows makes the changes and asks whether you want to keep them. In addition to these standard settings, you can click the Advanced Settings button to see any advanced configuration options that your display adapter and monitor provide. These settings are vendor specific, so you need to refer to your vendor documentation for details.

Defining the Problem Reports and Solutions settings

Opening the Problem Reports and Solutions applet of the Control Panel displays the Problem Reports and Solutions window, as shown in Figure 5-11. Windows automatically stores problem reports for you. Click See Problems to Check to see a list of existing problems that you haven't reported to Microsoft. Depending on your settings, Windows can also send the reports for you automatically. To send the reports manually and check for solutions, click Check for New Solutions. To change the level of automation this feature provides, click Settings.

As you can see, this window doesn't contain any solutions, but if the system shown in the figure had a problem and a corresponding solution, it would appear in the list shown in Figure 5-11. When you want to see the problems and solutions from the past, click View Problem History. The history can become lengthy. If you decide that you want to remove the entries, click Clear Solution and Problem History. Unfortunately, this is an all-or-nothing proposition, and the results are permanent. Windows asks whether you're sure that you want to clear all the history. Click Clear All to complete the action.

Figure 5-11:
The
Problem
Reports and
Solutions
window
makes it
easy to
report
Windows
problems
and get
answers.

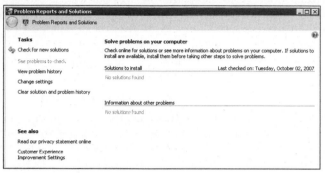

Defining the Regional and Language Options settings

In some cases, you may have to change the regional and language options for the server by opening the Regional and Language Options applet in the Control Panel. For example, you may have to change the keyboard layout or the format of any information on-screen. Figure 5-12 shows the Regional and Language Options dialog box you use to perform this task.

Figure 5-12:
Configure
the regional
and
language
options for
your needs.

Each of these tabs helps you configure a regional or language option. Regional needs express the requirements of a particular area of the world. For example, even if you speak Spanish, you need to format numbers in a certain way when working in the United Kingdom. You also use a specific monetary indicator. Regional options are different from language options. A language option defines the characteristics of your language, such as the characters you use to express idea and the layout of the computer keyboard. The following list provides a description of each tab:

✦ **Formats:** Defines the formatting used for numbers, currency, time, and date. You'll likely find a region that matches your needs in the Current Format drop-down list. If you determine that Windows doesn't provide a predefined region for you, choose the region that matches most closely and click Customize This Format. You see the Customize Regional Options dialog box, where you can customize every aspect of the regional formats. If you find that you make a mistake, you can always return to the starting point by clicking Reset in the Customize Regional Options dialog box.

✦ **Location:** This tab simply specifies the country. Oddly enough, it doesn't provide any method for adding new countries, so if your country isn't in the list, choose the closest match.

✦ **Keyboards and Languages:** Windows can adapt the layout of your keyboard to match the language you use. For example, you can change the $ symbol over the number 4 to match the currency for your country. You can also gain access to all the special characters that your language uses. Click Change Keyboards to choose a different keyboard layout for your language. In addition to configuring the keyboard, you can display Windows prompts in your language. However, you need to install the language to obtain this benefit in some cases. Click Install/Uninstall Languages to perform this task.

✦ **Administrative:** Most applications today support Unicode, which is a system of displaying the correct characters for a particular language without having to make any changes to the system. However, a few applications still rely on locale, a method of loading a particular character set to support a language. The tab contains the locale setting for your computer — all you need to do is choose the appropriate language. In addition to setting the locale, you see an option for copying your settings to the reserved accounts on the server. These accounts include the default user, local system, local service, and network service.

Defining the Taskbar and Start menu settings

The Taskbar and Start menu options you use are very important because they affect your productivity. Some people prefer what Microsoft now calls the Windows standard menus, while others, like me, prefer the classic menus. There isn't a wrong or right choice — simply the choice that you prefer. To access the settings that control the Taskbar and Start menu settings, right-click the

Taskbar and choose Properties from the context menu. You can also open the Taskbar and Start Menu applet in the Control Panel. Figure 5-13 shows the Taskbar and Start Menu Properties dialog box, which you use to configure these features.

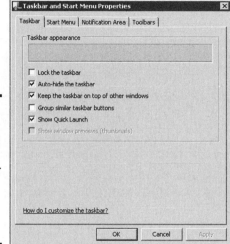

Figure 5-13: Set up the Taskbar and Start menu to meet your particular working requirements.

The Taskbar tab contains the settings that determine how the Taskbar appears on-screen. After you configure the Taskbar as you like it, check Lock the Taskbar so that you don't accidentally change the configuration. In most cases, you want to keep the Taskbar on top of other windows, to ensure that you can always access it. Some people automatically hide the Taskbar so that they regain the screen real estate it uses. The only time you need to group similar buttons is when you use applications, such as Office, that display a window for each document. You can also choose to show the Quick Launch toolbar, which contains icons for applications you commonly use.

The Show Window Previews (Thumbnails) option is available only when you use the standard menus and have the Desktop Experience feature installed. You can't access this feature when using the classic menus. This particular feature shows a preview of the documents you have open, to make it easier to locate the document you want to edit — it's unlikely to make your experience of working with a server much better unless you also use your server as a workstation.

The Start Menu tab, shown in Figure 5-14, shows the two main Start menu options you can choose. When you choose a particular Start menu look, click Customize for that option to configure how it looks. For example, you can choose whether you want to see the Administrative Tools folder and determine whether Windows should expand the Control Panel as a set of menu options.

Try out the various configuration options to determine which ones work best for your particular needs.

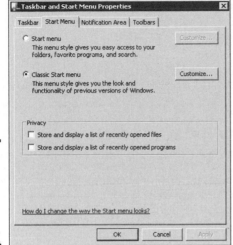

Figure 5-14: Choose a main Start menu look and then customize it.

The check boxes in the Privacy group determine whether Windows tracks the applications and documents you use most often. Most administrators will want to clear these check boxes to reduce the amount of information about the server that an outsider can obtain. Although these features can prove useful on a client system, they aren't particularly helpful on a server because there really isn't a pattern for using applications or documents on a server.

The Notification Area tab contains options for configuring the Notification Area of the Taskbar. You can choose which standard icons Windows displays in the Notification Area, such as time and network status. The Hide Inactive Icons option determines whether Windows hides any icons you don't use very often.

The Toolbars tab contains a list of toolbars you can add to the Taskbar. Of course, every toolbar uses up a little more space on the Taskbar, so you need to exercise care. The standard toolbar selections include Address, Links, Desktop, and Quick Launch. In most cases, you find that the Quick Launch toolbar is quite helpful and you may even want the Desktop toolbar when you define a lot of icons on the Desktop. Unless you perform a lot of browsing with your server, you'll probably find that the Address and Links toolbars don't provide much value for the space they consume.

Book III
Chapter 5

Performing Standard Maintenance

Configuring the Windows performance options

Windows provides a number of performance options, but you find them all over the interface. For example, you previously discovered the Effects dialog box in the "Defining the personalization settings" section of this chapter. You'll find other performance options in other areas of this book. This section discusses another kind of performance option. When you click Settings in the Performance section on the Advanced tab of the System Properties dialog box (refer to Figure 5-1), you see the Performance Options dialog box, as shown in Figure 5-15.

The Visual Effects tab contains options that can make your display more interesting or usable. When you choose the Let Windows Choose What's Best for My Computer option, Windows enables the Smooth Edges of Screen Fonts and Use Visual Styles on Windows and Buttons options. These two options definitely seem to make the display more usable. You can also choose to adjust the display for best appearance (all of the options) or best performance (none of the options) or a custom setup. Many people prefer a custom setup so that they can create a balance between fancy on-screen features and system performance.

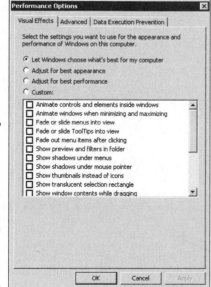

Figure 5-15:
Set performance options that make the display usable while making the system run faster.

The Advanced tab contains settings that control how Windows works with applications. The default setting for a server is to give background tasks priority so that client requests come first. If you're using the server as a workstation, you may want to choose the Programs option instead. Clicking Change on this tab also displays the Virtual Memory dialog box, where you can determine the size of the paging file that Windows uses for virtual memory. Windows uses virtual memory in place of physical memory, in many cases, to answer all the memory requests that applications make. In most cases, unless you have performance or hard disk concerns, you want to let Windows manage the virtual memory.

The Data Execution Prevention (DEP) tab determines how Windows controls access to application memory. A strict policy (the default in Windows Server 2008) can greatly reduce the potential for damaging virus activity in your system. However, a strict policy can also prevent some applications from running properly. You can learn more about DEP at `http://support.microsoft.com/kb/875352`.

Understanding How UAC Affects Maintenance Tasks

When working with Windows Server 2008, you often see the User Account Control (UAC) dialog box appear, which asks whether you really intend to perform a particular action. Although this dialog box can become quite annoying, it serves a useful purpose in alerting you of actions from viruses and other nefarious applications. Whenever you see the UAC dialog box and know that you've started a particular action, simply click Continue, and Windows Server 2008 continues the action (assuming that you have the proper rights).

The UAC features of Windows serve to increase security by reducing the chance that an application can perform any act on the user's behalf, without the user's knowledge. Windows Server 2008 assumes that all users — even administrators — are standard users. If you have an administrator account, you must elevate your privileges from standard user to administrator to perform many tasks. In most cases, this means clicking Continue when the UAC dialog box asks whether you really mean to perform a particular task.

Let's just say that the feature is incredibly annoying for anyone who spends the day performing administrative tasks, but it does serve a useful purpose and you may want to keep it enabled when your server has access to the Internet. Used correctly, UAC ensures that no one can perform an action on your behalf without your knowledge. Given that administrators have considerable power, this feature is especially useful to administrators who might become targets of nefarious individuals. After all, you don't want to suffer the embarrassment of being the source of viruses, adware, or spyware on the very network that you're supposed to protect.

**Book III
Chapter 5**

**Performing
Standard
Maintenance**

However, UAC goes much further than simply asking whether you want to perform a particular task. In some cases, it can actually prevent you from performing tasks, despite your having an administrator account. For example, you'll find that Windows Server 2008 severely hampers your access to the Windows and System32 folders even with an administrator account. Windows Server 2008 meets any attempt to change anything in the folders with disapproval that is seemingly impossible to overcome. The same holds true for the root directory of the boot drive. Network drives are nearly impossible to access as well. In fact, except for your personal data folders, Windows Server 2008 is locked down so tight that many administrative tasks are all but impossible to perform, even with an administrator account. The bottom line is that Windows Server 2008 is all about security. Microsoft has thrown backward compatibility out the window to achieve some level of additional security.

To see how to disable UAC on your system, check the "Disabling UAC on the Server" section in Book III, Chapter 2. However, before you disable UAC completely, check the "Understanding and Using the User Account Control (UAC)" section of Book V, Chapter 3.

Adding and Removing Standard Applications

Windows Server 2008 takes a different approach when it comes to applications than previous versions of the operating system. If you want to add or remove a Windows Server 2008 role or feature, use the Server Manager (see the "Using the Server Manager Console" section of Book II, Chapter 1 for details). However, when you want to work with third-party applications, you open the Programs and Features applet in the Control Panel, as shown in Figure 5-16.

Figure 5-16: Manage third-party applications using the Program and Features applet.

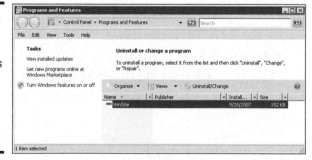

Of course, you install the third-party product using the setup application provided by the vendor, just as you always have. The display shown in Figure 5-16 is for managing the application. Whenever you select an application in the list, the toolbar changes to show actions you can perform with the application. In this case, you can either change or uninstall the program.

The Tasks list includes three entries for other activities you can perform. When you click View Installed Updates, the list shown in Figure 5-16 changes to show the Windows updates you have installed. You can use this display to manage your updates, much as you manage third-party applications.

Clicking Get New Programs Online at Windows Marketplace takes you to the Web site at `http://www.windowsmarketplace.com`, where you can purchase Microsoft products. Clicking Turn Windows Features On or Off displays Server Manager, where you can configure Windows Server 2008 roles and features.

Measuring Reliability and Performance

Knowing how your system is performing is the first step in locating problems of all sorts. Performance and reliability information can help you assess both the hardware (physical) and software status of your system. It can also help you locate problem areas and even predict when failures might occur based on trends. Of course, before you get any of this information, you must actually monitor the system by using the Reliability and Performance Monitor console, as shown in Figure 5-17.

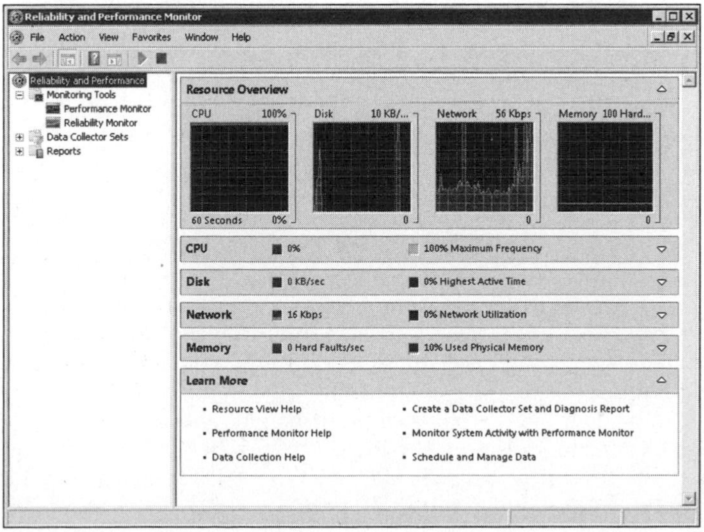

**Book III
Chapter 5**

**Performing
Standard
Maintenance**

Figure 5-17:
Get a quick overview of your system in this Resource Overview window.

The initial display you see provides you with a quick overview of the resources on your server. In many cases, this overview is all you need to determine whether you need to dig further into the system performance information. At some point, you begin to recognize how your system normally performs and you can use this display to see when something is wrong. When you do suspect a problem, you likely need to dig further using the features in the Performance Monitor and Reliability Monitor folders, described in the following sections.

Using the Performance Monitor

The Performance Monitor presents a display of performance information as you configure it. Figure 5-18 shows a typical display. The focus of this display is the graph, which contains colored lines for each of the items you're monitoring. The Performance Monitor also provides a histogram and report view, which you can use when the line graph doesn't work. Press Ctrl+G to switch between the graph types. Below this graph are simple statistics that tell you about maximum, minimum, and average values. Finally, you see a legend that describes what the display is monitoring.

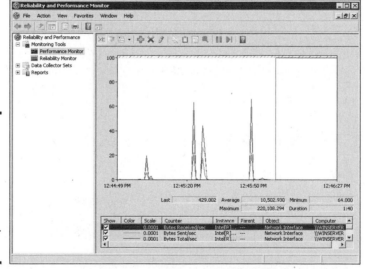

Figure 5-18: Performance monitoring shows how the values of the data change over time.

The basis of the Performance Monitor is very simple. The system installs a special piece of software called a counter. A *counter* does precisely what its name implies — it counts something. The counter may count the number of times an event occurs per second or calculate the percentage of memory used over time. However, the idea is to monitor the system and report on a particular event over a specific time interval. The system includes hundreds of counters, and you'll find that many applications include them as well.

To remove one of the counters from the list shown in Figure 5-18, highlight its entry in the list and press Delete. To highlight a counter so that you can see it better, highlight it in the list and press Ctrl+H. To add a new counter, you press Ctrl+I. In this case, you see the Add Counters dialog box, as shown in Figure 5-19.

The entire display is organized to make finding a particular counter easier. You begin by selecting a computer. Depending on your network setup, you can actually monitor the same counter from several computers so that you can create a centralized display of information.

After you select a computer, you choose a performance object on that computer. Figure 5-19 shows two objects: Job Object Details and LogicalDisk. The object contains a number of counters. These counters describe the performance characteristics of the object. You can select all the counters for an object by clicking the object, or you can click the plus sign next to the object to display individual counters and choose those individual counters from the list. Figure 5-19 shows the % Disk Read Time counter selected.

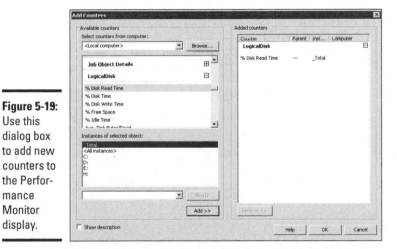

Figure 5-19: Use this dialog box to add new counters to the Performance Monitor display.

A counter has to measure something. In some cases, the counter has only one item it can measure, but this is the exception rather than the rule. Figure 5-19 shows a more typical example. In this case, the counter can measure the performance for all hard drives or a particular hard drive. A single measure, such as _Total or C:, is an instance of the counter.

When you finish choosing the computer, object, counter, and instance, click Add. The Performance Monitor adds the new counter to the list of counters in the left pane. You can add as many counters as needed to monitor your system for a particular need. Of course, too many counters make the display hard to read, so you have to balance your need for information against the readability of the display. When you finish adding counters, click OK and you see the new counters displayed on-screen.

Using the Reliability Monitor

The Reliability Monitor is more of a static display than the Performance Monitor. It's a kind of specialized log, as shown in Figure 5-20. The display begins with a stability report. The stability of your server is rated from 1 to 10, with higher numbers providing better stability. The stability for the selected day appears to the right of the chart. You can choose a particular date by clicking its entry.

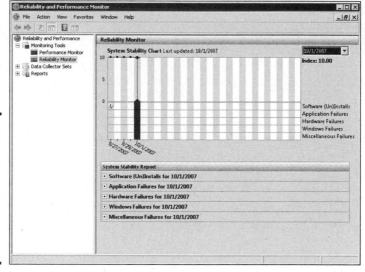

Figure 5-20:
The Reliability Monitor helps you understand the stability of your system.

The chart also includes little boxes that can contain a number. For example, if you uninstall a piece of software on a particular date, you see the number 1 in the box where the Software (Un)Installs entry crosses the date of interest. You can use this tabular data to determine which of the dates to select. When you find a date with an entry, you can see the details of the event in the report that appears below the chart.

The report includes a number of entries that help you quickly determine how the event affects your system. For example, a software installation includes the name of the software, version, activity (install or uninstall), activity status, and date of the event. You can usually find additional information about the event in the event logs.

Protecting System Data

The data on your server is probably worth more than just about anything on your computer system. Data is the basis of everything you do in your business, and it's irreplaceable in many situations. Consequently, you'll want to back up the data and have it ready for a restore when necessary. Of course, before you can perform a backup, you need to install the Windows Server Backup features. To start a backup or recovery, you open the Windows Server Backup console, found in the Administrative Tools folder. You see the Windows Server Backup console, as shown in Figure 5-21. The following sections assume that you have the required support installed.

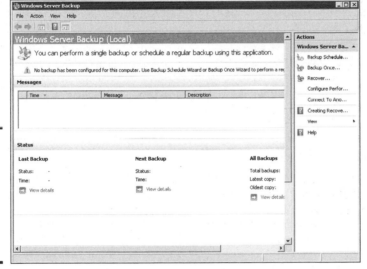

Figure 5-21: Use the Windows Server Backup console to perform backups.

Performing a system backup

The Windows Server Backup console provides two techniques for performing a backup. You can either back up manually using a one-time backup or schedule a backup to run at regular intervals. The following sections describe both backup types.

Performing a one-time backup

A one-time backup lets you back up the system manually. You can perform such a backup immediately before you install a new piece of software or perform a major configuration task. It's never a good idea to back up manually all the time — reserve manual backups for special situations. The following steps describe how to perform a manual backup:

1. **Click Backup Once in the Actions pane of the Windows Server Backup console.**

Windows Server Backup displays the Backup Options dialog box of the Backup Once Wizard. The first time you use this wizard, you must define the backup settings. However, after the first time, you can choose whether you want to use the previous settings or create new settings.

2. **Select the Different Options option if you want to create a backup using different options, and then click Next.**

When you choose Different Options, you see a warning message that you'll lose your previous backups if you don't restore the catalog first. The purpose of this message is to warn you that you need to restore any old data that you need before you create the new backup. If this is your first backup, you don't have any old data, so using the Different Options option won't cause any problems. Click Yes if you want to create a new backup or No if you want to restore some old data first.

After you make a choice about restoring the collection, you see the Select Backup Configuration dialog box. This dialog box lets you choose between performing a full backup or backing up only some of the information on your hard drive. Windows Server Backup doesn't provide the functionality of NT Backup, so you can't select individual folders, as you did in the past. If you choose the Full Server option, go to Step 4.

3. **Choose Custom and click Next.**

You see the Select Backup Items dialog box, shown in Figure 5-22. Place a check mark next to any of the volumes you want to back up. When you select Enable System Recovery, you must include the minimum number of volumes required to perform a complete system recovery. Using this option can increase the size of the backup significantly on multiboot hard drives but ensures that you can perform a complete recovery.

4. **Click Next.**

You see the Specify Destination Type dialog box. You can choose to store the backup on a local drive, including a DVD drive, or on a shared remote drive.

5. **Choose a destination type and click Next.**

The wizard displays either the Specify Remote Folder dialog box or the Select Backup Destination dialog box, depending on your choice of destination type. In both cases, you must provide the destination for the backup.

6. Specify the destination for the backup and click Next.

You see the Specify Advanced Options dialog box. This dialog box requires that you choose a Volume Shadow Copy Service (VSS) option. Although this option sounds complicated, all it really does is ask whether you want to tell the hard drive that the files are backed up or leave the file attributes as is so that you can use a third-party application to perform a backup of your server applications. If your only backup method is Windows Server Backup, choose the VSS Full Backup option; otherwise, choose the VSS Copy Backup (Recommended) option.

7. Choose a VSS backup option and click Next.

You see a confirmation dialog box, where you see the options you've selected.

8. Verify the options you've selected and click Backup.

The Backup Once Wizard shows you the progress of the backup.

9. Click Close when the backup completes.

The backup appears at the destination, in a folder named WindowsImageBackup.

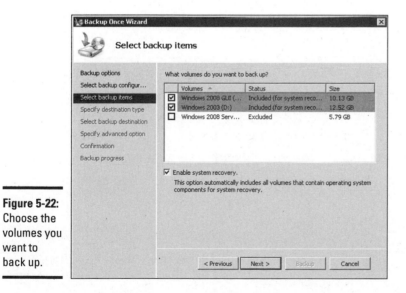

Figure 5-22:
Choose the
volumes you
want to
back up.

Performing a scheduled backup

Creating a scheduled backup is essentially the same as creating a one-time backup. The steps for using the Backup Schedule Wizard are essentially the same as using the Backup Once Wizard. The only two differences are that you must include all the drives required for a system restore when making a scheduled backup and you have to provide a time for the backup. In fact, you can select multiple backup times, as shown in Figure 5-23.

A scheduled backup assumes that you have a disk specifically set aside for the purpose. If you try to use an existing disk, the system asks you to attach a disk that it can use to perform the backup. The Backup Schedule Wizard won't let you use a DVD or remote storage. Consequently, you may find that a scheduled backup has limited appeal unless you have the local hardware required to perform it.

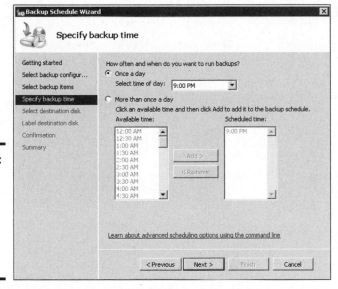

Figure 5-23:
Define the times you want to perform a scheduled backup each day.

Performing a system restore

You won't ever want to do it, but something can happen to your hard drive and you'll find a need to restore it. The Windows Server Backup console also provides a means to restore any backups you've created by using it. The following steps tell you how to perform this task:

1. **Click Recover.**

You see the Recovery Wizard. The Getting Started dialog box asks you to choose a source of data for the recovery. The default is to recover data from the current server. However, you can also choose a remote location. If you choose a remote location, you need to provide additional information about where to find the data.

2. **Choose a backup source and click Next.**

   If you've chosen a remote data source, you need to provide the remote location information. Otherwise, proceed to the next step, where you see the Select Backup Date dialog box, and choose the backup date and time you want to use:

   a. **Click Next.**

      The Recovery Wizard asks you to choose a location type. You can obtain data from a local drive or from a remote shared drive.

   b. **Choose a location type and click Next.**

      The wizard displays either a Specify Remote Folder dialog box or a Select Backup Destination dialog box, depending on your choice of location type. In both cases, you must provide the source of the backup.

   c. **Provide the backup source information and click Next.**

3. **Select a backup date on the calendar and then choose a backup time on that date. Click Next.**

   The Select Recovery Type dialog box asks you to choose what you want to restore. You can restore individual files and folders, entire applications, or the volume as a whole.

4. **Select a recovery type and click Next.**

   The steps you follow at this point depend on the kind of recovery you chose. For example, if you choose to recover individual files and folders, you need to choose which files and folders to recover. Likewise, you need to choose applications for an application recovery or entire volumes for a volume recovery. Eventually, you see a confirmation dialog box, where you see the results of your choices. The files and folders recovery presents an advantage in that you can recover the data to a different location from the original location, as shown in Figure 5-24.

5. **Verify the options you've selected and click Recover.**

   The Recovery Wizard shows you the progress of the restore.

6. **Click Close when the recovery process completes.**

   You find the files you restored in the expected locations.

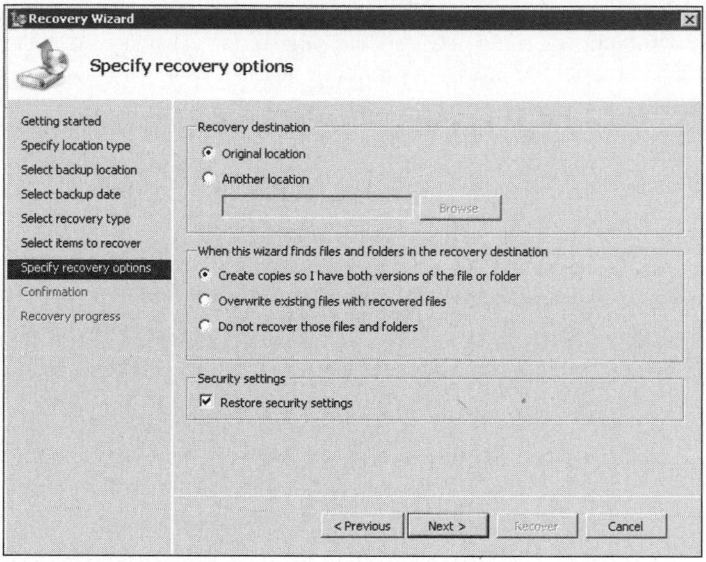

Figure 5-24: File and folder recoveries provide additional options for how the system performs the recovery.

Performing Disk Management Tasks

Managing your disk storage can make the difference between a server that everyone likes to use and one that fails to do the job. A server should have enough storage for everyone's basic needs, plus additional storage for growth and potential emergencies. The following sections describe a number of disk management utilities.

Performing share and storage management

The Share and Storage Management console helps you manage the shares on your server. You can determine with ease which resources are shared, how you've shared them, and who is using them. You can also define new shares and disconnect users from shares when necessary. This console provides a complete listing of shares on your system, as shown in Figure 5-25.

You can use this console to create new shares by clicking Provision Share in the Actions pane. The process for creating a share is essentially the same no matter where you create it. The "Sharing storage resources in the workgroup" section of Book II, Chapter 4 provides additional information about creating shares.

It's also possible to use this console to manage users. If you want to see all sessions that are using shares on the local machine, click Manage Sessions in the Actions pane. You see a list of every user who has some shared resource open on the system. Highlight a user and click Close Selected to stop that user from using resources. If you want to disconnect everyone, click Close All instead.

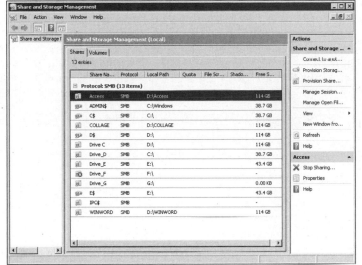

Figure 5-25: Manage the shares on your system to ensure that users have access and data remains secure.

When you need a little more control over share management, click Manage Open Files in the Actions pane. You see a list of all open files on the server, along with the name of the user who has opened them and how the files are opened (read-only, write-only, or read/write). The display even tells you how many locks each of the files has. As with the sessions display, you can select individual files and click Close Selected to close that file or click Close All when you want to close all open files.

In addition to working with users and opened resources, you can manage the shares. Highlight a share and click Properties in the Actions pane when you want to change characteristics of that share, such as the description, permission, and method of caching. If you simply want to stop sharing the resource, highlight it and click Stop Sharing in the Actions pane. Windows asks whether you're sure that you want to stop sharing the resource. Clicking Yes removes the share. It's important to note that most changes you make to a share take effect the next time the user logs in to the system.

Performing disk management

You can access the Disk Management console in a number of ways. The easiest method is to open the Computer Management console. You'll find the Disk Management functionality in the `Computer Management\Storage\ Disk Management` folder. If you want to preserve a little screen real estate, you can also open the Disk Management console using the DiskMgmt.MSC file. (See the "Accessing the Administrative Tools Folder" section of Book III, Chapter 1 for details on opening MSC files.) No matter which way you open it, you see a listing of the drives on your system, as shown in Figure 5-26.

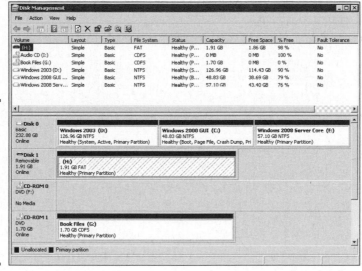

Figure 5-26: Disk management helps you configure and manage the drives on your system.

The main display shows the status of each of the drives on your system. The display includes flash drives, the hard drive, and CD/DVD drives. You won't see floppy drives listed. The top of the displays shows the status of each drive and includes information such as the amount of free disk space and the file system.

Whenever you click one of the drive entries in the upper display, you see it selected in the lower display. This lower display shows the physical media on which the drives exist. A single hard drive can contain multiple volumes, each of which appears as a drive to Windows. The physical media display also shows any free space that you can use for other purposes.

The display shown in Figure 5-26 doesn't make the management feature very accessible. The basic management tasks appear as icons in the toolbar. You can use these icons to display the console tree, obtain help, and display the Actions pane. In addition, you can refresh the display, see the selected drive properties, open the drive, or explore the drive. Finally, you can display the Settings dialog box, which is used to configure the Disk Management console appearance.

If you want to see the advanced management tasks you can perform with a particular drive, right-click its entry. The context menu contains a list of the tasks you can perform, which includes formatting the drive, setting its partition as active, changing the drive letter, extending the volume, shrinking the volume, or deleting the volume altogether. If you have the correct hardware, you can also mirror the drives to provide fault tolerance.

Defragmenting the hard drive

All hard drives eventually become fragmented as you use them. *Fragmentation* is a process where files appear in multiple locations on the hard drive rather than in a single location. A fragmented hard drive doesn't perform as well because the drive heads must move around a lot more to get work done. *Defragmenting* the hard drive is a process where you move the data around on the hard drive until all the files appear in contiguous clusters, making it possible to access them in a single long read rather than in multiple short reads.

To start the Disk Defragmenter console, choose Start⇨Programs⇨ Accessories⇨System Tools⇨Disk Defragmenter. Disk Defragmenter performs an analysis of your system and tells you whether it can improve performance, as shown in Figure 5-27.

Book III
Chapter 5

Performing Standard Maintenance

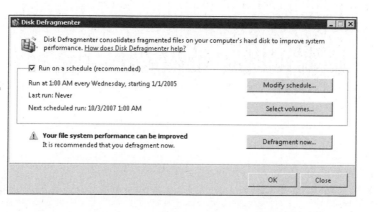

Figure 5-27:
Defragment your hard drives to improve performance.

Notice that you can set Disk Defragmenter to run automatically. You can choose a time that's unlikely to bother anyone and run Disk Defragmenter automatically so that your system is always optimized. Simply check the Run On a Schedule option and then configure the time to perform the task.

When you see that the hard drives require defragmentation, click Defragment Now. Disk Defragmenter asks you which disks to defragment. Place a check mark next to each drive that you want to work with and then click OK. At this point, Disk Defragmenter begins its task. You can stop the process at any time by clicking Cancel Defragmentation.

Some administrators complain about the time required to defragment a hard drive. One way to make defragmentation and virus scans faster is to free up as many machine resources as possible. Close as many open applications as you can, including those that appear in the Notification Area. In addition, sever network and Internet connections when you can. Anything you can do to make the machine work more efficiently speeds up both defragmentation and virus scanning.

Automating Diagnostic Tasks with Task Scheduler

Task Scheduler provides a means for running jobs automatically on the server. You use Task Scheduler to specify a particular time or event that tells Windows to begin doing work. For example, you can tell Task Scheduler to automatically defragment your hard drive. You open Task Scheduler by choosing Start➪Programs➪Accessories➪System Tools➪Task Scheduler. You see the Task Scheduler display, as shown in Figure 5-28.

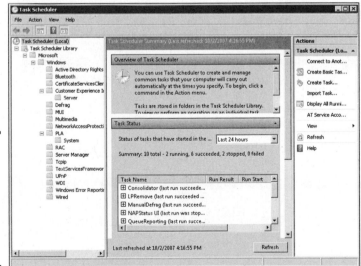

Figure 5-28: Use Task Scheduler to ensure that work is accomplished on your server.

Discovering the task status

The Task Status pane tells you how many tasks are running. You can go into the individual folders to determine the task status. The default setting shows you the last 24 hours of activity. You can change this default to anything from 30 days to 1 hour. When you change the status window, you see more or fewer tasks in the window.

Below the Task Status pane is the Active Tasks pane (not shown in Figure 5-28). This pane shows which tasks Task Scheduler has scheduled to run, including those that are currently running.

Using preconfigured tasks

Task Scheduler comes with a number of preconfigured tasks. You find them in the Task Scheduler Library, as shown in the left pane of Figure 5-28. If you want to use one of these tasks, highlight its folder. You see task entries, such as those shown in Figure 5-29. For example, you can defragment a drive manually or defragment it on a schedule, so Task Scheduler provides two templates you can use for the task.

To modify one of these templates, highlight its entry and choose Properties in the Actions pane. You see the task Properties dialog box, as shown in Figure 5-30. This Properties dialog box tells you everything about the task. For example, you can see the application name, how the task is run, and the security options for the task. These templates can tell you a lot about how to run your own tasks because you know that they're already debugged and ready to use.

Figure 5-29:
Task Scheduler comes with a number of precon-figured tasks.

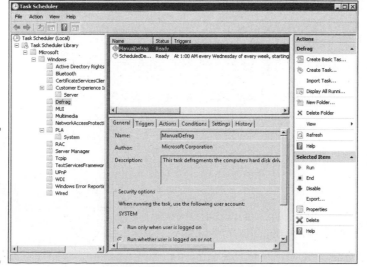

The Triggers tab, shown in Figure 5-30, is the one to use for starting the task. A *trigger* is an event that starts the task. You may think that the only trigger available is a scheduled time. However, you can also create triggers for various events, such as

✦ Logon for a particular user

✦ System startup

✦ Idle time

✦ When an event occurs the event gets logged into the event log

✦ Task creation or modification

✦ Connection to a user session

✦ Disconnection from a user session

✦ Workstation docking

✦ Workstation undocking

No matter how you approach the problem, you still need a trigger to start the task, which means modifying something on the Triggers tab. You can use a number of approaches when working with this tab. First, you can simply enable the default trigger that Microsoft provides. Highlight the trigger entry, click Edit, check Enabled in the Edit Trigger dialog box, and click OK. You're ready to go at this point. Second, you can create a new trigger. Simply click New and you see the New Trigger dialog box, where you can configure the trigger to meet your needs.

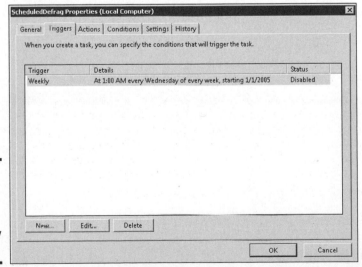

Figure 5-30:
Set the time
to run the
task and
you're ready
to go.

Creating your own tasks

In some cases, you need to create your own tasks for an application that isn't part of Windows. You have two options for creating a new task. The first option is to create a basic task. The "Attaching tasks to event logs and custom views" section of Book III, Chapter 1 shows you how to use this approach. You can also create a task by using the Create Task dialog box. To use this option, click Create Task. You see a dialog box that looks similar to the one shown in Figure 5-30. The only difference is that you need to supply the entries for it. The templates show you how to create a task by using this approach.

Working with Remote Desktop

The Remote Desktop Connection application provides the means to connect to Windows Server 2008 for remote management. You need this application only when you want to access the server from your client machine, which may be the only option you have in some cases. The Remote Desktop Connection application is exceptionally useful because it lets you create a direct connection to the server. You can monitor events and manage the system directly, which reduces one potential cause of failure (making the remote connection every time you want to perform a task).

You must make any changes you want to the Remote Desktop Connection application configuration before you connect to the remote server. After you make the connection, you can't change the configuration. Consequently, it's always a good idea to create a complete configuration first, save it to disk, and then reopen it as needed for a particular server. Otherwise, you spend a lot of time reconfiguring Remote Desktop Connection every time you want to use it. Select Start⟹Programs⟹Accessories⟹Communications⟹Remote Desktop Connection to start the Remote Desktop Connection application. The following sections describe how to use this application.

Creating a connection

Before you can use the Remote Desktop Connection application (I refer to it simply as Remote Desktop from this point on), you need to set up Windows Server 2008 to provide Terminal Server connectivity. You'll find a complete discussion of this topic in the "Working with Terminal Server" section of Book IV, Chapter 3. When the server is ready for a connection, you must configure Remote Desktop to make the connection. The following procedure helps you make the connection:

1. **Start the application and click Options.**

The General tab shows the connection options, as shown in Figure 5-31.

2. **Type the server name or select it from the drop-down list in the Computer field.**

3. **Type your account name on the server in the User Name field.**

4. **Type your password in the Password field.**

   Make sure you use the password for your account on the remote system.

5. **Type the name of the server in the Domain field when using a workgroup setup. If you're using a domain setup, type the name of the domain in the Domain field.**

6. **Optionally, check Save My Password if you want Remote Desktop to save your password for future use.**

Figure 5-31:
Set the connection parameters for the connection you want to normally make.

7. **(Optional) Click Save As.**

   You see the Save As dialog box. If you want to save this setup as the default connection, click Save. Otherwise, type a name for the setup in the File Name field and click Save. You can save as many setups as needed for the servers you want to access. Use the default setup for the server you access most often.

8. **Click Connect.**

   You see Remote Desktop performing all the required connection tasks. Eventually, you see the Remote Desktop window, as shown in Figure 5-32.

After you create the initial connection, Remote Desktop opens with the default connection already set up. If you want to use the default connection, all you need to do is click Connect When Remote Desktop starts. Otherwise, you can click Options, click Open, choose the connection you want to use from the Open dialog box, click Open in the Open dialog box, and, finally, click Connect to make the connection. You won't need to create a setup more than once if you save it to disk.

It's also possible to double-click the Remote Desktop Profile (RDP) file containing a connection in Windows Explorer to make the connection to the server, so you can simply place the RDP file on your Desktop to make the connection instantly accessible.

Figure 5-32: The remote connection appears in a special Remote Desktop window.

Setting the display

The display settings you use affect not only how much screen real estate you have for performing tasks but also performance. Using a larger screen size gives you more space to work. However, a larger screen size also requires more network bandwidth to transmit the data. Consequently, you must weigh the need to see as much as possible on the remote server against the performance requirements for your task. Figure 5-33 shows the display settings.

The Remote Desktop Size slider lets you change the size of the window. The smallest size is 640 x 480 pixels, which is normally too small to work with a GUI system. If you want to use your entire display to work with Windows Server 2008, move the slider all the way to the right. The size changes to Full Screen, and the display takes up your entire display area. In fact, it looks like you're working directly at the remote console rather than using Remote Desktop.

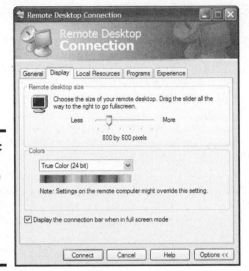

Figure 5-33: Define a display size that works best for the work you need to perform.

If you want to continue working with your local system while managing the remote system, make sure that you check the Display the Connection Bar When in Full Screen Mode option. Otherwise, you may need to log out every time you want to regain access to the local system.

Performance isn't affected by just the size of the screen. Notice that you can also modify the number of colors that Remote Desktop displays. More colors translate into a better display but also reduce performance because Remote Desktop has to transfer more data for the additional colors. Because Windows Server 2008 lacks much in the way of a GUI, you experience a performance gain by setting the number of colors to 256 colors. In most cases, you won't even notice the difference in appearance, but you will notice the difference in performance.

Accessing local resources

Remote Desktop makes it possible to map your local hardware to respond to events on the remote machine. Figure 5-34 shows the settings you can use to map resources as needed. The following list describes each of the resource mapping areas:

✦ **Remote Computer Sound:** Lets you bring sounds from the remote machine to your local machine. This setting has three options: You can choose to play the remote sound locally, not play the remote sound at all (effectively muting the remote system), or play the sound at the remote location.

Figure 5-34:
Perform
automatic
resource
mapping to
make local
resources
available for
use.

+ **Keyboard:** Controls the use of control-key combinations. For example, when you press Alt+Tab, this setting controls whether you switch between applications on the local machine or the remote machine. This setting affects Remote Desktop only when you have it selected when working in windowed mode. If you press Alt+Tab when Remote Desktop is working in a window and you don't have Remote Desktop selected, the Alt+Tab combination always affects the local machine even when you choose the On the Remote Computer option. Normally, any control key combinations go to the remote machine only when you use Remote Desktop in full-screen mode.

+ **Local Devices:** Determines which local devices you can access from the remote machine. This may sound like a very odd consideration, but when you're working with the remote machine, Remote Desktop shuts off access to local resources, such as disk drives, printers, and serial ports. Only your display, keyboard, and mouse are active on the remote machine, unless you tell Remote Desktop to perform the required mapping. Check any of these options to make the resources on your local machine available when working at the remote machine.

Running a configuration program

You may find that you want to run a configuration program on the remote machine when you create the connection. This program can perform any task, and you can use both batch and script files, in addition to standard applications. Figure 5-35 shows the Programs tab. The options work very much like a remote profile. When you want to use a remote program, check Start the Following Program on Connection, type the name of the application you want to use (including full path), and tell Remote Desktop which folder you want to use as a starting point.

Figure 5-35:
Use a configur-
ation
application
as needed
to automate
Remote
Desktop
tasks.

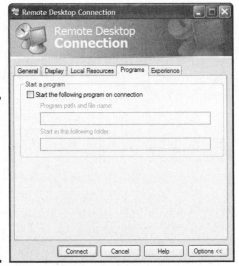

Optimizing performance

The connection you use to create a Remote Desktop is important. You can't expect the same performance from a dial-up connection as you do from a high-speed internal network. Consequently, Remote Desktop provides a method for telling it what to expect in the way of connection, to optimize connection performance, as shown in Figure 5-36.

Choosing one of the default options, such as LAN (10 Mbps or Higher), auto-matically sets the options that Remote Desktop uses — you don't need to do anything else. As an alternative, you can choose Custom from the list and configure the options you want to use. Windows Server 2008 works best with the Custom setting, even if you're working across a LAN.

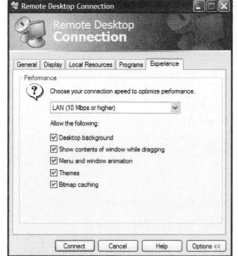

Figure 5-36:
Use only the resources you actually need to obtain good performance.

Creating a Windows Recovery Disc

You may find one day that your server won't boot or that it has some other serious problem. Of course, you already have your backup disk, but it isn't much good without some means of booting the computer. That's where a recovery disk comes into play. Creating one provides a means of recovering your system after a major failure. The following steps describe how to create a recovery disk:

1. **Insert a blank disk in the recordable DVD drive you want to use to create the recovery disc.**

2. **Choose Start⇨Programs⇨Maintenance⇨Create a Recovery Disc.**

You see the Create a Recovery Disc Wizard. The first step is to choose a DVD drive that has a blank disk in it.

3. **Choose the drive with the blank disk and click Create Disc.**

The wizard asks you to insert the Windows installation disk. If you have a second drive on your system, the wizard suggests using this second drive to make the process faster.

4. **Insert the Windows installation disk in the suggested drive and click Continue.**

   The Windows Recovery Disc Wizard begins creating the recovery disc. Get a cup of coffee while you wait because this process can take a while to complete. When the process is complete, you see complete instructions for using your recovery disc.

5. **Click Close twice to complete the task.**

Chapter 6: Working at the Command Line

In This Chapter

✔ Accessing the administrator command line

✔ Performing command line configuration

✔ Managing environment variables

✔ Getting help with command line utilities

✔ Using symbols at the command line

Some people associate the command line with DOS (the Disk Operating System used many years ago, before Windows arrived) or very old network operating systems. A few people associate it with modern operating systems, such as Linux, even though these operating systems have added a graphical user interface (GUI) over the years. However, the command line is still there and still useful. You can use it to automate tasks by using batch files, even if you aren't a programmer. In many cases, you can perform tasks faster at the command line than by relying on a GUI, as long as you know the *syntax* (the combination of arguments and command line switches) to perform the task. Even if you don't use the command line every day, administrators should know that it exists and have a basic idea of how to use it. Not knowing about the command line is like adding a screwdriver to your toolkit and leaving the hammer at home because you don't think you'll need it.

This chapter provides you with enough information to use the command line in Windows Server 2008. Some of the rules are different from previous versions of Windows, so you need this information even if you've worked at the command line before. For example, you'll find that you no longer have access to the root directory of your server and that you must open an administrative command line to perform useful work in many cases. These security restrictions can cause considerable problems for administrators who are used to working with older versions of Windows, but they really can help reduce potential security risks to your system. The level to which you customize your server depends on how much time you plan to spend working there.

Opening an Administrative Command Line

Opening a command line seems like an easy task, and it is — in older versions of Windows. However, Windows Server 2008 makes you jump through several hoops to gain the access you need. Unfortunately, when you open a command line, even as an administrator, you don't have all the access you require. If you type **WhoAmI /PRIV** and press Enter at the command line, you'll find that Windows severely curtails your rights. Notice that the command prompt shows that most of your rights are disabled. Use the following steps to overcome this problem:

1. **Open the System Configuration console, found in the Administrative Tools folder.**

2. **Select the Tools tab.**

You see a list of tools you can use, including one that disables UAC and another that enables it, as shown in Figure 6-1.

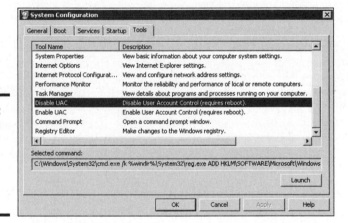

Figure 6-1: Locate the tools for enabling and disabling UAC.

3. **Highlight Disable UAC and click Launch.**

Windows displays a command prompt, runs the command, and shows the message "The operation completed successfully." The success message shows that you have your rights back.

4. **Type** Exit **at the command line and press Enter.**

The command prompt disappears.

5. **Reboot your system.**

You now have the rights you need at the command line.

Now that UAC can't interfere with your activities, you're ready to open an administrative command line. An administrative command line provides you with full rights at the command line. Without these rights, you'll find that many tasks are nearly impossible to perform. Use these steps to open an administrative command line:

1. Choose Start⇨Programs⇨Accessories.

You see the Accessories menu, which includes the Command Prompt shortcut.

2. Right-click the Command Prompt shortcut and choose Run As Administrator from the context menu.

Windows displays a command prompt that provides you with full access to system functionality.

At this point, you must take ownership of several directories and give yourself permission to use them. Use the following steps to give yourself permission to work at the command line:

1. Type Takeown /A /F C:\ **and press Enter.**

Windows displays the success message "SUCCESS: The file (or folder): "C:\" now owned by the administrators group." This command takes ownership of C:\ for the Administrators group. You must take ownership, or else any attempt to change the access rights for administrators will fail.

The commands provided in this section assume that you're using the C: drive as your boot drive. If you're using a different drive for your boot drive, replace the C: with the drive for your system, such as D:. The command will succeed only when you provide the correct drive letter.

2. Type ICACLs C:\ /Grant:r Administrators:F /T /C **and press Enter.**

Windows displays a message such as "Successfully processed 155 files; Failed processing 11 files." The fact that you can't gain access to some files is expected. For example, you can't gain access to the paging file and there isn't a good reason to do so. This command is successful when you gain access to the majority of the files.

You use this command to tell the ICACLs command to change the rights for C:\. The /Grant command line switch replaces the current rights for administrators (notice the :r entry) with full access. The /T command line switch indicates that the ICACLs is supposed to perform this replacement for all subdirectories and files and that it should ignore any errors it experiences. The Administrators group now has full access to the root directory; however, you don't have full access yet, even if you're a member of the Administrators group. You still don't have access to the Program Files or Windows directories. That's because Microsoft places additional restrictions on these directories.

An alternative to using Run As Administrator

If you always use the command line as an administrator, right-clicking the Command Prompt shortcut and choosing Run As Administrator from the context menu can get old quickly, especially if you forget to do it when you're busy. One way around this problem is to set the shortcut to always run in administrator mode. To make this change, right-click the Command Prompt shortcut and choose Properties from the context menu. When you see the Command Prompt Properties dialog box, select the Shortcut tab and click Advanced. Check Run As Administrator in the Advanced Properties dialog box and click OK twice. From this point on, every time you open the command prompt, you open it in administrator mode.

---

3. **Type** Takeown /A /F C:\Windows **and press Enter.**

4. **Type** ICACLs C:\Windows /Grant:r Administrators:F /T /C **and press Enter.**

   This particular command takes a long time to execute, even on the fastest machine, because the \Windows folder contains a significant number of entries.

5. **Type** Takeown /A /F "C:\Program Files" **and press Enter.**

   Make sure to include the double quotes or else the command won't work.

6. **Type** ICACLs "C:\Program Files" /Grant:r Administrators:F /T /C **and press Enter.**

   At this point, you should have the access required to perform administrative tasks (with the caveat that your system is also more exposed to a possible outside attack).

7. **Type** Exit **and press Enter.**

   Windows closes the command line.

You now have a workable configuration. However, you don't want to keep UAC disabled because it provides some protections for your server. The following steps describe how to enable the UAC:

1. **Open the System Configuration console, found in the Administrative Tools folder.**

2. **Select the Tools tab.**

3. **Highlight Enable UAC and click Launch within the System Configuration console.**

   Windows displays a command prompt, runs the command, and shows the message "The operation completed successfully." The success message shows that you have your rights back.

4. **Type** Exit **at the command line and press Enter.**

   The command prompt disappears.

5. **Reboot your system.**

   This act replaces your personal Access Control List (ACL) with the new one you created for the Administrators group. At this point, you can actually use the command line by opening an administrator command line whenever you need it. Be sure that you always open an administrator command line.

Configuring the Command Line

The command line starts as a smallish window with a black background and some grayish text. It isn't particularly appealing, and the window size is too small for some tasks. Fortunately, you can configure the command line to provide a little more pizzazz and a larger size (as well as a different font size, if you need it). You can access these features by clicking the box in the upper-left corner and choosing Properties from the context menu. If you want to make the changes permanent for all command lines you open, choose Defaults from the context menu instead. You see a properties dialog box with four tabs. The sections that follow describe each of these tabs.

Setting the window options

The Options tab, shown in Figure 6-2, defines how the command window reacts when you open it. The Cursor Size option controls the size of the cursor; small is the default. The Large option provides a block cursor that's very easy to see. The Display Options (refer to the "Missing options functionality" sidebar) determine whether you see the command window in full screen mode or as a window. Using full screen mode when you have a number of tasks to perform is easier on the eyes.

The command history is especially important. The Buffer Size option determines the number of commands the buffer will store. Every command requires memory, so increasing this number increases the amount of memory the command prompt requires. Increase this number when you plan to perform a number of complex commands. A smaller number saves memory for larger command line applications. The Number of Buffers option controls the number of individual histories. You need one history for each process (application environment) you create. Generally, the four that are shown work fine.

Missing options functionality

Older versions of Windows let you change the display mode through a property setting. However, Windows Server 2008 doesn't let you run the command window in full screen mode by changing the Display Options setting. This particular option is missing when you view the dialog box shown in Figure 6-2. In most cases, you don't want to run the command window in full screen mode when working with Windows Server 2008 because it's already possible to maximize screen real estate by maximizing the window. If you really must work in full screen mode, you must modify the registry to do it. To change this setting, locate the HKEY_CURRENT_USER\Console key. Change the FullScreen value from 0 to 1. You must restart the system for this to take effect. Other interesting console settings appear at `http://www.jsifaq.com/SF/Tips/Tip.aspx?id=0336`.

The Edit Options determine how you interact with the command window. Check QuickEdit Mode when you want to use the mouse to work with the entries directly. The only problem with using this feature is that it can interfere with some commands, such as Edit, that have a mouse interface of their own. The Insert Mode option lets you paste text into the command window without replacing the text currently there. For example, you might copy some information from a Windows application and paste it as an argument for a command.

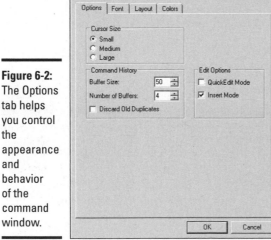

Figure 6-2: The Options tab helps you control the appearance and behavior of the command window.

Changing the font

The Font tab, shown in Figure 6-3, controls the font used to display text. The font size automatically changes when you resize the window, but you can also control the font size directly by using this tab. The raster fonts give the typical command line font an appearance that works well for most quick tasks. The Lucida Console font works better in a windowed environment. It's easier on the eyes because it's smoother, but you might find that some applications won't work well with it if they create "text graphics" using some of the extended ASCII characters. The extended ASCII characters include corners and lines that a developer can use to draw boxes and add visual detail.

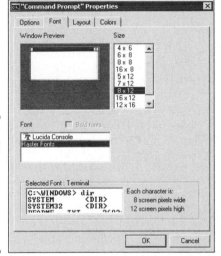

Figure 6-3:
Use the Font tab to control the size of the text in the command window.

Choosing a window layout

The Layout tab, shown in Figure 6-4, has the potential to affect your use of the command window greatly when working in windowed mode. The Screen Buffer Size setting controls the width and height of the *screen buffer*, the total area used to display information. When the Window Size setting is smaller than the Screen Buffer Size setting, Windows provides scroll bars so that you can move the window around within the buffer area and view all it contains. Some commands require a great deal of space for display purposes. Adjusting the screen buffer size and window size can help you view all the information these commands provide.

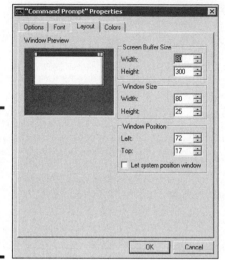

Figure 6-4:
Change the
size and
positioning
of the
command
window by
using the
Layout tab.

The window position determines where Windows places the command window
when you first open it. Some people prefer a specific position on the screen
so that they always know where a new command window will appear. However,
it's generally safe to check Let System Position Window to allow Windows to
place the command window on-screen. Each command window appears at a
different, randomly chosen, position on-screen.

Defining the text colors

Microsoft assumes that you want a black background with light gray letters
for the command window. Although DOS used this setting all those years
ago, many people today want a choice. The Colors tab lets you choose different foreground, background, and pop-up colors for the command window.
(Even though Figure 6-5 doesn't show the colors, it does present the dialog
box layout.) You can modify the window to use any of the 16 standard color
combinations for any of the text options. Use the Select Color Values options
to create custom colors.

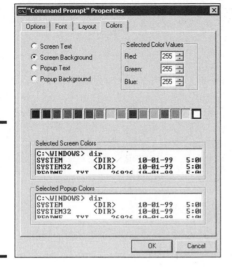

Figure 6-5:
Modify the
text colors
for an
optimal
display by
using the
Colors tab.

Setting Environment Variables

Some of the commands you can execute at the command line rely on environment variables. In addition, if you know the name of an environment variable, you can use it as input to a command in most cases. *Environment variables* are special repositories of data at the command line — they contain information such as the number of system processors or the default path information to use to locate a command or its data. You can always determine the value of an environment variable by typing Echo %VariableName%. Try it now by typing **Echo %UserProfile%** and pressing Enter. You see the starting location of your personal files on the hard drive.

Environment variables come in several different forms. You can create permanent environment variables for personal or global use. The personal environment variables appear as part of your settings, and no one else will see them. The global or system environment variables appear as part of HKEY_LOCAL_MACHINE in the registry and affect everyone who uses the machine. The difference between the two kinds of environment variables is that your personal environment variables contain information about you, and the global environment variables affect everyone.

You can also create temporary environment variables. These environment variables last only as long as you have the command line open. The moment you close the command line, the environment variable is gone as well. In addition, you won't see the environment variable in other command line windows, so the environment variable is local to the current command line and won't affect anything else. Use this kind of environment variable to provide information to a particular application, one that you don't use often and use only when you don't want to keep the environment variable values between sessions. The following sections describe how to create permanent and temporary environment variables.

Using the Environment Variables dialog box

The Environment Variables dialog box provides access to both your personal environment variables and the global ones. To access this dialog box, open the System applet in the Control Panel, click Advanced Settings to display the Advanced tab of the System Properties dialog box, and then click Environment Variables. You see the Environment Variables dialog box, as shown in Figure 6-6.

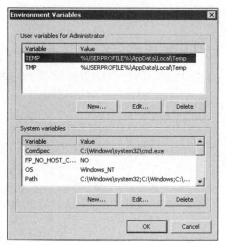

Figure 6-6:
Set permanent personal and global environment variables in the Environment Variables dialog box.

The upper list contains your personal environment variables, and the lower list contains the global environment variables. Windows Server 2008 defines a number of environment variables for you. For example, the TMP and TEMP environment variables in your personal section tell Windows where to store temporary variables. Applications use these temporary variable storage locations as well. Notice that the TMP and TEMP environment variables use %USERPROFILE% as the starting location for the temporary folders.

As you scroll through the lower list, you notice that the global settings also include the TMP and TEMP environment variables. If you type **Echo %TEMP%** at the command line and press Enter, however, you notice that Echo repeats the settings found in your personal section. Your personal environment settings always override the global environment settings, unless you actually log on under the SYSTEM account. (Policies usually prevent you from doing this.)

Each of the sections has three buttons. You can edit, add, or delete environment variables. Whenever you click New or Edit, you see a dialog box with two fields: Variable Name and Variable Value. The Variable Name defines the name you use to access the variable, and the Variable Value contains the actual environment variable content.

Clicking Delete removes the highlighted environment variable. You can remove any environment variable in the list, including the default environment variables that Windows requires to perform some tasks. Consequently, you want to delete environment variables with care. If you do remove one of the default permanent environment variables, you can always add it back in. The environment variables don't include any special hidden information that makes them unique.

Using the Set command

The Set command provides a means for setting temporary environment variables. These environment variables last only while the command line window is open. To set an environment variable, type **Set VariableName= VariableValue**. For example, if you type **Set MyVar=Hello** and press Enter, you create an environment variable with the name MyVar with a value of Hello. You can test this by typing **Echo %MyVar%** and pressing Enter.

The Set command also lets you display existing environment variables. For example, if you type **Set M** and press Enter, Set displays all environment variables that begin with the letter M. This feature comes in handy when you can't quite remember the name of an environment variable. If you want to see all the environment variables, type **Set** by itself and press Enter.

Microsoft has introduced a couple of command line switches to use with the Set command. The /A command line switch lets you use math expressions to create a value. For example, if you type **Set /A MyVar=1+2+3** and press Enter, Set stores a value of 6 to a variable named MyVar. Table 6-1 shows the operators what you can use with the /A command line switch in their order of precedence.

Table 6-1	Set /A Operators
Operator	*Description*
()	Grouping operators
! ~ -	Unary operators
* / %	Arithmetic operators
+ -	Arithmetic operators

continued

Table 6-1 *(continued)*

Operator	Description
<< >>	Logical Shift
&	Bitwise And
^	Bitwise Exclusive Or
|	Bitwise Or
= *= /= %= += -=&= ^= |= <<= >>=	Assignment
,	Expression separator

The order of precedence determines how Set interprets the values. For example, Set normally interprets multiplication and division before addition and subtraction, unless you use the grouping operators. If you enter 1+2*3 as the expression, the output is 7, even though the addition appears first in the list. However, if you enter (1+2)*3 as the expression, the output is 9 because the grouping operators tell Set to perform the addition first and then the multiplication.

You can also ask the user to supply a value for an environment variable by using the /P command line switch. In this case, Set prompts the user with the information that follows the variable name. For example, if you type **Set /P MyVar="Type a value: "** and press Enter, you see Type a value: at the command line. When you type a value and press Enter, Set assigns that value to MyVar. Give it a try — then type **Echo %MyVar%** and press Enter. You should see the value you typed at the prompt.

Obtaining Help at the Command Line

Windows doesn't provide a consistent way to obtain help at the command line. The first method you can try is to type **Help** and press Enter at the command line. You see a list of commands that are built into Windows. To obtain assistance with any of these commands, simply type **Help CommandName**. For example, if you want to learn more about the ChkDsk command, which checks your hard drive for errors, type **Help ChkDsk** and press Enter. You see a text display of information, as shown in Figure 6-7. (The "Understanding Command Line Symbols" section of this chapter describes how to interpret the symbols in the figure.)

Unfortunately, Help displays only a limited number of commands. If you want to learn about other commands, you need to know the command name. For example, you won't see the Windows Backup Administration (WBAdmin) command in the Help command list. To obtain help with this command, you type **WBAdmin /?** and press Enter. You see the help shown in Figure 6-8.

Most commands support the /? command line switch. This switch tells the command that you require help and it's always a safe option to use. Nothing will ever happen except that you obtain help when help is available.

Figure 6-7:
The Help command can help you obtain information about the commands it supports.

```
Administrator: Command Prompt                                    _ □ X
C:\Users\Administrator>Help ChkDsk
Checks a disk and displays a status report.

CHKDSK [volume[[path]filename]]] [/F] [/V] [/R] [/X] [/I] [/C] [/L[:size]] [/B]

  volume        Specifies the drive letter (followed by a colon),
                mount point, or volume name.
  filename      FAT/FAT32 only: Specifies the files to check for fragmentation
  /F            Fixes errors on the disk.
  /V            On FAT/FAT32: Displays the full path and name of every file
                on the disk.
                On NTFS: Displays cleanup messages if any.
  /R            Locates bad sectors and recovers readable information
                (implies /F).
  /L:size       NTFS only: Changes the log file size to the specified number
                of kilobytes.  If size is not specified, displays current
                size.
  /X            Forces the volume to dismount first if necessary.
                All opened handles to the volume would then be invalid
                (implies /F).
  /I            NTFS only: Performs a less vigorous check of index entries.
  /C            NTFS only: Skips checking of cycles within the folder
                structure.
  /B            NTFS only: Re-evaluates bad clusters on the volume
                (implies /R)

The /I or /C switch reduces the amount of time required to run Chkdsk by
skipping certain checks of the volume.

C:\Users\Administrator>_
```

Figure 6-8:
Use the /? command line switch when necessary to obtain help.

```
Administrator: Command Prompt                                    _ □ X
C:\Users\Administrator>WBAdmin /?
wbadmin 1.0 - Backup command-line tool
(C) Copyright 2004 Microsoft Corp.

---- Commands Supported ----

ENABLE BACKUP             -- Enable or modify a scheduled daily backup
DISABLE BACKUP            -- Disables running scheduled daily backups
START BACKUP              -- Runs a backup
STOP JOB                  -- Stops the currently running backup or recovery
GET VERSIONS              -- List details of backups recoverable from a
                             specific location
GET ITEMS                 -- Lists items contained in the backup
START RECOVERY            -- Run a recovery
GET STATUS                -- Reports the status of the currently running job
GET DISKS                 -- Lists the disks that are currently online
START SYSTEMSTATERECOVERY -- Run a system state recovery
START SYSTEMSTATEBACKUP   -- Run a system state backup
DELETE SYSTEMSTATEBACKUP  -- Delete system state backup(s)

C:\Users\Administrator>_
```

Notice that the WBAdmin command supports subcommands. Unfortunately, the Help screen shown in Figure 6-8 doesn't provide any information about these subcommands. Many complex command line utilities rely on subcommands. In most cases, you obtain help about the subcommand by typing it before the /? command line switch. For example, type **WBAdmin Enable Backup /?** and press Enter to obtain help about the Enable Backup subcommand.

TIP

It can be difficult to locate sufficient information about all the commands that Windows Server 2008 makes available to make administration pleasant, and documenting them would require an entire book. Fortunately, my book *Windows Administration at the Command Line* (Sybex, 2007), provides a complete listing of the commands Windows Server 2008 provides and tells you how to use them.

Understanding Command Line Symbols

The command line uses a number of odd-looking symbols. In addition, you also have access to a number of symbols. Knowing what these symbols mean is important if you want to use the maximum potential the command line has to offer.

The first set of command line switches are wildcard characters. These characters tell the Windows command that you want to perform a task on some unknown number of entities. The two common symbols are * (asterisk), which means to perform the task on an entity with any number of characters in its name, and ? (question mark), which provides a single unknown character. For example, if you type **Dir S*.EXE /S** and press Enter in the root directory, the Directory (Dir) command locates every executable file in the system that begins with the letter S. However, if you type **Dir S???.EXE /S** and press Enter, the Dir command locates only executable files with two to four letters in their name that begin with S. The Help files for most commands tell you whether they support wildcard characters. In some cases, the command help also tells you about other wildcard characters that you can use to obtain special effects.

The command line help often contains arguments (a value you provide as input to the command) or command line switches within [] (square brackets). Whenever you see an argument or a command line switch within square brackets, that argument or command line switch is optional — you don't have to provide it. In some cases, you even see the square brackets nested within each other. For example, if you saw Hello [FirstName [Last Name]] in Help, you would know that you could use the Hello command by itself, with a first name, or with a first name and last name. However, because the LastName argument is nested within the FirstName argument's brackets, you must supply a first name before you can supply a last name.

When working with the command line, arguments always appear without a slash, and command line switches appear with a slash. An *argument* is always an input value to the command that provides it with information needed to perform work. A *command line switch* determines how the command performs the work — it modifies the command's behavior.

In some cases, you see arguments in {} (curly brackets) and separated by | (the pipe symbol). For example, you might see {Yes | No | Maybe} as one of the inputs to the command. In this case, you would type Yes, No, or Maybe as an argument. However, you can type only one of these values, not all three of them.

Part IV

Networking

The 5th Wave   By Rich Tennant

"Good news! I found a place where the router works with the PC upstairs and the one in the basement."

Contents at a Glance

Chapter 1: An Overview of Windows Server 2008 Networking

In This Chapter

✓ Considering the new Windows Server 2008 networking features

✓ Working with the Network and Sharing Center

✓ Defining how UAC affects networking

✓ Understanding the new TCP/IP features in Windows Server 2008

✓ Understanding DHCP functionality in Windows Server 2008

✓ Understanding DNS functionality in Windows Server 2008

✓ Understanding WINS functionality in Windows Server 2008

*N*etworking can appear quite complicated and daunting. However, if you follow a few basic principles, you'll likely find that networking isn't nearly as difficult as it first appears. In previous versions of Windows, the administrator and user alike were immediately exposed to the complexities of the networking experience. Microsoft has changed all that in Windows Server 2008. In many cases, the networking functionality is able to figure out how to create the connection for you. When it doesn't work as expected, you can usually fix the problem by using a simple interface. Only when the problem is severe enough to require the services of a professional do you need to resort to the complex environment you used in the past.

Windows Server 2008 also introduces a number of new features. For example, Internet Protocol version 6 (IPv6) used to require a separate installation. Now you find IPv6 right alongside Internet Protocol version 4 (IPv4) in Windows Server 2008. The side-by-side approach is necessary because many organizations are just beginning their move to IPv6 and most public networks rely exclusively on IPv4. The transition promises to take a very long time to complete.

This chapter also introduces you to a number of standard technologies that you use with networking, including Dynamic Host Configuration Protocol (DHCP), Domain Name System (DNS), and Windows Internet Naming Service (WINS). Even though WINS is falling out of favor, you may need to install and use it on some occasions, so a brief overview of the technology is helpful.

Understanding the New Windows Server 2008 Networking Features

Microsoft has done a terrific job of making networking significantly easier under Windows Server 2008. You find not only that many tasks you used to perform by hand, such as installing Transmission Control Protocol/Internet Protocol (TCP/IP) support, are now automatic but also that Windows Server 2008 does a better job of repairing connections. In fact, the word you should use with Windows Server 2008 is *automatic,* as long as you don't require anything outside the Microsoft expectations for your server. For example, I was able to set up several configurations, including multiple network interface cards (NICs) and full router support, with very little effort. Here's a list of the new features you should expect to see in Windows Server 2008:

✦ Full IPv4 and IPv6 support as a standard feature. (Read the "Considering TCP/IP Configuration" section of this chapter for details.)

✦ Automatic tuning and optimization of network connections for maximum performance.

✦ Improved security for the host network. (See Book V, Chapter 4 for details.)

✦ Enhanced Internet Protocol Security (IPSec) support. (See the "Understanding IPSec" section of Book V, Chapter 4 for details.)

✦ Built-in support for hardware-based network offload and acceleration technologies.

✦ The Network and Sharing Center console, which makes configuring and managing your network significantly easier. (See the "An Overview of the Network and Sharing Center" section of this chapter for details.)

✦ Network Access Protection (NAP) support.

✦ New group policy settings for both wired and wireless network. (See Book III, Chapter 2 for details.)

✦ Enhanced Windows Firewall support that includes both inbound and outbound packet monitoring. (See the "Configuring the Windows Firewall" section of Book I, Chapter 4 for details.)

Not every change in Windows Server 2008 is for the better. Some network administrators rightfully complain about the additional steps you have to make to perform complex tasks. Yes, the new Network and Sharing Center is nice, but it hides settings, which make life harder for some administrators.

In the interest of protecting your server, Microsoft may also make it difficult to access. Administrators will find that they need to reduce some security features to get a usable server. Just how much you have to reduce security depends on how you use your server. Rather than look at this issue as a strict negative, however, you may want to view it as an opportunity to fix some of the security problems in your organization.

An Overview of the Network and Sharing Center

The Network and Sharing Center applet of the Control Panel provides you with easy access to common network functionality, as shown in Figure 1-1. In the upper-right corner, you see a picture of your network. Below this picture is a series of entries that tell you about the status of your network. Next comes a list of features you can configure, including network discovery, file sharing, public folder sharing, printer sharing, and password-protected sharing. On the left side of the display, you see a series of links to go to other network configuration windows.

The picture of your network does a lot more than you might think at first. If your network has a problem, you see a red X through that component. Click the red X and Windows Server 2008 attempts to fix the problem automatically; it succeeds regularly. When Windows Server 2008 can't fix the problem, it displays a dialog box that provides clues to how you can fix the problem yourself. Even if there isn't a problem, you can move your mouse cursor to any of those icons and it changes into a hand so that you can click on the item. For example, when you click on Internet, Windows opens a copy of Internet Explorer. Click the computer entry, and you see a copy of Windows Explorer open with the computer entry selected.

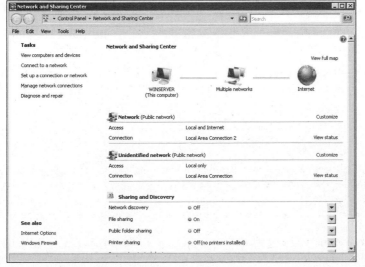

Figure 1-1: The Network and Sharing Center makes it easier for you to perform common tasks.

Book IV Chapter 1

An Overview of Windows Server 2008 Networking

Each of the NICs in your system receives a connection entry in the Network and Sharing Center. The network information includes the network type (public or private), the network name, and the connection name. The connections also contain two links: Customize and View Status.

When you click Customize, you see the Set Network Location dialog box, shown in Figure 1-2. You use this dialog box to provide a name for the network connection, determine whether the connection is public or private, and change the network icon. The choice between public and private is easier than Microsoft makes it sound. If someone can see your network using the connection, then it's public. Otherwise, it's a private connection. Consequently, if the connection goes directly to the Internet, you should choose public to help conceal your server.

When you click View Status, you see a Connection Status dialog box like the one shown in Figure 1-3. This dialog box provides access to a lot of information. When you click Details, you see a Network Connection Details dialog box, which contains everything you need to know about the network connection, including all the addresses a support person may request. Click Properties and you see a network connection Properties dialog box, where you can configure the connection with certain features and then manage the connection information (such as addresses). Don't worry too much about these details right now; Book IV, Chapter 2 discusses them in detail. If you suspect that a connection is causing problems, you can temporarily disable it by clicking Disable. Finally, when you want to verify that the connection is working properly, click Diagnose and Windows will perform a diagnostic on it. In most cases, Windows can fix any problems it finds.

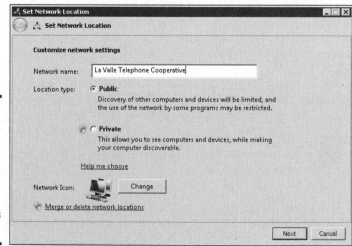

Figure 1-2:
Customize
the network
connection
information
to reflect
the
connection's
use.

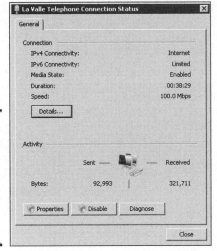

Figure 1-3:
Check
network
connection
status and
perform any
required
repairs.

You find the network features, such as network discovery (see the "Configuring networking" section of Book I, Chapter 4), spread throughout this book. All these networking features help you share something on the server. Of course, Windows enables some of these features by default. For example, when you share a drive or folder using Windows Explorer, Windows automatically turns on the File Sharing feature. Likewise, when you install and share a printer, Windows turns on Printer Sharing. As you can see, Windows sets many of these features automatically for you, and you don't need to worry about them unless you want to override the default setting.

The links on the left side of the display (refer to Figure 1-1) provide access to other network functionality. The following list provides a quick description of each of these locations — you find detailed descriptions as this book progresses:

✦ **View Computers and Devices:** Shows Windows Explorer with the Network folder selected.

✦ **Connect to a Network:** Displays the Connect to a Network Wizard, which you can use to connect to other networks (usually the Internet).

✦ **Set Up a Connection or Network:** Displays the Set Up a Connection or Network Wizard, which you can use to connect to other locations such as workplace.

✦ **Manage Network Connections:** Shows the Network Connections window, where you can perform configuration tasks on existing network connections.

**Book IV
Chapter 1**

**An Overview of
Windows Server
2008 Networking**

◆ **Diagnose and Repair:** After you click this link, starts a network diagnostic when you suspect a problem with your network. Windows often finds and fixes the problem automatically, even when the problem doesn't appear in the Network and Sharing Center window.

◆ **Internet Options:** Shows the Internet Options dialog box, where you can configure your connection to the Internet.

◆ **Windows Firewall:** Shows the Windows Firewall window, where you can set the Windows Firewall configuration.

Understanding How UAC Affects Networking

The User Account Control (UAC) doesn't seem like a Windows feature that would affect your ability to network, but it can. In fact, some network administrators will find it downright annoying because it prevents them from performing some tasks in an unsafe way. The biggest issue is that you can't provide access to the root directory of a hard drive in Windows Server 2008. Yes, you can create a share for the root directory, but you can't give anyone the rights to access it because of the way Windows is set up.

One way around the problem of complete hard drive sharing is to use the approach found in the "Opening an Administrative Command Line" section of Book III, Chapter 6, which is to give yourself access to the root directory. At this point, you can give everyone else access too. However, giving everyone access to the root directory isn't a good idea. They should have access only to the directories that contain data on the server. Many viruses target the root directory. By denying them access to the root directory, you can reduce the effectiveness of the virus and make it easier to remove.

The UAC also affects the user's ability to execute code on the server. Code that users download to their machines and execute isn't affected, but you may find that some applications execute code on the server in a way that makes this execution transparent to the user. The application may fail with odd error information that makes it hard to trace the source. If you have an application that worked fine under Windows 2003 and now fails to work properly under Windows Server 2008, you may want to look at where the code executes as a potential source of problems.

While working with Windows Server 2008 from a client system, you may notice other odd problems. In some cases, the problem occurs because Windows Server 2008 can't ask you to elevate privileges. This issue, in turn, prevents the application from executing properly. If you start seeing odd problems with an application such as Windows Explorer, you may want to try using the RunAs utility to execute it. For example, to open a file in the root directory of a mapped drive using Notepad, you might type **RunAs / User:WinServer\Administrator "Notepad I:\CPLFiles.TXT"** and press Enter.

This command line syntax would open the file using the credentials of the administrator on the machine named WinServer. Notice that you must place the command within quotes if it contains spaces.

Considering TCP/IP Configuration

The use of TCP/IP is a source of confusion for many people. It's actually a combination of two protocols. A *protocol* is a set of rules that a computer follows to perform a given task. Computers rely on a wealth of protocols to ensure that they can communicate and interact with other computers. The Transaction Control Protocol (TCP) is actually a transport protocol — it describes how a signal from your computer arrives at another computer on the network. Another familiar transport protocol is the User Datagram Protocol (UDP). You can use the Internet Protocol (IP) with either of these transport protocols; however, whereas TCP offers a reliable connection, UDP doesn't. On the other hand, UDP offers speed and simplicity.

IP defines the way your data is packaged for transport. It doesn't define the transport mechanism. The best way to view the combination of TCP/IP is that TCP is the mail carrier and IP is the envelope that the mail carrier carries. Your data includes the contents of the envelope. When you generate data on your machine and send it to another machine, the combination of TCP/IP ensures that the data arrives at the other machine. Of course, as with the post office, sometimes letters are sidetracked and, in some cases, they don't arrive at all; but generally the combination of TCP/IP is quite reliable.

At this point, you're probably wondering about IPv4 and IPv6. Although TCP doesn't have any constraints on size, IP does because it contains address information. The main difference between IPv4 and IPv6 from the perspective of this book is addresses. IPv4 uses 32-bit addresses, so you can address about four billion unique locations by using it. With all the cell phones, Blackberries, and other devices out there that need IP addresses, many people are concerned that we'll run out of IP addresses soon. IPv6 uses 128-bit addresses, which means it can address about 3.4×10^{38} unique locations. Hopefully, we won't run out of addresses any time soon.

This section provides everything you need to know about TCP/IP for this book. However, you may want to know additional information. You can find an excellent TCP/IP tutorial at http://www.w3schools.com/tcpip/default.asp. The original Request for Comment (RFC), a kind of specification, for IPv4 appears at http://www.faqs.org/rfcs/rfc791.html. If you want to know more about what makes IPv6 so special, check out the information on the IPv6 site at http://www.ipv6.org/.

Understanding DHCP

Chaos would result on a network if every machine had the same address because every machine would contact every other machine all the time and you couldn't send any unique messages anywhere. Imagine what would happen if everyone on your block had precisely the same address. The post office could never deliver the mail based on the address because the addresses aren't unique. Just as the city issues an address to your house, DHCP issues an address to your computer.

The role of the DHCP server is to ensure that every computer has a unique address. These addresses come from a pool of addresses that the administrator issues to the DHCP server. When your computer requests an address, the DHCP makes a reservation of a particular address for your computer. Your computer leases the address and obtains a new one when the lease expires.

In addition to the address, the DHCP server sends a default gateway, subnet mask, and DNS server address to your computer. The default gateway is the address of a router on your system that provides access to another network. The network could appear as another segment on your local network, or it could be the Internet. The subnet mask lets your local computer mask the network address portion of an IP address from the machine address. Every computer on the network has the same network address, but every machine must have a unique machine address. The DNS address provides access to a DNS server where your machine can find the addresses of other machines on the network.

 You know everything needed to work with DHCP in this book. However, there's a lot more you can discover about DHCP. For example, you can have only one DHCP server on a network, which means that if your router already provides this functionality, you don't need to provide it with Windows Server 2008. One of the better places to view information about DHCP is the Resources for DHCP site at `http://www.dhcp.org/`.

Understanding DNS

Think of DNS in the same way that you would picture a telephone book: You provide the name of a computer you want to find, and DNS provides the address. After you have the address, you can contact the other computer and communicate with it. Every URL you type into a browser is a host name that DNS translates into an address for you. If you know the address for a particular host, such as `www.microsoft.com`, you can simply type it into the browser instead. Because humans can remember names with greater ease than numbers, DNS provides an essential service. It helps make the entire Internet easier to use.

DNS actually relies on a tree-like structure based on zones. Each zone is a different network area. For example, your local network is a zone. The DNS server on your network maintains the mapping of host names to addresses for the zone that's your local network. When the DNS server sees a host name it doesn't recognize, it asks the next server in the hierarchy to map it from a host name to an address. In the case of smaller networks, the next DNS server in the hierarchy is probably that DNS server at the Internet service provider (ISP). The host name keeps traversing up the list of DNS servers until someone can provide an address or the request reaches the end of the line, at which time you receive an error message telling you that no one could find the address.

This chapter doesn't provide information on all the complexities of DNS. One of the better places to find additional information is the DNS Resources Directory at http://www.dns.net/dnsrd/. Pay special attention to the standards that define DNS as a technology. You can find the entire list of RFCs for DNS at http://www.dns.net/dnsrd/rfc/.

Understanding WINS

At one time, Windows relied on the Network Basic Input/Output System (NetBIOS) to provide identification on a network. Each machine supplies a name with, at most, 16 characters to identify itself. In the beginning, a machine using NetBIOS would register its name by outputting a packet asking the other machines on the network whether they were using that name. If no one answered, the machine could assume that the name was safe and use that name for connectivity on the network.

Waiting a few seconds for a response each time a machine logged on to the network was time-consuming, so developers came up with another method of working with the computer names: Using a name service, each computer stores these names with their mapped addresses and provides them to other computers as a service. It sounds a lot like DNS, and it is to an extent. The name of this service is the NetBIOS Name Service (NBNS), and WINS is the Microsoft implementation of that service. If you want to discover the details about NBNS, read the standards RFC 1001 (http://www.faqs.org/rfcs/rfc1001.html) and RFC 1002 (http://www.faqs.org/rfcs/rfc1001.html).

As networks grow in size, the decentralized nature of WINS introduces delays in the network. At some point, WINS becomes relatively slow, so Microsoft implemented DNS as part of Active Directory with Windows 2000. Of course, Microsoft maintains WINS for backward compatibility reasons. However, you need to implement WINS on your network only when you have very old clients that can't use DNS. In short, you won't use WINS on most modern networks.

**Book IV
Chapter 1**

**An Overview of
Windows Server
2008 Networking**

Chapter 2: Performing Basic Networking Tasks

In This Chapter

✔ Working with network properties

✔ Mapping your network as Windows Server 2008 sees it

✔ Creating a connection to another network

✔ Performing network connection management tasks

Microsoft has improved networking functionality in Windows Server 2008 considerably. Many tasks are performed automatically, and you'll definitely like the repair functionality. However, Windows Server 2008 can't read minds. You still need to perform some configuration tasks to get a fully functional operating system. For example, you may find that you need to reconfigure some network properties to obtain certain functionality. Windows Server 2008 doesn't set up an Internet Connection Sharing setup for you — you have to initiate that task on your own. It also doesn't detect that you don't want to use a particular NIC. It tells you that the NIC is unplugged, but it still installs software for it. You must manually disable the NIC when you won't use it.

To help you determine whether your network is working properly, you can use a new network mapping feature to display the computers and other resources on your network. Sometimes this map looks incomplete. In some cases, the incomplete entries represent problems that you need to fix manually because Windows can't fix them on its own. As far as Windows is concerned, the network is complete — only you know that the network isn't complete. However, the mapping feature lets you know that something is missing.

You also need to create connections to other networks, and you may need to configure an Internet connection as well. Wireless networks aren't automatic either — you need to create the connection manually. If you're getting the idea that much of this chapter focuses on network connectivity, you're right. Before you can do much with your network, you must have the required connections. All the connections are important, even those to devices such as printers.

Viewing the Network Properties

The Network and Sharing Center, described in the "An Overview of the Network and Sharing Center" section of Chapter 1 in this minibook, provides you with an easy way to perform many common tasks. However, it's far from complete. You still need to work with the connections directly. In this case, you want to click Manage Network Connections in the Network and Sharing Center to display the Network Connections window shown in Figure 2-1.

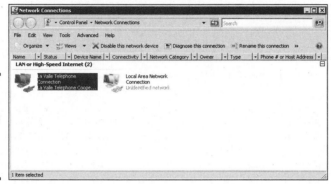

Figure 2-1:
Manage the connections for your network as needed.

Whenever you select a connection, the Network Connections window displays the tasks you can perform with that connection on the toolbar at the top of the window. In most cases, you have these options:

✦ **Disable This Network Device:** Makes the device inaccessible for use. The software remains in place and you don't lose any of your settings. However, users can't access the device. Disabling a network device has many uses. For example, your system may have the device installed, but may not use it. In addition, sometimes you can fix a problem with the network by disabling one connection so that Windows can focus on the second, broken connection.

✦ **Diagnose This Connection:** When a connection is broken, you may not be able to fix it on the first try from within the Network and Sharing Center. Highlighting the connection in the Network Connections window and clicking this link may provide additional answers, such as those shown in Figure 2-2. You can use these options to perform a detailed diagnostic on your system — essentially following step-by-step instructions to fix the problem.

If you attempt to reset a connection while working with Remote Desktop (Connection), Remote Desktop may temporarily lose its connection with the server. Be patient. It can require several minutes for the reset process to complete, at which time you regain the server connection.

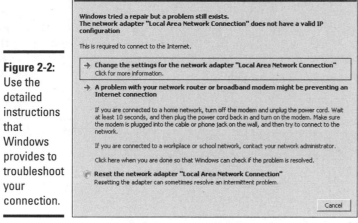

Figure 2-2:
Use the
detailed
instructions
that
Windows
provides to
troubleshoot
your
connection.

✦ **Rename This Connection:** The default names that Windows Server 2008
provides for your connections aren't very descriptive. When you have
multiple connections to maintain, the lack of distinctive names can make
management tasks significantly more difficult. Click this link to change
the name to something more descriptive.

✦ **View Status of This Connection:** Displays the connection Status dialog
box, where you can discover the connection settings, set the connection
properties, disable the connection, or diagnose connection problems.
You can read more about this option in the "An Overview of the Network
and Sharing Center" section of Chapter 1 in this minibook.

✦ **Change Settings of This Connection:** Displays the connection Properties
dialog box, where you can add, remove, and configure client, service,
and protocol features for the selected connection. The "Managing Network
Connections" section of this chapter tells you more about this option.

In addition to changing the connection settings, you can work with the connections in another way. Choose Tools➪Advanced Settings and you see the
Advanced Settings dialog box, as shown in Figure 2-3.

You should look at these advanced settings as a matter of preference. At the
top of the display, you see the connections for the current machine. When
you click on a particular connection, you see the bindings for it in the bottom
list. A *binding* is a method of saying that a particular connection will use certain protocols to create a connection to another machine. The connection is
required to use the protocols — the rules — you have specified.

**Book IV
Chapter 2**

**Performing Basic
Networking Tasks**

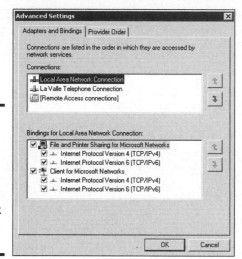

Figure 2-3:
Configure
the
advanced
settings to
ensure that
the network
behaves as
desired.

Figure 2-3 shows two networking features for Windows Server 2008: File and Printer Sharing for Microsoft Networks and Client for Microsoft Networks. These features determine which tasks the connection can perform. Below each of these features is a list of protocols for performing the task. If the feature doesn't have any protocols associated with it, the connection cannot perform the task because there aren't any rules for performing it.

The order of the protocols in the list determines the order in which the connection uses them. In this case, when the remote system supports TCP/IPv4, the server will use that protocol to converse with it. However, if the remote system doesn't support the protocol, the connection can use TCP/IPv6 to converse with it. When the remote machine lacks support for either protocol, the server can't converse with it at all — it's impossible to establish a connection because the two machines can't agree on a protocol to use.

You can change the order of any connection, feature, or protocol shown in Figure 2-3. Simply highlight the desired entry and click the up or down arrows as needed to change its precedence. Items higher on the list always receive priority treatment.

The Provider Order tab contains a list of providers. A *provider* is the software that supplies access to information. For example, when you create an application that requires access to a database, the provider is the intermediary that acts as a conduit between your application and the database. Likewise, when working with networks, a provider is the intermediary that acts as a conduit between two machines. All Windows Server 2008 systems will have the Microsoft Windows Network provider installed. If you also install a feature such as Remote

Desktop, you see the Microsoft Terminal Server Network Provider. This tab lets you control the priority of each provider so that the server knows which one should obtain access to remote systems first. Normally, you want to place the Microsoft Windows Network provider first to ensure best performance.

Displaying a Network Map

The Network Map feature is a combination of discovery, graphical view, and diagnostic tool all rolled into one. When you click View Full Map, you see a message saying that Windows is constructing the map, and then you see a map like the one shown in Figure 2-4 in most cases.

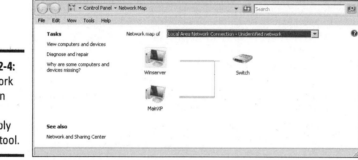

Figure 2-4:
A network map can be an incredibly helpful tool.

Although this technology will be very helpful eventually, it has a lot of problems today. To create an accurate network map, every machine on the network must run the Link-Layer Topology Discovery (LLTD) software. Unfortunately, Vista is the only product other than Windows Server 2008 that currently ships with LLTD. In addition, Vista doesn't even install the software by default, so you might not see the Vista machines on your network unless you take time to install LLTD. Windows XP doesn't even come with LLTD support. You can obtain this support from Microsoft, however, so you can also see Windows XP systems on your network. (See the instructions at `http://technet2.microsoft.com/WindowsVista/en/library/409fb2fa-8eb8-45af-b063-4f50f5a77b291033.mspx` for additional details.) If you have older systems on your network, you won't see them using this technology.

After you have everything working as you think it should work, you can begin using the display to view your network. The display shows any computers, switches, external connections, printers, and other hardware that the Network Map feature can detect. By placing your cursor over any of these hardware elements, you can determine the device's status, including its network address information and Media Access Control (MAC) address. The MAC address is important because it's a unique hardware address that resides within a chip on the NIC. The MAC address is always unique, and you can rely on it to identify any machine on your network, even if someone renames the machine.

The information that this display provides is important because it shows which machines are logged in to the system and which machines the server can see completely. Consequently, if you don't see a machine you expect or the machine has incorrect information, you at least have a starting point for diagnosing problems. Network problems can occur at many levels, and this display fills a gap in the information that Microsoft provided in the past by showing the hardware devices — assuming that you can get it working.

The links on the left side display various networking information. Clicking View Computers and Devices opens a copy of Windows Explorer with the Network folder selected. Click Diagnose and Repair when you suspect that a problem with the network is preventing the Network Map feature from working properly. If you think that a configuration issue is preventing you from seeing the entire network map, click the Why Are Some Computers and Devices Missing? link.

Connecting to Another Network

At some point, you'll want to connect to an external network. The network may be at work or an Internet connection you want to use from anywhere. The techniques can include wireless, broadband, or dial-up connections. Windows Server 2008 also provides support for Virtual Private Networks (VPNs). The basic criterion is that the remote system provides a connectivity option that Windows Server 2008 supports.

In many cases, Windows Server 2008 can detect an external connection automatically. To determine whether the connection is already available, click Connect to a Network. The Connect to a Network dialog box shows any current connections your server may have. It also displays any new connections that Windows Server 2008 has found. If you see such a connection, highlight it and click Connect. Windows Server 2008 completes any required connectivity for you automatically. When Windows Server 2008 can't find any additional connections, it displays a message to that effect. Click Cancel to close the Connect to a Network dialog box.

The fact that Windows Server 2008 can't find your connection isn't an indication that it doesn't exist. For example, Windows Server 2008 won't find VPN connections in most cases, and you'll find that you need to create any required dial-up connections. In this case, you need to use a wizard to create the connection. The wizard you use depends on the kind of connection you want to create. In all cases, you begin by clicking Set Up a Connection or Network to display the Set Up a Connection or Network dialog box, as shown in Figure 2-5. The following sections describe the process to configure each connection type.

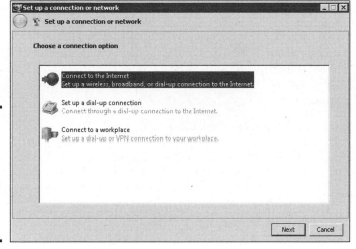

Figure 2-5: Choose a connection type from the Set Up a Connection or Network dialog box.

Connect to the Internet

You create an Internet connection when you want to work online. Use the Connect to a Workplace when you want to create a connection to your workplace (or a partner company) using a VPN over the Internet. This is the connection you'd use to access Web services, public Web sites, private Web sites, and other directly accessible locations on the Internet. The following steps describe how to perform this task:

1. **Highlight Connect to the Internet and then click Next.**

You see a How Do You Want to Connect dialog box. This dialog box shows the kinds of connections that Windows Server 2008 knows that you can make. For example, if you have a broadband connection available, then Windows Server 2008 will offer a broadband option. Likewise, you see options for wireless and dial-up connections. (If you already have a connection to the Internet and want to set up a redundant connection, you see a message saying you're already connected to the Internet. Click Set Up a New Connection Anyway.)

2. **Click a connection option.**

You see the dialog box shown in Figure 2-6. This dialog box contains all the information that your ISP requires to grant you a connection to the Internet.

Book IV Chapter 2

Performing Basic Networking Tasks

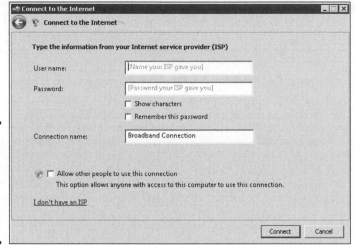

Figure 2-6:
Provide the
information
your ISP
supplied to
connect to
the Internet.

3. **Type the information your ISP provided in each of the fields.**

4. **Check Show Characters if you want Windows Server 2008 to display the password characters as you type them.**

Displaying the characters is unsafe because someone else could see your password. Even if this is a company connection that the entire company shares, you don't want employees knowing the password because they could use it for purposes you don't intend and share it with other people.

5. **Check Remember This Password if you want Windows to remember the password so you don't have to type it in each time.**

This option can save you time and effort. It should work fine as long as the server is in a secure location. However, if the server is in a public area, it's much better to type the password each time you want to make the connection.

6. **Type a connection name in the Connection Name field.**

The name you use will appear wherever the connection appears, so you want to use a meaningful connection name that everyone will understand. Using a meaningful connection name also makes it considerably easier to diagnose network problems.

7. **Check Allow Other People to Use this Connection if you want to share the connection using Internet Connection Sharing (ICS).**

The "Performing an ICS Setup" section of Book V, Chapter 2 describes ICS in greater detail.

8. **Click Connect.**

Windows tries to make a connection to the ISP using the information you provided. If the connection succeeds, Windows adds the connection to the list of available connections using whatever settings you provided. If the connection isn't successful, change any incorrect information and try the connection again.

Set up a dial-up connection

The Set Up a Dial-up Connection option provides a shortcut technique for creating a dial-up connection to another location. The prompts all tell you that this connection is for the Internet. Normally, that's what you use it for. However, you can actually use it for any dial-up connection, including a leased line connection between locations. Always use the Connect to a Workplace option when you need to create a secure connection between your current location and a workplace. The following steps describe how to perform this task:

1. **Highlight Set Up a Dial-Up Connection and click Next.**

If you see a message that Windows can't detect a dial-up modem, you'll want to click Cancel, fix the modem problem, and start this procedure again. Otherwise, you see the dialog box shown in Figure 2-7. Notice that you can enter any telephone number, username, and password. Consequently, you can connect to any other machine, not just to the Internet.

2. **Type the telephone number required to access the remote system.**

Click Dialing Rules to set up any outside access dialing rules. Make sure to include the complete number, including the area code, as necessary.

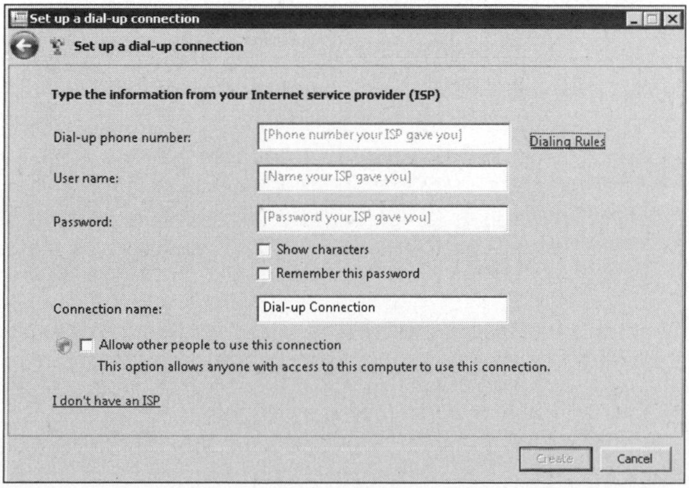

Figure 2-7:
Provide the information you need to make a connection to another system.

3. **Type your name and password in the User Name and Password fields.**

4. **Check Show Characters if you want Windows Server 2008 to display the password characters as you type them.**

   Displaying the characters is unsafe because someone else could see your password. Even if this is a company connection that the entire company shares, you don't want employees knowing the password because they could use it for purposes you don't intend and share it with other people.

5. **Check Remember This Password if you want Windows to remember the password so that you don't have to type it in each time.**

   This option can save you time and effort. It should work fine as long as the server is in a secure location. However, if the server is in a public area, it's much better to type the password each time you want to make the connection.

6. **Type a connection name in the Connection Name field.**

   The name you use appears wherever the connection appears, so you'll want to use a meaningful connection name that everyone will understand. Using a meaningful connection name also makes it considerably easier to diagnose network problems.

7. **Check Allow Other People to Use This Connection if you want to share the connection using Internet Connection Sharing (ICS).**

   The "Performing an ICS Setup" section of Book V, Chapter 2 describes ICS in greater detail.

8. **Click Connect.**

   Windows tries to make a connection to the ISP using the information you provided. If the connection succeeds, Windows adds the connection to the list of available connections using whatever settings you provided. If the connection isn't successful, change any incorrect information and try the connection again.

Connect to a workplace

Workplace connections commonly require additional security than a plain Internet connection provides. The security ensures that no one can eavesdrop on your connection with the company and give away company secrets.

You begin this process by highlighting Connect to a Workplace and clicking Next. Windows displays the connection options shown in Figure 2-8. These options offer you a VPN (secured) connection through the Internet or a direct dial-up connection through the telephone network. If you have some other kind of connection, you need special software to make the connection.

The vendor of the connection strategy normally provides this software, and you won't see it discussed in this book. The following sections describe the two connection types.

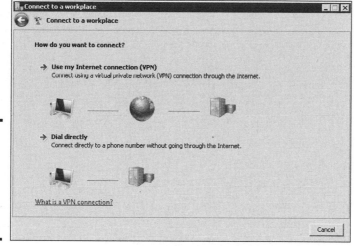

Figure 2-8:
Choose a connection strategy for your workplace connection.

Using an Internet connection to create a workplace connection

An Internet connection offers convenience because you use an existing connection to connect to your workplace. The connection also tends to provide reliability. However, because you're using the connection for multiple tasks, you may notice that it doesn't provide much in the way of speed (depending on the speed of your Internet connection). The following steps describe how to perform this task:

1. **Click Use My Internet Connection (VPN).**

You see the dialog box shown in Figure 2-9. This dialog box determines the connection settings for the workplace connection.

2. **Type the IPv4 or IPv6 address of the server used to make the remote connection.**

3. **Type a connection name in the Destination Name field.**

The name you use appears wherever the connection appears, so you'll want to use a meaningful connection name that everyone will understand. Using a meaningful connection name also makes it considerably easier to diagnose network problems.

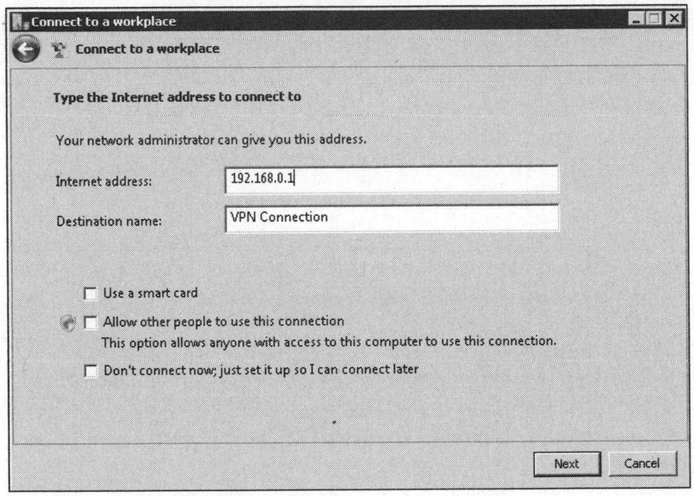

Figure 2-9:
Define the
workplace
connection
settings
when using
the Internet.

4. **Check Use a Smart Card if your company relies on smart card technology for identification purposes.**

If you check this option, the Next button changes to Create. You can't make the connection immediately because the remote server will require a smart card for each connection. In addition, the wizard automatically checks the Don't Connect Now option.

5. **Check Allow Other People to Use this Connection if you want to share the connection using Internet Connection Sharing (ICS).**

The "Performing an ICS Setup" section of Book V, Chapter 2 describes ICS in greater detail.

If you checked Use a Smart Card, click Create. Windows creates the connection for you and exits the wizard.

6. **Check Don't Connect Now if you want only to create a connection rather than use the connection immediately.**

7. **Click Next.**

You see the dialog box shown in Figure 2-10. This dialog box contains settings you use to identify yourself to the remote server.

8. **Type your name and password in the User Name and Password fields.**

9. **Check Show Characters if you want Windows Server 2008 to display the password characters as you type them.**

Displaying the characters is unsafe because someone else could see your password. Even if this is a company connection that the entire company shares, you don't want employees knowing the password because they could use it for purposes you don't intend and share it with other people.

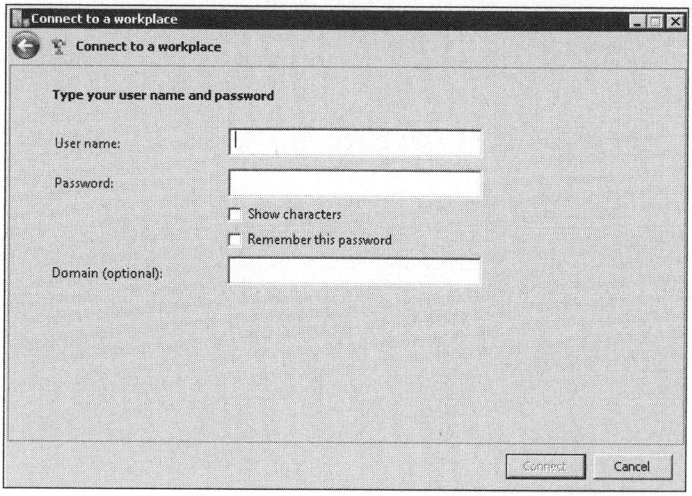

Figure 2-10:
Provide the
security
information
required to
make the
connection.

10. **Check Remember This Password if you want Windows to remember the password so that you don't have to type it in each time.**

This option can save you time and effort. It should work fine as long as the server is in a secure location. However, if the server is in a public area, it's much better to type the password each time you want to make the connection.

11. **Type the domain name for the remote server, if required.**

If you're connecting to a Windows server that's part of a domain, you usually need to provide that domain name as part of the connection information.

12. **Click Connect or Create.**

When the button says Connect, Windows tries to make a connection to the workplace by using the information you provided. If the connection succeeds, Windows adds the connection to the list of available connections by using whatever settings you provided. If the connection isn't successful, change any incorrect information and try the connection again.

When the button says Create, Windows creates the new connection for you. However, it doesn't actually test the connection and you won't be able to use the connection immediately.

Using a dial-up connection to create a workplace connection

Creating a dial-up connection to your workplace is essentially the same as creating an Internet connection. The only major difference is that rather than provide an IP address for the server, you supply a telephone number.

See the "Using an Internet connection to create a workplace connection" section of this chapter for details.

Managing Network Connections

There are many ways to display the properties of a connection. For example, you can choose the connection in the Network Connection window and click Change Settings of this Connection. You can also click Properties in the connection Status dialog box. Another method is to right-click the connection and choose Properties from the context menu. No matter how you open the connection Properties dialog box, you can use it to manage the connection, including adding or removing clients, services, and protocols. Figure 2-11 shows a typical connection Properties dialog box.

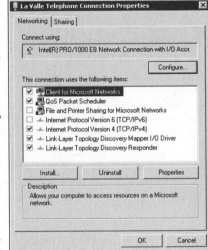

Figure 2-11: The connection Properties dialog box helps you manage connections.

Some network connections provide external connectivity that you can share, such as an Internet connection. In this case, you see a Sharing tab in the connection Properties dialog box. Use the procedure found in the "Performing an ICS Setup" section of Book V, Chapter 2 to share the connection.

Many of the network clients, services, and protocols don't have any settings you can configure. All you need to do is install them and let them do their job. If you highlight a client, service, or protocol and see that the Properties button is grayed out, the feature doesn't provide any user-configurable settings. The following sections describe other common configuration options. Some connection types may contain other options, and your selection of clients, services, and protocols may provide other options as well.

Working with Client for Microsoft Networks

The Client for Microsoft Networks client provides basic access to the Windows network. Unless you have the only Windows system on the network, you need to have this client installed. If you need to connect to a different kind of a network, you need another client. Windows Server 2008 can support as many clients as are needed to make the connections you require.

When you click Properties, you see a Client for Microsoft Networks Properties dialog box that contains a single setting, Name Service Provider. This provider defines the method used to access the name directory for Remote Procedure Calls (RPCs). An *RPC* is a technique of accessing code on one machine from another, and it's a common Windows requirement for networking.

In most cases, you'll want to use the default Windows Locator setting. However, when the need arises, you can also use the DCE Cell Directory Service (in which case you must also provide an address for the server). The DCE Cell Directory Service is an older technology that you need to worry about only when working with Windows NT servers.

Understanding the Internet protocol settings

The IP settings you use can make or break your network. If you use the wrong settings, you might not even get a connection to another machine. In some cases, IP misconfiguration is exceptionally hard to find, so you must make the settings choices carefully. Book IV, Chapter 1 discusses many of the issues surrounding IP configuration from a theoretical standpoint. The following sections put the theory into practice.

Configuring IPv4

Most of the Internet is still using IPv4. In addition, most local networks are using it. A few people have even stated that there's no overriding reason to use IPv6, but the address space of IPv4 will eventually run out and governments are moving ahead with IPv6 configuration. In the meantime, you always need an IPv4 protocol setup. When you click Properties after highlighting Internet Protocol Version 4 (TCP/IPv4), you see a dialog box like the one shown in Figure 2-12.

**Book IV
Chapter 2**

**Performing Basic
Networking Tasks**

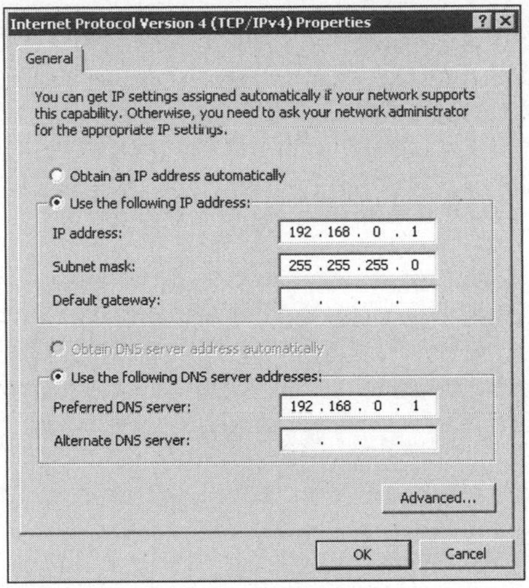

Figure 2-12:
Most
networks
today
require an
IPv4 setup.

When your network has a DHCP server or relies on an external DHCP server, you choose the Obtain an IP Address Automatically option. This option tells Windows Server 2008 to request an address from the DHCP server. The DHCP server provides your server with an IP address, subnet mask, and default gateway as a minimum. If you also select the Obtain DNS Server Address Automatically option, the DHCP server provides this value as well. This is the normal setup for a domain. Every computer except the DHCP server will use automatic settings, and you don't need to worry about anything.

If you're working at the DHCP server, installing the DHCP and DNS support will automatically configure the connection Properties dialog box for you. You see settings similar to those shown in Figure 2-12, except that the addresses reflect the addresses you choose for your network. In some rare cases, you may have to configure an alternative default gateway setting to connect to another network. In this case, make sure to get the appropriate address from the administrator of the secondary network. You may also have a need to configure the DNS server information.

Installing an ICS setup also changes the settings in this dialog box automatically. In fact, Figure 2-12 shows an ICS setup. The server that provides the connection sharing also provides DHCP and DNS support. Unlike with a domain controller, however, you won't install DHCP and DNS support separately. The support comes as part of the ICS package, and you don't have to worry about either DHCP or DNS support.

This book doesn't discuss, for a couple of reasons, the advanced settings you access by clicking Advanced. Normally, you never need to change these settings because they truly are advanced and you use them for unique situations. In addition, changing these settings can cause an otherwise correctly configured connection to fail. Consequently, unless you have a compelling reason to click Advanced, you may want to forget that it even exists.

Configuring IPv6

IPv6 is the upcoming protocol to use on the Internet. However, no ISP currently uses IPv6 exclusively, and many don't provide any support for it. Whether you need to configure IPv6 at all depends on whether your network uses it or you connect to a network that uses it. In some cases, you can gain a performance boost by uninstalling this protocol until you actually need it. The "Uninstalling network features" section of this chapter describes how to perform this task.

Configuring an IPv6 address is very much like configuring an IPv4 address, and the same automatic configuration scenarios apply. See the "Configuring IPv4" section of this chapter to learn about these defaults. The main difference between IPv4 and IPv6 configuration is that rather than use a subnet mask, IPv6 uses a subnet prefix length. This value determines how many bits of the 128 bits that IPv6 uses support the network address. The remaining bits support the individual machine address.

Installing new networking features

If you have an all-Windows network and don't need any fancy features, the default configuration you receive with Windows Server 2008 will do everything you want. Of course, the world doesn't provide this perfect scenario all the time, and you may find that you need to configure additional clients, services, and protocols to support other kinds of systems.

You always add a client, service, or protocol to a specific connection and not to the network as a whole. To begin this process, you click Install in the connection Properties dialog box. You see the Select Network Feature Type dialog box, as shown in Figure 2-13.

At this point, you highlight Client, Service, or Protocol and click Add. You see a feature selection dialog box, similar to the one shown in Figure 2-14. Windows Server 2008 provides access to any locally supported client, service, or protocol. Click Have Disk when you have a third-party disk containing additional network features.

**Book IV
Chapter 2**

**Performing Basic
Networking Tasks**

Figure 2-13:
Choose the kind of network feature you need to install for the selected connection.

Figure 2-14:
Select from the list the driver you want to install, or use a third-party disk.

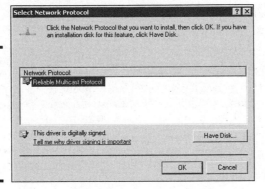

Notice that the highlighted driver is digitally signed in Figure 2-14. Although you might be able to use an unsigned driver to support auxiliary hardware on your system, you should never use an unsigned driver for the network because all kinds of terrible things can happen (including data loss, security breaches, intermittent connections, and things too gruesome to consider).

After you find the client, service, or protocol that you want to install, click OK to install it. Follow any directions that the installation program provides. Use the Client option when you want to install a connectivity option for another network, such as Novell Network. The Service option is useful when you want to install a new network service, such as file and printer sharing. Finally, use the Protocol option when you want to install a new set of connectivity rules, such as TCP/IPv4.

Uninstalling network features

At some point, you'll find that you want to uninstall networking features. For example, if your ISP doesn't provide support for IPv6, there's little reason to retain this feature until the ISP supports it. By removing extra features from your network, you can improve efficiency, reduce overhead, enhance security, and make your network connections speedier.

Removing a feature you actually need causes the network to develop problems, so remove features carefully. Always clear the check mark next to a network feature and test network functionality before you remove a feature. Testing ensures that your network won't go down and require a lengthy repair to fix it.

To remove the feature, highlight its entry in the connection Properties dialog box. Click Uninstall. Windows warns you about removing the feature. Click Yes and Windows removes it. You shouldn't have to reboot your machine in most cases to complete the removal process. Windows doesn't allow you to uninstall some features. In this case, the Uninstall button is grayed out.

Chapter 3: Accomplishing Advanced Networking Tasks

In This Chapter

✔ **Using Terminal Server to create and allow remote connections**

✔ **Using Remote Access Services (RAS) to provide remote connectivity**

✔ **Performing maintenance with the Network Shell (NetSH) command line utility**

*I*f you looked at previous chapters, you probably have the idea that the main job of servers is to provide connectivity — connectivity to the outside world, to other servers, to other users, and to application data. In fact, that's precisely how you use servers most often. Connectivity of all sorts is the most important job a server can perform. With this in mind, you won't be surprised to discover that this chapter contains still more information on connectivity.

The kinds of connectivity found in this chapter tend toward advanced tasks that you need to perform on some servers but not on others. For example, you need basic Terminal Server support to set up Remote Desktop, which is a common need. However, you may never need to configure a server for remote access by a client that needs to access the server for application and other needs. In fact, your organization may not have any of the *thin* clients (those with reduced or sometimes no processing power of their own) that normally rely on Terminal Services for this need.

You'll also find an interesting utility described in this chapter, NetSH. Many administrators avoid the command line because they think it's difficult to use. However, the command line is an essential tool for automation, and NetSH is one of the more important command line utilities you can discover because it offers so much flexibility for anyone who wants to automate tasks or simply accomplish them faster when working through a task manually.

Working with Terminal Server

When you choose to make Remote Desktop accessible in Windows Server 2008, you install a small subset of the Terminal Server functionality (see the "Enabling Remote Desktop" section of Book I, Chapter 4 for details. To obtain full Terminal Server functionality, however, you must install the Terminal

Services role. This role provides considerable additional functionality for your server, such as letting users access applications remotely. You can use this role to help thin clients access the applications they need. However, if you don't have thin clients and assume that the user will use local applications to modify data, installing this support really isn't necessary.

It pays to view the warning on the Terminal Services page of the Add Roles Wizard. You don't have to install Terminal Services if your only purpose is to allow administrative access to the server. In fact, if you plan to use Remote Desktop for other users, you simply have to add them to a list of people allowed to use Remote Desktop — you don't have to install Terminal Services. Installing Terminal Services opens another potential security hole on your server, so you should use this role only when necessary.

Carefully consider the Terminal Services features you need, and then install the Terminal Services features you require before you install any applications. If you install the applications first and then Terminal Services, the applications may not work correctly. The applications you share using Terminal Services must provide correct support for a multiuser environment. For example, database applications normally provide multiuser support, but a word processor may not. When you install Terminal Services after you install the applications, the multiuser support may not work properly. If this problem occurs, try uninstalling and then reinstalling the application to fix the problem.

Terminal Services on Windows Server 2008 also provides support for a new feature, Network Level Authentication (NLA). This feature works great as long as you have a network that solely supports Vista and Windows 2008 systems with the correct support installed. Most administrators need to install Terminal Services using the Do Not Require Network Level Authentication option.

When you reach the Role Services page of the Add Roles Wizard, choose the Terminal Services roles you need. Don't install all the roles unless you truly need them. Installing either TS Gateway or TS Web Access requires that you also install Internet Information Server (IIS), Network Access Protection (NAP), RPC over HTTP Proxy, and Windows Process Activation Services role services. You see Terminal Services abbreviated as TS in many places. The following sections describe the additional features you see when you install the Terminal Services role on your server. You can use the information in these sections to determine whether you actually need to install a particular Terminal Services role.

Using the default utilities

The Administrative Tools folder contains a subfolder named Terminal Services. Whether you simply install Remote Desktop or you provide a complete Terminal Services installation, you find these consoles available. The consoles won't have full functionality unless you install the required Terminal Services features. For example, the Terminal Services Configuration console lists only the RDP-Tcp connection until you install and configure other features. You also won't see any information when you select the Licensing Diagnosis folder. The following sections describe typical console functionality — you may see other features depending on how you configure Terminal Services.

Using the Remote Desktops console

The Remote Desktops console lets you configure connections to other Terminal Servers. When you initially open this console, you see essentially a blank window because you haven't configured any connections yet. Use the following steps to create a new connection:

1. **Right-click Remote Desktops and choose Add New Connection from the context menu.**

   You see the Add New Connection dialog box, shown in Figure 3-1.

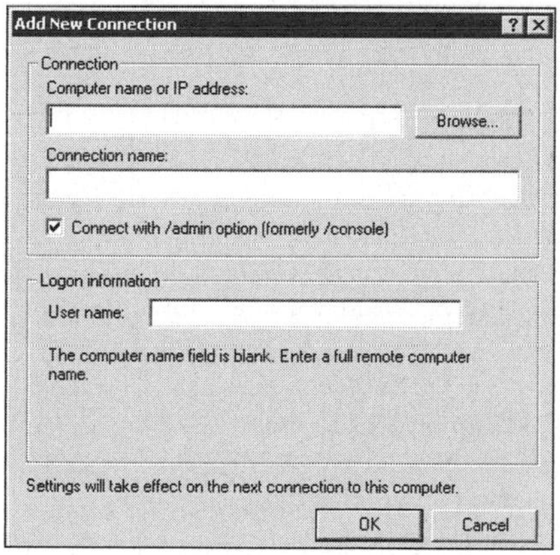

Figure 3-1:
Create new remote desktop connections as needed.

2. **Type the name or IP address of the remote server in the Computer Name or IP Address field.**

   If you don't know the name of the computer or its IP address, click Browse. Terminal Services automatically detects the presence of any other servers on the network and displays them for you. Highlight the name you want and click OK.

3. **Type a name for the connection in the Connection Name field.**

   Terminal Services normally suggests the name of the computer as the connection name. If you have only a few connections to worry about and a single connection to each computer, this strategy works fine. In most cases, you want to provide something a little more descriptive, especially if you have multiple connections for each Terminal Server.

**Book IV
Chapter 3**

Accomplishing
Advanced
Networking Tasks

4. **Check Connect with /Admin Option if you want to log in to Remote Desktop as though you're sitting in front of the real machine.**

   This is the same as the /Console option you used in the past. If you use this option, Windows Server 2008 logs out the person who's sitting in front of the machine. Of course, this isn't a problem if your machine is locked in a closet and you can't access it anyway.

5. **Type your username for the remote system.**

   Terminal Services asks you for your password or other credentials when you log on the first time.

6. **Check Allow Me to Save Credentials if you want to save time entering your password later.**

   Use this option if you're sure that no one else can access the Remote Desktop by using your system. Having to reenter the password every time is safer and reduces the risk of someone performing terrible tasks in your name.

7. **Click OK.**

   The Remote Desktops console creates the connection for you.

After you create a connection, you can use it by double-clicking it. Terminal Services attempts to contact the remote machine for you. After it creates the connection, Terminal Services asks you for your credentials. After the remote system verifies your credentials, you can begin working.

If you later decide to remove the connection, highlight its entry and click Delete on the toolbar. The Remote Desktops console won't ask whether you're sure that you want to remove the connection and there isn't an Undo feature, so be sure to choose the right connection.

It's also possible to change the connection properties. Right-click the connection and choose Properties from the context menu. You see a connection Properties dialog box like the one shown in Figure 3-2. The General tab looks just like the dialog box shown in Figure 3-1.

Figure 3-2 shows the Screen Options tab, where you can choose the size of the window that Terminal Services creates to the remote system. The Other tab contains options for starting an application when you log on to the remote system, change the authentication options, and redirect your local drives so that you can use them when working with the remote system.

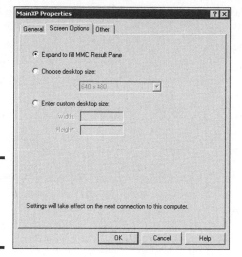

Figure 3-2:
Modify the
connection
properties
as needed.

Using the Terminal Services Configuration console

The Terminal Services Configuration console helps you create and maintain
the actual connection used for other machines. You can also use this console to perform general Terminal Server configuration tasks, such as determining whether a user can start multiple sessions. Finally, you can use this
console to determine whether Terminal Server has any licensing problems.

Working with the connection type

The server comes with one connection type. It's important to remember that
this connection type can support multiple connections, so you may need
only the type shown in Figure 3-3.

Before you can create new connection types, you need to provide either a
different connection type (the default is Microsoft RDP 6.1) or a different
transport protocol (the default is TCP). The Windows Server 2008 installation
comes with only one of each, so you need to acquire and install other types
before you attempt to create another connection. Follow the vendor instructions for installing the new connection type or transport protocol and then for
creating the new connection.

You can configure each connection type in the list. Right-click the connection
type entry and choose Properties from the context menu. You see a connection type Properties dialog box like the one shown in Figure 3-4.

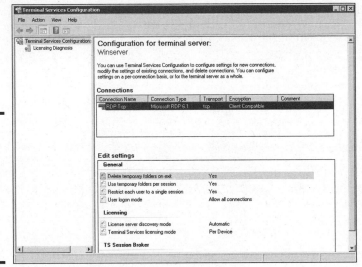

Figure 3-3:
In many cases, you need only a single Terminal Services connection type.

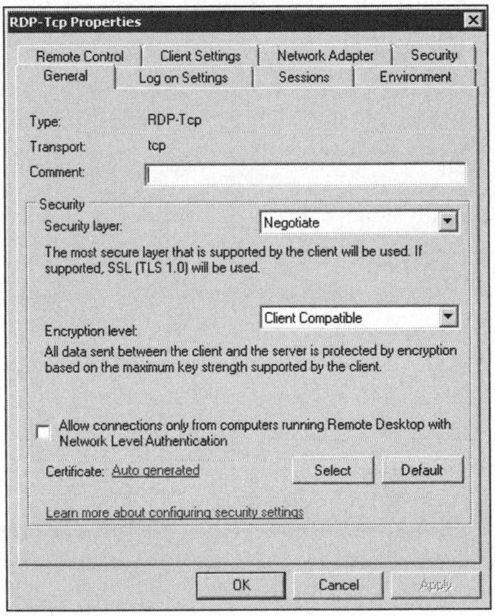

Figure 3-4:
Each connection type has a number of settings you can change.

The vast majority of these settings match those found with the Remote Desktop application, described in the "Working with Remote Desktop" section of Book III, Chapter 5. (You can see how to enable this support in the "Enabling Remote Desktop" section of Book I, Chapter 4.) The settings you see here let you override the user settings based on company policy. For the most part, these settings defer to the user's requirements.

The default settings do limit a few client items. For example, when you select the Client Settings tab, you can choose to limit the color depth and the potential for redirection. By default, Terminal Server limits the user to using a 16-bit color depth to improve performance. In addition, the user can't redirect audio in the interest of compatibility.

The only configuration setting that's unique to the connection Properties dialog box is the Security tab. When you click this tab, you see a pop-up dialog box that tells you to make most of your security changes to the Remote Desktop Users group. This is good advice because most users will be part of this group. You won't want to change the administrator settings in most cases, unless you truly want to limit the administrator's ability to manage the server. The security settings you see on the Security tab, shown in Figure 3-5, look and act like those you use in other places on Windows.

Performing general configuration tasks

Beneath the Connections section of the Terminal Services Configuration console (refer to Figure 3-3) is an Edit Settings section. These settings show the Terminal Services configuration. For example, the default configuration deletes all temporary folders for a session when the session is disconnected. You can change any of these settings by double-clicking its entry. Figure 3-6 shows the General tab of the Properties dialog box.

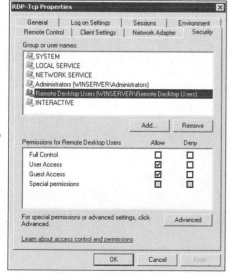

Figure 3-5: Change the rights that various groups have when using Terminal Server.

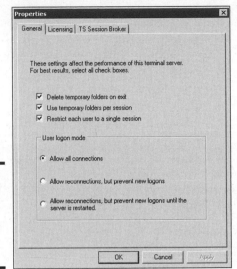

Figure 3-6:
Configure
Terminal
Services to
meet your
needs.

In most cases, you want to leave the performance options alone. For example, there really isn't a good reason to retain the temporary folders that a user generates between sessions. It also makes sense to restrict each user to a single session, for performance reasons.

The only set of configuration changes you may need to make appear on the Licensing tab. The Terminal Services licensing mode must match the licensing mode of your license (either per device or per user). Otherwise, Terminal Server indicates a licensing problem and disallows connection even when you have the proper licensing package installed. You can also choose to discover the licensing server automatically (normally the best option) or use a specific licensing server (the required option when you have multiple licensing servers on the network). If you don't configure the licensing option, Terminal Services displays a notice that you must configure it within the specified number of days or else it will stop working.

The TS Session Broker tab contains options for joining a server farm. You use this option when you want to use a number of servers to support users in a seamless way. The "Understanding TS Session Broker" section of this chapter provides additional information about this Terminal Services feature.

Performing license diagnosis

You may eventually run into a licensing problem after installing a new license or configuring Terminal Server incorrectly. When you select the Licensing Diagnosis folder, you see the status of any licensing configuration you performed. If you find that the licensing information isn't available, you need to configure a server that has TS Licensing installed. See the "Configuring and using TS Licensing" section of this chapter for details. After you perform the initial configuration, the Terminal Services Configuration console searches for licensing servers, locates any required configuration information, and displays the results on-screen. If there aren't any problems to report, you see a message to that effect.

Using the Terminal Services Manager console

The main purpose of the Terminal Services Manager console is to help you manage users. You can see the users currently connected to the system, any active sessions, and the processes associated with Terminal Server sessions. The initial display shows any users who are logged in to the system through Terminal Server, including the server, username, session, ID (a unique session number), state (such as active), any idle time, and the time that the user logged in to the system. The idle time value is the important one to consider when working with this console because it can indicate sessions that have failed. Clearing the connection can free resources for other users logged in to the system.

The Sessions tab, shown in Figure 3-7, contains a list of active sessions. You normally see a minimum of three sessions. The sessions of interest, in most cases, are those that have a type of Microsoft RDP. These are client sessions that you can monitor. Right-click any of these clients and choose Status from the context menu to discover more information about how that user has configured their session. You can disconnect the session by right-clicking it and choosing Disconnect from the context menu. It's even possible to send the user a message by right-clicking their session and choosing Send Message.

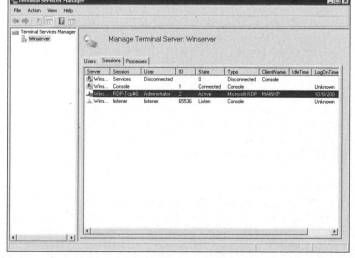

Figure 3-7: Monitor sessions to determine how users interact with the system.

Book IV
Chapter 3

Accomplishing Advanced Networking Tasks

The Console session in this list is the person who's working with the machine directly. Unless you have someone assigned to use the server as a workstation, this session won't show anyone logged in. You can take control of this session by right-clicking it and choosing Remote Control from the context menu. You also see a listener session that listens for new connection requests. Unless people are having a hard time logging in to the server, you should leave this session alone. To fix potential login problems, right-click the listener session and choose Reset from the context menu.

The Processes tab contains a list of processes associated with Terminal Server. The list looks very much like the one found in Task Manager. The difference is that the list is significantly longer, in most cases, because you're viewing the processes in use by a number of users, the system, and Terminal Server itself. To end an errant process, right-click the process entry and choose End Process from the context menu.

Configuring user-specific Terminal Services settings

Every user entry found in the Users folder of the Computer Management folder (or as part of Active Directory) contains several tabs that help configure that user's access to Terminal Server. (See the "Modifying users with the Computer Management console" section of Book II, Chapter 4 for details on other settings you can change.) To see these settings, right-click the user entry and choose Properties from the context menu. You see a user Properties dialog box like the one shown in Figure 3-8. The following sections describe the purpose of each of the three tabs related to Terminal Services.

Figure 3-8:
You can define various elements of the user's Terminal Server experience.

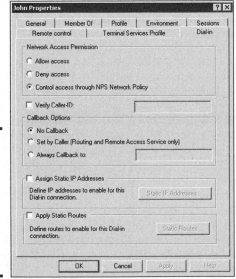

Setting the Remote Control tab

The Remote Control tab determines whether you can take control of the user's session. Checking Enable Remote Control lets you take control of the session. However, if you also check Require User's Permission, the user must first provide permission to give up control of the session. In most cases, you won't want these options checked for an administrator's account because the results may be unpredictable, depending on the low-level activity the administrator is performing at the time.

This tab also defines the level of control the system allows. The default setting lets you interact with the session, which means that you can perform tasks as though you're sitting in front of that computer. A second level of control lets you view the session, but not interact with it.

Setting the Terminal Services Profile tab

The Terminal Services Profile tab controls where the user's configuration data and home folder appear on the server. The settings on this tab serve the same purpose as the settings on the Profile tab, except that they're Terminal Server specific. A special check box on this tab denies the user permission to log on to Terminal Services, even when the user is a member of a group that has been granted access.

Setting the Dial-in tab

The Dial-In tab (refer to Figure 3-8) contains settings that affect how the user logs in to the server by using a dial-up connection. The default setting requires that the user log in to the system through the Network Policy Server (NPS). However, you can bypass this requirement when you don't have an NPS available.

This tab also contains a number of safety features. For example, when you enable the Verify Caller ID option, the server verifies the user's telephone number. If the user attempts to log in from a telephone number other than the expected number, the server denies access. This option can pose problems with unlisted numbers because they won't identify themselves through caller ID unless the user provides the correct dial-in code first. To avoid this problem, you can also choose to use a callback. In this case, the server hangs up immediately after the user dials in, and then the server calls the user back at a predefined number.

After the user completes the dial-in, you can configure the connection. The two options let you configure a static IP address for those users with special connectivity needs (an application on the client machine is expecting a particular IP address). When working with the Routing and Remote Access Service, you can also configure the user's account to rely on a static route. In most cases, you won't need to create a static route because you'd have to configure the server to use demand-dial routing. You can learn more about this particular feature at `http://technet2.microsoft.com/windowsserver/en/library/4bc0b6c7-7bb4-4721-a4e7-bda9c9504d1c1033.mspx`.

Configuring and using TS Licensing

The TS Licensing Manager console helps you manage licensing on your server. You can either rely on a remote server to perform the task or use the local server. When working with the local server, you need to authorize it before you can perform any other tasks. Consequently, when you initially open the TS Licensing Manager console, you see a display similar to the one shown in Figure 3-9. The following sections tell you how to configure and use this server.

Figure 3-9:
The initial TS Licensing Manager display shows that the server isn't activated.

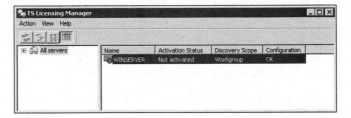

Activating the Terminal Server licenses server

Before you can perform any other licensing steps, you must configure and activate the server. The following steps describe how to perform this process:

1. **Right-click the server entry and choose Activate Server.**

You see the Activate Server Wizard.

2. **Click Next.**

The Activate Server Wizard displays the Connection Method dialog box, where you choose a connection method for your server. Generally, you want to use the Automatic Connection option. You also have the option of choosing a Web browser (Internet) or telephone (dial-up) connection.

3. **Choose an activation method and click Next.**

You see a Company Information dialog box like the one shown in Figure 3-10. You see fields for entering your first name, last name, company name, and country.

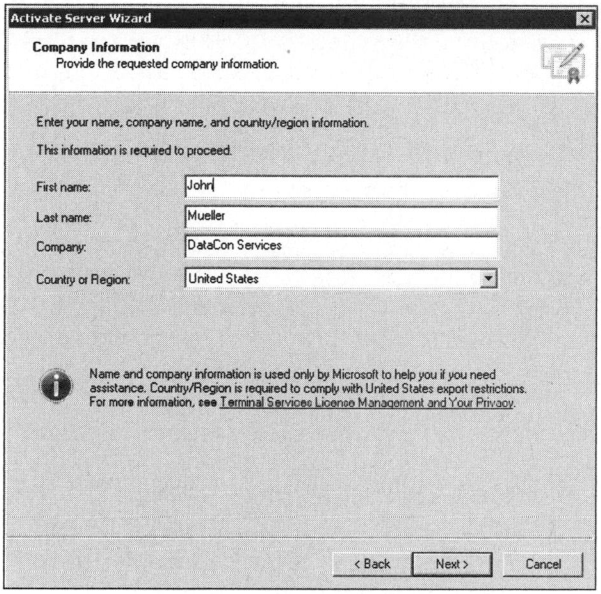

Figure 3-10:
Provide any
required
company
information.

4. **Fill in the required information using the name of the person responsible for maintaining the Terminal Services setup, and click Next.**

   The Activate Server Wizard displays another screen of company information, as shown in Figure 3-11. This information is optional, and you need to provide only enough information to identify your organization completely. The optional information includes an e-mail address, an organizational unit name, an address, a city, a state, and a postal code.

5. **(Optional) Fill in any information needed to identify your organization completely, and click Next.**

   The Activate Server Wizard activates the server. When the process is complete, you see a success message. At this point, the server is activated, but it isn't started, so no one can use it.

6. **Check Start Install Licenses Wizard Now when you have licenses to install and click Next.**

   If you don't have any licenses to install, you've finished the process for now and will need to install licenses later. Otherwise, follow the steps for installing licenses in the "Installing Terminal Server licenses" section of this chapter.

**Book IV
Chapter 3**

**Accomplishing
Advanced
Networking Tasks**

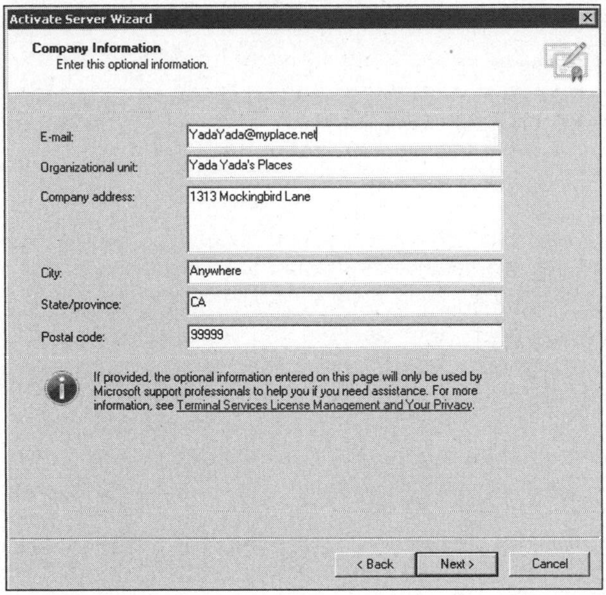

Figure 3-11:
Include any
optional
information
required to
identify your
company
completely.

If you ever need to deactivate your server, you should right-click the server entry and choose Advanced⇨Deactivate Server from the context menu. The server becomes unavailable after you perform this step. Sometimes, the server fails to perform as anticipated. In this case, you can usually fix the problem by right-clicking the server entry and choosing Advanced⇨Reactivate Server.

Installing Terminal Server licenses

At some point, you need to install licenses to use Terminal Server. Microsoft provides a number of licensing agreements, but the basic process is the same for all of them. You can also reach this section of the chapter directly from the Activate Server Wizard or through the interface later. When you arrive here from the Activate Server Wizard, the Activate Server Wizard performs Step 1 for you and displays the Install Licenses Wizard.

1. **Right-click the server entry and choose Install Licenses from the context menu.**

   You see the Install Licenses Wizard.

2. **Click Next.**

   The Install Licenses Wizard locates the server and then displays a License Program dialog box. Microsoft provides a number of licensing packages, so you need to choose carefully the licensing package you want to use.

3. **Choose a licensing option in the License Program field.**

The bottom of the dialog box shows the licensing information required for each program. For example, if you choose License Pack (Retail Purchase), you need to enter a series of five, 5-digit entries. An open license requires that you provide an authorization number and a license number.

4. **Click Next.**

Figure 3-12 shows a typical license entry display. Make sure that the display you see matches the product you purchased.

5. **Type the license code found on the licensing pack into the fields provided and click Next.**

The Install Licenses Wizard displays a Product Version and License Type dialog box like the one shown in Figure 3-13.

6. **Choose the product version in the Product Version field.**

7. **Choose the kind of licensing in the License Type field.**

8. **Type the number of licenses you purchased in the Quantity field and then click Next.**

You see a success message when the server accepts the licensing information you provided.

9. **Click Finish.**

The Install Licenses Wizard completes the installation.

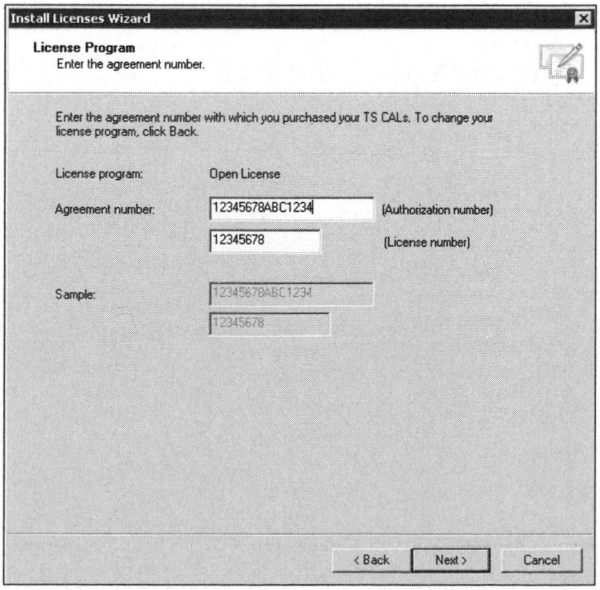

Figure 3-12: Provide the required licensing information for your package.

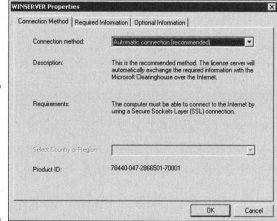

Figure 3-13:
Choose the
appropriate
product
options for
your
license.

Configuring Terminal Server license properties

At some point, you may need to change the configuration for your Terminal Server licensing server. To change the TS Licensing Manager properties for a particular server, right-click the server entry and choose Properties from the context menu. You see the server Properties dialog box, as shown in Figure 3-14.

Figure 3-14:
Reconfigure
your server
as
necessary
to provide
the support
you need.

These entries should look familiar. They work precisely the same as they did for the initial configuration. Each tab progresses just as the Activate Server Wizard did. Select the tab that contains the information you need, modify the information, and click OK to complete the task.

Understanding TS Session Broker

You can install the Terminal Services Session Broker on domains only when working with a domain controller. This Terminal Services feature helps you manage a server farm where multiple servers work together to respond to specific user needs. The only time you need this feature is when you have a very large installation. The technique you use to create the server farm, the software you install to manage functionality such as load balancing, and the specifics of your installation all control how you set up this feature. In most cases, you work with a consultant and a third-party vendor to create the complete setup. Consequently, this book doesn't discuss this topic in-depth.

Make sure that you work with a reputable consultant and a third-party server farm vendor when configuring this option. You can find a step-by-step guide for configuring load balancing for Terminal Services at `http://technet2.microsoft.com/windowsserver2008/en/library/6e3fc3a6-ef42-41cf-afed-602a60f562001033.mspx`. You can discover the host of special requirements for working with the TS Session Broker at `http://technet2.microsoft.com/windowsserver2008/en/library/902a6081-9ecd-45ec-96ee-f51097d71c8c1033.mspx`.

Working with Remote Access Services

You may wonder why Windows Server 2008 has so many connection technologies and it sometimes becomes confusing to figure out which technology to use. Of course, there are the general connectivity options, provided through the File Server and Print Server roles. Terminal Services provides access to the server in the same manner that terminals accessed mainframes. In this case, the client activities occur on the server rather than on the client. Finally, there are Remote Access Services (RAS) that let the user connect to the server from a remote location to use server resources as a service. The data-manipulation and -generation activities occur on the client, not on the server. The server provides access only to the resources required for the activity. The following sections describe services and servers that help you implement server access no matter which connection technology you rely on to get the job done.

Network Policy Server (NPS)

The Network Policy Server console appears within the Administrative Tools folder. It helps you configure the server portion of a Network Access Protection (NAP) or Remote Access Dial-In User Server (RADIUS) setup.

When you first open this console, you see an overview window, like the one shown in Figure 3-15, where you can perform standard or advanced configuration tasks. It's normally a good idea to perform the standard configuration first and then move on to the advanced options shown in the Advanced pane beneath the Standard pane.

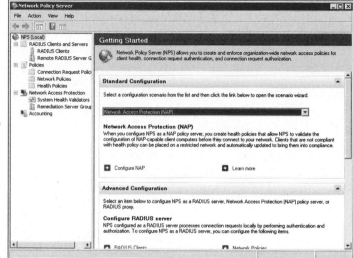

Figure 3-15: Configure external connections as needed for server resource access.

Both NAP and RADIUS configurations rely on wizards that make life significantly easier for the administrator. Simply select the configuration you want to perform in the Standard Configuration pane and click Configure NAP, Configure VPN or Dial-Up, or Configure 802.1X, as appropriate. The NAP configuration is especially important because this feature helps protect your server from external sources of corruption (namely, remote clients that haven't updated their systems in years). Use these steps to configure a NAP policy for your server:

1. **Choose Network Access Protection (NAP) and click Configure NAP in the Standard Configuration pane.**

   Windows starts the Configure NAP Wizard, as shown in Figure 3-16. The figure shows the various kinds of connections you can protect. Beneath the connection type list, you find the Policy Name field, which you use to define a policy name for the NAP connection.

2. **Choose the kind of connection you want to protect.**

   You'll notice that the wizard automatically suggests a policy name. In addition, you see an Additional Requirements link appear at the bottom of the dialog box in most cases. Clicking this link takes you to a Help page that contains a checklist of additional tasks you must perform after you create the NAP policy.

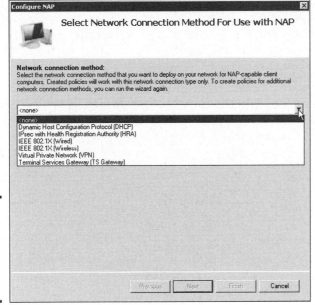

Figure 3-16:
Define the
kind of
connection
you want to
secure.

3. **Type a name for the policy you're creating and click Next.**

   In most cases, you see a dialog box asking you to supply the names of
   RADIUS clients to add to the policy, as shown in Figure 3-17. The exception
   is the TS Gateway policy, where you add a list of TS Gateway servers to
   the list. You can add clients or servers to the list later, so you don't have
   to provide the list when you create the policy.

4. **Use the Add, Edit, and Remove buttons to configure a list of RADIUS
   clients or TS Gateway servers. Click Next.**

   You see the Configure User Groups and Machine Groups dialog box,
   where you add users and machines to the list of entities that can access
   the server. The configuration options appear in two separate lists (one
   for machines and another for users). Add groups to the list that match
   the kind of entity you want to grant access. When you grant access to a
   machine, anyone who uses that machine gains access to the system as
   long as they have the proper rights. When you grant access to a user,
   the user may log in from any machine as long as the user has the proper
   rights to do so. The wizard doesn't offer any protection against placing a
   machine group in the user area or vice versa. Make sure you choose
   your selections carefully.

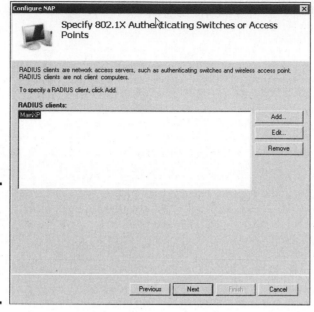

RADIUS clients are network access servers, such as authenticating switches and wireless access point. RADIUS clients are not client computers.

To specify a RADIUS client, click Add.

Figure 3-17:
Add, edit, or remove clients or servers as needed for the policy.

5. Add user groups and machine groups as necessary by clicking Add User or Add Machine. Click Next.

You see the Configuration Authentication Method dialog box, where you choose the authentication techniques used to verify the caller. The top of this dialog box contains the certificate you send to the caller. The bottom of the dialog box contains the technique you want the caller to use for authentication — either a secure password or a smart card (or other certificate). In both cases, the server uses Protected Extensible Authentication Protocol (PEAP) to secure the caller credentials.

6. Choose the authentication methods you want to allow, and click Next.

You see the Configure Virtual LANs (VLANs) dialog box. The dialog box contains options for configuring an organizational network and a restricted network. Both options have default settings. However, if you're using a custom product, you want to click Configure and choose the vendor on the Vendor Specific Attributes tab of the Virtual LAN (VLAN) Configuration dialog box.

7. Perform any required VLAN configuration and click Next.

You see the Define NAP Health Policy dialog box, similar to the one shown in Figure 3-18. The only validator you normally see is the Windows Security Health Validator, shown in the figure. The wizard requires that you select a health validator, so you normally keep this entry selected unless you install a third-party validator.

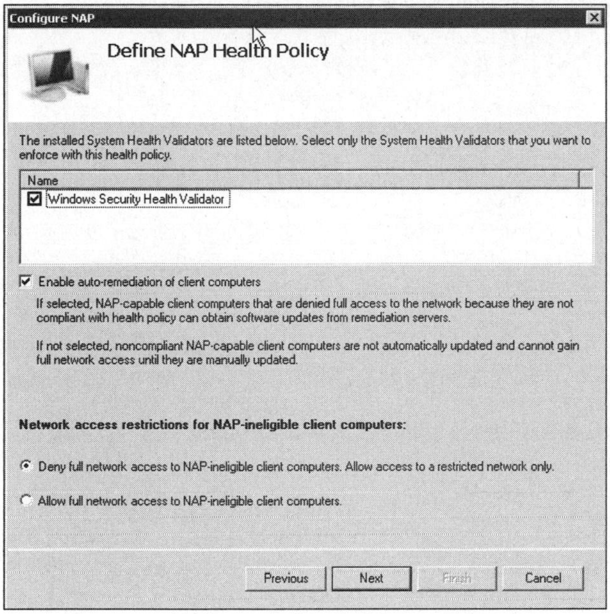

Figure 3-18:
Set a health
policy for
NAP.

8. **Choose a health validator from the Name list.**

9. **Check Enable Auto-Remediation of Client Computers if you want to allow Windows to attempt to update the client.**

The client downloads updates from the remediation server. However, even with the remediation server updates, the client may not meet all compliance requirements and the server will continue to deny it full access.

10. **Choose an access restriction policy for computers that fail to meet the NAP requirements.**

The main reason to use this feature is to keep clients from contaminating your server. Consequently, the default first option of Deny Full Network Access to NAP-Ineligible Client Computers is the best option to choose.

11. **Click Next.**

You see a summary dialog box, where you can view all the selections you made.

12. **Verify the selections and click Finish.**

The wizard performs the required policy configuration for you. You can see these policies in the various Policies folders shown in Figure 3-15. If you configured any RADIUS clients during this process, you see their entries added automatically to the RADIUS Clients folder. Likewise, any TS Gateway servers you configure appear as part of the Remote RADIUS Server Groups folder.

**Book IV
Chapter 3**

**Accomplishing
Advanced
Networking Tasks**

Understanding secure wireless access through the IEEE 802.11 standard

Windows implements both wired and wireless security using Institute of Electrical and Electronics Engineers (IEEE) standards. In the case of secure wired access, Windows relies on the IEEE 802.3 standards found at `http://www.ieee802.org/3/`. If you think that this list of standards is amazing, you should check out the IEEE 802.11 standards, found at `http://www.ieee802.org/11/`. The point is that these standards control just about every aspect of wired and wireless communication, including the security.

Wired security has a long history with Windows, and you'll find that the basic security features work well with it. Wireless security is a newer addition, and it presents a number of issues you need to consider. The main issue is that you can protect the data in a wire — at least within reason. Wireless implied some type of transmission through the air, where it becomes nearly impossible to secure the data completely. However, Windows does try within the confines of IEEE 802.11.

To secure your wireless connection completely, you must implement any security features that the hardware vendor provides for your wireless device. You must also make some configuration changes to the Wireless Network (IEEE 802.11) policies found in the Group Policy Management Console (GPMC). In some cases, the GPEdit.MSC file that you open using the Run dialog box doesn't provide access to this policy. (See Book III, Chapter 2 for details on working with group policies.) When this issue occurs, open a copy of MMC and use the Group Policy Object Editor snap-in to gain access to the required policies. The "Creating the RSM console" section of Book II, Chapter 2 tells you how to create a custom console.

The specifics of setting a policy for wireless networking depend on the device you're working with. By default, Windows Server 2008 doesn't set any policies for wireless networking, so you must perform this configuration task to secure your server. When you set the policies, Windows Server 2008 automatically downloads them to the wireless clients that are members of the domain. The TechNet article at `http://technet2.microsoft.com/windowsserver/en/library/5bd33ef2-51e9-4128-f45-850f6f1a162f1033.mspx` provides some tips on performing the configuration. You'll also want to view the article at `http://technet2.microsoft.com/windowsserver/en/library/1f52744d-02d1-421d-bc85-af90cc0ddb261033.mspx`.

Health Registration Authority (HRA)

The HRA validates the health of the client. It reviews the certificate request that the client provides and gives the client a certificate based on the client's health. When the client is missing important security features, such as Windows updates, the server limits the client's ability to perform most tasks. This safety feature helps prevent infection of your server, but it can also limit server accessibility. Of course, this feature also gives users a good reason to update their machines or request that the administrator perform the task for them.

When you install the HRA, you must also install a number of IIS-related role services. Interestingly enough, these role services involved IIS 6, the version of IIS found on previous versions of Windows. Windows Server 2008 supports both IIS 6 and IIS 7. Some features require IIS 6 in order to work properly, so make sure that you use the IIS 6 functionality when working with this feature.

In addition to the IIS 6 support, you must also provide the location of a Certificate Authority (CA). When working in a workgroup, the current server will probably provide CA services. If you don't already have the software required for a CA installed on the server, you can tell the Add Roles Wizard to perform this task for you. You can also use another machine to provide the certificates. Microsoft recommends this option for large networks and further recommends that you provide a machine dedicated to issuing HRA certificates. Otherwise, users may find that they experience trouble logging in to the system.

Installing the HRA normally promotes your server to a domain controller because you can't load a local CA otherwise. If you can access a remote HRA, your server is probably already part of a domain. Unfortunately, Microsoft doesn't tell you about this little change. When you reboot your server, you may find that your workgroup configuration is completely trashed and that you need to configure Active Directory to get anything done. (Your only clue is that you see Active Directory as one of the configuration headings, so you want to watch out for this heading when you perform other configuration tasks.) As a result of these changes, no one can access the server because promoting your server to a domain controller also changes the network addresses. Consequently, you need to configure all your workstations as well. In short, install HRA only if you really need it.

Host Credential Authorization Protocol (HCAP)

You need to install the HCAP only when you work with Cisco products that use the Cisco Network Access Control. You use this feature to integrate NAP with the Cisco technology. This feature lets the NPS perform authentication of the Cisco Network Access Control clients. Because this feature is relatively specialized and you must have the Cisco documentation to use it, you won't find it discussed in this book. You can find the generic Cisco documentation for HCAP at `http://www.cisco.com/warp/public/732/bbip/ pdfs/bbip_v7.02.pdf` and `http://www.cisco.com/application/ pdf/en/us/guest/netsol/ns628/c664/cdccont_0900aecd8034fa7f. pdf`. The Microsoft documentation for HCAP as it applies to NPS appears at `http://technet2.microsoft.com/WindowsServer2008/en/library /d347e8aa-3d9b-43a5-8a4a-0faf4c5baf141033.mspx`. Microsoft expects to provide additional documentation at a later date (the expected date isn't definite as of this writing).

Using the NetSH Command Line Utility

The Network Shell (NetSH) command line utility provides for your network the essential service of letting you perform most configuration tasks without using the graphical utilities that Microsoft provides. You can use NetSH for general configuration tasks. In addition, NetSH replaces several of the common Microsoft Management Console (MMC) snap-ins at the command line. For example, you can use it to configure these essential snap-ins:

✦ NPS

✦ HRA

✦ NAP

✦ RAS

✦ Routing and Remote Access

✦ Wireless Local Area Network (WLAN)

✦ Wireless Internet service provider (WISP)

Understanding the NetSH benefits for wireless configuration

It's easy to disregard some of the benefits of using a command line utility, especially if you haven't worked extensively with them. When working with NetSH, you gain a number of benefits that you can use to work with wireless networks. For example, you can configure mixed mode support with greater ease. It's possible to configure a client to support multiple security options. A client could support both the Wi-Fi Protected Access (WPA) and Wi-Fi Protected Access version 2 (WPA2) authentication standards.

You can also use NetSH to block undesirable networks. All you need to do is configure a list of denied networks by using NetSH. Likewise, adding corporate wireless networks to the allowed list provides quick access for the networks you want to work with.

Don't worry that NetSH won't support newer technology. For example, it can configure Wired Network (IEEE 802.3) policies, which would normally require you to use the Group Policy Management Console (GPMC). These settings affect Windows Vista clients that you equip with network adapters and the drivers that support the Wired AutoConfig Service. You'll find all the settings normally found on the General and Security tabs of the GPMC for Wired Network (IEEE 802.3) policies.

In some cases, you'd have to perform some configuration tasks using group policies as well. Consequently, using this command line approach can save you time and effort working with multiple consoles. Of course, you have to know how to work with the NetSH command line utility, which means learning some new skills in most cases.

The NetSH utility is essentially an extensible command processor — akin to the CMD processor in some respects and to the FTP command line utility in others. You access the functionality that this utility provides by loading a helper DLL. Each helper DLL places the NetSH utility into a different context. The use of helper DLLs theoretically makes it possible for third-party vendors to add NetSH functionality as part of their network product installations. One of the essential commands to know for NetSH, because it's so flexible, is NetSH Show Helper. This command displays a list of helper DLLs installed on your machine, which may differ from the list shown in Figure 3-19, based on the operating system features you have installed.

Figure 3-19: Obtain a list of helper DLLs for your setup using the NetSH Show Helper command.

Notice the hierarchy of contexts displayed in Figure 3-19. To access the IP context at the command line, you must type **NetSH Interface IP** and then the command you want to use. Likewise, if you want to access the 6To4 context, you must type **NetSH Interface IPv6 6To4** at the command line. Typing any context by itself (or followed by a question mark [**?**] or **Help**) displays the list of commands for that context.

Type a command to see the list of subcommands or the instructions for using that command. Type a subcommand to see the instructions for using that subcommand. For example, to discover how to add a new IP address, type **NetSH Interface IP Add Address** at the command prompt and press

Enter. You see a Help display explaining the command, as shown in Figure 3-20. Figure 3-20 shows the Windows Server 2008 view of the Help information for this command. If you're familiar with previous versions of Windows, you'll notice that the Windows Server 2008 Help is an improvement.

Figure 3-20: The multilevel command structure provided by NetSH provides you with help at each step.

The NetSH utility provides access to a broad range of networking functionality by using contexts. Each context represents a different functional network area, such as configuring the firewall or modifying security. You can interact with NetSH at the command line, in an interactive environment, and by using scripts. In this case, a *script* file is simply a list of commands that you want NetSH to perform. You place these commands in a text file and pass them to NetSH to execute. The NetSH utility uses this syntax: `NetSH [-a AliasFile] [-c Context] [-r RemoteMachine] [-u [DomainName\]UserName] [Command | -f ScriptFile]`. The following list describes the command line arguments:

✦ **-a AliasFile:** Specifies the alias file to use. An *alias* file contains a set of strings and their associated NetSH equivalents. You can use the alias in place of the corresponding NetSH command. This feature also allows you to map older commands to the appropriate NetSH command.

✦ **-c Context:** Defines the context of the command you want to run. A *context* refers to a specific helper DLL.

✦ **Command:** Specifies the NetSH command to execute. The command is helper-DLL-specific.

✦ **-f ScriptFile:** Specifies the name of a script file that contains NetSH commands. You can use the pound (#) symbol followed by text to create script file comments. Use the NetSH Dump command to display a sample script. Because the script is long, you might want to use redirection to send the output to a file.

✦ **-r RemoteMachine:** Defines the name or IP address of a remote machine to use to execute NetSH commands. This feature helps you manage remote systems.

✦ **-u [DomainName\]UserName:** Specifies the credentials to use to log in to a system. Windows Server 2008 prompts you for a password when logging in to another system.

The various helper DLLs provide contexts that you can use to perform specific tasks. You can access some of these contexts directly from the command line by using a command. Table 3-1 describes each of the top-level contexts.

Table 3-1	Standard NetSH Contexts	
Context Name	*Windows Version*	*Description*
Bridge	Windows XP and above	Shows configuration information for network adapters that are part of a network bridge. You can also use this context to enable or disable Level 3 compatibility mode.
Diag	Windows XP and above	Performs network diagnostic commands. For example, you can use this context to display network-service status information or perform diagnostics similar to the Ping utility. A special NetSH Diag GUI command displays a Web page in the Help and Support Center that provides access to the network diagnostics.
Firewall	Windows XP and above	Provides complete access to Windows Firewall. You can use this context to add and remove configuration information as well as to display the current firewall state.
Interface	Windows 2000 and above	Provides access to the network interfaces installed on your machine, which normally include IP, IPv6 (Windows XP and above), and standard port proxies. You can use this context to configure the TCP/IP protocol, including addresses, default gateways, DNS servers, and WINS servers.

(continued)

Table 3-1 *(continued)*

Context Name	Windows Version	Description
RAS	Windows 2000 and above	Provides access to the Remote Access Server (RAS) and all its configuration information. For example, this context provides access to the Authentication, Authorization, Accounting, and Auditing (AAAA) subcontext where you perform security setups.
Routing	Windows 2000 and above	Helps you configure the routing features of the system by using a command line interface rather than relying on the Routing and Remote Access console. The biggest advantage of the command line interface, in this case, is speed. You can access and manage remote servers much faster over a large network, especially wide area networks (WANs), by using NetSH than you can by using the graphical equivalents. In addition, because these configuration tasks can become quite complex, you gain the advantage of scripting them once rather than going through every required step each time you perform the task.
WinSock	Windows XP and above	Shows Windows Socket (WinSock) information for the current system. You can also use this context to dump the WinSock configuration script.

The default context is the root context, the NetSH utility itself. You can use specific commands from this context to perform configuration tasks or access other contexts. The following list describes the command line arguments, which differ according to the version of Windows you use and the networking features you have installed:

✦ **add:** Adds a configuration entry to the list of entries. When working at the root context, you can add new helper DLLs to the list.

✦ **bridge:** Sets NetSH to use the bridge context.

✦ **cmd:** Creates a command window where you can enter NetSH commands manually.

✦ **comment:** Executes any commands accumulated in offline mode.

✦ **delete:** Deletes a configuration entry from the list of entries. When working at the root context, you can remove a helper DLL from the list.

✦ **diag:** Sets NetSH to use the diag context.

✦ **dump:** Displays a configuration script. The script is quite long, so you want to use redirection to store the script to a file.

✦ **exec:** Executes the specified script file.

✦ **firewall:** Sets NetSH to use the firewall context.

✦ **flush:** Discards the commands accumulated in offline mode.

✦ **interface:** Sets NetSH to use the interface context.

✦ **offline:** Sets the current mode to offline. In Offline mode, the utility accumulates any commands you issue and executes them as a batch. Using this second approach on remote servers can greatly enhance performance without any loss of functionality. Use the Show Mode command to display the current mode.

✦ **online:** Sets the current mode to Online. In Online mode, which is the default for all previous versions of NetSH, the utility executes immediately any command you issue. Use the Show Mode command to display the current mode.

✦ **popd:** Removes a context from the NetSH stack.

✦ **pushd:** Pushes a context onto the NetSH stack.

✦ **ras:** Sets NetSH to use the RAS context.

✦ **routing:** Sets NetSH to use the routing context.

✦ **set:** Updates the configuration settings. Most versions of NetSH allow you to set the machine name only when working at the root context.

✦ **show:** Displays NetSH configuration information. Most versions of NetSH provide commands to display both the list of aliases and the list of helpers installed on the system.

✦ **winsock:** Sets NetSH to use the winsock context.

This chapter doesn't discuss the specifics of each context because they vary according to the operating system version and the helpers you have installed. Unfortunately, there isn't any documented resource from Microsoft for standard contexts in Windows Server 2008, but you can use the Windows 2003 resource as a guideline. The contexts for Windows 2003 appear at `http://technet2.microsoft.com/WindowsServer/en/Library/552 ed70a-208d-48c4-8da8-2e27b530eac71033.mspx`. You can find additional NetSH utility documentation in the Microsoft Knowledge Base article at `http://support.microsoft.com/?kbid=242468` and the Cable Guy article at `http://www.microsoft.com/technet/community/ columns/cableguy/cg1101.mspx`.

Book IV
Chapter 3

Accomplishing
Advanced
Networking Tasks

Chapter 4: Diagnosing and Repairing Network Connection Problems

---

In This Chapter

✔ **Working with the Diagnose and Repair feature**

✔ **Checking and fixing an individual connection**

✔ **Looking for common configuration errors**

✔ **Ensuring that users have the correct settings**

*N*o one wants to have a problem with their network. Such problems are often difficult to find because they could exist on the client system, the server, or anywhere in-between. In addition, network problems can be of an intermittent nature (the problem appears today, you try to troubleshoot it, and it goes away), which makes them even more frustrating to fix. A network is also influenced by outside sources, software and hardware from multiple parties, and a host of other issues that don't affect problems on the local machine. Given the number of sources for potential problems, it's amazing that networks are as worry free and stable as they are.

Microsoft has made a significant effort in Windows Server 2008 to make it easier to locate problems. For example, you now see an indicator when your network cable is unplugged, and running a simple diagnostic can fix many of the software errors a network can encounter. This chapter focuses on the ways in which Windows Server 2008 can help you locate and determine a course of action for a network repair.

You also find some additional rules of thumb in this chapter for locating problems with your network. These rules of thumb help you locate the problems with greater ease. However, they're just rules of thumb — sometimes they work and sometimes they don't. In many cases, the information you find online also falls into the rule-of-thumb category, so don't be disappointed when you need to try multiple methods to fix a particularly stubborn problem.

This chapter doesn't provide every answer to every networking problem that you'll ever encounter. Not only would such an attempt prove futile, but the resulting book would probably also be thousands of pages long. It's probably not possible for anyone to say that they have seen it all. Even after all the years I've worked with networks, I know I haven't seen it all. Actually, if you do encounter a particularly interesting problem, I'd love to hear about how you fixed it, at `JMueller@mwt.net`. With your permission, I'll publish the problem and its fix on my blog. The following sections address the common Windows Server 2008 networking problems you'll encounter.

Using the Diagnose and Repair Feature

In some cases, the repair for a problem is obvious. For example, if you see a message telling you that a cable is disconnected, you already know what's wrong (see the later section "Repairing Individual Connections" for additional information). However, most problems don't fall into this category. What you'll see is that the network has suddenly stopped working in some respect.

When you can't identify a problem, except to know that it's there, you can always try the Diagnose and Repair feature. When you click this link in the Network and Sharing Center (shown in Figure 4-1), you see a message saying that Windows is identifying the problem. Theoretically, Windows is checking all your connections for potential problems. In some cases, you see a dialog box telling you there aren't any problems. Of course, this doesn't mean that you're imagining things; it simply means that Windows didn't find a problem. The odd issue is that you might see an X on a particular connection (showing that the connection is bad), and it goes away after running the Diagnose and Repair feature. The problem existed, but it was one of those transient problems that sometimes plague networks.

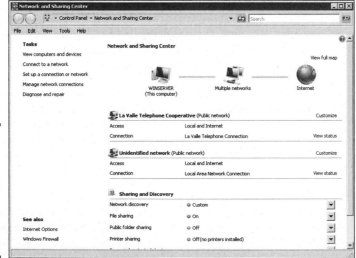

Figure 4-1:
The Network and Sharing Center provides the first level of diagnostics.

What happens, though, if the network problem still exists? At this point, you need to click Manage Network Connections to open the Network Connections window, shown in Figure 4-2. Locate the connection that you feel is the source of the problem and choose Diagnose from the context menu. Windows again performs a diagnosis, but this time it concentrates on that connection. In some cases, Windows finds the source of the problem and fixes it.

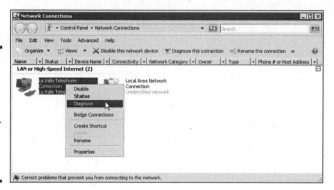

Figure 4-2: Try performing individual-ized trouble-shooting when necessary.

When Windows can't fix the problem, it can at least recommend a course of action in most cases, as shown in Figure 4-3. The order of the suggestions indicates the order that Microsoft recommends. Of course, after you get to know your system, you may find that a different order works better. For example, a system may have a modem that appears to lose contact with the ISP regularly, so unplugging the modem, waiting ten seconds, and plugging it back in may be the best solution, even though it appears second in the list. One thing to consider is that many modems have an actual power switch and some have a reset button as well. Try resetting the modem first because that route requires less recycle time. If that doesn't work, turning off the modem by using the switch is less likely to cause problems than unplugging it.

Always wait for the modem to recycle before you attempt the test again. The Microsoft Help screen doesn't tell you this requirement, but it can require up to a minute for the modem to recycle in some cases. Sometimes, it's best to turn the modem back on and then go get a cup of coffee. The minute or two you take won't hurt — it's better to ensure that the modem is up and running again.

The Microsoft Help system doesn't tell you this, but sometimes you have to recycle switches and routers as well. That's because these devices include intelligence that can become befuddled by daily networking tasks. A hub (sometimes called a *passive switch*) never requires recycling because it's a passive device that lacks intelligence.

**Book IV
Chapter 4**

Diagnosing and
Repairing Network
Connection
Problems

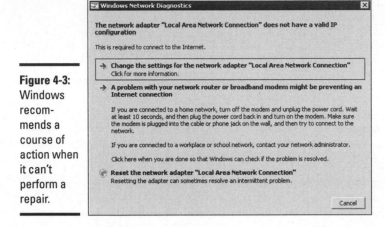

Figure 4-3:
Windows recommends a course of action when it can't perform a repair.

Repairing Individual Connections

In some cases, an individual connection is going to fail. The problem may be something as simple as a disconnected cable. Of course, *disconnected* also includes the possibility that someone has severed the cable or pulled on it too hard and caused the connector itself to fail or a myriad of other problems. One person told me about a user who rolled over a cable with a chair after pulling the cable out from under the desk while looking for something. The cable ended up wrapped around the chair wheel (breaking the connection), and the user seemed surprised that this kind of treatment could cause problems. A failed NIC sometimes shows up as a failed cable as well. It depends on where the NIC fails.

Your first indication of a connection problem is the usual red X in the Network and Sharing Center window. Running the network diagnostics in this case will probably tell you that the system can't find a Domain Name System (DNS) server or other useless information, as shown in Figure 4-4. A call to the other end of the line will tell you whether their server is up and running. If it is, this information really isn't helpful.

Don't waste a lot of time trying to pursue the error message shown in Figure 4-4. Instead, click Manage Network Connections. The Network Connections window, shown in Figure 4-5, provides significantly more useful information. In this case, you see that the problem is a disconnected cable. Of course, the message tells you only that the cable is disconnected. You need to locate the actual source of the disconnection.

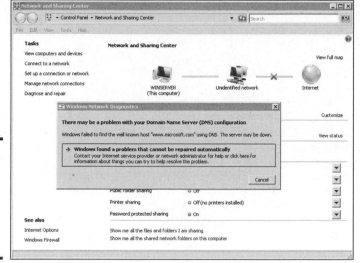

Figure 4-4:
Sometimes the information Windows provides isn't helpful.

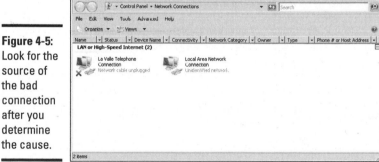

Figure 4-5:
Look for the source of the bad connection after you determine the cause.

Don't always assume that the fact that the cable is plugged in means anything. Connectors go bad, so you must actually check the connector to ensure that it's still in good shape. In addition, the NIC normally has a light that shows a good connection, and you don't see this light when the connection is bad. In fact, you should look at these locations for the source of the problem, (the order of this list is only a suggestion, and you can check the items in any order you think is useful, depending on past experience):

✦ NIC connection

✦ Switch or hub connection

✦ Network cable

✦ Both connectors

**Book IV
Chapter 4**

Diagnosing and
Repairing Network
Connection
Problems

✦ NIC

✦ Switch or hub

The troubleshooting problem can become complex. Make sure that you run the diagnostic that comes with your NIC. In some cases, you need to provide a loopback connector to perform the test completely — check with your vendor for details. A network cable can look perfectly healthy yet contain problems. Use a Time Domain Reflectometer (TDR) to check the cable. Some cable testers include this feature, and others don't, so you need to check the tester specifications before you buy it.

It's important to understand how a TDR works before you use it. You can find a technical discussion of this functionality at `http://en.wikipedia. org/wiki/Time-domain_reflectometer`. If you really want to get into the nuts and bolts of a TDR, check out the Web site at `http://web-ee. com/Schematics/TDR/tdr.htm`. You'll find instructions on how to build your own TDR, should you desire to do so.

Hubs generally don't provide any sort of testing functionality. You can normally switch cables between two connections to see whether the problem moves from one connection to the other. (Make sure to contact the workstation at the end of that cable before you perform the test.) In some cases, you may find it easier to simply replace the hub. Switches often provide testing functionality that you access through Telnet. Consult the vendor documentation for details on switch testing features.

Overcoming Common Configuration Errors

Many administrators think in total network failure terms, but that's a mistake. Because networks rely on security, ports, and all kinds of other issues, you can't look for a total network failure in every situation. A transient error is the hardest problem to fix, but it can also prove to be the most important problem to fix because transient problems often result in lost data.

Some configuration problems are somewhat obvious. Right-click a connection and choose Properties to view its Properties dialog box. Figure 4-6 shows a typical example. You can quickly detect any clients, services, and protocols with settings that you can change by highlighting the entry. If Windows enables the Properties button, you can change that setting. The "Managing Network Connections" section of Book IV, Chapter 2 tells you how to work with these settings. If you're having a problem with the network, it always pays to validate these settings.

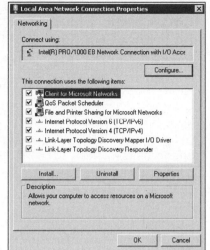

Figure 4-6:
Check each client, service, and protocol that has settings, to ensure that everything is correct.

Some administrators stop at this point. However, notice that Figure 4-6 includes a Configure button. When you click Configure, you see the NIC's Properties dialog box. Select the Advanced tab and you're likely to see a host of other settings that can create everything from total failures to intermittent problems. Figure 4-7 shows a typical example of the Advanced tab. The settings you find on this tab are NIC-specific, so you need to consult the documentation for your NIC before you make any changes here. Don't just try settings until you find the right one. Doing so can require hours, or perhaps even days, before you hit on the correct sequence of settings that will fix the problem (assuming that the settings are even the source of the problem).

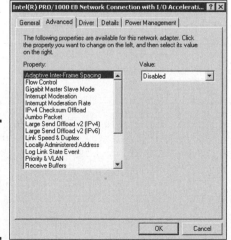

Figure 4-7:
The Advanced tab contains settings you should check.

**Book IV
Chapter 4**

**Diagnosing and
Repairing Network
Connection
Problems**

Make sure to check all NIC settings. An administrator once researched a problem for weeks only to find that the Power Management tab settings were incorrect and there was a fault in the server's power management strategy. The server kept turning off the NIC to conserve power and then refused to turn it back on until someone rebooted the system. Drivers can become outdated as well, and checking the Details tab can provide clues to what's troubling the NIC in your system.

Not shown in Figure 4-7 is the Diagnostic tab. Some NICs provide such a tab to use for running diagnostics on the NIC. In other cases, the vendor provides a separate application for performing the task. Less expensive NICs tend not to come with any testing functionality, which means that you must swap the NIC with a known good NIC to determine whether the NIC is the problem.

Configuring the User Settings Correctly

One problem in determining the source of a failure in a network connection is deciding where to begin looking. All you usually know when you start the task is that the network isn't working. You can ask any user with a network problem and they'll tell you it isn't working — beyond that, you're on your own. It shouldn't be too much of a surprise to discover, then, that many network problems affect a single user and you can usually chase the connectivity problem down to a few errant settings.

Most administrators know to check the user's security. It's important to determine whether the user has the rights required to access resources on the network. After you make this determination, you also check the user's share settings. The combination of network security and share settings determines what the user can do on the server. This two-tier strategy may seem cumbersome, but it serves a useful purpose in ensuring that the user receives only the required access. In addition, the two tiers serve to separate access gained through Terminal Services from access gained directly through the network. Book V, Chapter 1 tells you how Windows security works, and Book V, Chapter 2 describes how shares work.

The settings that seem to elude many administrators when it comes to connectivity are those found in the user's account. The user's profile, environment, and sessions settings can make a considerable difference in the level of connectivity that the user obtains. For example, an incorrect setting on the Profile tab can redirect the user to an area of the hard drive for which the user lacks rights. From the user's perspective, the problem looks and acts very much like a network connectivity problem. In a way, the problem is one of network connectivity because the user can't access any network resources in the current location.

The location of the user settings depends on your network settings. When working with Active Directory, you find them in the Active Directory-related consoles. When working with a workgroup, you find them in the Users folder of the Computer Management console. In either case, you open the user's account by right-clicking its entry and choosing Properties from the context menu. The following sections describe the connectivity concerns for these three tabs.

Setting the Profile tab

The Profile tab, shown in Figure 4-8, controls how the user connects to the network. An incorrect setting in any of these entries can send the user to a location that doesn't provide the correct rights or that even contains incorrect information for that user.

One way to avoid problems with this tab is not to use it. If you set up shares for specific folders on the network for the user, you've already controlled the user's access to the server. Placing shortcuts to specific project folders on the user's desktop further reduces access and tends to reduce the need to direct the user to a specific place by using the Profile tab settings.

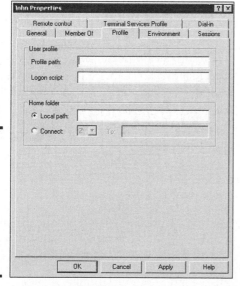

Figure 4-8:
Make sure that the user's profile is correct and points to an area they can access.

**Book IV
Chapter 4**

Diagnosing and
Repairing Network
Connection
Problems

Of course, despite the best configuration techniques available, you still need to configure some options on the Profile tab. For example, most companies use the logon script to ensure that the user receives required updates and configuration changes. In addition, the logon script configures part of the user's environment by setting up drive mappings, and so on. When you do make entries in either the Profile Path or Logon Script fields, make sure to use Universal Naming Convention paths that include one of the following forms:

- ✦ \\ServerName\ProfilePath\Username
- ✦ \\ServerName\ProfilePath\GroupName
- ✦ \\ServerName\ScriptPath\Username
- ✦ \\ServerName\ScriptPath\GroupName

Using group options whenever possible reduces configuration complexity and also makes it more likely that you'll find potential problems early. In addition, group settings make maintenance easier because you need to address changes in one location only. Of course, the trade-off for all these benefits is that you also lose some level of flexibility because the profile and script you create must address the needs of the group as a whole.

When choosing a Home Folder option, consider using a network drive in most cases. Using a network drive lets the user roam between different machines and always have the same home folder available. In addition, using a network drive makes it possible to back up those user settings so that you can restore them later.

A local drive has some advantages if you can ensure that the user will always use the same machine to connect to the network. The user receives a small performance boost because requests for home folder information doesn't have to go to the network. In addition, if the user relies on a laptop, the home folder goes with the user from place to place. The important issue is to ensure that the user won't have to go without home folder data because it can appear as a network connectivity failure to some applications.

Setting the Environment tab

The Environment tab, shown in Figure 4-9, affects Terminal Services sessions. These settings provide defaults that the user will use when connecting to the network through any form of Terminal Services.

The Starting Program section determines whether the system runs a starting program when the user logs in to Terminal Server. The starting program need not be an executable. You can always use a batch file or script as a starting program. The batch file or script can contain instructions for setting up drive mappings, configuring the environment, running standard executables, and performing other startup tasks the user may require. The more complex these startup tasks become, the greater the possibility that one or more of them will fail and cause network connectivity problems. Consequently, if you use a startup program to configure the user's setup, you need to test it fully in every environment the user will use.

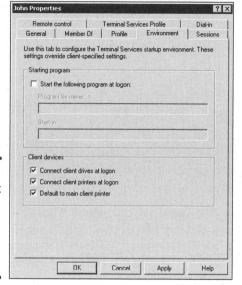

Figure 4-9:
Environment problems are often subtle and difficult to locate.

The Client Devices section contains options for making client resources available as part of the Terminal Services session. Figure 4-9 shows the default configuration, which makes all the client resources available while working in Terminal Services. This configuration works best for users who connect to the network from a remote location. A user printing in a Terminal Server application will expect the output to appear locally, because going all the way to work to retrieve it makes little sense. As with many network issues, printing to the remote system may actually appear as a network connectivity issue to the user even when everything is working precisely as you configured it.

The setup shown in Figure 4-9 can become a problem when the user is connecting through Terminal Services locally. In this case, an application may look for a client printer or hard drive and not find it. The user will wait as Terminal Services valiantly retries the operation to the point where the user will likely fall asleep waiting for the computer to respond. At this point, the computer tells the user that there's an error in trying to use a non-existent device. Again, the user will assume there's a network connectivity problem, even though Terminal Services and the associated Terminal Server are working precisely as planned.

Setting the Sessions tab

The Sessions tab, shown in Figure 4-10, can prove quite troublesome when configured incorrectly. In fact, the user may find that it's impossible to log in to the system when you configure this tab incorrectly, or at least, inconveniently.

Consider the scenario where you set Terminal Services to automatically end an idle session after 15 minutes. The user attempts to save the document

Book IV
Chapter 4

Diagnosing and
Repairing Network
Connection
Problems

they edited before lunch, and the application refuses because the session was terminated. The user automatically assumes that the network has connectivity problems and rather than save the document locally, simply closes the application in disgust. At this point, the data the user created before lunch is gone and the user blames you, of course, even though the company policy is to save data and exit the session before going to lunch or meetings. The lesson to learn in this case is to ensure that users know not to close their applications in the event of a network failure.

Now consider another scenario. You set the End a Disconnected Session option to Never. The user, who commonly loses their connection, loses it again today. Given that you recently set the number of sessions that a user can have to 1, the user can't log in to the system. The system shows that the user already has a connection because the disconnected session was never ended. The user assumes that there's a network connectivity problem and rants until you fix it. Unless you know to manually end the user's disconnected session, you can search for this particular problem for a very long time. The lesson to learn in this case is to automatically end disconnected sessions after a reasonable length of time.

Of the settings shown in Figure 4-10, the one that makes the least sense in today's computing environment is Active Session Limit. This feature makes sense only when you have a large number of people participating on a server with very limited resources. The goal of this setting is to force people using Terminal Services off the Terminal Server after a specific amount of time, to free resources for someone else to get their fair share of time. In most cases, you'll want to keep this setting at Never.

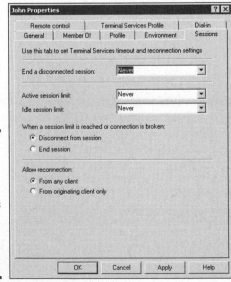

Figure 4-10:
A user may have session expectations that their settings don't consider.

Part V

Security

The 5th Wave
By Rich Tennant

©RICHTENNANT

"Don't be silly—of course my passwords are safe. I keep them written on my window, but then I pull the shade if anyone walks in the room."

Contents at a Glance

Chapter 1: Understanding Windows Server 2008 Security

In This Chapter

✔ Understanding basic Windows security

✔ Understanding .NET security

✔ Setting file and folder security

✔ Defining a local security policy

✔ Working with the Security Configuration Wizard

*W*indows Server 2008 has a number of new security features. For example, the User Account Control (UAC) feature is a nice addition to Windows Server 2008 that will keep your server safer. However, some new features are actually different implementations of existing features. You always had the resources required to lock everyone out of the root directory of the hard drive. In fact, you could easily convert Windows Server 2003 so that it works the same as Windows Server 2008 in this regard. The difference is that the root directory comes out of the package *locked,* which means that you don't have to do anything special to receive the protection that such a measure provides. In short, Windows Server 2008 uses a combination of old and new to obtain a higher level of security.

This chapter describes the basic security features that Windows Server 2008 provides. In many respects, you'll find that there really isn't much in the way of new basic security in Windows Server 2008, but Windows Server 2008 does use these security features in new ways. If you consider yourself a security guru already, you could probably skip the introductory material in this chapter, but then you'd miss out on a few bits of information that tell you how Windows Server 2008 differs.

If nothing else, make sure to visit the sections on setting security. You need to know this information as the book progresses because there are some differences in implementation that make life difficult if you don't. For example, you really do need to know that Windows Server 2008 plays by different rules when it comes to offering access to certain parts of the drive — setting security in one area doesn't necessarily give you access at a lower level any longer. If you're new to Windows security, the following sections provide a good overview of everything you need to know to secure your system successfully. Because security is so important, you'll want to refer back to this chapter as you progress through the other chapters in this minibook.

Working with Basic Windows Security

The security configuration process for Windows Server 2008 begins with basic Windows security. This is the form of security that prevents you from accessing the root directory of your hard drive. It's also the form of security that grants access to your personal folders while denying you access to the folders above this level. In short, basic Windows security is the first form of security that you see when using Windows Server 2008.

The theory behind Windows security is simple: Windows views every server resource as an object. A printer is an object, as are the directories on the hard drive, and even the system time. Every object has a lock, and every object requestor (normally users, but requestors can also include the operating system, services, or anything else that requires access to system resources) has a key. If the requestor's key fits the lock, the requestor gains access to the object and to the resources it provides. This is *token-based* security. The user's token is their key to resources on the local machine, the network and intranet, and even the Internet.

So much for the simple view of Windows security — although the simple lock and key analogy works well, it doesn't describe every aspect of basic Windows security. The following sections describe some of the complex issues surrounding this simple technology. You may not have known that all these actions are taking place in the background, but Microsoft performs them to ensure that your server remains safe.

Understanding the concepts of authentication

Authentication asks the question "Who are you?" When you see the login dialog box, Windows is asking who you are. It then matches the name and password (and, optionally, a domain) that you provide (your credentials) against a list of users who can access the server. When Windows finds your information in the list of those who can access the server, it gives you a token that contains a list of all the things you can access on the server. The authentication list resides either on the local server or as part of the Active Directory database, but it works the same in both cases.

It's important to understand that authentication merely identifies you to the system — it doesn't grant you access to anything. Users can have access to the system without having permission to use any of its resources (making the authentication a waste of time and effort). Many administrators confuse authentication with authorization. Authentication always occurs first, and it always provides you with a user token, but it doesn't provide anything else.

Of course, authentication is very important. Without the user token, you can't open the locks to any resources. The user token you obtain as part of the authentication process provides access to the resources you need.

Some people ask why there's a two-step process. The authentication process is important because it provides an additional layer of security. Until you authenticate with the server, you don't have any access to it. In short, the server blocks you before you can do anything to it and demands to know who you are. If you fail this test, you can't access any part of the server except to try to authenticate again.

In modern systems, you can authenticate using a number of technologies. Of course, there's the old standby of passwords. However, many systems now offer smart cards (those credit-card-size bits of plastic you slide through a reader) as an alternative. The advantage of smart cards is that they can use complex passwords that are definitely harder to guess, but a user can also lose a smart card, making it easier for someone to get unauthorized access in some cases. Laptops and other devices also come with thumbprint or other biometric-based security. Of course, you can't lose your thumb, but some people have demonstrated an ability to override this form of security as well. The point is that authentication identifies you to the computer, no matter how you perform the task.

Understanding the concepts of authorization

Authorization always happens after authentication. A user has a token that identifies the resources they can access. Of course, the token itself can be quite complex because it contains both individual user rights and those of the groups to which the user belongs. An administrator can also explicitly deny access to resources through individual or group entries in the token, so the token can include four major kinds of entry. The token must also specify specific rights. You may have the right to read a file, but not to modify it in any way.

User-level access depends on a security ID (SID). When the user first logs in to the system, Windows assigns an access token to the user and places the user's SID (stored on the domain controller or other security database) within it. The user object carries around both the access token and the SID for the duration of the session. An access token also contains both a Discretionary Access Control List (DACL) and a System Access Control List (SACL). (You may also see SACL defined as Security Access Control List.) The combination of Access Control Lists (ACLs) and SID within the access token is a key that allows the user access to certain system resources. Because this access lasts the entire session, the user must log out and then back in to the system whenever the administrator makes a change to security; otherwise, the user won't gain additional rights that the administrator provides.

A key is no good without a lock to open. The lock placed on Windows resources is a *security descriptor.* In essence, it tells which rights the user needs in order to access the resource. If the rights within the Access Control Lists (ACLs) meet or exceed the rights in the security descriptor, the lock opens and the resource becomes available. Figure 1-1 shows the content of the ACL and the security descriptor used for token-based security.

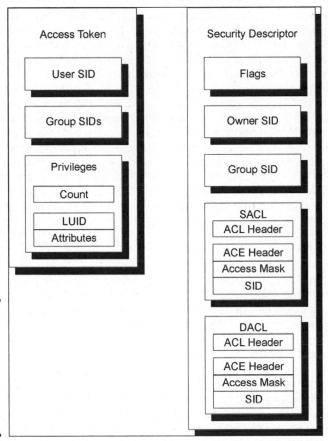

Figure 1-1:
Token-based security relies on ACLs and security descriptors.

Understanding access tokens

There are two ways of looking at a user's rights under Windows: individual rights and group rights. The user's SID is the account number that Windows assigns to the user during login. The access token that holds the SID also contains other structures that identify the groups the user belongs to and what privileges the user has. Each group entry also has a SID. This SID points to other structures that describe the group's rights. To understand the user's rights, you need to know both the user's individual rights and the rights of the groups that the user belongs to. You'd normally use the Local Users and Groups or the Active Directory Users and Computers Microsoft Management Console (MMC) snap-in to change the contents of this access token.

The privileges section of the access token, shown in Figure 1-1, begins with a count of the number of privileges that the user has — the number of special privilege entries in the access token. This section also contains an array of privilege entries. Each privilege entry contains a locally unique identifier (LUID) — essentially a pointer to the entry object — and an attribute mask. The attribute mask indicates which rights the user has to the object. Group SID entries are essentially the same. They contain a privilege count and an array of privilege entries.

One thing you need to know as part of working with some kinds of objects is that object rights flow down to the lowest possible node unless overridden by another SID. For example, if you give the user read and write privileges to the `\Temp` directory on a hard drive; those rights also apply to the `\Temp\Stuff` directory unless you assigned the user specific rights to that directory. The same holds true for containers. Assigning a user rights to a container object, such as a Word document, gives the user the right to look at everything within that container — even other files, in most cases. It's important to track a user's exact rights to objects on your server using security surveys, because you can inadvertently give the user more rights than needed to perform a certain task.

Understanding security descriptors

At this point, you have a better idea of how the access token (the key) works. It's time to look at the security descriptor (the lock). Figure 1-1 shows that each security descriptor contains five main sections. The following list describes each section:

✦ **Header and flags:** The header consists of version information and a list of control flags. The flags tell you the descriptor status. For example, the SE_DACL_PRESENT flag indicates the presence of a DACL. If the DACL is missing, Windows allows everyone to use the object. The basic security descriptors haven't changed since Windows 2000, so you can see a list of basic security descriptors at `http://www.microsoft.com/technet/prodtechnol/windows2000serv/reskit/distrib/dsce_ctl_qxju.mspx`. (Windows Server 2008 adds some security descriptors, but you don't really need to know them at this point because you won't normally need to modify them directly.) The overviews at `http://www.microsoft.com/technet/prodtechnol/windows2000serv/reskit/distrib/dsce_ctl_ajfg.mspx` and `http://msdn2.microsoft.com/en-us/library/ms679006.aspx` provide additional information about Windows security flags.

✦ **Owner SID:** Tells who owns the object. This doesn't have to be an individual user; Windows allows use of a group SID here as well. The limiting factor is that the group SID must appear in the token of the person changing the entry. In other words, you can't assign ownership to a group where you don't have membership.

✦ **Group SID:** Tells which group owns the object. This entry contains only the main group responsible for the object and won't contain a list of all groups with access to the object.

✦ **SACL:** This section controls the Windows' auditing feature. Every time a user or group accesses an object when the auditing feature for that object is on, Windows makes an entry in the audit log. There's more than one entry in this section, in most cases, so Windows stores the information in an array.

✦ **DACL:** This section controls object use. Windows assigns groups and users to a specific object. There's more than one entry in this section, in most cases, so Windows stores the information in an array. A DACL can contain a custom value, a default value, or a NULL (empty) value or not appear in the security descriptor at all. (This last option is rare and dangerous.) You normally find more objects with default values than any other DACL type.

Understanding ACLs

As previously mentioned, a security descriptor relies on an SACL and a DACL to control the security of an object. Both elements use the same basic ACL data structure, but for different purposes. An ACL consists of two entry types. The first is a header that lists the number of access control entries (ACEs) in the ACL. Windows uses this number to determine when it has reached the end of the ACE list. (There is no end-of-structure record or another way to determine the size of each ACE in the structure.) The second entry is an array of ACEs.

An ACE defines the object rights for a single user or group. Every ACE has a header that defines the type, size, and flags for the ACE. It includes an access mask that defines the rights a user or group has to the object. Finally, there's an entry for the user or group SID.

There are four main ACE header types. Windows currently uses three of the four main ACE header types. The following list tells you about each of the main header types:

✦ **General Access:** This header type appears in the DACL and grants object rights to a user. Use it to add to the rights a user already has to an object on an instance-by-instance basis. For example, you might want to prevent the user from changing the system time so that you can keep the machines on the network synchronized. However, there might be

Working with .NET Security **519**

Book V
Chapter 1

Understanding
Windows Server
2008 Security

one situation — such as daylight savings time — when the user would need this right. You could use an access-allowed ACE to allow the user to change the time in this single instance.

✦ **Object Access:** This header type helps Windows assign specific security to software objects and sub-objects. A developer must provide special code to provide this access. For example, the developer could use this type of ACE to assign security to the property of a COM object. To use this type of ACE, the developer needs to obtain or create a globally unique identifier (GUID) for the object in question. After the developer adds the required code, application settings could allow the administrator to control access to particular application features at runtime.

✦ **System Audit:** This ACE header type works with the SACL. It defines which events to audit for a particular user or group. There are system audit header types for both general and object use. The .NET Framework doesn't provide a specific auditing feature, so you can use this feature when you want to know who's accessing a particular Web site feature and when they access it. This feature requires that the user log on to the system. Yes, it works with anonymous access, but all you see is the anonymous user information.

✦ **System Alarm:** This is the currently unused ACE type. It enables either the SACL or DACL to set an alarm when specific events happen.

Working with .NET Security

The .NET Framework is a relatively new feature for Windows, and it isn't fully integrated into the server yet. In fact, it may take Microsoft quite a few years to complete this task because the entire operating system would need to rely on the .NET Framework. In short, Windows would need to become a managed application and there really isn't any way to accomplish that task just yet. Consequently, you may never run into .NET security while using Windows Server 2008.

Some parts of Windows Server 2008 do use .NET security. For example, the new Internet Information Server (IIS) 7.0 relies on managed code and provides complete support for .NET security. Consequently, you find that IIS provides support for .NET users, .NET roles, and other .NET security features.

The main benefit of .NET security is that it provides better coverage of the problems that could overtake your computer. Rather than just secure the user, as token-based security does, .NET security also secures the code, which means that even if someone manages to access an application, they can't force it to perform acts that it shouldn't perform. You also find that

.NET security provides flexible security based on zones and more levels of security than the basic Windows security does. The following sections describe .NET security in greater detail.

Considering the .NET security features

The .NET security features help you overcome some of the security issues inherent within Windows. Microsoft actually started this move with a technology called Component Object Model Plus (COM+). COM+ did (and still does) support role-based security (see the material that follows for an explanation of role-based security), but .NET security provides significantly more.

The managed environment also maintains better control over resources that tend to create problems in the unmanaged Windows environment. This form of security is Code Access Security (CAS) — it controls what an application can do with any resource it can access. The combination of role-based and code access security, along with the object-oriented programming strategy of the .NET Framework, strengthens server security considerably. The following list summarizes what you'll find as security enhancements in the .NET Framework. (The "Understanding role-based security" and "Understanding code access security" sections of this chapter provide additional details about these features.)

✦ **Evidence-based Security:** This feature determines which rights to grant to code based on information gathered about it. The Common Language Runtime (CLR) (pronounced "clear") examines the information it knows about an assembly (.NET executable file) and determines which rights to grant that code based on the evidence. Managed code doesn't run without CLR, so CLR is the final authority on what the code can and can't do. Using the information it has obtained, CLR matches the evidence against a security policy, which is a series of settings that define how the administrator wants to secure a system. The code can perform tasks only when the evidence shows that it has followed the proper security policies.

✦ **Code Access Security:** Essentially, this feature controls what the code can do, even before the user can interact with the application. CLR uses this feature to determine whether all the assemblies (a basic code element on the same order as a DLL) in a calling chain have rights to use a particular resource or perform a particular task. Imagine it this way: An application wants to display a dialog box, so it calls on the assembly that contains the code for the dialog box to display it on-screen. Both the application and the assembly it calls must have the proper rights to perform a task. Otherwise, CLR generates a security error that the system uses to detect security breaches. The purpose of this check is to ensure that someone can't intercept rights that they don't deserve.

✦ **Defined Verification Process:** Before the Just-in-Time (JIT) compiler accepts the Microsoft Intermediate Language (MSIL) assembly, it checks the code that the assembly contains for errors. These checks include everything from the way the developer has written the code to the kinds of data the assembly manipulates. This verification process ensures that the code doesn't include any fatal flaws that would keep it from running. The checks also determine whether an external force has modified strongly named code. After JIT performs these checks, it compiles the MSIL into native code. CLR can run a verified assembly in isolation so that it doesn't affect any other assembly (and more importantly, so that other assemblies can't affect it).

✦ **Role-based Security:** Rather than assign security to individuals or groups, you assign it based on the role that an individual or group will perform. The Windows SID security is limited in that you can control entire files, but not parts of those files. Role-based security still relies on identifying the user through a logon or other means. The main advantage is that you can ask the security system about the user's role and allow access to program features based on that role. An administrator will likely have access to all the features of a program, but individual users may have access to only a subset of the features. Most importantly, a user's role can change. An administrator may not always be in the administrator role. Likewise, a user may have rights temporarily elevated to perform administrator-like tasks.

✦ **Cryptography:** The advantages of cryptography are many. The concept is simple — you make data unreadable by using an algorithm, coupled with a key, to mix up the information. When the originator supplies the correct key to another algorithm, the original data is returned. Over the years, the power of computers has increased, making old cryptology techniques suspect. The .NET Framework supports the latest cryptographic techniques, which ensures that your data remains safe.

✦ **Separate Application Domains:** A developer can write .NET code in such a way that some of the pieces run in a separate domain. It's a COM-type concept where the code is isolated from the other code in your program. Many developers use this feature to load special code, run it, and then unload that code without stopping the program. For example, a browser could use this technique to load and unload plug-ins. This feature also works well for security. It helps you run code at different security levels in separate domains to ensure true isolation.

Understanding role-based security

When Microsoft started designing .NET, the world of computing was moving from the local area network (LAN) and wide area network (WAN) to the Internet. The individual user and group approach used by Windows didn't necessarily reflect the best way to pursue security in a distributed environment. In addition, the current environment was too open to potential attacks from outside.

Microsoft had actually begun working on the whole issue of one-size-fits-all security sometime earlier with COM+. In COM+, an administrator could configure applications to provide specific levels of access based on a user's role. You created roles, assigned users to those roles, and defined the applications and methods that the role could access. Consequently, a manager could have access to methods that a general user didn't. However, the COM+ version of role-based security didn't always work very well with the Internet and it wasn't as flexible as administrators would have liked. In addition, developers had to use convoluted tactics to make COM+ security work properly.

The following sections describe how .NET role-based security reflects its COM+ heritage and where it differs. More importantly, the following sections describe how you can work with role-based security to improve the overall security of your system. You'll also find out about some of the tools that Microsoft provides for working with role-based security.

Defining membership and evidence

For many people, the word *evidence* brings up the vision of a court with judge and jury. The term is quite appropriate for the .NET Framework because any code that wants to execute must present its case before CLR and deliver evidence to validate any requests. CLR makes a decision about the code based on the evidence and decides how the evidence fits within the current policies (laws) of the runtime as set by the network administrator. Theoretically, controlling security with evidence as CLR does allows applications built on the .NET Framework to transcend limitations of the underlying operating system. Largely, this view is true. However, remember that CLR is running on top of the underlying operating system and is therefore subject to its limitations. Here's the typical evidence-based sequence of events:

1. The assembly demands access to data, resources, or other protected elements.

2. CLR requests evidence of the assembly's origins and security documents (such as a digital signature and other credentials).

3. After receiving the evidence from the assembly, CLR runs the evidence through a security policy.

4. The security policy outputs a permission based on the evidence and the network administrator settings.

5. The code gains some level of access to the protected element if the evidence supports such access; otherwise, CLR denies the request.

Note that the assembly must demand access before any part of the security process occurs. The Win32 API normally verifies and assigns security at the front end of the process — when the program first runs. (A program can request additional rights later or perform other security tasks, but the initial verification usually provides sufficient security for the program to do its work.) CLR performs verifications as needed to enhance system performance. An assembly receives only enough permission to perform the current task — it must then request additional permission to perform other tasks. With correct programming, permissions last only the duration of the task, rather than the entire time the assembly runs.

CLR defines two kinds of evidence: assembly and host. Any custom evidence resides within the assembly as assembly evidence. CLR also ships with seven common evidence classes that cover most needs. These seven classes provide host evidence because Microsoft implemented them as part of the host (CLR):

+ ApplicationDirectory
+ Hash
+ Publisher
+ Site
+ StrongName
+ URL
+ Zone

The ApplicationDirectory, Site, URL, and Zone classes show where the code came from. The Publisher and StrongName classes tell who wrote the code. Finally, the Hash class defines a special number that identifies the assembly as a unique entity — it also shows whether someone has tampered with the content of the assembly.

Understanding permissions

So far, you've read about the kinds of security you can use, how the system uses evidence, and how to determine membership in a particular code group. All these facts help you understand how security works, but your application still doesn't have permission to perform any tasks. When CLR loads an assembly, the assembly lacks any rights — it can't even execute code. Consequently, the first task CLR must perform with the assembly is to use the evidence and the code group memberships to determine which permissions the assembly has. To perform this task, CLR must run the evidence through the policies set up by the network administrator.

The developer and the administrator must work together to assign permissions to an application. The developer begins by declaring security requirements for the application within the code. These declarations tell the administrator what the application must have in order to run. For example, the application may require access to a particular folder on the hard drive to use for data storage. In addition, the application user must also have access to this directory so that the application and the user can perform required tasks. Declarations in the application code make this requirement known to the administrator.

Meanwhile, the administrator must also configure the application to respect certain policies. For example, the administrator may give permission to use a particular subdirectory, but not the parent directory that contains it, to promote separation of applications running on the server. The network administrator sets these policies using the Microsoft .NET Framework 2.0 Configuration console.

It's possible to view the existing set of permissions using the Permissions Calculator utility (`PermCalc.EXE`). Earlier versions of the .NET Framework relied on the Permissions View utility (`PermView.EXE`), which works almost exactly the same as the Permissions Calculator utility, except that it has fewer command line options. If you want to get the developer eye view of permissions, the excellent short article at `http://www.codeproject.com/useritems/Permviewexe.asp` provides a good start.

Understanding zones

The zone from which code loads determines a basic level of security. For example, code contained on your local machine is generally safer than code downloaded from the Internet. Knowing the original location of code can help you determine its trustworthiness. By default, CLR defines five different zones (most of which look familiar to anyone who uses Internet Explorer):

✦ **MyComputer:** Anything that resides on the local machine is in the MyComputer zone. The MyComputer zone has maximum privileges, which means that applications in the MyComputer zone typically have to request fewer rights to perform correctly. Unfortunately, when you try to execute such an application from a network drive, it often fails to execute unless the developer has tested it thoroughly in both zones.

✦ **Intranet:** The Intranet zone normally includes any code downloaded using a Universal Naming Convention (UNC) location, such as `\\ServerName\Drive\Folder\Filename.TXT` (Windows Server 2008 defaults to viewing network drives in Windows Explorer as part of the Internet zone until you change this functionality). CLR also uses the Intranet zone for code downloaded from a Windows Internet Name Service (WINS) site rather than a standard IP site, such as a local Web server.

✦ **Internet:** The Internet zone provides a moderate level of privileges, in most cases, but usually not enough to execute an application successfully. Anything outside the MyComputer and Intranet zones is in the Internet zone.

✦ **Trusted and Untrusted:** Initially, the Trusted and Untrusted zones are empty. However, the network administrator can place sites that are normally in the Internet zone into either the Trusted zone (to raise its confidence level) or the Untrusted zone (to lower its confidence level). The Trusted zone normally has nearly the same execution privileges as the MyComputer zone (sometimes they're equal). The Untrusted zone typically reduces rights to none at all. However, you can view content in some cases.

✦ **NoZone:** The NoZone zone is a temporary indicator for items that CLR has yet to test. You should never see this zone in use.

Don't get the idea that these zones are unchangeable. If an application in the MyComputer zone accesses data in the Internet zone, it will work with that data as though it were executing in the Internet zone. Consequently, someone from the Internet zone can't try to trick a MyComputer zone application into performing tasks for which it lacks sufficient rights. As an administrator, you need to be aware of zones because users may try to work in multiple zones and find that some data access fails. Obviously, the worst thing you can do is reduce the requirements for the other zone in order to get the application to work. However, you can place that particular data source in another zone.

Understanding code access security

As previously mentioned, code access security checks the credentials of the code to perform a task rather than to interact with the user. You use code access security to ensure that the code can't perform any tasks that you wouldn't normally allow the user to perform and that the code shouldn't perform on the user's behalf. For example, you probably won't want anonymous users to access the company database to obtain a list of products. However, you can allow the code to perform that task on the user's behalf.

Reading the database shouldn't pose a problem. Writing to the database could present a problem, however, so you should use code access security to ensure that the code can read the database on the user's behalf, but not write to it. The use of code access security is important because it restricts applications from performing tasks incorrectly, even when someone tries to use an application flaw to force the code to perform the task. The following sections tell you more about the details of code access security.

Why use code access security?

Before you proceed any further, it's important to realize that the .NET programs you use always include both code access and role-based security. Even if the developer doesn't include a single line of security code in the program, .NET provides default levels of security for the application. Therefore, the advantage in asking the developer to add security code to the application isn't one of adding security — it's already there. The real advantage is controlling security, which is what everyone should be worrying about now.

You probably have a good understanding of user issues, but code access security can present a problem because no one has had to work with it in the past. At one time, every piece of code you ran on a computer came from one source. There was no need to worry about online connections, e-mail, and nefarious individuals knocking on your firewall door. Today, users face a deluge of code from a myriad of sources. Sometimes the code enters a system without anyone knowing. Code can also enter from a welcomed source, such as a Web service, and cause considerable damage to your system because someone has compromised the third-party source. In short, code could be trusted, at one point, but you don't have that luxury any more.

Systems are also more complex today. The advances in computer speed and resources have fueled unheard levels of development. This places a burden on you, as an administrator, to protect users of your code. The second reason you want to use code access security is to ensure that no one incorrectly uses the code in the applications you support. Code access security defines how someone can use the code and more importantly, what types of tasks they can't use the code to perform. For example, if you decide that your code should never access the hard drive, you can tell .NET that you don't want it to perform that task.

One of the special features that you probably won't see mentioned a lot is that your code can insist that a user have a digital signature. In addition, a vendor can provide a digital signature as evidence for gaining access to specific resources. The application code can actually check for a particular strong name. Although digital signature technology probably has flaws, it's considered very reliable. Using a digital signature is an option only when the developer adds the correct code to the application, which means the developer has to become proactive.

Another good reason to declare security requirements is error handling. When the developer doesn't define the security requirements for the code, CLR will assume that the current environment meets all the code requirements when it runs the application. Unfortunately, the environment varies by user and mode of access and a number of other characteristics that the developer can't determine when writing the application.

When to use code access or role-based security

It's important to consider when you should use a particular mode of security. One of the tendencies that developers have today is to create a secure user environment by restricting user activities to the point where the user can't do much at all. However, by restricting both the user and the code, an application can provide flexibility and secure access. The user's restrictions represent what the user can normally perform, but the code access restrictions represent what the user can do in a particular environment (such as accessing your network from the Internet).

Look at the issue of code access security versus role-based security from this perspective. If you know that the developer has signed all the code on your system, then any unsigned code probably came from a nonsecure source and you shouldn't execute it. This is an oversimplification of the problem, but it often helps to look at issues from this perspective. Because any code you execute can check for the security of other .NET code, it becomes possible to maintain good security even when the user downloads a virus from the Internet.

Configuring File and Folder Security

File and folder security is an essential security element for Windows because you use files and folders whether you have a workgroup or a domain. This level of security defines access to objects. In fact, you'll find modified forms of the file and folder security features used to secure all kinds of objects. When you set security for a printer, you'll find that the dialog box looks similar to the one used for file and folder security. Likewise, the security for sharing an Internet connection looks remarkably like the security for sharing files and folders. Consequently, the techniques you discover in this section work well in other places, too. The following sections describe how to set file and folder security, and also how to save user encryption certificates. (A system can have more than one.)

Setting file and folder security

Even though files and folders are very different kinds of objects, the way you set their security is about the same. The only significant difference is that setting security for a folder applies those settings to all the files that the folder contains unless you specifically set the security for a file. In addition, setting security for a top-level folder lets you flow those rights down to any subfolders that the top-level folder contains.

To set the security for a file or folder, right-click the entry in Windows Explorer and choose Properties from the context menu. Select the Security tab and you see the information shown in Figure 1-2.

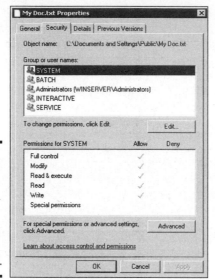

Figure 1-2:
Display the rights that groups and users have to an object by using the Security tab.

When you highlight a group or user in the Group or User Names list, the security information for the group or user appears in the Permissions list. A light gray check mark shows that the administrator or system has granted the right to the file or folder at a higher level and that this right has flowed down to the file or folder. A dark gray check shows that the administrator or system has granted the right for this particular object. When the object is a folder, the right can flow down to files and folders contained within the folder. What you're seeing in the Permissions list is an overview of the DACL for that group or user.

Assigning basic rights

If you want to assign basic rights to a group or user, click Edit. You see a Permissions dialog box that looks similar to the Security tab, shown in Figure 1-2. The difference is that you see check boxes for each of the permissions. Checking a permission in the Allow column grants that access to the group or user. Checking a permission in the Deny column specifically denies that right to a group or user even if the group or user has that right at a higher level.

When you want to remove access to a particular object for a group or user, highlight that group or user entry in the Group or User Names list and click Remove. Windows removes the access of the currently selected object for the group or user even when they have access at a higher level.

It's also possible to add new groups or users to the list. Click Add and you see the Select Users or Groups dialog box, shown in Figure 1-3. Type the name of the group or user and click OK. Windows shows the new entry in the Permissions dialog box, where you can assign rights to the group or user. Remember that you can grant or deny access to a particular group or user — this isn't a one-way feature.

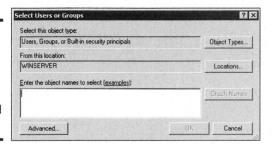

Figure 1-3:
Give new groups or users DACL entries for the selected object.

Assigning detailed rights

In some cases, the rights granted in the overview of the DACL don't sufficiently define the user's access requirements. In this case, you need to click Advanced on the Security tab, shown in Figure 1-2. You see the Advanced Security Settings dialog box, shown in Figure 1-4. This dialog box is considerably more elaborate than the one described in the "Assigning basic rights" section of this chapter, but it also provides considerably more flexibility.

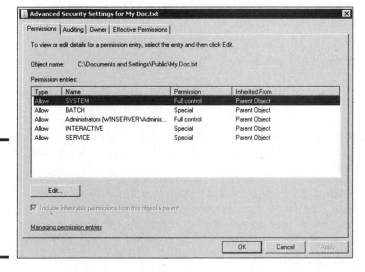

Figure 1-4:
Provide detailed configuration for users who need it.

The basic process works the same as described in the "Assigning basic rights" section of this chapter. The display shown in Figure 1-4 provides you with a listing of all groups and users who have rights to the object (either granted or denied). If you want to modify any group or user, click Edit. You see another dialog box that looks similar to the one shown in Figure 1-4 with the addition of buttons for adding, editing, and removing groups and users. Even though you see more rights listed (because this view provides better granularity), the process is the same as before. The dialog box shown in Figure 1-4 has three additional tabs, as described in the following list:

✦ **Auditing:** The Auditing tab is the only place where you can set the SACL for the selected object. Unlike the DACL settings (those shown in Figure 1-4), you won't see any default SACL settings. As with the DACL display, you click Edit to add, remove, or edit any group or user settings. The audit settings determine whether the system tracks successful or failed actions for the object. In addition, you find that the list of actions matches the list of rights for the DACL. Consequently, you can audit (track) failed attempts to traverse a folder or execute a file. Before you can use auditing, you must enable the auditing policy. See Book III, Chapter 2 for details on working with policies.

✦ **Owner:** The Owner tab determines who owns a particular file or folder. If you own the file or folder, you can change rights to it at any time. In most cases, the System account or Administrators group owns all the system-level files and folders on the hard drive. Individual users own files or folders that they create. However, if you have the proper rights, you can take ownership of files or folders as needed. The "Opening an Administrative Command Line" section of Book III, Chapter 6 shows how to perform this task at the command line.

✦ **Effective Permissions:** Because of all the levels at which you can grant or deny rights, it's possible to become confused about which rights the group or user actually has. The Effective Permission tab helps you discover precisely what a group or user can do with the selected object. All you need to do is provide the group or user name, and the display shows the results.

Managing user encryption file certificates

Windows Server 2008 adds additional protection to files in the form of encryption. The files are unreadable unless you have the key to open and decrypt them. The system manages these keys for you, so normally you don't have to worry about them. At some point, you need to reformat the drive or perform other maintenance that could affect the user accounts. When this situation occurs, you'll want to back up all the user certificates. Otherwise, the users will lose access to their files. You can't re-create the certificates after they're lost. Even if you re-create the user, the user will have a different SID, and the system will treat the re-created user account as a different user.

Some companies now use smart cards for security tasks. It's possible to store the user's certificates on the smart card. If you use this approach, then the certificates are stored there and you don't need to back them up. The user always has their certificates with them as part of their smart card. A problem with this approach is that if the user loses their smart card, they also lose access to all their encrypted files. Consequently, even though using a smart card as a storage location is convenient, it isn't always the best option when working with users who are prone to losing things.

You need to open the User Accounts applet of the Control Panel to begin the process. Click the Manage Your File Encryption Certificates link to start the Encrypting File System Wizard. The following steps describe how to use this wizard to save your certificates:

1. **Review the information in the initial dialog box and click Next.**

If your system doesn't have a certificate installed, it means that you haven't encrypted anything and don't need to worry. You can create a new certificate if you want to encrypt files later, or you can click Cancel to exit the wizard. Otherwise, you see your certificate listed in the Certificate Details list. If you're using a smart card to store the certificates, select a certificate from the smart card.

2. **Choose a certificate and click Next.**

You see a Back Up the Certificate and Key dialog box, where you can define the certificate backup details.

3. **Choose Back Up the Certificate and Key Now.**

4. **Type a location for the backup in the Backup Location field.**

You can, optionally, click Browse to find the backup location on disk graphically.

5. **Type a password in the Password and Confirm Password fields.**

6. **Click Next.**

You see an Update Your Previously Encrypted Files dialog box, which contains a list of all drives and folders on your system.

7. **Check each of the drives and folders you want to back up and click Next.**

You see a summary dialog box, telling you that the backup has completed successfully.

8. **Click Close.**

Creating a Local Security Policy

When working with a workgroup, you won't use the Group Policy Editor (described in Book III, Chapter 2) to create policies. What you use instead is the Local Security Policy console, shown in Figure 1-5, to perform the required security policy configuration. You can find this console in the Administrative Tools folder.

Figure 1-5:
Use the Local Security Policy console for workgroup policies.

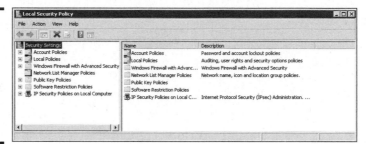

If you're thinking that this group of folders looks familiar from Book III, Chapter 2, you're correct. The Local Security Policy console provides access to a subset of the features provided by the Group Policy Editor. In fact, the settings are precisely the same. You can change any of the areas shown in Figure 1-5.

The lack of functionality shown in Figure 1-5 doesn't mean that you can't use the features in the Group Policy Editor. You'll be surprised to find that many of the administrative templates work fine in a workgroup setting. However, not all the settings work because some are designed for a domain setting, where you're using Active Directory.

When working with security in a workgroup setting, use the Local Security Policy console to make changes first. If you can't find a policy you need, try to make the change using the Group Policy Editor, as described in Book III, Chapter 2. Be aware, however, that not all policies will work. You need to make the change, reboot the system, log back in, and test the change to verify that it works as anticipated.

Using the Security Configuration Wizard

Some very simple networks can make use of the Security Configuration Wizard, found in the Administrative Tools folder, to start configuring security for their systems. The only problem is that the Security Configuration Wizard can be as potentially confusing as making the settings changes manually. In addition, these settings configure only the server policy and not groups and users. Consequently, consider the Security Configuration Wizard as a starting point in the security process. The following steps tell you how to use this wizard:

1. **Open the Security Configuration Wizard, found in the Administrative Tools folder.**

You see the Welcome dialog box.

2. **Click Next.**

The wizard displays a list of options for working with the security policy on your system. You can create a new security policy, edit an existing security policy, apply an existing security policy, or roll back the security policy that you applied previously. When you apply or roll back a security policy, the task is quite simple. You provide the name of a file (for applying a policy), choose a server, and let the wizard do the rest. The steps that follow apply to creating a new security policy or editing an existing policy.

3. **Choose Create a New Security Policy or Edit an Existing Security Policy. When you choose the Edit an Existing Security Policy option, you must also provide the name of the file that contains the security policy. Click Next.**

The wizard asks you to supply the name of the server that will receive the new policy.

4. **Type the name of the server you want to work with and click Next.**

The wizard tells you that it's processing the security configuration database. After a few seconds, you see a Processing Complete message. Clicking View Configuration Database shows you the content of the database. You can see the current settings, but you can't make any changes to them at this point.

5. **Click Next twice to bypass the Role-Based Service Configuration dialog box.**

You see the Select Server Roles dialog box, as shown in Figure 1-6. The list shows the roles that the server is fulfilling as a default. However, you can choose other default settings or check options yourself. Checking an option opens ports and starts services (when available) for that role. Consequently, you normally leave this option set to Installed Roles, as shown.

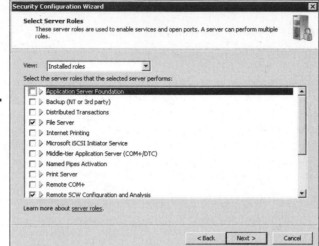

Figure 1-6:
Most settings you configure with the wizard require simple checks.

6. **Choose the roles you want the server to fulfill and click Next.**

   You see the Select Server Features dialog box, which works and acts just like the Select Server Roles dialog box.

7. **Choose the features you want the server to have and click Next.**

   You see the Select Administrative and Other Options dialog box, which works and acts just like the Select Server Roles dialog box.

8. **Choose the administrative and other types of options you want to use with the server and click Next.**

   You see the Select Additional Services dialog box, which works and acts just like the Select Server Roles dialog box.

9. **Choose any additional services you want the server to provide and click Next.**

   The wizard asks how you want to handle unspecified services — those you didn't select from any of the previous dialog boxes. If a service starts without your requesting it, it could represent unwanted activity on the server by outsiders. On the other hand, you may simply need to start the service to support activities that the server should support. Consequently, the default policy is to retain the current service starting mode and to start the service when requested. If you're in an environment where someone may try to access the server in this way, choose the Disable the Service option instead. Choosing this option may mean that some activities that you actually want to support won't start, which means changing your security policy to allow them. However, you also gain some additional security.

10. **Choose a service startup option and click Next.**

The wizard displays the Confirm Service Changes dialog box, where you can see any changes made by option selections in the previous dialog boxes.

11. **Review the list of changes carefully. If you don't see any changes you need to make, click Next. Otherwise, click the Back button and change the policy choices you made to match the server requirements.**

You see the Network Security welcome dialog box. At the bottom of this dialog box, you see a Skip This Section option. If you check this option and click Next, you go directly to the Registry Settings welcome dialog box (see Step 13).

12. **Choose whether you want to skip this section and click Next.**

The wizard displays the Network Security Rules dialog box, as shown in Figure 1-7. Checking an option imposes that rule on network security. You can also add, edit, or remove rules. When you add or edit a rule, you see the Add Rule or Edit Rule dialog box, where you can make rule changes. When you highlight a rule and click Remove, the wizard removes it without asking you for confirmation, so make sure to choose the correct rule.

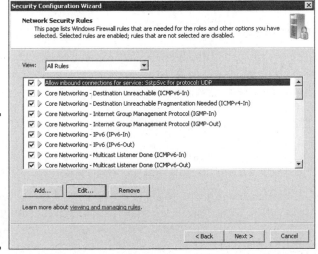

Figure 1-7:
Verify that the list of rules match those that you want to enforce for the network.

13. **Add, remove, and edit rules as necessary. Click Next.**

You see the Registry Settings dialog box. At the bottom of this dialog box, you see the Skip This Section option. If you check this option and click Next, you go directly to the Audit Policy welcome dialog box (see Step 19).

14. Choose whether you want to skip this section and click Next.

The wizard displays the Require SMB Security Signatures dialog box. The Server Message Block (SMB) security feature reduces the probability that someone can tamper with messages going between the client and the server. If your server has the extra capacity required, keep this option enabled.

15. Choose an SMB policy and click Next.

The wizard displays a list of outbound authentication methods that the server can use to authenticate on remote systems. You can choose from domain security, local accounts on the remote machine, or Windows 9x-era security (which has significant security problems). The default setting doesn't allow the server to authenticate, which is fine for a standalone server, but probably won't work for a multiserver setting. If you have multiple servers, choose Domain Accounts when working with a domain or choose Local Accounts on the Remote Computers when working with a workgroup. You may need a combination of settings depending on the complexity of your network.

16. Choose an outbound authentication strategy and click Next.

The wizard displays a list of inbound authentication methods. These are the methods that a client can use to authenticate with the server.

17. Choose an inbound authentication strategy and click Next.

You see the Registry Settings Summary dialog box, where you can check the changes you made.

18. Review the list of changes carefully. If you don't see any changes you need to make, click Next. Otherwise, click the Back button and change the policy choices you made to match the server requirements.

You see the Audit Policy dialog box. At the bottom of this dialog box, you see the Skip This Section option. If you check this option and click Next, you go directly to the Save Security Policy dialog box (see Step 22).

19. Choose whether you want to skip this section and then click Next.

The wizard displays the System Audit Policy dialog box. You can choose not to audit anything, audit successful activities, or audit both successful and unsuccessful activities. The default action is to audit successful activities, which can generate a huge amount of traffic on your server and fill the event log to bursting quite quickly. It's usually best to avoid setting the audit policy using this wizard and set it as needed using the Local Security Policy or Group Policy Editor consoles.

20. **Choose an audit policy and click Next.**

The wizard displays the Audit Policy Summary dialog box, where you can check the changes you made.

21. **Review the list of changes carefully. If you don't see any changes you need to make, click Next. Otherwise, click the Back button and change the policy choices you made to match the server requirements.**

You see the Save Security Policy dialog box.

22. **Click Next.**

The wizard displays the Security Policy File Name dialog box, where you type the name and location of the file that will hold the security policy. It's important to understand that saving the policy file doesn't automatically apply it to your server. You must separately apply the policy.

23. **Provide a name and description for the new security policy. Click Next.**

The wizard displays the Apply Security Policy dialog box.

24. **Choose whether you want to apply the security policy now or later. Click Next.**

The wizard displays a completion dialog box.

25. **Click Finish.**

The wizard saves the security policy to disk. If you chose to apply the security policy immediately, the wizard applies the security policy for you. You have to restart the server, in most cases, to complete applying the security policy because the server needs to start some services and stop others.

Chapter 2: Configuring Shared Resources

*S*haring resources is an essential part of networking. The share gives an external entity (another computer, an application, or a user or other entity) permission to use a resource from a remote location. It also describes how the external entity can interact with the resource. A share isn't security; the two differ in important ways. Some administrators find it difficult to understand how shares differ from security, so the first section of this chapter addresses this concern.

Server resources can cover a lot of ground. The most common resources are storage media (hard drives, CDs, DVDs, flash drives, read-only memory in various forms, and other media used to store data) and printers. Of course, modern servers include many other sharable resources. It's important to know how to share these various kinds of resources and which best practices to use when creating the share.

One of the resources that some servers have to share is an Internet connection. The simple way to share an Internet connection is by using the Internet Connection Sharing (ICS) feature of Windows Server 2008. This feature adds a lot of functionality in the background, such as Domain Name System (DNS) support. In some cases, the additional background functionality makes it impossible to use ICS, so this chapter discusses these concerns as well.

The latest version of Active Directory also provides some sharing solutions you need to consider. The final section of this chapter helps you understand these new solutions and how they can help you create a better server environment. The Active Directory Federated Services (AD FS) provide an identity access solution that makes it considerably easier to determine who's requesting resources over an Internet connection. The higher level of security makes it easier to share sensitive resources by using an Internet connection. The Active Directory Rights Management Services (AD RMS) makes the data itself secure by helping you implement usage polices. These policies move with the data, so you can let users download data resources without giving up the security that these data resources require.

Comparing Shares with Security

Some administrators confuse the functionality of a share with security settings. Consequently, some network resources have the wrong settings and end up having hidden security holes or don't provide the level of access that the user requires.

A *share* determines remote access to a resource, while *security* determines the local access to a resource. The combination of a share and security determines the access that a user ultimately sees when using a resource from a remote location. For example, if the share is set to full access yet the user's security for the resource doesn't allow any access, then the user still doesn't have any access. Likewise, if the user's security setting provides full access to the resource but the share provides read-only access, the user sees only read-only access.

It's important to remember the difference between a share and security. You may want to give the user full access to a resource locally but limit that access when the user works from a remote location for security reasons. An Internet connection doesn't always provide the best security, and you may want to add safeguards for sensitive resources by restricting share access. Windows always views the security settings first and then the share settings. Consequently, when the security settings disallow access, changing the share settings won't help.

Administrators may not see potential share problems because they usually rely on local access to perform work. For example, when an administrator uses Remote Desktop to access a server, the Remote Desktop connection provides local access to server resources. In fact, you must map the client computer's resources in order to use them. The administrator sees the security settings, but not the share settings when working in this mode. The reason that administrators use Remote Desktop is that it works the same as using the server console. With the correct setup, an administrator can work at several server consoles all without leaving the client machine.

Share settings also reside on a different tab than security settings do, so an administrator may not think to look at them. The "Sharing Resources" section of this chapter discusses the different locations of share settings for various kinds of resource, such as storage media and printers. The security settings always reside on the Security tab. Figure 2-1 shows a typical example of a Security tab. Compare this tab with the share settings also described in the "Sharing Resources" section of this chapter.

Figure 2-1:
Security
settings
reside on
the Security
tab of the
Properties
dialog box
for most
resources.

The bottom line is that an administrator must carefully set resource security first, test these settings locally using an application such as Remote Desktop, and then set the share using company guidelines. Otherwise, you can end up with security holes or improper resource access.

Improper resource access doesn't always manifest itself as an access-denied error on the user machine. Sometimes, improper access shows up as intermittent errors or odd application behavior. When you exhaust other potential sources of application errors, always consider improper resource access as a source of the problem.

Sharing Resources

As mentioned in the "Comparing Shares with Security" section of this chapter, it's important not to confuse sharing with security. Shares normally appear on a special tab of the Properties dialog box for the resource you want to share. The following sections describe how to share two common resources on your server. In addition, you receive some tips on sharing less-common resources.

Working with storage media

Microsoft provides a number of ways to share storage media. You usually want to adapt one technique, however, to ensure that you share resources consistently. The most common way to share storage media resources is to open a copy of Windows Explorer. Right-click the storage media you want to share, and choose either Share or Properties from the context menu. The sharing information appears on the Sharing tab of the resource, as shown in Figure 2-2.

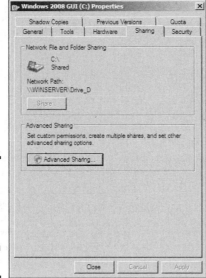

Figure 2-2:
The Sharing tab provides access to the sharing features of a resource.

The precise display you see depends on your server configuration. In this case, the server has the Sharing Wizard disabled (as is common for most servers). The figure also shows that the administrator has shared this resource. The following steps tell how to share a storage media resource:

1. **Click Advanced Sharing.**

You see the Advanced Sharing dialog box, as shown in Figure 2-3. Figure 2-3 shows a resource with a share already in place. When working with a resource that doesn't have a share in place, the Share This Resource (folder, drive, or other resource) option is cleared and all the other entries are grayed out. It's possible to create as many shares as needed to support a particular resource fully.

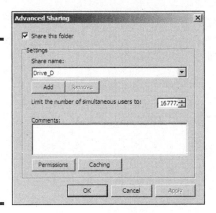

Figure 2-3:
Create as
many
shares as
needed to
provide
optimal
sharing
function-
ality.

2. **Check the Share this Resource (folder, drive, or other resource) option when necessary.**

   Windows enables the share features shown in Figure 2-3.

3. **When a share already exists for the resource, click Add.**

   You see the New Share dialog box. This dialog box contains the same options as the initial share for the resource, so filling it out is precisely the same process.

4. **Type a descriptive name for the share in the Share Name field.**

   Keep the share name relatively short to make it easier for users to map local drive letters to the share. Older versions of Windows don't work well with share names that have spaces — use an underscore in place of spaces as needed.

5. **Type a description for the share in the Description field.**

   Make the description as long as necessary to describe the share fully. It pays to create a company policy on descriptions so that all administrators describe shares in the same way.

6. **(Optional) Provide a number of simultaneous users for the resource.**

   The default value is the maximum allowed for the server. Limiting the number of users for a resource can help improve performance. However, the performance boost comes at the cost of availability; resources with limits may not be available to all users who need it.

7. **Click Permissions.**

   You see a Permissions For *share name* dialog box, as shown in Figure 2-4. This dialog box lets you add or remove users from the list. The initial display normally contains the Everyone group. To remove a user or group from the list, highlight the entry and click Remove.

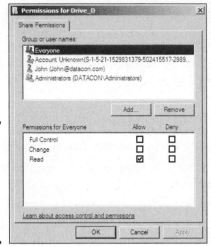

Figure 2-4:
Add or
remove
users and
groups as
needed
from the list.

8. **Click Add.**

You see a Select Users, Computers, or Groups dialog box.

9. **Type the name of the user, group, or computer that you want to share the storage media resource.**

10. **Click OK.**

Windows adds the user, group, or computer to the Group or User Names list (refer to Figure 2-4). The new entry you added is highlighted.

11. **Check share options for the new user or group you added in the Permissions for Username or Group Name list.**

The default setting is Read. You can allow or deny actions for the share as needed. Permissions include

- **Full Control:** The user or group can perform any task that the security settings allow.

- **Change:** The user or group can change information in the shared resource, but can't add or delete files or folders.

- **Read:** The user or group can read files, but can't modify them in any way.

12. **Click OK.**

Windows adds the new share to the Advanced Sharing dialog box.

13. **Click OK and then Close.**

The new share is ready for use.

Working with printers

Sharing a printer is considerably easier than sharing storage media because printers are simpler devices from a sharing perspective. A user can only write data to a printer. At the most, errant input results in wasted paper, not the lost data that can occur with a storage media resource. The following steps describe how to share a printer:

1. **Open the Printers applet in the Control Panel.**

You see a list of printers installed on the local machine.

2. **Right-click the printer you want to share and choose Sharing from the context menu.**

You see the Sharing tab of the printer's Properties dialog box, as shown in Figure 2-5.

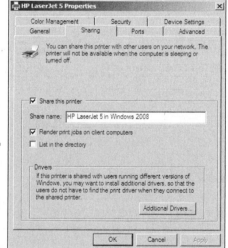

Figure 2-5:
Share printers as needed with the server's clients.

3. **Check Share This Printer.**

4. **Type a share name in the Share Name field.**

Make the share name descriptive so that users can recognize the printer quickly, but not so long as to make connecting to it cumbersome. When working with older clients, make sure that you use an underscore in place of a space. Older systems tend not to recognize spaces and can function improperly when they see spaces in the share name.

5. **(Optional) Check Render Print Jobs on Client Computers.**

Choose this option when working with smart clients. This option trades some network bandwidth for the processing performance that the client can add. Overall, you normally notice an improvement in server performance when using this option, especially when the client produces long or complex print jobs.

6. **(Optional) Check List in the Directory.**

This option is useful only when working with Active Directory. To make management easier, Windows doesn't list printers in the Active Directory database by default. Checking this option ensures that the printer appears in the Active Directory database.

7. **(Optional) Click Additional Drivers.**

You see the Additional Drivers dialog box. This dialog box contains a list of drivers that you can install for other platforms. Installing the additional drivers makes it easier for the client to connect to the server. However, the additional drivers also consume resources such as hard drive space.

    a. **Check any driver options that you want to install on the server.**

    b. **Click OK.**

        Windows installs the additional drivers you selected.

8. **Click OK.**

Windows creates the printer share.

Sharing other resources

You can share many resources on the server. After all, the main purpose behind installing a server is to share resources that require centralized control (such as a database) or incur a high cost that you want to spread across multiple systems (a printer). In some cases, you share resources to aid in collaboration (a hard drive) or to make management tasks easier. No matter what reason you have for sharing resources, a server usually provides the means.

This chapter examines two kinds of sharing. Because storage media provides a complex sharing model, you see that it also requires more work to share. Printers provide the ability to output data in printed form only, so sharing is easier when working with a printer. Most resources fall within the two extremes you see in this chapter for storage media and printers. The settings for shares normally appear on the Sharing tab of the resource's Properties dialog box.

Applications are a special case in sharing. An application that provides sharing normally includes some built-in functionality to manage the sharing. For example, the sharing features of a database can become quite complex. You choose not only precisely which tables to share but also how to share the tables, and then include checks to ensure that data remains safe during sharing.

Some applications perform sharing tasks automatically. For example, when you try to open a Word document that someone else already has open, Word asks whether you want to create a read-only copy of that document. Many applications have similar features to make sharing easier and automatic.

An administrator shares many server resources in many ways. One of the newer methods for sharing resources is to use Web services. This book can't address every sharing strategy. However, sharing normally requires some type of authentication, authorization to use the resource, and monitoring of that use. It doesn't matter what kind of sharing you perform, these three principles are always in place.

Performing an ICS Setup

ICS is a boon for workgroup administrators. An ICS setup provides simple Domain Name System (DNS) and Dynamic Host Configuration Protocol (DHCP) support. You don't even have to configure this support; ICS performs all required configuration automatically. However, ICS works only for workgroups. If you have a domain controller, you can't use ICS because the DNS support that ICS provides will conflict with the DNS server setup that Active Directory requires. If you want to share a connection in a domain controller setting, you must set up a Routing and Remote Access connection. The following steps describe how to perform an ICS setup:

1. **Open the Network and Sharing Center applet on the system providing the Internet connection.**

   You see the Network and Sharing Center window.

2. **Click Manage Network Connections.**

   You see the Network Connections window. This window contains all connections available on the local machine.

3. **Right-click the Internet connection and choose Properties from the context menu.**

   You see the connection Properties dialog box.

4. **Select the Sharing tab.**

   You see the Internet Connection Sharing option, as shown in Figure 2-6.

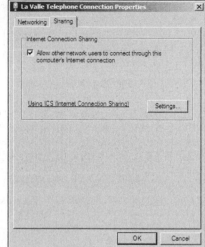

Figure 2-6:
Make it
possible for
others to
use your
Internet
connection
through ICS.

5. **Check the Allow Other Network Users to Connect through This Computer's Internet Connection option.**

6. **(Optional) Click Settings.**

You see the Advanced Settings dialog box, as shown in Figure 2-7. This dialog box comes with standard services you can share, such as the FTP server or an Internet mail service. To share a service, you must install the required support on your server. You must also provide access to the service through your firewall, provide shares for any service resources, and perform any required configuration.

Figure 2-7:
You can use
ICS to
provide
external
access to
services on
your server.

You can add services that don't appear in the list by clicking Add or remove any services that you add by highlighting the service and clicking Delete. (You can't remove any of the default services.) Highlight any service and click Edit to modify its settings. (Microsoft limits the settings changes you can make to a default service.)

a. **Check any services you want to share.**

b. **Verify the settings for the services by highlighting the service entry and clicking Edit.**

You see the Service Settings dialog box, as shown in Figure 2-8. Default services provide limited service-setting changes. Any service you install provides full access to service settings.

Figure 2-8:
Change the service settings as needed.

c. **Make any required changes and then click OK.**

d. **Repeat Steps a through c as needed for any additional services.**

e. **Click OK.**

Windows accepts any advanced service settings you make.

7. **Click OK.**

Windows activates ICS and makes your Internet connection accessible to others on the network.

Configuring an Access Solution with Federated Rights Management

Creating a share is all about remote access. Almost all access to a server is remote. The server console accepts local logins, but local logins at the server are the exception rather than the rule. Consequently, an administrator can log in directly to the console or use an application such as Remote Desktop to create a local connection. Likewise, a user might rely on Terminal Services to create a dumb-terminal-like connection from the client machine to the server that provides a local connection. Far more common is a remote connection that relies on mapping remote resources, such as storage media, to local drives.

A problem with almost all remote access is determining who's at the other end of the connection. Although a login authenticates the caller and the server authorizes the caller to use specific resources, you still aren't completely certain about the identity of the caller. In addition, even with great security, it's possible for a third party to perform tasks on behalf of the caller without the caller's or server's knowledge (such as a man-in-the-middle attack). Windows Server includes the new AD FS feature that helps with identity issues.

Even if you know and trust the person at the other end of the connection, you can't always trust them with your data. The person who obtains the data may not abuse it in any way, but you must consider what happens when the person who downloads the data gives it to someone else. The third party could abuse the data in some way. Consequently, you must also secure the data. The AD RMS feature of Windows Server provides the functionality required to secure the data and maintain that security as the downloader moves the data from place to place. The following sections describe these two Active Directory features in detail.

Working with Active Directory Federated Services (AD FS)

AD FS is a new identity technology that helps browser-based clients access resources, even when those resources appear on different servers or are managed by different organizations. In some respects, AD FS is the replacement for Passport technology that Microsoft used in the past, but it provides additional functionality and doesn't rely on Microsoft as the holder of user identification information.

Users find it annoying to have to enter their credentials more than one time, and in many cases, multiple logins promote bad use habits, such as the use of simple passwords. What normally happens is that the user logs in to a central Web site and that Web site authorizes the user, but only for that central location. When the user goes to another location to use an application, the secondary site must also authorize the user. The user sees another login page before the secondary server authorizes the user to work with the application. The use of AD FS lets the user bypass the secondary login by providing Single Sign On (SSO) capability. The use of SSO means that the user logs on to the server only once.

Businesses can also set up trust relationships to make SSO work between them. Each business in a business-to-business (B2B) relationship can create the required trust relationships. The user may not even be aware that different applications reside on servers managed by different businesses because the security requirements occur in the background. Of course, the B2B relationship must exist before SSO becomes a reality. Otherwise, what you really end up with is a big security hole by using this technology.

Organizations can manage AD FS at several levels. An organization that authorizes users need not always provide the required resources as long as a secondary organization provides the trust relationships required for the resources. In fact, you can install as many of the AD FS role services described in the following list as needed to meet your specific requirements:

✦ **Federation Service:** A Federation Service is a service on the server that provides access to a common trust policy. The federation servers route authentication requests from external locations to the local server. For example, when a user requests access to resources on Server A, then Server B, the federation server, may provide the required authentication. Server B may not even know the location of Server A — all it cares about is authenticating the user requesting the access, so the request can come from anywhere on the Internet.

✦ **Federation Service Proxy:** The Federation Service Proxy provides access to the Federation Service for the user using the WS-Federation Passive Requestor Profile (WS-F PRP) protocols. The use of a proxy avoids direct access to the Federation Service and potential corruption by external sources. The Federation Service Proxy collects the user credential information, verifies it, and then sends it to the Federation Service. Consequently, the user doesn't have any knowledge of which server is providing the authentication required to authorize access to resources. (The user doesn't normally care about the authentication process unless there's an ulterior motive, such as corrupting the server or gaining unwarranted access to resource.)

✦ **Claims-aware agent:** The claims-aware agent resides on a Web server that hosts one or more claims-aware applications. These applications query AD FS security tokens to authenticate a user's identity. Currently, all claims-aware applications rely on ASP.NET as their underlying technology. The ASP.NET application relies on the AD FS security token to make authorization decisions, such as the user's role. The user's role and other security information help personalize applications. For example, a manager may have access to enhanced application functionality or perform tasks that a standard user can't perform.

✦ **Windows token-based agent:** The Windows token-based agent resides on any Windows-based Web server. This security feature relies on standard Windows security features, so you can use it with any application that relies on standard Windows security. The difference is that the agent makes it possible for the standard Windows application to query the AD FS security token as an impersonation token. The result is that the application sees the user security as an impersonation level, just as it normally would for local resource access.

This chapter doesn't provide complete information on installing, configuring, and managing AD FS, because an AD FS often requires individual server settings and Microsoft hasn't provided full information on those settings as of the time of writing. See the article at `http://technet2.microsoft.com/windowsserver2008/en/library/a018ccfe-acb2-41f9-9f0a-102b80a3398c1033.mspx` for more information on AD FS installation. This article also contains links to other sources of information about AD FS that Microsoft will update as it becomes available. For example, you can see how to use AD FS with Office SharePoint Server 2007 at `http://technet2.microsoft.com/Office/en-us/library/61799f9a-da01-4c11-b930-52e5114324451033.mspx`.

Working with Active Directory Rights Management Services (AD RMS)

In most cases, the moment data leaves your personal possession, you no longer control it. The data circulates on its own and becomes a potential source of security problems for your organization. Many administrators control data by locking it up and letting only authorized people view it, but these authorized people often provide the greatest source of security leaks, so the data still gets out of the administrator's control. Unfortunately, the administrator receives the full brunt of any security breach problems, so it's in the administrator's best interests to lock up data so tightly that no one even knows it exists, which makes the data useless. As someone once said, the best way to keep a secret is to tell no one about it.

AD RMS is an alternative to keeping data locked so securely that no one can see it — it works by attaching a security policy to the data that prevents misuse. The concept behind this technology is a good one. Everyone would agree that keeping data so secure that no one can see it is self-defeating because it makes the data worthless. Attaching a security policy makes the data available under controlled conditions, at least as long as someone doesn't breach Microsoft's security technology. Unfortunately, breaches occur with relative frequency. You can probably use this technology for data that has short-term secrecy requirements or isn't of such a sensitive nature that a breach will cause permanent company damage. The best security policy is still one in which you treat data as a resource you must keep under lock and key. AD RMS provides multiple benefits to organizations, but it also has multiple requirements to obtain those benefits, as described in the following list:

✦ **Safeguard Information Automatically:** It's possible to enable applications to provide AD RMS functionality. When a user has an AD RMS-enabled application, it's possible to set a security policy on the documents the application creates to prevent their misuse. The only problems with this particular benefit is that no one except Microsoft produces AD RMS-enabled applications, and you must use the same application to read the AD RMS encrypted document. For example, if you use the AD RMS feature of Word to encrypt a document, you must use Word to read the document because third-party readers can't perform the required decryption (at least, not as of this writing).

✦ **Persistent Protection:** Firewalls, authentication, authorization, roles, code access security, and other security features all protect data. It's possible to view AD RMS as just another level of security, at least when using it within an organization where you have direct control over every aspect of data exchange. After you start working with third parties, AD RMS becomes a requirement that the third party must observe to interact with you. If the Web site provides protected, public access of data (such as a downloadable book for which the reader must pay), AD RMS can become a support nightmare because you can't depend on buyers to have the proper software or to even read about the access requirements.

✦ **Customizable Technology:** Developers can create applications that work with AD RMS. Microsoft makes the required Application Programming Interfaces (APIs) available through the .NET Framework. Of course, you must use a .NET language to write your application. In addition, you must use the application on a Windows machine because current .NET alternative technologies, such as Mono (`http://www.mono-project.com/Main_Page`), don't provide AD RMS support, at least, not as of this writing.

You install AD RMS support on your server as an Active Directory service role. The roles you install determine the level of AD RMS support that your server can provide. The following list details the AD RMS service roles available on Windows Server 2008:

✦ **Active Directory Rights Management Services:** You must install the Active Directory Rights Management Services role to obtain any AD RMS support. This service provides the basic support for AD RMS on the server. When you install this service role, the server can publish and consume rights-protected content. This level of support lets you work with a LAN, but not with external or remote parties with any ease.

✦ **Identity Federation Support:** The Identity Federation Support service role provides additional functionality for an AD RMS setup. In this case, the server can link AD RMS to AD FS to allow external parties to publish and consume right-protected content. If your goal is to serve rights-protected content to users on the road, B2B relations, or the public at large, you must install this service role to support the required identification services.

This chapter doesn't provide complete information on installing, configuring, and managing AD RMS because an AD RMS configuration often requires individual server settings and Microsoft hasn't provided full information on those settings as of the time of writing. See the article at `http://technet2.microsoft.com/windowsserver2008/en/servermanager/active directoryrightsmanagementservices.mspx` for more information on AD RMS installation. You also see links for a wealth of other AD RMS requirements on this Web site. Microsoft is continually providing additional AD RMS information as the technology develops, so make sure that you visit this Web site often.

Chapter 3: Configuring Internal Security

In This Chapter

✔ **Understanding Network Access Protection (NAP)**

✔ **Considering the User Account Control (UAC) feature**

✔ **Working with user passwords**

✔ **Working with user certificates**

✔ **Changing the startup and recovery options**

*Y*ou can build the highest virtual wall in the world and someone will have a virtual ladder tall enough to scale it. Of course, that's what internal security is all about — building a virtual wall that no one can scale. Every time someone creates a ladder to scale the wall, someone else builds the wall a bit higher. The context is an uneven one because building the wall takes considerably more effort than scaling it, which may make you wonder why you should an employ a wall around your network at all. Walls are good at keeping most people out, which means that you have only a few people to worry about. In short, walls reduce your workload as an administrator and that's the reason vendors keep building the walls higher.

Windows uses several rings of walls. You have the outside wall of standard Windows security that keeps most people at bay (see Book V, Chapter 1). Then there's the secondary wall around your shared resources (see Book V, Chapter 2). This chapter discusses the inner wall — the one that provides a final layer of protection for the server against external threats. This is the latest wall that Microsoft has built, and you'll find it quite imposing. Sometimes, it's actually too imposing to let honest people accomplish any work. (The chapter discusses this issue as well.) There's a final wall — the great wall imposed against the meandering hordes of the Internet. You'll find it discussed in Book V, Chapter 4.

This chapter visits three essential kinds of security. First, you discover the new technology that Microsoft provides to block machines with potentially bad code installed on them. The Network Access Protection (NAP) feature scores a client's health before it lets the client access the server. If the client's health fails, it doesn't gain access. Second, you find out how the User Account Control (UAC) feature locks down the system and provides another layer of authorization to the server. This new layer makes it hard for even an administrator to accidentally do something to compromise the server. Third, you see how Windows Server 2008 improves authentication and makes it easier to work with features such as passwords and certificates.

The final section of this chapter discusses startup and recovery options. Although these options have appeared in every version of Windows since Windows NT, they're an essential part of the inner wall of protection for your server. These features protect the server from errant code and the unexpected, to an extent. Setting this feature according to enterprise policy is extremely important if you really want the server to start up and recover properly. You'll be surprised to find out that Microsoft has made a few changes in this area, and you need to set some of the settings differently than you did in the past.

Working with Network Access Protection (NAP)

Is the client healthy? That's the question that Network Access Protection (NAP) asks. You find this feature on Windows XP, Vista, and Windows Server 2008. The basic purpose for using NAP is to ensure that computers that don't meet certain health requirements also don't have access to the network. It's a seemingly simple idea, but the implementation is complex. For example, you must consider whether the offending client should lose all access, or simply access to sensitive features. You also need to consider issues such as whether you want to update the unhealthy client automatically to bring it into compliance. NAP helps you answer these and many other questions through policies. To implement a survey of client health, NAP offers these four areas of functionality:

- ✦ **Health Policy Validation:** The initial level of functionality is health policy validation. The server ensures that the client is healthy by comparing the client's state to the state expressed by a policy. The policy determines issues such as the patches the client must have installed to gain access to the server. Clients that don't meet the health policy requirements are unhealthy and aren't granted complete access to the server. The level of access they obtain depends on the network access limitation policy you set.

- ✦ **Network Access Limitation:** You don't want to allow unhealthy clients access to the server. The client could have viruses, adware, and other issues associated with it. The problem is that you won't know about these problems until it's too late to do anything about them. Of course, you also want to present an opportunity to the client to clean itself up, so you have to allow some level of access. The server uses a policy that you set to determine just how much access a client can have to the server when it's in an unhealthy state.

✦ **Automatic Remediation:** In an enterprise environment, you probably want to perform some level of automatic remediation on a client that's unhealthy. A user could call in after being on the road for several days and require the update to gain access to the server. Perhaps a salesperson has sales to upload but can't do so until their machine is clean. This is the time that automatic remediation is helpful and even necessary to the proper functioning of your business. However, there are also times where you won't want to use automatic remediation. For example, a partner company may call in to your server and request information. When the client is unhealthy, in this case, automatic remediation isn't the proper choice — you must tell the partner company about the problem and let their IT department fix it.

✦ **Ongoing Compliance:** Even healthy computers require maintenance and care. You can create an ongoing compliance policy that performs this maintenance for you by updating clients with the latest updates as they connect to the server. You can almost view this policy as a grace period for the client. Yes, the client is technically unhealthy, but not so unhealthy that you fear a substantial risk to the server, so you bring the client back into a fully healthy state while allowing full access to server resources.

The use of NAP for locally attached machines is easy to understand. Because these machines connect to the network every day, you can maintain their health on a daily basis. When someone goes on vacation, their machine remains off for the duration. After the user arrives back from vacation, their machine is automatically updated with the latest patches before it's allowed to access the network again. Consequently, there's never a time when a local machine has access without having the proper updates installed.

Roaming laptops also have the proper updates installed, but perhaps not on a daily basis. The updates occur whenever the user logs in to the system. Depending on how long the user waits between company contacts, a roaming laptop may have to go through a remediation process every time the user logs in. Again, the idea is to prevent an unpatched system from connecting to the server.

The most dangerous client is the home computer. Many employees now work from home at least one day a week and sometimes more. A sick employee can work from home without infecting everyone else in the office and is usually more productive than if they came into the office because they're in a relaxed environment. No matter what reason you have for allowing home computers to connect to your network, they do represent the most dangerous form of client. In this case, updates and patches can help considerably, but NAP isn't a complete solution. If the client already has a virus or adware installed (you never know where a home system has been), it can still end up on the server. Consequently, when working with home computers, you must combine NAP with other forms of functionality. For example, you might want to run a virus check as part of the user's login.

No matter which scenario a client fulfills, the process for using NAP is the same. A health server performs the original validation of the client's health. Because the health server is used only for health validation, you don't expose your data servers to undue risk. When the health server finds a client with a health problem, a remediation server comes into play to fix the health problem and bring the client into full compliance. A client that's healthy obtains a health certificate that it can use to access the network. The components of a NAP setup appear in Table 3-1.

Table 3-1: NAP Components

Component	Type	Description
Enforcement Client (EC)	Enforcement	It provides access to network access devices. This component performs negotiations on the client's behalf.
Health Registration Authority	Enforcement	After a client passes the required health check, this component issues a health certificate that the client can use to access network resources.
Network Access Device	Enforcement	The EC negotiates with this component for access to the network by the client. This component provides an endpoint that the client uses to gain access to the network. The endpoint can include all the usual network endpoints, which includes switches or a wireless access point.
Quarantine Agent (QA)	Platform	This component coordinates the efforts of the SHA and the EC. It reports the client's health status so that the system can determine whether the client requires remediation.
Quarantine Server (QS)	Platform	When a client is unhealthy, this component restricts the client's access to the network based on the policies you set. These policies appear as part of the SHV.
Remediation Servers	Health	Depending on the automatic remediation policies you set, this component can install the patches, configuration settings, and applications necessary to bring the client to a healthy state. The amount of remediation depends on the client's current health status and the policies you set for it.

Component	Type	Description
System Health Agents (SHA)	Health	This component actually defines the health status of the client. It checks for issues such as patch state, system configuration, the kinds of applications installed, virus signature, and other policies that you set. The overriding consideration is whether the client has the potential to cause damage to the server, so you must make the policies relatively strict to gain full advantage of this component.
System Health Servers	Health	The SHA looks to this component to actually define the requirements for a healthy client. The system health server is where you place the policies that affect most of the other components in this table.
System Health Validators (SHV)	Health	A system of this complexity requires validation. This component certifies the declarations made by health agents as correct. Validation is an important step because someone could have tampered with the health agent to gain access to your network. If you relied only on the health agents, the system would have a single point of failure that someone with evil intent could exploit.

Understanding and Using the User Account Control (UAC)

User Account Control (UAC) was one of the most contentious additions to Vista. Many Vista users simply turned it off and rejected any claims that UAC provided anything of benefit in the way of protecting the system. Of course, UAC does provide some security benefits, and many Vista users have discovered them since Vista has been released. Although UAC is beneficial to Vista users because they're using it as a workstation, you may wonder why Microsoft also added this feature to Windows Server 2008. The fact of the matter is that many of today's servers end up accessing the Internet in the same way that users do and the servers require protection for that reason.

The problem for administrators is that UAC runs the administrator at the same privilege level as a common user, which tends to slow down tasks on the server. Consequently, while there really isn't a good reason to disable UAC on a Vista system, disabling it on a Windows Server 2008 setup may have some potential benefits. You must weigh the inconvenience of using UAC with the benefits it provides when your server has external contacts.

The following sections describe UAC in greater detail and tell you how to work with it and how to disable UAC when it's beneficial to do so.

Using UAC to protect your server

It's important to realize that many of the tasks you perform as an administrator don't require administrator privileges. For example, you can perform many configuration tasks without using administrator rights. It's also possible to install well-behaved software without administrator rights and perform some server maintenance (such as defragmenting the hard drive) as well. The only time you really need administrator privileges is when you're actually performing administrator-level activities. In some cases, this means that you may not even see the UAC messages on your server for days, perhaps even weeks.

The time that UAC becomes annoying on your server is when you begin performing security tasks, working at the command line, or making major changes to the server functionality. In many cases, you perform these tasks before the server goes live and has an Internet connection, so turning off UAC may not be a bad idea to speed up the configuration process considerably. Just don't forget to turn it back on, or else you may find a nasty bit of software on your lovely new server.

UAC works by alerting you to activities that a normal user wouldn't perform, such as installing a piece of software that changes certain parts of the registry or tries to overwrite a system DLL. The activities usually signal something else — something evil. Consequently, you see a message asking whether you initiated the activity. At that point, you can give your permission to perform the task. It's a little time-consuming when the software needs to make a lot of changes, but not overly so in many cases. (Microsoft has worked with UAC to make it considerably less invasive than it originally was in Vista, so you can ignore those early Vista warnings that you may have read.)

Another question to ask is whether you perform most of your configuration tasks at the server or by using a Terminal Services product such as Remote Desktop. Many of the consoles discussed in this book offer the option of connecting to a remote machine. You can use this feature to your advantage by performing all but the essential configuration tasks from your workstation using a console connected to the server. In fact, most command line utilities also support this option. UAC doesn't show up when you use this approach to management, so there isn't a good reason to turn it off.

Testing with the product, available at the time of writing, shows that the UAC dialog box also doesn't appear when no one is logged in to the server directly. Consequently, you don't have to worry about UAC interfering with normal server activities as long as you don't log in to the server. In fact, even when it does show up, such as when someone's logged in to the server using Remote Desktop, the background tasks on the server continue as normal. In short, UAC is a good feature for helping to keep your server safe from harm while imposing only a moderate inconvenience during certain activities.

Running tasks as an administrator

One feature that most administrators have overlooked because they didn't need it in the past is the ability to tell Windows that you want to run a task in administrator mode. You've already seen this feature in a couple of places in this book, such as in the "Using the boot method of permanently disabling signed driver checking" section of Book I, Chapter 2, the "Preparing a forest for installation" section of Book I, Chapter 3, and the "Opening an Administrative Command Line" section of Book III, Chapter 6. The technique works for any task you want to perform within the GUI. Simply right-click the application you want to start and choose Run As Administrator from the context menu.

Using the Run As Administrator approach is actually safer than you might think. You continue to work as a standard user, but the application runs in administrator mode. Consequently, you don't see the UAC warning messages when you run the application, but you see the UAC warning messages when another application starts and tries to perform an administrative-level task. If you're performing just one task as an administrator, this approach is preferable to turning off UAC.

When working at the command line or if you want to elevate privileges automatically within a shortcut, you can use the RunAs utility. This utility appears in places such as the "Understanding How UAC Affects Networking" section of Book IV, Chapter 1. Essentially, the effect is the same as using the Run As Administrator option, except that you have additional methods of validating your access to the administrator mode. This utility uses the following syntax:

```
RUNAS [ [/noprofile | /profile] [/env] [/netonly] ]
    /user:<UserName> program
RUNAS [ [/noprofile | /profile] [/env] [/netonly] ]
    /smartcard [/user:<UserName>] program
```

You use the command line syntax that best matches the task you want to perform. The two essential entries are the name of the program and your credentials to run it as a particular person. Here are the command line options for the RunAs utility:

✦ **/noprofile:** Specifies that you don't want to load the RunAs user's profile when running the application. The benefit of using this setting is that the application loads more quickly. In addition, this setting acts as a safety feature because the application you want to run is less likely to corrupt the RunAs user's settings. However, using this feature can prevent some applications from running, especially when they rely on settings in the user profile to perform certain tasks.

✦ **/profile:** Specifies that you want to load the RunAs user's profile when running the application. This is the default setting.

✦ **/env:** Specifies that you want to use the current environment, rather than the RunAs user's environment, to run the application. This feature is useful when the local environment is different from the environment that the RunAs user normally relies on to run applications.

✦ **/netonly:** Specifies that the credentials supplied for the RunAs user apply to remote access only.

✦ **/savecred:** Uses the credentials previously saved by the RunAs user instead of obtaining a new copy of the credentials.

✦ **/smartcard:** Specifies that the RunAs user credentials appear on a smart card.

✦ **/user:*UserName*:** Specifies the username. You must supply the username in one of two forms, User@Domain or Domain\User. When working in a workgroup setting, use as the domain name the name of the machine on which you want to authenticate. Always use the username as it appears on the machine that will run the application.

✦ *program*: Specifies the application you want to run as well as any command line switches the application requires to run. When the program argument includes spaces, enclose the entire program argument in double quotes. For example, you might want to open a copy of Notepad with a file already loaded, which means enclosing the Notepad application name and the filename in double quotes, like this:

```
RunAs /User:WinServer\Administrator "Notepad
    I:\CPLFiles.TXT"
```

Understanding automatic privilege elevation

You can set the UAC feature to automatically elevate administrator privileges. The "Using the local security policy" section of this chapter tells how to perform this task. Using automatic privilege elevation means that an administrator will never see the UAC warnings. However, the downside is that the effect of automatic privilege elevation is the same as turning off UAC for the administrator. (Non-administrators can't use automatic privilege elevation.) Although this feature is useful on workstations, it isn't very useful on a server because everyone who accesses the server likely has an administrator account.

Overriding the UAC settings

There are a number of ways to override or disable the UAC. In fact, you've already seen one of them, in the "System Configuration" section of Book III,

Chapter 1. The System Configuration applet provides a tool for enabling and disabling the UAC for a limited timeframe. You can see how this feature works in the "Opening an Administrative Command Line" section of Book III, Chapter 6. However, the System Configuration applet technique is really meant only for short-term disabling of the UAC, and it doesn't do the job completely. The following sections describe how you can perform the task on a more permanent basis and even control the amount of UAC functionality that you disable.

Using the User Accounts applet

When you have the proper permissions, you can turn UAC on or off for your account, without affecting any other account on the system. This is an all-or-nothing setting, so you can't provide just a partial change. The following steps tell you how to perform this task:

1. **Open the User Accounts applet in the Control Panel.**

You see a list of user account settings, as shown in Figure 3-1.

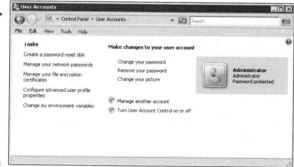

Figure 3-1: Open the User Accounts applet when you want to control UAC for just your account.

2. **Click the Turn User Account Control On or Off link.**

You see the dialog box shown in Figure 3-2.

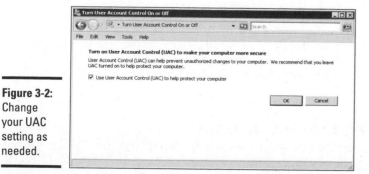

Figure 3-2: Change your UAC setting as needed.

3. **Clear the Use User Account Control (UAC) to Help Protect Your Computer option and click OK.**

   Windows informs you that you must restart the computer to make this change permanent.

4. **Make sure that no one else is using the server, and then click Restart Now.**

   The system restarts. When the reboot process completes, your account no longer has UAC enabled. You have to restart the computer again if you want to restore UAC later. Consequently, it's important to complete all tasks that require you to have UAC turned off before you turn it back on again.

Using the local security policy

Most methods for turning UAC on or off are like switches — UAC is either on or off, but you don't really have any control over it. When you open the Local Security Policy console, found in the Administrative Tools folder, you gain some added flexibility in working with UAC. Choose the `Security Settings\Local Policies\Security Options\` folder, shown in Figure 3-3. Near the bottom of the list, you see a series of User Account Control settings. These settings control how the system works with UAC, and by studying them, you gain a new appreciation for the number of tasks that UAC performs.

Figure 3-3:
Change the UAC settings as needed to make your server easier to use.

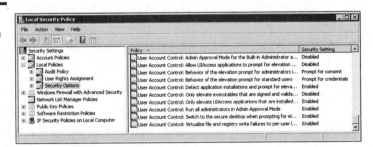

Double-clicking any of these entries displays a dialog box with settings for that particular policy. The dialog box contains two tabs, as shown in Figure 3-4. The Local Security Setting tab contains the settings for the policy.

When you don't understand a particular policy, you can click the Explain tab. The explanations that Microsoft provides are relatively clear, and the explanations contain details about each of the settings. If you still don't feel comfortable making a change, you can click the link near the bottom of the dialog box to obtain additional information from the Microsoft Web site.

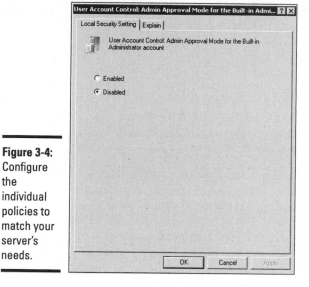

Figure 3-4:
Configure
the
individual
policies to
match your
server's
needs.

The various policies affect how UAC works on your system. For example, the default setting for the default Administrator account doesn't actually use UAC. You would need to enable the User Account Control: Admin Approval Mode for the Built-In Administrator Account policy to gain UAC protection for the Administrator account.

When an administrator is in Admin Approval mode, the default setting simply prompts them for consent when performing an action. However, you can change this setting to Elevate without Prompting or Prompt for Credentials using the User Account Control: Behavior of the Elevation Prompt for Administrator in the Admin Approval Mode policy. Standard users have a similar policy, except that they have only the choice of Prompt for Credentials or Automatically Deny Elevation Requests. Make sure to check the User Account Control: Run All Administrators in the Admin Approval Mode policy as well — it's enabled by default.

You can always make UAC more repressive in its action. For example, the User Account Control: Only Elevate Executables that are Signed and Validated policy is disabled by default. If you don't want to run any unsigned applications on your server, you can always enable this policy. Given that most applications aren't signed, you may find that your server's protected to the point that it can't run any applications at all if you choose to enable this policy. Of course, at some point, vendors have to sign their applications to meet new Microsoft requirements, so you may eventually need to enable this policy to protect your server.

Even if you aren't planning to change any of the current UAC policies, checking the entries in the Local Security Policy console is enlightening because it gives you a better feel for what UAC does. For example, many people don't realize that many applications must use the secure desktop (a desktop that doesn't permit outside access) to perform certain actions. In some cases, this will break the application, but you'll find that the secure desktop is a good security feature that protects your system from adware and viruses by keeping them from contacting their home server on the Internet.

Managing User Passwords

One major issue for administrators is the seemingly endless array of ways in which users can somehow lose or mangle their passwords. In fact, the issue is so common that some administrators actually keep a coin jar by their desk for password resets (the money goes for a company picnic or other function supported by users who lose their passwords). Unfortunately, as Windows becomes more complex, the loss of a password has some very real consequences. With common use of features such as encryption for files, a lost password can also mean lost data. Consequently, you need a way to guard the user's access to the system.

To get started with the user password tasks, open the User Accounts applet of the Control Panel (refer to Figure 3-1). The following sections describe in greater detail the user password management features provided by Windows Server 2008.

Creating a password reset disk

Many administrators imagine that it would be nice if they never again had to reset a password for a user. The password reset disk makes this possible by creating a disk the user can use to log in to the system after they forget their password. All the user needs to do is insert the disk to log in to the system and then reset their password to something new. This feature doesn't actually make the password accessible to anyone.

Theoretically, this option is safe because you can make it only when logged in to that user's account. However, this feature is also unsafe because anyone who possesses the disk can use it to log in to that user's account. If you decide to use this approach to managing user passwords, you'll want to create a locked area that only the user can access to store the disk. Of course, it's hard to maintain such an environment. A user who is careless with their password is also likely to be careless with a password disk. In addition, it's easy to imagine a scenario where the user doesn't bother to remember their password at all and simply relies on the disk to provide them with access.

Creating a password reset disk may be a good option for home users, especially if you can keep the disk locked up somewhere. Imagine someone who needs to call into the office from home, but finds out that they've forgotten the password to their home system. Keeping all these caveats in mind, follow these steps, which describe how to create a password reset disk:

1. **Click the Create a Password Reset Disk link in the User Accounts window.**

   Windows starts the Forgotten Password Wizard.

2. **Click Next.**

   The wizards asks where you want to create the reset disk. You have an option to use either a flash disk or a floppy disk. Interestingly enough, the wizard doesn't appear to support CD or DVD drives. Even rewriteable disks don't appear on the list. For most users, this means that you have to have a flash disk to use this option because many modern computers lack a floppy disk drive.

3. **Choose a storage location for the password and click Next.**

   You see a Current User Password dialog box.

4. **Type your current password into the space provided and click Next.**

   The wizard creates the password reset disk. You see a progress indicator. Proceed to the next step only when the progress indicator shows 100%. The resulting UserKey.PSW file on the flash drive or floppy disk is encrypted, so no one can see anything about your name or password in it.

5. **Click Next.**

   You see a success dialog box.

6. **Click Finish.**

   The wizard closes. Remove the password reset disk and store it in a safe location. You must repeat this process every time the password changes.

Managing your network passwords

You can tell Windows to store passwords that are required to access network locations of all kinds. Storing the password means that Windows supplies it to the network location each time you access it and you don't have to remember the password for that location. This feature works in three different scenarios:

+ Remote machine on the network
+ Local or remote application
+ Any Web site that requires you to provide a password

You begin using this feature by clicking the Manage Your Network Passwords link in the User Accounts window. The Stored User Names and Passwords dialog box looks like the one shown in Figure 3-5.

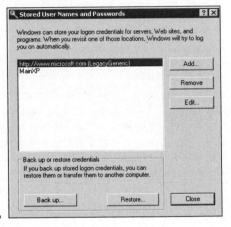

Figure 3-5:
Manage network passwords using the Store User Names and Passwords dialog box.

Of course, if you don't type the password very often (or at all), you tend to forget it. Consequently, you actually need to perform three kinds of tasks when using this feature:

✦ Add or edit password entries.

✦ Remove entries you no longer need.

✦ Back up or restore entries as needed.

Of the three, backing up the entries you make is possibly the most important because you could lose access to important network locations otherwise. The following sections describe how to perform these three tasks.

Adding and editing password entries

When you want to add a new entry, click Add in the Store User Names and Passwords dialog box. Click Edit when you want to modify an existing entry. In both cases, you see a dialog box similar to the one shown in Figure 3-6. (The editing dialog box disables some of the features, so you can't change the network location or type.)

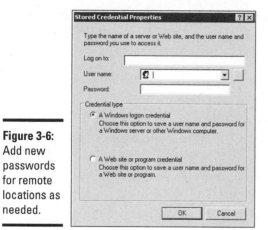

Figure 3-6:
Add new
passwords
for remote
locations as
needed.

Notice the two options at the bottom of the display. You choose A Windows
Logon Credential when you want to log on to a remote machine. Likewise,
you choose A Web Site or Program Credential for Web sites or applications
that you want to access. It's important to choose the correct option or else
Windows won't save the password for you. The dialog box doesn't change
when you choose a different option, so there's no visual cue to tell you when
you've selected the correct option.

After you choose a logon option, type the name of the machine, Web site
URL, or application name in the Log On To field. Supply your name and password in the User Name and Password fields, and then click OK. That's all you
need to do to create a new entry. Now, every time Windows detects the
machine, URL, or application you provided, it sends your username and
password.

Removing password entries

At some point, you find that you no longer access a particular machine, Web
site, or application. Keeping passwords hanging around that you don't need
may not seem problematic. However, if you get enough of them stacked up, it
takes longer for Windows to check each location you visit and you could
possibly notice a delay. In addition, a long list of locations makes it harder
for you to maintain your list. Consequently, it pays to remove old entries.

To remove an old entry, highlight it in the list and click Remove. You see a
dialog box telling you that Windows will remove the entry from the list. Click
OK to complete the process.

Backing up and restoring password entries

Performing a backup of your passwords every time you make a change to the list is essential. If you don't perform a backup and you forget the password you provided in the past, you may find that you can't access the remote location with any ease. Most locations provide a means of resetting your password, but doing so can be painful, and it's usually easier to create a backup instead. The following steps tell you how to perform this task:

1. **Click Back Up in the Store User Names and Passwords dialog box.**

You see a dialog box that asks where you want to store your usernames and passwords. It's important to select a location that the system automatically backs up to tape or disk for you, because you want this file saved somewhere safe.

2. **Click Browse.**

The wizard displays a Save Backup File As dialog box. The location defaults to your Documents folder. The system normally performs a backup of this folder, but you can choose any other location. The default extension for this file is CRD (credential), and you probably won't want to change it to something else.

3. **Choose a location to store the file and type a name for the file in the File Name field. Click Save.**

The wizard returns you to the original dialog box.

4. **Click Next.**

At this point, you see an odd instruction. The wizard tells you to press Ctrl+Alt+Delete to continue the backup by using the secure desktop. This feature ensures that nothing outside the machine can read the passwords as the system encrypts them and stores them in the file. You can disable this feature, but doing so isn't a good idea. (See the "Using the local security policy" section of this chapter for details on configuring UAC features.)

5. **Press Ctrl+Alt+Delete.**

You see the secure desktop appear. It has a black background. Absolutely nothing else is accessible at this point except for the dialog box that asks you to provide a password for the backup.

6. **Type a password in the Password and Confirm Password fields, and then click Next.**

The wizard displays a success dialog box. Notice that you're still at the secure desktop. It still isn't possible to do anything else.

7. **Click Finish.**

The wizard returns you to the standard desktop and closes. You now have a backup of your names and passwords for remote locations.

Eventually, you'll need to restore a backup when you lose your usernames and passwords for remote locations. The process for restoring a backup is nearly the same as for backing it up. The only real difference is that you select an existing file as a first step rather than create a new one.

Managing User Certificates

One of the hidden consoles on your machine is CertMgr.MSC. To open this console, you choose Start⇨Run, type **CertMgr.MSC** in the Open field, and press Enter. Figure 3-7 shows a typical view of this console with a certificate selected.

Figure 3-7:
The CertMgr console makes it possible to work with all the certificates on your machine.

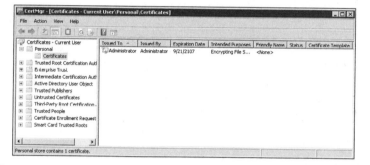

You can perform two tasks in this console. First, you can view any of the certificates it contains. Simply locate the certificate you want to view and double-click it. The resulting Certificate dialog box tells you everything there is to know about the certificate. Second, you can export any certificate to store it on disk. Use the following steps to perform this task:

1. **Right-click the certificate entry and choose All Tasks⇨Export from the context menu.**

You see the Certificate Export Wizard dialog box.

2. **Click Next.**

For certificates you own, you see the Export Private Key dialog box. If you don't own the certificate, proceed to Step 4. A *private* key is the key you keep to yourself for encrypting content. The *public* key is the key you send to others to decrypt the content, so the certificate always contains this key. The public key is safe to send anywhere because you can't use it to encrypt the file. You can export your certificate to other people with just the public key so that they can decrypt files you send them. Keeping the private key safe is essential, so save only the private key when you're making a backup of the certificate for your own use.

3. **Choose whether you want to export the private key and click Next.**

   The wizard displays the Export File Format dialog box, as shown in Figure 3-8. Notice that only some of the options are enabled in this dialog box. The export file format options you have depend on whether the file will contain a private key. If the file contains a private key, the options shown in Figure 3-8 are disabled and the lower options are enabled.

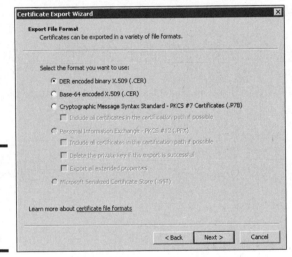

Figure 3-8: Choose a file format for saving your certificate.

The file format you choose depends on the person receiving the certificate. You have only one storage option for storing a private key, but the file can contain more or less information about the certificate. (Always store everything Microsoft has to offer for a backup.) There are three certificate options for files with public keys. In most cases, you'll want to use the DER Encoded Binary X.509 (.CER) option for sending a certificate to someone else. However, the other party may need one of the other two formats.

4. **Choose a file format from the list of associated file options (if any), and click Next.**

   For certificates that contain a private key, you see the Password dialog box. If the file has a public key, proceed to Step 6. The password encrypts the file so that no one can steal your private key.

5. **Type a password in both the Password and Type and Confirm Password (Mandatory) fields. Click Next.**

   The wizard displays a File to Export dialog box.

6. **Type the name and location of the file you want to use to store the certificate. Click Next.**

   You see a completion dialog box.

7. **Verify all the information provided in the summary and click Finish.**

   Windows exports the certificate for you.

Configuring Startup and Recovery Options

Microsoft makes certain startup and recovery options available to you, to ensure that the system starts properly and recovers from errors as you expect it to. Unfortunately, you can't access these options directly. Instead, you must follow these steps:

1. **Open the System applet of the Control Panel and click the Advanced System Settings link.**

   You see the Advanced tab of the System Properties dialog box.

2. **Click Settings in the Startup and Recovery section of the dialog box.**

   You see the Startup and Recovery dialog box, as shown in Figure 3-9.

Figure 3-9:
Set the startup and recovery options for your system.

Microsoft must have learned something from its Vista experience because Windows Server 2008 provides a method for changing the startup of your system without relying entirely on BCDEdit (see the "Configuring the Startup Options with BCDEdit" section of Book I, Chapter 4 for details). The options let you choose a default operating system when you have more than one installed, the length of time the system waits for you to choose an operating system before it automatically boots the default, and the length of time it displays any recovery options (when needed).

The System Failure section of Figure 3-9 shows the recovery options. You can choose whether to automatically reboot the operating system when a failure occurs. Normally, this is a good idea and you should keep this option selected. However, some viruses actually depend on this behavior, so you need to know how to shut off automatic reboots if a virus infects the server.

You can also choose whether to save debugging information as part of the reboot process. The debugging information can help a vendor locate a problem with software on your machine. Of course, it's not always convenient to store the file due to space limitations, and some administrators consider the debugging file a security risk, so you can choose not to store it at all. In some cases, you may find that a small dump file works fine and there's an option to create a small file as well. Unless you have an overriding reason to save multiple debugging files, always overwrite the existing file before creating a new one.

Chapter 4: Working with the Internet

In This Chapter

✔ **Working with the Windows Firewall feature**

✔ **Performing advanced security setups for Windows Firewall**

The Internet presents an interesting challenge for security because you must provide enough access to allow everyone to interact with it fully, yet not so much access that you have to worry about users dragging every virus and adware onto the network with them. In addition, you need to keep the walls around your network high enough to discourage outside predators.

The Windows Server 2008 Firewall monitors access on the network in two directions. Past Microsoft attempts at a firewall provided only one-way (incoming) protection. The firewall provided with Windows Server 2008 is substantially better than the initial Microsoft offering and lets you control both incoming and outgoing access so that your network doesn't leak data. You also have substantially greater control over the network configuration using the Windows Firewall with Advanced Security console.

Sometimes you need to pass data to someone else through the Internet. In most cases, you begin with a secure connection, as described in the "Connecting to Another Network" section of Book IV, Chapter 2. However, you may not always have the luxury of a secure connection. Sending financial information to an online vendor when you want to make a purchase falls into this category. In this case, you'll rely on other technologies, such as Internet Protocol Security (IPSec) to provide the security you need.

This chapter discusses all three components of a secure Internet connection: high walls, incoming and outgoing data monitoring, and impromptu security when necessary. Of course, these measures are only one of the walls you should have in place around your network. Chapters 1 through 3 of this minibook describe the other rings of protection you should use to create a secure network environment. Make sure that you also add monitoring to all four security levels. No network in the world is secure enough to keep everyone out, so constant monitoring is part of your security tasks.

Configuring the Windows Firewall

The Windows Firewall provides both incoming and outgoing protection for your server when you have it properly configured. In fact, you'll find, as you install or remove standard Windows Server 2008 features, that the operating system will automatically perform many configurations for you and you won't need to do anything more than verify the settings. You can use the Windows Firewall applet, found in the Control Panel, to perform most basic configurations. The Windows Firewall window that appears when you open the applet provides basic configuration information, as shown in Figure 4-1.

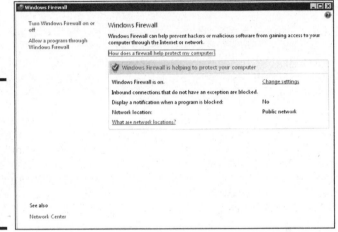

Figure 4-1: Use the Windows Firewall applet for most common configuration tasks.

The Windows Firewall window has a number of links, but the majority of them lead to the same Windows Firewall Settings dialog box, shown in Figure 4-2. You can also open a Help file with additional information about Windows Firewall and the Network and Sharing Center window as needed.

Turning Windows Firewall on or off

The General tab, shown in Figure 4-2, lets you turn Windows Firewall on or off. The only reason you might want to turn Windows Firewall off is when you have a third-party firewall that you want to use. Even if you don't have an outside connection for this system, you'll want to keep the Windows Firewall on, to help protect your server from other, potentially infected, machines on the network.

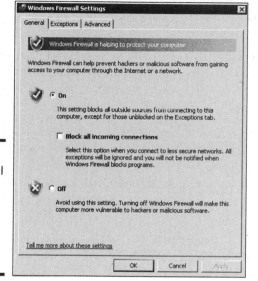

Figure 4-2:
The General
tab helps
you turn
Windows
Firewall on
or off as
needed.

Notice the Block All Incoming Connections option shown on the General tab. When you check this option, you essentially shut off the server from the rest of the world. This feature is helpful when you need to perform configuration tasks that may leave the server vulnerable to attack. Of course, you have to work directly at the server because this option also shuts off access for applications such as Remote Desktop.

Setting standard application and port exceptions

The Exceptions tab, shown in Figure 4-3, lets you open and close ports as needed on your server. It also helps you determine which applications can access the Internet. Microsoft provides standard entries for all the Windows Server 2008 roles and features. Many applications also add entries when you install them. In this case, all you need to do is check the entry to enable the port or application it supports. If you find that an application isn't communicating properly, this is one of the first places you should look for a misconfiguration.

Sometimes you need to add a new application or port to the list. When working with applications, click Add Program. You see the Add a Program dialog box, as shown in Figure 4-4. To unblock an application, highlight its entry in the Programs list and click OK. Windows Firewall adds the program to the Exceptions list. In many cases, you won't see the application you want to add. In this case, click Browse to display the Browse dialog box, locate the application on disk, and click Open.

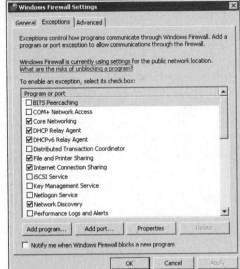

Figure 4-3:
Enable or
disable
applications
and ports as
needed for
proper
communi-
cation.

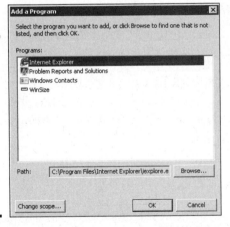

Figure 4-4:
Add
applications
to the
Exceptions
list to
specifically
allow that
application
through the
firewall.

Windows Firewall includes a concept called *scope*. You don't need to open a port or application for complete access to every location. When you click Change Scope (see Figure 4-4), you see the Change Scope dialog box. The default scope opens a port or application for access to the entire Internet. However, you can also restrict an application to the local subnet or a custom list of IP addresses. Consequently, when you add a new application or port to the list, make sure to set the scope to provide just the level of access needed.

When you need to open a port for general use, such as a special Web site on the server, you click Add Port rather than Add Program. In this case, you see the Add a Port dialog box, as shown in Figure 4-5. To use this feature, provide a name for the port entry, the port number, and the port type (TCP, Transaction Control Protocol, or UDP, User Datagram Protocol). The difference between opening a program and opening a port is that the port is available for all applications to use, so you must open ports with extreme care. Someone with bad intentions can scan for open ports and use them as a method for gaining access to your network and doing terrible things. As with an application, you can set a port to have a specific scope to limit its visibility.

Figure 4-5:
Add ports
to the
Exceptions
list when
you have a
general
access
need.

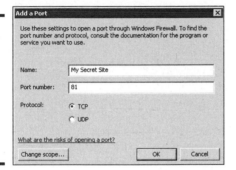

Assigning Windows Firewall to connections

The default Windows Firewall setup is to use Windows Firewall for all network connections. Consequently, it protects against both Internet and local network threats. You can set Windows Firewall to protect only certain connections by changing the settings on the Advanced tab. By default, all the connections have a check mark next to them. Clear the check mark from any of the connections that you don't want to protect.

Configuring Windows Firewall with Advanced Security

The Windows Firewall with Advanced Security console, located in the Administrative Tools folder, is an extension of the Windows Firewall applet, described in the "Configuring the Windows Firewall" section of this chapter. When you open this console, you see an overview of Windows Firewall support in Windows Server 2008 as a whole, as shown in Figure 4-6.

Figure 4-6:
Use this
console to
perform
advanced
Windows
Firewall
configu-
ration.

As Figure 4-6 shows, using this console, you have separate control over inbound and outbound rules. When you check the BITS Peercaching entry in the Windows Firewall Settings dialog box (see Figures 4-2 and 4-3), what you're really doing is choosing a number of rules that include

✦ BITS Peercaching (Content-In)

✦ BITS Peercaching (RPC)

✦ BITS Peercaching (RPC-EPMAP)

✦ BITS Peercaching (WSD-In)

✦ BITS Peercaching (Content-Out)

✦ BITS Peercaching (WSD-Out)

The Windows Firewall with Advanced Security console lets you set each of these rules individually rather than as a package. In addition, the Windows Firewall Settings dialog box enables these rules at only the Public profile level. If you want to enable them at the Private or Domain profile levels, you must use the Windows Firewall with Advanced Security console to do it. As you can see, Windows Firewall with Advanced Security provides finer control over the settings you make to the firewall inbound and outbound rules. Of course, you have to make more settings changes to obtain the same effect as you would in using the Windows Firewall Settings dialog box.

Now that you have a better idea of what Microsoft means by *advanced*, it's time to delve further into the features that the Windows Firewall with

Advanced Security console provides. The following sections provide a description of the various features you can configure.

Working with the profile settings

You may have wondered about the hubbub surrounding the public and private network settings in the Network and Sharing Center (see the "An Overview of the Network and Sharing Center" section of Book IV, Chapter 1 for details). When you click Customize next to one of the connections, you can choose between a public and private network. Part of the effect of that choice is the way in which the Windows Firewall works. In fact, you'll find that Windows Firewall actually supports three profiles:

✦ **Domain:** Settings that affect an entire network domain. You use these settings with Active Directory — they don't affect workgroups.

✦ **Private:** Settings that affect your private network — the one that doesn't have any connectivity to the outside world.

✦ **Public:** Settings that affect the public network — the one that does have connectivity to the outside world.

The Windows Firewall with Advanced Security console lets you configure these profiles individually. In addition, you'll find that the profiles play a central role in the rules you configure for allowing communication through the firewall. To see these profiles, right-click the Windows Firewall with Advanced Security entry console tree and choose Properties from the context menu. You see the Windows Firewall with Advanced Security dialog box, as shown in Figure 4-7.

Figure 4-7:
Modify the settings for each of the profiles on your machine.

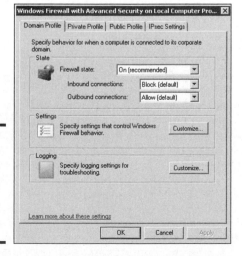

Figure 4-7 shows the default settings for the profiles on the server. Microsoft sets Windows Firewall to On for each of the profiles by default. The firewall blocks all incoming communication but allows all outgoing communication. From a security perspective, you'll want to change the Outbound property to Block to prevent applications on the server from sending output data without the proper permissions. Otherwise, any adware or virus that appears on the server can communicate freely with the outside world, which is always a bad idea.

When you click Customize in the Settings area, you see the Customize Settings dialog box, where you can configure the settings for a particular profile, as shown in Figure 4-8.

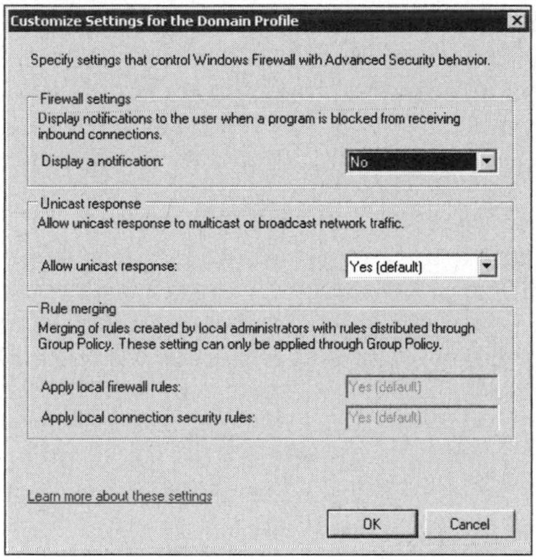

Figure 4-8: Change the settings for a particular profile.

The Display a Notification setting determines whether Windows Firewall tells you when it blocks an application from using a port. Normally, it's a good idea to set this value to Yes on a workstation so that you can reconfigure the Windows Firewall as needed for optimal performance. However, on a server, you'll want to keep this setting set to No because no one will see any messages that Windows Firewall displays (unless you're using the server as a workstation).

The Allow Unicast Response setting affects how your server interacts with responses from other computers as the result of a multicast message. For example, your server might send a multicast message to every other computer on the network that essentially asks whether everyone is OK. The message is multicast because it goes to more than one computer. Each computer on the network then sends a message back to the server (unicast because it goes to only one location) stating its status. If you don't enable this feature, some advanced management applications will fail to work properly. Windows Firewall waits up to three seconds for the unicast responses before it closes off the channel used to receive the messages, so this feature isn't available unless the server has sent a multicast message first.

Notice that the Rule Merging section of the dialog box contains entries but doesn't allow you to change them. To change these settings, you must modify a policy using the Group Policy Editor consoles. These entries tell you about the current policy only. See Book III, Chapter 2 for additional information on working with group policies.

Understanding IPSec

IPSec is an important part of secure communication on the Internet. To guarantee that no one's snooping on your communication, you must secure the packets between two endpoints (a client and a server, in many cases). Whenever a communication relies on IPSec, four events must occur:

1. The endpoints secure the communication channel.

2. The endpoints mutually authenticate each other using a digital certificate.

3. The first endpoint (usually the server) provides a public key that the second endpoint uses to encrypt information. Only the first endpoint has the private key required to decrypt information that the second endpoint sends to it.

4. The second endpoint sends a public key to the first endpoint to allow two-way encrypted communication.

IPSec is an optional part of IPv4. However, given the increasing complexity and uncertainty of the Internet, IPSec is a mandatory part of IPv6. Consequently, in the future, the Internet will use encrypted transmissions for all communication. However, today, when working with IPv4, someone can snoop on your communication unless you specifically secure it by using IPSec.

Although you don't have to worry about it much in Windows Server 2008, it provides two security modes. Windows Server 2008 automatically chooses the correct mode based on the task you want to perform. These two modes include

✦ **Transport:** This mode encrypts only the content of the IP packets. The header information (which tells the network where to send the packet along with other information) remains unencrypted. You typically use this mode when working directly with another host, such as a Web site.

✦ **Tunneling:** This mode encrypts the entire IP packet. The encrypted packet appears as part of an unencrypted packet, which provides routing information. In other words, the unencrypted packet acts as a tunnel for the encrypted packet between two locations. You typically use this mode when working with a Virtual Private Network (VPN).

You also see mention of the Internet Control Message Protocol (ICMP) when working with IPSec in certain circumstances. For the most part, Windows uses ICMP to send error messages. A client may request a service that the server can't provide, which generates an error on the server. The server makes the client aware of this error by using ICMP. When the endpoints of an IP communication must check for ICMP, the communication suffers a performance loss. Microsoft makes it possible to disregard ICMP, which means that the first party doesn't send the message and the second doesn't listen for them. Of course, disregarding ICMP also means that you won't receive error information and must assume that everything has gone as planned (not necessarily a good idea for any network).

For something that sounds seemingly so simple, actually implementing IPSec requires considerable effort. The details of making this work are quite complex and you have multiple methods of implementing them. The site An Illustrated Guide to IPsec, at `http://www.unixwiz.net/techtips/iguide-ipsec.html`, provides everything you need to know in detail. Because every machine must be able to communicate with every other machine using IPSec, you'll find that vendors follow the standards closely. You can find all of the standards in the following list at the Internet RFC/STD/FYI/BCP Archives site at `http://www.faqs.org/rfcs/`.

RFC	Title	RFC	Title
2367	PF_KEY Interface	2403	The Use of HMAC-MD5-96 within ESP and AH
2404	The Use of HMAC-SHA-1-96 within ESP and AH	2405	The ESP DES-CBC Cipher Algorithm With Explicit IV
2410	The NULL Encryption Algorithm and Its Use With IPsec	2411	IP Security Document Roadmap
2412	The OAKLEY Key Determination Protocol	2451	The ESP CBC-Mode Cipher Algorithms
2857	The Use of HMAC-RIPEMD-160-96 within ESP and AH	3526	More Modular Exponential (MODP) Diffie-Hellman groups for Internet Key Exchange (IKE)
3706	A Traffic-Based Method of Detecting Dead Internet Key Exchange (IKE) Peers	3715	IPsec-Network Address Translation (NAT) Compatibility Requirements
3947	Negotiation of NAT-Traversal in the IKE	3948	UDP Encapsulation of IPsec ESP Packets

RFC	Title	RFC	Title
4106	The Use of Galois/Counter Mode (GCM) in IPsec Encapsulating Security Payload (ESP)	4301	Security Architecture for the Internet Protocol
4302	IP Authentication Header	4303	IP Encapsulating Security Payload (ESP)
4304	Extended Sequence Number (ESN) Addendum to IPsec Domain of Interpretation (DOI) for Internet Security Association and Key Management Protocol (ISAKMP)	4306	Internet Key Exchange (IKEv2) Protocol
4307	Cryptographic Algorithms for Use in the Internet Key Exchange Version 2 (IKEv2)	4308	Cryptographic Suites for IPsec
4309	Using Advanced Encryption Standard (AES) CCM Mode with IPsec Encapsulating Security Payload (ESP)	4478	Repeated Authentication in Internet Key Exchange (IKEv2) Protocol
4543	The Use of Galois Message Authentication Code (GMAC) in IPsec ESP and AH	4555	IKEv2 Mobility and Multihoming Protocol (MOBIKE)
4621	Design of the IKEv2 Mobility and Multihoming (MOBIKE) Protocol	4718	IKEv2 Clarifications and Implementation Guidelines
4806	Online Certificate Status Protocol (OCSP) Extensions to IKEv2	4809	Requirements for an IPsec Certificate Management Profile
4835	Cryptographic Algorithm Implementation Requirements for Encapsulating Security Payload (ESP) and Authentication Header (AH)	4945	The Internet IP Security PKI Profile of IKEv1/ISAKMP, IKEv2, and PKIX

Configuring the IPSec settings

In many cases, you'll accept the default IPSec settings for Windows Firewall because they work with most servers and provide a moderate level of security. However, when you need to provide enhanced security (or if you're simply curious), you'll want to review the IPSec settings that Windows Firewall provides. To see the IPSec settings, right-click the Windows Firewall with Advanced Security entry console tree and choose Properties from the context menu. You see the Windows Firewall with Advanced Security dialog box, as shown in Figure 4-9. Notice that the IPsec Settings tab appears in the figure.

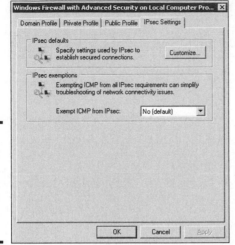

Figure 4-9:
Modify the
ICMP
settings as
required for
perfor-
mance.

Notice that this tab contains a Customize button you use to customize the IPSec settings and an ICMP setting. Normally, you want to receive the error messages that ICMP provides (see the "Understanding IPSec" section of this chapter for details). However, when performance is at a premium, you can change the Exempt ICMP from IPSec setting to Yes. You gain additional performance, but at the cost of error messages that you may need in order to diagnose problems on the network.

When you click Customize, you see the Customize IPsec Settings dialog box, as shown in Figure 4-10. These settings let you control the algorithms used to perform the key exchange, protect the data, and authenticate the secure environment. The defaults provide a moderate level of security that should be compatible with most systems. You'll want to change the settings only when you can control the settings on all machines involved with the data exchange.

The settings can become quite particular. For example, when working with authentication, you can choose to authenticate both the computer and the user. In fact, you can go so far as to authenticate only certificates from a particular Certificate Authority (CA). When you make the CA your own Certificate Server, only users who have a certificate from your server have access to your network. Of course, these strict settings can backfire when you start working with third parties who might not meet your certificate needs.

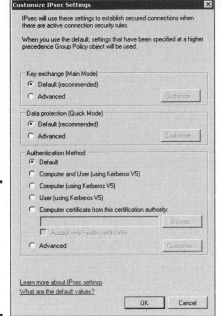

Figure 4-10:
Modify the
IPsec
settings as
required for
your
security
needs.

When working with the encryption settings, you must choose the Advanced option and then click Customize. Figure 4-11 shows the settings you can choose for key exchange. Notice that the default setting that Microsoft provides is at the low end of the scale, but it does provide moderate security with high compatibility. When you choose the strongest option, Elliptic Curve Diffie-Hellman P-384, you may find that older systems can't exchange keys with your server. The server becomes so secure that no one can access it with any reasonable assurance of success.

Notice the Security Methods list on the left side of the display in Figure 4-11. These methods appear in a number of situations. The defaults provide maximum compatibility with moderate protection. When you choose an entry and click Remove, the system no longer honors that method of securing data. Of course, removing a method also introduces compatibility problems and makes your server harder to access, so you need to ensure that anyone accessing your server will have the required security method installed as well.

Clicking Add or Edit shows a list of acceptable security methods. The methods vary by the kind of security you're trying to create. Figure 4-12 shows a typical example of the security methods that Windows Server 2008 supports.

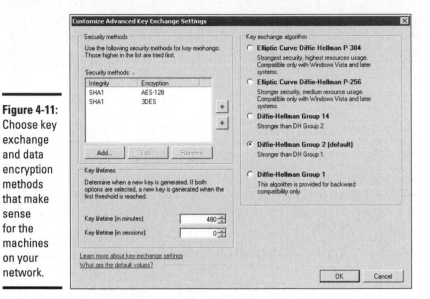

Figure 4-11:
Choose key
exchange
and data
encryption
methods
that make
sense
for the
machines
on your
network.

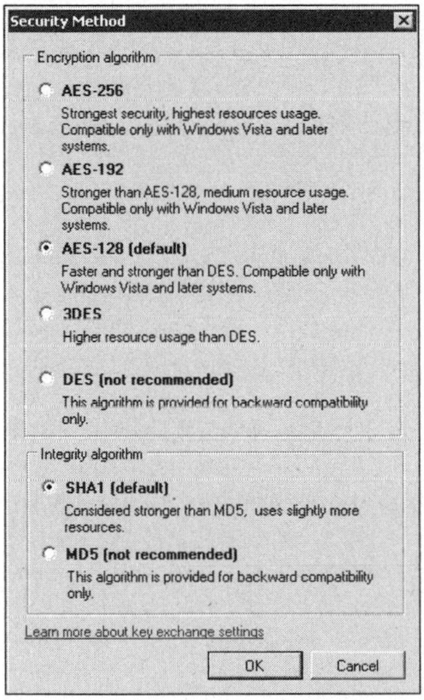

Figure 4-12:
Define the
security
methods
that your
server will
honor.

In this case, you must select both an encryption algorithm and an integrity
algorithm. The encryption algorithm supports two-way data exchange. One
machine encrypts the data, and the other decrypts and uses the data. The
methods that Windows Server 2008 uses rely on a public and private key

pair. The public key is known by everyone, and a recipient can use it to decrypt data encrypted by the private key. The recipient can also use the public key to encrypt data for the machine that has the private key. It's impossible to use the public key to decrypt data that's encrypted with the public key.

An integrity algorithm is a one-way encryption method. The system creates a unique number based on the data that the sender provides. The number acts as a means of identification, but doesn't transfer any information to the recipient. The system uses such an approach to send a password to the server from the client. The server doesn't need to know the actual password — it needs to know the unique number that the password generates when passed through the integrity algorithm. It's this number that the server stores, not the password. (Consequently, only you know your password, not the server, not the administrator, not anyone else — unless you share it, of course.)

When working with data, you must also choose a protocol for transferring the data. The Encapsulating Security Payload (ESP) encrypts just the data. The header remains unencrypted so that you can transfer the data using protocols such as Network Address Translation (NAT). The Authentication Header (AH) option also encrypts the header, which means that you can't use NAT. Windows Server 2008 typically uses only ESP for Windows Firewall to ensure that you can receive data from Web sites through NAT. You can discover more about the advantages and trade-offs of using ESP and AH at `http://www.tcpipguide.com/free/t_IPSecModesTransportand Tunnel-4.htm`.

Working with inbound and outbound rules

Windows Firewall uses rules to determine how to interact with incoming and outgoing traffic. These rules determine how Windows Firewall reacts to certain circumstances, such as information that arrives on a specific port for a particular application. The goal of both incoming and outgoing rules is the same — protect the server from unwanted information while allowing needed information to pass. You can see these rules when you choose either the Inbound Rules or Outbound Rules folders, as shown in Figure 4-13.

Microsoft provides a considerable number of rules with the default Windows Server 2008 configuration for roles and features that you can install with the product. Figure 4-13 shows just a few of these rules. In most cases, you don't ever need to edit these rules unless you want to make them stricter (which could cause the role or feature to stop working). However, it pays to look at the rules as a guide to creating custom rules that you'll need for applications you install. The following sections describe how to work with both inbound and outbound Windows Firewall rules.

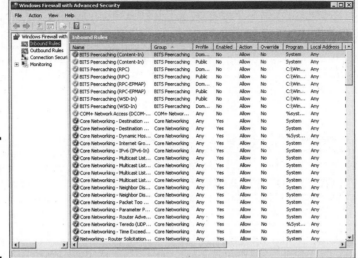

Figure 4-13:
Rules define
how your
server
reacts to
specific
situations.

Viewing and filtering rules

One of the first steps you must perform before you create a new rule is determining whether a rule for that need already exists. In some cases, you can modify an existing rule to address the needs of multiple applications, or you can at least use it as a template for creating a new rule. Unfortunately, you'll find that even a default Windows Firewall setup has a lot of rules and that your chances of finding a particular rule without filtering are slim. You can filter rules using the following criteria:

✦ **Profile:** Windows Firewall groups rules by their profile: public, private, or domain. See the "Working with the profile settings" section of this chapter for a description of the distinction between these settings.

✦ **State:** Rules are either enabled or disabled. You can filter out rules based on their current state.

✦ **Group:** Every rule belongs to a group. The group defines a number of related rules, such as those that control access for the BITS Peercaching feature. This form of filtering is helpful when you need to see rules that affect a particular built-in role or feature, or a custom port or application that you define.

To set a filter, right-click either the Inbound Rules or Outbound Rules folder, and choose one of the options on the Filter by Profile, Filter by State, or Filter by Group menus. When you want to clear a filter, choose Clear All Filters from the context menu. (The Clear All Filters option doesn't appear unless you have a filter in place.)

After you have a filter in place, you can further control the view by clicking any column shown in Figure 4-13. Clicking the column head sorts the list by that column. An arrow appears in the column you select. A down arrow signifies a descending order sort, and an up arrow signifies an ascending order sort. You can also change the number of columns that appear on-screen by right-clicking either the Inbound Rules or Outbound Rules folder and choosing View➪Add/Remove Columns from the context menu. You see the Add/Remove Columns dialog box, as shown in Figure 4-14.

Figure 4-14: Change the number of columns that the window displays.

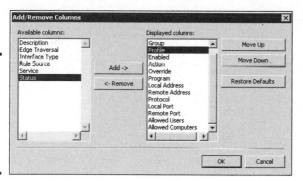

Use the Add and Remove buttons to add or remove columns from the Displayed Columns list, which controls the columns you see displayed on-screen. If a column appears in the wrong position on-screen, highlight its entry in the Displayed Columns list and use the Move Up or Move Down buttons to control the column's position. After you make the display appear as you want it, click OK and you see the changes on-screen. Click Restore Defaults if the display ever becomes messy and you want to restore it to its original appearance.

Adding a new rule

You'll eventually add a new application to the server that requires that you open a special port or provide direct Internet access. In the first case, you create a new rule for opening the port; in the second case, you create a new rule for providing the program with access. It's also possible that Microsoft's software will experience a problem at some point and you'll have to add access for a predefined role or feature manually. In very rare circumstances, you may have to create a custom rule that provides some combination of both port and programmatic access. No matter which kind of new rule you have to add, the following steps tell you how to do it (the screenshots show a new port rule for an incoming connection, but the other kinds of rules use approximately the same steps and look very much the same):

1. **Right-click either the Inbound Rules or Outbound Rules folder, and choose New Rule from the context menu.**

You see a New Rule Wizard dialog box, like the one shown in Figure 4-15. The precise name varies based on the kind of new rule you want to create, but the essential display is the same.

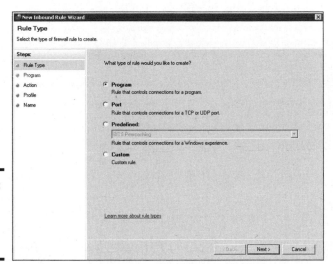

Figure 4-15:
Select the kind of rule you want to create.

2. **Choose the kind of rule you want to create.**

The steps change slightly according to the kind of rule you want to create. In all cases, you define an action. Program, port, and custom rules also require that you define a profile and a name for the rule. When working with a program, you define the name of the program or you create the rule for all programs. When working with a port, you find the port number or specify that the rule is for all ports. A predefined rule requires that you select the specific rules you want to work with. A custom rule requires that you specify both a program and a port, along with a special item, the *scope,* which defines the IP addresses to which the rule applies.

3. **Click Next.**

The dialog box you see at this point depends on the rule. However, what you see are the rule specifics, such as the program to work with or the port to use. Figure 4-16 shows a typical example for a program rule, but the other kinds of rules are similar.

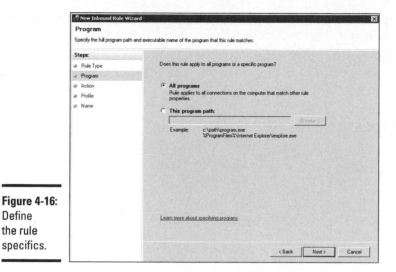

Figure 4-16:
Define
the rule
specifics.

4. **Define the rule specifics and click Next.**

   You may actually have to define several pages of rule specifics, depending on the kind of rule you want to create. At some point, you see the Action dialog box, as shown in Figure 4-17. This dialog box tells Windows Firewall what to do about the rule you created. You can allow the connection under all circumstances, allow the connection only when it's secure (you must also define what you mean by *secure*), or disallow the connection under any circumstance.

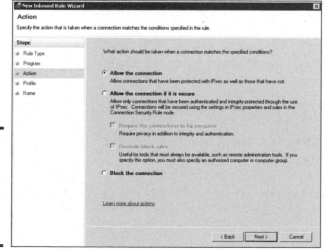

Figure 4-17:
Specify the
action you
want
Windows
Firewall to
perform.

5. **Determine which action you want Windows Firewall to perform and click Next.**

   At this point, you're finished with a predefined rule. Click Finish to create the rule. Otherwise, Windows Firewall displays the Profile dialog box, where you choose which of the three profiles use the rule (domain, public, and/or private).

6. **Choose one or more of the profiles and click Next.**

   The wizard displays the Name dialog box.

7. **Type a name and a description for the new rule. Click Finish.**

   The wizard creates and enables the rule for you.

If you ever find that you need to remove a rule you created, right-click its entry and choose Delete from the context menu. Likewise, you can edit a rule by right-clicking its entry and choosing Properties from the context menu. One entry that a predefined rule includes but you can't add to a custom rule is a group. Custom rules always have the group column as blank, and you can't add any information to it.

Editing a rule

You may need to edit one of the predefined or custom rules you create. To perform this task, right-click the rule entry and choose Properties from the context menu. Windows Firewall displays the Properties dialog box, as shown in Figure 4-18. This dialog box contains everything you specified when you created the rule using the wizard, as described in the "Adding a new rule" section of this chapter. It also includes some additional settings, such as the users and computers to which the rule applies and the rule's scope.

The settings on the Users and Computers tab apply only when you have the action set to allow only a secure connection. You can define specifically which computers and users Windows Firewall should monitor with the rule. When you grant an access with a rule, only the computers and users you choose will have the required access. Likewise, when you deny access, only the computers and users you choose will lack the required permission.

The Scope tab determines which IP addresses depend on the rule. In some respects, this tab is a lower-level version of the computer entries you can make on the Computers tab. The difference is that your server need not know about these computers in order to apply the rule. Windows Firewall differentiates between local and remote connections, so make sure to place the address in the correct list.

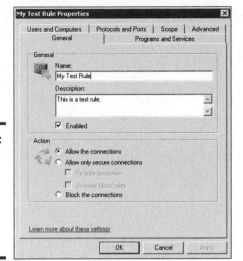

Figure 4-18:
The
Properties
dialog box
helps you
modify
existing
rules.

After you complete any edits, click OK. Windows Firewall checks the
changes you made and applies them immediately. However, the new rule
doesn't apply to anyone who is already logged in to the system. In this case,
the computer or user must log off and then log back in to the system.

Part VI

Windows PowerShell

The 5th Wave — By Rich Tennant

"It's Web-based, on demand, and customizable.
Still, I think I'm going to miss our old sales
incentive methods."

Contents at a Glance

Chapter 1: An Introduction to Windows PowerShell

In This Chapter

✔ Understanding what Windows PowerShell can do for you

✔ Working with PowerShell effectively

✔ Installing PowerShell on your server

✔ Considering how security affects the use of PowerShell

✔ Performing simple PowerShell tasks

✔ Getting help when working with PowerShell

✔ Working with PowerShell from remote locations

*W*indows PowerShell (often called simply PowerShell) is a new kind of command prompt. If you've worked with the command prompt before, you know it hasn't changed much since the days of DOS. In fact, some of the commands you use at the Windows Server 2008 command line have been around since the days of DOS. To an extent, the longevity of these commands bespeaks their original power and usability, but the commands have gotten outdated. You use one command line syntax with some commands and use a different syntax with other commands. In addition, the old command line features have security issues. Microsoft has good reason for introducing the new command line you find in PowerShell.

This chapter introduces you to PowerShell. You'll discover why PowerShell is such a great new Windows feature and how you can use it to work faster and more effectively. This chapter helps you get PowerShell installed so that you can work with it. (Microsoft doesn't install it on Windows Server 2008 by default.) Of course, all this information gets you set up to use PowerShell.

The next few sections of the chapter show you how to work with PowerShell. You'll discover how to perform simple tasks and how to obtain help when working with PowerShell. In fact, help in PowerShell is a real treat to use, so you may find that you want to spend some time looking at this feature alone. The chapter ends with a section on working with PowerShell from remote locations. Being able to perform tasks from a remote location is important when working with a server, because you'll perform many tasks from your workstation rather than directly from the server console.

An Overview of PowerShell

Of course, the first question that comes to mind when viewing PowerShell is what it is. Although Microsoft hasn't made a statement on the matter, many industry experts view PowerShell as a highly extensible equivalent to the many Unix shells on the market. Under Unix, many graphical utilities simply provide a convenient way to use the well-defined command line utilities. Working at the command line is the main event, and the graphical environment serves to make working with the command line utilities easier for those who need the additional help.

The second most common question is why anyone would need PowerShell. If the Unix shell approach is the direction that Microsoft is taking, you may eventually see all the old, poorly documented, and virus-prone utilities disappear from Windows and be replaced by PowerShell equivalents. So far, the company hasn't taken that approach in products such as the Server Core version of Windows Server 2008, so PowerShell may not arrive in force for a while. However, at some point, Microsoft has to face the fact that its old command line utilities have seen better days and require replacement — if for no other reason than the security issues surrounding them.

Of course, the basic issue that many administrators are concerned about is what PowerShell provides that the old command line doesn't provide. The "Using PowerShell Effectively" section of this chapter discusses in detail why you would want to use PowerShell. However, here are some issues to consider:

✦ **Reliability:** PowerShell provides a greater level of reliability than the command line.

✦ **Security:** Using PowerShell improves security because you need the required credentials in order to execute commands.

✦ **Managed Code Access:** PowerShell helps the administrator obtain the full resources of the .NET Framework without becoming a programmer.

✦ **Ease of Use:** In many cases, the commands are easier to remember and use because they use human readable terms. (The older commands are also available, for the most part, if you decide to use them.)

✦ **Scripting Support:** Scripting is considerably more powerful in PowerShell, albeit not always as easy as working at the old command prompt.

✦ **Complex Data Support:** Rather than use plain text for data, PowerShell uses .NET objects, which means that you can obtain the consistent output of complex data.

These basic reasons for using PowerShell also tell you what Microsoft is trying to accomplish. If you take a hard look at Windows Server 2008, many of the low-level operating system features still don't rely on the .NET Framework, but many of the higher-level features do. For example, you can no longer talk about IIS without also talking about the .NET Framework. The .NET Framework also makes an appearance in security, graphics, and communications. Consequently, it isn't any surprise that PowerShell also has a very heavy connection to the .NET Framework.

In general, you'll find that Microsoft is moving more and more in the direction of using the .NET Framework for the majority of operating system features. This change in focus means that you really do need a .NET Framework connection at the command prompt to get useful work done today and that the connection will only get stronger as time passes.

Using PowerShell Effectively

Microsoft doesn't throw out old technology very quickly. The fact that DOS hung around for so many years after Windows arrived is proof of that fact. In fact, in some respects, DOS is still around, in the form of the old command line. However, Microsoft does throw out old technology. In fact, Microsoft is already doing some serious housecleaning at the command prompt by removing old commands from Vista and Windows Server 2008, and you need to keep on top of them. You may eventually find that a command line tool that you've used often in the past doesn't appear in a future version of Windows — leaving you with PowerShell as the only alternative.

However, you have many reasons other than the eventual need to use PowerShell. In fact, you may very well find that PowerShell is one of the better productivity aids in your toolkit after you discover how to use it. Here are some of the ways that PowerShell can make you more efficient and effective as an administrator:

✦ It provides better automation features so that you can do more with less effort.

✦ You can create scripts more quickly in many cases.

✦ Scripts created with PowerShell tend to execute faster for a given task than performing the task at the old command line.

✦ Using PowerShell reduces potential mistakes.

✦ You get more information from PowerShell than you do from the command line utilities of the past.

✦ It's easier to obtain usable help in PowerShell than it is at the command prompt (which sometimes provides no help at all).

You may be wondering why you'd want to use a command prompt of any kind (old or PowerShell) when you have a host of graphical utilities to perform work. The problem is one of speed: You can automate the command line — automating a GUI tool is nearly impossible unless that tool provides the required automation. In addition, you can perform tasks in a single step at the command line when it requires a number of clicks in the GUI tool. Command line tools are easy to script and use within batch files — a feature not found in GUI tools. The trade-off for all this speed is an increase in errors. The GUI helps prevent errors and ensures that you enter correct data more often than not. Using PowerShell is the option you should try when you truly know how to perform a particular task.

Of course, the list in this section begs the question of whether you should just throw away that old command prompt. Unfortunately, you can't do that either. Many individuals and most companies have a significant base of existing batch files and scripts that they don't want to throw away. Unfortunately, this established base might not run very well under PowerShell for the very reasons that you want to use it — improved security and reliability. Consequently, during this transitional phase, you'll probably have to use both the command line and PowerShell for maximum productivity. To make the transition smoother, you may want to begin moving those old batch files and scripts to PowerShell as time permits.

Installing the PowerShell Feature

Windows Server 2008 comes with PowerShell as a feature. However, Microsoft doesn't install this feature by default; you must install it as a separate item. The following steps help you install and configure PowerShell as a feature on your server:

1. **Open the Server Manager console found in the Administrative Tools folder.**

2. **Select the Features folder and click Add Features.**

You see the Select Features dialog box of the Add Features Wizard, as shown in Figure 1-1. Notice that Windows PowerShell doesn't require that you install .NET Framework 3.0. This is perfectly normal, and you don't need to install the additional .NET Framework functionality unless you have an application that requires it.

3. **Check the Windows PowerShell option and click Next.**

The wizard displays the Confirm Installation Selections dialog box. Verify that you have selected the Windows PowerShell feature.

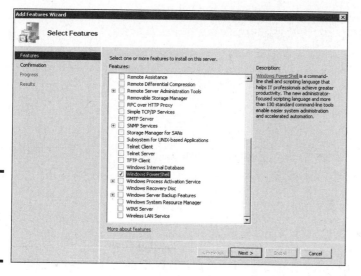

Figure 1-1:
Choose the
Windows
PowerShell
option.

4. **Click Install.**

The Add Features Wizard performs the required installation tasks for
you. After the installation is finished, you see the Installation Results
dialog box.

5. **Click Close.**

You're ready to begin working with PowerShell. (Even though the wizard
states that you may have to restart Windows to start using this feature,
you never do unless you install another feature that requires a restart.)

Now that you have PowerShell installed, you can begin using it to perform
tasks. To open a copy of PowerShell, choose the Start➪Programs➪Windows
PowerShell 1.0➪Windows PowerShell command. You see the command
prompt, shown in Figure 1-2. Notice that this command prompt shows that
you started Windows PowerShell and that it has a slightly different prompt
from the standard command prompt.

Configuring the Windows PowerShell window is the same as working with
the older command prompt. You can access these features by clicking the
box in the upper-left corner and choosing Properties from the context menu.
Figure 1-3 shows the resulting Windows PowerShell Properties dialog box.
Configure this option precisely as you would configure the command line
using the information found in the "Configuring the Command Line" section
of Book III, Chapter 6.

Figure 1-2:
PowerShell
looks very
much like
the standard
command
prompt,
but the
functionality
it provides is
different.

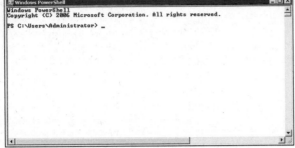

Figure 1-3:
Configure
PowerShell
before you
begin
using it.

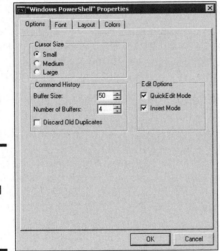

One difference you notice when working with PowerShell is that it defaults to a display that's 120 characters wide rather than the 80 characters used by the command prompt. The wider display accommodates the added information that PowerShell provides. However, you can configure PowerShell to use a narrower display using the Screen Buffer Size options on the Layout tab of the Windows PowerShell Properties dialog box. Of course, setting the display to use a smaller size may mean that you can't easily read some of the output from the commands you issue. Whenever possible, you want the display to remain 120 characters wide or even make it larger. Testing shows that using a 132-character-wide display actually works better than a narrower display does for displaying command output and Help information.

Although PowerShell uses a relatively large font and a 120-character screen size by default, the figures in this minibook use a somewhat smaller font and an 80-character screen size. The reason for this change is to ensure that you can see the text within the book. Using the larger number of characters would tend to make the text unreadable in the book, defeating the purpose of including screen shots. PowerShell also uses a black background with white letters by default — this minibook uses a white background with black letters to make the text more readable in the book.

Understanding the Security Issues of Using PowerShell

Microsoft has made the claim that Windows Server 2008 is more secure than any previous versions of Windows. In fact, if you use all the Windows Server 2008 features and don't disable the features that Microsoft includes for system protection, you find that the entire environment is more secure. The changes will be welcome in a world filled with all kinds of nefarious individuals and adware, viruses, and spyware. (These nefarious individuals are always looking for ways to get into your system or to trick you into providing them with sensitive information.)

Security, from a PowerShell perspective, is a relatively simple proposition. The plus side is that you might not have to worry as often about novice administrators shooting themselves (and everyone around them) in the foot by performing tasks that they really don't have the skill to perform. The negative side is that some of those old scripts and batch files might not work as anticipated, when they work at all. PowerShell adheres to all the standard Windows security policies that you've used in the past. In addition, it provides support for the role-based and code access security provided by the .NET Framework. Consequently, PowerShell is considerably more secure than anything you used in the past, but it comes with the price of not letting you do everything you did in the past.

One of Microsoft's goals for PowerShell, the command line interface for Windows Server 2008, is to keep batch files and scripts working as they always have. However, this goal is the direct opposite of good security, in some cases, because many of those old batch files and scripts performed tasks in an insecure manner. For example, deleting all temporary files on a drive might seem like an innocuous task, and it is. However, what happens when a nefarious individual changes that script, just for fun, and now it deletes all executable files on the hard drive? The script is no longer benevolent and requires some level of control. The old command line simply deleted the executable files and you had a mess on your hands.

Working with PowerShell, you see a message about the pending deletion. If you're like many advanced users, the warning is incredibly annoying, and you might simply disregard it. PowerShell attempts to protect you from shooting yourself in the foot, but you can override the features it provides. After all, there's a point at which you can't protect someone from their own actions. Consequently, you need to expect Windows Server 2008 security to be different and react appropriately to it. When you see a message from the operating system, don't get annoyed; make sure that you really want to do the task that the operating system is warning you about.

Performing Simple Tasks with PowerShell

Microsoft has tried hard to make as many of the older DOS commands as possible available in PowerShell. For example, you'll find that the CD (*change directory*) command is still available. These commands don't actually exist as real code. Instead, they exist as an alias for the managed code that Power-Shell does provide.

The CD command is actually the Set-Location *Cmdlet* (literally "a little command") in PowerShell. A Cmdlet provides the same functionality as utilities and commands do in the old command prompt — you use a Cmdlet to perform tasks at the command line. For now, you can use these aliases for compatibility features, but you should begin finding out how to use the new commands as soon as possible. The "An Overview of the Common Scripts and Cmdlets" section of Book VI, Chapter 3 provides a listing of common scripts and Cmdlets you'll use with PowerShell.

You'll also find that the CD command behaves differently than in the past. For example, in the past, to change directories to the root directory of a drive, you may have typed **CD**. Because using this syntax is imprecise and can lead to errors, Microsoft no longer supports it. In fact, you see the following error message:

```
The term 'CD\' is not recognized as a cmdlet, function,
 operable program, or script file. Verify the term and try
 again.
At line:1 char:3
+ CD\ <<<<
```

To change directories to the root directory of the drive, you must type **CD ** (with the space, to show that you mean to change directories to the root directory). The CD command can do more than it did previously. Type **CD D:** and you arrive at the root directory of the D: drive.

If you're used to writing your own scripts and batch files, you find a significant number of other changes at the command line. For example, you may want to locate all temporary files on your system and place the results in the Temp.TXT file. Using the old method, you typed **Dir *.TMP /S >> Temp.TXT** and pressed Enter. This technique doesn't work under PowerShell. What you see is the following error message:

```
Get-ChildItem : Second path fragment must not be a drive or
  UNC name.
Parameter name: path2
At line:1 char:4
+ Dir  <<<< *.TMP /S >> Temp.TXT
```

Rather than use the /S command line switch, you type **Dir -Include *.TMP -Recurse >> Temp.TXT** and press Enter. As an alternative, you can type **get-childitem -Include *.TMP -Recurse >> Temp.TXT** and press Enter. In both cases, the results are similar: The syntax is completely different from the Dir command you used at the command line. The Dir command also outputs information differently under PowerShell. The output appears in Figure 1-4. Notice the use of the get-childitem command. You could substitute **Dir *.TXT** and obtain the same results.

Figure 1-4:
The output
of the
directory
command,
no matter
which
syntax
you use,
differs in
PowerShell.

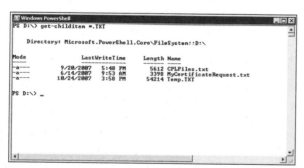

Obtaining Help for PowerShell Commands and Utilities

Working at the PowerShell command line shell is intrinsically different from working at the CMD.EXE command line. One of the first things you notice is that using the /? command line switch doesn't work for many commands and utilities. For example, if you type **Dir /?**, you see nothing at all. The insertion point simply moves to the next line.

When you want to find out about the Dir command, you must type **Help Dir** and press Enter. The command line help is also significantly different. Some people feel that they're reading a programming manual rather than a Help listing. Figure 1-5 shows a typical example. You see immediately that Power-Shell doesn't provide the same command line help you used in the past.

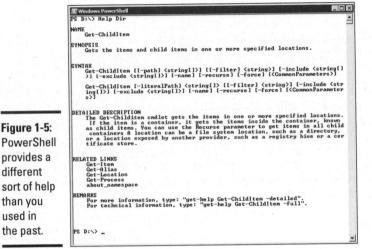

Figure 1-5:
PowerShell provides a different sort of help than you used in the past.

PowerShell uses a wealth of new names for old commands. For example, the CD command from days past is now the set-location command. You can see a list of PowerShell commands by typing **Help *** and pressing Enter. Figure 1-6 shows part of the list. This list might look a little daunting at first. However, it represents a major change in the way that the command shell works with commands from ancient Unix to a more modern object-oriented methodology. The bottom line is that PowerShell provides a vast wealth of commands, many of which don't appear in the old command prompt but require you to find a new way of working with those commands.

Notice that Figure 1-6 shows entries from both the Alias and Cmdlet categories. The Alias category entries aren't actual commands — they represent convenience entries that Microsoft has provided to help administrators make the changeover to PowerShell. The Cmdlet categories entries are the actual code provided by PowerShell. The Synopsis column of the output provides the name of a Cmdlet for an alias but provides an explanation of the task that the Cmdlet performs for a Cmdlet.

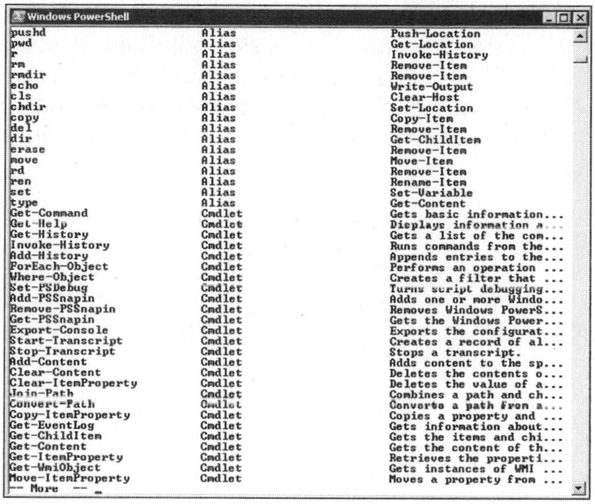

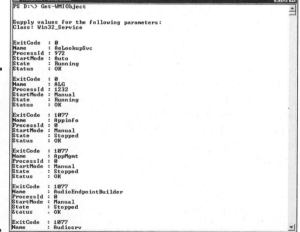

Figure 1-6:
Before you
begin using
PowerShell
in earnest,
you'll want
to review the
command
list.

In some cases, PowerShell Help requires that you provide additional information, rather than overwhelm you with information you don't need. In fact,
it provides prompts to help you use the command. For example, when you
type **Get-WMIObject** and then press Enter to obtain the status of services on
your system, you see a prompt for the class you want to use. If you type
Win32_Service and press Enter, you see a list of services, as shown in
Figure 1-7. Even though the Get-WMIObject Cmdlet has additional arguments you can supply, this command line represents the minimum that will
work. The point is that you don't get stuck trying to figure out why a command no longer works, because PowerShell provides you with clues.

Figure 1-7:
PowerShell
usually tries
to help you
provide the
minimum
information
necessary
to use a
Cmdlet.

A number of people are starting to compare the PowerShell interface to the interface provided with Linux. You can find an interesting article on the topic at `http://arstechnica.com/guides/other/msh.ars`. Most people who've used both PowerShell and Linux agree that Microsoft has taken a significant step in the right direction by making the command line easier to use overall and more object-oriented. The result is that you have a more consistent interface to work with, even if it's significantly different from what you used in the past.

Understanding the Remoting Difference

You may have noticed that many command line commands and utilities use odd methods for performing tasks on remote systems. The most common method is to supply the name of the remote system, your username, and your password at the command line. Unfortunately, sending your password in the clear is one certain way to invite people to steal it. To overcome this problem, many administrators resort to using the Remote Desktop application through Terminal Services. Although this technique works, it doesn't provide much in the way of automation.

PowerShell provides a significant difference in working with remote systems. For one thing, you provide only the name of the remote system without divulging your username or password. For another, PowerShell handles logging you in to the remote system automatically. Of course, if your credentials don't work on the remote system, you may not really be authorized to work on it. If you're authorized to work on it, PowerShell provides other techniques to obtain the credentials you need. Consider an example where you want to start a service on another system. Here's the command line you might use to do it (even though this command line appears on multiple lines in the book, you use only one line when working with the server):

```
Get-WmiObject -computer Remote -credential
  (Get-Credential Domain01\User01) Win32_Service -Filter
  "Name='Alerter'" | Start-Service
```

This command looks complex, but it really isn't, compared to some of the command line commands you probably used in the past. In this example, you use the `Get-WmiObject` Cmdlet to obtain a list of services on the remote machine. You're looking specifically for the Alerter service, so you use the –Filter command line switch. The name of the remote machine is Remote, and you specify it using the –computer command line switch.

You don't have access to the remote machine, so you must specify the –credential command line switch. To obtain the input for the –credential command line switch, you use the `Get-Credential` Cmdlet, which outputs a secure managed credential that the other machine can use to authenticate you.

After you're authenticated and the `Get-WmiObject` Cmdlet verifies that the Alerter service does indeed exist on the remote system, the command line pipes the result to the `Start-Service` Cmdlet. This second Cmdlet starts the service on the remote system. At no time have you exposed your credentials to anyone. In addition, you can put this command line in a batch file and not worry about anyone compromising your system. It really is a better and easier way to perform the task than the methods you might have used in the past.

It's also possible to place credentials in a system variable. For example, if you type **$C** = **Get-Credential**, the $C variable contains the credential in an unreadable form. When you use `Get-Credential` in this manner, you see the Windows PowerShell Credential Request dialog box, as shown in Figure 1-8. Simply type the name and password you want to use to access the remote system.

Figure 1-8:
Obtaining credentials is completely flexible when using PowerShell.

You may be wondering what happens when someone tries to use the Echo command to display the content of the variable. Try typing **Echo $C** after you create the credential and you'll see something unhelpful, like the output shown in Figure 1-9. Your credentials are safe when working with PowerShell.

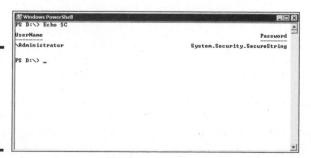

Figure 1-9:
Checking a credential displays no useful information.

Chapter 2: Understanding the .NET Framework

You may be wondering what a chapter about the .NET Framework is doing in the middle of a discussion about Windows PowerShell. After all, the .NET Framework is a tool for developers to create applications. However, when it comes to PowerShell, the .NET Framework is also a tool for administrators. Unlike the command line you used in days past, Power-Shell provides considerable access to the .NET Framework, which means that administrators can now create tools of any complexity that exist at the command line. Before you can exercise this newfound power, though, you need to have some idea of what the .NET Framework is all about.

This chapter can't provide you with a complete reference to the .NET Framework. After all, Microsoft has expended whole forests to give the .NET Framework even a modicum of coverage. What this chapter does is help you understand what the .NET Framework can do for you, how to manage it, and where to find the details you need to write applications. As this minibook progresses, you also see examples of how you can use the .NET Framework to write your own applications. The .NET Framework is really packed with a lot of features, so you should feel empowered at this point to do just about anything.

The .NET Framework also includes a host of tools. This chapter doesn't cover all of them, but by the time you're finished, you'll know enough about the essential tools to perform a number of important tasks, such as fix problems with the .NET Framework itself. You'll also have a better idea of how the modular approach used by the .NET Framework makes it easy for you to find out about just the pieces you need. You can build fully functional programs without knowing a lot about how the .NET Framework functions — just the pieces you need to know about today.

Understanding the .NET Framework Versions

PowerShell requires only that you have the .NET Framework 2.0 installed. If you don't want to work with any other version, that's fine when it comes to PowerShell. Custom-made applications may require other versions of the .NET Framework, and new Windows Server 2008 features may require .NET Framework 3.0. You should install .NET Framework 3.0, however, only when a system feature calls for it. Because the .NET Framework 3.0 is a special case, you find it discussed in the "Understanding the .NET Framework 3.0 Additions" section of this chapter. The following sections describe the version of the .NET Framework that you commonly use for features other than new Windows Server 2008 features.

Locating the .NET Framework on your system

The .NET Framework is Microsoft's technology for running applications based on the same tokenized technique that other modern development environments, such as Java, use. Compiling the program into tokens that rely on the Microsoft Intermediate Language (MSIL) means that the application can theoretically run on multiple platforms. In fact, products such as Mono (http://www.mono-project.com/Main_Page) make this possible, but Microsoft hasn't made cross-platform functionality a priority. Given that the .NET Framework represents an entirely different method of working with applications, Microsoft decided to place it in a different location on your hard drive. You normally find it in the \Windows\Microsoft.NET\ Framework folder of your system.

Because applications produced with the .NET Framework differ from those produced with standard application development technology, developers have had to create terminology to describe both application types. A .NET application relies on the Common Language Runtime (CLR) to execute based on the .NET Framework libraries. On the other hand, a native executable (application) relies on the Windows libraries located in the \Windows\ System32 directory to execute. All versions of Windows can run native executables, but older versions of Windows require that you install the .NET Framework to run .NET applications. If your system has PowerShell installed, it must have the .NET Framework installed as well. Here's a list of a few of the more important .NET Framework URLs:

✦ **.NET Framework 2.0:** http://www.microsoft.com/downloads/ details.aspx?FamilyID=b44a0000-acf8-4fa1-affb-40e78d788b00

✦ **.NET Framework 1.1:** http://msdn.microsoft.com/netframework/ downloads/framework1_1/

✦ **.NET Framework 1.1 Service Pack 1:** `http://www.microsoft.com/`
`downloads/details.aspx?familyid=a8f5654f-088e-40b2-`
`bbdb-a83353618b38`

✦ **.NET Framework 1.0:** `http://www.microsoft.com/downloads/`
`details.aspx?familyid=d7158dee-a83f-4e21-b05a-`
`009d06457787`

You'll find that Windows Server 2008 comes with several versions of the
.NET Framework. The version that most applications use appears in the
`\Windows\Microsoft.NET\Framework\v2.0.50727` folder. The .NET
Framework entries in the `\Windows\Microsoft.NET\Framework\`
`v1.0.3705` and `\Windows\Microsoft.NET\Framework\v1.1.4322`
folders are there for compatibility purposes only.

You might ask yourself why all these versions are important. A .NET application works better when it has access to the version of the .NET Framework
used to write it. The "Understanding the concept of side-by-side versions"
section of this chapter tells how you can maintain several versions of the
.NET Framework on your system and know that you'll never run into the
compatibility problems you encounter when working with Windows
applications.

Because Windows Server 2008 comes with basic .NET Framework functionality installed (you must install the .NET Framework 3.0 separately), you find
some additional folders under the `\Windows\Microsoft.NET\Framework`
folder. Each of these folders represents a different version of the .NET Framework and contains similar utilities. For example, the `\Windows\Microsoft.`
`NET\Framework\v1.1.4322` folder contains the 1.1 version of the .NET
Framework, and the `\Windows\Microsoft.NET\Framework\v2.0.`
`50727` folder contains the 2.0 version of the .NET Framework. The last
number in the folder, 4322 or 50727, can change depending on updates
that Microsoft provides.

The utilities in a particular .NET Framework version folder are for that version and support that version. For example, if you want to add support for
an ASP.NET application that relies on the .NET Framework 1.1 to IIS, you
must use the utilities in the `\Windows\Microsoft.NET\Framework\`
`v1.1.4322` folder, not those found in any other folder.

To access the utilities for a specific version of the .NET Framework from anywhere on your system, you must add the folder for that version to your path
statement. Avoid adding more than one version to the path because you'll
find that Windows stops with the first path it finds anyway, and the first path
might not contain the utilities you want to use. In fact, this is a good time to
use a batch file to add the path when you open the command prompt. Create

the batch file shown in Listing 2-1 by using Notepad and name it `Framework.BAT`. Place this file in your `\Windows\System32` folder so that you can access it at the command line. To use this batch file, simply type **Framework.BAT** at the command line.

Listing 2-1:   Adding the .NET Framework to Your Path Statement

```
@ECHO OFF

REM Add .NET Framework support as needed.
@ECHO Add .NET Framework Support
@ECHO.
@ECHO 1) Version 1.1
@ECHO 2) Version 2.0
@ECHO 3) Don't Add Support
@ECHO.
CHOICE /C:123 Select a .NET Support Option

REM Act on the selection.
IF ERRORLEVEL 3 GOTO :EOF
IF ERRORLEVEL 2 GOTO :Add20
IF ERRORLEVEL 1 GOTO :Add11

REM Add the .NET Framework 2.0
:Add20
SET PATH=%PATH%;%WINDIR%\Microsoft.NET\Framework\v2.0.50727
GOTO :EOF

:Add11
SET PATH=%PATH%;%WINDIR%\Microsoft.NET\Framework\v1.1.4322

@ECHO ON
```

As you can see, this menu system relies on the Choice command to request input from the user. Whenever you run this batch file, you see the .NET Framework choices you have. Select the choice that you want to use, and the batch file does the rest. The choice you make chooses one of the two path statement additions at the end of the batch file.

Some versions of Windows have the .NET Framework 3.0 installed. You can also install the .NET Framework 3.0 manually (download the installation package from `http://www.microsoft.com/downloads/details.aspx?FamilyID=10CC340B-F857-4A14-83F5-25634C3BF043`). If you have the .NET Framework 3.0 installed on your system, you want to add it to the batch file shown in Listing 2.1. The listing shows the common options found on most systems.

Understanding the concept of side-by-side versions

In the past, a Windows application would tell Windows that it required a certain DLL, and Windows would respond by loading it. Unfortunately, Windows would load whichever version of the DLL appeared in the `\Windows\System32` directory. The version of the DLL that the developer used to create the application might differ from the version that appeared on the hard drive. If the developer had to overcome a problem with the previous DLL by writing code that used its peculiar functionality, the application might break if Microsoft fixed that behavior in the new DLL. In short, applications of the past normally required a certain version of the DLL, but didn't have any means to request it from Windows.

Applications created with the .NET Framework are different from those created for Windows. Microsoft calls these applications *managed* because they run using the special Common Language Runtime (CLR) engine that controls the application environment and manages resource use. These applications include a *manifest*, which tells CLR (pronounced "clear") everything there is to know about the requirements for the application. The manifest contains a listing of the libraries that the application requires, along with the library versions, so that CLR loads the correct library to run the application. If you're really curious about seeing this manifest yourself, you can obtain the Intermediate Language Disassembler (ILDASM). You can obtain this tool as part of the .NET Framework 2.0 Software Development Kit (SDK) at `http://www.microsoft.com/downloads/details.aspx?FamilyID=FE6F2099-B7B4-4F47-A244-C96D69C35DEC` for the x86 (32-bit) version or `http://www.microsoft.com/downloads/details.aspx?familyid=1AEF6FCE-6E06-4B66-AFE4-9AAD3C835D3D` for the x64 (64-bit) version.

The important idea to grasp in this section is that you finally have the resources required to understand why an application isn't working properly. When you have a Windows application that suddenly stops running correctly, you usually have to guess the cause, and you can't verify the required DLL version numbers unless you request the information from the vendor. In short, native executables are very hard to troubleshoot. Using ILDASM (you can see a simple demonstration of this tool at `http://www.csharphelp.com/archives/archive23.html`), you can take apart any .NET application with relative ease, diagnose precisely what it needs to run correctly, and fix it without spending hours doing it. When you run across a .NET application that doesn't run correctly and eliminate the resource files as the cause of the problems, you're left with a few small things to check before you call the vendor and ask for help with an application error or usage anomaly that you're pretty certain is a bug.

Side-by-side version support also means that you don't have to worry about a host of native executable issues, such as DLL hell (see the article at

Book VI
Chapter 2

Understanding the
.NET Framework

`http://msdn2.microsoft.com/en-us/library/ms811694.aspx` for details). When you find that an application fails to run because you have the wrong version of the .NET Framework installed, you can simply download the version you need and install it. No longer will you have concerns about breaking another application when you perform the required installation. Although the .NET Framework is far from perfect, it's a step in the right direction, and knowing how to interpret .NET applications makes your job considerably easier.

Understanding the .NET Framework 3.0 Additions

Windows Server 2008 has the pertinent portions of the .NET Framework 1.0, 1.1, and 2.0 installed by default. However, you must install the .NET Framework 3.0 as a separate feature. The reason for this difference is that the contents of the `\Windows\Microsoft.NET\Framework\v3.0` folder are for new Windows Server 2008 features, such as

+ Windows Communication Foundation (WCF)

+ Windows Workflow Foundation (WWF)

+ Windows Presentation Foundation (WPF)

The .NET Framework is new to all client systems other than Vista. You can, optionally, install it on Windows XP and Windows Server 2003. If you need to install the .NET Framework 3.0 on a client system for server support or want to see other resources that Microsoft provides for it, check out the Web site at `http://www.microsoft.com/downloads/details.aspx?Family Id=10CC340B-F857-4A14-83F5-25634C3BF043`.

Some parts of the .NET Framework 3.0 will probably never see use on a server. For example, WPF is the part of Vista that provides features such as Aero Glass. Many administrators will work only with servers from a remote location, so the server user interface isn't as important as the one on their client machine. In addition, there probably isn't a better way to waste processing cycles than to spend them on eye candy.

The WCF, on the other hand, will likely see a lot of use of servers that rely on Microsoft-based Service Oriented Architecture (SOA) applications. When you think about SOA, think Web services. It's more than that, but for many administrators the Web service is the bottom line for SOA today. Given that Web services provide an extremely flexible method for sharing data through an Internet connection, you can expect to see WCF take a future role on your server, even if it doesn't take a role today. You can discover more about the WCF at `http://msdn2.microsoft.com/en-us/library/ms731082.aspx`.

You may eventually use WWF on your server. This is a new .NET Framework addition for managing workflow applications — essentially, long-running applications that control processes. Each process has a number of activities that must occur to complete the process. In other words, WWF attempts to model an application based on the way your application works. You can discover more about the WWF at `http://msdn2.microsoft.com/en-us/library/ms731082.aspx`.

Because the .NET Framework 3.0 is so specialized and you don't need to know anything about it to use any of the Windows Server 2008 features, this chapter doesn't discuss it in any detail. The only things you really need to know are that the .NET Framework 3.0 is an optional installation that you must have in order to use some Windows Server 2008 features and that the Server Manager tells you about this need automatically.

Book VI Chapter 2

Understanding the .NET Framework

Viewing the Global Assembly Cache

The .NET Framework introduces a number of new terms. One of the more important terms to know about is assembly. An *assembly* is any executable file. As with native executables, assemblies can include files with both EXE and DLL extensions. When you take apart a .NET application, you see why the term *assembly* is appropriate: The compiler assembles the application from a number of components (building blocks) that include forms, classes, and other features. The concept of an assembly isn't new, but because of the way the .NET Framework interacts with assemblies, developers needed a new name for the DLLs used for native applications.

Although it's just fine that applications can locate a public assembly, you often need to find them as well. The `\Windows\assembly` folder contains a special view of the Global Assembly Cache (GAC) that you can use to manage the public assemblies. Figure 2-1 shows a typical view of the `\Windows\assembly` folder.

The display shown in Figure 2-1 contains several essential pieces of information that you need to know about to manage the assembly correctly. The first piece of information isn't actually available. Every file in this list is a DLL. Consequently, the Accessibility entry is `Accessibility.DLL`.

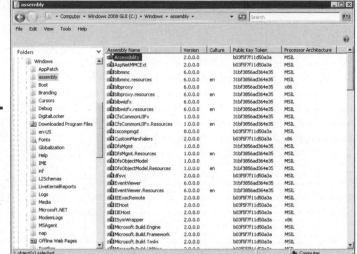

Figure 2-1:
Look in the
GAC for
any public
assemblies
you need to
make your
application
run.

Understanding assembly privacy

Assemblies are either private or public. Private assemblies are essentially inaccessible unless they appear in the same directory as the application that requires them or unless the application creates a specific reference to them. Developers use private assemblies in situations where other applications won't require code or resources that the assembly contains. You won't ever have a need to work with private assemblies unless they're part of an application you need to manage.

All public assemblies appear in the GAC. No matter where on the hard drive the public assembly physically appears, an application can find it by looking in the GAC. Any managed application can access any public assembly.

An overview of the GAC entries

In some cases, the \Windows\assembly folder shows two files with the same name. For example, you might see two Accessibility entries. Normally, a folder can't contain two files with the same name. It's essential to remember that the \Windows\assembly folder isn't a standard folder; it's a view into the GAC. The GAC can contain two files with the same name as long as the files differ by some criteria, such as version number.

Not every assembly in the GAC is associated with the .NET Framework. For example, if you install SQL Server 2005 on your system, you see a number of SQL Server-related assemblies in the list. In addition, any third party that produces a .NET application or resource can add an assembly to the GAC. Consequently, you should assume that only files that appear in the

`\Windows\Microsoft.NET\Framework` folder are part of the .NET Framework.

The assembly version number is next in the list. The assembly version number need not match the .NET Framework version. In fact, for the .NET Framework 1.1, the numbers definitely don't match. If the assembly is for a specific language, the next column contains a cultural code, such as en for English, as shown in Figure 2-1. You may see other two-letter designations, such as fr for French, depending on how you configure your system and which applications you install.

The public key token comes next. This is the most important piece of information for an administrator looking for modified files. Unlike with a Windows DLL, a developer must sign a .NET assembly before adding it to the GAC. The public key token is the developer's signature, and it uniquely identifies a particular developer.

Most references call the process of signing an assembly "giving it a strong name." The point is that this digital certificate is your guarantee of knowing who signed a public assembly. Because the token value for an assembly is unique, the system can tell you about security problems with the assembly. If someone makes any change to the assembly, the token is no longer valid and the GAC won't accept the assembly. If someone makes a change using devious means, CLR still won't run the assembly because the values inside the assembly no longer match the token value. In short, no one can modify a .NET assembly file without leaving a fingerprint behind and making it very easy for you to detect the change.

If you ever doubt the validity of a .NET assembly, you can always verify the token with the vendor. The token doesn't give away any information about your machine; every machine that has a particular version of an assembly installed has the same token. Consequently, it's very easy to check token numbers with the vendor to ensure that you have an unmodified assembly installed on your system.

The final column shows the target processor for an assembly. Most assemblies target the MSIL, which means that they should run on any platform that supports the .NET Framework. A few assemblies can contain code that won't run on just any platform, so they provide a platform-specific target. If you see no target, you can assume that the developer targeted the assembly at MSIL.

Removing an assembly using Windows Explorer

At some point, you may have to remove an assembly from the GAC. The need to remove an assembly is rare, however, and you should do it with extreme care because any assembly you remove from the GAC becomes unusable to applications that rely on the public version of the assembly. To perform this task, right-click any assembly and choose Uninstall from the context menu.

Selecting Uninstall removes the assembly from the GAC. However, the assembly is still available on the system. You can use the GACUtil utility, described in the "Placing assemblies in the GAC" section of this chapter, to reinstall an assembly that was removed accidentally. In fact, this information is essential when you have curious users who might damage their systems by cleaning up assemblies they think they no longer need.

Viewing assembly properties using Windows Explorer

Assemblies have properties, just like every other object managed by Windows. To display the assembly properties, right-click the assembly entry and choose Properties from the context menu. You see a Properties dialog box like the one shown in Figure 2-2.

Figure 2-2:
The Properties dialog box provides you with additional information about an assembly.

The General tab provides essentially the same information as you saw in Figure 2-1. The "An overview of the GAC entries" section of the chapter tells you more about these entries.

The Version tab is where you find additional assembly information. Notice that the File Version field doesn't match the assembly version. In this case, the number you see is the .NET Framework version number. The file version helps you match an assembly to the .NET Framework version that supports it (assuming that the assembly is part of the .NET Framework). You can always verify that an assembly is part of the .NET Framework by looking at the Product Name field. This field contains Microsoft .NET Framework for any assembly that's part of the .NET Framework.

Always look at the Comments field for an assembly if you think that you have the wrong support installed. A production system, one that you aren't using for development, should always have a retail version of the assembly installed. The Comments field tells you which kind of assembly you have installed when working with .NET Framework assemblies.

Working with Common .NET Framework Utilities

The .NET Framework comes with a number of utilities. These utilities appear in the version folder for the version of the .NET Framework you want to work with under the `\Windows\Microsoft.NET\Framework` folder. It's best if you can use the version of the utility that supports a particular version of the .NET Framework. In many cases, you can safely use a newer utility to modify a setting for an older version of the .NET Framework, but never use an older utility to manage a newer version of the .NET Framework. For example, don't use a version 1.1 utility to manage a 2.0 setup. The following sections contain common .NET Framework utilities that you need.

Placing assemblies in the GAC

Any assembly with a strong name — one that the developer has signed — can appear in the GAC. When you place the assembly in the GAC, it becomes available for public use. Some applications can't locate the assembly unless you make it public, so when an application stops working after working for a while, make sure that all the public assemblies it requires in order to run appear in the GAC as they should.

It's important to remember that the Global Assembly Cache Utility (GACUtil) appears as part of the .NET Framework SDK you download from Microsoft. (See the "Understanding the concept of side-by-side versions" section of this chapter for details.) The utility appears in the `\Program Files\ Microsoft Visual Studio 8\SDK\v2.0\Bin` folder of your hard drive after the installation. Because this utility is so important, you should consider downloading the SDK to have it.

You use the GACUtil to register an assembly in the GAC or to remove it from the GAC from the command line. It's also possible to remove an assembly from the GAC by using Windows Explorer. (See the "Removing an assembly using Windows Explorer" section of the chapter for details.) The GACUtil uses the following syntax:

```
GACUtil /i <assembly_path> [/r [{assemblyName |
    assemblyPath}]] [/f] [/nologo] [/silent]
GACUtil /il <assembly_path_list_file> [/r [{assemblyName |
    assemblyPath}]] [/f] [/nologo] [/silent]
GACUtil /u <assembly_display_name> [/r [{assemblyName |
    assemblyPath}]]
GACUtil /uf <assembly_name> [/nologo] [/silent]
GACUtil /ul <assembly_display_name_list_file>
    [/r [{assemblyName | assemblyPath}]] [/nologo] [/silent]
GACUtil /l [<assembly_name>] [/nologo] [/silent]
GACUtil /lr [<assembly_name>] [/nologo] [/silent]
GACUtil /cdl [/nologo] [/silent]
GACUtil /ldl [/nologo] [/silent]
```

As you can see, there are many ways to use the GACUtil to perform tasks on your system. The following list describes each of the command line arguments:

- **/i assembly_path:** Installs the specified assembly to the GAC. You must provide the assembly name and path. For example, if the MyAsm.DLL file appears in the D:\Temp folder, you type **GACUtil /i D:\Temp\MyAsm. DLL** and press Enter.

- **/il assembly_path_list_file:** Installs the list of files provided in a separate file. You must provide a text file that has one assembly listed per line. Simply create the list using Notepad. As with the /i command line switch, you must include both the assembly name and path.

- **/u assembly_display_name:** Removes the specified assembly from the GAC. You must use the display name of the assembly as it appears in the \Windows\assembly folder. Don't use the filename and path. For example, to remove MyAsm.DLL from the GAC, you type **GACUtil /u MyAsm** and press Enter. If you provide a partial assembly name, the utility removes all assemblies that match the partial name.

- **/uf assembly_name:** Forces the system to remove an assembly from the GAC by removing all traced references to the assembly. The only exception is when the Windows Installer has a reference to the assembly. Using this option can cause applications to stop responding.

- **/ul assembly_display_name_list_file:** Removes the list of assemblies provided in a separate file. You must provide a text file that has one assembly listed per line. Simply create the list using Notepad. As with the /u command line switch, you provide only the assembly name as it appears in the \Windows\assembly folder.

✦ **/l [assembly_name]:** Lists the contents of the GAC. Use the optional assembly name input to reduce the list size. Specifying a partial assembly name lists all assemblies that match the specified criteria.

✦ **/lr [assembly_name]:** Lists the contents of the GAC including all traced references to the assemblies. Use the optional assembly name input to reduce the list size. Specifying a partial assembly name lists all assemblies that match the specified criteria.

✦ **/cdl:** Deletes the contents of the download cache. The download cache is where a vendor places an assembly that you download from the Internet for use with Internet or local applications.

✦ **/ldl:** Lists the contents of the download cache.

✦ **/r [assemblyName | assemblyPath]:** Specifies a traced reference to an assembly that you want to install or uninstall. The traced reference includes a schema type, an identifier, and a description. You must use the same options to uninstall an assembly as you use to install it. This feature helps overcome problems where uninstalling an application doesn't necessarily remove it from the GAC or vice versa. For example, you might install an assembly using the FILEPATH schema type with `/r FILEPATH c:\MyProject\MyApp.EXE "My Application"` as the arguments.

✦ **/f:** Forces the utility to install the assembly in the GAC even when there's another assembly with the same name, version, and token information.

✦ **/nologo:** Suppresses the display of the GACUtil banner. This option is helpful when creating batch files where you don't want to disturb the user.

✦ **/silent:** Suppresses all utility output. This option is helpful when creating batch files when you don't want to disturb the user.

Registering assemblies before using them

The Component Object Model (COM) is the basis for many of the applications on your server. COM applications require registry entries, rather than the GAC, to locate DLLs that they need. When working with native executables, you use the RegSvr32 utility to register the executable as a component in the registry. The registration process adds registry entries that make the executable accessible from other applications. By reviewing the registry entries, a calling application can locate the component on disk and use the code it provides.

A .NET application doesn't always require access to the registry to locate a component because it has the GAC to consult. When working with a .NET component, the application can locate the required files and know how to use the component without relying on the registry. However, native executables that require access to the .NET component still require registry entries. The RegAsm utility performs the same task as RegSvr32 for .NET components. This utility uses the following syntax: RegAsm AssemblyName [/unregister] [/tlb[:FileName]] [/regfile[:FileName]] [/codebase] [/registered] [/asmpath:Directory] [/nologo] [/silent] [/verbose]. The following list describes each of the command line arguments:

✦ **AssemblyName:** Specifies the name of the assembly you want to register. You must include the full assembly filename as a minimum. For example, if the `MyAsm.DLL` file appears in the `D:\Temp` folder, you type **RegAsm D:\Temp\MyAsm.DLL** and press Enter.

✦ **/unregister:** Removes the registry entries for the .NET component.

✦ **/tlb[:FileName]:** Creates a type library for the .NET component. Normally, you won't need a type library unless you're writing an application. However, you might find that you need the type library in some cases, such as when you register the component with COM+ for use in COM+ applications. Type libraries always have a TLB file extension.

✦ **/regfile[:FileName]:** Generates a REG file that contains the .NET component registry entries instead of placing the entries in the registry. This option is useful when you need to register the .NET component on multiple machines using a batch file. You can't use this command line switch with the /unregister or /tlb command line switches.

✦ **/codebase:** Sets the code base for the component in the registry. In most cases, you won't need to use this command line switch unless you're working with a Web application that employs COM technology. The code base entry appears as part of the `<Object>` tag. The Web site at `http://www.w3schools.com/tags/tag_object.asp` provides an interesting tutorial about the `<Object>` tag.

✦ **/registered:** Specifies that the utility should reference only type libraries you've already registered.

✦ **/asmpath:Directory:** Specifies the path that the utility should use when looking for .NET components to register.

✦ **/nologo:** Suppresses the display of the RegAsm banner. This option is helpful when creating batch files where you don't want to disturb the user.

✦ **/silent:** Suppresses all utility output. This option is helpful when creating batch files where you don't want to disturb the user.

✦ **/verbose:** Displays additional information during the registration process. The amount of additional information depends on the .NET component.

Chapter 3: Working with Scripts and Cmdlets

In This Chapter

✔ Considering the common scripts and Cmdlets

✔ Working with the common scripts and Cmdlets

✔ Working from a remote location

*W*orking with PowerShell is all about using scripts and Cmdlets. As described in the "Creating a PowerShell Script" section in Chapter 4 of this minibook, a *script* is a series of textual instructions that you write yourself and the system interprets for you, and a *Cmdlet* is compiled code that a developer normally creates for you and compiles into an executable form. In both cases, PowerShell loads the required code into memory and then acts on the instructions within the code within the limits of your permissions and those of the code.

An Overview of the Common Scripts and Cmdlets

Using PowerShell is a different experience from working with the command line in a number of ways, not the least of which is how PowerShell provides functionality. Rather than emphasize individual utilities, Microsoft is placing a strong emphasis on Cmdlets and scripts, which let you access the power of the .NET Framework in a secure manner. Because you're working with the .NET Framework directly, you have potential access to thousands of commands. Table 3-1 shows a list of the common Cmdlets and scripts available as part of PowerShell.

Table 3-1	Common Cmdlets and Scripts Supported by PowerShell	
add-content	add-history	add-member
add-pssnapin	clear-content	clear-item
clear-itemproperty	clear-variable	compare-object
convertfrom-securestring	convert-path	convertto-html
convertto-securestring	copy-item	copy-itemproperty
export-alias	export-clixml	export-console

(continued)

Table 3-1 *(continued)*

export-csv	foreach-object	format-custom
format-list	format-table	format-wide
get-acl	get-alias	get-authenticodesignature
get-childitem	get-command	get-content
get-credential	get-culture	get-date
get-drive	get-eventlog	get-executionpolicy
get-help	get-history	get-host
get-item	get-itemproperty	get-location
get-member	get-pfxcertificate	get-process
get-psdrive	get-psprovider	get-pssnapin
get-service	get-tracesource	get-uiculture
get-unique	get-variable	get-wmiobject
group-object	import-alias	import-clixml
import-csv	invoke-expression	invoke-history
invoke-item	join-path	measure-command
measure-object	move-item	move-itemproperty
new-alias	new-item	new-itemproperty
new-object	new-psdrive	new-service
new-timespan	new-variable	out-default
out-file	out-host	out-null
out-printer	out-string	pop-location
push-location	read-host	remove-item
remove-itemproperty	remove-psdrive	remove-pssnapin
remove-variable	rename-item	rename-itemproperty
resolve-path	restart-service	resume-service
select-object	select-string	set-acl
set-alias	set-authenticodesignature	set-content
set-date	set-executionpolicy	set-item
set-itemproperty	set-location	set-psdebug
set-service	set-tracesource	set-variable
sort-object	split-path	start-service
start-sleep	start-transcript	stop-process
stop-service	stop-transcript	suspend-service
tee-object	test-path	trace-command

update-formatdata	update-typedata	where-object
write-debug	write-error	write-host
write-object	write-progress	write-verbose
write-warning		

As you can see, this is an impressive list of commands. You also have access to a number of other features to assist you in creating scripts. Book VI, Chapter 4 discusses these additional features and tells you how to create your own scripts.

Remember that you can easily get help with any common PowerShell script or Cmdlet by typing **Help** plus the command name, and then pressing Enter. (See the "Obtaining Help for PowerShell Commands and Utilities" section of Book VI, Chapter 1 for details.) If you find that you really dislike the command line reference, Microsoft also provides graphical help. You can learn more about the graphical Help application at `http://www.microsoft.com/technet/scriptcenter/topics/winpsh/pschm.mspx`.

Sometimes a good book on a topic can help significantly. If you want to explore the standard Cmdlets further, check out *Professional Windows PowerShell,* by Andrew Watt, and *Professional Windows PowerShell Programming: Snapins, Cmdlets, Hosts and Providers,* by Arul Kumaravel, Jon White, Naixin Li, Scott Happell, Guohui Xie, and Krishna C. Vutukuri (both published by Wrox). The second book delves into the intricacies of programming, so you definitely want to get the *Professional Windows PowerShell* book first.

Executing a Common Script or Cmdlet

You execute a common script or Cmdlet just as you would do at the command line of old. There are obviously some differences, but the basic idea is the same. However, PowerShell normally adds some expanded capability to what you could do in the past. For example, you might need to review a complex directory setup.

An overview of command line and PowerShell comparable activities

When working at the Windows command line in the past, you used the Dir command to obtain a directory list. PowerShell also supports the Dir command, but as an alias for the Get-ChildItem Cmdlet. You can type either command and obtain the same result in PowerShell. However, if you type **Dir /S** to obtain a list of subdirectories, as you did at the command line, PowerShell displays an error message. You must use the PowerShell form of Dir /Recurse to perform the same task.

The output from a Dir or Get-ChildItem command can be unwieldy. In the past, you needed to send the output to a text file and hope for the best. Now you also have the option of sending the output to an easier-to-work-with HTML file by typing **Dir | ConvertTo-HTML > Directory.htm** and pressing Enter. When you open the resulting file in Internet Explorer, you see a display similar to the one shown in Figure 3-1.

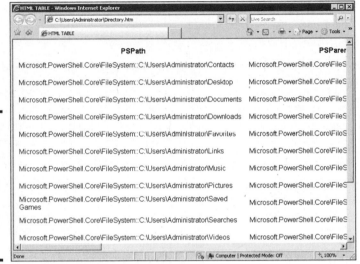

Figure 3-1:
You can use scripts and Cmdlets to create HTM files that you can view in a browser.

Notice that this display provides you with considerable detail about the contents of the directory. If you worked at the command line in the past, you already know about the pipe symbol (|), which is used to send the output of one command to the input of another. In this case, you send the output of the Dir command to the ConvertTo-HTML command. The old command line also supports redirection. The output redirection symbol (>) sends the output of the command to a file. At this point, the comparison between the old command line and PowerShell is over.

Working with COM objects in PowerShell

You may have opened Internet Explorer by double-clicking the `Directory. htm` file in Windows Explorer. That approach works, but it's inconvenient. It would be better if you could open Internet Explorer from within PowerShell. Unfortunately, you can't simply type **IExplore.exe** and press Enter. Typing **Directory.htm** and pressing Enter doesn't work either. These methods don't work within PowerShell because PowerShell is a managed environment.

When working in PowerShell, you work with objects. Internet Explorer is a COM object, so you create it as a COM object and interact with it as a COM object. Of course, you must then know the COM program identifier for Internet Explorer, which is `InternetExplorer.Application`. You can see a list of common COM program identifiers, as well as a means of finding the program identifiers associated with your application, at `http://www.winscripter.com/WSH/COM/61.aspx`. To open `Directory.htm` in Internet Explorer, you need to use the following steps:

1. **Type $ie = New-Object -ComObject InternetExplorer.Application and press Enter.**

   This step creates a variable named $ie. You discover more about this variable in a moment. However, what you need to know for now is that it contains a copy of Internet Explorer that you can bend to your will. Yes, that's pretty exciting!

2. **Type $ie.Visible = $true and press Enter.**

   You see a copy of Internet Explorer appear in the Taskbar. If you were to type **$ie.Visible = $false** and press Enter, the copy of Internet Explorer would disappear, but it would still exist. So this step doesn't create the copy of Internet Explorer; it simply makes it visible.

3. **Type $ie.Navigate('C:\Users\Administrator\Directory.htm') and press Enter.**

   Make sure to use the path for your user directory. It's also important to place the location within single quotes or else PowerShell registers an error. If you provided the right location, you see a directory listing similar to the one shown in Figure 3-1.

You may wonder where the `$ie.Visible` and the `$ie.Navigate` steps came from. Whenever you create an object in PowerShell, you can use the Echo command to display information about it. Type **Echo $ie** and you see information about the Internet Explorer object shown in Figure 3-2. This listing tells you about the Internet Explorer properties that you can work with. If you want to remove the Address Bar, you can simply set the AddressBar property to $false.

If you want to see a complete list of Internet Explorer members, you must use the Get-Member Cmdlet to do it. Type **$ie | Get-Member** and press Enter to see the list of members shown in Figure 3-3. Notice that you now see a listing of both methods and properties. The methods tell you what you can do with the object, such as navigate to another location or go to the user's home page. The properties contain values you can change.

Figure 3-2:
The variable
you create
tells you a
lot about
Internet
Explorer.

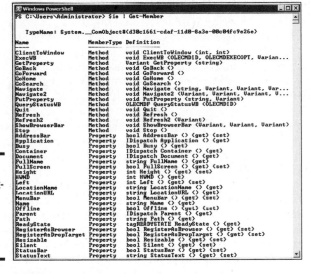

Figure 3-3:
Use the Get-
Member
Cmdlet to
see object
details.

As with many objects you encounter, some Internet Explorer objects
also contain properties and methods. For example, type **$ie.Document |
Get-Member** to see the list of properties and methods shown in Figure 3-4.
This impressive list of methods and properties tells you what you can do to
the Internet Explorer document. Consequently, you can control how the user
sees any Web page you present in the browser.

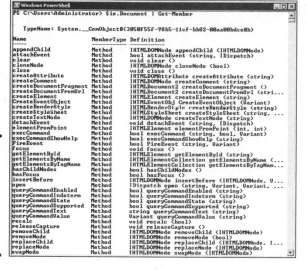

Figure 3-4:
Most objects you use have many levels of detail to explore.

Of course, this is a quick overview of a more complex topic. You can delve into any object you create in significant detail and control it in ways that you couldn't even imagine using the old command prompt. Of course, it also requires more time to create scripts to perform this level of interaction. As with all programming tasks, the flexibility you gain with PowerShell requires a payment of increased complexity.

Combining multiple steps

You can create command lines of just about any complexity in PowerShell. In fact, you can perform every task described so far in this section as a single command by separating individual actions with a semicolon (;). In this case, obtaining the local directory, saving it as HTML, and then displaying it in Internet Explorer would look like this (you type everything on a single line, even though it appears on multiple lines in the book):

```
Dir | ConvertTo-HTML > Directory.htm; $ie = New-Object
-ComObject InternetExplorer.Application; $ie.Visible = $true;
 $ie.Navigate('C:\Users\Administrator\Directory.htm')
```

When you press Enter after typing this entire string, you see a copy of Internet Explorer open with the directory listing displayed. Of course, you don't want to type long command lines such as this one very often. Book VI, Chapter 4 shows you how to combine these long statements into a file and then execute them whenever needed.

Of course, sometimes you might want to combine multiple steps for other reasons. For example, you might want to create a shortcut with the entire script right there in the Target field of the Shortcut tab. You may also want to perform a task by using the Run dialog box. In both cases, you have a single field in which to place everything you want to do. Of course, this technique also requires a little extra fiddling — you can simply put a `Dir` command in there of the sort discussed in this chapter.

In this case, you must specify `PowerShell.EXE` as part of the command line. Of course, PowerShell executes the command and exits immediately, which means that you see Internet Explorer quickly appear, display the directory listing, and then disappear. If you look fast, you might get to see something, but chances are that you won't. To make the display stick around, you need to use the –NoExit command line switch. PowerShell uses the following command line syntax:

```
PowerShell[.EXE] [-PSConsoleFile <file> | -Version <version>]
    [-NoLogo] [-NoExit] [-NoProfile] [-NonInteractive]
    [-OutputFormat {Text | XML}] [-InputFormat {Text | XML}]
    [-Command { - | <script-block> [-args <arg-array>]
                  | <string> [<CommandParameters>] } ]
```

Interestingly enough, you can't execute `PowerShell.EXE` from within PowerShell. The following list describes each of these command line switches.

✦ **-PSConsoleFile Filename:** Loads the file you specify as a PowerShell console. A PowerShell console file provides a means of re-creating an existing console later. You save the console settings by typing **Export-Console -path MyConsole** and pressing Enter, where MyConsole is the name of the console you want to save. Later, to restore the console, you type **PowerShell -PSConsoleFile MyConsole.PSC1** at the regular command prompt and press Enter. The command prompt changes to a PowerShell command prompt. When you finish using the console, type **Exit** and press Enter — the normal command prompt returns.

✦ **-Version VersionNumber:** Starts the version of PowerShell with the specified version number. You can use this feature when you have multiple copies of PowerShell installed on the same system. This feature ensures that you don't run into compatibility problems later, when Microsoft has a number of PowerShell versions available.

✦ **-NoLogo:** Starts PowerShell without displaying the copyright banner. This option is useful when you want to perform tasks in the background without disturbing the user.

✦ **-NoExit:** Starts PowerShell, performs any commands you request, and then leaves PowerShell running. You can use this feature to start

PowerShell, perform any required automatic setup, and then perform any additional required commands manually. This option is also important when you want to review the result of any tasks that PowerShell has performed.

✦ **-NoProfile:** Starts PowerShell without loading the user profile. This feature comes in handy for generic scripts that you want to exit without the interference of user options (such as a system-level task).

✦ **-Noninteractive:** Starts PowerShell and performs the requested command without presenting an interactive prompt to the user. This feature prevents the user from accidentally interfering with the command. You can use this option for background tasks. Of course, you must ensure that the task really doesn't require any user interaction to complete.

✦ **-OutputFormat {Text | XML}:** Specifies the default output format for any data you present on-screen. You can always override the default using the required commands, including ConvertTo-HTML. The two valid arguments for this command line switch are Text and XML.

✦ **-InputFormat {Text | XML}:** Specifies the default input format for any data you provide to PowerShell to execute commands. The two valid arguments for this command line switch are Text and XML.

✦ **-Command { - | <script-block> [-args <arg-array>] | <string> [<CommandParameters>]:** Executes the specified command and then exits unless you specify the –NoExit command line switch. You have three options for providing commands:

   • The first command option is to specify the hyphen (-). In this case, PowerShell waits for you to provide the command information by using the standard input device, which is normally the keyboard. You can redirect the standard input device, however, to any device capable of providing text input to PowerShell.

   • The second option is to create a script block. A script block can contain any number of commands you want. Always place a script block with curly braces ({}). For example, if you use **PowerShell -NoExit -Command {$ie = New-Object -ComObject InternetExplorer. Application; $ie.Visible = $true; $ie.Navigate('http://www. microsoft.com')}** as a command, the system opens a copy of Internet Explorer and displays the Microsoft Web site.

   The first script block form doesn't work in the Open field of the Run dialog box or as part of a shortcut. In this case, you must surround the command with double quotes and use the execution operator (&). The second form is **PowerShell -NoExit -Command "&{$ie =**

New-Object -ComObject InternetExplorer.Application; $ie.Visible = $true; $ie.Navigate('http://www.microsoft.com')}".

- The third option is to specify the command directly as the last element of the input string. This method is the one you use at the command line in most cases. Simply type the command string with associated arguments directly after the –Command switch.

Working from Another Location

In some cases, you need to work with PowerShell in a remote location. For example, you may want to interact with the server from your client machine. In this case, you need to begin by testing the command or script locally, if possible. After you know that the command or script works locally, you'll modify it to meet remote location requirements.

The method you use to access a remote location depends on the command you want to use. For example, when working with the Get-ChildItem Cmdlet, you can simply specify the remote path. Type the Uniform Naming Convention (UNC) path to the item you want. If you have a server named MainXP with a shared drive named Drive_D and you want to access the information on it, you type **Get-ChildItem \\MainXP\Drive_D** and press Enter. You don't need to map a network drive or anything else to use this technique because Windows PowerShell finds the shared drive using the UNC specification you provide.

In some cases, the command won't offer a direct method of working with resources. In this case, the command usually provides a special command line switch, such as –computer. The Get-WmiObject Cmdlet is a good example of a command in this category. To obtain the status of the Alerter service on MainXP, you type **Get-WmiObject -computer MainXP Win32_Service –Filter "Name='Alerter'"** and press Enter. If you also need the credential of someone named John on that system to execute the command, you type **Get-WmiObject -computer MainXP -credential (Get-Credential MainXP\ John) Win32_Service –Filter "Name='Alerter'"** and press Enter.

The current version of Windows PowerShell (1.0) has some limitations when it comes to remoting. In some cases, you see the dreaded "The RPC server is unavailable" error message for no apparent reason, among other issues. You often have to perform extra work to accomplish a specific task, and not all Cmdlets work as well as they should on a remote system. Microsoft plans to fix many of these issues in Windows PowerShell 2.0 and add some other goodies. You can read more about these proposed updates at http://searchwinit.techtarget.com/originalContent/0,289142,sid1 gci1270125,00.html. If you use Windows PowerShell, make sure to get the 2.0 update when it becomes available.

Chapter 4: Creating Your Own Scripts and Cmdlets

In This Chapter

✔ Adding a new shell extension to PowerShell

✔ Writing and using your own PowerShell script

✔ Considering script security

✔ Writing and using your own Powershell Cmdlet

You can perform an impressive number of tasks by using the built-in Cmdlets and scripts supplied with PowerShell. However, at some point, you find a task that you can't easily perform using the built-in features. The defaults provide you with access to commonly used .NET Framework functionality, but the .NET Framework provides significantly more functionality than the default settings let you see. For example, you can interact directly with the ports on your system or manipulate XML files on the hard drive. It's possible to visit a Web service, download and modify some data, and then display the data to the user. In fact, if you can think of it, you can probably do it, but you can't do it all the time with the built-in Cmdlets and scripts. The solution to this problem is to create your own scripts and Cmdlets.

This chapter provides an overview of how to customize PowerShell to meet your needs. Of course, achieving this goal means delving further into the .NET Framework and learning some new skills. In this case, you'll discover how to create scripts and then Cmdlets. Most administrators will never need to create a Cmdlet because PowerShell scripts provide amazing flexibility. It's still a good idea to know how to create both kinds of applications.

Creating a New Shell Extension

You can create extended command shells for the PowerShell environment. The Make-Shell utility (also know as the make-kit) helps you create these extensions. You use this utility to add the Cmdlets you create to the shell so that you can execute them directly from the command line, as you would execute any other command. The Make-Shell utility always creates an executable file as output.

The Make-Shell utility used to appear as part of the PowerShell installation program. However, Microsoft moved this utility to the Windows SDK because most users create snap-ins for PowerShell rather than create their own shell. To obtain the Make-Shell utility, you must download the Windows SDK at `http://www.microsoft.com/downloads/details.aspx?FamilyId=C2B1E300-F358-4523-B479-F53D234CDCCF`. The Windows SDK includes

✦ Shell examples using C#

✦ All the required reference assemblies

✦ `Make-shell.EXE`

✦ The required templates (`Format.PS1XML` and `Types.PS1XML`)

✦ The documentation (getting-started guide, programmer's guide, conceptual help, and managed reference)

Part of the reason you want to know about this utility is that it helps you understand how you can modify PowerShell, even if you don't intend to modify it yourself. For example, you might choose to use a custom authorization manager (the part of PowerShell that verifies the user's identify) — one that meets company policy. The authorization manager could provide additional restrictions based on your network setup or other requirements. You also find a wealth of other items you can change in this section. Consequently, it's helpful to go through the list of command line switches provided with this utility even if you never plan to create a new shell extension yourself.

Now that you have an idea of what you need in order to work with this utility, it's time to look at how it works. This utility uses the following syntax:

```
make-shell -out n.exe -namespace ns
    [-lib libdirectory1[,libdirectory2,..] ]
    [-reference ca1.dll[,ca2.dll,...] ]
    [-formatdata fd1.format.mshxml[,fd2.format.mshxml,...] ]
    [-typedata td1.type.mshxml[,td2.type.mshxml,...] ]
    [ -source c1.cs [,c2.cs,...]]
    [ -authorizationmanager authorizationManagerType ]
    [ -win32icon i.ico ] [ -initscript p.PS ]
    [ -builtinscript s1.PS[,s2.PS,...] ]
    [ -resource resourcefile.txt ] [ -cscflags cscFlags ]
    [-verbose] [ -? | -help ]
```

Of all these arguments, you must provide the output information and the namespace information. Of course, to get usable output, you must provide a list of source files or other code for the utility to use when creating a shell extension. The following list describes each of the command line arguments.

✦ **-out n.exe:** Specifies the name of the shell that you want to produce. You must specify the path as part of this argument. The Make-Shell utility automatically appends .EXE to the filename if you don't specify it.

✦ **-namespace ns:** Specifies the namespace to use for the RunspaceConfiguration table and the main() function that the Make-Shell utility generates and compiles for you. The main() function is the entry point for the executable.

✦ **-lib libdirectory1[,libdirectory2,..]:** Specifies the directories to search for .NET assemblies that your Cmdlet requires in order to run. You don't need to specify this command line switch for assemblies that appear in the Global Assembly Cache (GAC) or in the current directory. You may need to use this command line switch for any PowerShell assemblies you reference.

**Book VI
Chapter 4**

Creating Your Own
Scripts and Cmdlets

Always include this argument for assemblies that you access with the -reference command line switch unless the assemblies appear in the GAC. You must also provide directory entries for any assemblies that a main assembly references that don't appear in the GAC.

✦ **-reference ca1.dll[,ca2.dll,...]:** Specifies the assemblies you want to include in the shell. Don't include system or .NET Framework assemblies in this list; the Make-Shell utility finds these assemblies automatically. Reserve this command line switch for special assemblies that the Cmdlet requires to run, that contain the Cmdlet, and that contain resources used by the Cmdlet. If you don't include this command line shell, the resulting executable contains only the intrinsic Cmdlets (those produced by the PowerShell team). You may specify the references using a full path. Otherwise, use the -lib command line switch to provide the path information as needed.

✦ **-formatdata fd1.format.mshxml[,fd2.format.mshxml,...]:** Provides a comma-separated list of format data to include as part of the shell. If you don't include this command line switch, the resulting shell contains only the intrinsic format data (those produced by the PowerShell team). The current shell provides formatting for text and serialized XML.

✦ **-typedata td1.type.mshxml[,td2.type.mshxml,...]:** Provides a comma-separated list of type data to include as part of the shell. If you don't include this command line switch, the resulting shell contains only the intrinsic format data (those produced by the PowerShell team).

✦ **-source c1.cs [,c2.cs,...]:** Specifies the names of the source files to use to create the shell additions. The source code must appear as C# code. The code can provide any functionality that you want to include at the command line.

In addition to the code required to provide the new shell functionality, the code may include an Authorization Manager implementation that overrides the default Authorization Manager. You can also supply the Authorization Manager information (when you want to override the Authorization Manager) by using the -authorizationmanager command line switch. The code can also include a number of assembly informational declarations, including the overrides in the following list:

- AssemblyCompanyAttribute
- AssemblyCopyrightAttribute
- AssemblyFileVersionAttribute
- AssemblyInformationalVersionAttribute
- AssemblyProductAttribute
- AssemblyTrademarkAttribute

✦ **-authorizationmanager authorizationManagerType:** Defines the type in a source code (C#) file or a compiled assembly that the new shell should use as an Authorization Manager. The new shell will use the default Authorization Manager when you don't specify this command line switch or include an Authorization Manager as part of the shell source code. When you do specify a new type, you must include the full type name, including any required namespaces.

✦ **-win32icon i.ico:** Specifies the name of the file containing the icon you want to use for the new shell. (The icon file can contain multiple icons, one for each major resolution, if desired.) The new shell will use the C# compiler icon (if any) when you don't specify this command line switch.

✦ **-initscript p.PS:** Specifies the startup profile for the new shell. The Make-Shell utility doesn't verify this file in any way. Consequently, a faulty profile can prevent the new shell from running. A user can always override the default shell that you provide using the -NoProfile command line switch for the PowerShell utility. Therefore, you shouldn't assume that the profile you provide is absolute, even when the profile works as anticipated.

✦ **-builtinscript s1.PS[,s2.PS,...]:** Defines a list of built-in scripts for the shell. The new shell discovers these scripts before it discovers scripts in the path. The scripts you provide as part of this command line switch are absolute; the user can't change them.

The Make-Shell utility doesn't validate the scripts in any way. Consequently, even though an errant script won't keep the new shell from running, it causes problems when the user attempts to run the script.

✦ **-resource resourcefile.txt:** Specifies a text file containing the resources that the shell uses. You must name the first resource ShellHelp. This resource contains the Help text that the user sees when using the -help command line argument. It's possible to use this feature to add specific help for your custom Cmdlets and scripts. The ShellHelp resource doesn't affect the output of the Help command used to display Help for a particular shell command.

The second resource is ShellBanner. This resource contains the text and copyright information that appears when the user invokes the shell in interactive mode. The new shell uses a generic help banner when you don't provide these overrides.

✦ **-cscflags cscFlags:** Determines which flags the C# compiler (CSC.EXE, located in the .NET Framework directory) receives as part of compiling the new shell. The Make-Shell passes these command line switches to the compiler unchanged. Always surround this command line switch with quotes. Otherwise, the Make-Shell utility may not pass all the C# compiler command line switches and the compilation process will fail.

✦ **-verbose:** Displays detailed information during the shell creation process. The Make-Shell utility created the detailed information, so the output won't include any details of the C# compilation. If you want to see details of the C# compilation, you need to include additional command line switches for the C# compiler.

Creating a PowerShell Script

PowerShell supports both scripts and Cmdlets. A *script* is a series of commands contained in a text file that PowerShell interprets. It's possible to execute scripts from the command line or make them part of the shell using the Make-Shell utility, described in the "Creating a New Shell Extension" section of this chapter. A *Cmdlet* is a compiled executable in DLL format. As you do with the script, you begin with a text file containing commands that the C# Compiler (CSC) turns into an executable. To use a Cmdlet, you must make it part of the shell by using the Make-Shell utility.

This chapter doesn't provide a description of the PowerShell scripting language or its programming elements, but it shows you how to use them to create a script. You can find a listing of commands and some usage details in Book VI, Chapter 3. The authoritative resource for the PowerShell scripting language is the current documentation available from Microsoft at http://www.microsoft.com/downloads/details.aspx?FamilyId=B4720B00-9A66-430F-BD56-EC48BFCA154F. In fact, you may want to review the entire list of Microsoft resources for PowerShell at http://www.microsoft.com/technet/scriptcenter/hubs/msh.mspx.

Most administrators will want to start working with PowerShell scripts before they move on to working with Cmdlets. The following sections describe how to create a basic script and run it at the command line. If you want to add the script to the shell, add it by using the -initscript or -builtinscript command line switches of the Make-Script utility. The scripts then become part of the shell, and you can use them whenever you want.

Working with scripts and shells

Scripts and shells represent two different levels of working with PowerShell. When you create a script, you don't need to compile it. The system interprets the script, and you work with it interactively at the command line. Unless you build a script into the shell, you can change it in an ad hoc manner until you get it right. Scripts consist of simple text that PowerShell executes for you. They replace the batch files and JavaScript scripts that you used in the past. Unlike these older alternatives, however, PowerShell scripts are quite functional and powerful. You have the full functionality of the .NET Framework readily available.

A *shell,* on the other hand, is executable code. A shell contains a number of intrinsic (built-in) commands supplied by the PowerShell development team. A shell also includes any number of extrinsic commands that you create as Cmdlets. You add a Cmdlet to PowerShell by building a new shell to house it. Only after you create the new shell can you test the Cmdlet. PowerShell doesn't know anything about the Cmdlet until you perform both a compilation and a shell creation process.

Unlike the command line of old, scripts and Cmdlets aren't necessarily mutually exclusive. You can build a script, test it for a while, add functionality as needed, and eventually turn it into a Cmdlet if you want. In other words, you can now follow a distinct process to progress from quite simple and ad hoc to complex and part of the shell. Unlike the old static CMD.EXE, PowerShell.EXE is fully extensible, so you can create the environment you want rather than live with the environment that Microsoft thinks you need. Consequently, scripts and shells require a different viewpoint in PowerShell because what you build today can easily become part of the environment tomorrow.

Creating a simple script

As with most scripts, a PowerShell script is simply a series of executable statements that the system interprets to perform tasks. However, a Power-Shell script is built on a combination of the C# language, special objects that the PowerShell developers create for you, the .NET Framework, and any special Cmdlets you create. You can find a great overview of the language on the ars technica Web site at http://arstechnica.com/guides/other/msh.ars. If you want the short version, check out the basic list of elements on Arul Kumaravel's WebLog at http://blogs.msdn.com/arulk/archive/2005/02/24/379732.aspx.

Script files are text files with a PS1 file extension. The file must have a PS1 extension to execute it as a script. If you give the file some other extension and load it, PowerShell doesn't execute it.

A PowerShell script can include a wealth of features. As with any command line script, you can include any command that the command interpreter supports as well as calls to utilities. In addition, PowerShell scripts support all the same statements that full-fledged programming languages do, including both conditional and looping statements. Unlike in JavaScript, PowerShell scripts also include the concept of data type.

It's time to look at a scripting example. Remember that scripts are essentially commands linked together, so any of the examples in the other chapters of this minibook can also work as scripts. Listing 4-1 shows how to map a network drive by using a PowerShell script.

Listing 4-1: Mapping a Network Drive with PowerShell

```
#Input arguments Local Drive and Network UNC location.
Param ($DriveLtr - "", $UNCName = "")

# Detect the correct number of input arguments.
if (($DriveLtr -eq "") -or ($UNCName -eq ""))
{
    # Detect a request for command line help.
    if ($DriveLtr -eq "/?")
    {
        # Display the help information
        [system.console]::Out.WriteLine(
            "Usage: MapNetwork <letter> <UNC target>")

        # Exit the script and provide an error level of 1 to
        # indicate a help request.
        return(1)
    }
    else
    {
        # Ask whether the user wants to continue.
        [system.console]::Out.WriteLine(
        "No input provided! Provide it interactively? [Y | N]")
        $Answer = [system.console]::In.ReadLine()

        # If the user doesn't want to continue, display help
        # and exit. Use an exit code of 2 to indicate a data
        # entry error.
        if ($Answer -eq "N")
        {
```

(continued)

Listing 4-1 *(continued)*

```
        [system.console]::Out.WriteLine(
            "Usage: MapNetwork <letter> <UNC target>")
        return(2)
    }

    # Input the drive letter.
        [system.console]::Out.WriteLine(
            "Type the local drive letter (X:).");
        $DriveLtr = [system.console]::In.ReadLine();

    # Input the UNC drive on the remote machine.
        [system.console]::Out.WriteLine(
            "Type the UNC location (\\MyServer\MyDrive).");
        $UNCName = [system.console]::In.ReadLine();
    }
}

# Define the network object used to map the drive.
$oNetwork = new-object -COM WScript.Network

# Attempt to create the connection.
Trap [Exception]
{
    # Display an error when the task fails.
    [system.console]::Out.WriteLine("Couldn't map the drive!")
    [system.console]::Out.WriteLine($_.Exception.Message)
    return 3
}

# Perform the drive mapping function.
$oNetwork.MapNetworkDrive($DriveLtr, $UNCName);
```

As with any script, you can provide input arguments for a PowerShell script. In this case, the input arguments include the drive letter you want to assign and the Universal Naming Convention (UNC) path to the remote path. The user must provide both input values to map a drive — just as you provide these values when working with the IDE.

Notice the way that this example creates the input arguments. Rather than access an argument list as you might do with JavaScript, this example simply places the values directly in the variables, which ends up saving time because you don't have to check the argument list several times before you can even create the variables.

The example uses the pound sign (#) for comments. Always make sure that your code includes plenty of comments, or else you might not be able to figure out how your script works later.

In addition, you might notice the odd method of performing logical operations with `-eq` (for equals) and `-or` (for or). You'll find a complete list of these logical operators in the Getting Started document provided as part of the PowerShell documentation. All variables in a PowerShell script must begin with the dollar sign ($), as shown in the example.

For anyone who has worked with the .NET Framework, the `[system.console]::Out.WriteLine()` method call will look familiar, and that's precisely what it is. The example makes a call to the console class of the system namespace. The console class contains an `Out` property that's actually a container for the standard output stream. The stream object includes the `WriteLine()` method that the example uses to output text. You can use any .NET Framework feature in precisely the same way, which means that PowerShell has a very large list of language features from which to choose.

One feature that differs from standard .NET application coding is the lack of a try...catch structure. When working with PowerShell, you use `Trap` instead. It relies on the .NET Framework exception classes. After you set a trap, it remains in effect until it either goes out of scope or you set another trap. To access the data that the exception provides, you use the `$_.Exception` property, followed by the exception property that you want to access. The example simply displays the Message property so that the user knows what happened during an attempted drive mapping.

PowerShell can use COM objects, just as JavaScript scripts do. In this example, the script creates the `WScript.Network` object. To perform this task in PowerShell, you must use the `new-object` Cmdlet and call it with the -COM command line switch. The result is the `$oNetwork` object that calls the `MapNetworkDrive()` method using the same syntax as you would when working with JavaScript. The `Trap` statement that appears before the `MapNetworkDrive()` method call provides error-trapping in this case.

**Book VI
Chapter 4**

Creating Your Own Scripts and Cmdlets

Running the script

You're ready to try a script. However, running a script with PowerShell is nothing like running a script under the old command line. You can't simply type the script name and let the process take over. This section assumes that you're testing the script shown in Listing 4-1. Create the script using Notepad and save it to disk as `MapNetwork.PS1`. The following steps describe how to perform this process:

1. **Type** get-content MapNetwork.PS1 **and press Enter.**

This first step loads the script into memory. You must load the script in order for it to work. Now that you have the script loaded into memory, you can execute it.

2. **Type** ./MapNetwork **and press Enter.**

At this point, you're probably seeing the error message shown in Figure 4-1. The default PowerShell setting doesn't allow you to execute any scripts. You have to make a decision now. The issue is which level of script to allow on your system. Before you disable the protection that PowerShell provides, consider using the security to your advantage and set the system to execute only signed scripts.

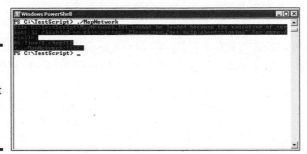

Figure 4-1: PowerShell scripts don't run without the proper permission.

3. **Type** Get-ExecutionPolicy **and press Enter to see the current execution policy.**

The default setting is restricted. If your system has some other setting, make sure to return your system to that setting after you complete this chapter.

4. **Type** Set-ExecutionPolicy Unrestricted **and press Enter.**

You have set your system to run any kind of script. Of course, you want to use this setting only on a test system where outside forces can't access it. See the "Defining a Script Policy" section of this chapter for a description of the various policies you can use for scripts.

Now that you have the permission problem solved with PowerShell, try running the script again. This time, the script tells you that it requires input. You can add the required input and map a drive. The script also accepts the input arguments from the command line. Try entering incorrect arguments and you'll find that the exception handling works fine, too.

Defining a Script Policy

You might think that the default PowerShell setup of not running any scripts is terrible. However, consider how many users have downloaded scripts from the Internet and run them without having any idea of what the script could do or even that they were downloading a script. It's important to consider how scripts running amok on user machines create infections that waste everyone's time and energy, not to mention that damage both systems and data. In fact, you might have been involved in cleaning up such a problem at some time in the past. Consequently, you need to weigh this factor against the few minutes required to sign your script so that the system knows that it's safe to execute. Most companies today have a zero-tolerance policy regarding executable content because it has become too expensive to continually clean infected machines.

Generally speaking, you should maintain the default Restricted policy of not running any scripts for all users on the network. If users don't run scripts, you don't need to worry about them loading something that will destroy their machine even accidentally. The following list describes the policy levels you can use to run scripts:

✦ **AllSigned:** When you must allow the user to run scripts, set the policy to AllSigned. With the policy at the AllSigned level, the user can't run a script unless someone you trust signs it. You can set the policy so that only scripts signed by someone at your company run on the user machine. Using only signed scripts on user machines ensures that you know who created the script and understand the potential pitfalls of using the script.

✦ **RemoteSigned:** Administrators and developers will likely want to share code from time to time. You should still ensure that someone has signed the code. Consequently, setting the policy to RemoteSigned can make sense for those who have more knowledge about Windows and need to execute code that someone else created. In most cases, you want to use this level with care because anyone can send you a signed script and your system will execute it, even if the individual used fake credentials.

✦ **Unrestricted:** The final level of script policies that let you execute a script is Unrestricted. Using the Unrestricted level is the same as returning to previous versions of Windows, where you don't have any protection. PowerShell allows you to shoot yourself in the foot, but why do it? Always keep your system safe by using signed code.

Creating a PowerShell Cmdlet

PowerShell uses an object-oriented strategy for running code. Part of that strategy is the use of scripts — the method you use to write the vast majority of your applications. However, sometimes a script won't answer the requirement. You might want to create an application that performs complex tasks and can therefore benefit from compilation rather than wait for the command line to interpret it at runtime. The second type of PowerShell application is a Cmdlet. Unlike with a script, you always create a Cmdlet as compiled code, and it always appears as part of the shell. Consequently, a Cmdlet represents a significant investment in additional coding time.

Many administrators want a quick overview of the PowerShell scripting language and want to know how it compares to the existing Windows Scripting Host (WSH) technology. You can find an excellent overview of this topic at http://arstechnica.com/guides/other/msh.ars/2. One feature that most administrators will find interesting is that all Cmdlets inherit the same base class, which means that they all use the same methods, parse the arguments in the same way, and output data using the same PowerShell framework. Consequently, Cmdlets offer a significant level of consistency over other scripting technologies.

The following sections describe tasks you must perform in addition to creating a C# file containing the Cmdlet code. Showing how to create a C# application is outside the scope of this book. However, if you know how to create a C# console application, you also know how to create a PowerShell Cmdlet. You can't use script code to create a Cmdlet.

Compiling the Cmdlet executable

Before you can do anything with the Cmdlet, you must create an executable. You can perform this task as part of the Make-Shell utility, but it's easier to perform the compilation as a separate step. Start this section at the Power-Shell command line.

The first task you need to perform is to create an alias for the C# compiler. This compiler appears in the .NET Framework folder on your machine. Creating an alias makes the compiler accessible by typing a simple command, CSC, as the command line. Here's the command for creating the alias on my system; you need to change the directory for CSC.EXE to match your system. Remember to use the .NET Framework 2.0 version of the CSC command; the older versions won't work (even though the entry appears on two lines in the book, you must type them on one line):

```
set-alias csc
 C:\WINDOWS\Microsoft.NET\Framework\v2.0.50727\csc.exe
```

The next step is to create a variable to reference the required libraries for your Cmdlet. Here's the command for creating a reference variable (even though the entry appears on two lines in this book, you must type them on one line).

```
$ref = "C:\Program Files\Microsoft Command
    Shell\v1.0\System.Management.Automation.Dll"
```

A Cmdlet can use any number of libraries. You must provide a single reference that lists all libraries for your Cmdlet. Separate each of the references with a semicolon.

At this point, you can compile the executable by using the C# compiler. You need to tell the compiler the following information:

✦ The kind of output you want to create (a library or DLL in this case)

✦ The name of the input file

✦ The name of the output file

✦ The names of any libraries that the Cmdlet needs

as shown in the following example (even though the entry appears on two lines in the book, you must type them on one line).

```
csc /target:library /out:MyCmdlet.dll MyCmdlet.cs /reference:
    $ref
```

The compiler displays a logo as a minimum. If the file contains errors or you miss a library reference, you also see error messages. In general, you can now create a new shell with the resulting library.

Using the Make-Shell utility to create the shell

It's time to create the new shell. You use the Make-Shell utility to perform this task. The following command line creates the new shell for this example (even though the entry appears on two lines in the book, you must type the entire entry on one line):

```
make-shell -out NewShell -ns MyCompany.Cmdlets
 -reference MyCmdlet.dll
```

This command line represents a minimal implementation. You must specify the output filename, the namespace for the shell, and the list of any DLLs you want to add as Cmdlets. The output is an executable named NewShell.EXE.

Before you can use the new shell, you must provide a registry entry for it. You can perform this task at the command line, but it's easier to use the Registry Editor to perform it in this case. Select Start⇨Run. You see the Run dialog box. Type **RegEdit** and click OK. You need to add a new key to the HKEY_LOCAL_MACHINE\SOFTWARE\Microsoft\PS\1\ShellIds key. In fact, you have to add a new key every time you create a new shell.

Let's say that you use a namespace of MyCompany.Cmdlets and a shell name of NewShell. To add the required registry entry, you create a key named MyCompany.Cmdlets.NewShell. This key contains two values, both of which are strings. The first value, ExecutionPolicy, contains one of the values described in the "Defining a Script Policy" section of this chapter. The second value, Path, contains the path to the new shell you just created. It's best if you place the new shell and any associated DLLs in the `\Program Files\ Microsoft Command Shell\v1.0` folder, if possible. The Path value on my system points to the `C:\Program Files\Microsoft Command Shell\v1.0\NewShell.EXE` folder.

Now that you have the registry values in place, you can start the new shell. You can choose one of two techniques. The first is to double-click the executable for the new shell you created. The second method is to type the name of the shell at an existing command line prompt. The system creates a new shell, and you can begin using it immediately. In either case, you should be able to execute your Cmdlet.

Part VII

IIS

The 5th Wave   By Rich Tennant

"We've got a machine over there that monitors
our quality control. If it's not working, just
give it a couple of kicks."

Contents at a Glance

Chapter 1: Understanding the New Interface

In This Chapter

✔ **Using the Start page**

✔ **Understanding application pools**

✔ **Considering the FTP site configuration differences**

✔ **Understanding the new IIS icons**

The first view you'll see of Internet Information Server (IIS) 7 is a completely new interface. In fact, the interface is so different that you may think you opened the wrong console. Microsoft has completely revamped the IIS 7 interface to make it easier to use. However, after offering essentially the same interface for IIS versions since IIS 4, the change will elicit a negative response from administrators who know the well-entrenched methods of performing tasks. Don't worry: The new interface is an improvement, and you'll find that you'll make the transition quickly. This situation is one of the few in which Microsoft has made an interface change that's easy to make — and that nets you a quick productivity bonus because it's so straightforward.

You may wonder why Microsoft decided to change an IIS interface that has obviously worked well for many years. The reasons are many, but the basic reason is that IIS 7 supports the .NET Framework directly. No longer will you find yourself performing odd rituals to get your ASP.NET applications to run correctly. IIS 7 supports managed applications of all types directly out of the package.

A second important reason for the change is performance in the form of security, reliability, and speed. IIS 7 improves security by embracing the additional security supported by the .NET Framework. IIS 7 improves reliability by using a modular approach to load only the features you're using at any given time — fewer parts translates to improved reliability. Finally, because IIS 7 improves security and enhances reliability, while loading only what you need, you find that it runs a given application package significantly faster than the same configuration under IIS 6.

Understanding the Vista difference

Vista also includes IIS 7. Unfortunately, it's not quite the IIS 7 that you see in Windows Server 2008. Most features are the same. For example, when you configure an ASP.NET application in Vista, it's the same as configuring the application in Windows Server 2008. So, if you've already begun learning to use IIS 7 in Vista, you haven't wasted your time, but you need to discover a few new features to transition to Windows Server 2008.

Most of the new settings provide security that people felt is missing from Vista. For example, the Windows Server 2008 version of IIS 7 includes a new Machine Key icon for controlling the encryption and hashing settings for ASP.NET applications and services. The IPv4 Address and Domain Restrictions icon helps you control server access by allowing or denying access by specific IPv4 addresses or domains.

Some new settings control content. The HTTP Redirect icon lets you redirect a target destination to another location on the server. You can also add new response handlers to the output of your server by using the HTTP Response Handlers icon. You'll also find a new Compression icon you can use to control how IIS 7 compresses files of all types. File compression can save considerable space on the server.

A few settings fall into the administration category. The Logging icon helps you control the log files on the server. The Output Caching Rules icon provides settings that can make your server run faster by keeping certain pages in memory for faster access. The IIS Manager Permissions and IIS Manager Users icons control who can administer the server and their permissions while managing it. The Management Service icon controls how users access IIS 7. Finally, the Shared Configuration icon lets you use a configuration from another server to configure the current server. Any changes on that remote server also appear on the local server, so you end up managing just one server.

All these changes will eventually appear in Vista. In fact, you should probably look for additional changes to IIS 7 as Microsoft releases service packs. In addition, Microsoft will eventually need to add FTP management to the IIS 7 interface. Because the IIS 7 interface is so new, you can count on it to change for now.

This chapter explores the new IIS 7 interface. You get an overview of what makes IIS 7 different from its predecessors. The remaining chapters in this minibook provide you with basic usage details — everything you need to configure your IIS 7 installation and provide basic application support. Unfortunately, describing IIS 7 in detail requires an entire book. If you need a complete description of IIS 7, along with detailed, low-level, usage details, you should obtain my book *IIS 7 Implementation and Administration* (Sybex, 2007).

Working with the Start Page

The place to begin working with IIS 7 is the Internet Information Services (IIS) Manager console, found in the Administrative Tools folder. IIS 7 includes a new start page that helps you get to where you need to go quite quickly. Figure 1-1 shows the start page. In this case, it has the IIS News feature enabled. The default setting has the IIS News feature disabled. Click the Enable IIS News link to enable IIS News. You see the latest IIS 7 information every time you start the Internet Information Services (IIS) Manager console.

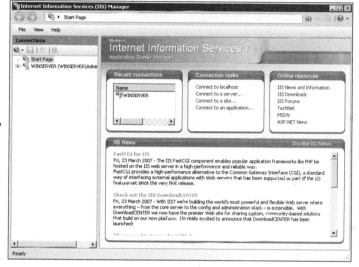

Figure 1-1: Choose the language and input options for using Windows Server 2008.

The left side of the display contains a hierarchical view of the entire server. You can use it to drill down to any level of the server. The right side of the display contains several panes for making quick connections, as described in the following list:

✦ **Recent Connections:** Contains a list of the servers you've recently managed.

✦ **Connection Tasks:** Contains a number of connection task links. Clicking a link displays a wizard that helps you create the required connection.

✦ **Online Resources:** Displays a series of links to Help information online.

✦ **IIS News:** Updates automatically to show the most recent information Microsoft provides about IIS 7. The news display often tells you about free products you can obtain. In some cases, the products are completely free, but in many cases, the products are free for a specific number of sites. If you want to use the products for an additional number of sites, you must pay a fee that varies by product.

Considering Application Pools

Every Web server has one or more application pools that it uses to run applications. You can find the list of application pools in the `<Web Server Name>\Application Pools` folder, as shown in Figure 1-2.

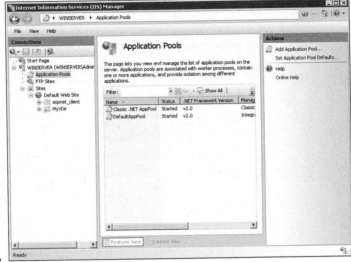

The default IIS 7 installation comes with two pools:

✦ Classic .NET AppPool, where the server runs ASP.NET applications

✦ DefaultAppPool, where the server runs static applications and other traditionally unmanaged code

The idea behind application pools is a good one. The applications on your server execute within a particular area of memory defined by an application pool. Applications from different application pools don't interact and, consequently, can't cause damage to each other. In addition, because each application can have its own application pool, you can control, among other things, the memory used by that application. In short, application pools provide an environment in which applications can execute safely, reliably, and efficiently.

IIS 7 isn't the first version of IIS to use application pools. They first appeared in IIS 6. You can read about the IIS 6 application pools at `http://www.microsoft.com/technet/prodtechnol/WindowsServer2003/Library/IIS/93ddbb51-5826-4ebd-a434-24c5fd103d3a.mspx`. IIS 6 application pools are the beginning of a solution to a problem where applications run in a single, large memory space. In this environment, an application with memory problems can easily overwrite the memory used by another application, causing it to crash. The problem can continue, causing a cascade reaction until the server simply gives up and freezes. Immediately after the reboot, the whole process can begin anew.

You'd think that Microsoft would come up with a foolproof way of fixing the problem, but it really hasn't. Memory errors still occur. However, the combination of the managed environment and application pools make memory corruption unlikely — someone would have to make an effort to make it occur. The immediate benefit of using a combination of managed applications and application pools then is to ensure that one application can't cause another application to crash, at least through memory corruption. Separating one application from another is a very good idea.

Understanding FTP Site Configuration

You won't find your FTP site in the Internet Information Services (IIS) Manager console. Instead, Microsoft has chosen to continue using the IIS 6 model for FTP servers. Consequently, you manage FTP sites by using the Internet Information Services (IIS) 6.0 Manager, as shown in Figure 1-3. If this console looks familiar, it is. The same procedures you use to manage an FTP site in IIS 6 running on Windows 2003 also work on Windows Server 2008.

Figure 1-3:
FTP server management hasn't changed in Windows Server 2008.

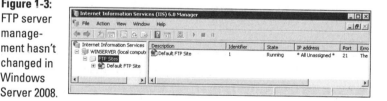

Considering the IIS Icons

Working with IIS 7 is all about knowing which icon to use to access a particular feature. You no longer have to drill down multiple levels to find a feature — it appears as an icon, as shown in Figure 1-4. Notice that the icons appear in groups, such as ASP.NET, by default. The Internet Information Services (IIS) Manager console lets you group the icons by using the Group By list.

Figure 1-4:
IIS 7 doesn't bury configuration settings, making it easier to find what you need.

The icons also appear at various levels. Each level controls a particular aspect of your server. Deeper levels provide control over the details of a site, and upper levels provide configuration for the server as a whole. IIS 7 supports the following configuration levels:

✦ **Web server:** Configures all the Web sites on the server and the server itself. You use this level to provide an overall policy for the Web server and to delegate certain features to lower levels.

✦ **Web site:** Configures every aspect of a particular Web site. However, this level doesn't affect any other Web site on the system. Each Web site has its own configuration information. Any changes you make at this level override changes made at the Web server level. However, to make a change, the administrator in control of the Web server must delegate authority to make the change at this level.

✦ **Application or directory:** Controls the functionality of an application or the features that a directory provides. This level overrides the settings at the Web site level. The default setup doesn't provide any settings at this level, and normally you do most of your configuration at the Web site level.

In addition to the icons found in Features view, each level also has Content view, which shows you the folders and files at that level. You can use Content view to configure folder and file permissions as well as to discover more about the folder or file you selected. Content view doesn't let you edit files as you would in Windows Explorer — you must perform certain tasks by using Windows Explorer or the command line.

Double-clicking an icon shows the settings for that particular feature. For example, when you double-click .NET Compilation, you see the settings for compiling ASP.NET applications at the selected level. The following sections describe each group and the icons (features) within each group.

An overview of the ASP.NET features

The features exposed by the ASP.NET icons work together to define the functionality, security, and management of ASP.NET applications. Microsoft has placed considerable emphasis on ASP.NET in IIS 7. Even though you can continue to build other application types, IIS 7 places considerable emphasis on ASP.NET and makes it quite easy to perform any level of configuration your application might require. The following sections describe each of the ASP.NET icons in detail.

.NET Compilation

When a developer creates a .NET application, the application itself remains in code form unless the developer precompiles it. When the first person requests the application from the Web site, the system compiles the code into an executable form. Subsequent requests use the executable rather than recompile it. Using this approach means that the user always sees an application compiled for the host machine rather than for the developer's machine.

Opening the .NET Compilation icon presents a list of configuration options for .NET applications, as shown in Figure 1-5. Some of these options control the application output, such as the Maximum File Size setting, which determines the maximum executable size (1 MB for the default setup). Developers use some of the settings, such as Debug, to correct application errors. It's also possible to control the assemblies that the application uses for resources, the default application programming language (Visual Basic), and the location of the temporary directory used for the compile process.

If you set the Temporary Directory field to use a different hard drive, the system can usually compile the application faster because it's using two different channels for the information it needs. However, you need to make sure that the second drive is physically different from the first drive. Using a different partition on the same hard drive won't yield any gain in compilation speed.

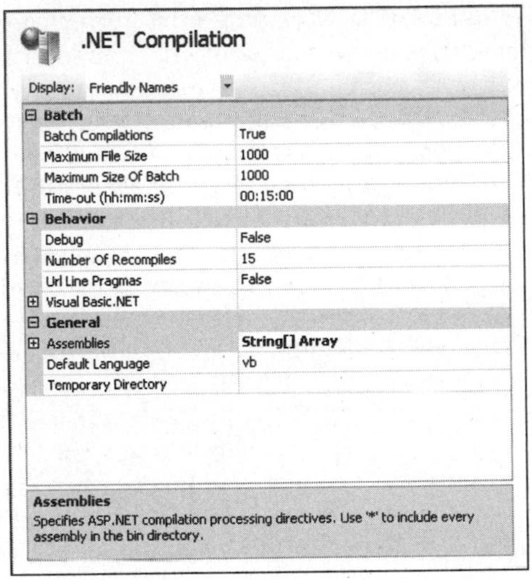

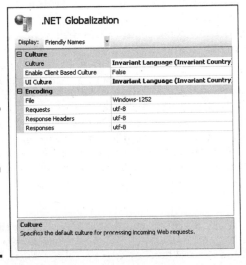

Figure 1-5:
Set the compilation settings to provide best application performance.

.NET Globalization

The .NET Globalization icon helps you configure the use of languages for the .NET application. The settings control how the server reacts to incoming requests and cues the application about the user's language so that it can provide the appropriate text strings. All language-specific features appear in the Culture group, as shown in Figure 1-6. If you set the Culture group settings as shown, IIS passes the user's culture information to the ASP.NET application and lets it determine how best to handle the user's language.

Figure 1-6:
Configure the globalization for your server to match the needs of the users.

As shown in Figure 1-6, globalization affects more than just the user's language and method of presenting information, such as numbers. Globalization also affects how the system encodes data for transmission. The most common encoding method is the Unicode Transformation Format (UTF), which commonly comes in two forms, UTF-8 and UTF-16. The Unicode Transformation Formats: UTF-8 & Co. Web site at `http://www.czyborra.com/utf/` tells you more about the UTF. Encoding comes in a vast array of forms, including Windows, International Business Machines (IBM), Code Page (CP), and International Standards Organization (ISO) forms. You can find an excellent tutorial on character sets and encoding at `http://www.cs.tut.fi/~jkorpela/chars.html`.

.NET Profile

The .NET Profile icon provides access to per user settings. A *per user* setting is a configuration option that affects one user but not another. You can set the configuration options by groups as well. For example, you might give all administrators a special setting that lets them control the debug feature of an application. A global setting, one that applies to everyone, might record the last person who made a change to the application configuration from within the application.

Settings rely on specific data types. For example, an application can't store a number in a date property. In addition, the settings are normally usable only by users who are logged in to the system, but you can make them available to anonymous users as well. Finally, you can make settings read/write or read-only. The read-only settings provide configuration, and the read/write settings provide the means to record state or other information.

.NET Roles

The .NET Roles icon displays a list of roles. A *role* describes a task that the user performs or a position that requires special application functionality. For example, a developer role might describe any number of positions within a company, but all these positions perform some type of application development task. An administrator role might describe anyone who manages the Web server in some way, even though the actual titles for these people differ.

The application must provide support for the roles it uses, so the developer generally creates the .NET roles for you. However, you should work with the developer to create roles that make sense for your organization.

.NET Trust Levels

The .NET Framework introduces the idea of code trust. Rather than place the full burden of security on the user, the .NET Framework also examines the code running on the system. When the code is fully trusted, it has complete access to the server and all its resources. Unfortunately, this level of trust is about the same as turning off the code-based security completely. In fact, the only time you should use the default setting of Full is when you're working with IIS on a development machine that has no outside access. Table 1-1 shows the .NET trust levels that IIS supports.

Table 1-1		.NET Trust Levels
Level	*Environment Where Used*	*Description*
Full	Only for development and local Web services needs	Provides no security for connected scenarios.
High	For connected scenarios within a firewall	Can be used within an intranet to serve content for people within your company. Using this setting provides minimal security, but prevents some actions that would compromise your system.
Medium	For applications that require good resource access on a private network	Possibly used on a network that provides connectivity only to trusted third parties. This setting provides moderate network protection, but doesn't provide enough for a public setting. Someone with talent, and given enough time, could probably bypass your security measures and gain access to your network.
Low	For working in a public access scenario	Provides good network protection. However, using this setting can also choke your application because it can't gain access to all the resources it needs unless both the developer and administrator work to configure the application correctly.
Minimal	Can also be called the paranoid setting	Used when you can't trust anyone or anything. It's so strict that you'll find that most applications don't even run. However, it ensures that your server remains safe.

.NET Users

Don't confuse the settings in the .NET Users icon with those used for standard Windows security. You use the options in this icon to configure .NET users, those that can access .NET applications. The user entries work with the .NET Framework's role-based security in that you assign users a role after you configure them.

Application Settings

Developers can create custom code that reacts to settings the administrator provides as part of an Application Settings icon entry. The entries for this icon consist of a name and value pair. The code reads the setting value by name and performs tasks based on the value provided. Even though this setup may seem simple, you can perform complex tasks with it, given the right environment.

Connection Strings

The Connection Strings icon provides information that tells applications how to connect to a database. IIS 7 uses a considerably easier method to create connection strings than previous versions of the product.

When you open the Connection Strings icon, you see a LocalSqlServer entry that IIS uses for authentication and other purposes. Don't change this connection. You also see options to add, remove, and edit database connections. When you add a new connection, you specify some very simple arguments to tell IIS where to find the database.

IIS also provides the means to define the credentials used to access the database, or you can choose to use Windows integrated security. Using custom strings lets you define complex database connectivity.

Machine Key

People who want to gain access to your data or your server will use any means possible to find out more about it. Any data you leave lying around, even temporary data, is a potential source of information for nefarious individuals or organizations. A machine key provides the means for hashing and encrypting data for application services. Using these security techniques keeps your system, its applications, and its data safer. When you open this icon, you see a display like the one shown in Figure 1-7.

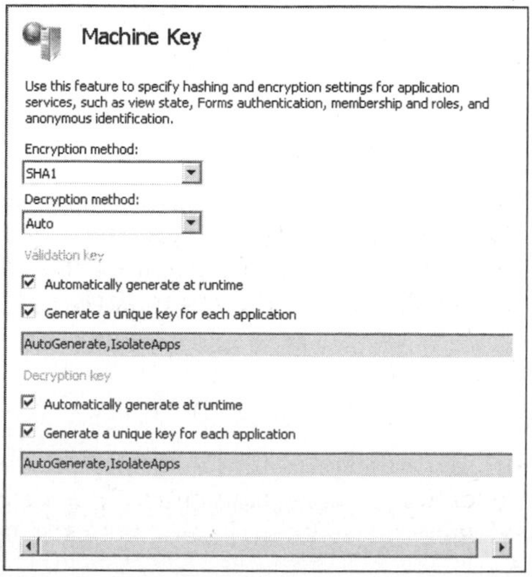

Figure 1-7:
Set your system to make even temporary data unreadable.

Machine Key

Use this feature to specify hashing and encryption settings for application services, such as view state, Forms authentication, membership and roles, and anonymous identification.

Encryption method:

| SHA1 | ▼ |

Decryption method:

| Auto | ▼ |

Validation key

☑ Automatically generate at runtime

☑ Generate a unique key for each application

| AutoGenerate,IsolateApps |

Decryption key

☑ Automatically generate at runtime

☑ Generate a unique key for each application

| AutoGenerate,IsolateApps |

All these settings control how the system works with the machine key to encrypt and hash data. *Encryption* is a two-way process where you make the data unreadable using one key and readable using another. *Hashing* is a one-way process where a piece of data is converted to a unique number. The sender performs the hash and sends the number to a recipient, who then compares the sender's number to one stored locally. The recipient knows that the data is correct without ever seeing the data. This technique is often used with passwords so that the sender need not expose the password to potential compromise.

Pages and Controls

The Pages and Controls icon works with new ASP.NET 2.0 features to provide your ASP.NET applications with a robust appearance. You can use this feature to define the master page and theme used for an application, as shown in Figure 1-8. In fact, you can use this feature to control many aspects of the ASP.NET 2.0 user interface.

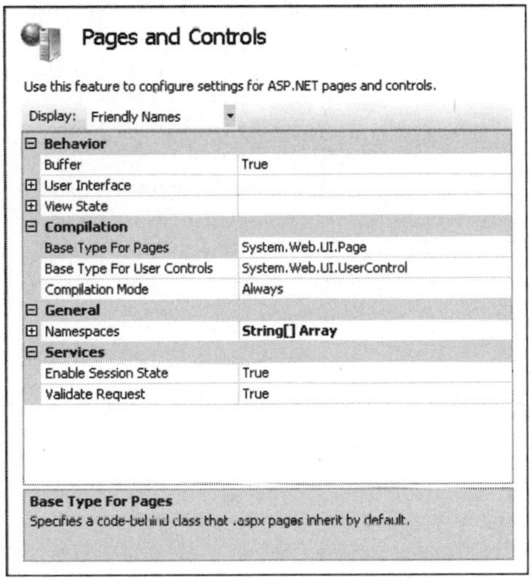

Figure 1-8:
Configure
the ASP.NET
2.0 features
by using this
dialog box.

[Pages and Controls dialog box screenshot]

Use this feature to configure settings for ASP.NET pages and controls.

Display: Friendly Names

Behavior	
Buffer	True
User Interface	
View State	
Compilation	
Base Type For Pages	System.Web.UI.Page
Base Type For User Controls	System.Web.UI.UserControl
Compilation Mode	Always
General	
Namespaces	**String[] Array**
Services	
Enable Session State	True
Validate Request	True

Base Type For Pages
Specifies a code-behind class that .aspx pages inherit by default.

Providers

A *provider* is a means of connecting a database to an application or another IIS feature. You begin with a connection string and then couple the connection to the application. The Providers icon contains a number of these entries by default, including those used for the .NET users, .NET roles, and .NET profiles.

The connection you create won't provide database connectivity of the usual sort — you won't use it for storing data. Instead, this provider helps you create a connection to a source of users, roles, and profiles for your application.

Session State

HTTP doesn't maintain any session information. When a user makes a request, the connection begins and ends with the request. The response is an entirely different communication, and any follow-up on requests are individual communications as well. Consequently, developers have created a number of different ways to maintain information about the conversation between the user and the server. Otherwise, you couldn't have applications, such as shopping carts, that require a means of tracking individual purchases. The information that defines the communication is called *state,* and the server maintains it for one communication stream called a *session*. The Session State icon, shown in Figure 1-9, provides access to the means of maintaining the session state on IIS.

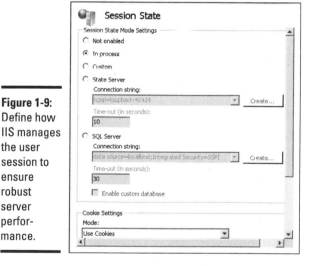

Figure 1-9: Define how IIS manages the user session to ensure robust server performance.

TIP

Some administrators miss an opportunity to improve the performance of their servers. If the Web site is only serving static data, the user doesn't need to maintain any type of session state. You can obtain a performance boost by setting the Session State Mode Settings option to Not Enabled.

Notice that you can modify features such as the means to maintain the state. For example, you can choose to use cookies to maintain the information. It's also possible to define how the server manages session state. For example, you could place the data within a database, but the default setting uses local memory for the task. Using memory increases consumption of this resource, but makes the application run faster.

Choose the server state settings with care. For example, you can use cookies only when you know that the client will have cookies enabled. A safer option for public Web sites is to detect the browser's ability to store cookies automatically or simply place the information within the Uniform Resource Identifier (URI).

SMTP E-mail

The SMTP E-mail icon helps you create connectivity between the server and the people administering it. The setup uses e-mail to send messages to the administrator, as shown in Figure 1-10.

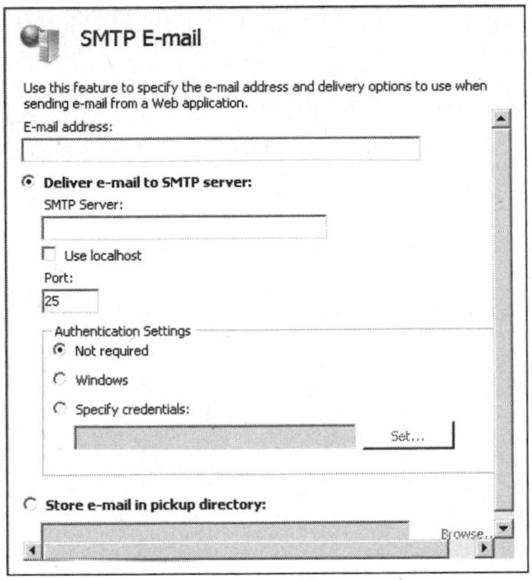

Figure 1-10: Create e-mail settings in IIS so that applications can send e-mail as needed.

The E-mail Address field contains the From portion of the e-mail message. The address tells the administrator that the message is authentic and not to reply to it because the server won't pick up the e-mail. You can also choose from several delivery methods, including

+ External server

+ Local server

+ E-mail folder on the server

Make sure to provide the proper credentials when using either an internal or an external Simple Mail Transfer Protocol (SMTP) server. Otherwise, the system simply generates error messages saying that it couldn't deliver the e-mails telling the administrator that something is wrong with the system.

An overview of the IIS features

The IIS icons control overall IIS functionality and provide support for non-ASP.NET applications. You use these icons much as you used the configuration features of previous versions of IIS. Although the positions of many of these configuration items have changed, you'll definitely notice some similarities as well, as described in the following sections.

ASP

Active Server Pages is a scripting language that lets you create moderately complex Web pages that include a level of intelligence. Even though ASP seems like it should be the predecessor to ASP.NET, the two technologies have little to do with each other. ASP.NET uses a few holdovers from ASP, but you really wouldn't recognize the similarities in most cases.

The ASP icon helps you configure ASP applications. Don't confuse these settings with those used for ASP.NET, because the two are completely different, as shown in Figure 1-11.

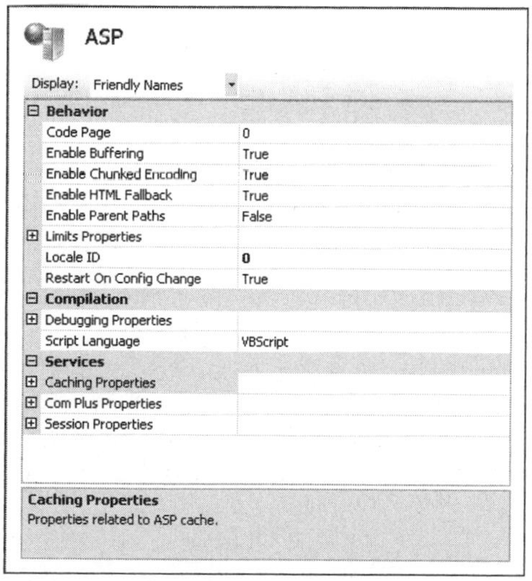

**Book VII
Chapter 1**

*Understanding the
New Interface*

Figure 1-11: Define the appropriate settings for your ASP applications.

You need to define how ASP presents information to the user. The code page (CP) defines the character set that ASP uses, which in turn affects the display of special characters used by many languages. A list of code pages that Windows uses appears at `http://www.microsoft.com/globaldev/reference/WinCP.mspx`. The Locale Identifier (LCID) identifies the user's location and controls the presentation of information, such as monetary amounts and dates. You can find a complete list of LCIDs for Windows at `http://krafft.com/scripts/deluxe-calendar/lcid_chart.htm`.

ASP provides extensive debugging configuration. This is because, unlike with ASP.NET, you won't have the Visual Studio .NET debugger help you locate errors. Many of the debugging features for ASP are on by default because you don't know when an error will occur.

Besides behavior and debugging issues, you can configure the services that ASP relies on to present information to the user. The default services include caching (to improve performance), COM+ (to provide business logic and database connectivity), and session (to control how the server interacts with the user).

Authentication

The Authentication icon controls how IIS performs security checks. The default setting of Anonymous doesn't perform any security checks — the server never knows who is accessing it. Users of older versions of IIS will recognize the basic, digest, and Windows authentication methods as three techniques that do determine who is accessing the system, but at varying levels of safety. The basic security level sends the username and password in clear text, which is almost like having no security because anyone can determine the required credentials using a simple *sniffer* (an application to read network packets). The Windows security method is most secure because it encrypts the user information and provides other checks to ensure that no one is spoofing the server.

IIS 7 defaults to using Anonymous Authentication mode. This mode performs no authentication of the user and leaves your server wide open to attack. A good first step in configuring IIS is to disable Anonymous Authentication and enable Windows Authentication (at least until you have everything set up).

IIS 7 adds ASP.NET impersonation and forms authentication. These two authentication methods can provide you with good alternatives to the old standbys when it comes to determining who is at the other end of the line. ASP.NET impersonation provides the same functionality as an ASP.NET application would provide, which means a combination of role-based and code-based security. The forms authentication method relies on multiple Web pages and redirection to perform its task. Forms authentication also sends the user information in clear text, but you can encrypt it using Secure Sockets Layer (SSL).

Authorization Rules

The Authorization Rules icon determines who can access what on the server. You can make the rules very specific by setting the authorization rules at the correct level. For example, you can enable access to one application or folder but disable access to another. The use of verbs helps you control precisely which kind of access the user and request, such as the ability to post data to the Web site but not get any data from it. It's important that you consider the level of configuration as well as the use of verbs when working with authorization rules.

IIS 7 defaults to letting anyone do anything anywhere they want. One of the first configuration tasks you should perform is to restrict access by removing All Users from the list and providing a list of trusted users who have the proper levels of access to the various Web server connections.

CGI

The Common Gateway Interface (CGI) is one of the oldest methods available for running applications on a Web server. To use this feature, you write scripts that perform actions on the user's behalf on the server. The CGI icon provides the few configuration options that IIS supports for CGI, including the ability to timeout when the script fails and a setting that controls CGI security.

Compression

The speed at which a Web server operates often hinges on the amount of bandwidth available and the efficiency with which the server uses the bandwidth to transmit data. The network bandwidth is often the performance bottleneck that makes or breaks a Web site. Using compression reduces the size of responses that the server sends to the caller. By using compression, the server can improve the efficiency of transmission and therefore make less bandwidth go further. The Compression icon controls how the server uses compression to improve performance.

Default Document

The Default Document icon provides a means of specifying the default document the user sees after providing just the domain and possibly a folder as the URL. You can also disable the use of default documents, in which case the user must enter the specific document name before seeing it on-screen.

Default documents can open security holes, in some cases, because they present information to others that may help them discover more about your Web setup. However, most public and private Web sites provide a default document to make it easier for the user to select content.

Directory Browsing

The Directory Browsing icon lets you control directory browsing (the ability to see folders and files) on the Web server. Normally, IIS 7 disables this feature due to the security risks. Anyone who can browse the directory structure of your server might find a way to circumvent your security.

The directory browsing feature provides benefits when you want to provide a download directory or other functionality where directory browsing is a requirement. The directory-browsing feature also lets you control what the user sees. The display elements include

+ Time
+ Size
+ Extension
+ Date
+ Long date (when available)

The user always sees filenames and an icon for each of the files. The icon identifies the file type and therefore the file extension. Most administrators frown on the use of directory browsing, and your Web server gains a security benefit when you don't enable it.

Error Pages

Whenever the server or an application encounters an error, the error generates an error code. The error code in turn triggers a specific response page on the server so that the user can see the error and react to it. The Error Pages icon lets you control the error pages that IIS uses to present error information.

IIS 7 hasn't changed its method of handling errors because the static Web page system seems to work fine. However, you don't have to continue using this method. You can also perform an action based on an error or redirect the user to a new URL. Because IIS provides great support for ASP.NET, you can now use ASP.NET applications to provide intelligent handling of errors.

The Error Pages icon provides support only for responses based on error codes. Applications often create their own error pages or use error codes that IIS doesn't understand natively. Make sure that you configure the server to handle unknown error codes, but don't defeat applications in their attempt to provide custom error responses.

Failed Request Tracing Rules

A failed request signifies that the server couldn't respond to a user request. In fact, the server generally provides an error page to signal the event. This particular error can happen for any reason, including a typo made by the user. In sum, a failed request need not signal a security failure (however, it can signal such an event). Most administrators don't track failed requests unless a user makes a complaint about not finding a particular resource or the administrator suspects that something is happening with the server.

IIS 7 doesn't come with any failed request tracing rules in place, so you need to add them using the Failed Request Tracing Rules icon. When you click Add in the Actions pane, you launch a wizard that takes you through the steps of configuring a failed request tracing rule. You can use these rules to track all content, ASP.NET, ASP, or custom content. The rule can check for a particular error code or even a request that takes too much time to complete (making it possible to use this technique to look for performance problems as well). Finally, you can configure the providers used to track the request and define the amount of information they provide.

Handler Mappings

A Web server doesn't know by instinct how to handle user requests — you must provide this information as a handler mapping. The mapping tells the server to use a particular application to answer a request based on the request's file extension. The Handler Mappings icon provides a way to support any file type as long as you have an application to support it.

The Handler Mappings window provides methods for enabling and disabling file extensions. This means that you can tell the server about a particular file extension and then insist that the server not handle it. Disabling extensions can provide a security benefit for your server by blocking requests that you never intended the server to support. An outsider, by simply making the right request could use known vulnerabilities to get your server to perform tasks that it normally wouldn't perform.

HTTP Redirect

Sometimes an administrator moves content from one location to another to better support an application or for other reasons. The administrator doesn't want a user who has the old URL to be disappointed, so the old location has a redirection set on it. Entering the old URL places the user automatically at the new location to obtain a response. The HTTP Redirect icon provides the means to redirect someone at any level. You can even redirect an entire server and send the user somewhere else.

HTTP Response Handlers

HTTP response headers tell a caller something about the server. For example, you might set a response header to tell the caller that your server normally uses ASP.NET as an application platform. You can see many of the standard response headers at `http://www.w3.org/Protocols/rfc2616/rfc2616-sec14.html`.

You use the HTTP Response Handlers icon to create custom response headers for your server. The default setup includes one custom header that tells the world that your server is powered by ASP.NET. Depending on how you work with IIS, you may want to remove this default header as either not reflecting the technology you use to develop Web sites or as a potential security risk.

IPv4 Address and Domain Restrictions

In some cases, you won't want to allow specific IPv4 or domains access to your server. Perhaps the callers from this address have caused problems in the past or you simply don't want to service requests from the location. The IPv4 Address and Domain Restrictions entry lets you create Allow and Deny entries that either allow or deny access to your server based on the IPv4 address or domain name.

Even though the Add Allow Restriction Rule and Add Deny Restriction Rule dialog boxes tell you that you can enter a domain name as a restriction, you can't enter one by default. You must enable this feature by clicking Edit Feature Settings and checking the Enable Domain Name Restrictions option in the Edit IP and Domain Restrictions Settings dialog box. However, using domain names is very expensive because the server must perform a reverse DNS lookup for every request to determine the IP address of the domain. It's far more efficient to enter the IP address rather than the domain name.

ISAPI and CGI Restrictions

IIS 7 requires you to enable both Internet Server Application Programming Interface (ISAPI) and CGI applications before you use them by using the ISAPI and CGI Restrictions icon. In short, because these technologies are old and untrusted, you must specifically tell IIS 7 to use them, which means that you must know about the application before anyone can use it. This restriction makes IIS significantly safer than ever, even while it lets you continue using older ISAPI and CGI applications when needed.

ISAPI Filters

ISAPI applications come in two forms: ISAPI extensions and ISAPI filters. An *ISAPI extension* handles requests, much like an ASP script, CGI script, or ASP.NET application does. All it provides is another method of performing the task. An *ISAPI filter* performs a different service for the server — one that isn't easy to replace with other technologies. Rather than answer requests, the ISAPI filter actually filters the content. For example, you could tell an ISAPI filter to review login requests for certain criteria and reject those that look like they might be from unreliable sources. Interestingly enough, the .NET Framework uses an ISAPI filter to look for ASP.NET requests. This filter is the only one that you find configured in IIS 7 by default.

To use any ISAPI filter, you must configure it using the ISAPI Filters icon. Click Add and you see a simple dialog box that asks for the filter name and executable name. When you click OK and restart the Web site, the filter becomes active and silently performs its task in the background. Generally, you don't have to configure ISAPI filters by hand because vendors who use them configure them for you as part of the installation routine.

Logging

Your server automatically logs many operations that take place. For example, every time someone requests a Web page, the server logs information about the request. These logs help you locate potential problem areas on your server and also monitor the activities of individuals with less than honorable intent. The Logging icon shows you the settings that IIS 7 uses for logging activities, as shown in Figure 1-12.

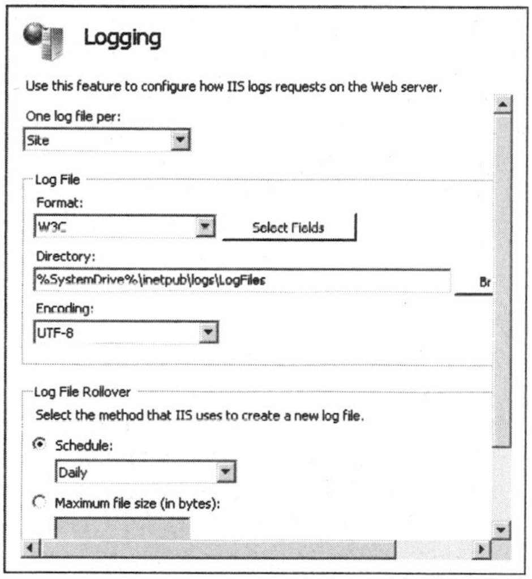

Figure 1-12: Control the logging used on your server.

The Logging window entries shown in Figure 1-12 help you control a host of settings. For example, you can set IIS 7 to log requests based on the entire server or on individual sites. You can choose a log format that matches any reporting utilities you use. Placing the log on another drive can improve system performance by giving the server multiple channels to use for data writing. It's also possible to control how often IIS 7 creates a new log.

MIME Types

A Multipurpose Internet Mail Extension (MIME) entry defines how the Web server tells the client to handle a particular file type. The technology was originally used in e-mail to help the e-mail reader know what to do with a particular file type that the user received as an attachment. The technology spread to Web servers as part of the response to a client request. The browser on the client machine can use the MIME type to launch a helper application to handle the file. Microsoft is even using MIME in Windows to help handle file extensions consistently — you find the entries with the file definitions in the registry. As you might imagine, the number of MIME file types for IIS 7 is extensive because modern Web sites use a considerable number of file types.

Adding a new MIME type isn't always easy, and it's not something you need to do very often. When you click Add in the Actions pane, IIS asks you to provide the file extension (which isn't hard to discover) and the MIME type (which can be quite hard to discover). Fortunately, IIS comes with a number of common MIME types predefined. In addition, when you install an application that requires a special type, the installation routine normally adds the required information for you. The Web site at `http://www.webmaster-toolkit.com/mime-types.shtml` provides an extensive list of MIME types that you'll find helpful.

Modules

IIS needs to know where to find the code it requires to perform tasks. Because IIS 7 is based on the .NET Framework, you'll find that it needs a combination of .NET (managed) and native code modules to function. A *managed* code module is one that relies on the .NET Framework and contains tokens. The Common Language Runtime (CLR) compiles these files into a native executable and then runs them. A *native code module* is already in machine code form — the form that your processor can understand without any special support. The Modules icon contains a list of native and managed code modules when you install IIS.

IIS requires two different procedures to install a module. When you click Add Managed Module to add a new managed code module to IIS, you see an Add Managed Module dialog box where you must supply a module name and type. You can also choose to load the module only when an application or handler requests the services of the module. When you click Add Native Module, you see the Add Native Module dialog box, where you choose one or more native module types. To change the specifics of the native module, you click Edit. IIS lets you change the name and the path to the executable.

Output Caching Rules

A server can realize a performance boost by updating content only as needed to keep it current. If someone requests a report from your server and then a second person requests the same report five minutes later, the chances that the report is outdated are small. Rather than regenerate the report, you can simply send a copy of the report from the first person. The Output Caching Rules icon lets you create output caching rules that control how IIS 7 recycles content. You can choose to recycle the content based on file change notifications (an actual change to the file that contains the content) or a time interval. It's also possible to tell IIS 7 not to use output caching for specific content, even if the content of that type normally relies on output caching.

Server Certificates

Digital certificates answer the question of how someone can know whether your Web site is actually the one they want. A digital certificate added to SSL ensures that your communication with a user remains secure. To implement the security features that digital certificates provide, you must create an entry in the Server Certificates icon.

Past versions of IIS were definitely limited in how they worked with digital certificates — your only option was to install one. IIS 7 makes things considerably easier by offering other options. You can use any of the options shown in Table 1-2 for creating a certificate on your system.

Table 1-2	Server Certificate Creation Techniques	
Technique	*Use*	*Description*
Import	Any Web site	This is the old standby option. You obtain a certificate from a third-party source, such as VeriSign, and then import it into your server. All you need to do is supply the location of the certificate and the password required to open it.
Create Certificate Request	Intranets or trusted private networks	In this two-part process, you begin by creating a request and sending it to a third party, such as VeriSign. The third party eventually responds, and you use the Complete Certificate Request action to install the certificate. It's a bit like using the Import option, except that you don't have to do the work of creating the request on a Web site and then extracting and installing the certificate manually.
Create Domain Certificate	Intranets or trusted private networks	Using a domain certificate server was a messy and error-prone process in the past. You ended up spending time using a Web interface to contact the server and, hopefully, obtain a digital certificate that you installed manually into IIS. Now you can use this option to create a certificate that works great for an intranet or in a private Web site where trusted third parties participate. Using this approach saves the time, money, and effort of using a third party and provides a perfectly acceptable means of identification.

(continued)

Table 1-2 *(continued)*

Technique	Use	Description
Create Self-Signed Certificate	Localized development or testing	Developers often require server certificates for test purposes. This option provides a certificate that works fine for testing and probably for a small network, but may not be a good choice, even for a private network, because anyone can generate this certificate if they have access to IIS. Previous versions of IIS didn't even consider this need, which often left developers looking for a digital certificate to use. Because a company would be ill advised to install its public certificate on a test server, the developer often had to resort to odd testing strategies and command line tools to accomplish the task.

All these certificate options mean that there's no longer a good reason not to have one installed on your server. After you install the certificate, you can begin working with SSL and securing your setup to make it harder for outsiders to gain unauthorized access.

SSL Settings

Anyone who has used the HyperText Transfer Protocol Secure sockets (HTTPS) protocol knows something about SSL. Using SSL means that you can encode the communication between client and server so that no one can eavesdrop on your conversations. SSL sees use for a number of tasks, including public uses, such as shopping cart applications and password entry screens. You can use SSL exclusively on a private Web site to ensure the integrity of any communications you perform.

Microsoft sets the SSL Settings feature delegation to Read Only in the default configuration. This setting means that you can't change the SSL Setting at any level because this setting isn't available at the Web server level and none of the other levels can access it. Because SSL security is a mandatory feature for secure transactions today, make sure to use the Feature Delegation setting to change the SSL security setting to Read/Write.

Before you can begin working with SSL, you need to create a server certificate (see the "Server Certificates" section of this chapter for details). After you have a server certificate, you can create a Web site that's bound to the SSL protocol. It's even possible to add this binding to a current Web site by clicking Bindings in the Action pane. After you create a Web site that uses the SSL protocol, you can redirect the user to it using the HTTPS protocol.

Use 128-bit SSL security whenever possible to improve Web site security. Although SSL is relatively secure at any level of encryption, doubts have recently surfaced about the 40-bit encryption level. Someone with the proper equipment can probably break the 40-bit level in a day, assuming you have something valuable enough to use an entire day to break. Most browsers also support the 56-bit level, which is considerably more secure. When you reach the 128-bit level, you can be sure that no one will break the encryption unless they have thousands of years to do it. However, you also give up some compatibility with older browsers. See the VeriSign PDF at `http://www.verisign.com.br/static/032932.pdf` for additional insights into using SSL.

Worker Processes

The Worker Processes icon answers the question of which processes are running on your server. You can determine whether individual processes are running, discover the amount of memory they're using, and see the amount of processor time they require. It's also possible to view the current requests for this process.

An overview of the Management features

For the most part, management features appear at the server level. They help you control access to the server for administrative purposes. You use the management features to determine who can change settings and precisely what they can change. The following sections describe the various management features. Only the IIS Manager Permissions icon appears at the Web site level — every other icon appears only at the server level.

Feature Delegation

IIS places strict control over the use of features in your hands. You can choose to delegate the feature and determine how the delegation occurs. When the Web server administrator decides to remove delegation, a Web site administrator can't even see the feature. You control all this functionality by using the Feature Delegation icon.

The trick is to provide the right level of delegation. If you provide too much access to Web server features, you might endanger the Web server integrity. However, when you provide too little delegation, the Web site administrator can be hindered in an effort to protect the individual Web site. As with many issues, you must provide a good balance of access for your particular setup.

Book VII Chapter 1

Understanding the New Interface

IIS Manager Permissions

The IIS Manager Permissions icon displays a list of users who have permission to perform management tasks at the site level. Adding a user to the list gives the user access to the Web server as a manager.

IIS Manager Users

Normally, IIS 7 is configured to allow connections from systems with Windows credentials for the purpose of performing administrative tasks. However, you can add users who have access to IIS, but not to the Windows server. This security feature is intended for hosted Web sites where you want someone to manage their Web site but not gain access to your server. The list of users you provide must supply their names and passwords to gain access to their individual Web sites.

Management Service

Use the Management Service icon to configure how IIS 7 controls client access to the Web server. Normally, you must have a Windows credential to perform remote management tasks. However, when you start the Management Service (WMSVC), you can configure IIS 7 to support IIS Manager credentials. These credentials let someone perform remote administration without having an account on the Windows server.

Shared Configuration

If you're managing an entire server farm, you don't want to configure each server individually. When a number of servers in the server farm use the same configuration, you can set the configuration using just one server. Set all other servers to use that server's configuration through the Shared Configuration icon.

Chapter 2: Performing Basic Configuration Tasks

In This Chapter

✓ **Managing the SMTP feature**

✓ **Sending requests to alternative locations**

✓ **Configuring responses to HTTP requests**

✓ **Creating, configuring, and using various kinds of data**

✓ **Working with the Internet Server Application Programming Interface (ISAPI)**

✓ **Delegating authority to perform management tasks**

Installing the Web Server (IIS) role is straightforward, so I won't belabor the point in this chapter. The "Adding roles" section of Book II, Chapter 1 provides you with details on performing this task. The only issue you need to consider is which role service to install — you need to install those role services that match the applications you want to run, but you shouldn't install role services you don't need. At some point, you have a shiny new IIS 7 installation on your hard drive and begin to wonder what you should do next. This chapter answers that question by describing some of the basic configuration tasks you perform in addition to moving your applications to the server.

One of the more important features from an administration viewpoint is setting up Simple Mail Transfer Protocol (SMTP) on your server so that IIS 7 can send you status messages. The server will now alert you to major problems so that you don't have to guess the status of your Web server or check it manually. Overall, this is a nice feature, but you must configure it before you can use it.

Depending on how you move applications to the new server, you may need to redirect some old URLs to new URLs on IIS 7. The redirection feature makes this task relatively easy. Of course, you want to make the transition seamless so that the user sees only the new content you've provided in the new locations.

Most Web applications today rely on a wealth of data types. A user may want to download a PDF containing the latest product information or video demonstrating how to perform a task. You'll want to include various media types to dress up the content on your Web site. The use of fonts and technologies such as Cascading Style Sheets (CSS) all has to work flawlessly to present the Web site you think the user wants to see. All these activities depend on defining the right kinds of content for the Web server.

Even though IIS 7 is highly modular and relies heavily on managed code (through the .NET Framework), you find that it still supports ISAPI extensions and filters. Configuring the ISAPI extensions and filters that your Web site requires is part of the entire configuration process. The special features of your Web site may not work without this configuration.

Finally, before you can turn over control of the individual Web sites to others in your organization or to the administrators of hosted sites, you must decide on what they can do. That's where the Feature Delegation icon comes into play. You use this feature to ensure that others on your Web server can manage the Web site features they need and nothing else.

Installing and Configuring SMTP Support

The Simple Mail Transfer Protocol (SMTP) comes as part of the basic IIS 7 installation, so you don't need to do anything special to get it. The use of SMTP, in this case, is for administrative tasks, not for e-mail in general, as you might expect. Your application may require the use of SMTP to send confirmation or status information when you're away from the office, or at least out of touch with the server. The following sections describe the SMTP support in more detail.

Understanding the purpose of SMTP in IIS 7

IIS 7 provides an option to configure an SMTP e-mail address for use by your application. The configuration identifies the application, not the recipient. In other words, the configuration tells IIS 7 how to identify the application to you as the message sender. You must still provide recipient information, such as your e-mail address, just as you always do as part of your application. The purpose of identifying the application is to help you identify the sender.

Creating identification for your applications doesn't necessarily guarantee the safety of the information you send. Someone can spoof your sender information, making it appear that their information is coming from your application, even though it isn't. However, having the information in place does add a little extra security because most outsiders won't take the time to research this information, so it's worth having. In addition, at least the administrator will know where a message is from, rather than see a blank sender entry in an e-mail. Because the sender information also helps the e-mail make it through firewalls and virus detectors, it does have a purpose, but you shouldn't rely on it heavily.

It's easy to configure an e-mail address for the Web server as a whole, individual Web sites, applications, or even folders. The level at which a user makes a request determines the e-mail address that IIS 7 chooses. When the user is in an application, IIS 7 chooses the e-mail address for that application when you've configured one. Otherwise, IIS 7 looks one level at a time until it finds an e-mail address to use. If it finds a Web site e-mail address, IIS 7 uses it for communication. However, if you don't have a Web site e-mail address configured, IIS 7 looks for a Web server e-mail address. Configuring an e-mail address for each level is important because individual level addresses help you know where an application made a request.

To display the e-mail information for any level, select the level you want to change in the Connections pane and double-click the SMTP E-mail icon in Features view. You see the SMTP E-mail pane, as shown in Figure 2-1.

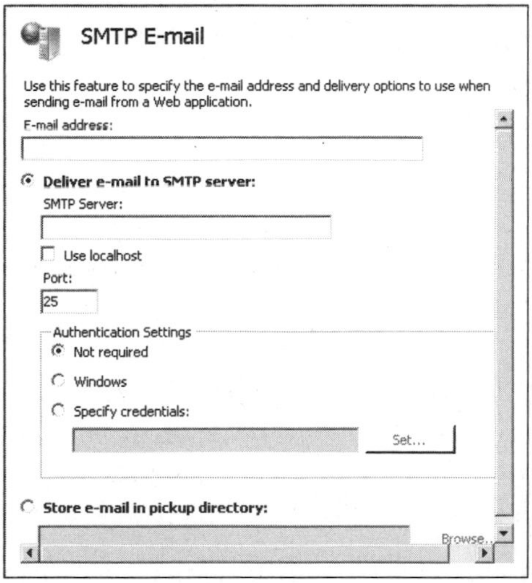

Book VII Chapter 2

Performing Basic Configuration Tasks

Figure 2-1: Configure SMTP e-mail settings for applications that need it.

IIS 7 provides two methods to send an e-mail: Use an SMTP server or store the e-mail locally. When you use the SMTP server, IIS sends the e-mail immediately. On the other hand, storing the e-mail locally lets an application pick it up later. You can use this second approach with a custom application to make it easier to perform custom processing on the data. In both cases, you begin the process by providing an e-mail address in the E-mail Address field.

Configuring an SMTP server

The upper half of the SMTP E-mail window, shown in Figure 2-1, contains the SMTP server settings. The following steps describe how to configure this option:

1. **Select the Deliver E-mail to SMTP Server option.**

2. **Type the URI for the SMTP server you want to use or check the Use Localhost option.**

IIS automatically provides the URI for the SMTP server when you choose the Use Localhost option.

3. **Provide a port number to use in the Port field.**

IIS provides the default setting of 25 for you. Configure this option only when your SMTP server has a special setup.

4. **Choose an authentication type in the Authentication Settings area.**

When you choose Not Required, IIS doesn't send any authentication information. About the only time this setting works is when you use Localhost. The Windows option sends your Windows credentials to the SMTP server and normally works only with an SMTP server on your network. For all other servers, you must use the Specify Credentials option.

   a. **When you choose the Specify Credentials option, click Set.**

     You see the Set Credentials dialog box.

   b. **Type your name and password as needed. Click OK.**

5. **Click Apply to make the settings active.**

Configuring a pickup directory

You normally use a pickup directory for local distribution of e-mail with a custom application. It's possible that you can encounter other situations where this option is helpful, but most administrators won't ever use it. The following steps describe how to configure this option:

1. **Select the Store E-mail in Pickup Directory option.**

2. **Type the location of the pickup directory.**

Click Browse if you need to search for the pickup directory on your hard drive.

Make sure that everyone who requires access to the e-mail can access the pickup directory. In addition, some administrators make the mistake of not giving IIS proper access to the pickup directory, which can prove fatal to your application.

3. **Click Apply to make the settings active.**

Redirecting Web Sites

There are many reasons that you may need to redirect a Web site. You may have reorganized your site, focused it, and moved some content to another domain, or changed it as a result of a change in your company. No matter what reason you have for redirecting a Web site, IIS 7 makes the task easy to perform.

The essential issue is to choose the right level for the redirection. If you want to redirect only an application or other resource on a Web site, make sure that you choose that level in the Connections pane of the Internet Information Services (IIS) Manager console. In fact, because a redirection can disrupt people using your Web site, you want to double-check your selection before you do anything. The following steps help you redirect a Web site:

1. Double-click the HTTP Redirect icon.

You see the HTTP Redirect window, as shown in Figure 2-2.

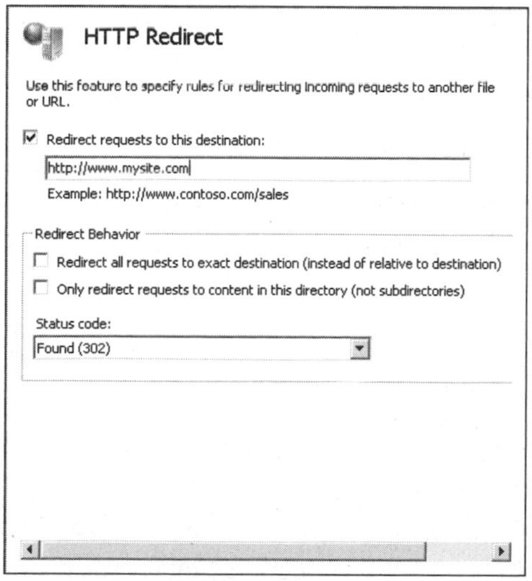

Book VII
Chapter 2

Performing Basic Configuration Tasks

Figure 2-2:
Set the redirection arguments for the current level.

2. Check Redirect Requests to This Destination.

3. Type the URL for the new location.

4. (Optional) Check Redirect to the Exact Destination.

Normally, IIS 7 uses relative redirection so that the user sees the same content in the new location. Relative redirection assumes that you duplicated the content in the new location to match that of the old location.

When you don't provide precise duplication, you need to redirect the user to the exact destination you provide so that the browser displays the content you intended rather than an error message saying that the server couldn't find the content. You should also use this option to display an error message or a content-moved Web page.

5. **(Optional) Check Only Redirect Requests to Content in This Directory.**

Use this option when the subdirectories for a Web site are still functional and only the content at an upper level has changed. In most cases, you don't use this option.

6. **Choose one of the Status Code options.**

The status code you choose determines how the browser interacts with the redirection and which information you see. You have the following status code options (you can see a complete list of standard HTTP status codes at `http://www.w3.org/Protocols/rfc2616/rfc2616-sec10.html`):

- **Found (302):** Tells the browser that the server has found the required content in another location but doesn't indicate whether the change is permanent or temporary.

- **Permanent (301):** Tells the browser that the server has found the required content in another location and that the change is permanent. In some cases, the browser prompts the user to update their bookmarks to the new location.

- **Temporary (307):** Tells the browser that the server has found the required content in a temporary location but that the content should appear in the old location sometime in the future.

7. **Click Apply to make the settings active.**

Handling HTTP Responses

The HTTP response headers you send with a response to a request help determine how the client reacts to the information. In some cases, the response header can request additional information or tell the client which forms of input the server supports. You can use custom responses to provide the client with special information about your Web site.

The important thing to remember about response headers is that they don't appear in the browser. The user won't see anything special by simply looking at the Web page with a browser. If the user views the source for your Web page, they see the special headers, but most users won't perform this task. In general, the browser must know how to work with the response header, or you must use a special application designed to react to your custom headers to make the response headers useful.

IIS 7 supports both standard and custom response headers. You can see the standard response headers at `http://www.w3.org/Protocols/rfc2616/rfc2616-sec6.html`. The information at `http://www.w3.org/Protocols/rfc2616/rfc2616-sec14.html` tells you about formatting these response headers. (IIS 7 usually does a good job of performing this task for you as long as you provide the right information.) It's also important to view the list of response headers that Microsoft supports at `http://msdn2.microsoft.com/en-us/library/ms537417.aspx`. The following sections tell you how to configure standard and custom response headers.

Configuring a standard response header

IIS 7 supports only two of the many standard response headers directly: HTTP Keep Alive and Expire Web Content. If you want to set any other standard header, you must do it as a custom response header, as shown in the "Configuring a custom response header" section of this chapter. The following steps describe how to set a standard response header:

1. **Double-click the HTTP Response Headers icon.**

   You see the HTTP Response Headers window.

2. **Click Set Common Headers in the Actions pane.**

   You see the Set Common HTTP Response Headers dialog box.

3. **(Optional) Check Enable HTTP Keep Alive.**

   IIS enables this option by default. Using this option improves server performance significantly and there isn't a good reason to disable it. An HTTP keep-alive ensures that the connection between the client and server remains open when the server must send multiple elements to the client. Most modern Web pages include multiple elements. The Web page itself is an element, as is every graphic and any other content contained within the Web page. Opening a new connection every time the server has to send one of these elements can consume considerable time and doesn't serve any useful purpose.

4. **(Optional) Check Expire Web Content.**

   Use this option to force the browser to update information from the Web server rather than use cached data on the server. This feature is important when the content on your Web site changes frequently, even though the URL doesn't. If the content is completely *static* (doesn't change), clearing this option can save considerable server resources and improve performance. If you check this option, you also need to choose one of the following update intervals:

   • **Immediately:** Use this option if you want the client to refresh its data from the server with every request.

   • **After:** Use this option when the content changes regularly but not constantly. For example, if the information on your Web site changes once a day, the client needs to update its local cache only once a day. Setting the interval correctly can save server resources and improve performance.

- **On:** Use this option when you know that the content on your Web site will change at a specific date and time. For example, you can use this setting to ensure that the client sees an announcement of a new product on a Web page that normally contains only static data.

5. **Click OK.**

IIS 7 closes the Set Common HTTP Response Headers dialog box. You don't see any changes in the HTTP Response Headers window.

6. **Click Apply to make the settings active.**

Configuring a custom response header

A custom response header can contain any information. The client must know how to handle the information, but otherwise there are no limits on what you can include. The following steps tell how to create a custom response header:

1. **Double-click the HTTP Response Headers icon.**

   You see the HTTP Response Headers window.

2. **Click Add.**

   You see the Add Custom HTTP Response Header dialog box.

3. **Type the name of the custom response header in the Name field.**

   When working with a standard header that IIS 7 doesn't support directly, make sure to type the response header name precisely to ensure that the client responds to it.

4. **Type the value of the custom response header in the Value field.**

   When working with a standard header, make absolutely certain that you type the value correctly. The common practice is to separate multiple values with a semicolon (;). Don't type quotes around the value — IIS 7 adds them for you.

5. **Click OK.**

   You see the custom response header added to the list of headers in the HTTP Response Headers window.

6. **Click Apply to make the settings active.**

You may eventually need to edit or remove custom response headers. To edit a response header, highlight its entry in the list and click Edit in the

Actions pane. To remove a response header, highlight its entry in the list and click Remove in the Actions pane. Any changes you make to the response headers list appear the moment you click Apply in the Actions pane.

Working with Data

Data management is an essential part of most modern Web sites. Imagine viewing a Web site that doesn't contain any graphics and uses a plain font. Most users will find such a Web site boring to the extreme. Of course, no one decided one day to create the multimedia extravaganzas presented by some Web sites today. Media and other data types have evolved as the Internet has grown. Consequently, you may sometimes find the rules for working with data on your Web site confusing and even contradictory at times. This section helps remove some of the confusion for you. You see how to work with data in three ways:

✦ **Multipurpose Internet Mail Extensions (MIME):** Provides the caller with identifying information about the content that the server is sending. A MIME type tells the caller how to handle the data. The server also uses MIME types to discover how to handle data coming from the caller.

✦ **Request handlers:** Simply because the caller provides a MIME type doesn't mean that the server knows how to handle the resulting input. A server must have a request handler that knows how to work with the data in question. You can install request handlers for any data type as long as the handler is written to support IIS 7.

✦ **Response modules:** The server must also know how to send specific kinds of media to the caller. A response module tells the server how to perform this task in a standardized way (one in which the caller can react, assuming that the caller has the required capabilities). As with a request handler, you can install a response module to handle any kind of output as long as the module is written to support IIS 7.

Configuring MIME types

The MIME type for a document originally started as a way for e-mail programs to handle files that they didn't natively support (read the history at `http://www.tcpipguide.com/free/t_MIMEMessageFormatOverview MotivationHistoryandStand.htm`). However, because MIME was originally introduced as a means of overcoming the limitations of text-based e-mail, it has found its way into a variety of applications, including the browser and even Windows. In short, setting the MIME type correctly is critical if you want IIS to provide the right support to the client. If you want to read about the internal workings of MIME, you can find the standard at `http://www.faqs.org/rfcs/rfc2049.html`. The following sections describe working with MIME in detail.

Understanding the basic MIME types

From the administrator's perspective, MIME types include a file extension and a string that tells what kind of application to use to handle the file. For example, the PDF file extension has a MIME type of application/pdf. The first part of the MIME type tells you that the system uses an application to handle the file, and the second part tells you that the application is the type assigned to the PDF file extension.

As another example, a WAV file, which contains a sound bite in most cases, uses the MIME type audio/wav. The first part specifies that this is an audio file and that the system should use the application responsible for WAV files to handle it. There's a very definite pattern to creating a MIME type — the file type comes first, followed by the handler type. The file types normally fall into the following categories:

Application	Audio	Example	Image
Model	Message	Multipart	Text
Video			

Even though you define the MIME type within IIS, the user never actually sees it because the MIME type appears as part of the response header (see the "Handling HTTP Responses" section of this chapter for details). A Web server always provides a complex response header that includes multiple MIME types because Web pages contain more than one kind of information. You can read more about how these response headers work at http://www.tcpipguide.com/free/t_MIMEBasicStructuresand Headers.htm.

As previously mentioned, IIS defines a considerable number of common MIME types for you. To see the list of existing MIME types, select the connection you want to work with in the Connections pane and then double-click the MIME Types icons. You see a list of MIME types, as shown in Figure 2-3.

However, you might have to work with some uncommon MIME types. In this case, you can rely on a number of alternative sources to determine the MIME type to add to IIS. The first source you should consider is the vendor responsible for creating the file extension. Often, a vendor provides the information as part of the documentation for an application.

When a vendor source doesn't exist, you can always check the registry. Choose Start⇨Run, type **RegEdit** in the Open field, and then click OK. Locate the file extension you want to add in the HKEY_CLASSES_ROOT hive. The Content Type value in the right pane contains the MIME types for the file extension you choose.

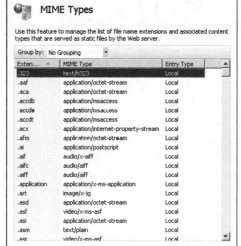

Figure 2-3:
Locate the
MIME type
for your file
extension by
reviewing
the list
in IIS.

In some cases, you won't have a local resource you can use. If the vendor
who created the file extension has a Web site, you might be able to find the
information there. You could also find the MIME type defined on one of
many Web sites that provide a list of standardized MIME types, such as
Internet Assigned Numbers Authority (IANA) at `http://www.iana.org/`
`assignments/media-types/` and LANTech at `http://www.ltsw.se/`
`knbase/internet/mime.htp`.

**Book VII
Chapter 2**

Performing Basic
Configuration Tasks

If you truly can't find a MIME type for a particular file extension, you should
register it with IANA at `http://www.iana.org/cgi-bin/mediatypes.pl`.
This group verifies that the MIME type doesn't exist and adds it to its list if
necessary. In no case should you ever make up a MIME type of your own and
attempt to use it with a Web application. If everyone used this approach,
chaos would result because each file could have multiple MIME types associated with it.

Defining a new MIME type

Despite all the help IIS provides, you may eventually need to add a MIME
type to the list. Make sure to use a valid MIME type for the file extension or
else users of your Web site will experience problems. Use these steps to add
a new MIME type:

1. **Select the connection you want to use in the Connections pane.**

2. **Double-click the MIME Types icon.**

    You see the display shown in Figure 2-3.

Understanding handler functionality

A request is always in the form of a file. You define the request in the form of a path. If you include only the file specification, the handler applies to all requests of that type at the level you specify. A file specification can include wildcards, so you could provide a handler for all ASP files by using the *.asp file specification. If you want the handler to apply to all requests, you simply provide the * (asterisk) wildcard character. IIS also lets you specify a folder as a path when you specify a folder, without providing a file specification.

A request can include more than one handler. For example, the *.ashx path requires two handlers. In fact, you'll notice that several paths require two or more handlers to complete the response. IIS passes the request to each of the enabled handlers in turn. IIS skips any disabled handlers, so you never have to uninstall a handler when you simply want to keep it from working with the requests for testing or other reasons.

IIS lets you set the order of the handlers on the system. However, because this functionality is open to anyone, you can't always assume that the handlers will appear in a certain order. To change the handler order, click View Ordered List in the Actions pane. The list changes to show the handler order. Highlight the handler you want to change and click Move Up or Move Down to change the handler's order in the list. IIS calls handlers at the top of the list first and then moves down. Consequently, when you have two handlers for the same path, the first handler works with the request first and then the second. When you've placed the handlers in the order you want, click View Unordered List to return to Standard view.

You can modify handler functionality by using several techniques. It's possible to enable and disable handlers as needed (see the "Enabling and disabling handlers" section of this chapter for details). IIS also lets you change handler permissions so that the handler will work in some situations but not in others. For example, you can set a handler to perform tasks when the user requests a folder but not a file. In addition, you can set restrictions on the verbs that the handler affects, such as GET, HEAD, POST, and others. The "Changing handler restrictions" section of this chapter describes handler restrictions in detail.

3. **Click Add.**

You see the Add Mime Type dialog box.

4. **Type the file extension you want to use, complete with initial period, in the File Name Extension field.**

5. **Type the registered MIME type in the MIME Type field.**

Make sure to include the file type (or category, depending on which resource you use), followed by a slash, followed by the file handler type. For example, application/wav is valid, but wav alone is not. MIME types don't typically include any spaces — application /wav isn't valid either.

6. Click OK.

IIS adds the new MIME type to the list in alphabetical order by file extension.

Associating a MIME type with an application

Setting the MIME type in IIS doesn't ensure that there's a program to handle the file type. The registry contains a number of file extensions that lack a corresponding application. Consequently, when an application sees the file extension, it won't know what to do with the file even though it has an associated MIME type. Theoretically, Windows asks the user to look for an application to handle the file either locally or online. However, you can also help the user to set the correct handler. Use these steps to associate an application with a file type in Vista and Windows Server 2008:

1. Open the Default Programs applet of the Control Panel.

You see the Default Programs window, which contains options for setting the default programs on your system.

2. Click Associate File Type or Protocol with a Program.

You see a list of file extensions, such as those shown in Figure 2-4.

Figure 2-4: Create a direct correlation between the file extension and the application.

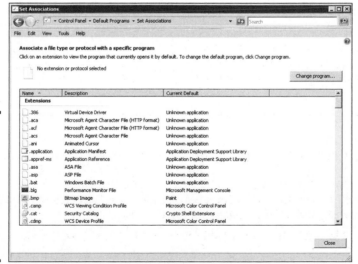

3. Highlight the file extension you want to change.

4. Click Change Program.

You see an Open With dialog box. If you try to change a system file extension, such as .386, Windows Server 2008 warns you that the file is an executable and encourages you not to associate an application with it. If you still want to associate an application with the file extension, click Open With and you see the normal Open With dialog box.

5. **Choose the application you want to associate with the file and then click OK.**

Windows creates the file association and uses the application to handle files of that MIME type.

Editing and deleting MIME types

You may run into a situation where you have to modify a MIME type. In very rare cases, you might have to edit one to correct it for mistakes. The MIME types that you obtain with IIS should be correct, as are those from IANA. However, you might obtain a bad MIME type from the registry (rare, but it could happen during an application installation), the vendor, or a third-party Web site. The steps for editing a MIME type are similar to those used to add one. The only difference is that you click Edit rather than Add. See the "Defining a new MIME type" section of this chapter for details.

You may decide that you don't want the server to support a particular MIME type. For example, the MIME type may not exist on your server and shouldn't exist under normal circumstances. Removing the MIME type could alert you to problems with content that others are placing on the Web site or to the changes an outsider is making to your files. Normally, you don't want to remove standard MIME entries that someone could legitimately use to ensure that the output from the Web site is correct. When you want to remove a MIME type, highlight the entry and click Remove.

Configuring handlers

A *handler* is a DLL or other executable that responds to a particular request from a client. IIS receives the request, locates the appropriate handler for the request, and then passes request information to that handler. You can view the handlers for IIS by choosing the connection you want to work with in the Connections pane and then double-clicking the Handler Mappings icon. You see the Handler Mappings window, as shown in Figure 2-5. The following sections describe handlers in detail.

Enabling and disabling handlers

A handler is functional only when you enable it. IIS provides the means for enabling and disabling handlers as needed. You can install a handler, but decide not to use it for requests until needed. A handler can provide special functionality, such as debugging, or it might represent a security risk in certain circumstances.

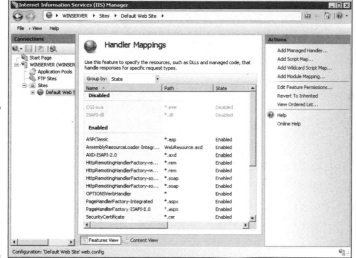

Figure 2-5:
Use the Handler Mappings window to manage request handlers on your system.

Book VII Chapter 2

Performing Basic Configuration Tasks

IIS disables two handlers by default: CGI-exe and ISAPI-dll. In both cases, modern Web sites don't commonly use the functionality they provide and they both have security issues. You must enable the CGI-exe handler if you want to use CGI scripts on your server. Likewise, you need the ISAPI-dll if you want to use ISAPI extensions (as contrasted to ISAPI Filters) on your Web site. IIS doesn't offer a choice of which handlers to enable. You enable both these handlers by enabling one of them.

IIS enables and disables handlers based on the permissions you provide to a specific level of the hierarchy. In fact, IIS provides the three levels of permissions shown in Table 2-1 for handlers.

Table 2-1		IIS 7 Request Handler Permission Levels
Level	*Use*	*Description*
Read	The read permission simply gives the handler permission to read data.	Only a few handlers require just read permission. In fact, in a default IIS configuration, you can rely on only three handlers to work with just the read permission: OPTIONSVerbHandler, TRACEVerb Handler, and StaticFile. The important handler at this level is the StaticFile handler because it lets the Web server provide a default document, allows the user to perform browsing, and provides the means to serve static content. Even though you can separately enable the scripts permission and make many handlers active, the loss of the StaticFile handler will almost certainly affect the user's ability to interact with your Web site.
Scripts	The scripts permission lets script files, but not executables, run at the designated level.	This permission enables the ASPClassic handler, along with a host of others, but not the StaticFile handler. The interesting issue here is that you could set up the Web site such that the user can access only the scriptable items, such as ASP files. The user would need to know the precise URL for accessing the entry point, but then you could provide links in the Web pages to move from page to page. The user wouldn't even know that you had all the features provided by the StaticFile handler unless they tried to access the Web site without using a precise URL.
Execute	The execute permission lets the handler perform the full range of executable tasks.	Some handlers, such as CGI-exe and ISAPI-dll, require permission to execute code. To set this permission, you must also enable the Scripts permission. However, you don't need to enable the read permission. Consequently, you can still obtain a little added security when using the CGI-exe and ISAPI-dll handlers by disabling the read permission.

Besides opening security holes in your Web site, enabling the execute permission also places a performance penalty on your Web site. Use the execute permission only when absolutely required. The following steps describe how to change the permission for a particular level (and therefore enable or disable handlers):

1. **Select the level you want to change in the Connections pane.**

2. **Double-click Handler Mappings.**

You see the Handler Mappings window.

3. **Click Edit Feature Permissions in the Actions pane.**

You see an Edit Feature Permission dialog box. By default, IIS enables the read and scripts permissions.

4. **Change the permissions as needed and click OK.**

IIS changes the permission for the selected level. Because the server, Web sites, and every folder can have different permissions, you should set the permissions as needed at the lowest possible level.

Adding a managed handler

A managed handler relies on managed code developed by using the .NET Framework. The Common Language Runtime (CLR) compiles and runs the code. A managed handler relies on a specific .NET Framework class as a base class — the class that defines the initial or starting characteristics of the managed handler.

IIS comes with all default-managed handlers configured. Normally, the only time you need to add a managed handler is when a developer creates one based on one of the other .NET Framework classes. You may also need to add a managed handler when you want to configure an existing handler to work with a new path. The following steps describe how to add a managed handler:

1. **Select the level you want to change in the Connections pane.**

2. **Double-click Handler Mappings.**

You see the Handler Mappings window.

3. **Click Add Managed Handler in the Actions pane.**

You see the Add Managed Handler dialog box.

4. **Type the new path in the Request Path field.**

5. **Choose one of the handler classes from the Type field.**

6. **Provide a human-readable name for the handler in the Name field.**

7. **(Optional) Click Request Restrictions to configure the handler restrictions.**

See the "Changing handler restrictions" section of this chapter for details.

8. **Click OK.**

IIS adds the new handler to the list.

Book VII
Chapter 2

Performing Basic
Configuration Tasks

Adding a script map

A *script map* is a connection to an unmanaged handler of some type. In most cases, the hander is an EXE or DLL file. You use a script map to provide support for older native code handlers. For example, you use a script map to create a handler entry for your ISAPI extension.

IIS requires that any EXE files you enter using a script map conform to the CGI specification. You can find this specification at http://www.w3.org/CGI/. Any DLL files you enter using a script map must conform to the requirements for ISAPI extensions. See the ISAPI extension overview at http://msdn2.microsoft.com/en-us/library/ms525172.aspx. The following steps describe how to add a script map:

1. **Select the level you want to change in the Connections pane.**

2. **Double-click Handler Mappings.**

   You see the Handler Mappings window.

3. **Click Add Script Map in the Actions pane.**

   You see the Add Script Map dialog box.

4. **Type the new path in the Request Path field.**

5. **Type the name and location of the executable file in the Executable field. (You can also use the Browse button to locate the file.)**

6. **Provide a human-readable name for the handler in the Name field.**

7. **(Optional) Click Request Restrictions to configure the handler restrictions.**

   See the "Changing handler restrictions" section of this chapter for details.

8. **Click OK.**

   IIS adds the new handler to the list.

Adding a module mapping

It's important to know the difference between modules and handlers. A module processes every request, no matter what the user is requesting. A handler works with specific files. For example, you can add an authentication module to the server, Web site, or folder that authenticates all incoming requests. The type of request doesn't matter — the module always performs the authentication. A module mapping performs the additional task of mapping specific files to a module. Before you can use this feature, you must first create the module entry. The "Configuring modules" section of this chapter describes how to work with modules in detail.

Module mappings tend to refine how a module works rather than determine the handling of a particular file. For example, select the OPTIONSVerbHandler entry in the list and click Edit. You see that the module mapping uses the * path to check all requests. The module type is ProtocolSupportModule. If you don't go any further, you never see why this mapping is necessary. Click Request Restrictions and choose the Verbs tab. The reason for the mapping becomes clear at this point. The only verb that this mapping reacts to is the OPTIONS verb. The selection of verb refines how the module works, in this case, rather than determines which file the module handles. The following steps describe how to add a module mapping:

1. **Select the level you want to change in the Connections pane.**

2. **Double-click Handler Mappings.**

   You see the Handler Mappings window.

3. **Click Add Module Mapping in the Actions pane.**

   You see the Add Module Mapping dialog box.

4. **Type the new path in the Request Path field.**

5. **Choose the module you want to use from the list in the Module field.**

6. **Provide a human-readable name for the handler in the Name field.**

7. **(Optional) Click Request Restrictions to configure the handler restrictions.**

   See the "Changing handler restrictions" section of this chapter for details.

8. **Click OK.**

   IIS adds the new handler to the list.

Editing handler settings

Whenever you need to modify the settings for a handler, choose the handler from the list and click Edit. IIS automatically opens the correct editor (managed handler, script map, or module mapping) to edit the handler settings. After you complete the changes, click OK and IIS automatically implements them.

Renaming handlers

IIS allows you to rename only handlers that you add. The default handler names are permanent. To rename a handler, highlight the handler you want to change and click Rename. IIS turns the handler name into an edit box where you can type a new name. Press Enter when you finish changing the name, to make the name permanent.

Book VII
Chapter 2

Performing Basic
Configuration Tasks

Removing handlers

In most cases, you remove only handlers that you added to IIS. Removing default handlers can cause problems for the server. When you need to remove a handler, choose the handler from the list and click Remove. IIS asks whether you're sure that you want to remove the handle. Click Yes. The handler becomes unavailable for use immediately.

Changing handler restrictions

No matter which type of managed handler, script map, or module mapping you create, you can restrict how the entry works by adding a restriction to it. A restriction affects the entry in three ways:

✦ **Mapping:** Determines the request level of the entry. You can choose files or folders or both. The unselected, or default, setting is Both. When the user requests a file, the entry must have the file mapping level selected in order to react to the request and provide a response. Some entries react only to files, such as the ASPClassic script map.

✦ **Verb:** Determines the action the request is making. A verb defines some type of action, such as getting a Web page or deleting a file. Limiting the number of verbs that an entry supports can have security and performance implications. The more verbs an entry supports, the greater the performance hit and the more likely it is that someone will break into the system using a flaw in the entry code.

✦ **Access:** Determines the precise level of access given to the selected handler. You can choose between None, Read, Write (which implies Read as well), Script, and Execute. Each level you move up in the list gives the handler additional rights.

IIS supports a number of verbs. These verbs describe the kind of request that the client is making. For example, the client may want to GET the specified resource, which is normally a file. The number of verbs available to you depends on the applications you have installed and the capabilities of the handlers you provide. The most common verbs include

GET	HEAD	POST	DEBUG	TRACE
PUT	DELETE	CONNECT	OPTIONS	

These nine verbs appear as part of the HTTP 1.1 standard found in RFC 2616 (`http://www.faqs.org/rfcs/rfc2616.html`). However, this is just the tip of the verb iceberg. For example, if you're working with Web Document Authoring and Versioning (WebDAV), you also have WebDAV verbs, such as PROPFIND and MOVE, available to you. The article "Distributed Authoring and Versioning Extensions for HTTP Enable Team Authoring" at `http://www.microsoft.com/msj/0699/dav/dav.aspx` provides a better description of the WebDAV verbs.

Many verbs have known security issues. In fact, these issues have been around since IIS 4.0. Limit the verbs you use to just those that the user requires. For example, rather than provide all the verbs when a user needs to see only a static page, support GET alone. As another example, when a user needs to upload a form to your Web site, allow only the PUT verb, not the other verbs that IIS supports. Support the DELETE verb only when you truly want the user to delete files on your server.

To change the restrictions for an entry, click the Request Restrictions button in any dialog box that supports it. You see the Request Restrictions dialog box, as shown in Figure 2-6. You can select the Mapping, Verbs, and Access tabs as needed to add restrictions to the handler. Click OK twice and IIS makes the required changes to the entry's restrictions.

Figure 2-6:
Define
restrictions
for the entry
so that it
processes
only the
requests
that you
want it to
process.

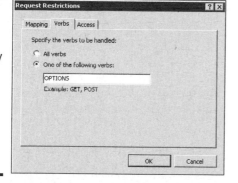

Configuring modules

For some people, IIS is a black box: The requests come in, the server locates the desired resource, and the response goes back to the caller — nothing could be simpler. Of course, it isn't actually that simple. Various requests have differing needs. To service each of these requests, the server must have software that understands the request and provides the desired response. That's the purpose of response modules. IIS calls a response module based on the user's request. The response module handles the details.

To display the response modules for a Web site, select the Web site in the Connections pane and double-click the Modules icon in Features view. You see the standard list of response modules, as shown in Figure 2-7, along with any special response modules you installed. The following sections describe how to perform various response module management tasks.

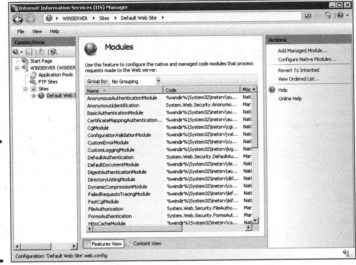

Figure 2-7:
Response
modules
provide the
answers to
incoming
requests.

Adding a native module

Native code modules use older languages that produce an executable that IIS can read directly. The following steps describe how to add a native module that comes with IIS:

1. **Click Configure Native Modules.**

You see the Configure Native Module dialog box. The modules you see are the additional modules that come with IIS.

2. **Place a check next to any of these modules as needed to assist in processing data on your server.**

3. **Click OK.**

IIS installs the module.

Adding a managed module

Managed modules rely on code that a developer creates using the .NET Framework. Whenever a caller requests a resource that this module can provide, IIS transmits the request through the Common Language Runtime (CLR, pronounced "clear"), which in turn compiles the module and starts it. After this initial communication, the managed module works much like the native code version. Consequently, you can obtain all the benefits of working with a managed module without incurring a significant performance penalty. The following steps describe how to add a managed module:

1. **Click Add Managed Module in the Actions pane.**

You see the Add Managed Module dialog box.

2. **Type a name for the managed module in the Name field.**

3. **Choose a managed module type from the Type field.**

IIS provides a number of type entries that don't already appear in the modules list. For example, you can add additional support for mobile devices by adding the appropriate managed module.

4. **(Optional) Check the Invoke Only for Requests to ASP.NET Applications or Managed Handlers.**

You can choose to let the module service only ASP.NET applications or managed handlers. This choice makes sense when your server runs mostly ASP.NET applications and the module won't work with other content. Checking this option can save system resources and improve performance slightly.

5. **Click OK.**

IIS installs the managed module.

Editing module settings

You may eventually need to edit one of the module entries you created. To perform this task, highlight the entry in the list and click Edit in the Actions pane. IIS displays the appropriate native code or managed module dialog box. Make any required changes and click OK. The "Adding a native module" and "Adding a managed module" sections of this chapter provide details about the dialog boxes.

Never edit a module entry that Microsoft provides with IIS unless told to do so by product support. Changing a module entry can have unexpected results and may even cause a server crash (or worse). Always record edits you perform so that you can return the module information to its original state if the edit fails.

Removing a module

When you no longer need a module, you can remove it from the list. Simply highlight the entry you want to remove and click Remove in the Actions pane. IIS no longer uses the module for processing incoming requests. IIS doesn't actually delete the module from the machine. The module reappears in the appropriate list for native code or managed modules on the machine. You can add the module back in by re-creating the entry.

Never remove a module entry that Microsoft provides with IIS unless told to do so by Product Support. Removing a module entry can have unexpected results and may even cause a server crash (or worse). Fortunately, you can overcome this particular problem by adding the module back in by using the techniques described in the "Adding a native module" and "Adding a managed module" sections of this chapter.

Changing a module priority

IIS calls the modules in a particular order. Modules earlier in the list receive the first opportunity to satisfy the request and send a response. On the other hand, modules later in the list may not see the request when an earlier module satisfies the need. Consequently, the order in which your server processes requests is very important; and you should order the modules by the probability that they'll satisfy the request. You can see the module priority by clicking View Ordered List in the Actions pane.

To change the order of a particular item, highlight its entry in the list and click Move Up or Move Down as needed. When you complete the required changes, click View Unordered List in the Actions pane to return to the standard view.

Understanding and Using ISAPI

Microsoft originally introduced ISAPI as a means of making IIS easier to work with. Developers could create new modules as needed, and administrators could install the new modules without a lot of help. It's still a good idea, but the technology is getting outdated. As developers work on new ways to improve modularity, the techniques used in ISAPI look less appealing because you have to write complex code to implement them. In addition, ISAPI tends to suffer from viruses and other problems.

ISAPI comes in two forms. ISAPI extensions provide improved functionality and data processing. ISAPI filters monitor the flow of data and manipulate it as needed. The following sections describe both forms of ISAPI.

Working with ISAPI extensions

Developers originally created ISAPI extensions using C and then C++. The technology was supposed to replace CGI, and it did in many ways. ISAPI extensions offer many features not found in CGI applications. One of the most important considerations for using ISAPI with IIS 7 is that it's more efficient — you don't have to create a new process for every caller. The article at `http://msdn2.microsoft.com/en-us/library/ms525913.aspx` provides a good comparison of various IIS development technologies, including a comparison of both ISAPI and CGI.

Microsoft also relied heavily on ISAPI extensions at one point. Most applications in IIS 6 rely on ISAPI extensions to perform tasks. The technology has changed for IIS 7. Now many of the applications that run in IIS use the .NET Framework instead, which provides a significant number of security, reliability, and performance benefits. You can read an excellent comparison of how Microsoft has changed from ISAPI to the .NET Framework in the article at `http://weblogs.asp.net/scottgu/archive/2007/04/02/iis-7-0.aspx`. The bottom line is that even though you can continue to use ISAPI extensions, the mainstream of IIS 7 development is headed toward use of the .NET Framework for server extensions.

Security is considerably pickier when working with IIS 7 than it was for previous versions of IIS. You must make certain that the user has access to the executable and all configuration files to make the ISAPI extension work as intended. Unlike with a script-based solution, however, you can often get by with giving the user access to the executable and not to the entire folder. In some respects, the less-intensive access requirements actually make ISAPI a little more secure than script-based solutions, such as ASP. Of course, ISAPI extensions don't share the security features of managed executables, so you still make some tradeoffs to use them.

You use ISAPI extensions differently from script-based solutions. In most cases, you won't move the ISAPI extension to a new folder on the system; you simply redirect the pointer to the ISAPI extension as needed. For example, when a user accesses your ISAPI extension for a particular resource, you create a handler mapping by using the technique found in the "Adding a script map" section of this chapter.

Managing ISAPI filters

ISAPI filters work very much like their name implies: They monitor the data stream between the client and the server and filter it as necessary. Unlike with ISAPI extensions, you can't call an ISAPI filter directly, but must configure it to monitor the data stream in particular ways. To display the ISAPI filters for a Web server or Web site, select the Web server or Web site in the Connections pane and double-click the ISAPI Filters icon in Features view. You see the standard list of ISAPI filters in the ISAPI Filters window, along with any additional ISAPI filters you installed. The following sections discuss how you configure ISAPI filters on IIS 7.

Adding ISAPI filters

Normally, any third-party product you install also installs any required ISAPI filters for you. However, you might need to install a custom ISAPI filter or a special ISAPI filter that you obtained from a third-party source rather than as part of an application. The following steps tell how to install an ISAPI filter:

Understanding CGI and ISAPI extension security risks

CGI and ISAPI are both older technologies that you may have used in the past, but may eventually want to replace with newer technologies that promise better security. The risks posed by both CGI and ISAPI extensions are real. CGI resides on just about every Web server, not just on IIS. Consequently, the security issues for CGI affect not just IIS but also many other servers, such as Apache. You can find a wealth of information about CGI security risks online, including the FAQs at `http://www.w3.org/Security/Faq/` and `http://www.irt.org/articles/js184/index.htm`.

Even though ISAPI extensions don't exist on all computer platforms, nefarious individuals have targeted them in the past due to some poor security decisions made by Microsoft when the technology first appeared on the scene. To learn more about possible ISAPI extension risks, read the articles at `http://msdn2.microsoft.com/en-us/library/ms525338.aspx`, `http://www.microsoft.com/technet/security/Bulletin/MS01-004.mspx`, and `http://www.microsoft.com/technet/security/Bulletin/MS01-023.mspx`. In fact, you'll find a considerable number of articles online about security risks for both technologies — you should use them only in a safe environment and only when necessary for backward compatibility.

1. **Click Add in the Actions pane.**

You see the Add ISAPI Filter dialog box.

2. **Type the name of the ISAPI filter in the Filter Name field.**

3. **Provide a location for the executable (either a DLL or EXE file) in the Executable field. You can also use the Browse button to locate the executable file on disk.**

Make sure that you choose the correct ISAPI filter executable. IIS doesn't perform any checking on the ISAPI filter when you install it. The executable you choose could literally contain any information.

4. **Click OK to complete the process.**

5. **Restart the Web server or Web site to ensure that the new ISAPI filter is in the processing loop.**

Editing ISAPI filter settings

If you choose the wrong ISAPI filter executable or you have an updated version of the ISAPI filter you want to use, you can easily modify the entry as needed to correct it. Modifying an existing ISAPI filter is similar to adding one. Highlight the ISAPI filter you want to change and click Edit in the Actions pane, and you see the Edit ISAPI Filter dialog box. Make the required changes and click OK to complete the process. You can't change the name of the ISAPI filter by using the Edit option.

Removing an ISAPI filter

At some point, you probably need to remove an ISAPI filter that you added previously. Remove only ISAPI filters that you add manually. Your setup requires the default IIS ISAPI filters in most cases. In addition, third-party products normally remove ISAPI filters as part of the uninstall process.

To remove an existing ISAPI filter, highlight the ISAPI filter in the list and click Remove in the Actions pane. IIS asks you to confirm that you want to remove the ISAPI filter. Click Yes to complete the process. Restart the Web server or Web site to ensure that IIS removes the ISAPI filter from the processing loop.

Renaming an ISAPI filter entry

You may decide to rename an ISAPI filter entry so that it better reflects the purpose of the ISAPI filter. To perform this task, highlight the ISAPI filter entry you want to change and click Rename in the Actions pane. IIS turns the ISAPI filter name entry into an edit box. Type the new name and press Enter to complete the process.

Understanding and Performing Feature Delegation

Feature delegation is a touchy subject in IIS 7. On one hand, you control the overall flexibility of the server with this feature. Web site administrators must have a feature delegated to them before they can use it. On the other hand, every feature you delegate to Web site administrators increases the risk of security, reliability, and even speed problems. You must delegate some features, and the default IIS setup provides these features to Web site administrators by default. Some features you don't want to delegate for any reason because they could cause significant problems. To access the Feature Delegation pane, as shown in Figure 2-8, choose the Web server entry in the Connections pane and double-click the Feature Delegation icon.

The settings you delegate depend on the kind of applications you plan to run on the server. For example, if you don't plan to run CGI applications, you should remove the delegation from that feature because setting up CGI incorrectly can cause all kinds of security and reliability problems. In addition, CGI applications tend to use resources inefficiently. A Web site administrator could decide to install and use a CGI application without permission when you provide the required delegation. The following sections describe various forms of feature delegation.

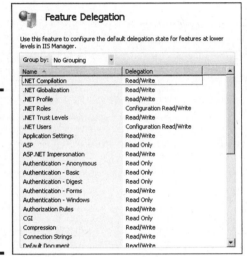

Figure 2-8:
Delegating features wisely can provide flexibility while preserving performance.

Changing the overall level of delegation

In most cases, you need to make some feature delegation choices as part of the initial server setup. Whenever you highlight one of the features in the list shown in Figure 2-8, the Actions pane choices change to reflect the levels of delegation you can provide for that feature. Simply click the link in the Actions pane that reflects the level of delegation you want to provide for that feature.

Changing the custom delegation for a Web site

In some cases, one Web site requires different functionality from others on your server. When this situation occurs, you can create a custom delegation setup for that Web site. To perform this task, click Custom Site Delegation in the Actions pane. You see the Custom Site Delegation window, which looks similar to the one shown in Figure 2-8, where you can choose the Web site you want to manage. After you select the Web site, you can highlight individual features as you normally do and choose the level of delegation you want to provide in the Actions pane.

Correcting delegation mistakes

It's possible that you'll assign the wrong delegation to a particular feature or to the Web site or server as a whole. When you find that the delegation setup you created is a hopeless mess, click Reset All Delegation in the Actions pane. Using this option returns IIS 7 to its default configuration. Of course, you have to start delegating features from scratch.

When you find that you modified a particular feature incorrectly but don't remember the setting you should use, highlight that feature in the list and click Reset to Inherited in the Actions pane. IIS 7 returns that feature to the state it inherited originally.

Chapter 3: Working with Scripted Applications

In This Chapter

✔ Considering IIS 7 support for scripted applications

✔ Installing and configuring CGI applications

✔ Installing and configuring ASP applications

✔ Defining a secure scripted application environment

Scripted applications cover a lot of ground. In fact, it would be easy to write entire books about scripted applications, and people have done it. Even though scripted applications may seem passé in light of new development platforms such as ASP.NET, many Web sites still use this technology because it's both tested and reliable. In addition, developers can easily find just about any code they need online rather than have to create it themselves, and you don't need to worry about connectivity or new drivers when working with scripted technologies. In some respects, scripted technologies are easier to use because they're familiar.

This chapter doesn't argue the case of whether you should use scripted applications. You won't find a discussion of all the technologies that IIS 7 supports, either, because there are simply too many to discuss for a single chapter. What you'll find is installation and configuration information for the two most common IIS 7 scripted application technologies: Common Gateway Interface (CGI) and Active Server Pages (ASP). You'll discover how IIS 7 supports these applications, how to install and configure them, and then how to secure them so that no outsiders spring nasty surprises on you.

Understanding the Scripted Application Support

When working with older versions of IIS, you found scripted application support provided as part of the package. However, that's no longer the case in IIS 7. To get scripted application support, you must install the correct role service. You'll find separate role services for CGI and ASP as part of the Application Development role service.

This new feature makes IIS 7 more flexible. You install only the amount of support you need, which means that the server runs faster and is less susceptible to external probing. The modular nature of this new support also means that you're more likely to see support for other kinds of scripted languages in the future, so IIS 7 has the potential to provide a significant level of scripted application support to everyone.

Installing the correct role service is only the first phase of the setup, however. Book VII, Chapter 2 discusses request handlers. Although you find that the ASP handler is enabled by default, the CGI handler isn't. In addition, if your scripted application relies on an ISAPI extension, you must also enable support for it. The "Configuring handlers" section of Book VII, Chapter 2 tells you how to work with the request handlers that IIS 7 provides.

After you have an interpreter installed that can read and understand the caller requests, and a mapping that passes requests from the server to the interpreter, you have the means to support whatever scripted language you want. People are already using IIS 7 to support a broad range of scripted languages that include PHP Hypertext Processor (PHP) (also known as Personal Home Page). As time passes, you'll find more languages supported, so if you don't see your language supported today, you'll probably find it supported tomorrow.

Working with CGI Applications

Unlike many new technologies, CGI applications have been around since the beginning of the Internet. CGI applications were once the cornerstone of Web applications. You could count on seeing them used with most of the older servers to perform a significant number of tasks. Some people confuse CGI with a language or a special technology. A *CGI* application is actually one that conforms to a particular communication protocol instead of using a specific language or technology. You can create CGI applications on IIS using a broad range of languages, including: C/C++ and Visual Basic.

CGI does suffer from a number of problems in IIS 7. The problem that you're likely to notice first is that most of the CGI resources on the Internet rely on scripting languages, such as Practical Extraction and Report Language (PERL), rather than on the language you're likely to use with IIS 7. You can partially overcome this problem by looking for script examples on Web sites such as ScriptSearch (`http://www.scriptsearch.com/`).

You also experience a performance hit using CGI. The standard technique for working with CGI is to create a new process for every call. Creating new processes costs the server a lot of time, making your CGI application slower than other solutions, such as ISAPI and ASP.NET. In fact, Microsoft optimized IIS 7 to provide the best performance when you create ASP.NET applications. That said, CGI still offers the best language support and greatest flexibility of any solution you might try on a Web server.

In most cases, CGI applications don't require much configuration. You can rely on the simple XCopy utility to move your application into place. Any configuration information is application specific, so you need to refer to your vendor documentation for any application configuration options. As mentioned, you need to install the required role services to provide CGI support. In addition, you need to enable the CGI handler. (See the "Understanding the Scripted Application Support" section of this chapter for additional information.)

Working with ASP Applications

Configuring your ASP application environment in IIS 7 differs from the process used in previous versions of IIS. Microsoft has centralized the settings and made them easier to maintain. It's important to set the ASP configuration at the proper level rather than try to set the configuration globally and risk a security breach. To display the ASP settings at any level, select the level you want to use (Web server, Web site, or folder) in the Connections pane and double-click the ASP icon in Features view. You see the standard list of ASP configuration settings, as shown in Figure 3-1.

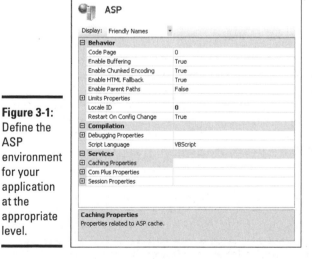

Figure 3-1:
Define the ASP environment for your application at the appropriate level.

You can divide the ASP settings into three functional areas: Behavior, Compilation, and Services. The settings you make at an upper level affect all lower levels unless you make a specific change at the lower level. For example, if you set code page 0 as the default at the Web server level, all Web sites and their folders also use code page 0 until you set another value at one of these levels. The following sections describe each of the three functional areas and tell how you can modify the associated settings to meet specific needs.

Understanding CGI better

Any thought that language plays a part in CGI at all limits the protocol. It's possible to implement a CGI solution using nearly any language as long as you can find a handler to support the language and create the application so that it meets CGI requirements. In addition, CGI isn't even a Microsoft technology — it exists on many platforms. Consequently, if you create a CGI solution for Apache running on Linux, it may be possible to move that solution to IIS on Windows. You can learn about CGI as a technology from The Common Gateway Interface (overview): `http://hoohoo.ncsa.uiuc.edu/cgi/overview.html`; The CGI Resource Index: `http://cgi.resourceindex.com/`; CGI Made Really Easy: `http://www.jmarshall.com/easy/cgi/`; and cgiExpo.com: `http://www.cgiexpo.com/`.

Changing the application behavior

The Behavior area modifies how the application interacts with the user. Changing a property here modifies the way the application performs its task. Table 3-1 describes each of the properties in this area and describes how you can work with them.

Table 3-1	ASP Application Behavior Settings	
Setting	*Subsetting*	*Description*
Code Page		A *code page* is the set of characters that IIS uses to represent different languages and identities. English uses one code page; Greek, another. Setting the code page to a specific value helps your application support the language of the caller. You can find a wealth of information, along with all the standard code page numbers at `http://www.i18nguy.com/unicode/codepages.html`. IIS understands only the Windows code pages defined at `http://www.i18nguy.com/unicode/codepages.html#msftwindows`. The default setting of 0 requests the code page from the client, which may or may not be a good idea, depending on the structure of your application. If you plan to support specific languages using different parts of your Web site, always set the code page to obtain better results.

Setting	Subsetting	Description
Enable Buffering		*Buffering* is the process of using a little memory to smooth the transfer of data from the ASP application to the caller. Using this technique makes the application run more efficiently, but costs some additional memory to gain the benefit. Generally, you'll find that buffering is a good investment on any machine that can support it, and you should keep this setting set to True (the default state).
Enable Chunked Encoding		*Chunked* transfers convert the body of a Web page into small pieces that the server can send to the caller more efficiently than it can send the entire Web page. In addition, the caller receives a little of the Web page at a time, so it's easier to see progress as the Web page loads. You can learn more about this HTTP 1.1 technology at `http://www.w3.org/Protocols/rfc2616/rfc2616-sec3.html`. Look at Section 3.6.1 of the specification to get the details. This value defaults to True.
Enable HTML Fallback		Sometimes your server gets busy. If the server gets too busy to serve your ASP application, you can create an alternative HTML file that contains a static version of the ASP application. The name of the HTML file must contain `_asp`. For example, if you create an ASP application named `Hello.ASP`, the HTML equivalent is `Hello_asp.HTML`. This value defaults to True.
Enable Parent Paths		Depending on the setup of your Web server, you might want an ASP application to reference a parent directory rather than the current directory by using the relative path nomenclature of `..\MyResourse`, where `MyResource` is a resource you want to access. For example, the ASP application may reside as a subfolder of a main Web site folder. You may want to access resources in that main folder. Keeping the ASP application in a subfolder has security advantages because you can secure the ASP application folder at a stricter level than the main folder. In most cases, however, the resources for the ASP application reside at lower levels in the directory hierarchy. Consequently, this value defaults to False.

(continued)

**Book VII
Chapter 3**

Working with Scripted Applications

Table 3-1 *(continued)*

Setting	Subsetting	Description
Limits Properties		This setting defines application limits within ASP. The main use for the Limits Properties is to ensure that the server performs well — that everyone receives the resources they need and resource waste is kept at a minimum. In some respects, these limits also help reduce potential security problems, but you shouldn't count on them playing a major role in security. For example, by limiting the body length, you ensure that no one uses too many resources, but you also reduce the risk of someone uploading a lengthy script to your server. Even so, some very small scripts cause significant system damage, so limiting request size is only a small part of a much larger solution.
	Client Connection Test Interval	Your server might experience heavy loads where the caller gets tired of waiting and disconnects. If the server still processes the client request, the time is wasted because there isn't anyone to receive the response. By verifying that the caller is still waiting after a long wait interval, the server can cut out some of this wasted time. If the caller has disconnected, the server simply deletes the request from the queue. The default setting for this property is three seconds. However, you can tune the setting to better balance caller expectations and server performance. Checking for the caller too often wastes time too, so you don't want to check too often.
	Maximum Requesting Entity Body Limit	Most initial ASP application requests for information won't have an entity-body as defined by the RFC 2616 standard. (See http://www.w3.org/Protocols/rfc2616/rfc2616.html for details.) However, when the user fills out a form and posts the data to the server, the form can have an entity-body that contains the data from the form. Use this setting to control the maximum size of the entity-body. The default setting of 200,000 bytes might be too large, depending on your application. For example, if your application requires authentication, the application must receive up to 200,000 bytes before it can send a response that requests a name and password from the caller, resulting in wasted time and network bandwidth. In addition, a large entity-body gives potential intruders lots of

Setting	Subsetting	Description
		space for scripts or other nasty input. This setting doesn't affect the size of the entity-body for any response you send to the caller. Try to maintain a reasonable entity-body size limit, to promote better server performance and reduce the risk of infection. The discussion at `http://msdn2.microsoft.com/en-us/library/aa364621.aspx` provides additional information about the inner workings of the server.
	Queue Length	This property determines the maximum number of requests that the server can place in the queue. It's important to remember that each request consumes resources, such as memory and processing time. In addition, allowing too many requests in the queue can result in a lot of wasted processing time spent determining whether the caller is still connected. Consequently, you must maintain a balance between allowing enough queue entries to handle peak server requests and allowing for server request handling capacity and resources.
	Request Queue Timeout	You can somewhat mitigate the need to contact a caller about a request by defining a limit on the amount of time that a request can wait in the queue. The default setting of `00:00:00` means that the request can wait forever, which isn't an efficient way to handle the requests. Tuning this value to allow a certain number of client connection tests and then terminating the request even if it hasn't been fulfilled usually guarantees that the server won't become completely bogged down by requests it can't satisfy. The time limit you place depends on your server's activity level and the probability that it will catch up with old requests during less-busy times. A value three or four times the Client Connection Test Interval usually works well.
	Response Buffering Limit	Response buffering, controlled by the Enable Buffering setting, makes data transfers more efficient. However, it also uses memory, and you don't want to use too much memory to gain this advantage. This setting controls how much memory IIS sets aside for buffering; IIS flushes (sends) the data when the buffer is full. The default setting uses 4,194,304 bytes (4 MB) of memory for buffering.

(continued)

**Book VII
Chapter 3**

Working with
Scripted
Applications

Table 3-1 *(continued)*

Setting	Subsetting	Description
	Script Timeout	A script, even one that is debugged and usually runs fine, can experience an error and continue running despite the failure. This setting determines the length of time that a script can run before IIS terminates it. The default setting of 1 minute and 30 seconds is usually enough for any moderately complex script. However, if your application works with databases and performs complex processing, you may need to increase the timeout value, or else IIS may terminate the application too early. Likewise, if you have a script that is short and should finish quickly, you might want to set a shorter interval to release resources earlier for a script that fails.
	Threads Per Processor Limit	This setting determines the number of worker threads that IIS can create to handle ASP requests. It's important to remember that this setting defines the number of threads per processor. Consequently, if your server contains two dual core processors, IIS sees four processors. The default setting of 25 means that IIS can create up to 100 worker processes to handle ASP requests. Normally, an ASP script and the Visual Basic objects it creates run on the same thread. So, theoretically, having up to 100 worker processes means that IIS can handle up to 100 requests simultaneously. However, it's important to remember that every out-of-process Component Object Model (COM) object requires another thread, so the actual number of requests that the server can handle varies based on the complexity of your application.
Locale ID		The Local Identifier (LCID) indicates the country in which an application is used (contrasted to the language of the person using the application, which you set using the Code Page property). The LCID helps your application define formatting, such as date, and units of measure, such as currency. The default setting is 1033, which equates to United States English. You can find a complete list of LCIDs at `http://krafft.com/scripts/deluxe-calendar/lcid_chart.htm`.

Setting	Subsetting	Description
Restart on Config Change		Normally, when you make a change to your ASP application, IIS recompiles it immediately. The change is available to new callers immediately, which means that your changes take effect almost as soon as you make them. Because most people want this behavior, Microsoft normally sets this property to True. However, if you have an exceptionally large application or you need to make changes to other part of the server before implementing these changes, you might want to set this value to False. When you set this value to False, you must restart the server to see the changes you made, but you also have better control over when the changes take effect.

Compiling the application

Even though you're using script to create your ASP application, the system compiles it at some point to run it. Compiling the application makes it run faster and lets you add features related to debugging. The way in which you compile the application affects performance. You normally find the compiled applications in the `\inetpub\temp\ASP Compiled Templates` folder on your hard drive. Each application appears in a folder that has the Program Identifier (PID) as part of the code, such as `PID3164.TMP`. When you shut down IIS or the application changes, IIS cleans up the folder.

Adding debugging code slows down the application but helps you locate problems. You can see the debugging features for ASP in Figure 3-2. Obviously, you use a debugging mode until you're sure that the application runs properly and then remove the debugging features.

As shown in Figure 3-2, you should set the Script Language property to match whatever scripting language you're using. The default setting is VBScript, as shown. However, you can use a number of other scripting languages, including JScript, which is very close to JavaScript in features and structure. You can find the Microsoft VBScript language reference at `http://msdn.microsoft.com/library/en-us/script56/html/ddfa5183-d458-41bc-a489-070296 ced968.asp` and the JScript language reference at `http://msdn.microsoft.com/library/en-us/script56/html/29f83a2c-48c5-49e2-9ae0-73 71d2cda2ff.asp`. Table 3-2 describes each of the debugging properties in this area and describes how you can work with them.

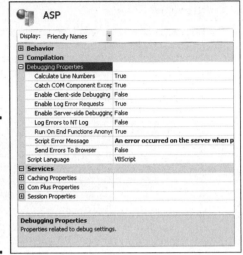

Figure 3-2:
Use the debugging features to locate and squash bugs in your application.

Table 3-2	ASP Application Debugging Settings
Setting	*Description*
Calculate Line Numbers	It's normally a good idea to know the line number of the piece of code that causes an error so that you can find it more quickly within the source file. This setting uses a small number of processing cycles and memory, but hardly enough to make any difference in the processing capability of your server. This value defaults to True.
Catch COM Component Exceptions	If your application uses COM components, those components can generate errors. This setting tells IIS to trap those errors so that your application can handle them. In some cases, such as providing an incorrect input value, your application can recover and continue processing. When you set this value to False, IIS doesn't trap the error, and another level of the application (such as the VB Script processor or the worker process) handles it. In most cases, setting this value to False means that the application terminates whenever it encounters a COM error. This value defaults to True.
Enable Client-side Debugging	Debugging can occur in two locations: the client and the server. The client sends requests to the server, and the server generates a response. This setting enables debugging on the client so that you can check issues such as input processing. It doesn't let you see how the application runs on the server, so you can't check to determine how the server handles the input data. Because debugging consumes a considerable number of processing cycles and other resources, this setting is set to False by default.

Setting	*Description*
Enable Log Error Requests	Normally, IIS writes any ASP errors to both the client browser and the Application event log on the server. This information can help you diagnose problems without spending as much time debugging the application. In fact, good error information can help you find the location of an error with no debugging, especially if you encountered the error previously. This value defaults to True.
Enable Server-side Debugging	This setting enables you to see how the server processes input data. You can step through each processing task to determine the source of errors. This setting doesn't enable client-side processing, which helps you discover input and output processing errors. (See the Enable Client-side Debugging setting for details.) Because debugging consumes a considerable number of processing cycles and other resources, this setting is set to False by default.
Log Errors to NT Log	This setting tells IIS to write detailed error information to the Application event log on the server. The detailed information includes the filename, error, line number, and description. Normally, the log entry tells you simply that an error of a specific type occurred. This value defaults to False to preserve hard drive space.
Run On End Functions Anonymously	ASP provides for some default processing of scripts. These functions appear as part of the global functions on the server. This setting determines whether the server runs the `SessionOnEnd()` and `ApplicationOnEnd()` global ASP functions anonymously. If you set this value to False, IIS won't run the functions.
Script Error Message	One of the biggest problems with getting error information is that users don't know where to send it. Even if your company policies provide this information, it's unlikely that the user will take time to look it up. Consequently, you should customize this message to tell the reader what to do when an error occurs and especially where to send the error information. The default message isn't helpful because it tells users what they already know — an error has occurred.
Send Errors to Browser	This setting tells IIS to write detailed error information to the client browser. The detailed information includes the filename, error, line number, and description. This value defaults to True to ensure that the client receives complete error information.

Configuring application services

As you might imagine, the Services area contains settings that affect how the application uses services that IIS offers. IIS divides these services into three areas: Caching, COM+, and Session, as shown in Figure 3-3. Table 3-3 describes each of the settings you find in this area.

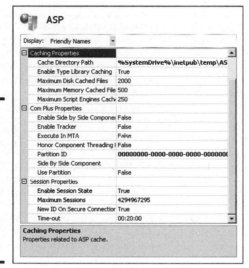

Figure 3-3: Configure application services as needed to ensure that your ASP application works properly.

Table 3-3		ASP Application Services Settings
Setting	*Subsetting*	*Description*
Caching Properties		Caching makes it possible to access resources faster. The resource is in a ready-to-use form that the server can access quickly. Consequently, even though the first person to request the resource waits the full length of time to access it, subsequent requests require far less time. Some administrators speed the process even faster by making the first request themselves using a process known as *touching* (an automated application requests each resource one at a time).
	Cache Directory Path	Use this setting to change the default location for storing the compiled ASP templates. As mentioned, the default cache directory is \inetpub\temp\ASP Compiled Templates. You can improve server performance by placing the cache on a different physical hard drive (rather than on a different partition on the same hard drive) from the Web server.

Setting	Subsetting	Description
	Enable Type Library Caching	Type libraries describe the content of COM components. Caching the type library makes accessing and using the component faster. Of course, caching always exacts a price in processing power and memory, but normally the performance benefit far outweighs any cost. This value defaults to True.
	Maximum Disk Cached Files	Every time you cache an ASP template, it consumes an amount of hard drive space. The amount of space used depends on the complexity of the ASP application. Unfortunately, Microsoft doesn't provide a means of specifying the maximum cache size based on memory; rather, it relies on the number of templates. The default setting is 2,000. You may have to tune this number depending on the size and complexity of your application and the number of incoming requests.
	Maximum Memory Cached Files	IIS allows you to set the number of precompiled ASP script files to cache. A single ASP application may contain multiple script files, so this number doesn't necessarily reflect the number of applications that IIS caches. Set this value to 0 when you don't want to cache any script files. Likewise, set this value to 4,291,967,295 when you want to cache all the script files. Use this property to tune the performance of your server. The actual results depend on the amount of memory installed on the server. The default setting is 500.
	Maximum Script Engines Cached	Every time someone makes a request that opens an ASP script file, the server must start an instance of the script engine to process that file. If a file uses an include statement to add a number of external files, those files are treated as part of the original script file and IIS doesn't start a new script engine. However, when the file isn't part of an include, IIS does start a new script engine. This setting determines the number of script engines that IIS can cache. The default setting is 250.
COM+ Properties		COM+ (shown as Com Plus) is a service-side COM technology that provides access to business logic, databases, and other server resources. The essential technology is COM, but it runs within a special environment. You also find a number of special applications in this environment, such

Book VII Chapter 3

Working with Scripted Applications

(continued)

Table 3-3 *(continued)*

Setting	Subsetting	Description
		as Queuing Services. It's even possible to turn COM+ applications into Web services (see the article at `http://www.devsource.ziffdavis.com/article2/0,1759,1627474,00.asp` for details). You can gain a better understanding of COM+ at `http://msdn2.microsoft.com/en-us/library/ms685978.aspx`. A complete description of the inner workings of COM+ is outside the scope of this book. However, this very powerful technology can make your applications perform tasks that you never thought possible. The settings in the Com Plus properties subgroup determine how your applications interact with COM+.
	Enable Side By Side Component	ASP applications can suffer from a problem known as *DLL hell,* where two applications require two different versions of the same DLL or COM component. (Read the article at `http://msdn2.microsoft.com/en-us/library/ms811694.aspx` for more information about DLL hell.) This setting enables the COM+ side-by-side component feature with an ASP application and defines which version of a DLL or COM component it wants to use. Because most applications don't have these entries defined, Microsoft sets this value to False by default. You shouldn't set this value to True unless you plan to include versioning information in all your ASP applications.
	Enable Tracker	The COM+ Tracker gives the administrator the ability to perform advanced debugging of ASP applications. However, as with all debugging, this feature uses a considerable number of resources. Consequently, you shouldn't enable this feature until you need it to debug an application. The default setting is False.
	Execute In MTA	ASP applications normally run in a Single Threaded Apartment (STA), where each thread has its own execution space. An STA application has performance penalties and uses more resources, but it's inherently safer from an execution (reliability) perspective than using a Multi-Threaded Apartment (MTA), because there aren't any concurrency requirements.

Setting	Subsetting	Description
		This setting lets you set IIS to execute your ASP applications in an MTA to gain the performance benefits that an MTA can provide. You can learn more about the COM+ MTA model at `http://msdn2.microsoft.com/en-us/library/ms686448.aspx`. You'll also want to read the detailed Knowledge Base article at `http://support.microsoft.com/kb/q150777/`. The default setting is False.
	Honor Component Threading Model	Components normally contain information about the threading model that the developer intended for them to use. However, MTA components can run quite successfully in the default STA model used by ASP, so IIS normally won't check the component to determine whether it can use some other model. This setting lets you change the default behavior so that IIS examines the component and runs it in the threading model that the developer originally intended. Using this approach doesn't always result in a performance benefit because the system encounters performance penalties when switching threading models. The default setting is False.
	Partition ID	This property defines the Globally Unique Identifier (GUID) for COM+. You must use a tool such as GUIDGen (`http://www.microsoft.com/downloads/details.aspx?familyid=94551f58-484f-4a8c-bb39-adb270833afc`) to create the GUID and ensure that it's unique. Set the Use Partition property to True to enable the GUID. You can learn more about COM+ partitions at `http://msdn2.microsoft.com/en-us/library/ms686110.aspx`.
	Side By Side Component	This property defines the name of a COM+ application to use as a side-by-side component. To use this feature, you must set the Enable Side By Side Component property to True. This feature assumes that you have a single COM+ application that interacts with your ASP application. Normally, you set this option only at the folder level because it's unlikely that other ASP applications will all require the same COM+ application interaction (and you can set them individually when they do).

(continued)

Table 3-3 *(continued)*

Setting	Subsetting	Description
	Use Partition	Application isolation, the act of placing each application in a separate container so that the applications won't interact, provides an increased level of reliability for your applications, but does incur a performance penalty. When you enable this feature, the ASP applications all execute in their own COM+ partition. To use this feature, you must define a GUID by using the Partition ID property. The default setting is False.
Session Properties		The session is the unique communication between one caller and one ASP application instance. The caller may maintain multiple sessions with multiple instances of the same ASP application, but IIS treats each instance as a unique session. The session properties define how IIS treats each ASP session. For example, the caller may choose to end a session prematurely, so IIS has to terminate the session locally so that it can recover the resources used by the session.
	Enable Session State	HTTP is a *stateless* protocol, which means that every request made by the caller is a new request. Maintaining state information is necessary for most applications because the user will want to move from one step in a process to another (such as filling a shopping cart with items). IIS uses session state to maintain the caller information. Maintaining state information incurs a performance penalty, but most modern applications won't work without it. The default setting is True.
	Maximum Sessions	This setting determines the maximum number of sessions that your Web server can maintain. Most Web servers fail long before they reach the default value of 2,147,483,647 sessions. You'll want to set this value to a more reasonable number to help avoid potential security issues, such as a Distributed Denial of Service (DDoS) attack. Even if no one attacks you, you'll want to set this number to a value that your Web server can handle to maintain the Quality of Service (QoS) for your application.

Setting	Subsetting	Description
	New ID On Secure Connection	It's important to maintain the confidentiality of your connection to the user to avoid man-in-the-middle (`http://en.wikipedia.org/wiki/Man_in_the_middle_attack`) and other forms of online attack. This setting tells IIS to issue a new cookie (the form of identification for the caller) every time the server switches from Nonsecure to Secure mode. The default setting is True.
	Timeout	A caller can make a number of requests during a particular session. This value determines the length of time that IIS holds on to the state information for a session. When the timeout expires, IIS frees the resources that the session information required. The default value for this property is 00:20:00.

Considering Scripted Application Security

It's important to do everything you can to secure your scripted applications and make them less vulnerable to attack by outside forces. Of course, your first line of defense is to control access to your Web server. Make sure that you

✦ Use firewalls to control access.

✦ Monitor input data to ensure that no one is sending you a virus.

✦ Authenticate everyone who wants more than casual access (especially on a public Web site).

✦ Authorize outsiders to do only the tasks they actually need to do.

Unfortunately, all the latest security features that you see for IIS 7 rely on the .NET Framework, which means using managed code. Yes, Microsoft is touting the high security that IIS 7 provides, but you get it only if you want to do things the Microsoft way, which means using ASP.NET for your applications. The additional security that IIS 7 provides for scripted applications is small. For example, by loading fewer modules, IIS 7 reduces the risk that someone can gain access to the server through a common flaw. The use of managed code within IIS 7 itself means that IIS 7, the server, is more secure. However, in the long run, your scripted application must still provide good internal security to make the grade today.

Despite all the precautions you take, nefarious individuals can still gain entry to your server. The following sections help you provide a second and third line of defense. Of course, someone who is determined can also breach these lines in time, so vigilance is your number-one way of protecting your server. Take time to know what's happening on your server and be sure to look for attacks to occur — never assume that outsiders won't break into your system.

Securing a CGI application

CGI applications are possibly the least-secure scripting technology you can use because you must give the caller execute rights to the folder holding the CGI scripts. It's possible to secure static resources by using standard Windows security and read-only rights from the Web server, but CGI requires that you open yourself to potential intrusions. When working with CGI, make sure to keep a strong hold on each directory — expose only those directories that the user must absolutely access to perform a task.

One way you can make CGI applications more secure is to rely on the RunAs utility (`http://www.microsoft.com/resources/documentation/windows/xp/all/proddocs/en-us/runas.mspx`) as often as possible. Using the RunAs utility, you can severely limit the user's rights to perform any task on their own. You rely on the RunAs utility to perform tasks in the user's stead. Consequently, the RunAs utility has the rights, not the user. This approach limits your security risks because the user can't use the RunAs utility in ways you hadn't intended if you set it up properly.

Securing an ASP application

ASP applications are a little easier to secure than CGI applications. For one thing, you need to provide an ASP application with only scripting rights, rather than execute rights, in most cases. If you must execute an application, don't let the user perform the task directly. Use techniques such as the RunAs utility to run the executable indirectly and keep user rights to a minimum.

As with CGI applications, you have only Windows security to rely on to secure resources. Make sure that you give users access to only the folders they need, give them only the rights they require, and block access to everything else. Because of the way ASP works, you can potentially place everything you need in a single folder and significantly reduce your exposure. If the user needs access to external data, make sure to place that data in a location that the user can reach only through your application. Keep the user away from anything that doesn't require direct access. This means keeping the folder you use for your ASP application free from anything other than the actual ASP file the user requires to run the application.

Defining ISAPI extension and CGI restrictions

Not every ISAPI extension or CGI application has to run on your system. In fact, you'll find that they can't run unless you enable them in some way. The first method of enabling an ISAPI extension or CGI application is to create a handler and enable the handler. Using handlers restricts the executable somewhat in that it works for only a specific resource. You can learn more about handlers in the "Configuring handlers" section of Book VII, Chapter 2.

The sections that follow discuss the second method of enabling an ISAPI extension or a CGI application. In this case, you enable or disable the executable on a global basis — for all the Web sites on a particular server. This approach lets you add support for alternative scripting languages or other features that can affect the server as a whole rather than an individual Web site. To display the restrictions for the Web server, select the Web server in the Connections pane and double-click the ISAPI and CGI Restrictions icon in Features view. You see the standard list of restrictions, as shown in Figure 3-4, along with any additional ISAPI filters you installed.

Figure 3-4:
Use restrictions to specifically enable or disable ISAPI extensions or CGI applications.

**Book VII
Chapter 3**

Working with Scripted Applications

Unlike other executable setups, it's very likely that you'll add ISAPI extensions manually to IIS 7 to accommodate a special need, such as language support. However, any third-party application you purchase should make the required entries for you as part of the installation process. Most CGI applications will also make the required entries for you when they come with Windows-friendly installation programs. The following sections provide an overview of using restrictions and discuss how you configure them on IIS 7.

Changing the feature settings

You can simply open your server to any and every ISAPI extension or CGI application that anyone installs — creating a potential security breach. Microsoft should never have added this feature to IIS 7 because there's absolutely no reason to include it. When you use this feature, you open your server to all kinds of potential problems of such a dire nature that your only recourse might include formatting the drive and starting from scratch. In fact, you should probably stop reading now and go to one of the other sections. If you insist on letting anyone install any ISAPI extension or CGI application on your server, use the following steps to perform the required configuration:

1. **Click Edit Feature Settings in the Actions pane.**

You see the Edit ISAPI and CGI Restrictions Settings dialog box.

2. **Check the Allow Unspecified CGI Modules option if you want unfettered access to CGI applications.**

3. **Check the Allow Unspecified ISAPI Modules option if you want unfettered access to ISAPI.**

4. **Click OK.**

IIS makes the required changes to your server configuration.

It's possible to mitigate the potential for attack slightly by making specific entries in the restriction list and not allowing that executable to run. The only problem with this approach is that you have to know about the executable and it's almost certain that persons of ill intent won't send you an e-mail with the name and location of that executable. Security by exception doesn't work, especially in this case. It truly is better to add individual restrictions to keep your server secure.

Adding a restriction

The term *restriction* is misleading. You can use a restriction to enable or disable an ISAPI extension or a CGI application. The restriction is more of an entry in a database with an on-off switch that lets you tell IIS 7 how to treat the executable. Follow these steps to add a new restriction:

1. **Click Add in the Actions pane.**

You see the Add ISAPI or CGI Restriction dialog box, like the one shown in Figure 3-5.

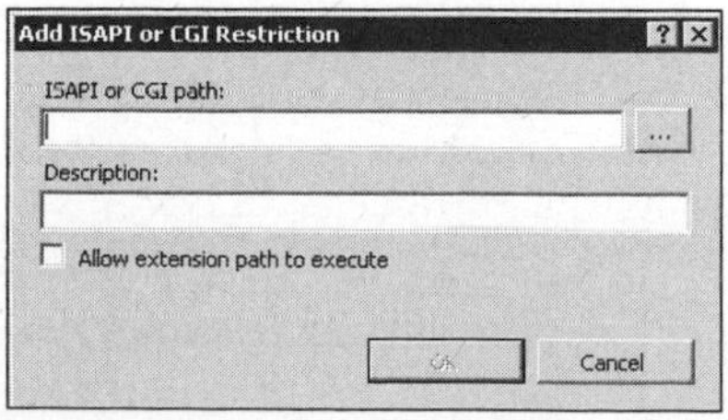

Figure 3-5:
Add a restriction to either enable or disable an executable on your system.

2. **Type the name and location of the executable in the ISAPI or CGI Path field.**

Click the Browse button if necessary to locate the file. The entry should include the full executable path.

3. **Type a human-readable name for the executable in the Description field.**

Make sure that you choose a name that won't conflict with other executables.

4. **Check the Allow Execution Path to Execute option if you want to enable the executable.**

5. **Click OK.**

IIS adds the new restriction to the list.

Denying or allowing a restriction

You may need to temporarily enable or disable an ISAPI extension or a CGI application. For example, you might use a particular executable only for maintenance purposes and not want to allow access to it normally. Alternatively, an application can experience an error, and you may want to disable it temporarily to allow time for repairs. In either case, IIS 7 makes it easy to enable or disable the executable. All you need to do is choose the executable you want to change and then click either Allow or Deny in the Actions pane. This setting is a toggle, so you see only the option you need in order to change the status of the executable.

Editing a restriction

Sometimes you need to change a restriction. For example, an updated ISAPI extension or CGI application might have a slightly different name than the original, or you might encounter a conflict with the human-readable name you chose. In either case, highlight the entry you want to change and click Edit in the Actions pane. You see the Edit ISAPI or CGI Restriction dialog box, like the one shown in Figure 3-5. IIS 7 provides full access to all the fields, so you can make any change required.

Removing a restriction

When you no longer need a particular restriction, it's better to remove it than to simply disable it. Otherwise, you end up with a number of disabled entries in your restriction list and have no idea where they came from. To remove a restriction, highlight the entry you want to remove and click Remove in the Actions pane. IIS 7 asks whether you're sure that you want to remove the restriction. Click Yes to complete the process.

**Book VII
Chapter 3**

Working with
Scripted
Applications

Chapter 4: Working with ASP.NET

In This Chapter

✔ **Considering how ASP.NET affects Web sites**

✔ **Working with database connections in ASP.NET**

✔ **Installing ASP.NET applications on the server**

✔ **Performing ASP.NET configuration tasks**

*I*IS 7 supports a considerable number of application types, but Microsoft is hoping that you'll use ASP.NET because it's the company's latest Web page development product. ASP.NET is becoming a mature technology — it has been around for several years now. As ASP.NET has matured, Microsoft has added more functionality to it so that you can now perform an amazing number of tasks with it and create truly dynamic Web sites with back-end (database and business logic) connectivity. Of course, just because ASP.NET is a newer technology, and provides so many bells and whistles that you could never use them all, doesn't mean that ASP.NET is the technology of choice for your application. Consequently, the first section of this chapter considers just what ASP.NET is as a technology and what it means to your organization.

One of the better features of ASP.NET is the level of database connectivity that it supports. You can create a connection to nearly any kind of database on the market and present the data within the database on-screen for the user. It's possible to create an application that provides full user interaction or restricts the user to simply viewing the data you want to display. Flexibility is the key in ASP.NET database connectivity.

Normally, the developer provides you with the software needed to install the ASP.NET application. However, you may find the need to perform some installation tasks when a server refuses to perform the task properly or when an update ends up creating more problems than it solves. You always need to configure your ASP.NET applications, and this chapter provides some details on how to perform that task. Of course, you always need to work with the developer to obtain a complete configuration because some configuration tasks are application specific.

Understanding ASP.NET

For many administrators, ASP.NET is a mystery of sorts. However, it really isn't all that mysterious. When you look at output from an ASP.NET application, what you see is standard HTML with some scripting added to perform various tasks on the client machine. In addition, you find some scripts that perform callbacks to the server and data used to maintain the state of the application. In short, the output isn't all that special — any application could generate it.

ASP.NET on the server normally consists of an ASPX file that contains a combination of HTML and ASP and special ASP.NET entries for controls and other features. In addition to the ASPX file, the Web page also includes a *code-behind* file that contains the code that makes the Web page active. When the user clicks a button, the code in the code-behind file responds to the event and does something. A code-behind file normally has a VB extension for Visual Basic code or a CS extension for C# code.

When a user calls on an ASPX file, the just-in-time (JIT) compiler combines the information in the ASPX file and the code-behind file to create an executable file. The resulting executable file responds to requests and outputs responses based on the developer's code. It's possible to create an executable directly by compiling the application using the ASPNet_Compiler utility found in the `\WINDOWS\Microsoft.NET\Framework\v2.0.50727` folder.

The interesting part about ASP.NET applications for administrators is that you can use `CONFIG` files to change the way the application behaves. In the past, administrators had to know how to modify these files directly, which means working directly with XML entries that aren't easy to understand in many cases. IIS 7 provides direct ASP.NET support, which means that the changes you make using the Internet Information Services (IIS) Manager directly change `CONFIG` files. You could make the same changes manually, but there isn't a good reason to do so.

Considering ASP.NET and Data Connectivity

One of the most common changes you make to an ASP.NET application configuration is database modification. You may need to use a different *provider* (a piece of software that provides access to the database from an application), change the location of the database, or modify how the application works with the database.

Because a developer won't use the production database when writing the application, you normally need to change the database setup after you install the application, to ensure that the application uses the production database. Otherwise, application users see the test data rather than the real data needed to perform tasks. The following sections describe how to work with database connectivity for ASP.NET applications. You'll find sections for managing providers and for changing the connection strings used to create a connection between the application and the database.

Managing providers

At one time, you had to create a connection string to perform just about any task using ASP.NET. Someone at Microsoft finally figured out that developers were spending a great deal of time re-creating the same connections repeatedly. A *provider* is also a special kind of service that manages certain kinds of data storage. For example, IIS relies on a provider to store role information for a user. Don't confuse an IIS provider with a database provider, which is a special kind of software that creates a connection between the application and the database manager. The following sections describe providers in detail and help you understand how they help you create a connection to your database.

Using providers to create access

Using providers can save developers a great deal of time. For example, when a developer adds login controls to a Web page to implement forms-based security, the login controls rely on the `System.Web.Security.Sql MembershipProvider` class as a provider in most cases. This class provides membership information using a SQL Server database. As an alternative, the developer can use `System.Web.Security.ActiveDirectoryMembership Provider`, which provides membership information from Active Directory. (It helps to think of Active Directory as a specialized kind of database in this context.) The point is that the developer simply uses the services of the provider instead of having to code the database connectivity by hand.

IIS includes some default providers. You can also add providers through applications. The providers you consider in this chapter fulfill three needs: .NET Roles, .NET Users, and .NET Profile. ASP.NET supports other providers. (See the "Adding new providers" section of this chapter for details.) You can add providers as needed to the Web Server, Web Site, or application.

To access the providers, select the level you want to work within the Connections pane and double-click the Providers icon. You see the Providers pane, as shown in Figure 4-1. The figure is showing the .NET Roles feature, but you can also choose to view the .NET Users or .NET Profile features. Each feature provides access to a particular IIS element.

**Book VII
Chapter 4**

Working with
ASP.NET

Figure 4-1:
Use the Providers pane to manage the providers on your Web site.

Understanding the purpose of a provider

Applications use connection strings that you create separately from a provider. The connection string tells the application where to locate the data that the application requires. Likewise, a provider requires a connection string as input to describe the connection to the database manager. All providers in IIS 7 are .NET classes. Providers fall into three groups:

✦ **.NET Roles:** This feature implements any role-based need. You find everything from the provider for the .NET Roles feature to providers used for role-based security. The default provider is the `System.Web.Security.SqlRoleProvider` class.

✦ **.NET Users:** This feature implements any user or membership need. If you were to create your own user database, such as for a forms-based application, the resulting provider would appear as part of this feature. The default provider is the `System.Web.Security.SqlMembership Provider` class.

✦ **.NET Profile:** This feature implements any profile storage. You can use it to store any global or group profile information. The default provider is the `System.Web.Profile.SqlProfileProvider` class.

Every feature has a default provider. When you select the default provider, IIS 7 tells you that it's the default provider (refer to Figure 4-1). You can't edit, rename, or remove the default provider because IIS 7 requires it in order to perform tasks. The default provider is also the one that applications are most likely to use for specific purposes, such as managing user accounts or working with roles.

Whenever a developer creates a .NET application with database requirements, Visual Studio provides the means to include the correct connection string within the `Web.CONFIG` file. However, you may find that the default providers don't appear as part of your IIS 7 installation or they become corrupted. You can re-create the database and its required tables by using the ASPNet_RegSQL utility with the -A command line switch. For example, if you want to re-create the database required for the `System.Web.Security.SqlRole Provider` class, you type **ASPNet_RegSQL -Ar** at the command line and press Enter. The ASPNet_RegSQL utility appears in the `\Windows\Microsoft.NET\Framework\v2.0.50727` folder of your hard drive.

Viewing connections associated with a provider

A provider isn't very helpful without connections. It's important to remember that the provider includes software only, not the actual connection. The connection string you create provides the information required to create the connection using the provider software.

To see the connections associated with a particular provider, highlight the provider in the Providers pane and click Connection Strings in the Actions pane. You see a list of connections like the one shown in Figure 4-2. You can use the techniques described in the "Managing connection strings" section of this chapter to change the connection information when necessary.

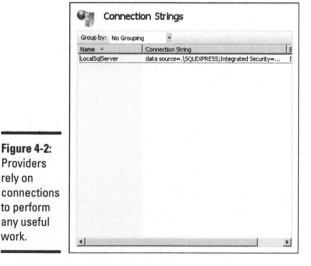

Figure 4-2: Providers rely on connections to perform any useful work.

Adding new providers

In some cases, you may need to add a new provider to IIS. For example, an application you want to install may use Active Directory, rather than SQL Server, to store .NET User information. Table 4-1 shows the standard providers used by ASP.NET and IIS. Third parties can create custom providers as well, so you may see other options in your IIS installation.

Table 4-1		Standard IIS 7 Providers
Provider Type	*Feature*	*Associated Classes**
Membership	.NET Users	`System.Web.Security.ActiveDirectoryMembershipProvider,System.Web.Security.SqlMembershipProvider`
Profile	.NET Profile	`System.Web.Profile.SqlProfileProvider`
Protected Configuration	N/A	`System.Configuration.DPAPIProtectedConfigurationProvider,System.Configuration.RSAProtectedConfigurationProvider`
Role Management	.NET Roles	`System.Web.Security.AuthorizationStoreRoleProvider,System.Web.Security.SqlRoleProvider,System.Web.Security.WindowsTokenRoleProvider`
Session State	N/A	`System.Web.SessionState.InProcSessionStateStore,System.Web.SessionState.OutOfProcSessionStateStore,System.Web.SessionState.SqlSessionStateStore`
Site Map	N/A	`System.Web.XmlSiteMapProvider`
Web Events	N/A	`System.Web.Management.EventLogWebEventProvider,System.Web.Management.SimpleMailWebEventProvider,System.Web.Management.TemplatedMailWebEventProvider,System.Web.Management.SqlWebEventProvider,System.Web.Management.TraceWebEventProvider,System.Web.Management.WmiWebEventProvider`
Web Parts Personalization	N/A	`System.Web.UI.WebControls.WebParts.SqlPersonalizationProvider`

*The class name is a single entry even though it appears on two lines in this table.

Make sure that you choose the correct provider type for any applications you install. The following steps tell how to add a new provider to the list shown in the Providers pane:

1. **Choose the provider type in the Feature field and click Add in the Actions pane.**

   When working with .NET Roles or .NET Profile, you see the Add Provider dialog box, as shown in Figure 4-3. The .NET Users feature shows the alternative view in Figure 4-4. As you can see, the .NET Users feature requires a few additional fields of input, but the overall process of creating the provider is the same as when working with either the .NET Roles or .NET Profile feature.

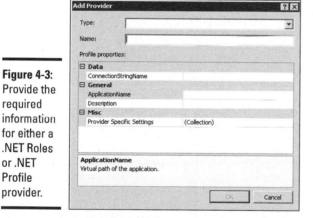

Figure 4-3: Provide the required information for either a .NET Roles or .NET Profile provider.

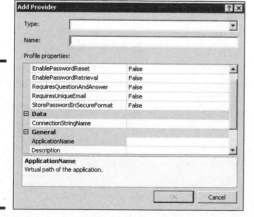

Figure 4-4: The .NET Users provider requires additional settings to work properly.

2. **Choose a provider class from the Type field.**

   The Type field contents changes according to the kind of provider you want to install. If you don't see the provider class you need, it means that you're installing the wrong provider type or that you haven't registered the provider on the current system. The provider must appear in the Global Assembly Cache (GAC) to appear in the list.

3. **Type a name for the provider.**

   The provider name is important because the developer may use it to reference the provider.

4. **Perform any special setup required for the .NET Users feature.**

   The following list describes each of the entries in the Behavior section:

   - **EnablePasswordReset:** This setting determines whether the application can reset a password using the provider's `ResetPassword()` method. The default setting is False. You should set this value to True when the application includes an administrator or a user feature to reset the password.

   - **EnablePasswordRetrieval:** This setting determines whether the user can ask the application to retrieve a password by using the `Get Password()` method. The default setting is False. You should set this value to True when the application requires automated password retrieval.

   - **RequiresQuestionAndAnswer:** This setting determines whether the user must supply an answer to a question. The default setting is False. In all cases, you should change this setting to True for any user activity.

   - **RequiresUniqueEmail:** Generally, forms-based security requires a unique e-mail address because otherwise multiple users could send their password information to a single e-mail address when retrieving it. The default setting is False. In all cases, you should change this setting to True for any user activity.

   - **StorePasswordInSecureFormat:** The SQL Server database used to store the password information normally stores it as a hash, which means that no one can read it. This technique ensures that the application can store the user's password without storing the human-readable form. The default setting is False. Always change this setting to True to maintain good Web server security.

5. **Type the name of the connection string in the ConnectionStringName field.**

   Don't type the connection string here — just the *name* of the connection string. You must configure the connection string separately. (See the "Managing connection strings" section of this chapter for details.)

6. Type, in the ApplicationName field, the name of the application (if any) that will use the provider.

When working with a provider in an application, you type that application's name. Don't include an application name when multiple applications will use the same provider. If you don't provide an application name, the provider defaults to using the value in the `HttpContext.Current.Request.ApplicationPath` property supplied as part of the caller request (making it possible to determine the application name when the application runs).

7. Type a description for the provider in the Description field.

A description may not seem very exciting or useful, but you really need to include one unless you expect other administrators to delete the provider accidentally. Only a properly documented provider has any chance of survival.

8. (Optional) Provide any required provider-specific settings.

Normally, you won't need to create any provider-specific settings for the default classes. Check with the application developer for any application-specific setting requirements.

9. Click OK.

IIS creates the new provider for you.

Editing existing providers

You may make a mistake when creating a new provider or find that you need to modify a setting to reflect changing environmental needs. IIS lets you edit any provider except the default provider, which you can never change. To edit a provider, highlight the provider's entry in the Providers pane and click Edit in the Actions pane. You see a dialog box similar to the one shown in Figure 4-3 (.NET Roles and .NET Profile) or Figure 4-4 (.NET Users). IIS lets you modify all settings except the Type and Name fields.

Removing unneeded providers

At some point, you may need to remove a provider you no longer need. You can remove any provider except the default provider. To remove a provider, highlight the provider entry in the Providers pane and click Remove in the Actions pane. IIS displays a dialog box asking you to confirm that you want to remove the provider entry. Click Yes to complete the process.

Managing connection strings

Before you can make a connection to a database, you need a connection string. Although it's possible to define the connection string within the application, it's a lot more flexible to define it within the `Web.CONFIG` file. By placing the connection string within the Web.CONFIG file, you can ensure that both developers and administrators have equal access to the connection string, making it far more likely that database changes will flow down to the application where the user needs them.

To access the connection strings, select the level you want to work within the Connections pane and double-click the Connection Strings icon. You see the Connection Strings pane. IIS 7 includes a default connection named LocalSql Server that it uses to store IIS configuration information. The following sections describe how to add, edit, rename, and remove connection strings.

Adding a new connection string

You can define a connection string using a number of techniques. The easiest method is to define a connection to SQL Server because you can do it with a few simple entries. The harder method applies to everyone else because you have to create the connection string by hand. After you become familiar with the methods your DBMS uses, creating a connection string by hand isn't hard, but the first few attempts at creating a connection string can prove troublesome.

Fortunately, the developer normally creates and tests the connection string as part of creating the application. Consequently, you won't normally need to create a new connection string, but you may have to edit a connection string to match a new database location or other requirements (such as password, timeout, or other requirements to gain access to the data). The following steps tell you how to create a basic connection string in IIS:

1. **Click Add in the Actions pane to create a new connection string.**

You see the Add Connection String dialog box, as shown in Figure 4-5.

Figure 4-5:
Define the connection string using the SQL Server defaults or a custom connection string.

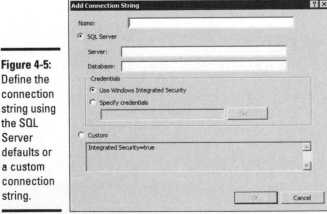

2. Type a name for the connection in the Name field.

The name has to match the connection that the application expects to use. If you don't provide the correct name, the application won't find the data it requires to perform tasks.

3. Select the SQL Server or Custom option.

The SQL Server option works only for SQL Server databases. You must use the Custom option when working with every other kind of database. When you choose the Custom option, type the connection string for the database and click OK to create the connection. Otherwise, continue to the next step of this procedure.

4. In the Server field, type the name of the server that has the data you want to use.

Notice that IIS automatically adds the Server property to the edit box in the Custom area for you.

5. Type the name of the database you want to use in the Database field.

Notice that IIS automatically adds the Database property to the edit box in the Custom area.

6. Choose Use Windows Integrated Security to pass the caller's credentials to SQL Server or choose Specify Credentials to provide specific credentials to SQL Server.

You must always specify the credentials when working with anonymous connections. Follow these additional steps when you choose the Specify Credentials option:

a. Click Set.

You see the Set Credentials dialog box.

b. Type the username.

c. Type the password twice.

d. Click OK.

IIS adds the credentials to the Specify Credentials field. Notice that IIS automatically adds the User ID and Password properties to the edit box in the Custom area and removes the `Integrated Security=True` entry.

7. Click OK.

IIS adds the new connection.

Editing existing connection strings

Editing a connection string is very much like adding a connection string. You still see the dialog box shown in Figure 4-5 when you edit a connection string and have all the same options to change except for the connection name. IIS won't let you change the connection name — see the "Renaming connection strings" section for details about renaming a connection string.

To edit the connection string, highlight the entry you want to modify in the Connection Strings pane. Click Edit in the Actions pane. Use the procedure found in the "Adding a new connection string" section of this chapter to modify the entry.

Renaming connection strings

IIS lets you modify the name of any connection string except the default connection string, LocalSqlServer. To rename a connection string, highlight the one you want to modify in the Connection Strings pane. Click Rename. (If you don't see the Rename action, you can't rename the connection string.) IIS turns the Name field into an edit box. Type the new name and press Enter to complete the process.

Removing connection strings

You can remove any connection string, including the default connection string (something you should never do). To remove a connection string, highlight the connection string entry in the Connection Strings pane and click Remove in the Actions pane. IIS displays a dialog box asking you to confirm that you want to remove the connection string. Click Yes to complete the process.

Installing ASP.NET Applications

ASP.NET applications won't execute unless you turn the folder or virtual directory that holds them into an application. This requirement isn't anything new; it already existed in previous versions of IIS. IIS 7 requires that you perform the same task; it just uses a different approach to perform the task. In addition, you have some additional issues to consider in IIS 7 because it provides a higher level of security and greater flexibility than IIS 6. The concepts and the goals are the same, but some of the details are different (changed for the better). The following sections describe when to create an application, how to create a new application, and how to convert an existing folder or virtual directory to an application.

Determining when to create an application

Normally, you won't need to create an application for ASP.NET. The application's installation program normally performs this task for you (along with creating required application pools, installing ISAPI filters, and performing other tasks). Even the Visual Studio IDE creates the required application folder for you when you test an application. However, you may find that you need to create an application in certain circumstances, as listed here:

✦ IIS forgets that the folder contains an application (can occur during updates).

✦ An administrator or developer configures an application incorrectly, requiring a reinstall and new configuration.

✦ You need to test a custom application on another machine.

✦ An organization sets up a server farm, requiring the same application configuration on multiple machines.

✦ Moving an application works out better than reinstalling it on the new machine.

Adding a new application

Adding a new application means creating a folder or virtual directory to hold it, as well as providing the correct configuration information for IIS. If you already have an application within a folder or virtual directory, you should follow the procedure in the "Converting a folder or virtual directory to an application" section of this chapter. You normally create a new application when you want to test a custom application on another server and don't already have a location for it on that server. The following steps describe how to create a new application:

1. **Right-click the Web site, folder, or virtual directory that will hold the new application and choose Add Application from the context menu.**

You see the Add Application dialog box, as shown in Figure 4-6.

Book VII Chapter 4

Working with ASP.NET

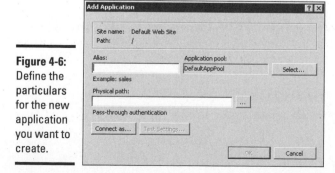

Figure 4-6: Define the particulars for the new application you want to create.

2. **Type a name for the application in the Alias field.**

   The user uses this name to access the application with a browser, so you should provide a name without spaces that the user will find easy to type.

3. **Click Select.**

   You see the Select Application Pool dialog box.

4. **Choose an application pool to use for this application. Click OK.**

5. **Type the physical path to the location of the data on the hard drive.**

   You can use a Universal Naming Convention (UNC) path, such as `\\My Server\MyDrive\Myfolder` when required. When you provide a UNC path, IIS automatically enables the Connect As button.

   a. **Click Connect As.**

      You see the Connection As dialog box.

   b. **Choose Specific User or Application User.**

      The default setting of Application User relies on the application user's credentials to make the connection. You can also choose to provide credentials for a specific user.

   c. **Click OK.**

      IIS creates the required connection credentials.

6. **Click OK.**

   IIS creates a new virtual directory with the name you provided that points to the remote location you specified.

Converting a folder or virtual directory to an application

You may have an existing folder or virtual directory that isn't an application. It may have even been an application at one time, but some type of error or failure has changed it back into a standard folder or virtual directory. You can change the folder or virtual directory directly back into an application using the following steps:

1. **Right-click the folder or virtual directory that you want to convert into an application and choose Convert to Application from the context menu.**

   You see the Add Application dialog box (refer to Figure 4-6). Notice that IIS fills in all the required information automatically.

2. **Change the application name found in the Alias field, if necessary.**

3. **Click Select to display the Select Application Pool dialog box.**

   You see the Select Application Pool dialog box.

4. **Choose an application pool to use for this application. Click OK.**

5. **(Optional) If the Physical Path field contains a UNC path, click Connect To and configure security as needed.**

   Don't change the Physical Path field entry, or else you lose your connection to the data source.

6. **Click OK.**

   IIS converts the folder or virtual directory into an application.

Configuring ASP.NET Applications

ASP.NET applications rely on CONFIG files to hold various application settings. Some of these settings affect any ASP.NET application, such as the ability to place the application into debug mode. However, a developer can also create custom settings that an administrator can then use to change the way the application behaves. The following sections describe how you can use the graphical interface to modify CONFIG file entries that change the way ASP.NET applications behave.

Changing application behavior with application settings

At one time, application developers made assumptions and configured an application in a certain way without regard to the needs of the people using it. This strategy didn't work at all, and developers soon found ways of exposing configuration settings to users. Unfortunately, the techniques often required the user to edit external files or fiddle with the registry. The open settings invited end users to make application tweaks that the administrator didn't want. In addition, using this approach required that the user make some kind of a decision, in some cases, so it didn't work very well, either.

Today, application developers have another alternative for IIS 7 as well: They can expose settings in IIS 7 in such a way that the administrator can use the Internet Information Services (IIS) Manager to change them without doing anything extra or odd. A developer must add configuration settings to the application code before you can change them using IIS. It's true that you can create settings yourself, but the application won't use them.

This section assumes that the developer has added settings to the application code that the administrator can use to configure the application. To configure a setting for a particular application, choose the application in the

Connections pane and double-click the Application Settings icon. You'll see a list of application settings when the application supports them.

Using the application variables is relatively easy. Any application variables that the developer has already defined appear in the list automatically. These variables have a Local entry type in most cases. Global variables that affect more than one application will have an Inherited entry type.

The task you perform most often is editing exiting variables. To perform this task, highlight the variable you want to change and choose Edit from the Actions pane. You see an Edit Application Setting dialog box. Don't change the name of the variable as it appears in the Name field. However, you can change the information in the Value field to meet a particular need. Always verify that you made the entry correctly because incorrect entries can result in a malfunctioning application.

When you need to make an application setting, click Add in the Actions pane. You see an Add Application Setting dialog box. Type the name of the variable as specified by the developer. Type an appropriate value in the Value field.

To remove a setting you no longer need, highlight the value in the Application Settings pane and then click Remove in the Actions pane. IIS asks whether you're sure you want to remove the setting. Click Yes to complete the action.

Managing session state

HTTP is a one-request protocol. The client makes a request, the server responds, and then everyone forgets that the conversation took place. Because there isn't any memory between requests, HTTP normally can't work for applications such as shopping carts or address application needs such as form-based security. However, developers have found many ways of overcoming this problem. The entire conversation between client and server becomes a session that can have one or more requests. Storing (remembering) the content of that conversation between requests is called the *session state,* and it relies on some form of application variable storage. The following sections describe how ASP.NET manages session state and how you can configure the technique you want to use from within IIS 7.

Changing the Session State mode

IIS 7 provides considerable flexibility when it comes to state information for ASP.NET applications. You can view state information by choosing the ASP.NET application in the Connections pane and double-clicking the Session State icon. Figure 4-7 shows the portion of the session state information for this section, the session state mode.

Figure 4-7:
Choosing
the correct
session
state mode
can make
your
applications
more
accessible.

The session state mode determines how IIS 7 tracks session state. The default option tracks the session state in process. In other words, the worker process actually tracks the state information as it fulfills the request of the caller. The disadvantage of this approach is that the session state information is lost when the system recycles the worker process. Of course, because the server lets the current worker process complete answering all requests in its queue, this problem may not affect your applications. However, when a user has to make many requests, such as working with a shopping cart application, it can be a problem.

You can also choose not to track session state. Simply select the Not Enabled option. The advantage of this option is that it increases application perform-ance when an application doesn't need to maintain session state. The downside is that it prevents applications from using session state even when they need it and a configuration error could cause your application to fail.

The Custom setting is usable only when an application developer creates a custom provider to support session state for ASP.NET applications. If your application doesn't include this feature, you don't need to worry about this setting. Normally, you find this setting only when working with custom appli-cations. Commercial applications normally use a standardized method for handling session state.

The final option is to store the state information in SQL Server. In this case, IIS stores the state information in SQL Server. This approach has the advan-tage of not storing state information in the worker process and making it vul-nerable to worker process recycling. The technique exchanges memory as a medium of storage for hard drive space. Consequently, the storage is also more permanent. As with the State Server option, you must decide on a time-out value that reflects the needs of your application. You shouldn't need to change the connection string. To enable this particular feature, you must run the `InstallSqlState.sql` script located in the `\Windows\Microsoft.NET\Framework\v2.0.50727` folder of your hard drive. If you decide that you don't want to use the standard configuration, you can check the Enable Custom Database option and create a custom setup. Generally speaking, you probably won't need this feature for anything but very large applications.

Controlling the use of cookies

One of the ways to store state information is cookies. Of course, you have to decide how to use cookies. For example, some Web sites insist that the caller use cookies even when the caller doesn't want to — the caller normally wins on a public Web site. You find the cookie settings in the Cookie Settings area, as shown in Figure 4-8.

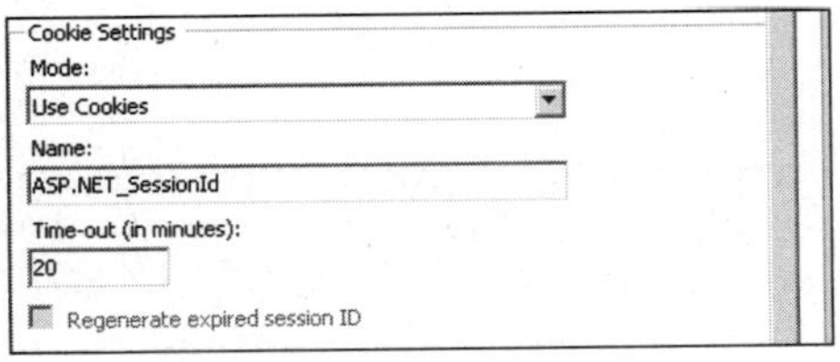

Figure 4-8:
Use the cookie settings to control how IIS works with cookies.

The first thing you have to determine is how you want your application to use cookies. The default is to use cookies even if the caller doesn't want to, and, as mentioned, the caller usually wins that argument by leaving your Web site. You do have other options, as described in the following list:

+ **Auto Detect:** You should use this setting whenever possible because it detects the caller's wishes and uses cookies only when the caller allows them.

+ **Use Cookies:** The default setting assumes that all users want to use cookies, whether they can support them or not. This setting irritates people who disable cookies on their browser because they find that they can't interact with your application unless they turn cookies on — they may choose to go somewhere else. More importantly, however, is that some devices *can't* support cookies, and using this setting locks them out of your application.

- ✦ **Use Device Profile:** If you choose to use cookies even when the user doesn't want them but you don't want to lock out devices that can't support the cookies, you can use this setting. IIS checks the caller first to determine what kind of device is making the request. When the device doesn't support cookies, IIS provides another means of storing the state information.

- ✦ **Use URI:** This choice avoids the whole issue of cookies. It stores the state information in the URI and then redirects the user to the original URL. The technique requires additional time and server resources to use. The caller waits a little while longer on complex Web pages, too. However, because this method doesn't require cookies, it works better when you have a public Web site.

The session identifier is a value that helps the application to detect different callers. It's a name-and-value pair, just like most cookies. To avoid giving the ne'er-do-wells of the world too much help, you can change the name of the session identifier from the default value of ASP.NET_SessionId. Doing so makes it harder for someone to search your Web pages for the value they need. Of course, you want to tell the developer about the change, too, because the application code may look for this value as well.

Considering impersonation requirements

Impersonation is an important feature of Windows. If someone's logging in to the system anonymously, you don't want them to have access to everything on your network, and that includes your SQL Server setup. However, when using certain kinds of session state management, the system has to access SQL Server. Because the anonymous user doesn't have access to SQL Server, gaining the required access could be a problem. That's where impersonation comes into play. The session can impersonate someone who does have the required access to gain access to SQL Server for the session state information. Because the impersonation is under the control of the system, there's no security issue with this approach. The anonymous user is still locked out, and the system is performing any required tasks on the user's behalf.

The Use Hosting Identity for Impersonation setting of the Session State window lets the system use the ASP.NET account or a Windows service account to gain access to SQL Server for the purpose of maintaining session state information. If your session state strategy doesn't rely on SQL Server, you can probably clear this option. You can also clear this option when your application depends on secured sessions, and you can use the user's identity to gain the required access. The time you need this option is when the user logs on anonymously or doesn't have sufficient rights to access the SQL Server setup.

It's important to set the timeout value as well. Some individuals will attempt to obtain the session identifier and then use it to gain access to the communication between the caller and the server. In some cases, the individual simply steals the session. Regenerating session identifiers by setting a short timeout value tends to reduce this problem. Of course, setting the timeout too short won't let you accomplish much and consumes many server resources. Microsoft recommends something shorter than the default of 20 minutes, but it doesn't tell you how much shorter to set the timeout value. A good rule of thumb is to consider the complexity of the data you're manipulating and the sensitivity of that data.

The final setting, Regenerate Expired Session ID, applies only to sessions that don't rely on cookies (the Use URI setting) unless you create specialized software to support this feature in other scenarios. Checking this option tells IIS to reject any session identifiers that don't have an active session in the database. IIS then reissues an identifier to the original caller.

Chapter 5: Configuring an FTP Server

In This Chapter

⌕ **Getting started using an FTP server**

⌕ **Performing management tasks using the graphical tools**

⌕ **Performing management tasks using the command line tools**

⌕ **Securing your FTP site**

A File Transfer Protocol (FTP) site may not seem like a very interesting addition to your server, but FTP still provides one of the easiest ways to share files with the outside world or with employees on the go. Tools such as FTP Explorer (`http://www.ftpx.com/`) make your FTP site look just like another Windows Explorer display. In short, FTP is a great technology for making files of all kinds accessible.

Companies typically make certain kinds of files available using FTP. For example, employees will likely use FTP to download forms or company policies. This kind of content can consume a lot of room and doesn't require a lot of explanation, so it's a perfect use for FTP. It's possible to create FTP links on your Web site, so you can also direct users to any files they need by using directions on your Web site. Some companies also use FTP sites to provide software updates, especially when the update files are large.

This chapter provides the basics of using FTP as a means for distributing files. As with many IIS features, you install a separate feature for FTP support. Unlike most other IIS features, FTP relies on the old IIS 6 Management console, now called Internet Information Services (IIS) 6.0 Manager. Consequently, if you already know how to work with FTP in Windows 2003, you also know how to work with it in Windows Server 2008 (although you might want to read about a few small twists in this chapter).

Understanding FTP Site Prerequisites

The FTP installation features appear in the FTP Publishing Service role service for the Web Server (IIS) role. You can install just the FTP Management Console or the FTP Management Console and the FTP Server. When you install the FTP functionality, Windows also automatically installs the Information Services

(IIS) 6.0 Manager. If you don't need FTP functionality, you can simply install the Information Services (IIS) 6.0 Manager console separately. The Information Services (IIS) 6.0 Manager console provides for both the local and remote management of FTP sites.

You may have noticed the FTP Sites entry in the Internet Information Services (IIS) Manager. This entry is actually a placeholder. Click the Click Here to Launch link and you open the Internet Information Services (IIS) 6.0 Manager. Microsoft will probably change this functionality sometime, but for now you can simply use the link to open the Internet Information Services (IIS) 6.0 Manager. It's also possible to open the Internet Information Services (IIS) 6.0 Manager console directly from the Administrative Tools folder of the Control Panel.

You won't see much when you initially open the Internet Information Services (IIS) 6.0 Manager, as shown in Figure 5-1. Rather than the setup you might have seen in earlier versions of IIS, the only feature that appears in the default configuration is the FTP site. In fact, the default setup won't even start the FTP site for you, and the service itself is in manual mode. This change from previous versions of Windows is a security feature designed to let you set security for your FTP site before you allow anyone to visit. To start the FTP site for a short time, select the FTP site in the left pane and click Start Item on the toolbar.

Figure 5-1: IIS doesn't start the FTP site by default; you must configure IIS to start it.

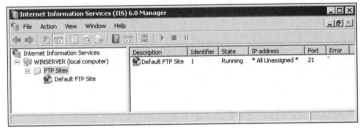

If you want to set the FTP site to start automatically, you need to configure the service manually. Use the following steps to perform the task:

1. **Open the Services console in the Administrative Tools folder of the Control Panel.**

You see a list of services, as shown in Figure 5-2.

2. **Locate the FTP Publishing Service in the list.**

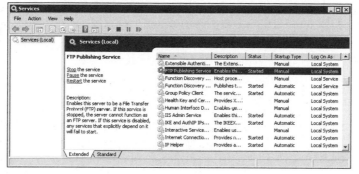

Figure 5-2:
Locate the FTP Publishing Service and set it to start automatic- ally.

3. **Right-click the entry and choose Properties from the context menu.**

   You see the FTP Publishing Service Properties dialog box.

4. **Click Start to start the service.**

5. **Choose Automatic in the Startup Type field and click OK.**

   Windows changes the FTP Publishing Service status to start automati- cally every time you start Windows.

Managing FTP Server with the Graphical Interface

Whether you have the FTP site running or not, you can perform configuration tasks on it. In fact, it's often a good idea to make changes with the FTP site stopped so that everyone is certain to receive the changes. The following sections describe how to configure the FTP server by using the graphical interface.

Accessing the FTP features

You can modify some server features directly, but not as many features as in past versions of IIS. To access the server features, right-click the server entry in the left pane and choose Properties from the context menu. One of the first changes you'll notice from previous versions of IIS is that you can still change the Enable Direct Metabase Edit and Encode Web Logs in UTF-8 settings as you did before, but IIS disabled the MIME Types options. The reason for the change is that Windows Server 2008 uses a different method for assigning MIME types. (See the "Configuring MIME types" section of Book VII, Chapter 2 for details.)

Generally, you work with FTP sites rather than with the server or the IIS con- figuration as a whole. To modify a particular FTP site, right-click the FTP site entry and choose Properties. You see the Default FTP Site Properties dialog box, as shown in Figure 5-3. You use this dialog box for local FTP settings.

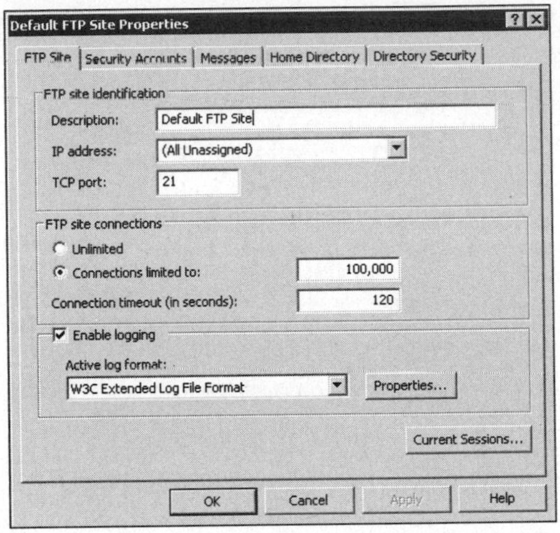

Figure 5-3:
The Default
FTP Site
Properties
dialog box
contains
settings for
your local
FTP site.

As with all hierarchical setups in Windows, you can also set properties for all FTP sites on a particular server by right-clicking the FTP Sites folder in the left pane and choosing Properties from the context menu. The FTP Sites Properties dialog box (the one used for global settings) doesn't include the FTP Site tab. In addition, you find a few features missing on the Home Directory tab.

The Directory Security tab doesn't work for IIS 7. Rather than use the Directory Security tab, your system must rely on a combination of account settings and permissions. The "Setting Security for Your FTP Site" section of this chapter describes how to set the permissions for your FTP site.

Modifying the FTP Site tab

As you can see from Figure 5-3, the FTP Site tab contains the FTP site description, IP address, and TCP port. The default setting is port 21. If this is a private FTP site, using a different port can reduce the chance of attack (or, at least, slow it down a little). Setting the security for your FTP site is essential. (See the "Setting Security for Your FTP Site" section for details.)

Make sure that you set the Connections Limited To and Connection Timeout (in Seconds) values to match the expected load for your FTP site. Setting the value too high can place a significant burden on the server. Setting the value too low can cause callers to receive errors messages when they try to download files.

The FTP Site tab also contains an option for logging all user access. The standard format is a World Wide Web Consortium (W3C) Extended Log File Format. You can also choose the Microsoft IIS Log File Format or Open Database Connectivity (ODBC) Logging (for any database that supports

ODBC). FTP for IIS 7 doesn't support all six log file formats found in IIS 6. You can see these logging formats at `http://www.microsoft.com/technet/ prodtechnol/WindowsServer2003/Library/IIS/bea506fd-38bc- 4850-a4fb-e3a0379d321f.mspx`.

Click Properties and you see a Logging Properties dialog box, like the one shown in Figure 5-4. The General tab has settings that determine the amount of time that IIS uses the same log and the location of that log. The default settings change the log daily and place it in the `\WINDOWS\System32\ LogFiles` folder. You can increase security by changing the default log location to another secure area of your system.

Figure 5-4:
Use extended log entry information to help identify anyone using the FTP site.

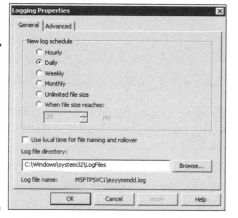

The Advanced tab contains a list of standard log entries. The standard settings don't tell you much about the person using your site. If this were a public site, you'd want to save log space by using the default entries. However, if this is a private site and log size isn't a problem, you should log as much information about the individual as possible.

Click Current Sessions at the bottom of the FTP Site tab, and you see the FTP User Sessions dialog box. It lists the name of the person (or persons) using the FTP site, the IP address of the remote connection, and the amount of time they have connected to the FTP site. You can use the Disconnect and Disconnect All buttons to remove users from the site as needed.

Modifying the Security Accounts tab

The Security Accounts tab controls access to your FTP site, as shown in Figure 5-5. Clear the Allow Anonymous Connections option if you want to restrict someone from logging in to the site anonymously. Unfortunately, this also causes problems because FTP passes the username and password in clear text. This means that someone with a network sniffer could gain access to the user's connection information. This tab also contains options that force IIS to use anonymous connections alone.

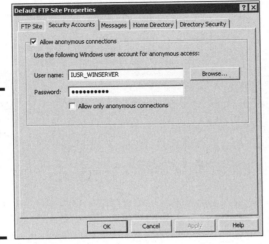

Figure 5-5:
Set the security for your FTP site to ensure proper access levels.

Modifying the Messages tab

FTP sites normally require the use of four messages for connecting users. IIS doesn't include any default messages, so visitors to your site see a blank screen until you define a message. The Messages tab contains these options:

✦ **Banner:** The message the user sees before logging in to the FTP site.

✦ **Welcome:** The message the user sees after logging in to the FTP site.

✦ **Exit:** The message the user sees after logging out of the FTP site.

✦ **Maximum Connections:** An error message that the user sees when the server reaches its maximum number of connections.

Modifying the Home Directory tab

The Home Directory tab, shown in Figure 5-6, controls the location and security settings for the home directory. Notice that you can use a local directory or a share (directory or drive) on another machine. The FTP Site Directory information includes the path to the directory and the rights the user has to the directory. Notice that you have only a choice of read, write, and log visits. The Directory Listing style is especially important. Many FTP utilities require the UNIX style of directory listing and don't show any subdirectories until you use it. If users have problems seeing the folders or files on your FTP site, you may need to make this change.

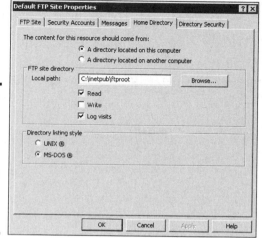

Figure 5-6:
The Home Directory tab controls the location and security settings of the root FTP directory.

Saving your configuration

After you take all the time required to create an FTP site configuration, it's time to save the configuration for later. (This technique also works for virtual directories.) You can use the configuration to create a new FTP site based on the file content or to restore a broken configuration. To save the configuration:

1. **Right-click the FTP site and choose All Tasks⇨Save Configuration to a File from the context menu.**

   You see the Save Configuration to a File dialog box.

2. **Type the name of the file you want to create in the File Name field.**

3. **Choose a location for the file in the Path field.**

   The default setting of `\Windows\system32\inetsrv` usually works fine.

4. **(Optional) Check Encrypt Configuration Using Password, type a password in the Password field, and confirm it in the Confirm Password field.**

5. **Click OK.**

   IIS saves the configuration for you.

Restoring your configuration

Eventually, you need the configuration information you stored. Follow these steps when you decide to use the configuration to create a new FTP site (or virtual directory):

1. **Right-click the FTP Sites or a specific FTP site and choose New⇨FTP Site (From File) from the context menu. When creating a virtual directory, choose New⇨Virtual Directory (From File) instead.**

   You see an Import Configuration dialog box.

2. **Type the path and name of the file that contains the configuration information.**

   This information appears in an XML file. Consequently, if you named your file Test earlier, you need to look for Test.XML now. The default configuration file storage directory is \Windows\system32\inetsrv.

3. **Click Read File.**

   You see the configurations within the file appear in the Select a Configuration to Import list.

4. **Click OK.**

   IIS asks whether you want to create a new site based on the data or replacing the existing site data.

5. **Choose a site creation option and click OK.**

   IIS creates or re-creates the FTP site (or virtual directory) for you.

Managing FTP Servers with the FTP Utility

At some point, you need to manage the content on your FTP site. You can perform this task manually using Windows Explorer or with a graphical utility, such as FTP Explorer. However, the problem with all these utilities is that you have to be present to use them — they don't provide automation.

You can automate many content management tasks by using the FTP utility, which is one of the easiest ways of transferring files to literally any system. This utility uses the following syntax: FTP [-v] [-n] [-i] [-d] [-g] [-s:<Filename>] [-a] [-w:<Buffer_Size>] [-x:sendbuffer] [-r:recvbuffer] [-b:asyncbuffers] [-A] [-?] [<Host>].

FTP uses case-sensitive switches. For example, -A isn't the same as -a. In addition, you must use the minus sign (–) and not the slash (/) when typing command line arguments. You need to type the command with these requirements in mind. Most of these switches also appear in the interface, so you can modify the behavior after you start the application. The following list describes each of the command line arguments:

✦ **-?:** Displays online help. Note that, at the time of this writing, there are typos in both the Help and Support Center document and the application-supplied help.

✦ **-a:** Tells FTP to use any available interface when creating a connection to the host.

✦ **-A:** Logs you in as an anonymous user. Note that this switch is the only one typed in uppercase.

✦ **-b:asyncbuffers:** Overrides the default number of asynchronous buffers (3 is the default).

✦ **-d:** Displays all FTP commands passed between the client and server. This switch enables you to debug script files.

✦ **-g:** Disables filename *globbing* (essentially, wildcard expansion), which permits the use of wildcard characters in local filenames and pathnames.

✦ **Host:** Contains the name or address of the host you want to connect to for a file download.

✦ **-i:** Removes interactive prompting during multiple file transfers. This switch enables you to automate the file transfer process.

✦ **-n:** Disables auto-logon on initial connection.

✦ **-r:recvbuffer:** Overrides the default received buffer size of 8,192 bytes.

✦ **-s:Filename:** Provides the name of a text file containing FTP commands. In essence, this switch enables you to create a script for your FTP download. Use this switch rather than redirection (>).

✦ **-v:** Disables the display of remote server responses. It comes in handy if you want the download to progress in the background without disturbing your foreground task.

✦ **-w:Buffer_Size:** Changes the data transfer buffer size. The default size of 4,096 bytes normally works well. However, you might want to decrease the buffer size if you experience errors on a connection or use a larger buffer size for local connections. A large buffer is more efficient, but you lose less data for each damaged packet when working with a small buffer.

✦ **-x:sendbuffer:** Overrides the default send buffer size of 8,192 bytes.

The FTP utility provides a surprising array of commands you can use after you run the utility. There are too many to list here, but you can get a list easily enough. All you need to remember is one command when working in interactive mode: the question mark (?). If you type a question mark in interactive mode, you see a list of all the things you can do with FTP. (You can obtain a similar list using the -? command line switch.)

Book VII
Chapter 5

Configuring an FTP Server

Setting Security for Your FTP Site

You can control access to your FTP site using the same techniques you use for any other part of the server. When working with an FTP site, you can set security at the FTP site, folder, virtual directory, and file levels. The FTP site, folder, and virtual directory levels all use the same technique for setting permission.

To change security for any of the FTP levels, right-click the entry you want to change and choose Permissions from the context menu. You see security options that look similar to those you set for a file or directory, as shown in Figure 5-7. However, you'll notice that this isn't the standard security dialog box. It provides additional levels of security, such as the ability to list the folder contents. Consequently, the security you set at these levels is refined without having to perform too many extra configuration steps.

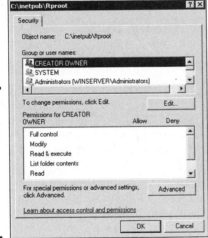

Figure 5-7: Set permissions for individual directories on your FTP site as needed.

The IIS_IUSRS user doesn't have any access by default. Consequently, even if you allow anonymous access to your FTP site, you must also provide to the IIS_IUSRS user the permissions required to access it. Microsoft added this extra step as a security feature to IIS 7. Use these steps to add the IIS_IUSRS user:

1. **Click Edit.**

You see the Permissions dialog box.

2. Click Add.

You see the Select Users, Computers, or Groups dialog box. In many cases, you need to change the From This Location entry.

    a. Click Locations.

        You see a Locations dialog box.

    b. Choose the machine that contains the FTP site and click OK.

        The location information changes so that you can enter the IIS_IUSRS user account.

3. Type IIS_IUSRS in the Enter the Object Names to Select field and click OK.

Windows adds the IIS_IUSRS account to the Group or User Names list in the Permissions dialog box.

4. Check the required access options in the Permissions for IIS_IUSRS list.

5. Click OK twice.

Windows applies the permissions you set to the FTP site, folder, or virtual directory.

Accessing file security in an FTP site is the same as in Windows Explorer. If you can't see the files, right-click the FTP site, folder, or virtual directory and choose Explore from the context menu. Right-click the file and choose Properties from the context menu. Select the Security tab. At this point, you can set security for the file just as you would do for any other FTP site entity.

**Book VII
Chapter 5**

**Configuring
an FTP Server**

Chapter 6: Configuring IIS Security

In This Chapter

✓ **Working with certificates**

✓ **Managing an SSL setup on IIS**

✓ **Managing the ASP.NET security features**

*I*t's easy to see the effects of some changes on your server. When you decide to add a new control to your Web page, you can see and work with it immediately — change a color and you see it immediately as well. Security is less visible. It really receives attention only when someone tries to do something with your server that you didn't expect or want. Sometimes, security is more annoying than helpful when it prevents someone from performing a legitimate task. However, for the most part, security simply isn't visible. Yet, security is potentially the most important part of your Web site — the part that you must address or nothing else you do is worthwhile. Without security, someone will come along and deface your Web site, at minimum, or cause untold damage to your data and reputation.

Security begins with the standard Windows security features. You begin securing your Web site by adding security to the folders and files that hold the data used to present information on your Web site. Consequently, before you begin this chapter, you should explore Book V and ensure that you have basic security in place for your Web site. You want to ensure that all the proper rights are in place and that you have locked down the entire Web site structure before you do anything else.

This chapter focuses on the next level of security. Your Web site will likely provide the point of entry for anyone of ill intent. Sure, you have a firewall in place to provide partial protection and you've secured the directory structure, but you really need a lot more than these basic security measures. This chapter explores the use of certificates to help secure your Web site. For example, you can use a certificate to lock down communications with Secure Sockets Layer (SSL).

You also find a discussion of ASP.NET security in this chapter. It may seem as though this book has spent an inordinate amount of time looking at ASP.NET, but this new technology really does have a lot to offer in the area of security. You can not only secure the directory structure, the files, and the user but also provide better authentication, improved authorization, and a significant improvement in Code Access Security (CAS) for your applications.

Never assume that you can build a security wall so high that someone can't scale it and damage your system. Being paranoid when it comes to security is a good way to keep your network protected. Yes, users may find your paranoia disturbing, even offensive, but watching the network for unexpected activity is the only way to ensure that your system remains safe. When a breach occurs, make sure to handle it quickly. Be sure that your company has procedures in place for handling data breaches because they will occur despite your best efforts.

Obtaining a Certificate

Digital certificates provide electronic identification that others can use to determine your company's identity and decide whether they want to interact with it. Much like a driver's license, a digital certificate provides essential information about your company. Someone viewing the digital certificate knows who has authenticated your company's identity (even when you've done so yourself using a self-signed certificate). The combination of information about your company and the third party who has authenticated the information gives the viewer confidence about your identity. The following sections discuss the important issue of certificates and how to work with them in IIS.

Understanding the importance of certificates

The term *certificate* is appropriate. A *server certificate* is a kind of document that identifies the server. Normally, this certificate comes from a third party that performs a verification process to determine that you are who you say you are. When someone makes a sensitive request for information from your Web site, you present the certificate to them so that they know you're actually the one receiving the information, rather than someone else posing as you. A third party that the caller trusts signs the certificate, so the caller trusts you as well because the trusted third party has vouched for you. Because the Internet is so impersonal, it's important to know whom you're working with at any time, making certificates an essential tool.

Digital certificates can appear in a number of situations. When someone creates a secure connection to your server, they see the digital certificate used to encrypt the data stream. If you provide a control that performs certain tasks for the user, the control receives your company's digital certificate as a signature. The signature ensures that the control comes from you and that no one tampers with the control while you send the control to the caller. A digital certificate can appear as part of the files you download to the user's machine and as part of the e-mails your company sends to the user. In all cases, the digital certificate serves to identify your company; in some cases, the digital certificate also provides a lock on content so that no one can tamper with it without raising an alarm.

Sometimes you don't need a trusted third party to vouch for you — all you really need is a certificate that identifies your organization in some way. For example, a partner company already knows and trusts your organization, but you want to be sure that they know they're working with you and not with someone else. Using a self-signed certificate can work, in this case, because the certificate is still unique and it specifically identifies your organization.

No matter how you create a certificate, you need certificates to perform some tasks in IIS. For example, if you want to set up an SSL connection, you need a certificate of some type to do it. The SSL protocol is based on the concept of creating a secure connection between parties based on a certificate that positively identifies at least one of those parties — normally the server. To access the server certificates, select the server entry in the Connections pane and double-click the Server Certificates icon. You see the Server Certificates pane, as shown in Figure 6-1.

Figure 6-1: Server certificates provide identification between two parties on the Internet.

Book VII Chapter 6

Configuring IIS Security

Importing an existing certificate

Whenever you receive a certificate from a third party, you must import it into your server in order to use it. In addition, you export and then import a certificate when you want to move a certificate from an existing server to a new one. The following steps show how to import a certificate:

1. **Click Import in the Actions pane.**

You see the Import Certificate dialog box.

2. **Type the path for the certificate you want to import.**

   You can also click the ellipses to display the Open dialog box, which you can use to locate the Personal Information Exchange (PFX) file containing the certificate.

   The PFX file format is the only one that IIS accepts. You can't use an alternative format, such as, PKCS #12 (P12), ARM, Privacy Enhanced Mail (PEM), or Distinguished Encoding Rules (DER). There's some confusion about whether PFX and P12 are two different versions of the same Public Key Cryptographic System (PKCS #12) standard, but the two file formats aren't the same. Consequently, IIS won't accept a P12 file in place of a PFX file even if both truly are following the same standard. You can see a list of all PKCS standards at `http://en.wikipedia.org/wiki/PKCS`. The PKCS FAQ at `http://www.drh-consultancy.demon.co.uk/pkcs12faq.html` attempts to make some sense out of the whole mess.

3. **Type the password for the certificate in the Password field.**

   The password must match exactly (even with capitalization).

4. **Check the Allow this Certificate to be Exported option if you want to allow someone to export the certificate.**

   This option is beneficial when working with a locally generated certificate. However, it's a good idea to secure your third-party certificate by clearing this check box and locking away the original file where no one but authorized personnel can get to it.

5. **Click OK.**

   IIS imports the certificate, and it appears in the Server Certificates pane.

Creating a certificate request

Before you can obtain a certificate from a third party, you must create a request for it. The certificate creation process generates a file that you send along with other information to the third party. The amount of information you must supply depends on the third party's requirements and the kind of certificate you request. The following steps describe how to create a certificate request:

1. **Click Create Certificate Request in the Actions pane.**

   You see the Request Certificate dialog box, as shown in Figure 6-2.

2. **Type a name for the certificate in the Common Name field.**

   Make sure that this name reflects the name that your organization wants to use for the certificate, because anyone who works with it will need to know the name.

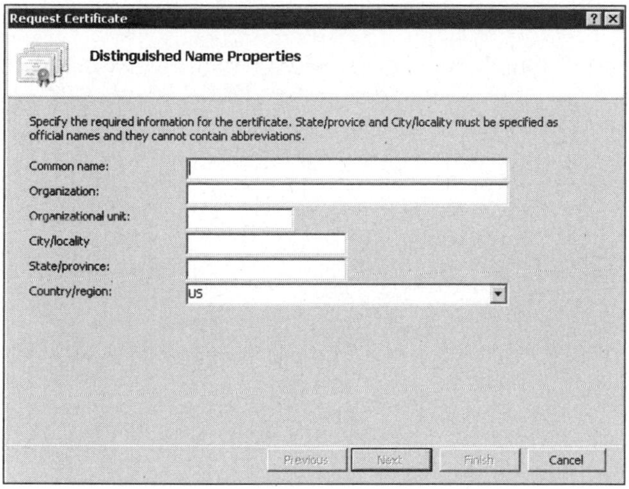

Figure 6-2:
Define a
name for the
certificate
and the
identifying
information
for your
organization.

3. Provide your organizational information.

You must use full names; no abbreviations. The certificate must contain full information in every one of the fields, including the Organizational Unit field. If you have a small company, you need to provide either your company name or a name, such as `main office`.

4. Click Next.

You see the Cryptographic Service Provider Properties dialog box.

5. Choose a cryptographic service provider.

The Microsoft RSA SChannel Cryptographic Provider works well in most cases. It provides support for hashing, data signing, and signature verification. You can provide a complete description of this cryptographic service provider at `http://msdn2.microsoft.com/en-us/library/aa386988.aspx`. In most cases, you want to use the default setting of Microsoft RSA SChannel Cryptographic Provider.

The Microsoft DH SChannel Cryptographic Provider provides support for a number of additional needs. The most important reason to use this cryptographic service provider is that you need to exchange private keys on a nonsecure network. However, you also find that this cryptographic service provider suffers from a number of flaws, one of which is speed. The other problem is that this cryptographic service provider supports only 512- and 1,024-bit keys. You can read more about this cryptographic service provider at `http://msdn2.microsoft.com/En-US/library/aa386984.aspx`.

6. **Choose a key length in the Bit Length field.**

   The rule of thumb here is that a longer key provides better security and a shorter key provides better performance. You need to choose a key length that reflects the security requirements for your organization. In most cases, the 1,024-bit key length for a Microsoft RSA SChannel Cryptographic Provider and the 512-bit key length for Microsoft DH SChannel Cryptographic Provider work well.

7. **Click Next.**

   You see a File Name dialog box.

8. **Type the name of the file you want to use to save the request.**

9. **Click Finish.**

   IIS generates a text file you can use to request a certificate.

Completing a certificate request

After you supply all the information that a third party requires to generate a certificate, you receive a Certificate (CER) file. You use this file to install the certificate on your server. The following steps help you perform this process:

1. **Click Complete Certificate Request in the Actions pane.**

   You see the Complete Certificate Request dialog box.

2. **Type the location of the CER file.**

   You can also click the Ellipsis button to display the Open dialog box, which you can use to locate the file.

3. **Type a friendly name for the certificate in the Friendly Name field.**

   Make sure that the friendly name reflects the actual certificate use.

4. **Click OK.**

   IIS imports the certificate, and it appears in the Server Certificates pane.

Creating a domain certificate

A domain certificate is very much like a third-party certificate, except that you use the domain certificate server to sign the certificate rather than rely on a third party. Consequently, you can use this certificate with partners who already trust you, but it isn't a good choice for a Web site where you must provide a certificate that callers who don't know you will trust. The following steps tell how to create a domain certificate:

1. **Click Create Domain Certificate in the Actions pane.**

You see the Create Certificate dialog box, which looks similar to the one shown in Figure 6-2 (except for the title bar).

2. Type a name for the certificate in the Common Name field.

Make sure that this name reflects the name your organization wants to use for the certificate, because anyone who works with it will need to know the name.

3. Provide your organizational information.

You must use full names; no abbreviations. The certificate must contain full information in every one of the fields, including the Organizational Unit field. If you have a small company, you need to provide either your company name or a name like `main office`.

4. Click Next.

You see the Online Certificate Authority dialog box. It identifies the certificate authority used to sign the certificate. When creating a certificate using a certificate server on your network, provide the location of the certificate server.

5. Type the name of the certificate authority on the server, followed by a backslash, followed by the server name.

As an example, if the certificate authority name (as you provided it during installation) is MyCA and the name of the server is MyServer, you type **MyCA\MyServer**. If you've forgotten the certificate authority name, open the Certificate Authority console found in the Administrative Tools folder of the Control Panel on the server. The certificate authority name appears directly after the Certification Authority entry in the Certification Authority console.

6. Type the friendly name for the certificate.

The friendly name is the name you use to reference the certificate on your machine. Use a name that reflects that this certificate is a domain certificate rather than one issued by a third party, such as VeriSign.

7. Click Finish.

Even on a lightly loaded system, the certificate signing process can require several minutes. Be patient because interrupting the process simply means that you have to start it over again. When the certificate is signed, it appears in the Server Certificates pane. In addition, you see the certificate information in the Issued Certificates folder of the Certification Authority console as a Web Server certificate. The certificate type appears in the Certificate Template column of the entry. The remainder of the entry tells about the certificate — who requested it, how long the certificate will last, and all the identifying information found in the original certificate request.

Domain certificates require additional maintenance that you won't encounter with other certificate types. The following sections describe these additional maintenance actions.

Exporting domain certification authority certificates

You must install the certificate authority certificate in the Trusted Root Certification Authorities store on the IIS server system before the system will trust the domain certification authority. To perform this task, you must export the certificate authority server certificate and then import the certificate into the IIS server. Use the following steps to export the certificate authority server certificate:

1. **Right-click the certificate authority name and choose Properties from the context menu.**

   You see a certificate authority Properties dialog box.

2. **Choose the General tab.**

   You see one or more CA certificates (normally just one).

3. **Highlight the certificate you want to use and click View Certificate.**

   You see a Certificate dialog box.

4. **Choose the Details tab and click Copy to File.**

   You see the Certificate Export Wizard.

5. **Follow the steps to create a domain certificate (CER) file.**

   Any of the output formats should work fine for this task. Now that you have a CER file, use the steps in the "Importing domain certification authority certificates" section of this chapter to import the certificate where needed.

Importing domain certification authority certificates

Working with a domain certification authority certificate is a two-step process. Before you can do anything, you must export the certificate by using the steps in the "Exporting domain certification authority certificates" section of this chapter. After you have a CER file to use, you need to install it on the IIS server. The following steps accomplish this task:

1. **Double-click the certificate entry in Windows Explorer from the IIS server.**

   Windows asks whether you're sure that you want to open the file.

2. **Click Open to see the certificate.**

3. **Verify that the information is correct and then click Install Certificate.**

   You see the Certificate Import Wizard.

4. **Click Next.**

You see the Certificate Store dialog box.

5. **Choose the Place All Certificates in the Following Store option.**

6. **Click Browse and choose the Trusted Root Certificate Authorities option.**

7. **Click OK.**

You see the store added to the Certificate Stores dialog box.

8. **Click Next.**

You see a summary dialog box.

9. **Click Finish.**

A Security Warning dialog box tells you that you're about to install a certificate from a certificate authority.

10. **Verify the information and click Yes.**

The domain controller now appears within the trusted list for the IIS server.

Renewing certificates

Unlike most of the certificates you see in the Server Certificates pane, a domain certificate includes an additional entry in the Actions pane. The Renew action lets you renew a certificate when it becomes outdated. The following steps describe how to review your domain certificate:

1. **Highlight the outdated certificate and click Renew in the Actions pane.**

If this action doesn't appear, the certificate you have highlighted isn't renewable using this technique. You see the Renew an Existing Certificate Wizard.

2. **Choose the Renew an Existing Certificate option and click Next.**

You see the Specify Online Certificate Server Authority dialog box.

3. **Type the name of the certificate authority on the server, followed by a backslash, followed by the server name.**

This field contains the same information as when you originally requested the certificate.

4. **Click Finish.**

After a long wait, IIS updates the certificate information in the Server Certificates pane.

On rare occasions, renewing a certificate directly fails. In this case, you can try creating a certificate request, handling it on the certificate authority server, and then installing it on the IIS server using the other options on the first page of the Renew an Existing Certificate Wizard. Use the Create a Renewal Certificate Request option to create the request and the Complete a Certificate Renewal Request option to install the certificate. If you still can't obtain satisfactory results, delete the old certificate and create a new one using the procedure in the "Creating a domain certificate" section of this chapter.

Renewing certificates normally won't work for third-party certificates because you have no direct connection to the certification authority server. Follow the third-party recommendations for renewing a third-party certificate.

Creating a self-signed certificate

A self-signed certificate is good for a number of tasks. If someone already knows you and simply needs to know that they're talking with you, a self-signed certificate can do the job. You also find self-signed certificates used for testing purposes. There isn't a good reason to purchase a certificate from VeriSign for your test server. In most cases, all you really need is something to let you test your applications. After all, you already trust yourself. The following steps tell you how to create a self-signed certificate:

1. **Click Create Self-Signed Certificate in the Actions pane.**

You see the Create Self-Signed Certificate Wizard.

2. **Type a friendly name for the certificate.**

The name should be something that positively identifies the certificate as self-signed so that you don't confuse it with another certificate.

3. **Click OK.**

IIS generates the certificate for you and automatically installs it in the Server Certificates pane.

Configuring SSL on IIS

One of the main reasons to obtain a server certificate is to create an SSL setup. In some cases, you secure the whole server, but in other cases, you secure only specific applications or even specific Web pages. What you secure depends on the situation. For example, a public Web site may secure only the Web pages used to log in for premium information, whereas a shopping cart application may use SSL for the entire shopping experience. A private Web site may secure the entire Web site to ensure that no one can intercept messages between the client and the server. No matter what reason you have for securing a Web site or its elements, the following sections will get you started.

Creating an HTTPS binding

Before you can use SSL, the Web site must support a Hypertext Transfer Protocol Secure Sockets (HTTPS) binding. The HTTPS protocol relies on SSL to secure the communication between the client and the server. Because the server encrypts the communication, no one can eavesdrop on your conversation.

Only the communication is secure when using HTTPS — you still need to include appropriate security to secure the Web site or application as needed. For example, when working with a shopping cart application on a public Web site, all you need to secure is the communication using HTTPS, but when working with a private Web site where access is limited, you also need to provide security. Of course, you must always consider ancillary elements as part of your strategy. Your shopping cart application will include customer databases that you must secure, even though these databases likely reside behind a firewall and the user never accesses them directly.

When you create a Web site, you normally assign it an HTTP binding. The default port for this binding is port 80, but you can use any port desired. HTTPS binding works the same way, except it has a default port of port 443. You can use another port number if desired for additional security. In this case, you're adding a second binding to an existing Web site. The following steps show how to add an HTTPS binding after you install a server certificate on the server:

1. **Select the Web site you want to modify in the Connections pane.**

2. **Click Bindings in the Actions pane.**

You see the Site Bindings dialog box, as shown in Figure 6-3.

3. **Click Add.**

You see the Add Site Binding dialog box, similar to the one shown in Figure 6-4.

Figure 6-3:
View the existing bindings for a Web site using this dialog box.

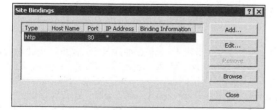

Figure 6-4:
Add the
HTTPS
binding to
the Web site
for secure
communica-
tions.

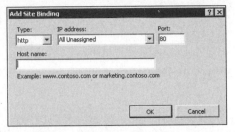

4. **Choose the HTTPS entry in the Type field.**

   The dialog box changes to include an SSL Certificate field. IIS also grays the Host Name field so that you can't enter a new host name.

5. **Provide an IP address in the IP Address field or use the All Unassigned setting as shown.**

6. **Choose a port for the secure communication.**

   The default setting is port 443.

7. **Choose an SSL certificate in the SSL Certificate field.**

8. **Click View.**

   You see the certificate.

9. **Verify that this is the correct certificate for the Web site in question.**

   You see a Certificate dialog box that contains all the certificate details.

10. **Click OK to close the Certificate dialog box.**

11. **Click OK.**

    IIS creates the new binding. You can see it in the Web Site Bindings dialog box.

12. **Click Close.**

    IIS closes the Site Bindings dialog box.

Defining the server settings

After you install a certificate and configure the appropriate bindings, you can't begin using SSL. Even though the entire infrastructure is in place, you still have to configure the Web site, folder, or application to use SSL. To perform this task, select the Web site, folder, or application you want to configure in the Connections pane and double-click the SSL Settings icon. You see the SSL Settings window, as shown in Figure 6-5.

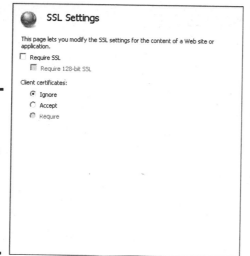

Figure 6-5:
Configure a
Web site, a
folder, or an
application
to rely on
SSL for
commun-
ication
security.

All you need to do is check the Require SSL option and then click Apply in the Actions pane to implement SSL. The default SSL provides 40-bit encryption, which works fine for most applications. It's important to remember that even 40-bit encryption slows the connection dramatically and uses more server resources. Theoretically, it's possible for someone to break 40-bit encryption, however, so you might need additional encryption.

When the situation requires tougher security, you can click the Require 128-bit SSL option. This option makes it incredibly unlikely that someone will intercept and decrypt your communication. However, it also presents problems for browsers that don't support 128-bit encryption and slows your server even more.

You can also require that the client provide a certificate to prove their identity. A client certificate provides an additional level of security because now both ends of the conversation have proof of the other's identity. You can either accept the client certificate when available or require the certificate as part of the SSL setup using the options shown in Figure 6-5. Using the client certificate provides a significant boost in security, but using the client certificate also impacts system performance even more than using 128-bit SSL encryption. You should require a client certificate in only the most secure communications.

Defining the client settings

The client also needs to make some changes to use SSL. If a client attempts to access an SSL page using the HTTP protocol, they receive error message 403.4, which signifies that IIS has forbidden access. On the list of the most likely causes for this issue, you find that enabling SSL ranks at the top. The client must access the Web page by directly typing HTTPS as the protocol because most browsers assume that the client will use HTTP.

Most browsers also display a message box when the user attempts to access the Web site for the first time. This message tells the user that the Web site uses SSL security and asks the user to accept the server's certificate after viewing it. Unfortunately, no matter how the browser developer words the message, most users just don't understand what's happening and refuse to accept the certificate. You can overcome this problem by pre-installing the certificate on the user's machine whenever possible.

When you require a client certificate, you need to ensure that the server knows about the client and that the client has the certificate installed using the procedures for their particular browser. Because only private Web sites are likely to require client certificates, you can make this procedure part of any Web site documentation for your organization. The important issue is that the client must have a certificate installed in the browser and not just on the machine. Browsers that support certificates provide the means for viewing existing certificates and installing new ones. If the user encounters problems accessing your application, ask them to view the certificate they have installed on their machine and ensure that it meets any access requirements for your server.

Configuring ASP.NET Security

ASP.NET security adds to the security that you define using the normal Windows methods. Consequently, the security you add using the techniques in this section is in addition to what you have already configured. It's important to think about the additive effect when you encounter a security problem, such as a lack of access. Configuring ASP.NET security consists of three essential tasks:

1. You must define the trust level of the application as a whole. This trust level determines what the application can do.

2. In many cases, you need to define roles for the application. The application must have code in it to work with the roles, so you can't simply arbitrarily add roles — you must work with the developer to add roles.

3. Add users to roles as needed. A user has certain rights within the application, depending on the role the user fulfills.

Defining trust levels

The .NET trust level determines how much trust you can place in the code for a particular application. This setting complements the code-based security settings defined by the developer. In some cases, the setting overrides the developer setting by placing greater restrictions on the code. The purpose of this setting is to restrict the code so that an outsider can't fool the code (by using an exploit or another trick) into performing a task that the original developer never intended.

To access the .NET trust level, select the application you want to configure in the Connections pane, and then double-click the .NET Trust Levels icon to display the .NET Trust Levels window. The setting is a single drop-down list box that defines how much trust you can place in the code in a given circumstance. Table 6-1 describes each of the settings.

Table 6-1	.NET Trust Levels	
Level	*Description*	*Special Restrictions*
Full	Gives the code unrestricted permissions, which means that it can do anything on the server. The application can perform any task and access any resource on the server unless the developer has included restrictions that reduce application trust or you configure the application using other means, such as the Microsoft .NET Framework 2.0 Configuration console. You should never use this setting for an application that has outside access, and you may not want to use it on internal applications unless required.	N/A
High	Provides the application with maximum access to system resources and allows it to perform most common tasks. This level of security normally works fine for internal networks and some applications on private networks. You don't want to use this setting with a public connection unless absolutely required because it still provides the application code with considerable access to the server.	Call unmanaged code using the Platform Invoke (P/Invoke) functionality, call serviced components, write to the event log, access Microsoft Message Queuing (MSMQ) service queues, and access Open Database Connectivity (ODBC), Object Linking and Embedding – Database (OLE-DB), or Oracle data sources

(continued)

Table 6-1 *(continued)*

Level	Description	Special Restrictions
Medium	Provides the application with a moderate level of access to system resources, but restricts actions that the application can perform to a greater degree. This level of security normally works well in private networks where outside access is questionable and can work on some public networks. However, when working with a public network, you must also work with the developer to ensure that all inputs are checked and that the application provides internal restrictions as needed to prevent unauthorized actions.	All the high-level additional restrictions, access files outside the application directory, access the registry, and make network or Web service calls (even internal Web services)
Low	Provides the application with restricted access to resources and considerable restraints on actions that it can perform. Use this level of security for public networks where you have no reason to believe that there's any chance of securing the application otherwise. About the only task this application can perform is serving data to the user.	All the medium-level additional restrictions, write to the file system, and call the Assert method (the Assert method is used by developers for debugging purposes)
Minimal	At this level, the application can only execute. You can't use it to serve data or perform other tasks. However, this level is useful for situations where you truly need the application to execute and rely on its internal data. For example, you can create an online game using this approach. The application can also store information on the user's machine using cookies, so it can still function and maintain state.	N/A

Managing roles

The roles you create for an application depend on the application itself because the developer must add code to the application to act on the roles. Consequently, you probably see the roles already configured when you install a new application, and you have to work with the developer before you can change any of them. To see the roles associated with an application, choose the application in the Connections pane and then double-click the .NET Roles icon to display the .NET Roles window.

It's important not to change any settings in the .NET Roles pane without understanding the consequences of doing so. For example, when you click Rename, IIS turns the Name field of the selected entry into an edit box and you can change the role name. Unfortunately, if the application doesn't have a similar change, it won't recognize the user's role and won't work as expected. Removing roles can have a similar effect and adding roles is useless when the application doesn't support the role.

This pane does have one particular feature that will appeal to administrators: You can highlight a role and click View Users in the Actions pane. IIS displays a .NET Users pane that's filtered to show just the users that fulfill the specified role. This view can prove useful when you need to make changes to every one of the users in a particular role or simply need to perform an inventory of them.

Managing users

The list of .NET users you create for a Web site or an application helps determine who can log on to the Web site or application. However, before you can add .NET users to your setup, you need to enable forms-based authentication. You should also disable any other form of authentication for an application or else the application may not work as anticipated.

Because the developer must create the application with forms-based authentication in mind, the application should make the required configuration changes when you install it. The process isn't hard, but the application will end up with a Login.ASPX file and some database entries that control user access. After you enable forms-based authentication and have a suitable application, you can begin adding users to the list. Choose the application you want to configure in the Connections pane and then double-click the .NET Users icon to display the .NET Users window. The following sections describe how to manage .NET users.

Resetting the password

You may have noticed the Reset Password action in the Actions pane. Clicking this action displays a dialog box that tells you that the user's question and answer are required in order to reset the password. As an administrator, you can't do anything with the password; the application that the developer creates must include the functionality required for the user to make this change. In fact, if you look at the user entries in the SQL Server database, you find that the .NET Framework encrypts much of the information, making it impossible for the administrator to peek at the information. The .NET Framework also supports functionality that lets a user recover a password. The user provides the answer to a question, and the application automatically sends the password to the user's e-mail account.

Adding users

One of the first tasks you perform with the new application is to add a list of users that can access it. Some applications include functionality for you to add new users by using the application itself. In fact, some applications may ask the user to provide their own information and gain acceptance through administrator approval. Theoretically, you may never see any of the user's information except for a name and other nonsensitive data. Follow these steps when you want to add the users directly from IIS:

1. Click Add in the Actions pane.

You see the Add .NET User dialog box.

2. Type the user's information in the various fields.

You must provide input for every blank. Make sure that the blanks contain valid information because you can't edit the information later. In fact, you can't see any of the information later, not even for verification purposes, so getting it right the first time is essential.

3. Click Next.

You see the .NET User Roles dialog box.

4. Check each of the roles that the user will fulfill in the organization.

5. Click Finish.

IIS adds the new user to the list.

Editing users

You can edit users for a particular ASP.NET application — you simply can't change much information about them. When you click Edit in the Actions pane, you see the Edit .NET User dialog box. This dialog box lets you change the user's e-mail address and set new roles for the user. Otherwise, you can't make any changes to the user's settings.

Removing users

Because of the restrictions placed on administrators, you'll likely need to remove a user at some point. Although the security restrictions that IIS places on administrators are warranted (and even good), user idiosyncrasies make it necessary to remove an account and then re-create it from time to time. To remove a .NET user entry, highlight the entry you want to remove and click Remove in the Actions pane. You see a dialog box asking whether you're sure that you want to remove the user. Click Yes to complete the action.

Part VIII

Services

The 5th Wave   By Rich Tennant

Contents at a Glance

Chapter 1: An Overview of Windows Server 2008 Services

In This Chapter

✓ **Defining how services differ from other application types**

✓ **Considering the basic Windows services**

✓ **Using the WMI interface to perform tasks with services**

✓ **Managing the WMI control properties**

*W*indows Server 2008 relies on a myriad of services. A *service* is a special kind of application that executes in the background and doesn't normally interact with the user in any way. Often, roles and features rely on services to perform tasks in the background. In most cases, the role or feature starts the service for you, but in a few cases, such as FTP support for IIS 7, you must start the service manually to obtain the functionality provided by the service.

Having an application that can't interact with the user may seem like a limitation, but you might be amazed at the number of tasks that services can perform. For example, when your system needs to access Windows Update, it relies on the Windows Update service to do it. When Windows Update needs to download a file to your system, it uses the Background Intelligent Transfer Service (BITS) to perform the task. Services are constantly performing tasks in the background to make the Windows computing experience better.

You may wonder why you need to worry about services, considering that they work almost automatically. An administrator needs to know about every application executing on Windows Server 2008, even the services. In some cases, Microsoft assumes that you need a particular service enabled when you really don't. For example, when you use some other means of updating your server, you really don't need the Windows Update and Background Intelligent Transfer Service enabled. These services are using processing cycles and can open potential security holes. (Yes, services present security holes too.)

One of the more important management services is the Windows Management Interface (WMI). You can use WMI to query a hierarchical database containing information about the server. In addition, by changing settings within this database, you can control the configuration of the server to an extent. By understanding how the Windows Management Instrumentation service works, you can begin to see the importance of working with services as an administrator.

Understanding How Services Work

Services are a special kind of application. However, you can't run a service from the command line — at least, not directly. The system normally starts services for you when it starts or in response to a command you provide. Unlike with most applications, you issue commands to a service by using the Services console, described in the "Using the Services Console" section of Book VIII, Chapter 2. Services normally respond to the commands in the following list:

- ✦ **Start:** Starts the service after you stop it. The service starts with a fresh copy of itself in memory and without any memory of tasks it performed previously.

- ✦ **Stop:** Stops the service from executing any other commands. This action also clears any memory that the service uses.

- ✦ **Continue:** Starts the service after you stop it. The service picks up where it left off in the processing cycle.

- ✦ **Pause:** Stops the service from executing any other commands. This action doesn't clear memory and lets the service later resume any activity it was performing.

- ✦ **Restart:** Performs a combination of a Stop and a Start command. The service restarts any processing it's supposed to perform. You can use this command to restart a service when it has frozen or become corrupted in some other way.

Not all services support all commands in the list. In fact, some services don't support any of the commands — you can't start or stop them. A few services don't provide much in the way of configuration settings either because Microsoft considers them essential to Windows Server 2008 operation. If you see a service that lacks both commands and configuration options, it's safe to assume that you should leave the service alone.

Normally, you never need to know anything more to use a service effectively. In fact, you can safely skip the rest of this section if you want, but you'll also miss out on some very interesting information about how services work.

Some services also support hidden commands. A user application may interact with the service and use these hidden commands to direct service actions. You should never use any technique to issue a hidden command unless directed to do so by a support person.

A service always appears as a DLL. Normally, you can use the RunDLL32 utility to run a DLL file, but services don't rely on this utility. Instead, a service relies on the SvcHost utility to run. Consequently, when working with services, you normally look for the SvcHost utility, rather than the service itself, as a starting point for learning more about the service. You find the SvcHost utility in the `\Windows\System32` folder of your system.

The SvcHost utility relies on registry entries to determine which DLLs to work with. The DLLs normally appear in groups and you tell SvcHost to execute a group by specifying the -k command line switch, along with the group name. For example, the Background Intelligent Transfer Service is part of the `netsvcs` group, which appears as a value in the `HKEY_LOCAL_MACHINE\ SOFTWARE\Microsoft\Windows NT\CurrentVersion\SvcHost` key of the registry. To start the Background Intelligent Transfer Service using SvcHost, type **%SystemRoot%\system32\svchost.exe -k netsvcs** (where %SystemRoot% is the location of the Windows folder on your system) and press Enter at the command line.

A group contains a number of strings that define registry entries containing additional entries for the service. For example, if you look at the `netsvcs` group, you notice that one of the entries is `BITS`. When you look at the `HKEY_LOCAL_MACHINE\SYSTEM\CurrentControlSet\Services\BITS` key, you find all the information needed to use the Background Intelligent Transfer Service. If you're looking for the DLL used to create the service, check the `Servicedll` value of the `HKEY_LOCAL_MACHINE\SYSTEM\ CurrentControlSet\Services\BITS\Parameters` key. You'll discover that the Background Intelligent Transfer Service resides within `QMGR.DLL`. This two-layer approach for working with the SvcHost utility is common in Windows — it's the technique you see most often for working with a service.

Malware often uses the complex set of registry entries used by services to hide in plain site. The malware creator simply designs the virus or Trojan as a service rather than as an application. Placing the service in a group, such as `netsvcs`, means that finding the rogue service requires a lot of administrator time. You can find out more about how services can appear as malware at `http://www.bleepingcomputer.com/tutorials/ tutorial83.html`.

An Overview of the Basic Windows Services

Windows comes with a wealth of services. You must start some services to see basic Windows functionality. For example, you can't use the server as a server without starting the server service. Likewise, if you want to interact with the server, you must start the Workstation service.

In some cases, Windows installs a service as the result of a role or feature you install. For example, you won't see the World Wide Web Publishing Service unless you install the Web Server IIS role. These optional services are part of Windows, so you don't have to do anything special to use them, but Windows won't install them unless you need them.

Microsoft installs some services automatically, but doesn't start them. For example, you don't need the COM+ System Application service running unless you're using a Component Object Model Plus (COM+) application. In fact, Microsoft disables some services because they're dangerous or simply not needed by most people. For example, the Routing and Remote Access service can open a security hole in your system, so Microsoft disables it unless you truly need it. Table 1-1 provides a list of the basic Windows services and describes their use.

Table 1-1	Basic Services Installed on Windows Server 2008	
Name	*Startup Type*	*Description*
Application Experience	Automatic	Monitors application launches. When the service detects a launch, it determines whether the application appears within the application compatibility cache and offers advice on using the application with Windows Server 2008. In some cases, you can set this service to manual to save processing cycles, but you may also experience compatibility problems.
Application Information	Manual	Elevates user privileges as needed. Some applications require that you have specific privileges in order to run. This service monitors the system for such applications and provides the required privilege-elevation dialog box when necessary. You can normally keep this service set to Manual on a server.

Name	Startup Type	Description
Application Layer Gateway Service	Manual	Lets you use third-party plug-ins with Internet Connection Sharing (ICS). You need to change only the startup type for this service when you're using third-party plug-ins with ICS.
Application Management	Manual	Helps you manage the installation and removal of applications that you want to distribute using a group policy. The service also lets you obtain a list of available applications. In most cases, you won't need this service on a server unless you plan to distribute server applications using a group policy.
Background Intelligent Transfer Service	Automatic (Delayed Start)	Performs file transfers in the background using idle network bandwidth (which lets the user continue working unimpeded). BITS also provides the means for starting and stopping downloads without losing track of the download status. You can even continue a download between reboots. Other services, such as Windows Update, rely on this service, so you shouldn't disable it without considering the consequences for other services and applications.
Base Filtering Engine	Automatic	Manages firewall and Internet Protocol Security (IPSec) policies. This service also comes into play for filtering user mode requests. It's a bad idea to stop or disable this service.
Certificate Propagation	Manual	Works with smart cards to distribute digital certificates for identification and other purposes. You don't need to start this service unless your organization uses smart cards.
CNG Key Isolation	Manual	Provides Cryptographic Next Generation (CNG) key process isolation. Windows hosts this service within the Local Security Authority (LSA) process. You can learn more about how this service works at `http://msdn2.microsoft.com/en-us/library/bb204778.aspx`.
COM+ Event System	Automatic	Supports the special COM+ application feature System Event Notification Service (SENS), which provides automatic distribution of events to subscribing Component Object Model (COM) components. You can

(continued)

Table 1-1 *(continued)*

Name	Startup Type	Description
		obtain overviews of SENS at `http://msdn2.microsoft.com/en-us/library/aa377599.aspx`. However, you may find the article about a use for SENS at `http://msdn.microsoft.com/msdnmag/issues/02/08/SENS/` more useful.
COM+ System Application	Manual	Helps you manage and configure COM+ applications. This service also tracks COM+ application status. Most COM+ applications won't run properly without this service, but the COM+ functionality in Windows starts the service automatically as needed, so you shouldn't need to modify this service's configuration.
Computer Browser	Disabled	Creates and maintains a list of computers and other resources (such as printers with direct network connections) on the network. The service supplies this information to other computers that the system designates as browsers. Using this service can speed the spread of resource information on a network. Microsoft disables this service for two reasons. First, this service won't work over an IPv6 network. Second, this service is associated with a named pipe security vulnerability you can read about at `http://www.microsoft.com/technet/security/Bulletin/MS05-007.mspx`.
Cryptographic Services	Automatic	Performs four cryptographic-related management tasks. The Catalog Database Service confirms the signatures of Windows files and lets you install new programs. The Protected Root Service adds and removes Trusted Root Certification Authority certificates from the computer. The Automatic Root Certificate Update Service retrieves root certificates from Windows Update and enables features such as Secure Sockets Layer (SSL). The Key Service helps enroll this computer for certificates. Never stop this service.
DCOM Server Process Launcher	Automatic	Lets the system launch Distributed Component Object Model (DCOM) processes. Never stop this service.

Name	Startup Type	Description
Desktop Window Manager Session Manager	Automatic	Provides all the eye candy associated with the new Windows interface. This service provides some theme support, transparency effects, and special features, such as Thumbnail view on the Taskbar. It's unlikely you need these features in a server, so disabling this service can net a small performance gain.
DHCP Client	Automatic	Registers and updates IP addresses. This service also updates Domain Name System (DNS) records for the computer using the Dynamic Host Configuration Protocol (DHCP).
Diagnostic Policy Service	Automatic	Provides policy support for problem detection, troubleshooting, and resolution for Windows components. You manage these policies through group policies on the local system or domain controller. Never stop this service.
Diagnostic Service Host	Manual	Performs the actual task of problem detection, troubleshooting, and resolution for Windows components. Windows automatically starts this service as needed to address errors detected by the Diagnostic Policy Service.
Diagnostic System Host	Manual	Works as part of the Windows Diagnostic Infrastructure (WDI) with the Diagnostic Policy Service and Diagnostic Service Host to present information about problem detection, troubleshooting, and resolution for Windows components. Windows automatically starts this service as needed to address errors detected by the Diagnostic Policy Service. You can learn more about WDI at `http://technet.microsoft.com/en-us/windowsvista/aa905076.aspx`.
Distributed Link Tracking Client	Automatic	Maintains links between NTFS files within a computer or across computers in a network. For example, you can create a file on Computer A and a link to that file on Computer B. When this service detects a change in location for the file on Computer A, it tells Computer B to update its information. Theoretically, you can stop this service if you never use links on your system.

(continued)

Book VIII Chapter 1

An Overview of Windows Server 2008 Services

Table 1-1 *(continued)*

Name	Startup Type	Description
Distributed Transaction Coordinator	Automatic (Delayed Start)	Coordinates transactions that span multiple resource managers, such as databases, message queues, and file systems. Never stop this service.
DNS Client	Automatic	Performs two DNS-related tasks. First, this service registers the full computer name for the local computer with the DNS server. Second, this service caches DNS information found on the DNS server to the local machine to make locating other network resources easier. Never stop this service.
Extensible Authentication Protocol	Manual	Provides network authentication for various 802.1x wired and wireless connections, Virtual Private Networks (VPNs), and Network Access Protection (NAP). The Extensible Authentication Protocol (EAP) service also provides Application Programming Interfaces (APIs) used by developers to create network applications.
Function Discovery Provider Host	Manual	Hosts the Function Discovery providers for various Windows features, such as Windows Media Center. You normally won't need to enable this service on a server.
Function Discovery Resource Publication	Automatic	Publishes a list of resources available on your computer to other computers on the network. This service helps other computers discover resources located on the local computer. Disabling this service doesn't appear to have any negative effect on network functionality.
Group Policy Client	Automatic	Applies group policy settings to the local computer. If you disable this service, group policies won't have any affect on the local computer. Never stop this service on any network using group policies.
Health Key and Certificate Management	Manual	Provides X.509 certificate and key management services for the Network Access Protection Agent (NAPAgent). Enforcement technologies that use X.509 certificates may not function properly without this service.
Human Interface Device Access	Manual	Supports any Human Interface Device (HID) hardware on your system, such as mice and keyboards. If you disable this service, the hardware still functions, but any special hot buttons or other HID features won't work.

Name	Startup Type	Description
IKE and AuthIP IPsec Keying Modules	Automatic	Hosts the Internet Key Exchange (IKE) and Authenticated Internet Protocol (AuthIP) keying modules. These keying modules provide support for authentication and key exchange in IPSec. Disabling this service will likely cause IPSec to fail on the local system.
Interactive Services Detection	Manual	Notifies users of new interactive services. This service also provides access to the dialog boxes provided by interactive services. If you disable this service, the user may not see required interactive service input and cause problems for the system as a whole.
Internet Connection Sharing (ICS)	Automatic	Lets the user share an Internet connection with others on the network. The ICS service provides Network Address Translation (NAT), addressing, name resolution, and limited intrusion prevention. You should disable this service on a network that has a DNS server.
IP Helper	Automatic	Provides automatic IPv6 connectivity over an IPv4 network. If this service is stopped, the machine has IPv6 connectivity only if it's connected to a native IPv6 network.
IPSec Policy Agent	Automatic	Enforces IPSec policies created through the IP Security Policies console or the NetSH IPSec utility. IPSec provides support for network-level peer authentication, data origin authentication, data integrity, data confidentiality (encryption), and replay protection. Never stop this service.
KtmRm for Distributed Transaction Coordinator	Automatic (Delayed Start)	Coordinates transactions between the Microsoft Distributed Transaction Controller (MSDTC) and the Kernel Transaction Manager (KTM). Never stop this service.
Link-Layer Topology Discovery Mapper	Manual	Provides support for the new network mapping functionality found in Windows Server 2008 and Vista. You can also add this service to Windows XP machines to obtain a complete map of your network. Windows starts this service automatically as needed.
Microsoft Fibre Channel Platform Registration Service	Manual	Registers the local system with all available Fibre Channel fabrics (used with network storage such as storage area networks or SANs), and maintains the registrations. You can disable this service unless you rely on network storage.

**Book VIII
Chapter 1**

An Overview of
Windows Server
2008 Services

(continued)

Table 1-1 *(continued)*

Name	Startup Type	Description
Microsoft iSCSI Initiator Service	Manual	Manages Internet Small Computer System Iinterface (iSCSI) sessions from this computer to remote iSCSI target devices. You can disable this service unless you rely on iSCIS storage.
Microsoft Software Shadow Copy Provider	Manual	Manages software-based volume shadow copies taken by the Volume Shadow Copy service. Windows starts this service automatically as needed. Applications such as Backup require this service. In addition, some third-party ghost image applications require this service.
Multimedia Class Scheduler	Manual	Prioritizes the work that the system must perform based on task priorities. The system normally uses this service for multimedia applications, so you won't usually need to enable this service on a server.
Netlogon	Manual	Maintains a secure channel between this computer and the domain controller for authenticating users and services. Never stop this service.
Network Access Protection Agent	Manual	Provides Network Access Protection (NAP) functionality on client computers.
Network Connections	Manual	Manages objects in the Network and Dial-Up Connections folder. These two folders provide views of both local area network (LAN) and remote connections.
Network List Service	Automatic	Creates a listing of connected networks. The service then collects and stores properties for these networks. After the list is complete, the service notifies applications about the connected resource. It also provides application notification whenever the network configuration changes. Never stop this service.
Network Location Awareness	Automatic	Collects and stores configuration information for the network and notifies programs when this information changes. Never stop this service.
Network Store Interface Service	Automatic	Delivers network notifications, such as interface additions and deletions, to user mode clients. Stopping this service causes loss of network connectivity.

Name	Startup Type	Description
Offline Files	Disabled	Performs maintenance activities on the Offline Files cache, responds to user logon and logoff events, and implements the internals of the public API. This service also dispatches interesting events to applications interested in Offline Files activities and changes in cache state.
Performance Logs and Alerts	Manual	Collects performance data from local or remote computers based on a preconfigured schedule. The service then writes the data to a log or triggers an alert. Windows starts this service automatically as needed.
Plug and Play	Automatic	Detects system hardware on startup. This service also registers changes in the hardware configuration. Never stop this service.
PnP-X IP Bus Enumerator	Disabled	Manages the virtual network bus, discovers network connected devices using the Simple Service Discovery Protocol (SSDP) or WS-Discovery protocols (where WS stands for Web Service), and provides access to them through Plug and Play (PnP). You normally keep this service disabled because it can open security holes in your system.
Portable Device Enumerator Service	Manual	Enforces group policy for removable mass-storage devices. Enables applications such as Windows Media Player and Image Import Wizard to transfer and synchronize content using removable mass-storage devices.
Print Spooler	Automatic	Caches data sent to the printer and outputs that data as the printer becomes ready to receive it. You can stop this service if you don't intend to do any printing.
Problem Reports and Solutions Control Panel Support	Manual	Supports viewing, sending, and deletion of system-level problem reports for the Problem Reports and Solutions Control Panel. Windows starts this service automatically as needed.
Protected Storage	Manual	Provides protected storage for sensitive data, such as passwords, to prevent access by unauthorized services, processes, or users. Windows starts this service automatically as needed.

(continued)

Table 1-1 *(continued)*

Name	Startup Type	Description
Remote Access Auto Connection Manager	Manual	Creates a connection to a remote network whenever a program references a remote DNS or Network Basic Input/Output System (NetBIOS) name or address. Windows starts this service automatically as needed.
Remote Access Connection Manager	Manual	Manages dial-up and virtual private network (VPN) connections from this computer to the Internet or other remote networks. Windows starts this service automatically as needed.
Remote Access Quarantine Agent	Manual	Restricts network access to remote clients until the client meets required authentication requirements. After the client meets these requirements, the service removes the validated client from the quarantine network. Windows starts this service automatically as needed.
Remote Procedure Call (RPC)	Automatic	Serves as an endpoint mapper (the end of a communication stream) for COM application. It also serves as the COM Service Control Manager. Never stop this service.
Remote Procedure Call (RPC) Locator	Manual	Manages the RPC name service database. Windows starts this service automatically as needed.
Remote Registry	Automatic	Lets a remote caller manage the registry settings on the local computer. You should consider disabling this service because it creates a huge security hole.
Resultant Set of Policy Provider	Manual	Provides a network service that processes requests to simulate application of Group Policy settings for a target user or computer in various situations and computes the Resultant Set of Policy settings.
Routing and Remote Access	Disabled	Provides routing services for both LAN and WAN connections. Windows enables this service when you use the Routing and Remote Access features; otherwise, you should keep it disabled for security reasons.
Secondary Logon	Automatic	Lets you start an application or other process using alternate credentials. For example, this service is the one that the RunAs utility uses to let you elevate standard user credentials to administrator credentials. Never stop this service.

Name	Startup Type	Description
Secure Socket Tunneling Protocol Service	Manual	Supports the Secure Socket Tunneling Protocol (SSTP) used to connect the local system to remote computers using VPN. Windows starts this service automatically as needed.
Security Accounts Manager	Automatic	Provides Security Accounts Manager (SAM) support to other applications. This service also signals other services that the SAM is ready to accept requests. Without this feature, applications and services can't perform certain secure tasks on the system. Never stop this service.
Server	Automatic	Supports file, print, and named-pipe sharing over the network for this computer. Never stop this service.
Shell Hardware Detection	Automatic	Provides notifications for AutoPlay hardware events. Never stop this service.
SL UI Notification Service	Manual	Provides Software Licensing activation and notification. If you disable this service, Windows doesn't start in Normal mode. Start Windows in Safe Mode, set the service back to Manual, and then reboot.
Smart Card	Manual	Manages access to smart cards read by this computer. You can disable this service if you don't rely on smart cards.
Smart Card Removal Policy	Manual	Lets you configure the system to lock the user desktop after smart card removal.
SNMP Trap	Manual	Receives trap messages generated by local or remote Simple Network Management Protocol (SNMP) agents and forwards the messages to SNMP management programs running on this computer. Windows starts this service automatically as needed.
Software Licensing	Automatic	Enables the download, installation, and enforcement of digital licenses for Windows and Windows applications. Never stop this service or else Windows will run in reduced functionality mode.
Special Administration Console Helper	Manual	Helps administrators remotely access a command prompt using the Emergency Management Services. Windows starts this service automatically as needed.

(continued)

**Book VIII
Chapter 1**

**An Overview of
Windows Server
2008 Services**

Table 1-1 *(continued)*

Name	Startup Type	Description
SSDP Discovery	Disabled	Discovers networked devices and services that use the SSDP discovery protocol, such as Universal Plug and Play (UPnP) devices. This service also announces SSDP devices and services running on the local computer. Microsoft disables this service because UPnP presents security risks. (See the article at `http://research.eeye.com/html/advisories/published/AD20011220.html` for details.)
Superfetch	Disabled	Maintains and improves system performance over time by placing commonly used applications in a cache. This service doesn't provide much value on a server. Read the material at `http://www.tomshardware.com/2007/01/31/windows-vista-superfetch-and-readyboost analyzed/` for additional details on how this service works.
System Event Notification Service	Automatic	Monitors system events and notifies subscribers to COM+ Event System of these events. Never stop this service.
Task Scheduler	Automatic	Lets you configure and schedule automated tasks on this computer. Microsoft has started to use the Task Scheduler for operating system needs. At one time, you could disable this service without a problem, but you may want to check which tasks Microsoft has scheduled before you disable it on Windows Server 2008.
TCP/IP NetBIOS Helper	Automatic	Provides support for the NetBIOS over TCP/IP (NetBT) service and NetBIOS name resolution for clients on the network. This service lets users share files, print, and log on to the network by using NetBIOS. You can stop this service if your network doesn't rely on NetBIOS or Windows Internet Naming Service (WINS).
Telephony	Manual	Provides Telephony Application Programming Interface (TAPI) support for programs that control telephony devices on the local computer and through the LAN. When working on a LAN, the remote computer must also run this service.

Name	Startup Type	Description
Terminal Services	Automatic	Helps users connect interactively to a remote computer. Remote Desktop and Terminal Server depend on this service. Clear the check boxes on the Remote tab of the System Properties applet of the Control Panel to disable this feature.
Terminal Services Configuration	Manual	Provides configuration support for Terminal Services and Remote Desktop functionality. It also supports session maintenance activities that require SYSTEM context, such as per-session temporary folders, TS themes, and TS certificates.
Terminal Services UserMode Port Redirector	Manual	Redirects printers, drives, and ports for Remote Desktop Protocol (RDP) connections.
Themes	Disabled	Provides user experience theme management.
Thread Ordering Server	Manual	Provides ordered execution for a group of threads within a specific timeframe.
TPM Base Services	Automatic (Delayed Start)	Provides access to the Trusted Platform Module (TPM) that offers hardware-based cryptographic services to system components and applications. You can normally disable this service if your motherboard lacks a TPM.
UPnP Device Host	Disabled	Lets the system host UPnP devices.
User Profile Service	Automatic	Loads and unloads user profiles. Never stop this service. If you stop or disable this service, users can no longer successfully log on or log off, applications may have problems obtaining user data, and components registered to receive profile event notifications will not receive them.
Virtual Disk	Manual	Provides management services for disks, volumes, file systems, and storage arrays.
Volume Shadow Copy	Manual	Manages the Volume Shadow Copies used for backup and other purposes. Windows starts this service automatically as needed.
Windows Audio	Manual	Manages audio for Windows-based programs. Unless your server has a sound card installed, you can disable this service.
Windows Audio Endpoint Builder	Manual	Manages audio devices for the Windows Audio service. Unless your server has a sound card installed, you can disable this service.

(continued)

Book VIII Chapter 1

An Overview of Windows Server 2008 Services

Table 1-1 *(continued)*

Name	Startup Type	Description
Windows Color System	Manual	Hosts the third-party Windows Color System color device model and gamut map model plug-in modules. These plug-in modules are vendor-specific extensions to the Windows Color System baseline color device and gamut map models. Disabling this service may result in poor color rendering between the screen and attached devices.
Windows Driver Foundation - User-mode Driver Framework	Manual	Manages user-mode driver host processes in managed environment. This is the next-generation driver model for Windows. You can learn more about this model at `http://whitepapers.tech` `republic.com.com/whitepaper.` `aspx?docid=166001`. Windows starts this service automatically as needed.
Windows Error Reporting Service	Automatic	Reports errors when programs stop working or responding and delivers any existing solutions. This service also generates logs for diagnostic and repair services. Windows starts this service automatically as needed.
Windows Event Collector	Manual	Manages persistent subscriptions to events from remote sources that support WS-Management protocol, such as Windows Vista event logs, hardware and Intelligent Platform Management Interface (IPMI)-enabled event sources. The service stores forwarded events in a local event log. Windows starts this service automatically as needed.
Windows Event Log	Automatic	Manages events and event logs. This service supports logging events, querying events, subscribing to events, archiving event logs, and managing event metadata. It can display events in both XML and plain-text format. Never stop this service.
Windows Firewall	Automatic	Helps prevent unauthorized users from gaining access to your computer through the Internet or a network. Never stop this service.
Windows Installer	Manual	Adds, modifies, and removes applications provided as a Microsoft Installer (MSI) package. Windows starts this service automatically as needed.

Name	Startup Type	Description
Windows Management Instrumentation	Automatic	Provides a common interface and object model to access management information about operating system, devices, applications, and services. Think of this service as a kind of database manager. Never stop this service.
Windows Modules Installer	Manual	Installs, modifies, and removes Windows updates and optional components. Windows starts this service automatically as needed.
Windows Process Activation Service	Manual	Provides process activation, resource management, and health management services for message-activated applications. Windows starts this service automatically as needed.
Windows Remote Management (WS-Management)	Automatic (Delayed Start)	Implements the WS-Management protocol for remote management. WS-Management is a standard Web services protocol used for remote software and hardware management. (See `http://www.dmtf.org/standards/wsman` for details.) You must configure the Windows Remote Management (WinRM) Service using the `WINRM.CMD` command line tool or through Group Policy for it to listen over the network. The WinRM service provides access to WMI data and enables event collection. Event collection and subscription to events require that the service be running. WinRM messages use HTTP and HTTPS as transports. The WinRM service does not depend on IIS but is preconfigured to share a port with IIS on the same machine. To prevent conflicts with IIS, administrators should ensure that any Web sites hosted on IIS do not use the `/wsman` URL prefix. You can disable this service if your network doesn't rely on WS-Management.
Windows Time	Automatic	Maintains date and time synchronization on all clients and servers in the network. Make sure that you synchronize at least one server to an external time source. Never stop this service, or else you may have Kerberos security problems on the network.
Windows Update	Automatic (Delayed Start)	Detects, downloads, and installs updates for Windows and other programs. Disable this service if you use another method of updating your server.

(continued)

Book VIII
Chapter 1

An Overview of
Windows Server
2008 Services

Table 1-1 *(continued)*

Name	Startup Type	Description
WinHTTP Web Proxy Auto-Discovery Service	Manual	Implements the client HTTP stack. This service also provides developers with a Win32 API and COM Automation component for sending HTTP requests and receiving responses. In addition, WinHTTP provides support for auto-discovering a proxy configuration using its implementation of the Web Proxy Auto-Discovery (WPAD) protocol. Windows starts this service automatically as needed.
Wired AutoConfig	Manual	Performs IEEE 802.1X authentication on Ethernet interfaces. Windows starts this service automatically as needed.
WMI Performance Adapter	Manual	Provides performance library information from Windows Management Instrumentation (WMI) providers to clients on the network. This service runs only when Performance Data Helper is activated.
Workstation	Automatic	Creates and maintains client network connections to remote servers by using the Server Message Block (SMB) protocol. Never stop this service.

Understanding the Windows Management Instrumentation (WMI)

Not everyone uses Windows systems, and not everyone manages a network that relies solely on Microsoft technology. Because networks often contain a host of machine types using different operating systems and configured with differing hardware, it's important to have some common way to manage them. The eventual result of a lot of discussion about the topic is Web-Based Enterprise Management (WBEM). (See `http://www.dmtf.org/standards/wbem/` for details.)

WMI is Microsoft's version of WBEM. It implements all the features required by the standard, including the Common Information Model (CIM). The *CIM* is essentially a hierarchical database that provides information about the system configuration. When someone needs to know about a particular system, they query the WMI database to discover the information.

The WMI database also includes configuration information. Consequently, when the system needs to perform a task, it consults the WMI database to discover how to do it. The WMI database may not contain every piece of configuration information about the system, but it contains most of the information that an administrator needs, such as the IP configuration of a network interface card (NIC).

WMI treats every entry in the database as an object. Of course, different objects have different characteristics. A NIC has different characteristics from a disk drive. In addition, a disk drive can have a quote assigned to it as well as security. Consequently, WMI must provide the means to interact with these various objects. The solution is to use a WMI provider — a special piece of software that understands the object and can act as an intermediary between it and WMI.

Any application that understands WMI can access the WMI database. You find WMI in many common administrator utilities, such as Systems Microsoft Management Server, Microsoft Health Monitor, and Microsoft Operations Manager. It's also possible to access the WMI database directly with command line utilities, such as Windows Management Instrumentation Command line (WMIC).

Interestingly enough, one of the many Windows features you can manage with WMIC is services. The Service object helps you interact with services in a lot of ways. Using WMIC, you can start, stop, pause, continue, and restart services. It's even possible to change some service characteristics when you have the proper rights. You'll discover that knowing about WMIC can save you considerable time because you can use WMIC to fully script many configuration activities.

Configuring the WMI Control Properties

There are two levels of WMI configuration: the WMI Control and the WMI database. The database contains all the information that describes the system. The WMI Control controls how WMI works — how it manages the WMI database.

The WMI Control appears as part of the Computer Management console in the `Computer Management\Services and Applications\WMI Control` folder. You can also access this control directly by using the WMIMgmt.MSC console. No matter how you access the WMI Control, you don't see anything at first because the pane normally containing information is blank. Instead, you right-click the control entry and choose Properties to display the WMI Control properties dialog box. The General tab of this dialog box tells you about your system. The remaining tabs help you perform specific tasks, as described in the following sections.

Performing a backup

The Backup/Restore tab contains two buttons that let you back up the WMI database and restore it later as needed. Creating a backup is important if you make substantial changes to your server, because restoring the WMI database can significantly reduce recovery time for a failed server. The following steps describe how to perform a backup:

1. **Click Back Up Now on the Backup/Restore tab.**

You see a Specify a Name for Your Backup File dialog box. Even though Microsoft recommends placing the file in the `\Windows\System32\WBEM\Repostory` folder on your hard drive, it's unlikely that your daily backup includes this file. Make sure to place the file in a folder that you back up regularly.

2. **Choose a folder for the backup.**

3. **Type a name for the backup file in the File Name field.**

Choose a filename that makes the purpose of the backup clear. Don't give the file an extension — the backup feature performs that task for you.

4. **Click Save.**

You see a dialog box telling you that the system is creating a backup. This dialog box disappears after a few moments. The backup is complete at this point. Make sure to include the file in your normal backup routine.

Performing a restoration

At some point, you need to restore the WMI database. The system may have failed, or a rogue application may have caused damage to your system. As with any database, you can also see damage from a number of other causes. The following steps tell you how to restore the backup:

1. **Click Restore Now on the Backup/Restore tab.**

You see a Specify Backup File to Restore dialog box.

2. **Choose the folder that contains the restore file.**

3. **Highlight the restore file in the dialog box.**

Remember that the file will have an REC extension. Consequently, if the original backup name is MyBackup, the file you want to restore is `MyBackup.REC`.

4. **Click Open.**

You see a dialog box telling you that the system is restoring the backup. The dialog box disappears after a few moments.

5. **Reboot your system.**

   Theoretically, the changes made by the restoration process should take effect immediately. However, rebooting your system ensures that the restoration actually works as intended.

Setting WMI security

The Security tab of the WMI Control Properties dialog box lets you set the security of the individual levels of the WMI database. Figure 1-1 shows a typical view of this database. Each of the folders shown in the dialog box is a separate storage level within the database, and you can control each level separately.

Figure 1-1:
The WMI database contains multiple levels, each of which can have different security.

To set security for a particular WMI database level, highlight that level in the dialog box and click Security. You see a Security dialog box such as the one shown in Figure 1-2. This dialog box looks and acts just like any other Security dialog box for Windows.

The rights you assign at each level determine who can perform a particular task. The following list describes the various rights you can assign:

✦ **Enable:** Lets the user read objects within the namespace.

✦ **Execute Methods:** Lets the user run objects that are exported from the CIM Object Manager.

✦ **Full Control:** Grants full read/write/delete access to all CIM objects, classes, and instances.

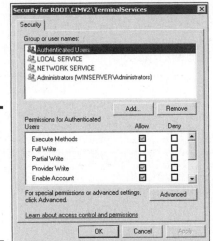

Figure 1-2:
Set the
security for
a particular
level by
using this
Security
dialog box.

+ **Partial Write:** Grants write access to static objects in the repository.

+ **Provider Write:** Grants write access to objects that are made available by the provider.

+ **Read Security:** Provides read-only access to WMI security information.

+ **Edit Security:** Grants read/write access to WMI security information.

+ **Remote Access:** Grants remote computers the same rights that are allowed when connecting from a local computer.

Changing the default namespace for scripting

Most administrators interact with the WMI database through some form of scripting. In fact, you'll find a host of scripts on the Internet. All these scripts have one thing in common: They help you configure your system in a particular way. The namespace that a script uses determines its starting point within the WMI database hierarchy. Look again at Figure 1-1 and you'll see this hierarchy — it begins at the root object and ends wherever the script needs to perform work.

Setting the default namespace to the correct location can make it easier to write scripts because you don't need to include the entire path for an object every time you try to do something. Most scripts rely on the default WMI setting of Root\CIMV2 as the default namespace. Consequently, you should never have to change the default. However, if you choose to change the default for some reason, click Change on the Advanced tab of the WMI Control Properties dialog box to display the Browser for Namespace dialog box. Highlight the namespace you want to use as a default and click OK.

Chapter 2: Monitoring and Configuring Services

In This Chapter

✓ Working with services using the Services console

✓ Working with services using the Task Manager

✓ Working with services using the SC utility

Services perform important tasks on your server. In fact, you wouldn't even have a server without them. A server relies on the various services to perform various tasks in the background. For example, you can serve up files to callers without the Server service. The Workstation service provides access to the server so that you can configure it in the first place. In fact, you'll find a wealth of services in your server, many of which are essential.

For the most part, services work in the background, and you don't have to worry about them much. In fact, services are so reliable that many administrators forget about them. Unfortunately, forgetting about the services on your system can pose problems. Running services you don't need can open security holes, use resources inefficiently, and even make the server behave oddly. Outsiders also stick viruses and Trojans onto your system by using services, so you need to know which services are running on your system and how they're supposed to act. Services are so important, in fact, that Microsoft provides three methods for monitoring and configuring them: the Services console, the Task Manager, and the SC utility.

Using the Services Console

The Services console provides you with a good overview of each of the services installed on your system. You can also use the Services console to perform most major tasks with the services and even perform some types of configuration. Figure 2-1 shows the Services console.

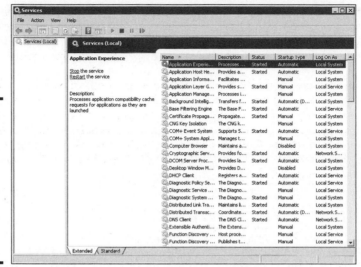

Figure 2-1:
The
Services
console
helps you
perform
most
services-
related
tasks.

The Services console contains two tabs. The information on both tabs is essentially the same. However, the Extended tab, shown in Figure 2-1, includes an additional area with a full description of the service you select and a list of actions you can perform, such as stopping or restarting the service.

Both tabs include a list of services that defines the name, description, status, startup type, and logon settings for the service. You can sort the display by any of these columns, which can come in handy when you need to perform configuration tasks. For example, you may want to check all the services that start automatically, to ensure that only the services you need start when the machine starts. Sorting by the Startup Type column provides this information.

You can change the number of columns shown in the display by right-clicking Services and choosing View⇨Add/Remove columns. It's also possible to change the features you see by right-clicking Services and choosing View⇨ Customize. The following sections describe how to use the Services console to perform configuration tasks.

Starting and stopping services

Starting a service means creating a new copy of the executable for that service and requesting that the executable create any new variables it needs and then perform any other required configuration. *Stopping* a service means telling the service executable to clear any memory that it's using and completely unload itself from memory. In short, starting and stopping a service represents a definite condition change for the service.

When working with a service, make sure that you actually mean to stop or start a service rather than pause or continue it. Administrators often make this mistake and find that the service loses status information that the system requires to overcome a fault or simply continue processing as before.

The Services console provides a number of methods for starting and stopping services. The easiest method is to highlight the service you want to start or stop and then click the Start or Stop link. You can also right-click the service entry in the list and choose Start or Stop from the context menu. The General tab of the Properties dialog box for a service also lets you start or stop the service. (See the "Working with the General tab" section of this chapter for details.)

Pausing and continuing services

Pausing a service means sending a command to the service that stops any processing. The service stays loaded in memory and continues to maintain its current state information. The most common reason to pause a service is to let you fix a problem on the server that prevents the service from working correctly and then continuing to perform any required processing after you fix the error. *Continuing* a service means sending a command to the service to resume any existing processing.

Most services let you stop and start the service. Fewer services let you pause and continue the service because the service must provide the code required to perform this task. In some cases, a developer can't add the code because doing so would leave the service in an unstable state.

As with starting and stopping, the Services console provides a number of methods for pausing and continuing a service. You can highlight the service and click the Pause or Resume links. It's also possible to right-click the service entry in the list and choose Pause or Resume from the context menu. Finally, the General tab of the Properties dialog box for a service also contains a Pause and Resume feature (see the "Working with the General tab" section of this chapter for details).

Working with service properties

When you right-click a service entry and choose Properties from the context menu, you see a Properties dialog box like the one shown in Figure 2-2. This dialog box normally contains the four tabs shown in Figure 2-2. In rare situations, you may see additional tabs, but these additional tabs are always vendor specific, and you should consult the vendor documentation for using them. The Properties dialog box lets you configure common service features, such as the service's starting state. If you need to change low-level service properties, you must rely on the SC utility (see the "Working with the SC Command Line Utility" section of this chapter) or the WMIC utility. The following sections describe the four tabs common to all services.

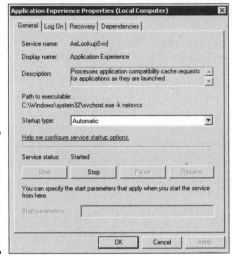

Working with the General tab

The General tab of the service Properties dialog box contains information about the service executable. You can see the service name, description, command used to start the service, startup type, and current status. In addition, the General tab provides buttons for issuing basic commands to the service, such as Start or Stop.

The command you see on the General tab starts the service. However, as explained in the "Understanding How Services Work" section of Book VIII, Chapter 1, the command describes how to start the group in which the service exists rather than start the service itself. Consequently, if you use this command, you start all services in the group, not just the single service that you may want to start. You must search through the registry to locate the specific command for starting the service.

Working with the Log On tab

The Log On tab, shown in Figure 2-3, contains information used to log the service in to the system. In most cases, the service uses the Local System, Local Service, or Network Service account. However, you can configure the service to use any legitimate account on the system.

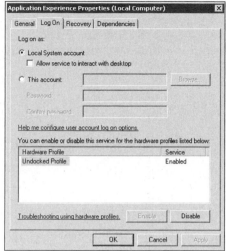

Figure 2-3:
The account the service uses to log on to the system determines which tasks the service can perform.

The account that the service uses determines what the service can do. For example, if you configure the service to log on using the Local Service account, the service is extremely restricted in the tasks it can perform. On the other hand, using the Network Service account provides considerable leeway in how the service interacts with the system. The article at `http://msdn2.microsoft.com/en-us/library/ms674946.aspx` describes the standard service accounts in detail.

Notice the Allow Service to Interact with Desktop option. In most cases, you won't check this option because it's highly unusual for a service to interact with the Desktop. Checking this option can open a security hole on your server, so check it only when the vendor says that you must check it for the service to work properly. Services normally communicate through logs, especially the event logs.

You can also use the Log On tab to configure the service for a particular hardware profile. For example, you may want to start a service when docked into your station at work, but not while working at home on your laptop. In this case, you can highlight the required hardware profiles and click Disable. If you later decide that you want to enable the service for a particular profile, highlight the hardware profile in the list and click Enable.

Working with the Recovery tab
Services fail from time to time. As with any other computer software, unexpected events and bugs in code cause problems for services. The fact that

vendors typically test services to a stricter standard doesn't mean that
services are perfect. However, you might not know that a failed service is
responsible for your lack of access to the Internet. In fact, services are the
last place that many administrators look for problems. Fortunately, services
can follow an automatic-recovery protocol, as shown in Figure 2-4.

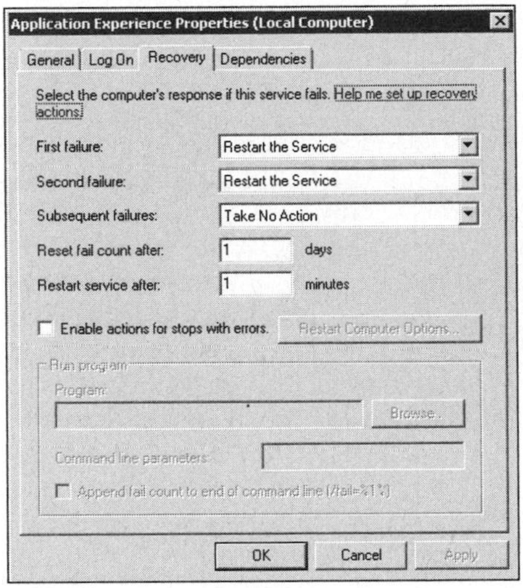

Figure 2-4:
Configure
services to
recover
according to
company
policies
and past
experi-
ences.

Every service on your system comes with a default recovery policy — the
policy that the vendor feels will work best. Figure 2-4 shows a typical example of such a policy. In this case, the system attempts to restart the service
twice and then ignores the problem. Although this approach has its merits,
most companies want to do more. You can define up to three different failure
policies for the first, second, and subsequent failures, as described in the
following list:

✦ **Take No Action:** The system ignores the problem. Essentially, this
head-in-the-sand approach isn't helpful because it doesn't accomplish
anything.

✦ **Restart the Service:** The system restarts the service automatically when
it detects a failure. This is a good rudimentary fix for service problems
because it doesn't require anyone to do anything. Of course, it's also a
very limited approach because no one knows there's a failure unless the
service notifies someone through the event log.

✦ **Run a Program:** The system runs a program to repair the problem. You
can run any kind of custom or standard application, including a batch
file that performs a number of tasks. For example, you can use the SC

utility to perform low-level management of the service and then rely on the EventCreate utility to record in the event log the actions you take. Using a batch file, it's possible to perform an entire automated repair sequence and even send an e-mail to the administrator (using a product such as sendEmail, `http://caspian.dotconf.net/menu/Software/SendEmail/`) with the results. Of course, all this customization means that you must spend the time required to create the batch file, simulate a failure, and debug the results. When you select this option, check Enable Actions for Stops with Errors and fill out the fields in the Run Program section of the dialog box.

✦ **Restart the Computer:** The system restarts the computer in an effort to resolve the problem with the service. All kinds of bad things can happen when you use this option. For example, the user can lose valuable data when the system suddenly reboots due to a service failure. If the source of the failure is a virus, rebooting the system can even cause the virus to activate itself. You should use this option as a last resort for services that are so critical that the system can't possibly work properly without them. When you select this option, check Enable Actions for Stops with Errors and click Restart Computer Options. You see the Restart Computer Options dialog box, where you can define the amount of time that passes before the system reboots the computer and a message to send to other computers on the network.

The system must track the number of failures. However, if the system never resets its counter, the failures would accumulate and the first action you specify would occur only once. The Reset Fail Count After field determines how long the system maintains the current count. When this timeframe expires without a failure event, the system sets the failure count to zero and begins with the first action again on the next failure. The default value of 1 Day seems to work well.

Some services require recovery time after a failure. If you try to reset them immediately, the reset fails and counts as another failure in the failure count. The Restart Service After field determines how long the system waits before it restarts the service. On most systems, finding the optimal length of time requires a little work on your part. The server load, resource availability, nature of the service, and other environmental factors can all play a part in determining how long you should wait to restart the service. Try using the vendor's default value first, and then change the value as needed when you see that the service is still failing to restart properly.

Working with the Dependencies tab

The Dependencies tab, shown in Figure 2-5, is one of the more important tabs in the Properties dialog box because it tells you about potential issues with starting or stopping a service. The upper window shows you services that you can't stop if you want the current service to run. If you stop the DCOM Server Process Launcher, the Remote Procedure Call (RPC) service also stops. In this case, stopping either service could be catastrophic.

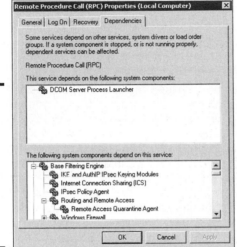

Figure 2-5:
Check depen-dencies before making any decisions that could ruin your day.

The lower window shows you all the services that depend on the current service. For example, if you stop the Remote Procedure Call (RPC) service, all services in the lower window also stop. In some cases, as with the Base Filtering Engine, the dependent services run several layers deep. The Services console always shows you the list of dependent services.

Windows always asks you about services you want to stop when other services rely on them, but some administrators don't quite understand the ramifications because Windows asks only about a single level of the hierarchy. For example, in Figure 2-5, Windows would tell you that stopping the Remote Procedure Call (RPC) service also stops the Base Filtering Engine service, but it mentions nothing about the Routing and Remote Access service. Therefore, it's always a good idea to look at the Dependencies tab to ensure that your decision to stop a service won't have unexpected results.

Modifying Service Status Using Task Manager

Many administrators will find a surprise with the new version of Task Manager. You can now use Task Manager to work with services directly. To display the Task Manager, right-click the Taskbar and choose Task Manager from the context menu. You can also press Ctrl+Alt+Del and click Task

Manager. When you see the Task Manager dialog box, select the Services tab. Figure 2-6 shows the Services tab of the Task Manager.

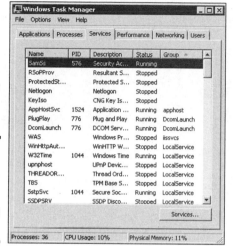

Figure 2-6: View, start, and stop services on the Services tab.

The Services tab of Task Manager shows all services currently installed on the machine, not just those that the system is now running. This listing makes the Services tab different from other Task Manager tabs because this tab provides you with complete information about the services installed on your system. You can see the entire list of services, the actual service name, the Process Identifier (PID) when the service is running, the description, the status, and the group (the group that appears on the General tab — refer to Figure 2-2), as shown in Figure 2-6.

You can also use the Task Manager to start and stop services as needed. Simply right-click the service of interest and choose Start Service or Stop Service from the context menu as needed. Consequently, you need not start the Services console when you're familiar with the service. However, to prevent unforeseen problems, when you're unfamiliar with a service, it's always better to view the Dependencies tab (refer to Figure 2-5) before you stop the service.

Services normally don't run independently on Windows. A special application named Service Host (`SvcHost.EXE`) provides a home for services. Consequently, when you see `SvcHost.EXE` on the Processes tab, you know that it has something to do with a service, but not *which* service. These methods help you see the relationship between services and process.

✦ To see which services the SvcHost.EXE entry affects, right-click the entry and choose Go To Service(s) from the context menu. Task Manager opens the Services tab with all the services hosted by that process highlighted.

✦ To see the SvcHost.EXE entry that hosts a service, right-click the service entry and choose Go to Process from the context menu. Task Manager opens the Processes tab with the process that hosts the service highlighted.

Not all services rely on `SvcHost.EXE`. For example, right-click the SamSs service and choose Go to Process from the context menu. You see that the service relies on the Local Security Authority Subsystem Service application (`LSASS.EXE`).

Working with the SC Command Line Utility

The Service Control (SC) utility helps you control services on your machine. The control is at a low level. Although you can start, stop, pause, and continue services using other utilities, this utility lets you perform additional tasks, such as query the service for detailed status information, send it a change of configuration message, or enumerate the services that the target service depends on. The SC utility provides substantially more information about services than does any other utility on your system.

The SC utility is exceptionally powerful. In fact, you should avoid using it, in most cases, and rely on the Services console instead. The Services console usually protects you from making terrible mistakes with your system. For example, you can use the SC utility to delete a service. Deleting the wrong service can have dire consequences for your system and may even cause it to stop working.

The SC utility uses this syntax: `sc [\\server] [command] [service name] [<option1> [<option2>...]]`. The following list describes each of the command line arguments:

✦ **\\server:** Specifies the server that runs the service you want to manage. The default assumes that you want to use the local machine. Make sure that you provide the Universal Naming Convention (UNC) form of the service name, such as \\MyServer.

✦ **command:** Specifies the command you want to execute. For example, if you want to stop a service, you issue the Stop command. Some commands can work alone or with a service name. To obtain a list of all services installed on a machine, type **SC Query** and press Enter at the command line. Because a system can have a lot of services, you normally add a pipe to the More command by typing **SC Query | More** and pressing Enter. Figure 2-7 shows typical results of using the SC Query | More command. Notice that the output includes both the actual service name and the human-readable form found in the Services console.

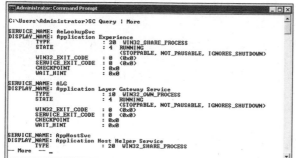

Figure 2-7:
Obtain a
list of the
services on
your system.

✦ **service_name:** Specifies the name of the service you want to manage. This name isn't the same as the name you see displayed in the Services console, located in the Administrative Tools folder of the Control Panel. The name also isn't the executable name for the service. This entry is the name that the service used for registration purposes. For example, to access the event log, you use the `eventlog` service. However, the display name for this service is Event Log, and the executable name is `Services.EXE`. You have two easy methods of obtaining the true service name:

- Type **SC Query** and press Enter at the command line to obtain a list of registered service names on the target system (either local or remote).

- Use the Services tab of the Task Manager (see the "Modifying Service Status Using Task Manager" section of this chapter for details) to obtain a list of registered services on the local machine.

✦ **option1 [option2...]:** Provides additional information required by some commands.

One focus of this utility is the command that you issue to a service. The command determines which tasks the service performs. For example, when you issue a stop command, the service stops whatever it's doing at the time. The following list describes the common commands for all services. Theoretically, a vendor can (and many do) introduce custom commands for a particular service. Refer to the vendor documentation to discover these custom commands.

✦ **config:** Changes the service configuration. Be very careful using this command. Changing the service configuration can cause the service to stop executing or applications that rely on the service to stop recognizing the server. In most cases, make changes only to the services based on input from the vendor's product support staff.

You must specify any changes you want to make by using the options in the following list — make sure that you include the space between the equal sign (=) and the value:

- **type={own | share | interact | kernel | filesys | rec | adapt}:** Defines the service type. Change this setting only if the vendor requests that you do so.

- **start={boot | system | auto | demand | disabled}:** Defines the method the system uses to start the service. The auto option always starts the service when the system starts, while the disabled option prevents the service from ever starting.

- **error={normal | severe | critical | ignore}:** Defines the method used to report service errors in the event log. Using the ignore option means that the system never reports errors for the service.

- **binPath=BinaryPathName:** Specifies the location of the service's executable on the hard drive.

- **group=LoadOrderGroup:** Specifies the service's group, which defines the order in which the service loads, among other things.

- **tag={yes | no}:** Specifies whether the system obtains a tag identifier from the CreateService( ) function call. The system uses tag identifiers for only the boot-start and system-start drivers.

- **depend=Dependencies:** Defines one or more dependencies for this service to start. The requested service must start before this service can start. Separate each of the dependencies with a slash (/).

- **obj=AccountName | ObjectName:** Specifies an account name or a driver object name to use to run the service. This entry defines the security for the service. The default setting is the LocalSystem driver object.

- **DisplayName=display_name:** Defines the name that the user sees in the Services console.

- **password=password:** Specifies a password that the service must use to log in to the system. You don't need to provide a password for the LocalSystem driver object.

✦ **continue:** Restarts the service after a pause. You can't issue this command for a stopped service; use the start command instead.

✦ **control Value:** Sends a control code to a service. Control codes generally ask the service to perform a task based on a change to the service.

For example, if you send a `paramchange` value to the service, the service looks for a change in one of its parameters and reconfigures itself as necessary to accommodate the change. The control code can be a standard value, such as `paramchange`, `netbindadd` (adds a network binding to the service), `netbindremove` (removes a network binding from the service), `netbindenable` (enables a network binding associated with the service), or `netbinddisable` (disables a network binding associated with the service). Many services also provide custom control codes. You must obtain these custom codes from the vendor documentation.

✦ **create ServiceName binPath= Path:** Creates a service by querying the executable and adding any required entries to the registry. You can use this feature to install a third-party service when necessary. This technique is also the one you'll probably need to use to install any special services created by developers at your company.

The creation process requires that you supply a service name and the path to the binary (executable) file. In addition, you can provide configuration options for the service as defined in the following list — make sure to include the space between the equal sign (=) and the value:

- **type={own | share | interact | kernel | filesys | rec | adapt}:** Defines the service type. Change this setting only if the vendor requests that you do so.

- **start={boot | system | auto | demand | disabled}:** Defines the method the system uses to the start the service. The `auto` option always starts the service when the system starts, while the `disabled` option prevents the service from ever starting.

- **error={normal | severe | critical | ignore}:** Defines the method used to report service errors in the event log. Using the `ignore` option means that the system never reports errors for the service.

- **binPath=BinaryPathName:** Specifies the location of the service's executable on the hard drive.

- **group=LoadOrderGroup:** Specifies the service's group, which defines the order in which the service loads, among other things.

- **tag={yes | no}:** Specifies whether the system obtains a tag identifier from the `CreateService()` function call. The system uses tag identifiers only for the boot-start and system-start drivers.

- **depend=Dependencies:** Defines one or more dependencies for this service to start. The requested service must start before this service can start. Separate each of the dependencies with a slash (/).

- **obj={AccountName | ObjectName}:** Specifies an account name or a driver object name to use to run the service. This entry defines the security for the service. The default setting is the `LocalSystem` driver object.

- **DisplayName=display_name:** Defines the name that the user sees in the Services console.

- **password=password:** Specifies a password that the service must use to log in to the system. You don't need to provide a password for the `LocalSystem` driver object.

♦ **delete ServiceName:** Removes a service from the registry, which means that the system won't activate it and that the service won't appear in the Services console. Use this command with extreme care. Removing a critical service can cause system instability or even make your server unbootable. Unlike using a wrong setting, adding a critical service back into your server is nearly impossible, and you may find that you have to reinstall the operating system from scratch.

♦ **description:** Changes the description of a service. Use the qdescription command to obtain the current description for the service.

♦ **enumdepend [BufferSize]:** Enumerates the dependencies (the list of services that must be running before the service can start) for a service. You can specify an optional buffer size argument for this command that defines the size of the buffer you set aside for the description. When the buffer is too small, the utility returns a value that tells you the minimum buffer size.

♦ **failure:** Specifies the action the system should take in case of a service failure. Setting this feature is infinitely easier using the Services console, and you should never use the SC utility to perform this task unless you have no other option. Use the qfailure command to determine the state of this feature. You specify the failure actions using the following options:

- **reset=interval:** Defines the length of time that the service must wait in seconds before the system can reset the failure count to 0. You may specify a value of `INFINITE` to keep the failure count from ever resetting. Use this setting with the `actions` option.

- **reboot=message:** Defines the message to broadcast before rebooting the system due to a failure.

- **command=command:** Defines the command you want to run after a failure.

- **actions={run | reboot | restart}/delay:** Specifies an action to take, along with the delay time, for executing the action in milliseconds. For example, run/5000 attempts to run the service again after 5,000 milliseconds. You must also specify a reset interval when using an action.

♦ **failureflag [ServiceName] [Flag]:** Modifies the failure flag to a new value. You can use this command to set special failure flags that define the special circumstances of a failure (such as environmental factors). Use the qfailureflag command to determine the state of this feature. The default value of 0 tells the Service Control Manager (SCM) to use the configured failure actions on the service only when the service terminates in a state other than SERVICE_STOPPED.

When you set this value to 1, the SCM performs the configuration failure actions whenever the service terminates with an exit code other than 0 (in addition to the actions performed with a flag value of 0). The system ignores this flag when the services lack configured failure actions. This feature registers as 1 when you check the Enable Actions for Stops with Errors option on the Recovery tab of the service's Properties dialog box (refer to Figure 2-4).

✦ **getdisplayname KeyName [BufferSize]:** Obtains the display name (the one shown in the Services console) for a service based on its key name. For example, when you enter a key name of event log, you receive a display name of Event Log. You can specify an optional buffer size argument for this command that defines the size of the buffer you set aside for the description. When the buffer is too small, the utility returns a value that tells you the minimum buffer size.

✦ **getkeyname "DisplayName" [BufferSize]:** Obtains the key name (the one used for most SC utility commands) for a service based on its display name. For example, when you enter a display name of Event Log, the utility returns a key name of event log. Make sure to enclose the display name in quotes. You can specify an optional buffer size argument for this command that defines the size of the buffer you set aside for the description. When the buffer is too small, the utility returns a value that tells you the minimum buffer size.

✦ **interrogate:** Queries the status of a specific service. The output from this command includes service name, type, state, Win32 exit code, service exit code, checkpoint, and wait hint.

✦ **pause:** Pauses the specified service. Pausing the service differs from stopping it. When you stop a service, the service returns all resources to the operating system and removes itself from memory. Pausing the service lets it maintain status information and the service remains in memory.

✦ **privs [ServiceName] [Privileges]:** Modifies the privileges required to run the service. This command can keep unwary users from starting the service (even accidentally or through an application). However, changing this setting incorrectly can also cause application or system failure when the user can't interact with the service properly. You can see a listing of common privilege constants at http://windowssdk.msdn. microsoft.com/en-us/library/ms718062.aspx. Use the qprivs command to determine the current privileges for the service.

**Book VIII
Chapter 2**

Monitoring and
Configuring
Services

✦ **qc:** Queries the specified service for configuration information. The output from this command includes service name, type, start type, error control, binary path name, load order group, tag, display name, dependencies, and service start name.

✦ **qdescription [BufferSize]:** Queries the description for a service. You can specify an optional buffer size argument for this command that defines the size of the buffer you set aside for the description. When the buffer is too small, the utility returns a value that tells you the minimum buffer size.

✦ **qfailure [BufferSize]:** Queries the actions taken by a service when a failure occurs. You can specify an optional buffer size argument for this command that defines the size of the buffer you set aside for the description. When the buffer is too small, the utility returns a value that tells you the minimum buffer size.

✦ **qfailureflag [ServiceName]:** Queries the failure actions flag of the service. You use this option for diagnostic purposes.

✦ **qprivs [ServiceName] [BufferSize]:** Queries the privileges required in order to run the service. You can see a listing of common privilege constants at `http://windowssdk.msdn.microsoft.com/en-us/library/ms718062.aspx`.

✦ **qsidtype [ServiceName]:** Queries the service's SID type.

✦ **query:** Queries the status of a service or enumerates the services installed on the computer. The output from this command includes service name, type, state, Win32 exit code, service exit code, checkpoint, and wait hint. You don't need to provide a service name with this command. You can filter the output of this command by adding optional information described in the following list — make sure that you include the space between the equal sign (=) and the setting:

• **type={driver | service | all}:** Specifies the kind of service to query. The default setting is a service.

• **state={inactive | all}:** Defines the state of the service to enumerate. The default setting is active.

• **bufsize=size:** Defines the size of the enumeration buffer in bytes. The default size is 4,096 bytes.

• **ri=index:** Specifies the resume index at which to begin the enumeration. This number starts the enumeration at a location other than the first entry. The default setting is 0.

• **group=group:** Defines which service groups to enumerate. The default setting is all groups.

✦ **queryex:** Queries the extended status of a service or enumerates the services installed on the computer. You can filter the output of this command by adding optional information, as explained for the `query` command. The output from this command includes service name, type, state, Win32 exit code, service exit code, checkpoint, wait hint, PID, and flags. You don't need to provide a service name with this command. Figure 2-8 shows how the output of this command differs from the `query` command.

```
Administrator: Command Prompt

C:\Users\Administrator>SC Query AeLookupSvc

SERVICE_NAME: AeLookupSvc
        TYPE               : 20  WIN32_SHARE_PROCESS
        STATE              : 4   RUNNING
                               (STOPPABLE, NOT_PAUSABLE, IGNORES_SHUTDOWN)
        WIN32_EXIT_CODE    : 0   (0x0)
        SERVICE_EXIT_CODE  : 0   (0x0)
        CHECKPOINT         : 0x0
        WAIT_HINT          : 0x0

C:\Users\Administrator>SC QueryEx AeLookupSvc

SERVICE_NAME: AeLookupSvc
        TYPE               : 20  WIN32_SHARE_PROCESS
        STATE              : 4   RUNNING
                               (STOPPABLE, NOT_PAUSABLE, IGNORES_SHUTDOWN)
        WIN32_EXIT_CODE    : 0   (0x0)
        SERVICE_EXIT_CODE  : 0   (0x0)
        CHECKPOINT         : 0x0
        WAIT_HINT          : 0x0
        PID                : 964
        FLAGS              :

C:\Users\Administrator>_
```

Figure 2-8: Obtain a list of the services on your system.

✦ **sdshow:** Displays the security descriptor for a service in Security Descriptor Definition Language (SDDL) format. You can learn more about SDDL at `http://msdn.microsoft.com/library/en-us/ secauthz/security/security_descriptor_definition_ language.asp`.

✦ **sdset SD:** Sets the service's security descriptor. You must provide the security descriptor in SDDL format. You can learn more about SDDL at `http://msdn.microsoft.com/library/en-us/secauthz/ security/security_descriptor_definition_language.asp`. Using this command incorrectly can cause the user or system to lose access to the service.

✦ **showsid Name:** Displays the SID string associated with a service based on the arbitrary name you provide as input. The name can be of an existing service or a service that doesn't exist on the local machine. The resulting string lets you query the security of a service.

✦ **sidtype [ServiceName] [{Unrestricted | Restricted | None}]:** Changes the service Security Identifier (SID) type of the service. This change affects the service's ability to interact with the system by increasing or decreasing its privileges. Using this command incorrectly can cause access problems that result in system instability or even the loss of functionality. Use the `qsidtype` command to determine the current SID type for the selected service. You can use any of the following values for the `sidtype` command.

**Book VIII
Chapter 2**

Monitoring and Configuring Services

- **Unrestricted:** The service's SID appears as part of the process token without restrictions. You can use this level only for Win32 user mode services.

- **Restricted:** Places the service's SID in the process token, but as a restricted token. You can learn more about restricted tokens at `http://windowssdk.msdn.microsoft.com/en-us/library/ms722922.aspx`.

- **None:** Doesn't add the service's SID to the process token.

✦ **start:** Starts the specified service.

✦ **stop:** Stops the requested service. Stopping the service differs from pausing it. When you stop a service, the service returns all resources to the operating system and removes itself from memory. Pausing the service lets it maintain status information and the service remains in memory.

The SC utility has three special commands that affect the services as a whole, so they don't require a service name. The following list describes the three commands:

✦ **boot {ok | bad}:** Determines whether the system saves the last boot information into the last-known-good boot configuration.

✦ **lock:** Locks the SCManager database. The command line displays a prompt that shows that the system has locked the database. The database remains locked until you press u to remove the lock.

✦ **querylock:** Returns the locked status of the SCManager database.

Chapter 3: Using Application-Specific Services

In This Chapter

✔ **Understanding application-specific services**

✔ **Finding application-specific services**

✔ **Managing application-specific services**

*W*hen you initially install Windows Server 2008, you see a host of services — all of which serve Windows. Even after you install roles and features, the new services you see are part of the operating system. These services all follow the rules, don't include any special configuration features, and perform as expected. In many cases, you won't need to perform any configuration other than setting the options on the Recovery tab of the services Properties dialog box. (See the "Working with service properties" section of Book VIII, Chapter 2 for details on working with the Properties dialog box.)

Applications often install services too. When working with a Microsoft product, you usually don't see any surprises because Microsoft has a specific way of performing tasks. One difference you'll probably see is that the service doesn't rely on `SvcHost.EXE` to support it, but rather uses a custom executable to perform the task. However, when working with third-party products, you might see some differences. For example, you may see special settings when working with the SC utility, have access to special commands through the SC utility, or find that the service varies from what you expect in other ways. This chapter can't tell you about every potential difference you see when working with application services, but it can help you understand some of the major differences so that these application-specific services don't take you by surprise.

One major difference is that application-specific services normally require more configuration than those used by the operating system. For example, you'll find that application-specific services require a special login in many cases. Depending on the service, you may also find that the standard start up option doesn't work in Windows Server 2008 and you have to change it before the service will work properly. Application-specific services also have special needs with regard to application access, and you may find that you must provide a special security configuration.

Defining an Application-Specific Service

An *application-specific* service is any service that supports an application that doesn't come as part of the operating system, rather than the operating system, a role, or a feature. For example, when you install SQL Server on the server, the installation program adds a number of services. In fact, depending on the features you install, a SQL Server 2005 setup can include up to nine services. All these services start with the SQL abbreviation, such as SQL Server (MSSQLSERVER). As with many application-specific services, you must perform special configuration to use them at times.

In the case of SQL Server, configuration comes in a number of forms. For example, you may have to change the logon credentials so that the service can access SQL Server correctly. Failures you see in the event logs may have less to do with a SQL Server or application error than the ability of the service to interact with SQL Server or the application. Consequently, you need to verify that the service has the proper credentials to do its work.

Some services don't start automatically. The SQL Server Agent service doesn't start automatically because it can present a security risk and not every organization uses the SQL Server Agent to perform tasks automatically. Consequently, you may find that your automation fails on a system if you don't set the SQL Server Agent service to start automatically.

Unfortunately, the question of starting and stopping services isn't as easy as simply starting a service with the right name in some cases. SQL Server installs a service for each instance of SQL Server on a system. Some organizations use multiple instances to ensure that the database works efficiently and to better spread the database load. Consequently, you may see two instances of the SQL Server Agent service, such as SQL Server Agent (MSSQLSERVER) and SQL Server Agent (MSSQLSERVER2). Starting the right instance is essential. Services always interact with a specific application instance, so the need to configure multiple services with almost the same name isn't all that unusual.

You may be surprised to find that the SQL Server services don't have a recovery plan. The default action in all cases is Take No Action, as shown in Figure 3-1. In addition, notice that the Reset Fail Count After field value is 0, which means that the service resets the value to 0 immediately and that the second and subsequent failures never occur. Many application-specific services come with this configuration because vendors can't guess about the policies your company has in place, and they tend to prefer to hide failures to make their products appear more reliable.

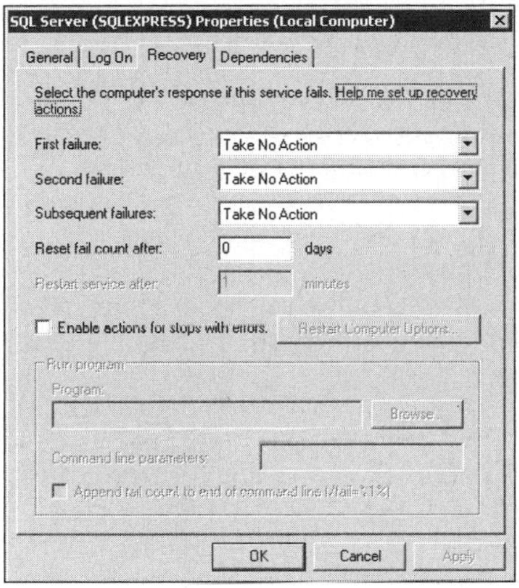

Figure 3-1:
Some
application-
specific
services
won't
include a
recovery
plan.

In the case of SQL Server, the Database Management System (DBMS) takes care of most recovery actions as part of the DBMS software. Even so, depending on the policies set by your company, you may have to set alternative recovery options for the application-specific service. In the case of SQL Server, company policy may require that you create a batch file that can help the system detect precisely how the service failed and determine whether the failure incurred any data loss. Other applications may require a different course of action. In some cases, all you need to do is restart the service when you know that no data loss occurs as the result of a service failure.

SQL Server services, as with most application-specific services, don't rely on the SvcHost.EXE file to run. Look at the General tab and you'll find that the Path to Executable field contains something like this:

```
"C:\SQL Server\MSSQL.1\MSSQL\Binn\sqlservr.exe" -sMSSQLSERVER
```

Notice that the service host actually appears in the SQL Server folder and that the host appears in SQLServr.EXE. The –s command line argument specifies the service instance. In this case, the service instance is for the MSSQLSERVER SQL Server instance.

All these cues define an application-specific service. By looking for these features, you can discover application-specific services very quickly. More importantly, you can learn enough about the service to begin managing it effectively. For example, when you have a problem with the application performing tasks, you may actually need to change the service start mode or logon type.

Locating Application-Specific Services

The Services console doesn't make it easy to locate application-specific services. You would literally need to look for the services one at a time, and that could consume a considerable amount of time when you're in a hurry. The SC utility described in Book VIII, Chapter 2 provides more information, and you could look for the information you need without quite as much difficulty, but the SC utility still isn't the best choice. It turns out that what you really need is the Windows Management Interface Command line (WMIC) command to locate the application-specific services on your system quickly and efficiently.

This chapter can't provide complete details about the WMIC command. In fact, you'd probably need an entire book to cover the topic fully. My book *Administering Windows Server 2008 Server Core* (Sybex, 2008), provides significant coverage of this utility, but even this book doesn't tell everything you can do with WMIC — the command is so complex that you need to work with it for a long time to master it. Even so, this section provides a description of how to use the Service alias to locate application-specific services on your machine.

You must open a copy of the administrator command prompt to use the WMIC command. WMIC relies on a special syntax to define which tasks to perform with it. In this case, you use the LIST or GET verbs to obtain information about the SERVICE alias. (WMIC has many aliases you can access.) WMIC requires that you define what to look for, unless you want extremely generic and mostly unusable output. For example, when you type **WMIC SERVICE WHERE "DisplayName Like 'SQL%'" GET DisplayName,Name, StartMode** and press Enter, you see a listing of SQL Server services, as shown in Figure 3-2.

Figure 3-2: Locate the SQL Server services using the display name.

It's important to break down this command into its components. The command line has these elements:

✦ **WMIC:** The name of the command. As with any other command or utility, you supply the WMIC entry as the first item on the command line.

✦ **SERVICE:** The alias you want to use. The SERVICE alias tells you all about service information stored in the WMI database. WMIC can access a considerable number of other aliases that don't appear in this book. To see a list of aliases, type **WMIC /?** and press Enter.

✦ **WHERE "DisplayName Like 'SQL%'":** Defines what to look for. In this case, you tell WMIC that you want to locate all entries where the DisplayName property begins with the word *SQL*. The % after SQL tells WMIC that the entry can have any number of characters after the word *SQL*. The Like keyword tells WMIC that you aren't looking for a precise match. You can always combine multiple search criteria to narrow a search.

✦ **GET:** Determines the action that WMIC performs. After you tell WMIC which alias to use and what to look for in that alias, you must tell WMIC what you want it to do. The GET verb (or action) obtains specific information about the entries that match the search criteria you define.

✦ **DisplayName,Name,StartMode:** Defines the output of the command. You see the properties output in the order you specify. The WMIC command adds white space as necessary to make the properties easy to see.

If you want basic information, the LIST verb is often a better choice. You can obtain a quick listing of the services using a command line that doesn't depend quite as much on an intimate knowledge of the WMI database structure. For example, when you type **WMIC SERVICE WHERE "DisplayName Like 'SQL%'" LIST BRIEF** and press Enter, you see the output shown in Figure 3-3. The LIST verb provides a number of preformatted output options. For example, if you replace BRIEF with FULL, you see all the information about every service entry that matches the search criteria in the output.

Figure 3-3:
Listing
services
don't
provide
precise
output but
require less
knowledge
of the WMI
database.

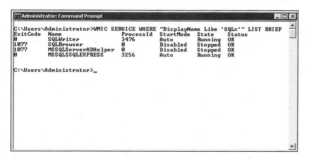

WMIC provides many ways to search for information. Sometimes you need to try multiple methods to ensure that you see everything the WMI database has to offer. For example, you might want to search for SQL in the name of the service, rather than the display name. The name is the actual name of the service, rather than what you see in the Services console. To see all SQL Server entries, you can type **WMIC SERVICE WHERE "Name Like '%SQL%'" GET DisplayName,Name,StartMode** and press Enter. The output is the same as shown in Figure 3-1, but the means of getting the output is different. In this case, you look for services that have SQL in their names. Notice that you must use %SQL% to indicate that SQL can appear anywhere in the name, rather than just at the beginning of the name, as when using the DisplayName property.

Sometimes an application-specific service won't use a specific pattern as part of its name or display name. In this case, you may need to look for some other characteristic, defined in the "Defining an Application-Specific Service" section of this chapter as search criteria. For example, the PathName property provides the perfect method of locating an application-specific service. To obtain the same result shown in Figure 3-1, type **WMIC SERVICE WHERE "PathName Like '%Microsoft SQL Server%'" GET DisplayName,Name, StartMode** and press Enter. Notice that you don't include the whole PathName property value or even the complete path. All you need is the full name of the application storage folder because no other services appear in that folder.

So far, you've seen WMIC output that consists solely of plain text. The WMIC command provides a number of formatting options that you specify with the /FORMAT command line switch. Two of the most useful formats are Comma Separated Value (CSV), which is useful for importing the data into a database, and HTML Format (HFORM), which is useful for displaying the data in a browser.

In both cases, you redirect the output using a redirection character. For example, to create a CSV file, type **WMIC SERVICE WHERE "DisplayName Like 'SQL%'" GET DisplayName,Name,StartMode /FORMAT:CSV > SQLServices.CSV** and press Enter. Likewise, to create an HTML file, type **WMIC SERVICE WHERE "DisplayName Like 'SQL%'" GET DisplayName, Name,StartMode /FORMAT:HFORM > SQLServices.HTM** and press Enter. Figure 3-4 shows the HTML output.

WMIC formatting varies by alias and action. The SERVICE alias provides a considerable number of formatting options, so you may want to review this list before you decide that WMIC doesn't support a format you need. To obtain the list of formats for the LIST verb, type **WMIC SERVICE LIST /FORMAT /?** and press Enter. Likewise, to obtain the list of GET verb formats, type **WMIC SERVICE GET /FORMAT /?** and press Enter.

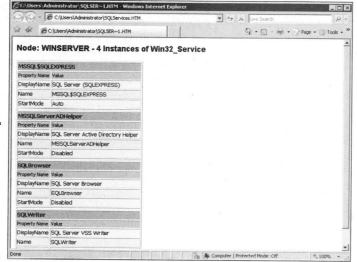

Figure 3-4:
WMIC
makes it
possible to
create nice-
looking
HTML
output.

Working with Application-Specific Services As Needed

Application-specific services don't include some of the safeguards that operating systems services provide. For example, you can stop an application-specific service in most cases, even when it doesn't make sense to do so. Using the SC utility, you can easily remove an application-specific service when the uninstall program for your application fails to remove it. (MySQL used to have this very bug, and you ended up with a MySQL service sitting on your system long after MySQL was gone.) The following sections describe the precautions and techniques you use for working with application-specific services.

Starting and stopping application-specific services

The act of starting and stopping application-specific services is the same as for any other service: You locate the service in the Services console, right-click its entry, and choose Stop or Start from the context menu. The SC command also makes it quite easy to start and stop services as needed. However, you need to take additional care when starting and stopping an application-specific service.

You can encounter many problems when starting or stopping application-specific services, but the major problem, the one that will make you lose sleep at night, is data loss. Stopping an application-specific service at the wrong time can cause the service to lose data and not record everything that you expect it to record. Oddly enough, starting an application-specific service can create similar problems. For example, if the application normally collects information, starts the service, and sends an e-mail with the information, starting the service early, before the application collects all the information, can result in an incomplete e-mail message. Consequently, you must know when to start or stop services to reduce the risk of data loss.

Many administrators wrongfully assume that stopping a service impacts only the application associated with the service. For example, if you stop the SQL Server database services, the associated SQL Server functionality becomes unavailable. However, some applications provide special functionality, and stopping the service can impact the server as a whole. For example, stopping the service associated with your UPS application can cause the application to assume that the server has lost power. After completing any required shutdown procedures, your entire service shuts down, potentially resulting in data loss. Never assume that stopping a service stops only the associated application.

The Dependencies tab, shown in Figure 3-5, is another source of potential problems for application-specific services. The information in the figure is correct, but it doesn't tell you the whole story. For example, when you stop the SQL Server (SQLEXPRESS) service, the SQL Server Browser service won't find the SQLEXPRESS instance of SQL Server on the system. Yes, the SQL Server Browser service still runs, but it can't accomplish the task set for it. In fact, unless you have another instance of SQL Server installed on the server, none of the other SQL Server application-specific services can perform their tasks either. They all work, but they all report that they can't find a database to work with. This is an example of how an application-specific service requires more thought when starting or stopping it — you can't always depend on the service information to provide complete information to you.

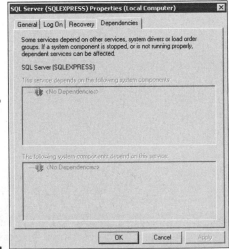

Figure 3-5: Don't rely on the Dependencies tab as a sole source of dependency information.

Configuring an application-specific service start-up

Configuring an application-specific service to start automatically or manually works the same as it does for any other service. The vendor normally
ensures that required services start automatically and that optional services
start only as needed or are disabled until you need them. When you
encounter a feature that doesn't work properly on the first try, you should
always check the associated service to ensure that it has started. The
vendor may feel that the service is optional and disable it during installation.
For example, Microsoft disables the SQL Server Browser service during
installation. You must start this service, however, to help some products,
such as Visual Studio, work with SQL Server properly.

One subtle problem that Windows Server 2008 has introduced is the need
for some services to start in a delayed state. You choose the Automatic
(Delayed Start) option in the Startup Type field, as shown in Figure 3-6.
Choosing a delayed start can solve problems in which the service doesn't
start when it should or displays errors when it does. In some cases, a service
must wait for other services to start before it can start itself. When you experience problems with services starting incorrectly, try the Automatic
(Delayed Start) setting to determine whether the new setting will fix the
problem.

Figure 3-6:
Use a
delayed
start when
a service
relies on
other
services
to start
correctly.

One consideration for application-specific services that is optional is that
you may not need to start them automatically. Setting such a service to
manual allows the application to start the service as needed. In some cases,
the application also automatically stops the service when the service is no
longer needed. As an alternative, you can manually start the service when

users require it by right-clicking the service entry and choosing Start from the context menu. Of course, manually starting services is time consuming, so you want to reserve this option for services that the user requires rarely or at a specified time. When the user requires the service at a specific time (say, for monthly reports), you can use the Task Scheduler to create jobs for starting and stopping the service. Simply use the SC utility to start and stop the service as described in the "Working with the SC Command Line Utility" section of Book VIII, Chapter 2.

Changing the application-specific service logon settings

Windows Server 2008 places additional security restrictions on applications of all types, including services. You may find that the logon settings that work on another system running a different version of Windows won't work on Windows Server 2008. The main symptom of this problem is error messages telling you that the service can't access something or doesn't have required permissions. You see that the service is running, that it isn't failing in any other way, but that it still can't seem to accomplish specific tasks. In this case, you must change the settings on the Log On tab to account for Windows Server 2008 security.

Because Windows Server 2008 places additional restrictions on services, you may think that using the Administrator account is a quick fix to the problem. It's true that the service will now work as expected, but using the wrong logon account also leaves your server open to attack. Rather than open your server to needless prying by outsiders, consider creating a special account for the service that provides just the rights that the service requires. Using this approach keeps your system safe, but also lets the service run as expected.

It's also important to remember that not every logon problem is the fault of Windows Server 2008. For example, when working with SQL Server, the service must normally log on using the Network Service account. Otherwise, the service can't access SQL Server databases on the network. Some services, such as SQL Server Browser, may not work at all. These issues occur on other versions of Windows as well, but may become amplified on Windows Server 2008 due to the enhanced security in this operating system. In short, an inconsistency in Windows 2003 may become a complete failure in Windows Server 2008, but the logon setting is still incorrect in both operating systems.

Modifying the application-specific service recovery features

Whether you need to configure recovery options on the Recovery tab of the service Properties dialog box depends on the service and on your company policies. For example, SQL Server provides some recovery features as part of the DBMS. In many cases, these recovery features are enough for the average setup, but may not be enough for your organization. You have to consider what Microsoft is providing and determine how to fill any gaps in recovery that Microsoft has left behind. The same consideration holds true for any application-specific service.

Microsoft does rely on automated recovery for the SQL Server Browser service, as shown in Figure 3-7. Notice that the answer to every problem is the same — restart the service. In fact, the strategy shown could lead to an endless loop of restarts on your server. Because the service isn't informing anyone about the problem, you could see a performance drop without discovering much of a reason for it. Consequently, when you see this kind of setup for an application-specific service, you want to reconfigure it to provide a more reasonable approach to recovery. The "Working with the Recovery tab" section of Book VIII, Chapter 2 provides some insights into recovery strategies you can use.

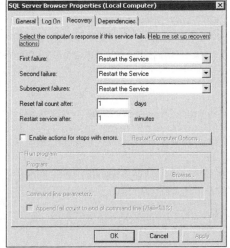

Figure 3-7: Restarting the service over and over doesn't accomplish much except killing server performance.

Understanding security required by application-specific services

Most of this chapter considers configuration tasks for the service. You change the startup type, logon account, recovery options, and so on to ensure that the service will run. In most cases, you won't need to perform any additional tasks to ensure that the service runs as anticipated. Because services run in the background and usually have special accounts suited to their needs, you may never see another problem with a service in Windows Server 2008.

Microsoft has become very security conscious, and some of the new features of Windows Server 2008, such as User Account Control (UAC), underscore this commitment. The need to sign code is another indication that Microsoft is changing when it comes to security. Finally, Microsoft has also locked down resources. Any of these issues can cause an older service to run incorrectly or not at all. In fact, the code signing requirement can cause a custom service to fail to install at all. The SC utility (or your custom installation program) will state that the service is flawed, usually with a message that tells you nothing about the real source of the problem. With this change in security in mind, here are some tips for services you want to install on your system:

✦ Sign all your custom code.

✦ Ask third-party vendors to sign their code.

✦ Verify that services can access the resources they require to run.

✦ Check logon accounts to ensure that the service can perform any required tasks.

✦ Ensure that all dependent services provide required access and run correctly.

✦ Determine whether managed services have any special security or configuration requirements.

✦ Check the event logs for any suspicious service entries.

✦ Check the event logs for any suspicious resource entries (including entries from dependent applications).

Considering special application-specific service configuration needs

Application-specific services can have special configuration needs. You may need to perform this configuration by issuing commands using the SC utility or create a configuration file on the hard drive. The settings won't appear as part of the service Properties dialog box, and vendors may not provide everything you need unless you ask about specific issues. Always consider the lack of special configuration as one of the reasons that a service refuses to work properly on your server.

Index